THE PAPERS OF
BENJAMIN FRANKLIN

SPONSORED BY

The American Philosophical Society

and Yale University

Benjamin Franklin

THE PAPERS OF

Benjamin Franklin

VOLUME 30 *July 1 through October 31, 1779*

BARBARA B. OBERG, *Editor*

ELLEN R. COHN AND JONATHAN R. DULL, *Senior Associate Editors*

DOROTHY W. BRIDGWATER, *Associate Editor*

KAREN DUVAL AND MARILYN A. MORRIS, *Assistant Editors*

CLAUDE A. LOPEZ, *Consulting Editor*

KATE M. OHNO, *Editorial Assistant*

New Haven and London   YALE UNIVERSITY PRESS, 1993

As indicated in the first volume, this edition was made possible through the vision and generosity of Yale University and the American Philosophical Society and by a substantial donation from Henry R. Luce in the name of Life Magazine. Additional funds were provided by a grant from the Ford Foundation to the National Archives Trust Fund Board. Subsequent support has come from the Andrew W. Mellon Foundation and the Pew Charitable Trusts through Founding Fathers Papers, Inc. Major underwriting of the present volume has been provided by the Florence Gould Foundation. Generous sponsors include the American Philosophical Society, Da Capo, the Kemper Educational and Charitable Fund, Mr. and Mrs. Malcolm N. Smith, and George F. Waters. Contributions from The Fort Wayne Journal-Gazette *Foundation, the Friends of Franklin, and the Friends of the Franklin Papers also help to sustain the enterprise.* The Papers of Benjamin Franklin *is a beneficiary of the generous and long-standing support of the National Historical Publications and Records Commission under the chairmanship of the Archivist of the United States. An award from the National Endowment for the Humanities, an independent federal agency, ensured the completion of this volume. For the assistance of all these organizations and individuals, as well as for the indispensable aid of archivists, librarians, scholars, and collectors of Franklin manuscripts, the editors are most grateful.*

Published with assistance from the National Endowment for the Humanities.

913.2
F831p
v.30

Contents

Foreign-language surnames and titles of nobility often run to great length. Our practice with an untitled person is to provide all the Christian names at the first appearance, and then drop them; a chevalier or noble is given the title used at the time, and the full name is provided in the index.

*Denotes a document referred to in annotation.

xxiv

List of Illustrations

Contributors to Volume 30

The ownership of each manuscript, or the location of the particular copy used by the editors of each rare contemporary pamphlet or similar printed work, is indicated where the document
appears in the text. The sponsors and editors are deeply grateful
to the following institutions and individuals for permission to
print or otherwise use in the present volume manuscripts and
other materials which they own.

INSTITUTIONS

American Philosophical Society
Archives de la Marine, Paris
Archives Départementales du
    Morbihan
Archives du Ministère des affaires
    étrangères, Paris
Archives Nationales
Bibliothèque municipale de Nantes
Columbia University Library
Harvard University Library
Henry E. Huntington Library

Historical Society of Delaware
Historical Society of Pennsylvania
Library of Congress
Massachusetts Historical Society
National Archives
New-York Historical Society
Pierpont Morgan Library
Princeton University Library
University of Pennsylvania Library
University of Virginia Library
Yale University Library

INDIVIDUALS

Stanley R. Becker, East Hampton,
    New York
M.D.A.F.H.H. Hartley Russell, on
    deposit in the Berkshire County
    Record Office, Reading, England

Philip H. and A.S.W. Rosenbach
    Foundation

Statement of Methodology

Arrangement of Materials

The documents are printed in chronological sequence according to their dates when these are given, or according to the date of publication in cases of contemporary printed materials. Records such as diaries, journals, and account books that cover substantial periods of time appear according to the dates of their earliest entries. When no date appears on the document itself, one is editorially supplied and an explanation provided. When no day within a month is given, the document is placed at the end of all specifically dated documents of that month; those dated only by year are placed at the end of that year. If no date is given, we use internal and external evidence to assign one whenever possible, providing our explanation in annotation. Documents which cannot be assigned a date more definite than the entire length of Franklin's stay in France (1777–85) will be published at the end of this period. Those for which we are unable to provide even a tentative date will be published at the conclusion of the series.

When two or more documents have the same date, they are arranged in the following order:

1. Those by a group of which Franklin was a member (*e.g.,* the American Commissioners in Paris)
2. Those by Franklin individually
3. Those to a group of which Franklin was a member
4. Those to Franklin individually
5. "Third-party" and unaddressed miscellaneous writings by others than Franklin.

In the first two categories letters are arranged alphabetically by the name of the addressee; in the last three, by the name of the signatory. An exception to this practice occurs when a letter to Franklin and his answer were written on the same day: in such cases the first letter precedes the reply. The same rules apply to documents lacking precise dates printed together at the end of any month or year.

Form of Presentation

The document and its accompanying editorial apparatus are presented in the following order:

1. *Title.* Essays and formal papers are headed by their titles, except in the case of pamphlets with very long titles, when a short form is substituted. Where previous editors supplied a title to a piece that had none, and this title has become familiar, we use it; otherwise we devise a suitable one.

Letters written by Franklin individually are entitled "To" the person or body addressed, as: To John Adams; To John Adams and Arthur Lee; To the Royal Society.

Letters to Franklin individually are entitled "From" the person or body who wrote them, as: From John Adams; From John Adams and Arthur Lee; From the Committee of Secret Correspondence.

Letters of which Franklin was a joint author or joint recipient are titled with the names of all concerned, as: Franklin and Silas Deane to Arthur Lee; Arthur Lee to Franklin and Silas Deane. "Third-party" letters or those by or to a body of which Franklin was a member are titled with the names of both writers and addressees, as: Arthur Lee to John Adams; The American Commissioners to John Paul Jones.

Documents not fitting into any of these categories are given brief descriptive headings, as: Extract from Franklin's Journal.

If the name in the title has been supplied from external evidence it appears in brackets, with a question mark when we are uncertain. If a letter is unsigned, or signed with initials or an alias, but is from a correspondent whose handwriting we know, the name appears without brackets.

2. *Source Identification.* This gives the nature of the printed or manuscript version of the document, and, in the case of a manuscript or a rare printed work, the ownership and location of the original.

Printed sources of three different classes are distinguished. First, a contemporary pamphlet, which is given its full title, place and date of publication, and the location of the copy the editors have used. Second, an essay or letter appearing originally in a *contemporary* publication, which is introduced by the words "Printed in," followed by the title, date, and inclusive page numbers, if necessary, of the publication. Third, a document, the manuscript or contemporary printed version of which is now lost, but which was printed at a later date, is identified by the words "Reprinted from," followed by the name of the work from which the editors have reproduced it. The following examples illustrate the distinction:

Printed in *The Pennsylvania Gazette*, October 2, 1729.

Reprinted from William Temple Franklin, ed., *Memoirs of the Life and Writings of Benjamin Franklin* . . . (3 vols., 4to, London, 1817–18), II, 244.

The Source Identification of a manuscript consists of a term or symbol (all of which are listed in the Short Title List) indicating the character of the manuscript version, followed by the name of the holder of the manuscript, as: ALS: American Philosophical Society. Since manuscripts belonging to individuals have a tendency to migrate, we indicate the year in which each private owner gave permission to publish, as: Morris Duane, Philadelphia, 1957. When two or more manuscript versions survive, the one listed first in the Source Identification is the one from which we print.

3. An editorial *Headnote* precedes some documents in this edition; it appears between the Source Identification and the actual text. Such a headnote is designed to supply the background of the composition of the document, its relation to events or other writings, and any other information which may be useful to the reader and is not obtainable from the document itself.

4. The *Text* of the document follows the Source Identification, or Headnote, if any. When multiple copies of a document are extant, the editors observe the following order of priority in determining which of the available versions to use in printing a text: ALS or ADS, LS or DS, AL or AD, L or D, and copy. An AL (draft) normally takes precedence over a contemporary copy based on the recipient's copy. If we deviate from

the order set forth here, we explain our decision in the annotation. In those instances where multiple texts are available, the texts are collated, and significant variations reported in the annotation. In selecting the publication text from among several copies of official French correspondence (*e.g.,* from Vergennes or Sartine) we use the version which is written in the best French, on the presumption that the French ministers used standard eighteenth-century spelling, grammar, and punctuation.

The form of presentation of the texts of letters is as follows:

The place and date of composition are set at the top, regardless of their location in the original manuscript.

The signature, set in capitals and small capitals, is placed at the right of the last line of the text if there is room; if not, then on the line below.

Addresses, endorsements, and notations are so labeled and printed at the end of the letter. An endorsement is, to the best of our belief, by the recipient, and a notation by someone else. When the writer of the notation has misread the date or the signature of the correspondent, we let the error stand without comment. Line breaks in addresses are marked by slashes. Different notations are separated by slashes; when they are by different individuals, we so indicate.

5. *Footnotes* to the Heading, Source Identification, Headnote, and Text appear on the pages to which they pertain. References to documents not printed or to be printed in later volumes are by date and repository, as: Jan. 17, 1780, APS.

Method of Textual Reproduction

1. *Spelling* of all words, including proper names, is retained. If it is abnormal enough to obscure the meaning we follow the word immediately with the current spelling in brackets.

2. *Capitalization and Punctuation* are retained. There is such variety in the size of initial letters, often in the same manuscript, that it is sometimes unclear whether the writer intended an upper or lower case letter. In such cases we make a decision on the basis of the correspondent's customary usage. We supply a capital letter when an immediately preceding period, co-

lon, question mark, exclamation point, or dash indicates that a new sentence is intended. If a capital letter clearly indicates the beginning of a new thought, but no mark of punctuation precedes it, we insert a period. If neither punctuation nor capital letter indicates a sentence break, we do not supply one unless the absence renders comprehension of the document nearly impossible. In that case we provide them and so indicate in a footnote.

Dashes were used for a variety of purposes in eighteenth-century personal and public letters. A dash within a sentence, used to indicate a break in thought, is represented as an em dash. A dash that follows a period or serves as a closing mark of punctuation for a sentence is represented as an em dash followed by a space. Occasionally correspondents used long dashes that continue to the end of a line and indicate a significant break in thought. We do not reproduce the dash, but treat it as indicating the start of a new paragraph.

When there is an initial quotation mark or parenthesis, but no closing one, we silently complete the pair.

3. *Contractions and abbreviations* are retained. Abbreviations such as "wd", "honble", "servt", "exclly", are used so frequently in Franklin's correspondence that they are readily comprehensible to the users of these volumes. Abbreviations, particularly of French words, that may be unclear are followed by an expanded version in brackets, as: nre [navire]. Superscript letters are brought down to the line. Where a period or colon is a part of the abbreviation, or indicates that letters were written above the line, we print it at the end of the word, as: 4th. for 4.th. In those few cases where superscript letters brought down to the line result in a confusing abbreviation ("Made" for "Mad^e"), we follow the abbreviation by an expanded version in brackets, as: Made [Madame].

The ampersand by itself and the "&c." are retained. Letters represented by the "y" are printed, as: "the" and "that". The tailed "p" is spelled out, as: "per", "pre", or "pro". Symbols of weights, measures, and money are converted to modern forms, as: *l.t.* instead of ℔ for *livres tournois*.

4. *Omissions, mutilations, and illegible words* are treated as follows:

If we are certain of the reading of letters missing in a word because of a torn or taped manuscript or tightly bound copybook, we supply the letters silently.

If we cannot be sure of the word, or of how the author spelled it, but we can make a reasonable guess, we supply the missing letters in brackets.

When the writer has omitted a word absolutely required for clarity, we insert it in italics within brackets.

5. *Interlineations* by the author are silently incorporated into the text. If they are significant enough to require comment a footnote is provided.

Textual Conventions

/	denotes line break in addresses and different hands in notations.
⟨roman⟩	denotes a résumé of a letter or document.
[*italic*]	editorial insertion explaining something about the manuscript, as: [*one line illegible*]; or supplying a word to make the meaning clear, as: [*to*].
[roman]	editorial insertion clarifying the immediately preceding word or abbreviation; supplies letters missing because of a mutilated manuscript.
(?)	indicates a questionable reading.

Abbreviations and Short Titles

AAE	Archives du Ministère des affaires étrangères.
AD	Autograph document.
Adams Papers	Robert J. Taylor, Richard L. Ryerson, *et al.*, eds., *Papers of John Adams* (8 vols. to date, Cambridge, Mass., 1977–).
ADB	*Allgemeine Deutsche Biographie* (56 vols., Berlin, 1967–71).
ADS	Autograph document signed.
AL	Autograph letter.
Allen, *Mass. Privateers*	Gardner Weld Allen, ed., *Massachusetts Privateers of the Revolution* ([Cambridge, Mass.], 1927) (Massachusetts Historical Society *Collections,* LXXVII).
Almanach des marchands	*Almanach général des marchands, négocians, armateurs, et fabricans de France et de l'Europe et autres parties du monde . . .* (Paris, 1779).
Almanach royal	*Almanach royal* (91 vols., Paris, 1700–92). Cited by year.
Alphabetical List of Escaped Prisoners	Alphabetical List of the Americans who having escap'd from the Prisons of England, were furnish'd with Money by the Commissrs. of the U.S. at the Court of France, to return to America. A manuscript in the APS, dated 1784, and covering the period January, 1777, to November, 1784.
ALS	Autograph letter signed.
Amer.	American.
APS	American Philosophical Society.
Archaeol.	Archaeological.

xl

Assn.

Auphan, "Communications"

Association.

P. Auphan, "Les communications entre la France et ses colonies d'Amérique pendant la guerre de l'indépendance Américaine," *Revue Maritime,* new series, no. LXIII and LXIV (1925), 331–48, 497–517.

Autobiog.

Leonard W. Labaree, Ralph L. Ketcham, Helen C. Boatfield, and Helene H. Fineman, eds., *The Autobiography of Benjamin Franklin* (New Haven, 1964).

Bachaumont, *Mémoires secrets*

[Louis Petit de Bachaumont *et al.*], *Mémoires secrets pour servir à l'histoire de la république des lettres en France, depuis MDCCLXII jusqu'à nos jours; ou, Journal d'un observateur* . . . (36 vols. in 12, London, 1784–89). Bachaumont died in 1771. The first six vols. (1762–71) are his; Mathieu-François Pidansat de Mairobert edited them and wrote the next nine (1771–79); the remainder (1779–87) are by Barthélemy-François Mouffle d'Angerville.

Balch, *French in America*

Thomas Balch, *The French in America during the War of Independence of the United States, 1777–1783* (trans. by Thomas Willing Balch *et al.;* 2 vols., Philadelphia, 1891–95).

BF

Benjamin Franklin.

BF's accounts as commissioner

Those described above, XXIII, 20.

BFB

Benjamin Franklin Bache.

Bigelow, *Works*

John Bigelow, ed., *The Works of Benjamin Franklin* (12 vols., New York and London, 1904).

Biographie universelle

Biographie universelle, ancienne et moderne,

xli

ou histoire, par ordre alphabétique, de la vie publique et privée de tous les hommes qui se sont fait remarquer . . . (85 vols., Paris, 1811–62).

Bodinier — From information kindly furnished us by Cdt. Gilbert Bodinier, Section études, Service historique de l'Armée de Terre, Vincennes.

Bodinier, *Dictionnaire* — Gilbert Bodinier, *Dictionnaire des officiers de l'armée royale qui ont combattu aux Etats-Unis pendant la guerre d'Indépendance* (Château de Vincennes, 1982).

Boudriot, *John Paul Jones and the Bonhomme Richard* — Jean Boudriot, *John Paul Jones and the Bonhomme Richard: a Reconstruction of the Ship and an Account of the Battle with ... Serapis* (trans. by David H. Roberts; Annapolis, 1987).

Bowler, *Logistics* — R. Arthur Bowler, *Logistics and the Failure of the British Army in America, 1775–1783* (Princeton, 1975).

Bradford, *Jones Papers* — James C. Bradford, ed., *The Microfilm Edition of the Papers of John Paul Jones, 1747–1792* (10 reels of microfilm, Alexandria, Va., 1986).

Burke's Peerage — Sir Bernard Burke, *Burke's Genealogical and Heraldic History of the Peerage Baronetage and Knightage with War Gazette and Corrigenda* (98th ed., London, 1940). References in exceptional cases to other editions are so indicated.

Burnett, *Continental Congress* — Edmund C. Burnett, *The Continental Congress* (New York, 1941).

Burnett, *Letters* — Edmund C. Burnett, ed., *Letters of Members of the Continental Congress* (8 vols., Washington, 1921–36).

xlii

Butterfield, *Adams Correspondence*	Lyman H. Butterfield, Richard L. Ryerson, *et al.*, eds., *Adams Family Correspondence* (6 vols. to date, Cambridge, Mass., 1963–).
Butterfield, *John Adams Diary*	Lyman H. Butterfield *et al.*, eds., *Diary and Autobiography of John Adams* (4 vols., Cambridge, Mass., 1961).
Case of Silas Deane	[Edward Ingraham, ed.,] *Papers in Relation to the Case of Silas Deane* (Philadelphia, 1855).
Chron.	*Chronicle.*
Claghorn, *Naval Officers*	Charles E. Claghorn, *Naval Officers of the American Revolution: a Concise Biographical Dictionary* (Metuchen, N.J. and London, 1988).
Clark, *Ben Franklin's Privateers*	William Bell Clark, *Ben Franklin's Privateers: a Naval Epic of the American Revolution* (Baton Rouge, 1956).
Clark, *Wickes*	William Bell Clark, *Lambert Wickes, Sea Raider and Diplomat: the Story of a Naval Captain of the Revolution* (New Haven and London, 1932).
Clowes, *Royal Navy*	William Laird Clowes, *The Royal Navy: a History from the Earliest Times to the Present* (7 vols., Boston and London, 1897–1903).
Cobbett, *Parliamentary History*	William Cobbett and Thomas C. Hansard, eds., *The Parliamentary History of England from the Earliest Period to 1803* (36 vols., London, 1806–20).
Col.	Column.
Coll.	*Collections.*
Commons Jours.	*Journals of the House of Commons* (233 vols. to date, [London,] 1803–); vols. I–LI are reprints.

xliii

Croÿ, *Journal*	Emmanuel, prince de Moeurs et de Solre et duc de Croÿ, *Journal inédit du duc de Croÿ, 1718–1784* (4 vols., Paris, 1906–07).
Cushing, *Writings of Samuel Adams*	Harry Alonzo Cushing, ed., *The Writings of Samuel Adams . . .* (4 vols., New York, 1904–08).
d.	*denier.*
D	Document unsigned.
DAB	*Dictionary of American Biography.*
DBF	*Dictionnaire de biographie française* (18 vols. to date, Paris, 1933–).
Deane Correspondence	*The Deane Papers; Correspondence between Silas Deane, His Brothers and Their Business and Political Associates, 1771–1795* (Connecticut Historical Society *Collections,* XXIII, Hartford, Conn., 1930).
Deane Papers	*The Deane Papers, 1774–90* (5 vols.; New-York Historical Society *Collections,* XIX-XXIII, New York, 1887–91).
DF	Deborah Franklin.
Dictionnaire de la noblesse	François-Alexandre Aubert de La Chesnaye-Dubois and M. Badier, *Dictionnaire de la noblesse contenant les généalogies, l'histoire & la chronologie des familles nobles de la France . . .* (3rd ed.; 19 vols., Paris, 1863–76).
Dictionnaire historique	*Dictionnaire historique, critique et bibliographique, contenant les vies des hommes illustres, célèbres ou fameux de tous les pays et de tous les siècles . . .* (30 vols., Paris, 1821–23).
Dictionnaire historique de la Suisse	*Dictionnaire historique & biographique de la Suisse* (7 vols. and supplement, Neuchâtel, 1921–34).
DNB	*Dictionary of National Biography.*

Doniol, *Histoire* — Henri Doniol, *Histoire de la participation de la France à l'établissement des Etats-Unis d'Amérique. Correspondance diplomatique et documents* (5 vols., Paris, 1886–99).

DS — Document signed.

Duane, *Works* — William Duane, ed., *The Works of Dr. Benjamin Franklin . . .* (6 vols., Philadelphia, 1808–18). Title varies in the several volumes.

Dubourg, *Œuvres* — Jacques Barbeu-Dubourg, ed., *Œuvres de M. Franklin . . .* (2 vols., Paris, 1773).

Dull, *French Navy* — Jonathan R. Dull, *The French Navy and American Independence: a Study of Arms and Diplomacy, 1774–1787* (Princeton, 1975).

Ed. — Edition or editor.

Edler, *Dutch Republic* — Friedrich Edler, *The Dutch Republic and the American Revolution* (*Johns Hopkins University Studies in Historical and Political Science,* ser. XXIX, no. 2; Baltimore, 1911).

Elias and Finch, *Letters of Digges* — Robert H. Elias and Eugene D. Finch, eds., *Letters of Thomas Attwood Digges (1742–1821)* (Columbia, S.C., 1982).

Etat militaire — *Etat militaire de France, pour l'année . . .* (36 vols., Paris, 1758–93). Cited by year.

Exper. and Obser. — *Experiments and Observations on Electricity, made at Philadelphia in America, by Mr. Benjamin Franklin . . .* (London, 1751). Revised and enlarged editions were published in 1754, 1760, 1769, and 1774 with slightly varying titles. In each case the edition cited will be indicated, e.g., *Exper. and Obser.* (1751).

Fauchille, *Diplomatie française* — Paul Fauchille, *La Diplomatie française et*

xlv

	la ligue des neutres de 1780 (1776–1783) (Paris, 1893).
Ferguson, *Power of the Purse*	E. James Ferguson, *The Power of the Purse: a History of American Public Finance* . . . (Chapel Hill, N.C., 1961).
Fitzpatrick, *Writings of Washington*	John C. Fitzpatrick, ed., *The Writings of George Washington* . . . (39 vols., Washington, D.C., 1931–44).
Force, *Amer. Arch.*	Peter Force, ed., *American Archives: Consisting of a Collection of Authentic Records, State Papers, Debates, and Letters and Other Notices of Publick Affairs* . . . , fourth series, March 7, 1774 to July 4, 1776 (6 vols., [Washington, 1837–46]); fifth series, July 4, 1776 to September 3, 1783 (3 vols., [Washington, 1848–53]).
Ford, *Letters of William Lee*	Worthington Chauncey Ford, ed., *Letters of William Lee, 1766–1783* (3 vols., Brooklyn, N.Y., 1891).
Fortescue, *Correspondence of George Third*	Sir John William Fortescue, ed., *The Correspondence of King George the Third from 1760 to December 1783* . . . (6 vols., London, 1927–28).
France ecclésiastique	*La France ecclésiastique pour l'année* . . . (15 vols., Paris, 1774–90). Cited by year.
Freeman, *Washington*	Douglas S. Freeman (completed by John A. Carroll and Mary W. Ashworth), *George Washington: a Biography* (7 vols., New York, 1948–57).
Gaz.	*Gazette.*
Gaz. de Leyde	*Nouvelles extraordinaires de divers endroits,* commonly known as *Gazette de Leyde.* Each issue is in two parts; we indicate the second as "sup."
Geneal.	*Genealogical.*

xlvi

Gent. Mag. — *The Gentleman's Magazine, and Historical Chronicle.*

Gruber, *Howe Brothers* — Ira D. Gruber, *The Howe Brothers and the American Revolution* (New York, 1972).

Hayes, *Calendar* — I. Minis Hayes, *Calendar of the Papers of Benjamin Franklin in the Library of the American Philosophical Society* (5 vols., Philadelphia, 1908).

Heitman, *Register of Officers* — Francis B. Heitman, *Historical Register of Officers in the War of the Revolution . . .* (Washington, D.C., 1893).

Hillairet, *Rues de Paris* — Jacques Hillairet, pseud. of Auguste A. Coussillan, *Dictionnaire historique des rues de Paris* (2nd ed.; 2 vols., [Paris, 1964]).

Hist. — *Historic* or *Historical.*

Idzerda, *Lafayette Papers* — Stanley J. Idzerda *et al.,* eds., *Lafayette in the Age of the American Revolution: Selected Letters and Papers, 1776–1790* (5 vols. to date, Ithaca, N.Y., and London, 1977–).

JA — John Adams.

JCC — Worthington C. Ford *et al.,* eds., *Journals of the Continental Congress, 1744–1789* (34 vols., Washington, 1904–37).

Jefferson Papers — Julian P. Boyd, Charles T. Cullen, John Catanzariti *et al.,* eds., *The Papers of Thomas Jefferson* (25 vols. to date, Princeton, 1950–).

Jour. — *Journal.*

JW — Jonathan Williams, Jr.

Kaminkow, *Mariners* — Marion and Jack Kaminkow, *Mariners of the American Revolution* (Baltimore, 1967).

L — Letter unsigned.

Landais, *Memorial* — Pierre Landais, *Memorial, to Justify Peter*

	Landai's Conduct during the Late War (Boston, 1784).
Larousse	Pierre Larousse, *Grand dictionnaire universel du XIXe siècle* . . . (17 vols., Paris, [n.d.]).
Lasseray, *Les Français*	André Lasseray, *Les Français sous les treize étoiles, 1775–1783* (2 vols., Paris, 1935).
Laurens Papers	Philip M. Hamer, George C. Rogers, Jr., David R. Chestnutt *et al.*, eds., *The Papers of Henry Laurens* (13 vols. to date, Columbia, S.C., 1968–).
Le Bihan, *Francs-maçons parisiens*	Alain Le Bihan, *Francs-maçons parisiens du Grand Orient de France* . . . (Commission d'histoire économique et sociale de la révolution française, *Mémoires et documents*, XIX, Paris, 1966).
Lee, *Life of Arthur Lee*	Richard Henry Lee, *Life of Arthur Lee, L.L.D., Joint Commissioner of the United States to the Court of France, and Sole Commissioner to the Courts of Spain and Prussia, during the Revolutionary War* . . . (2 vols., Boston, 1829).
Lee Family Papers	Paul P. Hoffman, ed., *The Lee Family Papers, 1742–1795* (University of Virginia *Microfilm Publication* No. 1; 8 reels, Charlottesville, Va., 1966).
Lewis, *Walpole Correspondence*	Wilmarth S. Lewis *et al.*, eds., *The Yale Edition of Horace Walpole's Correspondence* (48 vols., New Haven, 1939–83).
Lopez, *Mon Cher Papa*	Claude-Anne Lopez, *Mon Cher Papa: Franklin and the Ladies of Paris* (rev. ed., New Haven and London, 1990).
Lopez and Herbert, *The Private Franklin*	Claude-Anne Lopez and Eugenia W. Herbert, *The Private Franklin: the Man and His Family* (New York, 1975).

LS	Letter or letters signed.
l.t.	*livres tournois.*
Lüthy, *Banque protestante*	Herbert Lüthy, *La Banque protestante en France de la Révocation de l'Edit de Nantes à la Révolution* (2 vols., Paris, 1959–61).
Mackesy, *War for America*	Piers Mackesy, *The War for America, 1775–1783* (Cambridge, Mass., 1965).
Mag.	*Magazine.*
Mass. Arch.	Massachusetts Archives, State House, Boston.
Mazas, *Ordre de Saint-Louis*	Alexandre Mazas and Théodore Anne, *Histoire de l'ordre royal et militaire de Saint-Louis depuis son institution en 1693 jusqu'en 1830* (2nd ed.; 3 vols., Paris, 1860–61).
Meng, *Despatches of Gérard*	John J. Meng, *Despatches and Instructions of Conrad Alexandre Gérard, 1778–1780* . . . (Baltimore, 1939).
Métra, *Correspondance secrète*	[François Métra *et al.*], *Correspondance secrète, politique & littéraire, ou Mémoires pour servir à l'histoire des cours, des sociétés & de la littérature en France, depuis la mort de Louis XV* (18 vols., London, 1787–90).
Meyer, *Armement nantais*	Jean Meyer, *L'Armement nantais dans la deuxième moitié du XVIIIe siècle* (Paris, 1969).
Meyer, *Noblesse bretonne*	Jean Meyer, *La Noblesse bretonne au XVIIIe siècle* (2 vols., Paris, 1966).
Morison, *Jones*	Samuel E. Morison, *John Paul Jones: a Sailor's Biography* (Boston & Toronto, 1959).
Morris Papers	E. James Ferguson, John Catanzariti, Elizabeth M. Nuxoll *et al.*, eds., *The*

	Papers of Robert Morris, 1781–1784 (7 vols. to date, Pittsburgh, Pa., 1973–).
Morton, *Beaumarchais Correspondance*	Brian N. Morton and Donald C. Spinelli, eds., *Beaumarchais Correspondance* (4 vols. to date, Paris, 1969–).
MS, MSS	Manuscript, manuscripts.
Namier and Brooke, *House of Commons*	Sir Lewis Namier and John Brooke, *The History of Parliament. The House of Commons 1754–1790* (3 vols., London and New York, 1964).
Naval Docs.	William B. Clark, William J. Morgan *et al.,* eds., *Naval Documents of the American Revolution* (9 vols. to date, Washington, D.C., 1964–).
Neeser, *Conyngham*	Robert Walden Neeser, ed., *Letters and Papers Relating to the Cruises of Gustavus Conyngham, Captain of the Continental Navy 1777–1779* (New York, 1915).
NNBW	*Nieuw Nederlandsch Biografisch Woordenboek* (10 vols. and index, Amsterdam, 1974).
Nouvelle biographie	*Nouvelle biographie générale depuis les temps les plus reculés jusqu'à nos jours . . .* (46 vols., Paris, 1855–66).
Pa. Arch.	Samuel Hazard *et al.,* eds., *Pennsylvania Archives* (9 series, Philadelphia and Harrisburg, 1852–1935).
Pa. Col. Recs.	*Minutes of the Provincial Council of Pennsylvania . . .* (16 vols., Harrisburg, 1851–53). Volumes I–III are reprints published in Philadelphia, 1852. Title changes with Volume XI to *Supreme Executive Council.*
Palmer, *Loyalists*	Gregory Palmer, ed., *Biographical Sketches of Loyalists of the American Revolution* (Westport, Ct., 1984).

l

Patterson, *The Other Armada*   A. Temple Patterson, *The Other Armada: the Franco–Spanish Attempt to Invade Britain in 1779* (Manchester, Eng., 1960).

Phil. Trans.   The Royal Society, *Philosophical Transactions.*

PMHB   *Pennsylvania Magazine of History and Biography.*

Price, *France and the Chesapeake*   Jacob M. Price, *France and the Chesapeake: a History of the French Tobacco Monopoly, 1674–1791, and of Its Relationship to the British and American Tobacco Trade* (2 vols., Ann Arbor, Mich., 1973).

Proc.   *Proceedings.*

Pub.   *Publications.*

Quérard, *France littéraire*   Joseph Marie Quérard, *La France littéraire ou Dictionnaire bibliographique des savants, historiens, et gens de lettres de la France, ainsi que des littérateurs étrangers qui ont écrit en français, plus particulièrement pendant les XVIIIe et XIXe siècles* ... (10 vols., Paris, 1827–64).

Rakove, *Beginnings of National Politics*   Jack N. Rakove, *The Beginnings of National Politics: an Interpretive History of the Continental Congress* (New York, 1979).

RB   Richard Bache.

Repertorium der diplomatischen Vertreter   Ludwig Bittner *et al.*, eds., *Repertorium der diplomatischen Vertreter aller Länder seit dem Westfälischen Frieden (1648)* (3 vols., Oldenburg, etc., 1936–65).

Rev.   *Review.*

s.   *sou.*

Sabine, *Loyalists*   Lorenzo Sabine, *Biographical Sketches of Loyalists of the American Revolution* ... (2 vols., Boston, 1864).

Schaeper, *Battle off Flamborough Head* — Thomas J. Schaeper, *John Paul Jones and the Battle off Flamborough Head: a Reconsideration* (New York, Bern, Frankfurt am Main, 1989).

Schelle, *Œuvres de Turgot* — Gustave Schelle, ed., *Œuvres de Turgot et documents le concernant* (5 vols., Paris, 1913–23).

Schulte Nordholt, *Dutch Republic* — J. W. Schulte Nordholt, *The Dutch Republic and American Independence* (trans. Herbert M. Rowen; Chapel Hill, N.C., 1982).

Sellers, *Franklin in Portraiture* — Charles C. Sellers, *Benjamin Franklin in Portraiture* (New Haven and London, 1962).

Sibley's Harvard Graduates — John L. Sibley, *Biographical Sketches of Graduates of Harvard University* (17 vols. to date, Cambridge, Mass., 1873–). Continued from Volume IV by Clifford K. Shipton.

Six, *Dictionnaire biographique* — Georges Six, *Dictionnaire biographique des généraux et amiraux français de la Révolution et de l'Empire (1792–1814)* (2 vols., Paris, 1934).

Smith, *Letters* — Paul H. Smith *et al.*, eds., *Letters of Delegates to Congress* (19 vols. to date, Washington, D.C., 1976–).

Smyth, *Writings* — Albert H. Smyth, ed., *The Writings of Benjamin Franklin . . .* (10 vols., New York, 1905–07).

Soc. — Society.

Sparks, *Works* — Jared Sparks, ed., *The Works of Benjamin Franklin . . .* (10 vols., Boston, 1836–40).

Stevens, *Facsimiles* — Benjamin F. Stevens, ed., *Facsimiles of Manuscripts in European Archives Relating*

	to America, 1773–1783 (25 vols., London, 1889–98).
Taylor, *J. Q. Adams Diary*	Robert J. Taylor *et al.,* eds., *Diary of John Quincy Adams* (2 vols. to date, Cambridge, Mass., and London, 1981–).
Trans.	Translator or translated.
Trans.	*Transactions.*
Van Doren, *Franklin*	Carl Van Doren, *Benjamin Franklin* (New York, 1938).
Van Doren, *Franklin-Mecom*	Carl Van Doren, ed., *The Letters of Benjamin Franklin & Jane Mecom* (American Philosophical Society *Memoirs,* XXVII, Princeton, 1950).
Villiers, *Commerce colonial*	Patrick Villiers, *Le Commerce colonial atlantique et la guerre d'indépendance des Etats-Unis d'Amérique, 1778–1783* (New York, 1977).
W&MQ	*William and Mary Quarterly,* first or third series as indicated.
Ward, *War of the Revolution*	Christopher Ward, *The War of the Revolution* (John R. Alden, ed.; 2 vols., New York, 1952).
Waste Book	BF's accounts described above, XXIII, 19.
WF	William Franklin.
Wharton, *Diplomatic Correspondence*	Francis Wharton, ed., *The Revolutionary Diplomatic Correspondence of the United States* (6 vols., Washington, D.C., 1889).
Willcox, *Portrait of a General*	William B. Willcox, *Portrait of a General: Sir Henry Clinton in the War of Independence* (New York, 1964).
WTF	William Temple Franklin.
WTF, *Memoirs*	William Temple Franklin, ed., *Memoirs of the Life and Writings of Benjamin Frank-*

lin, L.L.D., F.R.S., &c . . . (3 vols., 4to, London, 1817–18).

WTF's accounts   Those described above, XXIII, 19.

Yela Utrilla, *España*   Juan F. Yela Utrilla, *España ante la Independencia de los Estados Unidos* (2nd ed.; 2 vols., Lérida, 1925).

Note by the Editors and the Administrative Board

As we noted in volume 23 (pp. xlvi–xlviii), the period of Franklin's mission to France brings with it roughly two and a half times as many documents as those for the remaining seventy years of his life. In the present volume once again we summarize a portion of his incoming correspondence in collective descriptions; they appear in the index under the following headings: commission seekers; emigrants, would-be; favor seekers; and intelligence reports.

A revised statement of textual methodology appeared in volume 28 and is repeated here. The original statement of method is found in the Introduction to the first volume, pp. xxiv–xlvii. The various developments in policy are explained in xv, xxiv; xxi, xxxiv; xxiii, xlvi–xlviii.

Two individuals make their final appearance as editors of *The Papers of Benjamin Franklin*. Marilyn A. Morris resigned to take up a teaching position in Texas. She was an Assistant Editor for three years, researching with a keen eye London newspapers and countless British printed sources for the annotation of letters from Franklin's British correspondents. Her expertise, as well as her wit and good sense, will be greatly missed.

Dorothy W. Bridgwater died at the age of ninety-one as this volume was in press. Her name appeared on the title page of sixteen volumes, on eight as Assistant Editor and on eight more as Associate Editor. She annotated Franklin's correspondence with his family, with his American and British friends, and with the American seamen taken prisoner by the British. Her energy for research is unmatched and her knowledge of the hidden resources of Sterling Memorial Library unsurpassed. Miss Bridgwater witnessed the arrival of William Mason's collection of Frankliniana at Yale in 1935, and from that time until the present she catalogued, tended, and cherished it as no one else could have. Successive generations of editors, the Yale community, and Franklin scholars are in her debt, and we, her friends and colleagues, will miss her deeply.

Introduction

July opened with a bang in Passy when Franklin commemorated the anniversary of American independence with a party on Monday the fifth.[1] Lavish food, patriotic toasts, stirring military music, dancing, and keepsakes (what could be more appropriate than French translations of *The Way to Wealth?*) marked this occasion. The festivity was an announcement of his ambassadorial "coming-of-age," a celebration of his own status and his nation's cause. Franklin's private social gathering, however, had a diplomatic purpose as well: it signaled to American and French guests the continuing importance for the United States of Franco-American friendship and alliance. Of the seven toasts offered, five honored France or the Bourbon family and only two mentioned the Americans. The Independence Day party was the reflection in a private sphere of public politics and international diplomacy. Franklin, in fact, possessed an uncanny knack for blending public and private occasion and for joining the serious business of serving as America's minister plenipotentiary to the Court of France to what the unknowing observer might characterize as a frivolous social whirl.

The July fourth capture of the rich, sugar-producing island of Grenada by Admiral d'Estaing was another occasion for celebration; it was "material and welcome News" indeed.[2] The victory's importance was more psychological than strategic. D'Estaing's record had been less than spectacular up until then: he had failed to destroy Howe's fleet at New York or to take Newport or St. Lucia. Now he finally seemed able to do something right, and in both France and the United States spirits and self-confidence rose. In Philadelphia bells were

1. See our headnote to Toasts at an Independence Day Banquet, printed under July 5.

2. Bordot to BF, Sept. 4. Rumors of the capture circulated in Paris as early as Aug. 10; see item XV in our headnote on the intelligence reports, printed under July 3. William Bingham described the event in his letter of July 20, below.

rung and the city's inhabitants celebrated in the streets.[3] In Paris thanksgiving masses were sung and the admiral's wife opened her estate to the village of Passy for fireworks, a ball, and supper (she was reportedly too shy to attend herself).[4] The naval action also captured the nation's attention in the most ephemeral of spheres—fashion. It precipitated the creation of an array of women's headdresses *à la Grenade*.[5]

In the weeks following the news of the island's fall Franklin received requests from British acquaintances who owned property there for assistance in dealing with the new regulations imposed by the French governor. His old friend William Alexander, whose daughter Mariamne married Franklin's great-nephew Jonathan Williams, Jr., on September 12 (Franklin acted as surrogate father to the groom), was one who sought aid.[6]

Requests like these were a small portion of the paperwork that crossed Franklin's desk at Passy. The American minister had remarked when the three-man commission was dissolved in February that he could handle affairs more efficiently on his own, and he accomplished just that.[7] He claimed to be a bad correspondent whose aversion to writing was increasing,[8] but with the exception of the myriad unsolicited requests for favors that came to him he answered his mail fully and

---

3. RB to BF, Aug. 6, below.

4. The masses were sung at Versailles on Sept. 11 and in Paris the following day: Bachaumont, *Mémoires secrets,* XIV, pp. 176–7. Mme d'Estaing's *fête* is described in the *Jour. de Paris* for Sept. 26.

5. One such hat, on which a ripe pomegranate (*grenade*) was encircled by a crown of laurel, representing victory, was designed and sold by Mademoiselle Saint-Quentin, "Marchande de Modes," rue de Clery: *Jour. de Paris,* Sept. 18. For another example see the illustration facing p. 119. John Paul Jones had also captured the designers' imaginations (as well as Marie-Antoinette's) and "chapeaux à la *Paul Jones*" became the new rage: Métra, *Correspondance secrète,* VIII, 288.

6. See our headnote to William Alexander's letter of Sept. 8, JW's letter of Sept. 13, and BF to Vergennes, Oct. 24. Other acquaintances seeking BF's intervention with the French government for themselves or on behalf of others were Thomas Digges, Thomas Oliver, and Benjamin Vaughan, all on Oct. 8, and Sir Charles William Blunt on Oct. 11.

7. XXVIII, 559.

8. To Lafayette, Aug. 17, below.

promptly. The issues confronting him ranged from such relatively minor ones as handling financial transactions for acquaintances, locating and supplying funds to the father of his old friend Richard Peters, or protesting the commission Jean-Daniel Schweighauser was charging on the delivery of cargoes of tobacco to a more time-consuming assortment of mercantile matters.[9]

As he had done before, Franklin protested that he would have preferred not to be troubled by these concerns.[1] But he dealt with them nonetheless. Among the more complex issues were requests to render judgments on prizes made by American privateers, principally those captured by the *Black Prince*. For several months the American minister resisted ruling on the legitimacy of the prizes, pleading his lack of authority and urging the admiralty courts in French ports to hold the trials that the regulations of September 27, 1778, had established as the proper method for determining the validity of the prizes. But when he learned that as America's representative in France he did possess such powers, he moved swiftly and effectively to issue rulings and to draft the required certificates of condemnation.[2] What sustained Franklin through the effort of managing the details of these maritime matters was the boost their successful resolution gave to one of his pet projects: the exchange of prisoners. For every British seaman taken by an American privateer, Franklin envisioned an American prisoner set free.[3]

Naval affairs were of a vastly different magnitude from mercantile or shipping concerns, and for the former Franklin had infinitely more patience. During the months covered by this

9. See, for example, BF's letters to Richard B. Lloyd and Richard Peters, both of July 12, and to Schweighauser of July 25.

1. See his letter to Schweighauser of Sept. 17 and to John Jay of Oct. 4–[28]. The Marine Committee apologized on Sept. 17, below, for having to divert his attention from affairs of more general importance.

2. BF expressed his reluctance to handle prize cases to Sartine on July 25 and Coffyn on Sept. 8. By Sept. 18 he had learned of his authority; see the certificate condemning prizes, printed under Sept. 18, and BF's letter to Torris, Sept. 19.

3. See, in particular, BF to Marchant, July 4; to Jones, July 8; and to Coffyn, Oct. 10.

volume he was deeply involved with naval matters, working closely with French naval minister Sartine and Le Ray de Chaumont, Franklin's landlord and the intermediary between the ministry and John Paul Jones, to supervise the operations of American captains Jones and Pierre Landais. The ultimate authority for issuing orders to the American captains was the French court, who had, as Franklin pointed out, outfitted and paid for the squadron.[4] Usually Franklin couched his directions to Jones and Landais in terms of deference to Sartine's requests or orders, but occasionally he issued his own commands.[5] Franklin joined readily in the work of directing the cruises, arranging for refitting ships, and providing for the prisoners held on shipboard in the Texel. He seemed buoyed by the successes of the privateers and encouraged by the prospects for Jones's squadron.

Supervising American naval actions in European waters entailed also mediating the disputes of Jones and Landais. From early on in their joint cruise Jones and Landais differed over whether Landais had been placed by Franklin under Jones's orders or operated under his own, a disagreement culminating in early October with Jones's grave charge that Landais had disobeyed orders in the Battle off Flamborough Head and deliberately fired on the *Bonhomme Richard*. At Sartine's directive, Franklin commanded Landais to appear at a hearing in Passy in November to justify his conduct.[6]

During the months covered by this volume Franklin's work load continued to increase. Moreover, in late July his French secretary, Nicolas-Maurice Gellée, quit.[7] Clearly there had been some sort of falling out between Franklin and the young man, and Franklin was left without a full-time French clerk.

4. BF indicated as much to Alexander Gillon on July 5 and to Jones on the 8th, below.

5. BF wrote Landais that if the *Bonhomme Richard* were delayed, he would "direct" him to cruise in the North Sea until the end of September and then proceed to the Texel to await "orders": BF to Landais, July 28, below. The close cooperation between Sartine and BF is evident in the letters to Jones of July 8, 14, and 19.

6. See BF to Jones, July 28, and Jones to BF, Oct. 3. Franklin informed both Jones and Landais on Oct. 15, below, that he had ordered the inquiry.

7. His letter of resignation was dated July 28, below.

Not until the following February did a replacement, Barbeu-Dubourg's nephew L'Air de Lamotte, arrive.[8] One of his first tasks apparently was to prepare a letterbook of the previous months' incoming and outgoing letters. The young and inexperienced secretary, whose English was far from perfect, produced severely flawed copies, often introducing errors of spelling and syntax and altering punctuation and capitalization. Regrettably, Lamotte's letterbook provides the only extant copies of much of Franklin's official correspondence dating from this period, and we publish them as they stand.

Franklin made the best of a bad situation, turning the lack of sufficient secretarial assistance into an opportunity to find new uses for the foundry and print shop he had established the previous spring.[9] From the Passy press over the next five years would issue a variety of official documents: passports in his own name as sole minister; forms for installment payments on loans from the French government; condemnations for prize ships; promissory notes for money he lent escaped prisoners to assist them in returning home; and copies of congressional resolutions. The most important of these documents merited careful design, a unique typeface, and paper of the highest quality. In the summer and fall of 1779 each of these elements took shape as Franklin experimented with the format and wording of the forms, ordered marbled wove paper from London, and consulted with the premier typefounder of Paris on a font of type to be cut exclusively for American government passports in France.[1] The first official Passy imprint—a passport for Thomas Burdy—appears in this volume.[2] The full flowering of these efforts would not appear until more than a year later, when the loan certificates were actually printed on the special imported paper and the preliminary proofs of the Franklin script were ready.

8. He also prepared duplicates of correspondence BF had last sent to America; see our annotation of BF to Lovell, Sept. 30.

9. XXIX, 726.

1. See our annotation to the French loan certificate, the letter from Simon-Pierre Fournier le jeune, both of Sept. 16, and BF to Fizeaux, Grand & Cie., Oct. 29.

2. Burdy's passport, below, is dated Aug. 2.

On one level the renewed enthusiasm for printing sprang from necessity—why copy all those forms by hand?—and from the pure pleasure to be had in printing something like the invitation to the Independence Day party. But on a more important level was the symbolic statement of the serious need to prepare official American documents equal in quality and formality to those produced by the governments of established nations. Just as Franklin's appointment as sole minister elevated him to a higher diplomatic rank than he had held as one member of a three-man commission, the elegantly designed and printed official documents signaled to the French government the seriousness and stature of the new United States government.

We detect in the months covered by this volume a deepening of Franklin's anger toward the British and their conduct of the war. While he continued to work with David Hartley on the prisoner exchange, he refused to be mollified by tentative propositions of peace offered by those who had no authority to treat,[3] and he expressed bitter thoughts of retribution, particularly when he received accounts of British atrocities in America. Jonathan Loring Austin reported on "cruel wanton Barbarities," and the Committee for Foreign Affairs pleaded with Franklin to retaliate for the "Burning of our beautiful Fairfield." The attacks on that and other Connecticut towns, confessed Franklin, "have at length demolish'd all my Moderation."[4]

The most likely prospect for bringing the realities of war home to the English came from a French expeditionary force waiting to invade the Isle of Wight. The scheme took on a particular significance for Franklin when Lafayette invited Temple Franklin to join the expedition as his own aide-de-camp. The Frenchman's letters express affection for the American minister fifty-one years his senior and eagerness to bring Temple along with him. He promised that Temple would be at his side in active duty and "see as much of the service" as he

3. BF to Thomas Digges, July 12, below.
4. Austin to BF, July 12; Committee of Foreign Affairs to BF, July 16; BF to James Lovell, Oct. 17.

did himself.[5] The arrangements were completed down to the smallest detail (Temple would report for duty only after the wedding of Jonathan Williams, Jr.). In mid-September, however, unfavorable winds and sickness of the crews forced the cancellation of the invasion and the return of d'Orvilliers' fleet to Brest.

Franklin continued to captivate the French and they continued to seek his participation in the intellectual and social life of the nation which he called "the civilest . . . upon Earth."[6] Numerous invitations to meetings, dinners, and other social gatherings attest to the demand for his presence, although the record often fails to reveal whether he attended. The occasions include a convocation at the Collège Mazarin to hear a dissertation on electricity dedicated to him; his masonic lodge's *fête académique;* the unveiling of H. Sykes's electrical machine; a meeting of the Société royale de médecine; a gathering of commissioners of the Académie des sciences to investigate Marat's experiments; a charity sermon sponsored by Madame Le Veillard and the curé of the parish church of Passy; and dinner with the botanist Denis-Claude Cochin to view his "most curious and uncommon plants."[7] In September Franklin was appointed by the Académie des sciences to a committee charged with inspecting the abbé Rochon's château La Muette to settle a dispute between the abbé and Le Roy over the lightning rod installed there.[8]

His circle of intimate friends remained the core of Franklin's social life. Madame Brillon wrote to him hardly at all in the four months covered by this volume (a temporary retreat; she will resume her frequent letters in the coming month), but Pierre-Jean-Georges Cabanis served as go-between for Franklin and the coy and mildly flirtatious Madame Helvétius, cen-

5. Lafayette extended the invitation for WTF to serve in the expeditionary army on Aug. 29, and BF forwarded the suggestion to Vergennes on the 31st, both below.

6. BF to Elizabeth Partridge, Oct. 11.

7. See Cadet de Vaux's letter of July 17 and the invitations extended by the abbé du Rouzeau [before Aug. 18]; by Sykes on Aug. 20; by Vicq d'Azyr on Aug. 21; by Marat on Aug. 22; by Clément Noguères and Mme Le Veillard [before Sept. 5]; and by Barbeu-Dubourg on Sept. 15.

8. *Procès-verbaux,* tome 98, fol. 276.

ter of a witty, vivacious circle nicknamed the "Académie d'Auteuil." The abbé Morellet enlivened their gatherings, singing in French Franklin's favorite Scottish ballads while the Doctor accompanied him on the glass armonica. For a dinner in honor of Franklin held sometime around Independence Day, the abbé toasted him in a highly complimentary song of his own composition with a heady refrain: "Le verre en main / Chantons nôtre Benjamin."[9]

From Philadelphia Franklin received from friends and family reports of parties and high living that followed the city's liberation (in June, 1778) from nine difficult months of British occupation. Sarah Bache declared that the winter of 1778–79 had been a "Season of Triumph" for the Whigs (patriots). The city took on an atmosphere of gaiety and celebration: balls, subscription assemblies, entertainments for French minister Conrad-Alexandre Gérard (who was exceedingly well-liked by Franklin's family) amused Philadelphia's social elite.[1] Underlying the appearance of wealth and well-being was the reality of sharply escalating prices and scarcity of food and other necessities that markedly affected the lives of the Baches and all other Philadelphia residents. For artisans, shopkeepers, and the laboring poor, the doubling and tripling of commodity prices was devastating. Popularly elected committees sought to arrest the inflationary spiral and redirect the distribution of goods by controlling markets and regulating prices. Efforts at economic change and political reform merged into what Thomas Bond described as "a great Revolution among us."[2]

Franklin's understanding of American economic conditions was at best partial. He had severely chided his daughter in June for desiring pins and feathers from Paris, enjoining her to practice frugality; her September response offers us a strik-

9. See BF and Mme Helvétius: An Exchange, printed at the end of August; BF to Cabanis, Sept. 19; and Morellet's Song in Honor of Franklin, c. July 5.

1. Sarah Bache to BF, Sept. 14.

2. Bond's letter is dated Sept. 24. The regulation of prices in Boston is discussed by Peter Collas on Oct. 12. Gourlade and Moylan on Sept. 6 reported efforts of the states to reduce prices on imported goods and domestic produce. See our annotation to their letter.

ing view of the domestic economy of a Philadelphia household in wartime.[3] Whereas the father held up a vision of republican economy based on industry, virtue, and simplicity, she recounted the difficulty in keeping up her spirits while she was "being drove about from place to place" and her worries about the winter approaching with "so many horrors." She confided to Temple that her patience, like her linen, was "quite wore out."[4]

To Franklin, however, the times called for national sacrifice. He believed that Americans were spending their money on tea and on "Gewgaws & Superfluities" when he was laboring to fill Congress' orders for military supplies, negotiating a loan from the French government, and working diligently to free as many American prisoners as possible.[5]

Perhaps Franklin had been away from Philadelphia too long. His home was now in France; there he understood life and there he was honored and adored. The most dramatic evidence of the recognition accorded this "citoyen vertüeux," as his friend the chevalier de Kéralio styled him, was the Salon of 1779, which opened on August 25.[6] While the American dignitary had been represented at the Salon of 1777 by Jean-Jacques Caffiéri's terra cotta bust, in 1779 he was a commanding presence. Three images of Franklin in three media were on display: an engraving by Louis-Jacques Cathelin after Anne-Rosalie Filleul's painting; a terra cotta bust by Jean-Antoine Houdon; and an oil painting by Joseph-Siffrède Duplessis, the leading portraitist of the French court.[7]

3. XXIX, 613–15. The response is her letter of Sept. 14, cited above.
4. Sarah Bache to WTF, Sept. 16.
5. BF to Jay, Oct. 4–[28].
6. Kéralio to BF, Oct. 17. For the opening of the Salon see the *Jour. de Paris* of Aug. 25, and for a discussion of the place of that biennial exhibition in eighteenth-century public life see Thomas E. Crow, *Painters and Public Life in Eighteenth-Century Paris* (New Haven and London, 1985), pp. 1–22 and *passim*. Sellers, *Franklin in Portraiture*, discusses the Salon of 1779 on pp. . 123–7.
7. The Duplessis portrait is the frontispiece of vol. 1 of this edition; the Caffiéri bust is reproduced in vol. 25, facing p. 266; the Cathelin engraving is the frontispiece of vol. 29, and the Houdon bust that of the present volume. For contemporary comments on the representations of BF on ex-

The historical tableaux and classical themes that dominated the Salon were intended to inspire wisdom, strength, and virtue. Philosopher of the enlightenment, defender of liberty against tyranny, statesman of the new world, and American "citoyen vertüeux," Franklin was the ideal representation of these classical themes translated into contemporary idiom. He was virtue, not in the guise of a Roman soldier but in the style of a simple man (VIR) in a plain fur collar. Franklin was heroic, but he was also human: Cathelin does not flinch from recording the moles on his subject's face.[8]

If the Salon was the most dramatic indication of the height to which Franklin's reputation had risen, the production and reproduction of prints, sculptures, miniatures, medallions, snuffboxes, and other keepsakes were the visible signs of the breadth his popularity had reached. The Franklin image, carefully cultivated during the almost three years that he had been in France, was almost universally known there. The "Paintings, Busto's, Medals & Prints" rendered his face "now almost as well known as that of the Moon," as he wrote to his sister Jane.[9] Like his Independence Day celebration, they served a public purpose. These images of Franklin demonstrated the strength and wisdom of the ages and the promise of the new world. They personified confidence and success, not simply in Franklin but for the American cause.

---

hibit see the *Jour. de Paris,* Sept. 27, which remarked that Houdon's bust of BF was recognizable at a glance. Bachaumont, *Mémoires secrets* echoed the compliments, and referred to Franklin as "législateur du nouveau monde": XIII, 230.

8. Sellers, *Franklin in Portraiture,* p. 123.

9. To Jane Mecom, Oct. 25.

Chronology

July 4: D'Estaing captures Grenada.

July 5: BF's Independence Day celebration.

July 6: Naval battle of Grenada.

c. July 13–c. September 3: C.G.F. Dumas visits Passy.

July 15: BF attends dissertation on electricity at Collège Mazarin.

July 15–25: Second cruise of the privateer *Black Prince*.

July 16: Congress sends BF list of supplies to be requested from French government. Gen. Anthony Wayne recaptures Stony Point on the Hudson.

c. July 20: *Milford* arrives at Nantes with second group of American prisoners from Britain.

July 23: Cadiz fleet arrives at rendezvous with combined fleet.

August 2–3: La Luzerne, JA arrive in Boston area.

August 14: Destruction of American fleet at Penobscot Bay.

August 14–October 3: Cruise of John Paul Jones's squadron.

August 15–23: Third cruise of the *Black Prince*.

August 16: Combined fleet in sight of Plymouth.

August 18: Installation of Houdon's bust of BF at Nine Sisters' *Séance académique*.

August 19: Maj. Henry Lee raids Paulus Hook, N.J.

August 24: WTF sent to Le Havre with Lafayette's sword.

August 25: Opening of the 1779 Salon, Académie royale de peinture et de sculpture.

September 3: D'Orvilliers' fleet recalled to port.

September 4: BF visits Bicêtre and La Salpetrière prisons; BF appointed to committee of Académie des sciences to investigate scientific dispute between Le Roy, abbé Rochon.

September 4–24: Fourth cruise of the *Black Prince*.

September 11–12: D'Estaing begins landing troops near Savannah.

September 12: jw and Mariamne Alexander are married.

September 16: BF receives 250,000 *l.t.* from French government as second of four loan installments.

September 21: La Luzerne arrives in Philadelphia.

September 23–24: Beginning of French/American siege of Savannah.

September 23 or 24: Battle off Flamborough Head; Jones's squadron captures *Serapis, Countess of Scarborough.*

September 27: Jay elected minister to the court of Spain; JA elected peace commissioner.

September 28: Samuel Huntington succeeds Jay as president of Congress.

September 29: John Laurens elected BF's secretary; Joshua Johnson elected commissioner to examine BF's accounts.

October 4: BF receives third loan installment from French government.

October 9: D'Estaing's unsuccessful assault on British defenses of Savannah.

October 15: BF orders Landais to Paris for inquest.

October 20: French at Savannah return to ships.

October 21: Congress selects Henry Laurens to negotiate a loan in the Netherlands.

October 25: British evacuate Newport, R.I.

October 26: Jay, Gérard sail for Europe on the *Confederacy.*

THE PAPERS OF

BENJAMIN FRANKLIN

VOLUME 30

July 1 through October 31, 1779

Editorial Note on Franklin's Accounts

Of the accounts discussed throughout the French period, the following still apply: VI, XII, XIII, XVI, XVII, XIX, XXI–XXIII. We offer here a summary of entries which have not found a place elsewhere in our annotation, but which provide insights into Franklin's private and public life during the course of this volume.

Account VI (XXIII, 21) records an Oct. 13 payment of 32 *l.t.* for Franklin's subscription to the *Mercure de France*.

Account XVI (Cash Book, XXVI, 3). The predominant entries for this period are the recurring expenses of running the foundry. It was headed by Hémery, whose weekly salary amounted to 24 *l.t.* Hémery was assisted by Beauville (at 12 *l.t.* per week), plus a woman and a boy at 3 *l.t.* each. Disbursements were made for lead, blankets, and wood. On July 28, Franklin purchased 162 *l.t.*'s worth of punches from Fagnion[1] and on September 26 he paid Fagnion 156 *l.t.* for punches and matrices.

A number of entries were marked C for charity. Some of those sums were for prisoners or former prisoners: on July 2, 48 *l.t.* went to Daniel Duchemin, "Officer who has been a Prisoner";[2] others for people in distress: 72 *l.t.* were advanced on August 2 to "Mr Stewart a young Gentleman of Baltimore in want of Money to get home"; a Polish *abbé* received 24 *l.t.* on August 21 while "Un pauvre Matelot François-Americain" got 24. An undisclosed sum was contributed on September 26 to the "Collector for the Sufferers by Fire." On October 24, "M. Mante, an Author in Prison"[3] received 24 *l.t.*

Franklin's personal expenditures included gratuities at the baths, including eau de Cologne, and to Vergennes' messenger on August 21. His wardrobe cost him 43 *l.t.* paid to Mme Grand for repairing his shirts and 30 *l.t.* to Mlle Bonnefoy "to buy Stuff for my Bedgown."

1. Jean-Charles Fagnion (Fagnon), Engraver of the *Imprimerie royale* since 1774: Marius Audin, *Les Livrets typographiques des fonderies françaises créées avant 1800* (Paris, 1933), pp. 29, 31. BF would continue to buy punches and matrices from him through the spring of 1780, and in April of that year purchased from him two printing presses. Three autograph visiting cards are at the APS: "Mr Fagnion graveur du Roi Rue Jeantizon en fasse de Lotelle d'espagne prais st germain loxerois a paris."

2. See XXIX, 319–20.

3. This was not the first time BF had given him money; see XXIX, 686n. See also Claude-Anne Lopez, "Benjamin Franklin and William Dodd: A New Look at an Old Cause Célèbre," APS *Proc.*, CXXIX (1985), 260–7.

And finally there was, on July 23, a payment of 3 *l.t.* "for returning Flore," presumably a house pet.

Account XXII (xxviii, 4). Franklin's personal account with F. Grand has few entries for this period. On July 16 he received five months' worth of dividends on the eight shares of the Caisse d'Escompte that he had purchased on February 19, *i.e.,* a sum of 680 *l.t.* On August 30 he bought two more of those shares for 6728.8.0 *l.t.*

Account XXIII (xxix, 3). In addition to the items mentioned elsewhere in this volume there are the customary household expenses: payments to Fremont the *maître d'hôtel,* expenses for the menservants François and Arbelot, 141.10.0 *l.t.* for Gombeau the carpenter's account, and 240 *l.t.* for Brunel the carpenter. On August 11 Franklin paid 33 *l.t.* to Ruault for books.

From Rodolphe-Ferdinand Grand

AL: American Philosophical Society

ce 1 Juillet [1779?][4]

Pour Celebrer LIndependance il faut etre Independant Et la mauvaise Etoille de Mr. Grand ne lui permet pas de l'etre, par des Engagemens pour ce jour la, qu'il ne lui est pas possible de rompre. Il prie monsieur Le Docteur Franklin, d'en agreer touts ses regrets, Et d'etre persuadé qu'il ne la Celebrera pas moins, in petto.

Addressed: a monsieur / Monsieur Le Docteur / Franklin / a Passy—

From John Hay, Jr.[5]

ALS: American Philosophical Society

Sir   1779 July 1st. Passy
   After the trouble already given to Your Excellency You may perhaps think it extraordinary to receive more from the same quarter— What I neglected mentioning to You when I waited on Your Excellency this morning was the strong desire the Concerned (in the expedition to which You have granted Your protection) have to know Your Excellency's opinion of the American Port in their entrance to which they would be least subjected to the interruption of Brittish Cruizers— It is in general the intention of the concerned to settle in Pensylvania but if in their run for the Delaware more danger was to be apprehended they would rather make any other Port to the north or South of it.

4. 1779 is the earliest possible year. There was, so far as we know, no public celebration in France of American Independence Day in 1777 and Grand, the commissioners' banker, did attend their party in 1778: Butterfield, *John Adams Diary,* II, 317. In late June, 1779, BF sent out printed invitations to Independence Day festivities to be held on Monday, July 5: XXIX, 726–7.

5. One of the group of Irish who wanted to emigrate to America, led by Jesse Taylor. Having received BF's encouragement but afraid to entrust a list of their names to the post, they sent Hay to deliver the list and to bring back a passport: XXIX, 158, 304–7. The passport is discussed in the annotation to his next letter, July 6.

Your Excellency's advice on this point is earnestly requested before I leave Passy which will be early tomorrow.

But if I depart before Your Excellency's leisure will permit You to answer this Your Excellency's note directed to Mr Nathaniel Wilson to care of Madam the Widow of Maths: Jaques at Rotterdam will come safe to the hand of Sir Yr. Excellency's most obedt: Servt: JOHN HAY.

Addressed: To / His Excy: Doctor Franklin / Passy.

Notation: Jonh Ray

From John Paul Jones

ALS: American Philosophical Society; AL (draft): National Archives; copies: Library of Congress, United States Naval Academy

On board the Bon homme Richard at Anchor
under the Isle of Groa [Groix] off L'Orient
Honored and dear Sir,   July 1st. 1779.

On the 19th. Ulto. the American Squadron under my command, consisting of the Bon homme Richard of 42 Guns, the Alliance of 36 Guns, the Pallas of 30 Guns, the Cerf of 18 Guns and the Vengeance of 12 Guns, sailed from hence with a Convoy of Merchant Ships and Transports with Troops &c. bound to the different Ports and Garrisons between this place and Bordeaux.— On the evening of the day following I had the Satisfaction to see the latter part of the Convoy safe within the Entrance of the River of Bordeaux; the rest having been safe escorted into the entrance of Nantes & Rochefort &c.— But at the preceding Midnight, while the Squadron & Convoy was laying too off the Isle Dieu the Bon homme Richard and Alliance got foul of one another and carried away the Head and Cutwater Spritsail Yard & Jib Boom of the former, with the Mizen Mast of the latter—fortunately however neither of the Ships received any damage in the Hull, nor have since been leaky.[6]

6. Capt. Pierre Landais of the Continental frigate *Alliance* blamed the collision on Jones's changing course without signaling. According to Landais'

In the evening of the 21st., Steering to the Westward from the entrance of Bordeaux, I sent the Cerf to Reconnoitre two Sail which appeared in the SW Quarter, and Captain Varage was so ardent in the pursuit that he had lost Sight of the Squadron next morning; and I am now told that he had a Warm Engagement with one of them a Sloop of 14 Guns, which he took, but was obliged to abandon on the approch of another Enemy of Superior Force. The Action lasted an hour and half and several Men were killed and wounded on board the Cerf. That Cutter is now refitting at L'Orient.— On the 22d. we had a rencounter with three Ships of War:— They were to Windward and bore down in a Line Abreast for some time; but seeing that we were prepared to receive them they hauled by the Wind, and by carrying a pressed Sail got clear in spite of our utmost endeavours to bring them to Action.— On the 26th. in the Night, it being squally with thick weather and Rain, we lost company with the Alliance and the Pallace.— I am at present unable to say where the blame lays, either with respect to this accident[7] or that of getting foul of the Alliance:— Both will be the subject of Courts of inquiry when the two Ships arrive, which I expect every Hour, and shall then communicate to you a more particular Account.— I gave the Ships a Rendezvous off the Penmark Rocks, but did not meet them there.

I anchored here yesterday at Noon, having had a Rencounter the Night before with two of the Enemies Ships of War in the offing in sight of this Island and of Belle Isle:— previous to this rencounter I had given the Vengeance leave to make the best of his way to this Road, so that the Enemy found me alone in a place where I had no expectation of a Hostile Visit.— They appeared for some time very earnest to Engage; but at last their Courage failed.— They Fled with precipita-

---

later testimony Capt. Denis-Nicolas Cottineau de Kerloguen of the frigate *Pallas* subsequently said that Jones was unfit to command a squadron: Landais, *Memorial,* pp. 19–21.

7. Landais said the separation occurred as a result of Jones's failure to signal his squadron: Landais, *Memorial,* p. 20. For further discussion of the cruise see xxix, 709n, and Schaeper, *Battle off Flamborough Head,* pp. 36–8.

tion, and to my great mortification, outsailed the Bon homme Richard and got clear.— I had however a flattering proof of the Marshal Spirit of my Crew, and I am confident that had I been able to get between the two Enemies, which was my intention, we should have beaten them both together.

In the course of this little Cruise I have endeavoured as much as possible to come up to the wishes of the King as communicated to me the 15th. of June in a Copy of a letter from M. De Sartine to M. De Chaumont.—[8] I have traversed the "Golphe de Gascogne" over and over both within and without soundings, from half a Degree to the southward of the entrance of Bordeaux to the Raz Passage in sight of Brest. I have fallen in with and chased various other Ships & Vessels which I believe were Enemies, but all such as I have been able to overtake have proved either Dutch Spanish or other nuteral Property.— Tho I am much concerned at the Seperation of the Ships, yet that circumstance is not unfavorable to the Object of the Cruise, and they have a better chance to meet with the Enemies Cruisers by being Seperate than together.

This Ship wants at least Fifty Tons of Ballast, and, unfortunately for me, is by no means equal to the account which I have had of her Sailing. Even the Pallas sails faster.

The Wind does not at present admit of entering the Port (Port Louis) therefore should it continue unfavorable, unless I find that the damage can in three or four days be repaired here, I shall in the meantime go out and see what passes in the offing.— If the Court is yet disposed to give me the Ship which they at first offered,[9] I think it possible, in the present situation of affairs, to make a Useful and Honorable Cruise that way with the force now under my Command, and after-

8. Chaumont, BF's landlord in Passy, was the liaison between Jones and French Naval Minister Sartine: XXIX, 240n. Jones was also receiving orders from Sartine via Antoine-Jean-Marie de Thévenard, the port commandant at Lorient: Charles H. Lincoln, comp., *A Calendar of John Paul Jones Manuscripts in the Library of Congress* (Washington, D.C., 1903), p. 90.

9. Probably the frigate *Indien* at Amsterdam, whose command had been promised to him (XXVI, 558); she had been built for the commissioners but sold to the French government: XXV, 208–9. Sartine had been seeking in vain to devise a way to bring her to France: Jan. 29, 1779, to the duc de La Vauguyon, the French ambassador to the Netherlands (AAE).

wards to bring that Ship out with the Crew I now have.— I am ready to enter with Cheerfulness upon any Plan or Service that is consonant with the Common interest and meets with your approbation; and if I fail it shall not be for want of attempting to Succeed where there appears an opening.

I am ever with sentiments of greatful Esteem & real Affection Dear Sir, Your very obliged Friend & most humble Servant   JNO P JONES

N.B. You will if you please communicate the account in this letter to M. De Sartine and M De Chaumont.

His Excellency Doctor Franklin

Notation: P. Jones isle de Groa 1st juillet 1779.

From Jonathan Williams, Jr.

ALS: American Philosophical Society; copy: Yale University Library

Dear & hond Sir.   Nantes July 1. 1779.

My Trial comes on tomorrow at 9 oClock.— As your Letter impowering these Gentlemen to examine my accot was addressed to all, and as according to the old saying "what ought to be taken care of by many is generaly taking care of by nobody" I apprehend this Letter is either mislaid, or perhaps left in the Hands of some one of the Gentlemen who are gone. I therefore request you to send me by return of post a Copy of this Letter, signed by you so that if these Gentlemen should have occasion to look at their authority, I may prevent any Delay by having it ready to produce.— You will please to observe that it is the second Letter to the second Sett of Gentlemen that I mean.—[1]

I beg your pardon for troubling you, perhaps it may be useless, but I take the precaution to prevent even the possibility of delay.—

---

1. Because of Arthur Lee's accusations of misconduct, JW's accounts were to be audited by a group of merchants at Nantes. BF's directive to them, dated April 8, is above, XXIX, 280–1.

I am ever most dutifully & affectionately Yours

J WILLIAMS J

The Hon Doctor Franklin.

Notation: Williams Jona. July 1. 1779.

From John Bondfield

ALS: American Philosophical Society

Sir   Bordeaux 2 July 1779

Mr Dhorman of Lisbon whose distinguish'd conduct at that City in favor of America and americans from whom I have received many personal accounts by them who stand indebted to his services,[2] having the honor of receiving his vissit in his road thro' this City for Paris I take the liberty of giving him the present to serve him as an introduction to your Excellence. I am informd his Conections are of such as entitles to every regard, his avowd principles and conduct have occationally drawn attention from the Governing powers of that Kingdom with whom by report he stands much considered. I have the Honor to be with due respect Sir your most Obedient Humble Servant   JOHN BONDFIELD

His Exellency Benj Franklin

From John G. Frazer[3]

ALS: American Philosophical Society

Sir,   Bordeaux, 2d. July 1779—

Inclosed is a Letter I recd from Mr. Geo: Anderson a young Gentleman of Virginia who was taken in a Vessell of his own by an English cruizer & carried into Lisbon, where he now is, at the House of Mr. Arnold Henry Dohrman the bearer of this, and who will have the Honour of delivering it to you himself.[4]

---

2. For the assistance rendered unfortunate Americans by the merchant Arnold Henry Dohrman see XXVI, 211; XXVII, 451; XXVIII, 545–8; XXIX, 682.

3. Six days earlier the former army officer had forwarded a letter from Cradock Taylor, an American prisoner in Aix: XXIX, 743–4.

4. Anderson himself had already written in praise of Dohrman: XXVIII, 545–9.

This Gentleman has been a particular Friend to all our unfortunate Countrymen that have been taken & carried into
Lisbon and still continues so to be—he is a Man of considerable Fortune, & connections, in that Country—and is very
capable of giving you any information respecting it—his in-
tegerity you may depend upon, every civillity shewn him by
you (which he merits) will be acknowledged as the greatest
Honour done Yr. Most Obt. & Mo. Hbl. Servt.

JNO. G. FRAZER

Addressed: His Excellency / Benjamin Franklin Esqr. / Plenipotentiary to the / United States of America / at Passy near /
Paris, / Mr. Dohrman

From Gourlade & Moylan

ALS:[5] American Philosophical Society

Honord Sir   L'Orient 2d July 1779
We beg leave to refer you to the inclosed letter from Cap:
Jones respecting the affaires of his fleet[6] and we join to this
extract from a letter we this day recd from Cap: John Green,
for your perusal.[7] We are respectfully Hond. Sir Your most
obt. & most humble Sts   GOURLADE & MOYLAN

The Honble. Doctor Franklin.

Notation: Gourlade et Moylan L'Orient 2. juillet 1779.

5. In the hand of James Moylan, an American merchant who in late 1778
had become a business partner of the Frenchman Jacques-Alexandre Gourlade; see XXVIII, 209n.

6. Above, July 1.

7. That extract, dated June 25, contained nearly the same information as
Green had written to BF on the same date (XXIX, 737–8). But to Gourlade
& Moylan, Green also included an account of British forces in New York,
which, he claimed, "dont exceed 7000." This was a considerable underesti-
mate; on May 1 more than twice this number were fit for duty: Mackesy,
War for America, p. 270.

From James Hopkins and James Corrick

ALS: American Philosophical Society

Vitré in Bretagne
May it Please your Excellency   July 2nd: 1779—
    We the underwritten being Natives of America (hearing there are Ships belonging to the united States at Nantes and bound for America) Pettiton your Excellency that you would gett us the Liberty to go in one of those Vessells in order for our proceeding to America and as we are able to engage in any office or Station onboard a Ship we hope your excellency will gett us the Liberty to proceed. We are on Parole Therefore it is not of Necessity but Volontarily So in expectation of your Excellency's Answer we Remain Your Excellency's devoted Servants   JAMES HOPKINS
                                        JAMES CORRICK

May it Please your Excellency to Direct for one of us on Parole Vitré in Bretagne.

Addressed: To his Excellency / Benjamin Franklin Esqr / Plenipotentiary from the / United States of America at / the Court of Versailles / Paris

Notation: Corrick James July 2d. 1779.—

From John Paul Jones
ALS: American Philosophical Society

Honored & dear Sir,   L'Orient July 2d 1779.
    I have the honor to acquaint you that this day arrived the Alliance & Pallas and joined me in the Road of Groa with a Brigantine belonging to Dublin and bound homewards from Bordeaux with a Cargo of Wine & Brandy.—[8] About noon the Wind changed and we have availed ourselves of the Opportunity to enter the Port. The Bon homme Richard & the Alliance are now at Anchor before L'Orient; the Pallas and the Vengeance remain at Port Louis neither of them having re-

---

8. The prize was the British ship *Three Friends,* which the *Alliance* captured on June 28: Landais, *Memorial,* p. 20.

ceived damage. This Prize which Captain Landais has taken, I cannot take upon me to release, tho had I been present when the Vessel was met with I believe I should have suffered her to proceed.— They have produced a passport signed by M. De Sartine in Octr. last for one Voyage only—but it is imagined that they have made more than one Voyage in that time— besides Captain Landais thinks the Prize is good because the Master can produce no passport from you.—[9] All that I have done in the matter is I have sent my Purser in company with the Purser of the Alliance to seal up every thing on Board, that in case the Vessel should be set at liberty they may not be able to say they have been plundered—or if the Prize be good there may be no Embezzlement.— I find it the General Opinion here that the Prize is good—but nothing shall be done in the matter further without your orders. Captain Landais is Very Urgent to have his Ship Careened which they tell me can be compleated in six days inclusive of the time for Loading and Unloading. I cannot oppose this as it is absolutely necessary that the Bottom of a Cruising Ship should be clean and as I find no Orders lodged for my future Government— The Bottom of the Bon homme Richard is also foul but I shall not now attempt to heave Down Unless the Surveyers should find it necessary before the damage of the Cutwater can be repaired.— I at present hope to be quite ready for Sea with each of the Vessels when your answer becomes due.— To Morrow at Day Break the Bon homme Richard's damages will be Surveyed and not an hour shall be lost in repairing them.

I see that both the Captains of the Pallas and the Vengeance have received letters from Paris Indorsed "De Sartine" on the Cover—but I do not yet know whither these letters are or are not Orders from the Minister.

I have the honor to be with Sentiments of real Affection Dear Sir Your very obliged Friend and most humble Servant

JNO P JONES

His Excellency Doctor Franklin.

---

9. Jones sent Landais a brief note approving of his conduct and ordering the prize sent into Lorient and placed under the care of Gourlade & Moylan: Bradford, *Jones Papers,* reel 4, nos. 663–4.

Addressed: His Excellency / Doctor Franklin / American Ambassador at the Court / of France / at his Hôtel at Passy / near Paris

Notation: Capt. Jones July 2. 79

From Richard Bennett Lloyd

ALS: American Philosophical Society

Dear Sir,   London 2d. July 1779—

I am somewhat distressed, as I begin to be fearful I shall be too troublesome—but as the business I wrote to you upon about three weeks or a month ago[1] is of such consequence, as to determine my remaining in Europe, or quitting it very soon—I therefore pray for the favour of your answer as soon as you conveniently can— and I flatter myself you will pardon the liberty I take, as you are the only person I know, who can put me into a road to get my remittances in the manner my Friends in America have thought on—. My Correspondent (Monsieur Girardot at Paris) informs me he sent my letter to you at Passy and I hope it got safe to your hands— In that letter I enclosed two copies of Letters I have received from Maryland—. It will make me very happy to hear that you enjoy the same good state of health as you had last Summer— and I am, with Mrs. Lloyd's and my best respects, your obliged and very obt. humble Servant   RICHARD B. LLOYD

Addressed: A Monsieur / Monsieur Franklin / à / Passy / hotel Colbert

Notations: R.B. LLoyd Londres 2. juillet 1779. / hotel Colbert

1. He had written on June 11, forwarding letters from his uncle and brother about remitting funds to him through bills of exchange: XXIX, 674. Lloyd wrote to WTF on July 15 that he was distressed at having received no reply to that letter, which M. Girardot informed him had been safely delivered. His situation was critical, and he entreated WTF to show his letter to his grandfather. APS.

From Antonio Francesco Salucci & fils

ALS: American Philosophical Society

Sir   Leghorn The 2 July 1779

We have been very unhappy in our Expedition into North America.[2] Our Captain Joseph Bettoja who Comanded our Tuscan Ship Called—La Prosperità—as your Excellency is Acquainted, has been Taken, near the Baye of Cheaspeak on the 20. April Last by two Sloops of War of New York, Where they pretend to have the Ship, and the Cargo confiscated. This Misfortune Which has been very Sensible to us, does not discourage Us from going on in this Comerce As Soon as the General Peace Shall be established,[3] and Since we Think it not very far, as Well as, the General Independency of The Unite Provinces, and That the first Expeditions Shall be the happiest, We humble beg Your Excellency to be So Kind, as to Acquaint us with it at its Time, in order to take the best of it, and restore our Losses. As our unhappy Captn. Bettoja Writes Us on The 4th: May from New York, that he proposed to pass in Some of The Unite Provinces, to take there Some acquintances, We dare to beg Your Excellency, to favour his deplorable Situation Sending him the inclose Letters, and to have him recomanded expecially in Virginia by Some Person of Authority, Who may help, and Secour him, and We profess, of Such a Grace, the most perfect acknowledgment to Your Excellency, and We will furnish the necessary Expences at any advice of it. We entreat your Excellency of this Kindness With the Strongest force we may, and we are Convinced, that his Royal Highness our Souverain[4] will Shew on this, his Royal Satisfaction.

2. On March 2 they had sent *La Prosperità,* in high hopes and with BF's blessing, from Cadiz: XXIX, 156, 250–1.

3. Indeed they did try again after the end of hostilities, sending two ships to Philadelphia in the spring of 1783, as attested by their letters of March 7 and June 6, 1783. APS.

4. Leopold, grand duke of Tuscany.

We are with The most humble respect Of Your Excellency Your most H & m O. Servants   ANTI: FRANS: SALUCCI & SON

Notation: Salucci & son Anti. Frans. 2. July 1779.

From John Torris

ALS: American Philosophical Society

Sir   Dunkerque 2d. July 1779.

The Letter I did myself the honnour to write your Excellency the 30th. ulto. Conveyd the Particulars of the Cruise of the Black Prince Cutter.[5] Her Cap. Mr. Stephen marchant, Sends me, recd. per yesterday mail, The List of his Prisonners deliverd in Morlaix, & also, a List of 21, equal number, of his men on Board of the 6 Prises, which, he has all reason to think, are retaken by the English Frigat that Chased them, & was Cruising Close to the French shore, where these Prises were Sent.[6] I Send your Excellency the Original Letter, & I warmly join my request for the Exchange therein mentionned, hoping your Excellency, guided by your Justice, will employ her generous offices to Procure this Exchange, as Soon as Possible, & prevail on the Minister of the French Navey, to order Immediatly all assistance be given in Morlaix, or Brest, where she Likely will always send her Prises, to grant all assistance to the good, honest, & Brave People of this Privateer the Black Prince, either to Procure men to Continue her Prosperous & finely begone Cruise, & to order some Kings ships to Cruise on the Coast, to Protect her & her Success, & deffend the French Shore from the attempt & arm done by our too Bold Ennemy.

5. XXIX, 783. Torris was part owner of the privateer cutter, which in June had made the first of her seven cruises. Details of these cruises are provided in Clark, *Ben Franklin's Privateers.*

6. Marchant had sent BF a similar list, naming both the prisoners he had captured and his own crewmen who had been captured by the British while manning the *Black Prince*'s prizes: XXIX, 721–2. BF had provided him with an American commission in hopes he would be able to capture prisoners to exchange for the American sailors being held at Portsmouth and Plymouth: XXIX, 495–6, 571–2.

I beg the favour of your Excellency to send your orders & account of your success to the destressed Cap. Stephen Marchant.

I am with respect Sir your most obedient most humbel Servant   J Torris

Notation: Mr. Torris July 2. 1779

From Jonathan Williams, Jr.

ALS: American Philosophical Society; copy: Yale University Library

Dear & honoured Sir.   Nantes July 2. 1779.

My Examination is begun & goes on very well, my Judges are compleat Merchants and their apparent Satisfaction pleases me. We have found the Letter I wrote you for last Post so you need not trouble yourself about it, but as you have incoporated Mr. Lees Answer to your desire, that he would "support his accusations, or give his further Reasons if he has any", in a private Letter to me, please to send me down either Mr. Lees original Letter or an attested Copy of it that it may be received as a piece of authority to remain with my Judges. This Letter must be about the beginning of last April.[7]

The Gentlemen have concluded to give Mr Lee Information that they are sitting, so as to leave no Excuse for hereafter saying he had not an Opportunity of supporting his Charges; the Letter will probably be sent to you, if so please to send it to Mr Lee by some person to put it into his own hand and let that Person return a certificate of its delivery specifiing the Day the hour & the place.[8] I shall give you a line every Post to let you know how affairs go on, but you may be very easy on my Account, for I shall come out of the Trial without a Stain, and I trust with honour & applause. I am ever with the greatest Respect Your dutifull & affectionate Kinsman

JONA WILLIAMS J

7. Lee to BF, XXIX, 132–4; BF to JW, XXIX, 284.
8. On July 6, at the request of the Gentlemen, JW forwarded to BF their letter to Lee. JW's cover letter is at the APS.

Mr Schweighauser has in writing declined sitting, and given his Health for an Excuse.— As this is the Case the number is reduced to four,[9] & least an Umpire should be wanted I have desired the Gentn. previously to name one & they have chosen Commodore Gillon, I shall therefore be obliged to you to give a Letter to them requesting them to add Commodore Gillon to the Number, which will give me the advantage of his Signature; otherwise I can't have it unless there is an Occasion for an Umpire. In expectation of this I shall desire the Commodore to sit during the whole examination. Please to answer by return of Post for time is precious to me now.

Notation: Williams Jona. July 2. 1779.

From Jacques Barbeu-Dubourg

AL: American Philosophical Society

Paris 3th. July 1779

Dr. Dubourg presents his dutifull civilities to his Excellency, no man will celebrate more gladly next Monday the anniversary of the Declaration of American Independency. He will bring with him his Refutation of the Morals of Chess, in order of submitt this little Piece to the judgment of his dear and respectable Master.

Addressed: A S.E. / M Le Docteur franklin / Ministre Plenipotentiaire / des Etats unis de l'Amerique / A Passy

Notation: Dubourg

---

9. The four merchants were Joshua Johnson, Jonathan Nesbitt, James Cuming, and Joseph Gridley: XXIX, 779n.

From Barbeu-Dubourg: Another Morals of Chess

AD (draft): American Philosophical Society

[*c.* July 3, 1779][1]

Autre Moralité des Echecs.

Le jeu des Echecs est moins un amusement qu'une vaine occupation, une frivolité penible, qui n'exerce point le corps, qui fatigue l'esprit au lieu de le recréer, qui desseche et endurcit l'ame. Ce n'est ni un jeu de societé, ni un lien d'amitié; c'est le simulacre de la guerre, de ce jeu cruel auquel la necessité seule peut servir d'excuse, parceque alimenter l'orgueil de l'un et mortifier l'amour propre de l'autre, est le moindre mal ou le plus grand bien qu'il puisse faire.

Les Joueurs d'echecs sont presque toujours inquiets, soucieux, ombrageux, inabordables, pointilleux, dedaigneux; la prosperité les enyvre et les enfle singulierement, l'adversité les atterre. Ils ne se pardonnent rien l'un à l'autre, et sont continuellement en defiance même des Assistans, lorsque l'ennuy qu'ils inspirent ne suffit pas pour ecarter tout ce qui les environne.

Une observation singuliere c'est que le jeu des echecs diminue la transpiration et augmente les urines, tandis que la pluspart des autres jeux portent moins aux urines qu'à la transpiration, ce qui est bien plus favorable à la santé. Mais c'est le moindre reproche qu'on ait à lui faire: ce que je ne saurois lui pardonner c'est que loin de developer des talens utiles, il semble etouffer dans les cœurs tout germe de vertu publique; la vue d'un echiquier fascine tellement quantité d'excellens esprits, que la Patrie ne trouve que des joueurs dans des sujets assez heureusement nés pour qu'elle eût cru pouvoir les compter au nombre de ses meilleurs citoyens.

---

1. Dubourg had characterized BF's "Morals of Chess" (XXIX, 750–7) as "pure pleasure" when he returned the manuscript on June 28. That pleasure had inspired in him certain reflections, he said, which he would set down on paper. By July 3 (see above), those musings had turned into a pungent "refutation" which Dubourg promised to bring to the party on July 5. This document, endorsed by BF, must have been what Dubourg brought to Passy, but we have no record of the response it provoked.

Les Amateurs des echecs ne se font ils point trop d'illusion à eux memes en se representant leur jeu favori comme l'image de la vie humaine, et se flattant que celui là leur apprendra à mieux connoitre et mieux remplir les devoirs de celle cy. Que de disparités de l'un à l'autre!

1°. Au jeu des echecs, le tems est compté pour rien. Dans le cours de la vie, il n'est pas indifferent de savoir prendre promptement son parti au besoin: connoitre le prix du tems est une des plus importantes siences de l'homme.

2°. Au jeu des echecs, on est sans cesse aux prises un à un. Dans le cours de la vie, chacun a souvent à se defendre de plusieurs à la fois, et toujours occasion aussi de s'aider de plusieurs, et de les aider réciproquement.

3°. Au jeu des echecs, la difference est toujours precisement de la perte au gain. Dans la vie humaine on peut faire de petites et de grandes pertes, de petits et de grands benefices, suivant qu'on se conduit plus ou moins bien, et qu'on se trouve dans des conjonctures plus ou moins favorables.

4°. Le jeu des echecs admet des milliers de combinaisons, mais toutes du même ordre, soumises au seul calcul et absolument independantes de la fortune. Dans le cours de la vie, le sort influe plus ou moins sur toutes les affaires; la sagesse et la fortune se joignent et se repoussent tour à tour, se mêlent, se demelent et se recombinent de tant de façons qu'il n'en resulte pas seulement une infinité de gradations, mais encore une infinité de nuances.

Le Piquet à ecrire est incomparablement plus vivant, plus social que les echecs, et plus propre si non à former, du moins à façonner des hommes; mais aucun jeu n'est fait pour nous apprendre l'employ de la vie; toute leur utilité se borne à en remplir innocemment quelques vides; et le plus heureux de tous les mortels est celui à qui il en reste le moins.

Endorsed: Jeu d'Echecs

From Joseph Gridley

ALS: American Philosophical Society

May it please your Excellency   Nantes 3d July 1779.

I hope it will not be thought impertinent, that I should inform your Excellency, there is now at this Place a Small Vessell & a Prime Sailor, fitted out for Philadelphia; she has all her Cargo on board & waits for nothing but her Dispatches & papers from the Minister of the Marine department.

This Circumstance I judged might not possibly have come within your knowledge; which knowing, you might be pleased to improve, in sending whatever Dispatches either Original or Duplicates, you might have for America.

The Capt. Monsr. Maurice Levesque Baumard, is a man I am well Acquainted with, being a fellow Passenger from Boston last Fall,[2] and from a more particular knowledge of him since, can answer for his Fidelity in the delivery of whatever Papers you may intrust him with, provided he does not fall into the Hands of the Enemy, in which Case, he will follow whatever directions you might please to give him, His Owner Mr. Nicholas Vaud[3] is a Merchant of known reputation & has fitted out several Vessells for the Indias, who will become answerable for his Conduct.

The Vessell is a Chasmaré, called the Furet, & mounts 12 pieces of Cannon for her defence against small Vessells & boats, if your Excellency should have any Dispatches you would choose should be imediately sent off, and think proper to send them in this Vessell, Your Excellency's application to the Minister for the necessary papers of Dispatch, will enable her to take her departure in Twelve hours after their Arrival, and will greatly oblige him, who has the Honor to be Your Excellencys, most obliged & most obedient & Very Humble Servant   JOSEPH GRIDLEY

Notation: Gridley Joseph 3. July 1779.

---

2. Gridley, now a merchant in Nantes, had arrived late in 1778 with mineral samples sent by his father: XXVII, 658–9; XXVIII, 239.

3. Or Viaud. He ranked 49th among Nantes merchants in trans-Atlantic trade during the war: Villiers, *Commerce colonial,* p. 406.

Intelligence from Bilbao and Other Places

D: National Archives

During the months covered by the present volume there was a considerable decline in the volume of intelligence collected by the chevalier de Kéralio and given to Franklin for eventual forwarding to Congress.[4] Kéralio was absent from Paris for much of the period and made arrangements to provide such information during his absence,[5] but from late August until the end of October the flow of information came to a complete halt. As in past volumes we provide the first of the intelligence reports as a sample and summarize the remainder; unless otherwise noted the items are in French and at the National Archives. The other items are the following:

(I) Bordeaux, July 6: This item reports on construction undertaken in the port for the French navy and relays information from the captain of a Spanish merchant ship that the Franco-Spanish squadron at La Coruña had sailed.[6]

(II) Cadiz, July 6: The Spanish fleet sailed from here on June 22 and it is said it will rendezvous with the French fleet off La Coruña. It is also said Gibraltar is blockaded by land and sea.[7]

(III) London (?), no date, but written on or after July 12:[8] Enclosed are two newspapers, which have raised our spirits. People take little notice of General Mathew's return from Virginia and his

---

4. The most recent intelligence reports are printed or summarized in XXIX, 11–15. An additional piece of intelligence which BF forwarded to Congress was provided by someone else; see our annotation of Samuel Wharton's July 25 letter.

5. XXIX, 11–12. None of the items in this volume are in his hand.

6. These ships were intended to form part of a great fleet assembling off Cape Finisterre in preparation for escorting a French expeditionary force from St. Malo and Le Havre to the Isle of Wight. Spain had demanded French participation in the expedition as part of her price for entering the war: XXIX, 382n, 559n, 714n.

7. The Cadiz fleet, delayed by contrary winds, did not reach the rendezvous off Finisterre until a month after its sailing: XXIX, 714n. By the end of July Gibraltar was blockaded by land and sea: W.M. James, *The British Navy in Adversity: a Study of the War of American Independence* (London, New York, and Toronto, 1926), p. 189.

8. This is a letter, unsigned, written in English. The information it gives about Mathew's Virginia expedition (for which see XXIX, 670n, 761) appeared in the London newspapers of that date (*e.g.*, the *General Advertiser, and Morning Intelligencer*).

silence regarding the supporters we have been told would rally to the king's standard. The public is indifferent to the danger of an invasion of Ireland, but I believe the government finally is thoroughly frightened. It is rumored we are now willing to negotiate on terms we rejected a short while ago.

(IV) Bayonne, July 13: A courier bearing dispatches from Admiral d'Estaing is expected to pass through here tonight or tomorrow. In late May his squadron contained nineteen ships of the line with five more under La Motte-Picquet expected; Admiral Byron's British squadron lacked supplies and had 1800 seamen sick.[9] Eight richly loaded ships from Havana have reached Cadiz. Don Antonio d'Arce has been dismissed from command of the Ferrol squadron.[1]

(V) Brest, July 14: This item reports the arrival of a convoy from Port-au-Prince, a dockyard fire, and other news of the port.

(VI) Morlaix, July 14: The Austrasie regiment has arrived here and has been ordered to embark for India.

(VII) Lorient, July 15: Captain Jones's squadron, having suffered some damage, entered the port for repairs; one of his ships is being careened, while the others are cruising off Belle-Isle for British privateers.

(VIII) St. Malo, July 15: News has been received from Bayonne and La Coruña. Cannon fire was heard off St. Malo the night of the 10th–11th, reportedly from the French privateer *Monsieur.* M. de Montbarey [the French war minister] left here yesterday for Brest. All is in readiness both here and at Le Havre [for the invasion of England]; all that remains to be done is to embark the troops and cavalry mounts.

(IX) Cadiz, July 23: The Cadiz fleet comprised of twenty-seven ships of the line has rendezvoused off La Coruña with d'Orvilliers' fleet. The combined fleet now contains sixty-five ships of the line and approximately thirty smaller ships.[2] Rumors of the safe arrival of the Jamaica convoy in England are unfounded; an outbound convoy for Jamaica has had to put back to the Thames.

(X) No location or date, but probably written in July: The Span-

9. La Motte-Picquet and a large convoy reached Martinique on June 27, giving d'Estaing's squadron a superiority in numbers over the British. Byron, moreover, had had to borrow soldiers in order to complete his crews: James, *British Navy in Adversity,* pp. 145–6.

1. He was, however, reinstated: Patterson, *The Other Armada,* p. 161.

2. A list of the ships in the fleet can be found in James, *British Navy in Adversity,* pp. 438–40. D'Orvilliers had brought the main French fleet from Brest and was overall naval commander of the expedition against England.

ish declaration of war against Britain was published in Madrid on June 28. The importation of English goods, even fish carried by neutral vessels, has been prohibited in Spain. All British subjects have been ordered to leave the country within fifteen days, merchants have been told to list all the English merchandise in their possession, and orders have been sent to seize English ships. A letter of June 30 from Barcelona reports the movement of troops to a camp facing Gibraltar and Venetian ships carrying supplies there have been seized. Preparations continue at St. Malo and Le Havre. Some officers from d'Estaing's squadron report the arrival of two ships of the line at Martinique.[3]

(XI) Lorient, August 1: The arming of the ship of the line *Ajax* is progressing. Two cutters and a number of barks sailed yesterday for the mouth of the Loire. Captain Jones's squadron is still in the roadstead; he is replacing the English sailors aboard his squadron with some 150 exchanged American sailors and sending the Englishmen back to prison.

(XII) Morlaix, August 1: A small American privateer has brought into this port the English packet boat *Dublin,* worth 100,000–150,000 *l.t.*[4] Twenty-four ships from Granville have arrived at St. Malo.

(XIII) St. Malo, August 3: We have no news of the British fleet, which reportedly contains only thirty-five ships of the line. The king [of France] has leased at least 500–600 ships in the various ports. Twenty-seven ships from Granville recently arrived here. The embarkation of cavalry mounts is commencing. We learn from Brest that there are twenty-two ships in the port loaded with provisions. According to the English papers there is much desertion from their militia.

(XIV) Brest, August 9: The frigate *Inconstante* arrived on the 6th and reported the combined fleet is off Cape Ushant. It is comprised of sixty-six ships of the line, twenty-three frigates and corvettes, two bomb vessels, and six fire ships. There were few sick on board the fleet.[5]

(XV) No location listed, August 10: The convoy from Jamaica

3. The *Fendant* and *Sphinx,* under the command of the marquis de Vaudreuil, which arrived on April 26: James, *British Navy in Adversity,* p. 145; Dull, *French Navy,* p. 125.

4. Actually the *Dublin Trader,* a prize of the privateer *Black Prince.*

5. In fact, the sickness which eventually crippled the combined fleet was already worsening: Patterson, *The Other Armada,* pp. 162, 168. One of its victims was d'Orvilliers' son, as was reported in the following item.

has safely reached port. The combined fleet is in the English Channel; d'Orvilliers says the Spanish ships are in the best condition in the world. It is rumored in Paris that d'Estaing has captured St. Vincent and Grenada.[6]

(XVI) Brest, August 11: The frigate *Aigrette* arrived on the 8th from the fleet in order to put ashore her captain, who is dangerously ill. She reports that four Spanish ships of the line have been detached. Ten supply ships have been sent to the fleet. Some ships are being readied to embark 2,000–3,000 horses.[7]

(XVII) Bordeaux, August 15: Two recently constructed warships have been given masts. According to letters from Cadiz a supply ship en route to Gibraltar has been captured. All is in readiness at the Spanish camp to begin in the autumn the siege of Gibraltar.

(XVIII) Brest, August 18: Nine provision ships left to join the fleet. Various prizes and cargo ships have arrived here.

(XIX) Morlaix, August 19: The cargo of the *Dublin* has been put ashore and is appraised at 40,000 *écus*. The privateer *Duchesse de Chartres* awaits a favorable wind to sail.

(XX) No location, [c. August 20]:[8] A London banker writes his correspondent in Paris that an English frigate entering port reports the combined fleet contains sixty-six ships of the line. A neutral ship brought the same news to a French port. The frigate *Iphigénie* has captured a British frigate. St. Malo is still ready to embark troops as soon as ordered. The frigate *Néréide* has been launched here.

(XXI) Toulon, August 20: The frigate *Aurore* returned here with four prizes she took off Algiers. Her captain asked the *bey* of Algiers not to furnish stores to the English squadron at Gibraltar.[9] The construction of warships here is proceeding with alacrity; work continues even on Sundays and feast days. A prize moored near here caught fire and exploded.

6. The islands were captured by the French on June 16 and July 4.

7. Immediately following this entry is an extract, dated August 10, giving war news from "Papiers Anglois," including that of a total British defeat in South Carolina.

8. A roughly correct estimate of the size of the combined fleet finally appeared in the English papers of August 18. We presume the London banker had the information shortly before and that his letter took a few days to reach Paris. Arguing for an earlier date, however, is the fact that the *Néréide* was launched at St. Malo on May 30: Dull, *French Navy,* p. 357.

9. Without apparent success, as small boats from Algiers continued to carry provisions to Gibraltar; see, for example, Jack Russell, *Gibraltar Besieged 1779–1783* (London, 1965), p. 124.

(XXII) Brest, August 25: The frigate *Junon* arrived here with the prize *Ardent,* 64;[1] she left the combined fleet off Plymouth, while the British fleet was off Lizard Point.

(XXIII) Extract from a letter from London, October 30:[2] The American privateer *General Glover,* captured by Admiral Byron, reported having seen d'Estaing's fleet off South Carolina. Byron is blamed here for not sending the prize directly to New York to warn of d'Estaing's approach, which could cause great trouble to General Clinton. As of September 17, 4,000 troops were being readied at New York for an expedition to the southward.[3] We are concerned about Jamaica. Admiral Rodney is preparing a fleet of four or five ships of the line and about thirty merchant ships.[4]

Bilbao, 3 Juillet [1779]

Un négociant arrivé depuis peu de Gibraltar où il a fait un Séjour de 4 mois rapporte que la garnison de cette Place est d'environ 4000 hommes tout compris; que le Gouverneur a fait afficher que ceux qui voudroient rester dans la Place, eussent à Se pourvoir de vivres pour trois mois; mais que cela étoit impossible dans l'exécution, le Peuple n'étant composé que de Genois, de Juifs et de quelques Ecossois tous misérables; et qu'enfin il étoit persuadé que cette Place ne pouvoit pas tenir plus de 4 mois, Si elle étoit bloquée exactement.[5]

1. The *Ardent* was captured on Aug. 17, after she stumbled by mistake into the combined fleet: Patterson, *The Other Armada,* p. 182.

2. Bearing a notation that it was received from BF on May 13, 1780. Apparently it was enclosed with BF's March 4, 1780, letter to the president of Congress: *JCC,* XVII, 428; Wharton, *Diplomatic Correspondence,* III, 534–7. It is in WTF's hand.

3. Gen. Clinton, commanding at New York, sent this detachment to Jamaica, but it turned back within a few days after learning d'Estaing was bound for North America: Willcox, *Portrait of a General,* p. 289.

4. Rodney and his squadron replenished Gibraltar, whereupon Rodney proceeded to the Caribbean: James, *British Navy in Adversity,* pp. 189–95.

5. Total strength of the garrison upon the outbreak of hostilities with Spain was 5,382 men. A 1777 census of the civilian population counted 519 British, 1,819 Roman Catholics from Genoa, Portugal, and Spain, and 863 Jews: Russell, *Gibraltar Besieged,* pp. 28–9, 163.

From Jean de Neufville & fils

ALS:[6] American Philosophical Society

High Honourable Sir.   [before July 4, 1779][7]

We begg leave to address oúr selfs again to Your Excellency, and to begg for her favoúrs by the personall appearance of oúr Worthy frend Mr. Dumas, the Worthy Agent for Congress—[8] He would be Kind enough to charge himself with this present, and we dare promitt oúr selfs from his frendship, that if yoúr Excellence already had some goodness for ús he will strenghten it.

We were favoúred with the sight of the Plan he is the bearer of, the prospect of its being determind upon, gave ús great pleasure, as we were not entirely Strange to it, may that time be not farr distant.[9]

We fúrther make free to referr to Mr. Dúmas about what we had already begged as a favoúr from yoúr Excellence to be honourd with so múch confidence as is required for Commis-

6. In the hand of the Amsterdam banker Jean de Neufville who had been trying on BF's behalf to raise a loan in the Netherlands. He and his son Leendert's firm had been communicating with BF about Dutch affairs since the end of May: XXIX, 586–7, 661–2, 692–5, 759–60, 761–3.

7. Based on the reference in the text to celebrating the anniversary of American independence. The subjects under discussion point to 1779 as the year.

8. Charles-Guillaume-Frédéric Dumas was preparing to leave for a visit to Passy: Dumas to BF, July 6. Dumas' friendship with de Neufville was not uncritical; he planned to discuss the banker with BF in person: XXIX, 705.

9. In September, 1778, William Lee and Jean de Neufville had drafted an American-Dutch commercial treaty. Dumas had been sent it by a mutual friend to make a fair copy and brought it to Passy with him: XXIX, 100, 126, 194–5. On July 28–Aug. 3 de Neufville wrote to the president of Congress announcing several minor changes in the draft treaty: Stevens, *Facsimiles*, X, nos. 939–40; *JCC*, XV, 1361. Henry Laurens took that letter as well as a copy of the draft treaty with him when he sailed for the Netherlands in 1780. When he was captured by the British, they used the draft treaty as an excuse to declare war on the Netherlands: Samuel Flagg Bemis, *The Diplomacy of the American Revolution* (rev. ed., Bloomington, Ind., 1957), pp. 160–1. When the British government released Laurens' papers to the press, the July 28–Aug. 3 letter was mistakenly published as being from de Neufville to BF; see, for example, the Dec. 22, 1780, issue of the *London Courant, and Westminster Chronicle* and the *Annual Register,* XXIII (1780), 365–6.

sioners for trade and Navigation and Treasúrers fr. Congress and every Private State of the United States of North America through the Seven United Provinces;[1]

We should likewise be glad to referr to his intercession aboút the proposed Loan, and this we most heartily do, bútt we múst here observe that as for the terms, it is more in the Mercantile way, then he himself perhaps should chúse to meddle with, that we wont faill to give yoúr Excellence as to the terms all satisfaction possible, and that we, if only we may be Súre the form will some thing agree with what we had the honoúr to propose we think there will be no objection bútt we flatter oúr selfs more and more that we shall succed to satisfaction. May the 4th. of this Month be happy again to America we propose to Celebrate this Anniversary of its Independence with all the Gentlemen belonging to the States; may the next involve the Connection of the Two Republicqs!

We remain with all devoted Regard High Honourable Sir! Yoúr most Obedient and faithfull Servants

JOHN DE NEUFVILLE & SON.

Notation: Neufville John & son

To John Bondfield

Copy: Library of Congress

Sir,   Passy, July 4. 1779.

This Morning some Bills drawn by you were presented to me amounting to 19800 livres which I declin'd accepting for want of advice. The Person who brought them was hardly out of the house before I found on my table unopened yours of the 29th past which advises of those Drafts.[2] I immediately Sent after him, but he was not overtaken; and not knowing from what house in Paris he came, I know not where to send the Notice that I will accept and pay them.— I hope this Accident will not be attended with any considerable Inconvenience

1. XXIX, 693n, 704–5.
2. XXIX, 764.

to you.— I thank you for the News contained in your late Letter, and are with much Esteem, Sir

M. Bondfield.

To Stephen Marchant   Copy: Library of Congress

Sir,   Passy, July 4. 1779.

I received yours with the Acct. of your Cruise,[3] in which I see you have been both diligent and successful. The Misfortune of having several of your Prises retaken was what you could not help.— You have done good Service in bringing in so many Prisoners. I cannot get the *particular* Exhange made which you desire;[4] but in the *general* Exchange which is going on your Men will be discharg'd in their Turn. In the mean time, as the Cartel Ship from England with 100 American Prisoners is soon expected,[5] you will be at liberty to take as many of them as you may want to make up your Loss and as Shall be willing to go with you.— Those Prisoners you have brought in are to be delivered to the Care of the Commissary of the Marine at Morlaix.— You should if possible have brought in all your Prisoners, except what were necessary to Sail the ransomed Vessel, because they serve to relieve so many of our Country-men from their Captivity in England:— The Necessity of the Case must be your apology for the present: But for the future hope you will do your utmost to fulfil your Instructions on that head, And if you should again be oblig'd to dismiss some, take their Engagement in writting to procure the Discharge of an equal Number from the Prisons

3. XXIX, 718–22.

4. The British had retaken several of the prizes from Marchant's recent cruise, along with 21 of the *Black Prince*'s men serving aboard them as prize crews. Marchant had proposed to BF exchanging his own 21 prisoners for the captured prize crews.

5. The *Milford* arrived at Portsmouth on June 25 to embark a second group of 100 American prisoners for exchange in France: XXIX, 732n. The first exchange had involved Americans from Mill Prison, Plymouth.

in England. With wishes for Success, I am Sir, Your most obedient.

Capt Merchant

From John Paul Jones

ALS: American Philosophical Society

Bon homme Richard L'Orient
Honored and dear Sir,   July 4th. 1779.

I had the honor to write you the 2d. an account of the arrival of the Alliance & Pallas with an Irish Brigantine which they brought in as a Prize.— Captain Landais has reported that Vessel as being destined for America, so that I shall suffer no further step to be taken without your approbation.

I have the satisfaction to inform you that the damage of the Bon homme Richard is of less consequence than I at first imagined— We are now lightening the forepart of the Ship and expect to make every thing secure without going into the Port.— I am of Opinion that our little Squadron will again be ready to proceed on Service when your answer becomes due. Altho the plan of our future Operation may be on the point of conclusion, if not altogether fixed, yet I cannot help observing that our Ships are very unfit to cruise after Privateers— We can get Sight of them it is true, but that is all; for we are unable to overtake them.— If therefore we would Employ our force usefully I think it would be expedient to pursue some of the plans which I hinted to M. De Sartine last Summer—or the Plan which was laid down between myself and M. Garnier when I took command of this ship.[6] Since the Commencement

6. The preceding July Jones had suggested a variety of plans to the commissioners and to Sartine—raiding into the Irish Sea, attacking the east coast of England and Scotland, intercepting various merchant fleets, or destroying the Greenland fishery: *Adams Papers,* VI, 261–3. In January, 1779, he seems to have discussed with his friend Charles-Jean Garnier (a former *chargé d'affaires* in London) making use of a squadron of five ships to embark 400 troops for some "unexpected Blow": Bradford, *Jones Papers,* reel 3, no. 507. For Jones's disappointment that Chaumont instead of Garnier was placed in charge of handling his squadron see Idzerda, *Lafayette Papers,* II, 253n.

of this War no time has appeared more favorable to put that Plan in execution; and I am sure that no plan that has been thought of, at an Equal expence, could if Successful have an equal effect.— I do not however think it could Succeed without Troops.— Had the Marquis embarked with me,[7] I should, *when at Sea,* have endeavoured to put him upon that Plan instead of the one which he communicated in Secret to M—— who told it *as a Secret* to almost all his acquaintances.—[8] On account of that intended expidition this Armament has cost much more than it otherwise would have done—and yet is calculated much less for the ordinary Services of Ships of War. This is not surprising when it is remembered that the Bon homme Richard and the Pallas were obliged to be calculated to serve as Transports which not only prevented me from Cutting away the Upper Deck of this Ship and lowering the Gunnels but also obliged me to have a Round House built for the accomodation of the General and his officers.— Had I been allowed to pursue my own Ideas, I should have mounted only one open battery of 30 Eighteen Pounders, which would have been of more Service than the 42 Guns that are now on board in proportion as 540 is to 508— And the ship would then have made much better way thro' the Water and required less Ballast. This alteration however may easily be made at any time after the Cannon have arrived here which I contracted for at Angouleme—[9] and the expence will be triffling both with respect to time & Money.—

I cannot however persuade myself to forego the hopes of Commanding the Ship in Holland that the Court first offered—[1] and I hope the present situation of affairs will admit of my going with this Ship to take Command of that, after

7. Lafayette, whose joint expedition with Jones had been canceled on May 22: XXIX, 549n, 561–2.

8. Lafayette had discussed with Chaumont arrangements for the joint expedition, and Jones specifically complained about Chaumont's inattention to security: Idzerda, *Lafayette Papers,* II, 260n, 264n; Jones to BF, July 9, below.

9. For Jones's labors to locate cannon for the *Bonhomme Richard* see XXIX, 68, 221, 261, 411n; Bradford, *Jones Papers,* reel 3, no. 524.

1. The *Indien.*

doing something by the Way.— You are the best Judge whither or not it will be proper to communicate this Idea to M de C——² He mentioned it to me while here oftener than Once.— I have not yet written either to him or to M de Sartine— because I think it my Duty to communicate my Ideas first to you— and because you can give them to the Minister if you please with more propriety and with due effect.

I have Saluted the Sun last evening & this Morning and shall again this Evening.— This I hope will be done to the latest posterity where ever the Flag of Freedom is Displayed!

I am ever with Sentiments of grateful Esteem & Real Affection Dear Sir Your very obliged Friend and most humble Servant JNO P JONES

His Excellency Doctor Franklin.

Notation: Capt. Jones July 4. 79

From David Moffett ALS: American Philosophical Society

Hond: Sir Vitre Bregtaiun [Bretagne] Jul 4th 1779

I make Bould to trubell you with this as I will Know you have the Intrest of america and its natifes so much at hearte which I happen to be one of them that has the messfortan to be a pressaner in france at presant and has bein for this 9 mounths past I Should have made applacton to your Honnr Befor but as I had some money Deuw to me in England I was in hopes of an Exchainge that I might have an opertounitey of getting it befor I indeverd to get home but as ther is no appireance of an Exchainge nor can I get aney supplaies from my frinds in Boston I ame verey much at a Loss what to Do at presant My father lived in Johns Street Boston new England and my Brother Lives ther at presant which I should be verey happey to see if your Honnar would precour me a passe for to go one Bourd aney marchant shipe ore Crousare Bound to america I should be for evar under the gratest obelatigons to your goodness and genarosatey and should I have the happ-

2. Chaumont, who had conferred with Jones at Lorient in May: XXIX, 410–11 and following.

ness to araive safe in my oun Contrea I shall Do my Endevar to serve it in what so evar Capasetey I may be thoght Cape-paell of and I troust your Honr will take my steat into Conse-dareton as I have no other frind hire to appley to but your Honr I was a passchanger in the shipe st peter of Livarpool which was taken on hir passesh to Jameaica wher I Lived four years with an unckel I have ther from Boston Should your Honr Condesand to wrait me an ansuer to this you will Con-far the greatest honnar emeganebell one honred Sir Your moust Devoted and moust Humbell Servant

DAVID MOFFETT

Addressed: The Honbl: Bengn: Francklon Esqr / ambasrder from the Congrass / of america in paris

Notation: David Moffett, Vitre Bregtaium July 4. 1779

From ——— Vigneron and Other Applicants for Emigration

LS: American Philosophical Society

The first two applicants for emigration in the course of the four months covered by this volume were quite demanding.[3] Vigneron, whose letter is printed below, wanted no less than a county named after him in one of the "warm colonies." Charles Epp, who had sent Franklin some political advice one year earlier,[4] writes on July 12 from Altorf, in Switzerland, to explain his wish: a fine, large country-seat situated near the water, moderately priced, where he could settle with his family and exchange the practice of law for life in the open air. Well-versed as he is in foreign languages and repub-lican institutions, he might be of use as a consul. His advice is not to allow foreign troops to tarry on American soil, as friction is un-avoidable.

Epp's request was forwarded by a fellow countryman serving as a second lieutenant in the Swiss Guard. This man urged Franklin for an answer on three occasions (July 30, August 14, August 27), always signing his name in such an illegible manner that it is en-

3. Unless otherwise mentioned, the documents in this group are all in French and located at the APS.
4. See XXVII, 22. His current letter is in English.

dorsed successively as Grigglang, Giggling, and Gigglang.[5] Franklin finally answered both men on August 27.[6]

Not agriculture but the desire to practice medicine and surgery in America, a nation he reveres, is the motivation of Dr. Joseph Pellegrini de Coli et Luciani who writes from Vienna on July 19. He was a fellow student and close friend of Dr. Kaufmann, whose recent death on the battlefield put an end to their project of sailing together to Philadelphia where Kaufmann had his practice. A thirty-year-old bachelor, Pellegrini is willing to go to Paris at his own expense. Will Franklin sponsor his voyage after that?

On July 22, young Cavallier, employed in the Palermo firm of Gamelin frères & Cavallier, begs Franklin to help him escape European decadence and tyranny in order to join the generous Americans. He wants to give up commerce to cultivate a plot of land, certain that he will in due course reimburse the advances made to him. A friend of his, J.J.S. Nicoud, a citizen of Geneva, adds a plea of his own. He, too, does not want his employers to know of his plans but entreats Franklin for advice.[7] He is twenty-eight.

From Leghorn comes the request of Pierre Martin who supposes that, while not remembering him in particular, Franklin must be well aware of his family's holdings in America. Parental authority and youthful indolence have prevented him so far from acting but now that the collapse of the family business grants him his freedom, he wants to emigrate, convinced that the honest American states will give him back the lands taken away by the English oppressors. He hopes his knowledge of the Dutch language will be of some use. His letter is dated July 23.

A cautious candidate from Liège (but writing from Brussels) explains on August 3 that he will merely sign himself *L'ami de la liberté*. Well in his forties, he has been studying America for fifteen years and wishes to settle there, along with a number of agriculturists and craftsmen. But first he has questions about transportation, land grants, housing, subsidies, supplies, etc. Only after they have been answered will he reveal his identity and come to Paris if necessary. He provides a fictitious name for the Doctor to send his answer to.

---

5. It looks to us like Godt de Gresslang. In the *Etat militaire ... pour l'année 1779*, p. 134, he appears simply as Godt.

6. See BF to Epp on that date, below. To Gresslang he simply apologized for the delay due to "Multiplicity of Business and the infinite Number of Letters with which I am Oppressed. . . ." Library of Congress.

7. The letter must have been remitted to BF by the banker Caccia (*Almanach des marchands*, p. 373) whose name and address appear in the margin.

The final application, sent on August 20, comes from Delfshaven in Holland. Writing in English, Thomas Guinea states he works as a gunsmith and stove-grate maker. He would like to emigrate but cannot afford the price of passage. Could Franklin procure him a berth on a ship about to sail for Maryland or Virginia? Or at least give him advice? He does not want to fight against England, his country, but his sympathies are with America. His brother, a sail maker, would also like to go.

Monsieur,   Beauvoir sur mer, Bas Poitou, 4. Juillet 1779.

La Paix, cette felicité, que les humains, Monsieur Le docteur, vont devoir, aux talens, aux qualités du Cœur et aux hauts sentimens dont le Createur, à bien voulu doüer votre grande ame! Cette paix enfin, longue, par votre ouvrage, heureuse par les liens puissants dont vous allés lier, la naissante amerique, avec les forces des paisibles Bourbons, Jette tous les françois dans un vœu d'Emigration.

Puis-je Monsieur l'ambassadeur, ici prendre la Liberté, de vous ouvrir les sentimens de mon Cœur agé de 35. ans; ayant femme, trois enfans dont deux filles commencent a croitre et un garçon agé de 3. ans; jouissant d'une fortune de prés de 200. mille livres en Esperant a peu près autant? dois je m'occuper d'une Emigration.

L'Edit de Nantes ayant traversé ma famille j'en ignore l'origine, je sçais que sortis de l'anjou, mes parents ont toujours vecu noblement; j'ay entendu parler d'un grand oncle autrefois président au parlement de Paris. Le frère de mon pere, à joui, d'une certaine Réputation, sous le nom du medecin vigneron de la chauvetrie, mon Pere enfin etoit major d'infanterie.

Je désirerois donc Monsieur, le premier printemps sitot la Paix, passer sous vos puissants auspices, dans vos Colonies chaudes, depuis philadelphie Jusqu'a la Caroline, le Croyant salutaire pour la goutte que j'ay du sang. Je demandrois un ascencement de 10. a 12. mille arpens de domaines, peu eloignés d'un port ou Riviere Navigable et d'une ville ou je voudrois faire Résidence, faisant une Expresse demande à Vôtre Excellence, que la terre que je compterois y deffricher fut erigée *en Comté de mon nom.*

Mon intention seroit, en partant, de vous Remettre Monsieur, mille louis d'or, dont vous voudriés bien me faire compter le surplus, a mon arrivée, de ce qui me reviendroit, le paiement fait de mon ascencement, son erection faitte en comté. Mon plan pris mes logemens preparés, mon intention seroit d'en partir au mois de 7bre. suivant, pour revenir prendre ma famille, des fonds, des cultivateurs, si *ce gouvernement* le permet, pour m'y fixer, avec toute Liberté de Religion, ainsi que vous l'avés annoncé.

Voila Monsieur l'ambassadeur, mes désirs, vous pressentés, qu'il faut un Eguillon, pour Emigrer les hommes; le mien est pour mes enfans, je souhaitte qu'il puisse convenir aux vües du Congrés, aux grands projets que vous avés formés, et aux grands sentimens que vous avés voüé à l'utilité publique et pour le bonheur des citoiens de l'amerique.[8]

Je Suis avec le Respect le plus profond Monsieur, Votre très humble et trés obeissant serviteur   VIGNERON

Monsieur Le Docteur franklin à Paris

Notation: Vigneron 4 Juillet 1779.

To Alexander Gillon

Copies: Library of Congress, Harvard University Library[9]

Sir   Passy, July 5. 1779.
I received the Honour of yours dated the 29th. past.[1] The Zeal you show for the Relief of Carolina is very laudable: and

8. In an undated follow-up, Vigneron stresses his competence in agriculture, in horse and cattle breeding, as well as in commerce. He will endeavor, if possible, to stop "la dégénération des bêtes" in America (he must have been reading the Abbé Raynal's *Histoire philosophique*). Even though he alludes to the personal intervention of friends on his behalf, he must not have received encouragement from BF, since he will write again on Oct. 15, 1783, this time under the name of Vigneron de la Jousselandière—still desirous to emigrate (APS).

9. Made by John Joyner, a captain in the S.C. navy, on Oct. 10, and certified by him to be a true copy. It bears two notations: "Letter from Dr. Franklin To Commodore Gillon respecting the Bon Homme Richard &c.—" and "July 5. 1779. he has no authority to direct the operations of the Little Squadron under JP Jones."

1. XXIX, 765–7. Commodore Gillon of the S.C. navy had asked that Jones's squadron be sent to the relief of South Carolina and Georgia. He

I wish it was in my Power to second it by complying with your Proposition. But the little Squadron which you suppose to be in my disposition, is not as you seem to imagine fitted out at the Expense of the United States; nor have I any Authority to direct its Operations. It was from the beginning destined by the Concern'd for a particular Purpose. I have only, upon a Request that I could not refuse,[2] lent the Alliance to it hoping the Entreprise may prove more advantagious to the Common Cause than her Cruise could be alone. I suppose too, that they are Sail'd before this time. Your other scheme for raising a sum of 1,800,000 livres by Subscription throughout france, to be advanc'd to the State of So. Carolina on an Interest of 7 per Cent &c. being mix'd with a Commercial Plan, is so far out of my way, and what I cannot well judge of. But in the present Circumstances, I should think it not likely to succed. However, as I am charg'd to procure a Loan for the United States at a Lower Interest, I can have no hand in encouraging this particular Loan, as it interferes with the other.[3] And I cannot but observe, that the Agents from our different States running all over Europe begging to borrow Money at high Interest, has given such an Idea of our Poverty and Distress, as has excedingly hurt the general Credit, and made the Loan for the United States almost impracticable.[4] With great Esteem I have the honour to be &c.

Mr. Ar. Gillon. Comme.

---

was in Europe to purchase frigates or arrange a loan for the state: XXVII, 118–19.

2. The request was from Sartine: XXIX, 345–6.

3. Attempts by the houses of Horneca, Fizeaux & Cie. and Jean de Neufville & fils to raise a loan for the United States in the Netherlands had thus far met with a cold reception, although the latter firm still expressed some optimism: XXIX, 662.

4. In April BF had advised Gillon that financial requests should be the prerogative of Congress: XXIX, 352. After an unproductive summer in France Gillon finally decided to go to the Netherlands in hopes of procuring either money or ships. On Sept. 27 BF drafted a certificate for him, testifying that his commission was in the hand of President of South Carolina Rawlins Lowndes and that it bore the S.C. seal (Hist. Soc. of Pa.). Arthur and William Lee signed similar certificates for Gillon: D.E. Huger

From Samuel Davison[5]

ALS: American Philosophical Society

Honord. Sr.   Masterland[6] Sweden July 5th. 1779.

I having saild from Norfolk Virginia the first of may with the Sloop Phianix Burthen 80 tons mounting 8 carrige Guns 20 men I purpose mounting four more & Shipping as many hands here as is necessary to fight her. She is ownd By Saml Cad Morris of Phila. henry & thos. of Norfolk[7] Mr. Brown having applyd at williamsburg for a commissn the Governor not having any Blanks by him from congress was obligd to Sail without a commission. If you can send me a commissn per post so as to arrive here by Middle of August Youll oblige Sr. your Most Obdt. humble Servt.[8]   SAML DAVISON

Addressed: To / The Honorible / Benjamin Franklin / Paris

Notation: Davison Saml. July 5. 1779.

Smith, "Commodore Alexander Gillon and the Frigate South Carolina," *S.C. Hist. and Geneal. Mag.* IX (1908), 192, 196.

5. Quite likely the Samuel Davison of Philadelphia who had served as a commodore in the Pa. Navy: Claghorn, *Naval Officers,* p. 85.

6. Marstrand, a free port on an island off the coastal city of Gothenburg. American vessels had been trading at the two ports since at least mid–1777: H.A. Barton, "Sweden and the War of American Independence," *W&MQ,* 3rd ser., XXIII (1966), 410–11. A consul there named Pierre Eckstrom forwarded the present letter with one of his own dated July 6, volunteering to relay to Davison any papers or documents BF might send him. APS.

7. Samuel Cadwalader Morris (1743–1820) was a Philadelphia merchant and political figure, as well as a former militia officer: Robert C. Moon, *The Morris Family of Philadelphia* (3 vols., Philadelphia, 1898), II, 437–41. Henry and Thomas Brown (whose full names are given in the next Davison letter, cited below) were prominent merchants and patriots from Portsmouth, Virginia: William J. Van Schreeven *et al.,* eds., *Revolutionary Virginia: the Road to Independence* (7 vols., Charlottesville, 1973–83), II, 89; IV, 353.

8. In a letter of July 10 (APS) Davison explained that on the 10th of June he had removed four casks of indigo and some provisions from the brig *Robert,* en route from London to New York. His disgruntled second mate reported this to the British consul at Marstrand, who demanded the return of the indigo. Davison wished BF to send a commission by the first post, addressing it to Henry Greg, a merchant at Gothenburg. The merchant, who spelled his name Greig, wrote a covering letter of the same date with

From David Hartley

Transcript: Library of Congress

July 5 1779

I send you for fear of accidents copies of two letters wch I have lately writ to you.[9]

I told you in my last that I hoped that our negotiation had done some good upon at least the minds of Men[1] they had not been immediately as effectual as I cd have wished. Perhaps you may incline to the same opinion when you see the last paragraph of the King's Speech viz that those *unhappy* provinces will not persist in preferring foreign alliances &c. to *Peace* & *Reunion* with the Mother Country.[2] Terms & phrases begin to soften. I live in hopes that better times & dispositions will come & I shall never keep my eye off of such expectation I am very strongly of opinion that many arguments wch I have urged upon the Consideration of Ministers have lost [left] a material impression I wish they had gone a little farther and that they wd have the experiment towards reconciliation upon a ten years peace for a good beginning.

---

more particulars on the case (APS). The want of a commission had prevented Davison's taking the whole ship as a prize. Now the British consul had petitioned the governor of the province to sequester the *Phoenix* as a pirate. Greig planned to supply Davison with more men, guns, and ammunition and believed him worthy of a commission. In a later undated letter (APS) Greig reported that the governor had granted sequestration of the ship into Greig's hands until he received the king's orders. We have no record of any response from BF to these letters.

9. Either his two letters of June 24 or one of the 24th and one of the 29th: XXIX, 731–3, 767–70. On Aug. 20, below, BF acknowledged receipt of the two of the 24th and the present letter.

1. XXIX, 767–8.

2. George III's speech at the close of the Parliamentary session, July 3: Cobbett, *Parliamentary History*, XX (1778–80), 1020. On July 9 Hartley wrote Lord North, repeating his desire for "Peace & Reunion" and enclosing terms of negotiation (almost identical to those he had proposed in Parliament on June 22 [*ibid.*, 907]). He asked the English minister to reconsider them and offered to postpone his departure for summer recess if it would facilitate peace. Not until Jan. 5, 1780, however, did Hartley forward to BF this communication with North. Both letters are at the APS.

From John Paul Jones

ALS: Princeton University Library

Honored & dear Sir,   L'Orient July 5th. 1779
I embraced the Opportunity which presented itself to write to you by the Captain of the Epervier who arrived here the day before, it is believed, from Martinico and as he went off express Undertook to deliver my letter to you at Passy on his way to Paris.—³
I have now the honor to forward a letter from Captn. Landais with Copies of the Papers that respect the Prize &c. for your particular information.—⁴ The Admiralty will this day put their Seals on the Hatches.— Yesterday being very stormy the Alliance touched the Ground a short while before High water but I think recd. no Damage.
I have the honor to be with real Esteem & Greatful Affection. Dear Sir Your very Obliged Friend and very humble Servant.   JNO P JONES

N.B. I have only this moment recd. the within

His Excellency Doctor Franklin.

From William Kentisbear⁵

ALS: American Philosophical Society

Aix in Provence
May it Please your Excellency   July 5th. 1779
Being now a Prisoner at this Place & on My Peroole of Honour, begs leave to address your Excellency on this present occasion, As Being a Subject to the United & Independent

---

3. The *Epervier* was a 16-gun corvette, commanded by the comte de Capellis, which had just returned from Senegal and Gambia: Asa Bird Gardiner, *The Order of the Cincinnati in France* . . . (Providence, 1905), p. 145; E. Chevalier, *Histoire de la marine française pendant la guerre de l'indépendance américaine* . . . (Paris, 1877), p. 133n. The preceding summer Jones had attempted to obtain her for the squadron he hoped to command: Bradford, *Jones Papers,* reel 2, nos. 359, 366, 379, 383–4, 386, 401.
4. Landais' letter of July 2 reporting the capture of the *Three Friends (ibid.,* reel 4, no. 663).
5. An American prisoner in France, he had already written BF three times: XXVIII, 86–7.

States of America, Sollicits your Honour to Use your interest & influence to Procure my Enlargement & Liberty As there being but two Unhappy Sufferers of Us natives of America puts Great confidence in our being Successful— Having received a Letter lately from Bourdeaux from Mr. Frasier Directed to My fellow Sufferer Mr. Taylor in which he intimates the nessesity of our Accquainting Your Excellency of the above.[6] Anxious Waiting for your approbation hoping Yr. Excellency Will take our Distressed situation in consideration Which Will be Gratefully Acknowledged by Sr. With Profound Respect Your most Obedient & humble Servant

WILLIAM KENTISBEAR

Your Excellency will Please to Observe that We Shall think it the most happy circumstance that can Occur to procure us Passes to proceed to Bourdeaux Or Nants & there to repair on Board Some American frigate Or Vessel of War as Your Excellencys Goodness shall think most Expedient

Addressed: a Son Excellence / Monsieur Le Docteur Franklin / ambassadeur des Etats unis de l'amerique / à la Cour de france / à Paris

Notations in different hands: William Kentisbear, Aix in Province July. 5. 1779 / aix

From Antoine-Raymond-Gualbert-Gabriel de Sartine

Copy: Library of Congress

Versailles le 5. Juillet 1779.

J'ai l'honneur, Monsieur, de vous envoyer une lettre que le Sr. Samuel Will[7] detenu à Carhaix m'a fait passer, et par la quelle il represente qu'ayant été pris par le Corsaire le Ranger au mois d'avril 1778. Il a été oublié dans l'Echange qui a été fait des Prisonniers Americains[8], et en conséquence il demande sa

---

6. See our annotation of Frazer's July 2 letter.

7. Actually Samuel Hill, surgeon of Jones's prize, H.M.S. *Drake,* who had been separated from his shipmates because of illness; see his letter of July 20.

8. Sartine is referring to the exchange made in the Loire the preceding April of nearly a hundred British prisoners for a comparable number of

liberté. Je vous prie de vouloir bien donner vos ordres pour faire verifier l'Exposé de ce Prisonnier, et me faire connoitre ce que vous aurez jugé a Propos de decider.

J'ai l'honneur d'être avec un sincere Attachement, Monsieur, votre très humble et tres obeissant serviteur

(signé) DE SARTINE.

M. Franklin

From John Walsh

ALS: American Philosophical Society

Honoured Sir   Vitré July the 5th. 1779

Sience the prisoners, who were detain'd on board the patience brig in Brest road, receiv'd the honour of your oblidging Answer to their Memorial. persuant to your Excellency's desire I did meself the honour of sending you an account of the provisions which were served us, and have not been so happy, as to know whether you receiv'd said account.—or a letter I took the liberty of sending you last Month from Fougeres[9] to Request your being Graciously pleased to allow me with Thomas Wilkinson pilot, William Sweeny, John Butcher, James Hay, and John Key as Necessary Evidences on a Court Martial to return to England on my promise there to use my Endeavours to get as many Americans Returned in Exchange for us: I have been inclined to think the reason of your Excell. not favouring me with an answer proceeded from som bad Idea Mr. Riou of Brest, might injust have given Your Excellency of me.— If I have Judged wright as to that matter, I would gladly have it in my power to Justify meself in person before your Excellency.— The french soldiers were constant witnesses of the Miseries we often laboured under while we were under his care, it was with the greatest relluctance we found ourselves Necessitated to aply to your Excellencys un-

---

Americans brought from Plymouth by the *Milford.* Among the returning British were most of the crew of the *Drake* (who had been brought from Brest aboard the *Alliance*): XXIX, 337, 353n, 573. For other sick and wounded from the *Drake* who were not included in the exchange see XXIX, 535, and the following letter.

9. Actually, May 28, XXIX, 572–4.

bounded Humanity. As I was the person whose duty it was to represent the grevances of my fellow prisoners on board said brig, so I was the one that Mr. Riou levelled his Mallice at, by Detaining me prisoner contrary to all Expectations.— I wrote John Paul Jones Esq. under whose Command we were taken, to Request he would interceed with your Excellency to obtain your permission for the aforesaid four men and me, to return to England. In answer thereto, he was pleased to send me the inclosed, which I take the Liberty of forwarding you, in hopes to convince you upon what good terms I have been with that Gentilman and how soon he would have rendered me that Justice which Mr. Riou Depriv'd me of, and which I now pray your Excellency to accord me.[1] My Lords commissioners of the Amiralty can not, in my humble oppinion, refuse to make Your Excellency Equal returns for us, in case your Excellency would condescend to grant me my present Resquest.

I have the honour of being with the greatest veneration & respect Your Excellencys very humble and obed. Servt.

JOHN WALSH
late Master of the Drake

N.B. if yr. Ex's Secritery's Name was known to me I would have wrote him, and [*not*] have troubled you on this occation. As on my court Martial Capn. Jones letter may serviceable to me lays me under the Necessity to request that said Letter may be Returned me.

To His Excellency the Honorable Bengimen Franklin one of the commissioners from the united states of America A Paris

Notation: John Walsh Vitre July 5th. 1779

1. Walsh had written to Jones on May 11; Jones's reply, of May 19, is at the APS. Jones regrets that Walsh and his party were not exchanged, and offers his written testimony, to be used if necessary at Walsh's court martial, that the *Drake* made a gallant defense and was disabled before surrendering.

Toasts at an Independence Day Banquet

Copy:[2] American Philosophical Society

The anniversary of American independence, which fell on a Sunday in 1779, was celebrated on both sides of the Atlantic on Monday, the fifth of July. While back in Philadelphia the French minister plenipotentiary, consul, local officials, and visiting dignitaries were being hosted by Congress,[3] in Passy Franklin was hosting Americans and French friends of the cause.

Even the preliminaries of the Passy celebration were ceremonious. Franklin had printed invitations on his newly established press.[4] The guest list included representatives for Vergennes and Sartine, *premier commis* Gérard de Rayneval and Baudouin; the marquis and marquise de Lafayette; the chevalier de Laneuville and "comte" Montfort de Prat, both officers in the American army; the banker Ferdinand Grand; French friends and neighbors the Chaumonts, Brillons, le Veillards, the abbés Chalut and Arnoux, and Barbeu-Dubourg.[5] Among the Americans invited were the Izards, Arthur Lee, Samuel Petrie, and Samuel Wharton. Altogether, according to a French account, there were forty at table.[6]

The party began with a banquet whose magnificence has left its traces in Franklin's account books. The rented tableware included 36 platters in silver-plated copper, 17 ornamental figures of porcelain, 20 vases, 24 dozen goblets, a number of decanters, ice buckets, double salt cellars, compote bowls, etc., from which enough items disappeared to raise the bill by 22 *l.t.* to the sum of 93 *l.t.* 3 *s.* 6 *d.* The impressive quantities of chickens ("gras," "communs," or "a la Reine"), ducks, turkeys, veal, lamb, quails, and two varieties of pigeons amounted to 121 *l.t.* 10 *s.* As to fruit and vegetables, they included vast amounts of gooseberries, strawberries, raspberries, cherries, pears, apricots, lemons, melons, figs, artichokes, carrots, turnips, onions, cauliflower, cabbage, lettuce, peas, mushrooms, cu-

---

2. In Gellée's hand.

3. A description of that entertainment, which included music, thirteen toasts, and an impressive display of fireworks, is in the *Pa. Evening Post,* July 9, 1779.

4. See XXIX, 726–7.

5. Of these, only Ferdinand Grand and the chevalier de Laneuville did‧ not attend; their respective regrets are dated July 1 and 7.

6. Métra, *Correspondance secrète,* VIII, 137.

cumbers, green beans, grape leaves, and "fines herbes." To wash it down, 136 "pintes" of wine were purchased on July 3, 4, and 5. And between July 1 and 6 the grocer Gautier furnished a wide range of goods including butter, sugar, eggs, coffee, vinegar, pickles, cooking oil, pepper, nutmeg, cloves, anchovies, orange blossom water, mustard, and rice, as well as products such as brooms, candles, paper, coal, a notebook, string, sieves, gravy boats, and two dozen lanterns, for a total of 421 *l.t.* 13 *s.* 3 *d.*[7]

The guests dined under the inspiring gaze of a full-body portrait of George Washington, shown holding the Declaration of Independence and the Franco-American Treaties of Alliance and Commerce, and trampling the British conciliatory bills. The portrait, painted by Louis Trinquesse, had been brought to France by Lafayette.[8]

Following the banquet and toasts there was singing, and the distribution of keepsakes. The poet Feutry had composed "Un Chant d'alégresse" especially for the occasion, and copies (printed at Franklin's expense) were handed out to the company. Sung by a "coryphée insurgent," the song extolled the bravery of all the allied parties in defending liberty, dearer than life itself, and predicted that the anniversary of the Declaration of American Independence would always be celebrated by future generations. Copies of "La Science du Bonhomme Richard" were distributed to the guests. A band of musicians played military music, and the whole was followed by a ball.[9]

[July 5, 1779]

I

The King of France, illustrious Protector of American Liberty.

Le Roi de France, illustre Protecteur de la Liberté Americaine.

---

7. These individual bills are collected as part of Account XXI (xxviii, 3).

8. The portrait is reproduced in Idzerda, *Lafayette Papers,* ii, 286; see also p. 287n.

9. A lengthy description of the event, including the texts of Feutry's song and the impromptu verse he composed for Mme de Lafayette, is in Métra, *Correspondance secrète,* viii, 137–40. BF paid the musicians 102 *l.t.* on the day of the party; Feutry was paid 15 *l.t.* on July 18 for the printing of his verses: Account XXIII (xxix, 3).

2

The Queen, and may they and their Posterity long reign over an affectionate and happy People.

La Reine puissent ils regner longtems eux et leur Posterité sur un Peuple heureux et affectionné.

3

The King of Spain and the Rest of the renowned Bourbon Family; with Success to their Arms.

Le Roi d'Espagne et toute l'illustre Famille des Bourbons. & Succés a ses Armes.

4

The Congress and may they always govern with the same Wisdom that has hitherto distinguished them.

Le Congrés. Puisse-t-il toujours gouverner avec la même Sagesse qui l'a distingué jusqu'a present.

5

The Marquis de la Fayette and all the brave Strangers who have hazarded their Lives in our Cause.

Le Marquis de la Fayette et touts les braves Etrangers qui ont risqué leurs Vies pour notre Cause.

6

Generals Washington, Gates, Arnold and all the valiant Americans who have fought in Defence of their Country.

Les Generaux Washington, Gates, Arnold et touts les vaillans Americains qui ont combattu pour la Defense de leur Patrie.

7

The combined Fleets of France & Spain, and may Fame swell their Sails, and Victory crown all their Enterprizes.

Les Flottes combinées de France et d'Espagne; Puisse la Renommée enfler leurs Voiles et la Victoire couronner toutes leurs Entreprises.

Notation: Feast on the 6th July

The Abbé André Morellet's Song in Honor of Franklin

Two AD: American Philosophical Society, Nationale Forschungs-und-Gedenkstätten der klassischen deutschen Literatur, Weimar[1]

A love of music was one of the many things that Franklin and Morellet discovered they had in common when the two first met at Lord Shelburne's estate in 1772. Their discussions of Morellet's recently published theories on the subject inspired Franklin, upon his return to London, to list fifty-one emotions which could be evoked by musical means. Morellet rendered the terms in French.[2] Years later, in Passy, the abbé translated seven of Franklin's favorite Scottish songs and ballads, and compiled them into a small songbook. Desperately proud of them, Morellet sang the French versions while the Doctor accompanied him on his glass armonica.[3]

Franklin's frequent dinners with his "Académie d'Auteuil" were often enlivened with singing, and Morellet seems to have composed songs in his honor for two kinds of occasions: birthdays and Independence Day dinners.[4] He noted, on the manuscript copy now in Weimar, Germany, that this piece was composed for a dinner in 1779 at the home of Mme Helvétius. The allusion in stanza nine to the invasion of England points to a date in the summer of that year. We suspect that Mme Helvétius hosted a dinner in honor of Franklin

1. The Weimar manuscript is entitled, "Chanson faite pour un diner donné à Benjamin Franklin chés Made. Helvetius à auteuil en 1779." The first page is reproduced as an illustration in Dorothy Medlin, Jean-Claude David, and Paul LeClerc, eds., *Lettres d'André Morellet* (1 vol. to date, Oxford, 1991–), p. 401.

2. See Ellen R. Cohn, "Benjamin Franklin and Traditional Music," *Reappraising Benjamin Franklin: A Bicentennial Perspective*, ed. J.A. Leo Lemay (Newark, Del., 1993), pp. 290–318. BF's list of emotions, with Morellet's notations, is at the APS.

3. M. Lémontey, ed., *Mémoires de l'abbé Morellet . . .* (2 vols., Paris, 1821), I, 290.

4. When the abbé, his memory by that time hazy, included this piece in his *Mémoires* (pp. 286–9), he guessed that it had to have been written for either one or the other occasion. Morellet wrote another song for BF's dinner of July 4, 1783, set to the same tune as this one (APS). For the relationship between the two men, and the "Académie d'Auteuil," see Lopez, *Mon Cher Papa*, pp. 243–301.

around Independence Day, and that Morellet toasted his friend with this "chanson à boire."[5]

[*c.* July 5, 1779?]
air des *Treize cantons*[6]

chanson

Que l'histoire sur l'airain
grave le nom de Franklin
pour moi je veux à sa gloire
faire une chanson à boire
le verre en main
Chantons nôtre Benjamin.

En politique il est grand
à table joyeux et franc
Tout en fondant un empire
Vous le voyes boire et rire
le verre en main &.c.

Comme un aigle audacieux
il a volé jusqu'aux cieux
et dérobé le tonnerre
dont ils effrayoient la terre
le verre en main &.c.

L'Americain indompté
conserve sa liberté
moitié de ce bel ouvrage
est encor de nôtre sage
le verre en main &c

5. Morellet tinkered with the wording over time. The song was first published in the Nov. 6 issue of the *Mercure de France* (pp. 57–9), where the sixth stanza ends with, "Franklin fait à l'Amérique / Boire du vin catholique," and the two subsequent stanzas were dropped. In the *Mémoires,* all twelve stanzas are printed (including the original version of the sixth), various lines are reworded, and Morellet replaced the refrain with individual couplets, each of which concludes with the word "Benjamin."

6. The melody, also known as "Lampons, camarades, lampons," was published in *Airs notés des quatre volumes des Chansons choisies,* (London, 1783–84), and reproduced in Medlin, David, and LeClerc, *Lettres d'André Morellet,* p. 401.

48

On ne combattit jamais
pour de plus grands interêts
ils veulent l'independance
pour boire des vins de france
le verre en main, &c

L'anglois sans humanité
vouloit les reduire au thé
il leur vendoit du vin trouble
et le leur vendoit au double
le verre en main &c

Le congrès a declaré
qu'il boiroit notre claré
et c'est pour notre champagne
que l'on s'est mis en campagne
le verre en main &c

Si vous voyes nos heros
braver l'anglois et les flots
c'est pour faire à l'amerique
boire du vin catholique
le verre en main &c

Ce n'est point mon sentiment
qu'on fasse un debarquement
que faire de l'angleterre
on n'y boit que de la biere
le verre en main &ca

Ces anglois sont grands esprits
profonds dans tous leurs ecrits
ils savent ce que l'air pèse
mais leur cuisine est mauvaise
le verre en main &c

On les voit assés souvent
se tüer de leur vivant
qu'y feront les moralistes
faute de vin ils sont tristes
le verre en main &c

Puissons nous domter sur mer
l'orgueuil de ce peuple fier
mais apres notre victoire
nous leur apprendrons à boire
le verre en main &c

Notation:[7] Abbé Morrellet's Song for B. F.

To the Abbé Morellet[8]

Reprinted from M. Lémontey, ed., *Mémoires de l'abbé Morellet . . .* (2 vols., Paris, 1821), I, 294–7; copy: American Philosophical Society

[after July 5, 1779?]

Vous m'avez souvent égayé, mon très-cher ami, par vos excellentes chansons à boire; en échange, je désire vous édifier par quelques réflexions chrétiennes, morales et philosophiques sur le même sujet.

In vino veritas, dit le sage. *La vérité est dans le vin.*

Avant Noé, les hommes, n'ayant que de l'eau à boire, ne pouvaient pas trouver la verité. Aussi ils s'égarèrent; ils devinrent abominablement méchans, et ils furent justement exterminés par l'eau qu'ils aimaient à boire.

Ce bonhomme Noé, ayant vu que par cette mauvaise boisson tous ses contemporains avaient peri, la prit en aversion; et

7. In WTF's hand.

8. This undated letter was inspired, we believe, by Morellet's drinking song, above. There can be no question that BF drafted it in French. It revolves around a string of untranslatable puns on the word *vin: deviner,* to soothsay; *divin,* divine. The perfect grammar of the final version is obviously not BF's own, though in this case, we do not know which of his friends served as linguistic advisor.

The only surviving MS of this letter is a contemporary copy in an unidentified hand. It bears Cabanis' notation, "Lettre de M Franklin a m. l'abbe," includes a footnote (quoted below) which did not appear in any of the later printed versions, and crudely reproduces the figures. The text is marred, however, by various slips of the pen, and erratic punctuation and capitalization. We therefore publish a printed version which was presumably taken from the ALS.

WTF published the letter, with an English translation, in *Memoirs,* III, 347–50, placing it with the Bagatelles. To the best of our knowledge, BF never printed it on the Passy press.

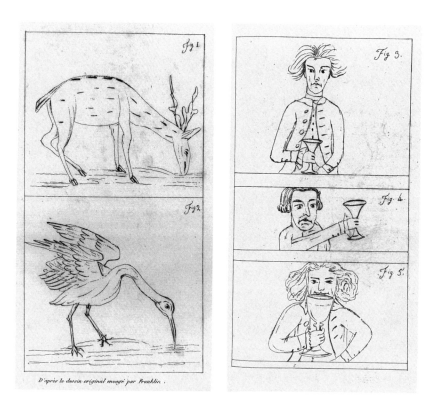

D'après le dessin original envoyé par Franklin.

William Temple Franklin's Illustrations

Dieu, pour le désaltérer, créa la vigne, et lui révéla l'art d'en faire le vin. Par l'aide de cette liqueur, il découvrit mainte et mainte vérité; et depuis son temps, le mot *deviner* a été en usage, signifiant originairement *découvrir* au moyen *du vin.*[9] Ainsi, le patriarche Joseph prétendait *deviner* au moyen d'un coupe ou d'un verre *de vin,* liqueur qui a reçu ce nom pour marquer qu'elle n'était pas une invention humaine, mais *divine;* autre preuve de l'antiquité de la langue française contre M. Gébelin.[1] Aussi, depuis ce temps, toutes les choses excellentes, même les déités, ont eté appellées *divines* ou *divinités.*

On parle de la conversion de l'eau en vin, à la noce de Cana, comme d'un miracle. Mais cette conversion est faite tous les jours par la bonté de Dieu devant nos yeux. Voilà l'eau qui tombe des cieux sur nos vignobles; là, elle entre les racines des vignes pour être changée en vin; preuve constante que Dieu nous aime, et qu'il aime à nous voir heureux. Le miracle particulier a été fait seulement pour hâter l'opération, dans une circonstance de besoin soudain qui le demandait.

Il est vrai que Dieu a aussi enseigné aux hommes à réduire le vin en eau. Mais quelle espèce d'eau? —*L'eau-de-vie;* et cela,

9. Footnote in the MS copy:

Scyphus dit son homme d'affaires par ses ordres *quem furati estis ipse est in quo bibit dominus meus et in quo augurari solet.* Genese 44. 5.

L'orateur Romain qui est bien connu par ses mauvaises poesies d'etre un buveur d'eau confesse franchement dans son livre de divinatione, peut-etre qu'il ne savoit pas deviner *quid futurum est non divino.*

BF is mixing erudition with fancy. The Latin quotation from Genesis can be translated, "What you have stolen is that in which my lord drinks and in which he is accustomed to divine." Scyphus, hardly a Biblical figure, is a kind of drinking cup. The second paragraph refers to Cicero and his *De Divinatione:* the poet, a drinker of water, admits that he might not be able to foretell the future. BF's disparagement of Cicero's drinking habits seems to derive from a brief passage near the end of *De Divinatione.* Following the extensive considerations of various methods of divination, Cicero discounts, in one brief sentence, the "countless delusions of drunk or crazy men", asking: who will not occasionally hit a mark if he shoots long enough? *De Divinatione,* II, 121.

1. A facetious allusion to their common friend, Antoine Court de Gébelin, author of *Le Monde primitif, analysé et comparé avec le monde moderne;* see XIX, 342n; XXVI, 131.

51

afin que par-là ils puissent eux-mêmes faire au besoin le miracle de Cana, et convertir l'eau commune en cette espèce excellente de vin qu'on appelle *punch.* Mon frère chrétien, soyez bienveillant, et bienfaisant comme lui, et ne gâtez pas son bon breuvage.

Il a fait le vin pour nous réjouir. Quand vous voyez votre voisin à table verser du vin en son verre, ne vous hâtez pas à y verser de l'eau. Pourquoi voulez-vous noyer la verité? Il est vraisemblable que votre voisin sait mieux que vous ce qui lui convient. Peut-être il n'aime pas l'eau: peut-être il n'en veut mettre que quelques gouttes par complaisance pour la mode: peut-être il ne veut pas qu'un autre observe combien peu il en met dans son verre. Donc, n'offrez l'eau qu'aux enfans. C'est une fausse complaisance et bien incommode. Je dis ceci à vous comme homme du monde; mais je finirai comme j'ai commencé, en bon chrétien, en vous faisant une observation religieuse bien importante, et tirée de l'Ecriture Sainte, savoir, que l'apôtre Paul conseillait bien sérieusement à Timothée de mettre du vin dans son eau pour la santé;[2] mais que pas un des apôtres, ni aucun des saints pères, n'a jamais conseillé de mettre de l'eau dans le vin.

P.S. Pour vous confirmer encore plus dans votre piété et reconnaissance à la providence divine, réfléchissez sur la situation qu'elle a donnée au coude. Vous voyez, figures 1 et 2, que les animaux qui doivent boire l'eau qui coule sur la terre, s'ils ont des jambes longues, ont aussi un cou long, afin qu'ils puissent atteindre leur boisson sans la peine de se mettre à genoux. Mais l'homme, qui était destiné à boire du vin, doit être en état de porter le verre à sa bouche. Regardez les figures ci-dessous: si le coude avait été placé plus près de la main, comme en fig. 3, la partie A aurait été trop courte pour approcher le verre de la bouche; et s'il avait été placé plus près de l'épaule, comme en fig. 4, la partie B aurait été si longue, qu'il eût porté le verre bien au delà de la bouche: ainsi nous aurions été tantalisés. Mais par la présente situation, représentée fig. 5, nous voilà en état de boire à notre aise, le verre venant justement à la

---

2. "Drink no longer water, but use a little wine for thy stomach's sake and thine often infirmities." 1 Timothy 5:23.

bouche. Adorons donc, le verre à la main, cette sagesse bien-
veillante; adorons et buvons.[3]

From the Baron de Bessel and Other Commission
Seekers ALS: American Philosophical Society

Of the ten people who applied for commissions in the Continental
Army between July 1 and October 31, 1779, four were German,
three were French, two were English, and one was a Frenchman
who had passed into German service.[4] While paying lip service to
America's struggle for freedom, most claim candidly that personal
advancement is their motivation. Baron de Bessel, for instance,
whose letter is published below, stresses that at age forty-five he is
at a dead end.

Writing from Watrouville near Verdun on July 13, the baron de
Sabardin explains that he has served the King of France for twenty-
six years but is now in an inactive post (*lieutenant des maréchaux de
France*). Once in America, he will accept no rank lower than that of
lieutenant-colonel and wishes to know what salary it entails.

Theodore Gursch strikes roughly the same note on July 21. After
active duty as an adjutant with Hungarian troops in the service of
the King of Prussia, he had been placed in the tobacco administration in Silesia where frustration drove him to illness and resignation.
In good health once again, he is unable to locate an acceptable military position and has come to Paris to visit Franklin in order to
discuss his case. His reading of Richard Price and others has convinced him of the justice of the American cause.

Pigault de Beÿmont, a young man of twenty-three, demonstrates
his mastery of English by writing in that language on August 7,
from Calais. He is vague about his curriculum: his family is one of
"some fortune and consideration"; he has had a few years of military employ as *lieutenant des maréchaux de France,* but hints at personal misfortunes that will require his absence for a few years.
Would Franklin give him a letter of recommendation to Congress,
stressing the military career of his brother and two of his uncles?

Admitting that he is animated by a very valid reason, an effort to

3. The accompanying figures, reproduced here, were engraved after the
original drawings by WTF.
4. Unless otherwise specified, the following documents are in French and
located at the APS.

"faire ma fortune par Vôtre gracieuse assistance," J.C. de Berger, a Saxon, explains that his future obviously lies with the American army where he wants "un avancement avantageux." His letter of August 10, from Münster in Westphalia, is accompanied by one he desires Franklin to forward to General Washington. He is a veteran of sixteen years in the army of Hanover. His cousin, a well-built young man with an understanding of mathematics, whose career is too slow to satisfy him, would also like to fight in America. He signs himself *Capitaine de Sa Majesté Britannique*. Believing that his letter has not reached Franklin, he writes again along the same lines on November 2.

Another baron, named de Heimenthal, addresses his plea, on September 20, from Valença-do-Minho in Portugal. He has been in the military since the age of twelve, first in the service of Württemberg and later in that of Portugal where his rank (first lieutenant of artillery) has remained the same since 1765. He wishes Franklin to grant him the rank of major and the command of a small artillery corps about which he goes into great detail, specifying that he demands the right to appoint officers and men, and have no commanding officer above him. In a postscript in English, he states that he has some knowledge of that language. Heimenthal's letter is accompanied by a three-page-long recommendation, quite warm, written in English by an anonymous person visiting Portugal who reveals only that "I am one of your friends of your club at Old Slaughters & the Swan which you will know we have since endeavour'd to keep up at different places, with a warm and respectful remembrance of you."[5] The writer points out that there are excellent officers to be found in Portugal, assembled by Count La Lippe[6] and now disgusted by the government or in fear of religious persecution. "Your country is now become the proper azylum of persecuted merit." Of all these officers, Heimenthal is, in his view and that of distinguished officers, the best qualified.[7]

On September 25 from Erlangen in Bayreuth, a former French

5. For the Old Slaughter's coffee house see XXII, 173. The writer, whose hand is not familiar to us, is probably alluding to the Club of Thirteen which met there for the purpose of preparing a philosophers' liturgy: XXI, 119–20.

6. For whom see XXVII, 102n.

7. Heimenthal wrote to JA from the same place on Feb. 5, 1780, repeating in an abridged form the content of his letter to BF. He also mentions the anonymous letter of recommendation, saying it came from "a competent Judge in Military affairs." *Adams Papers,* VIII, 317–18.

captain, a Protestant whose name at birth was de Rot, but who now signs himself de Flachenfeld, explains that he is a victim of the reforms of the comte de St. Germain.[8] He tried to salvage his career by moving to Germany but arrived unfortunately just as Prussia had concluded peace with Austria. He is now totally indigent, Franklin his only hope. What port should he head for?

A different voice in the chorus is that of Escudier fils who, on September 5, writes from Toulon to say that he is not of aristocratic descent, hence excluded by birth from serving his King. But he will not despair. What nature has refused, Franklin's clemency will grant him: the right to fight his master's enemies.

The letter sent from Ostend on October 18 is written in English by Richard Booth and John Brevitt. It explains that their parents' *over tenderness* kept them from the military line of life to which they aspired. Both "Articled to an Attorney of Eminence in London," they chafe at their inactive condition and are seized with a growing admiration for the "ever glorious American States." The spirit of their countrymen seems to them degenerate and they would gladly change "Dulce et decorum est pro patria mori" to "Dulce et decorum est pro libertate mori." Their project, for which they need Franklin's help, is to be appointed officers in the "Land Service of the American States." They are setting off for Paris on the following Wednesday in order to present their case.

There is no indication that Franklin answered any of the above.

Monsieur!   Hannovre ce 6m. Juilliet 1779

Parvenu â l'age de 45 Ans, apres avoir Servi Sa Majesté le Roi de Prusse l'espace de 30. ans et pendant l'avant dernière guerre en qualité de Major de Brigade et d'aide de Camp, et après avoir eu pendent 13 ans une Compagnie, des injustices et des affaires de famille m'ont forcé à donner ma demission que j'ai obtenu comme le prouve l'agrément du Roi ecrit de sa main ainsi que plusieurs lettres de sa part, Je me suis retiré à Hannovre où A. S. A. S. Msgr. le Duc de Mecklenbourg Streelitz m'a nommé Major de ses gardes pour en cas de guerre m'attacher en qualité d'aide de Camp general, à la personne du Prince Erneste son frere Lieutenant General des troupes Electorales d'Hannovre, mais il etoit stipulé que je chercherois fortune ailleurs en cas que la guerre n'eut point lieu.

Le service a été dés ma plus tendre jeunesse mon premier

8. For which see XXIII, 167.

point de vue, et je m'y suis livré avec un zéle analogue à mon caractère, Comme Vôtre Excellence pourra en juger par les deux ouvrages que j'ai mis au jour relativement à ma profession et à l'experience que j'ai aquise.[9] Il me reste encore un grand nombre d'exemplaires de ces ouvrages et Votre Excellence me rendroit un service des plus signalés de vouloir bien disposer de quelques uns.

Je suplie Vôtre Excellence de daigner faire des representations en ma faveur au congrès et au General de Wassingthon pour un placement convenable je suis bien persuadé que votre credit seul peut m'ouvrir une voie sure à mon avancement et J'ose Vous assurer d'avance que je ne dementirai jamais la bonne opinion que Vous pourrez donner de moi. Si j'avois le bonheur d'ètre agréé je prendrois des mesures pour pouvoir me présenter à Votre Excellence et recevoir ses ordres ulterieurs, que j'exécuterai avec tout le zele possible pour me rendre digne de plus en plus de ses bontés. J'attens cette grace de la bonté qui Vous caracterise, et suis dans les sentimens du plus profond respect. Monsieur! de Votre Excellence le plus humble, et obeissant Serviteur   FREDERIC GUILLAUME
                                                    BARON DE BESSEL

En suposant que Son Excellence daignera me faire repondre, j'ose la suplier d'adresser la lettre à Mr. Lefmann Isaac Hanau et Compe. à Francfort sur le main pour la faire passer à A. Ms. de Bessel, Major des Gardes de S. A. S. Mgr. le Duc de Mecklenbourg Streelitz *à Hannovre*

Notation: Bersel Baron de 6. Juillet

From Thomas Digges[1]   ALS: Historical Society of Pennsylvania

Dr Sir.   London 6 July 1779.
     I make use of the oppertunity by the under Spanish Secretary (who takes his departure today with the remaining

---

9. One of them was *Observations sur la tactique concernant l'infanterie*, which came out originally in German (n.d.) and was published in French, at the Hague, in 1781. Quérard, *France littéraire*.

1. Writing under one of his many aliases; see XXIX, 288n.

domestiques of the Ambassador) to forward you this;[2] in which I take the liberty to inclose one for Mr. Johnson at Nantes under a French direction & I am to beg the favor of you to cause it to be put into the common post as soon as may be. I also forward in my packet a letter from our friend, to which I refer for particulars.[3] He, as well as myself, have nothing now left but hopes; but we would not have You loose sight intirely of what we have been lately aiming at, and what may on some more fortunate day, be brought about. The Cloud is thickening a pace, & if appearances speak truth, almost every discription of Men among the thinking & great seem afraid it will soon burst with violence on this Country. In consequence of the impending mischeifs, there has been very great exertions in the naval department & many Seamen impressd, so that eight sail of the line *more* will be ready in about a fortnight to join the thirty one now cruising a few leagues west of Scilly.

I have got an answer from Mr Peters pressing me to draw on you, that He may get the much wanted supply.[4] I wrote you a few days ago that I shoud draw a bill on you payable at Grand's; I am advisd by the conversant in these matters to direct it to Grand himself marking it to be presented at Passy and so it will go by next mail—ie for Livres equivalent by the then Exchange to one hundd & ten pounds, payle at ten days sight to Messrs French & Hopson.[5] You understand the ten pounds is for another accot, and as soon as there is accots of the bill being paid Mr Peters shall have his £100 lodgd where he requested & the proper receipts forwarded to you. You will please to give the necessary orders about the bill when it may appear at Monsr. Grands.

I expect in a packet or two to forward You the whole

---

2. The secretary was José de Anduaga: xxix, 741n. The marques de Almodóvar had left London on June 18 after a virtual declaration of war against Britain: xxix, 651n.

3. Probably Hartley's of July 5, above.

4. In May BF had enlisted Digges's assistance in locating and transmitting funds to William Peters: xxix, 492, 736.

5. Whom Digges later identified as brokers: Elias and Finch, *Letters of Digges*, p. 215. They are listed as French & Hobson, merchants, in *Kent's Directory for the Year 1779* (London, 1779), p. 67.

printed Evidence of Cornwallis Grey & other officers respecting America; and also the very curious Evidence brought to counteract the others by Lord G. G of his now friend & new ally Mr Galloway.[6] This Gentn. has provd too much, & has compleatly done for himself in the opinion of all honest men even of his own Torey principles. He was treated as he deservd by some of the minority Speakers, & by attempting to prove the practicability of the American War, has innevitably fixd his ruin at home.

I begin to get more & more sick of these kind of Gentry and heartily tired of the Country. My business will lead me in a few months to Lisbon, but you shall have timely notice of my move; and I hope for your aid & recommendations when ever the day comes that any thing may be done in that Country favorable to my own. Your mentioning me even in a common way to those you write to at home will I am confident be highly servicable. It may seem odd that I have rejected three offers to attend Gentn whom you may guess at, as Secy;[7] & by such rejection appear cool in the cause they are engaged in: this is by no means the case; I was engagd in matters here, that I could not leave; & to speak truly I was afraid of joining intimately & cordially those who were engagd in disputes & quarrels which I ever disapprovd & carefully endeavourd to shun. I am sure no good can come of disunion, & that I have no prospect of comfort or satisfaction by living with a man or men who are apt to quarrel. I love quiet, & have no doubt I shall find it where I am going, because I am well-known & a little respected there. It will be a great additional happiness to me to have your approbation & friendship, for there is no one who esteems you more or wishes you better.

6. For the late parliamentary inquiry into the military conduct in America of the Howe brothers and for Joseph Galloway's testimony at those hearings see XXIX, 477n, 514, 531–2, 697n.

7. In January, 1778, William Lee had suggested Digges for the job of American commissioner in Portugal: Ford, *Letters of William Lee* I, 339–40. In late August of that year Digges was supporting Arthur Lee's charges that BF, Silas Deane, and Bancroft were mismanaging American affairs in Europe: Elias and Finch, *Letters of Digges*, pp. 11–14. A few weeks later Digges offered his services to BF: XXVII, 420.

I am happy to inform you the Milford Cartel Ship is again saild from Portsmouth with 119 Prisoners for Nantes, & will I hope be forwarded quickly back to Plymouth for the remainder there. There were 17 officers & 102 Men among the Officers Captns. Harris, Tew, Lunt, White, &ca.[8] They behaved very quietly & properly as they passd to the Ship, & by the joy & gifts of the people as they passd thro Gosport, there were strong indications that if Peace & accomodation could be brought about between that Country and America, the affections of Brethren and fellow Citizens would soon return. Leiut Knox, who Commands the Milford Cartel Ship is a very humane good Man, & gave a passage to a poor crippled Amn Woman, & to some other dischargd prisoners who had been in Haslar Hospital for cure. The general language of the lower class of People as the American Prisoners passd thro Gosport to embark was "they are fine fellows, God Bless them, & send them safe home".

I have thought it better to put the Nantes Letter into the Common post & therefore shall not Trouble you with it. I am with great regard Dr Sir Yr obligd & Obt. Servt

V——J——D——D

Addressed: To Docter Franklin

Endorsed: July 6

Notations in different hands: July 6. 1779. / July 6. 79

From Charles-Guillaume-Frédéric Dumas

ALS: American Philosophical Society

Monsieur, La Haie 6e. Juillet [1779]

On a eu besoin de moi ici pour répandre la note ci-jointe. La suspension a été accordée, à la priere de la ville d'Amst., qui, quoique la Province, par complaisance pour un grand

8. Capt. John Harris of Virginia, commander of the *Mosquito*, had been in Forton Prison since August, 1777 (XXV, 415–16n; XXVII, 92–4); Capt. James Tew of the *Swallow* (XXVIII, 389n) since January, 1778; Joseph Lunt of the *Rising States* (XXVII, 491n) since June, 1777; and Lt. Thomas White of Philadelphia since August, 1777: Kaminkow, *Mariners*.

personnage, n'eût pas accepté la médiation, n'a pas laissé d'intercéder, vendredi 8 jours, pour les villes souffrantes.[9] Vendredi matin ceux de Rotterdam avoient aussi demandé grace a l'hôtel de fce. par une Députation. Mr. l'Ambassadeur[1] n'avoit pas alors reçu encore la note. Il m'a dit qu'on ne s'est abstenu, dans cette note, de faire mention de la médiation & de son effet, que pour ne pas trop mortifier, &c.

Je pars dans un quart-d'heure pour Rotterdam. Je serai demain au soir s.p. à D. [s'il plaît à Dieu] à Anvers, Jeudi à midi Bruxelles, & arrivé à Paris j'obéirai à votre obligeant ordre, en me faisant conduire à Passy.[2]

Je suis avec un très-grand respect, Monsieur, Votre très-humble & très-dévoué serviteur   D.

Passy à S.E. Mr. Franklin M. Plénipotentiaire des E.U. &c.

La note suivante a été remise le 2e. Juillet par M. le Duc de la Vauguyon à Mr. le Conseiller Pensionaire des Etats d'Hollande, en le réquérant ministeriellement d'en donner une prompte communication à toutes les Régences des Villes de la Province.

9. Amsterdam and Haarlem supported proposals in the States of the Province of Holland and in the States General of the Netherlands for the Dutch Navy to provide convoy protection from British attack for ships carrying timber and naval stores to French ports. France therefore had exempted them from decrees which since March had rendered Dutch ships subject to capture and Dutch goods subject to increased custom duties; see XXIX, 5–7, and *passim*. This discrimination finally forced the remainder of the province to adopt Amsterdam and Haarlem's position; on June 25 the States of Holland voted to appoint a commission to prepare measures for protecting Dutch commerce if the States General continued to delay and to write a circular letter to the other provinces. France responded by extending the exemption to the remainder of Holland: Fauchille, *Diplomatie française*, pp. 136–44; Edler, *Dutch Republic*, pp. 126–7. The "grand personnage" is the stadholder, William V of Orange. For other political figures who appear in Dumas' correspondence and the code names and abbreviations he uses for them see XXVII, 31n; XXVIII, 21n; XXIX, 6n. For a sketch of the workings of the Dutch political system see *Adams Papers*, VI, 50–1n.

1. Paul-François de Quélen de Stuer de Caussade, duc de La Vauguyon, the French ambassador.

2. For several months Dumas had been planning to visit Passy (XXIX, 126 and *passim*). He was in Paris by July 13: XXIX, 195n.

Sa Majesté, informée de la Résolution que les Etats de la Province d'Hollande ont prise le 24 de Juin, a chargé Son Ambassadeur auprès des Etats-Généraux, de déclarer qu'Elle suspendoit jusqu'au 1er. Août, en faveur de la Province d'Hollande exclusivement, l'effet des Arrêts de son Conseil du 26 Janvier, du 27 Avril, & du 5 Juin: Qu'en conséquence tous les habitans de la dite Province pourroient jouir, jusqu'à la dite Epoque, des exemptions & avantages accordés exclusivement jusqu'ici à ceux d'Amsterdam & de Harlem, pourvu qu'ils se munissent d'un Certificat du Commissaire de la Marine à Amsterdam, ou de l'Agent de la Marine à Rotterdam: Qu'Elle a fait connoître ses intentions à cet égard à toutes les Amirautés de son Royaume, & qu'aussitôt que les Convois illimités auront été expédiés, Elle se propose de faire remettre aux habitans de la dite Province les sommes qui, en vertu des dits Arrêts, auront été perçues par les Préposés de ses Fermes.[3]

Sa Majesté se persuade, que ce nouveau témoignage de son affection fera de plus en plus connoître l'équité de son systême, qui ne tend qu'à maintenir la prospérité des Etats-Généraux, pourvu qu'ils ne s'écartent pas de l'impartialité absolue qu'ils sont si interessés à observer. Elle ordonne à Son Ambassadeur d'annoncer en même temps que, si à l'époque du 1er. Août les effets de la neutralité de la République ne sont pas assurés par la protection efficace des Convois illimités, conformément aux Loix de l'équité publique & aux stipulations des Traités, les dits Arrêts du 26 Janvier, du 27 Avril, & du 5 Juin recommenceront à être exécutés, sans qu'il soit besoin d'une nouvelle Déclaration de Sa Majesté.[4]

Addressed: à Son Excellence / Monsieur B. Franklin, Esqr. / Min. Plenipe. des Etats-Unis

Notation: Dumas. Juillet 6

3. *I.e.*, the agents of the farmers general, who collected the French monarch's taxes.

4. The French government issued an *arrêt* on July 3 suspending the ordinances; an English translation is given in Francis Piggott and G.W.T. Omond, eds., *Documentary History of the Armed Neutralities, 1780 and 1800* ... (London, 1919), p. 110.

From John Hay, Jr.

ALS: American Philosophical Society

Sir   Dunkirk 6th. July 1779

Your Excellency may perhaps wish to hear of the progress of a person, whose strong affection, for America, and the cause in which she is engaged, induced him to undertake so long a journey to visit a Gentleman so very respectable in his private character; and so very honorable, in his publick capacity. I left Paris at Midnight of the second instant since which I have not slept owing to the expedition of the Diligence in which I travel— This Evening at 7 Oclock I arrived here from whence I have resolved to proceed immediately home by route of Dunkirke and Ostende. Your Excellencys Passport has been but twice examined and is very good as it sets me off as an Americain—[5] If the Pacquet Boat in which I sail is taken I beg leave to use it to preserve my being made a Prisoner of war.

I again express for myself and the concernd our obligation for the Papers You were so obliging to commit to my charge: be assured they will never be used; but for the avowed purpose, on which they were solicited.

As several of the concerned will goe without having before them either relations or connections and will, from their attachment alone to the cause of liberty, desert that country wherein they retained certain and permanent possessions; it would be for them very desirable, to have Your Excellency's recommendation sent after them— In case You judge the expedition so worthy of Your attention as to make it the subject of any part of a public dispatch to the States; You will be

---

5. A draft of the passport in WTF's hand, with interlineations by BF, is at the APS, along with the list of thirty-four names which was indicated for insertion. The draft had originally stated that the persons named were "Natives of Ireland." That reference was marked for deletion, perhaps at Hay's request, and their nationality was left unspecified. The passport continued: "Being willing to encourage whatever is likely to prove beneficial to America, & knowing that these Undertakings are allowed & encouraged by the Government there," the minister plenipotentiary requested that the crew and passengers of the brigantine Elizabeth, 14 guns, commanded by William Stewart, be allowed to pass freely, and be given "every Succour in Case of Necessity."

advised of its sailing, when it will be sufficiently early for you to take such notice of it as you think it deserves.

I can not avoid acknowledging my particular obligation for Your extreme delicacy towards me in avoiding all manner of inquiry concerning the present state of that country which gave me birth and to which I must for a short time return— Perhaps the very high regard in which I hold Your Excellency had led me into indiscretion in conversing on that subject and likely the melancholy picture which in my own mind I have been accustomed to draw of it would have led You into error.

But I may say this much, that if (through a continuation of that ill directed policy in Brittain towards Ireland) the Inhabitants should have recourse to violent measures it will be happy for those to whom Your Excellency has granted Your protection that they will not be present at such a scene of distress as must ensue.

Discord sewd in deep rooted prejudices civil & religious must prevent that happy unanimity which has crowned America with success— The contest in that case would partake much more of the nature of Civil War than even Your Country has experienced—but to compare private characters with those that have been distinguished in the Annals of History although none of the friends to the expedition could in such a scene submit to the shameful inactivity of an Atticus it will be at least a blessing to be removed from a situation in which they would induced to follow at a humble distance the more noble but unfortunate conduct of Brutus— Indeed such differences have been spread by the wicked policy of the Brittish Court among all ranks & persuasions in Ireland that the probable effects of the contention hinted at would be to hasten the ruin of a Kingdom which till of late was gradually declining to the lowest ebb of insignificance— But by some small exertion of her own Spirit She has at last become an object of attention to Brittain.

By a continuation of that spirit Ireland may arrive at that stage when She will rather be considered as the Ally than the Subject and perhaps the ruling power taught by the conduct of America and it's consequence an awful lesson how dangerous it is to trample on the rights of mankind will avoid future strides toward unjust authority when the People may be happy in the enjoyment of their liberty and if not fitted as a nation to make requests it may still be so respectable in power as to avoid being subdued by foreign invasion and if for a moment I could suppose Brittain as thus described, & America to forget her well grounded resentment and Brittain her idle claim over that continent as her Colonies in times of danger to public liberty they together allied must form a sufficient guard for its protection— But I find immagination carrying me where I fear neither reason nor future consequences will be it's attendant. I fear I have spoken more on politicks than very high respect I entertain for Your Excellency & the very little knowledge You have of me will warrant.

In the name of myself & the concerned I request, that if any new matter strikes Your Excellency (as to the forwarding or delaying of the expedition and the quarter to which with least interruption it can proceed) that You may communicate it to Mr Nathl. Willson Belfast under cover to Messrs. H: I: Botermans & frs Negotiants a Anvers. In the mean time every matter shall be prepared to embrace the earliest and best opportunity to visit that country which we hold dearer than our own. I have the honor to be for Self & Concerned Yr Excys. Most Respl: Servt: J HAY JUNR:

Addressed: A Son Excellence / Son Excellence Doctour Franklin / Passy / Pres / Paris

Notation: John Hay, Dunk— 6 July 1779.

From Robert Montgomery

ALS: American Philosophical Society

Dear Sir   Alicante 6th: July 1779

I had the Honour of Addressing your Eccelly the 26th: ulto.[6] advising that by the officious Impertinence of the Assesor to this Governour I had been Arrested and my House Embargoed, notwithstanding I had Presented my Certificat and

---

6. XXIX, 746–7.

Pasport, Given by the Plenipotentiarys of the united States residing at Paris,[7] and also proved that I had always Subscribed my Self a Subject of those States in the Anual List taken of foraign Merchants Established here, which Confirm; but on my Representing the facts to the Conde de Ricla Ministre of war at Madrid, He Immediately dispatched a Courier Extraordinary with a Severe Repremand to the Govr, and Orders to suport the Americans and Protect them as freinds and Allies, so that I have been Redressed with Honour and all the Expidition Possible, the Express Come down in forty Hours, which by the Regular post is four days, wishing you Every Happiness and Success I am very Truly Dr Sir your Eccellys Most Obedt and Most Humble Servt   ROBT MONTGOMERY

Ben Franklin Esqr. Passy

Addressed: To / His Excellency / Benjamin Franklin Esqr / Passy / Paris

Notation: Robt Montgomery alicante 6. juillet 1779.

From Petre Sargét[8]   ALS: American Philosophical Society

⟨La Rochelle, July 6, 1779, in French: I left New Orleans on April 20 and arrived here June 19. The Americans had taken Illinois and Vincennes, but the post of Vincennes was retaken by the British last November. Col. [George Rogers] Clark has gone by land and sent troops by water to recapture it; there is every reason to believe he has been successful.[9] Natchez and

7. The merchant Montgomery had been residing in Alicante for more than two years. After he expressed his fears of being mistaken for a British subject in case of hostilities between Britain and Spain, the commissioners provided him documentation of his American citizenship: XXVI, 242–3. See also *Adams Papers*, VIII, 96. For Spanish actions against British merchants see above, 23–4.

8. Printed with a translation and editorial comments by Lewis J. Carey in "Franklin is Informed of Clark's Activities in the Old Northwest," *Mississippi Valley Hist. Rev.* XXI (1934–35), 375–8.

9. After an arduous march, Clark captured Vincennes and 79 prisoners on Feb. 24, 1779: Mark Mayo Boatner III, *Encyclopedia of the American Revolution* (New York, 1966), pp. 1192–3.

Manchac are well fortified. James Willing, who conquered them without resistance, should easily have been able to save them; to recapture Natchez will cost lives.[1] Pollock, the agent, is not a very honorable man. Col. Clark has bought many furs, giving letters of exchange on him. Pollock says he will honor them when Congress places funds at his disposal.[2] I have much to tell about their agreement. Bills of exchange are occupying me: more than 50,000 piastres of them have been protested, doing inexpressible injury to New Orleans. I fear business losses will keep merchants from aiding Col. Clark. I will come to Paris as soon as I finish my business here, which has prevented my coming sooner. My wife is from New York and I know the continent perfectly. I sailed from there to St. Domingue and Spain, stopping to recover my business affairs in New Orleans, where I always conducted myself like a true American.)

From Benjamin Vaughan   AL: American Philosophical Society

My dearest sir,   July 6h:, 1779.

I have this instant heard of this opportunity. I can put up nothing; scarcely this letter.

Every thing appears to me huddled and uncertain; we were a little up, but the apparent imbecillity of those to act against us, has let the spirit cool again very much. And danger made a cry for *unanimity* that did us mischief.

Your paper about the *aurora* has been a good deal controverted, which has made me very much exert myself.[3] I think we shall do, and you will receive pleasure at last from what I

1. James Willing and Oliver Pollock captured these Louisiana posts in early 1778, but left them unprotected; the British reoccupied them in May: Carey, "Franklin is Informed of Clark's Activities," p. 376.

2. Commercial agent Oliver Pollock had also asked BF's help: XXIX, 303–4.

3. BF's paper on the aurora borealis (XXVIII, 190–200) ran to six pages in Vaughan's 1779 edition of BF's writings. Vaughan's commentary, even though set in a reduced type size, was more than three times that length.

have gone through.— Poor Henly is dead;[4] suddenly, as you might expect.

I believe you were not aware that the air at less than 40 miles high is 10,000 times rarer than at the surface at the pole; the height & rarity going the one in an arithmetical the other in a geometrical progression; which you will see leads to consequences. Yours ever most devotedly.

In great haste.

I think it likely that a certain friend of mine will soon marry a niece of the Bedford family.

I sent a letter to you by Mr Barton of Bourdeaux the other day, inclosed to the Duke of Chaulnes?[5] Pray is it received?

Addressed: A Monsr / A Monsr. Franklin / a Passy / pres de Paris

Notation: B Vaughn July 6. 79

From the Chevalier de Laneuville

ALS: American Philosophical Society

Monsieur,   Paris ce 7. Juillet 1779

Je suis arrivé dimanche 4 de ce mois de la campagne, Votre Excellence pourroit me soupconner de peu d'Empressement a répondre a son honorable invitation pour célébrer le 5 l'indépendance Américaine,[6] si je ne lui expliquois pas les motifs qui m'ont privé de cet honneur.

Aÿant donné Ordre que l'on me fit passer au chateau de

4. The linendraper who had recently claimed that BF owed him money: XXVIII, 422; XXIX, 139.

5. On July 4, the duc de Chaulnes wrote the following note to BF: "M. de chaulnes recoit de M. Benjamin Vaughan la lettre cy jointe pour Monsieur francklin; il a l'honneur de lui faire bien ses complimens, et de la lui envoyer." APS. There is no way of telling which one the letter was; we only know that Vaughan's most recent surviving letter was dated June 17. John Barton was an Irish merchant at Bordeaux: XXV, 454n; XXVI, 325n.

6. Laneuville, formerly Gates's inspector general, had returned to France with Lafayette on the *Alliance*: XXIX, 57–8. He became a close friend and frequent correspondent of WTF.

Brueil les lettres qui me seroient adréssées a paris, je n'ai receu que ce matin la votre qui m'a eté renvoyée du paÿs d'ou je viens, et Je ne perds pas un moment pour vous témoigner combien je suis sensible a votre souvenir, combien j'ai de regrets de n'avoir pu avoir l'honneur de boire aux treize ètats unis de L'Amèrique, et combien je serois flatté dans toutes les circonstances de ma vie d'être dans le cas de leur montrer mon zele et mon affection.

Je suis avec respect, De Votre Excellence le tres humble Et tres obeissant serviteur LANEUVILLE

Notation: Laneuville 7. Juillet 1779.

To Laneuville

L (draft):[7] American Philosophical Society

[after July 7, 1779]

Dr Franklin regrets much M le Chevr de La neufville, not receiving his Invitation to Celebrate the anniversary of American Independence, 'till the Day appointed was past. He assures him however that he was not forgot when the Company drank, to the Brave Strangers who have hazarded their Lives in support of American Liberty.

If M. le Chevalier is not engaged Sunday next Dr. Franklin will be glad of his Company at Dinner.—

To John Paul Jones

LS:[8] National Archives; copies: Library of Congress (two)

Dear Sir, Passy July 8. 1779.

I received your Favours of the second and 4th Inst. I am sorry for the Accidents that have obliged your little Squadron to return & refit; but hope all may be for the best. Some Days since, Mr Chaumont handed to me the Substance of a Letter in French, which contained heads of the Instructions that M.

7. In WTF's hand.
8. In WTF's hand. One of the copies was certified by Thomas Hutchins at Lorient in August, 1780.

De Sartine wish'd me to give you. I had them translated & put into the Form of a Letter to you which I signed & gave back to Mr C. who I suppose has sent it to you.[9] I have no other Orders to give: For as the Court is at the chief Expence, I think they have the best right to direct. I observe what you write about a Change of the Destination: But when a thing has been once considered & determined on in Council, they don't care to resume the Consideration of it, having much Business on hand, and there is not now time to obtain a Reconsideration. It has been hinted to me, that the Intention of ordering Your Cruise to finish at the Texel, is with a View of getting out that Ship:[1] but this should be kept a Secret. I can say nothing about Capt. Landais Prize. I suppose the Minister has an Account of it; but I have heard nothing from him about it: If he reclaims it on Account of his Passport, we must then consider what is to be done. I approve of the Careenage proposed for the Alliance, as a thing necessary. As she is said to be a remarkable swift Sailer, I should hope you might by her means take some Privateers and a Number of Prisoners, so as to continue the Cartel, and redeem all our poor Countrymen.[2] My best Wishes attend you, being ever, with great Esteem, Dear Sir, Your affectionate Friend, & most obedt. Servant.

B Franklin

Honble: Capt: J.P. Jones Esq.

[*In Franklin's hand:*] If it should fall in your Way, remember that the Hudson's Bay Ships are very valuable. BF

Addressed: A Monsieur / Monsieur le Cape. Jones, / à L'Orient,

Endorsed: from His Excellency B. Franklin Passy July 8th. 1779. recd. L'Orient July 14th.

9. Jones had been ordered to circumnavigate the British Isles and cruise in the North Sea before sailing to the Texel, the great Dutch naval base at the entrance to the Zuider Zee: XXIX, 780–1.

1. The frigate *Indien.*

2. A favorite project of BF's; for Jones's eagerness to cooperate see XXIX, 406.

To Jonathan Williams, Jr.: Two Letters

(I) and (II) copy: Library of Congress

I.

Dear Jonathan,   Passy, July 8. 1779.

I received yours of the 1st. & 2d. Instand. Inclos'd I send as you desire Mr. Lee's original Letter declining any farther Concern with the Accounts. As it contains some malevolent Insinuations relating to them that are groundless, I think it right you should at the same time see my Observations on them, in the Drafts of a letter Intended to send him in Answer; but which on second Thougts I did not send, merely to avoid a continued Altercation, for which I had neither Time nor Inclination, and he abundance of both.

I am much oblig'd to the Gentlemen who have undertaken the Trouble of examining your Accounts and if they think fit to join Commodore Gillon to their Number, and he will be so good as to accept it will be very agreable to me. I am sorry that Mr. Schweighauser declines it, as he was put into our business by Messrs. Lee's and it was therefore I nam'd him in the request, tho' not an American.

I request you would make Enquiry concerning the Complaints contain'd in two Papers I inclose, which were handed to me from the spanish Ambassador.[3] I suspect that some of the English Cruizers do sometimes personate Americans to create Mischief. Let me know if Such Vessels realy went from Nantes. I am your Affectionate Uncle.

M. Williams.

---

3. The now-missing enclosures from Ambassador Aranda undoubtedly concerned the reported capture of the *Nuestra Señora de la Merced* (XXIX, 744n) and the two other Spanish merchant ships by American privateers. Documentation of the Spanish concern is provided in Yela Utrilla, *España*, II, 260–6. See also JW's response of July 13.

II.

Dear Cousin,   [July 8, 1779][4]

The Bearer, Mr. Genet junior,[5] a young Gentleman of excellent Character, goes to Nantes with an Intention of Spending a little time there in improving himself in the Englisch Langage by conversing among our Countrymen. I desire you would introduce him to their Acquaintance, and I recommend him warmly to all your Civilities, which I Shall esteem as done to myself. I am ever Your affectionate Uncle   BF

Jona. Williams.

From Charles Collins *et al.*

ALS: American Philosophical Society

Sir   pembrook preson July the 8 1779

Wee understand by Capt obrey that you are the gentelman aurthorized to hear & Redress the Complant and Grievances of the amrican presoners wee thearfore make bold to petition to you Sir on this head that you will be So Good as to hear & answer this our petition poor naked & Distitute as we are hear having bin plundred of all our Clothes & money by The Sailors on bord the Culloden officers & men without Distinction a Grat part of us having been taken out Halifax & Rhodisland prison against our will whear Some had been Confined upwords of two years when after being promsd to be Set on Shore again In a merica was broght hear So fair from home

---

4. Dated by its placement in the letterbook.

5. Edmond-Charles-Edouard Genet (1763–1834), the only son of BF's friend Edme-Jacques, was the future Citizen Genet who would become the first minister of the French Republic to the United States, befriend BFB, marry the daughter of George Clinton, and become an American citizen. Already at this young age he had distinguished himself as a talented translator of several languages. One of his projects, for the time he proposed to live at Nantes, was to work on a dictionary of English nautical terms for French sailors. *DAB; DBF;* Meade Minnigerode, *Jefferson, Friend of France, 1793: the Career of Edmond Charles Genet . . . 1763–1834* (New York and London, 1928), pp. 12, 24, 51–4.

Distitute of Evry thing hardly So much Clothes as will Cover our nakedness & as wee are In Such an out of the way place & not a nough prisoners hear for a Cartel thear being only 30 americans hear we Thearfore humbly beg that we may be Removed to Some more Convienient place whear wee may Expect a Speder Release then what at presant appears to us hear: Sir if we Cant be Removed from this place we beg & pray that you will be So kind as to Let us have Some Clothes to Cover our nakedness for if we Should Remain hear another winter we must Suffer Greatly for want of necessary Clothing: & as we hear that thear a Charitable Contribution In London for the Relief of the Distresed americans prisoners we thearfore Humbly beg that you will In Compasson to Distresed of your fallow mortles uise your kind & Genires Afforts That we may have a Shear In this Genires & Benifishet Charity & In So Doing we Shall In Duty bound for you Ever pray In the meantime we Remain Sir your most obeidant humble Sarvents   AMERICAN PRISONERS

Rote by CHARLES COLLINS a presoner at pembrook[6]

A letter I Rote to Mr Hudson when I was presner In Wales

From Arthur Lee

ALS: American Philosophical Society; AL (draft): National Archives

Sir,   Paris July 8th. 1779
I have just receivd a Letter from my Brother in Germany informing me of your having written to him, that— "When Capt. Lemaire came over last year & made known here the wants of Virginia, you found three different Merchants of ability, who offerd each of them separately to supply the whole"—[7]

6. Collins had been taken on Sept. 9, 1778, in the continental brig *Resistance.* On Dec. 15 he was put in Pembroke prison in Wales, from which he eventually escaped, made his way to France, and shipped on the privateer *Black Princess.* Collins to BF, March 29, 1780, APS.
    7. BF's letter is in XXIX, 232. Le Maire came to France to assist William Lee in procuring arms for Virginia: XXVI, 34–6; XXVII, 361–3.

I shall be very much obligd to you Sir if you will let me know the names of these Merchants, where they live, & what were the terms on which they proposd to supply the demands of the State of Virginia.

It will yet be of very great advantage, to that State & consequently to the common cause, if these Gentlemen will supply the things wanted, upon admissible terms. In all probability too these wants will increase every day, as the war now presses particularly on the State of Virginia. This consideration will I hope excuse the trouble, it will give you, to comply with what I request.

I have the honor to be with great respect Sir, Your most Obedt. Humbe Servt.   ARTHUR LEE

The Honble. Dr. Franklin

To Arthur Lee   Copy: Library of Congress

Sir,   Passy, July 9. 1779.

The Merchants alluded to in my Letter to your Brother, were Mr. Bayard, Mr. Monthieu, and M. Chaumont. The Terms I understood to be those proposed by Virginia. I have the honour to be with great respect, Sir Your most obedient and most humble servant   BF

honble. Arthur Read[8] Esq.

From George Leopold Besson and Other Favor Seekers

ALS: American Philosophical Society

The most obvious category of favor seekers is made up of people who simply want a handout and tell their hard luck story at greater or lesser length.[9] Most persistent among those was George Leopold Besson who penned eight appeals in the course of one year and whose initial plea, dated July 9, is printed below. He tries again on

8. An obvious mistranscription by the copyist.

9. Unless otherwise specified, the following documents are in French and located at the APS.

August 27, giving more information about the benefactors who helped him originally in his native Switzerland and enclosing copies of letters written in his favor: one sent from Montbeillard on August 3 by the baron de Goll, chevalier de l'Ordre de L'Aigle Rouge, to M. de Watteville de Belp, treasurer of Bern, and the latter's answer of August 25 stating that the Bernese authorities had decided to grant poor Besson two louis d'or, once and for all (*pro semel et semper*) since he really does not belong to Bern but to Neufchâtel. On November 25, Besson reminds Franklin of his previous plea, to which no answer has been made, and adds that he has been advised by someone in the King's good graces to appeal to the Doctor, so well known for his humanitarian views. He extends his good wishes on January 3, 1780, repeats his previous request almost verbatim, and asks Franklin to return de Watteville's letter. Another follow-up, written on February 20, expresses despair at the thought that he must have offended Franklin. He asks him once again to return de Watteville's letter. His next appeal, of April 8, 1780, is addressed to "Monsieur Le Premier Commis de la secretairerie de S.E.M. Le Docteur Franklin" and begs for that person's intervention on his behalf. He tries once more on June 4, with a different text in which he hints at the superior people in France and the Low Countries who have not disdained helping him in the past. His last letter, of July 29, is a true cry of despair; nobody is coming to his help anymore, he is doomed to perish. Much abridged here, his letters are all quite long and it seems obvious that Franklin never responded.

Other pathetic stories crossed the plenipotentiary's desk. Two of them came from fellow Masons. André Honoré writes from Paris on the fifteenth day of the sixth month (*i.e.,* August 15 in the Masonic calendar) to invoke the powerful bonds of brotherhood. He is near destitution, along with his numerous family. The meager subsidies he has received from other Masons are running out and he counts on Franklin's well-known humanity. Dubourg, who is to see the Doctor later in the day, will hand him a brochure about which Honoré himself says that it is not worth reading but will serve as an introduction.

The baron de Sabine explains that for a number of years he has been persecuted by fate and is now in the humiliating situation of having to beg for help. He has not had any bread (which he refers to in Masonic language as *pierre brute*) for more than forty hours, In another message, sent twice in almost identical form, he states that

74

he is a former captain many times wounded whose wife has been ailing for the last four years. They don't even have a fire.[1]

On August 17, two pages of convoluted Latin were sent from Lutetia, *i.e.,* Paris, by one Tirsius Tellejus who calls Franklin his generous supporter, his Maecenas, and thanks him for his help on two previous occasions. The lot of writers is a hard one and he wonders whether, in the Republic made illustrious by the Doctor's merits, there is a place for exiled professors. He will come again to pay his respects.[2]

Charles Blankenberg is "an unhappy young German who, by a marriage contrary to his family, is reduced through a chain of continual misfortunes to the most pitiful condition," as he relates on August 26. He had flattered himself to find honest employment in Paris (he speaks German, Latin, French, and Italian, and his letter is in fluent English) but is now penniless and indebted; his wife is in despair, their clothes are pawned. He will present himself at Passy the following morning, putting all his hope in Franklin's "infinite humanity and Generosity."[3]

Another needy couple sends an appeal from Paris on September 22. Their name is de Samson and the husband identifies himself as an unemployed architect. The cause of their misery is a lost lawsuit. Any help Franklin extends them will be further proof of his well-known kindness. "Obliger est la loi, du héros, et du Sâge."

Victor Breda, born in Lausanne, sends an undated letter to explain that his situation is desperate. He claims that he was captured during the battle of Trenton ("Trintanne"), carried off to England, and eventually sent back to Switzerland, a country he had left at such a young age that he has no more connections in it, his parents having died during his absence. He has lived fourteen years in America, his brother and sister are there and he hopes to return. But he is penniless and hungry.[4]

An officer by the name of de St. Firmin writes on August 2 to explain that he came to Paris in order to find a position in the army but it took so long that he switched plans and obtained the rank of

1. None of his letters bears a date. We guess at 1779 at the earliest since BF was *Vénérable* that year.
2. On or after Aug. 21 BF gave 12 *l.t.* to a "Poor Author," maybe this one: Cash Book (Account XVI, XXVI, 3).
3. In late August BF gave 6 *l.t.* to "a young German." Cash Book.
4. BF sent him 24 *l.t.* on July 10: Cash Book.

first lieutenant of volunteers on the *Brave Normand*. Alas, a two-week illness deprived him of the little money he still had to reach Caen, there is no time to procure the sum from his family, and his last best hope lies in Franklin's generosity.

Also from Paris comes the imploring letter of August 7 from the widow de Courcy, *veuve d'un insurgent*, as she dubs herself. Her husband embarked for Boston eighteen months previously, but the frailty of his constitution and the sorrow of leaving his fatherland led him to the grave. She would like Franklin to procure his death certificate and also to give her the means of subsisting until then. She hopes he will grant her an appointment in Passy or Paris. Being of high birth, she cannot possibly see how she might cope *honnêtement*.

After a widow, a wife. The chevalier de Sauseuil, too embarrassed to explain the "unhappy circumstances" into which he has fallen, entrusts his wife, Franklin's countrywoman, with the task of paying a visit to him and appealing to his "tenderness and sensibility."[5] Sauseuil's letter, written in English, is dated Paris, September 3. He refers vaguely to the possibility of employment.

Only one man, in a refreshing change, really wants to work for his money. Gautray le Jeune, from Bordeaux, throws himself, as he says, at Franklin's feet on October 30. He loves to work and would accept any position fit for his feeble talents, be it in some financial office or as secretary in France or America. He would even consider the army in which his family has served with honor. Anything rather than go on being a burden to his parents. He worked in Nantes for six years in the commercial line until the war forced him to go home where he feels bored and desperate. He knows Franklin's goodwill towards the French and puts his trust in him.

One correspondent wished Franklin would help him not merely to find a humble occupation but to earn serious sums in business. G[erv]ais Charles, who sends his plea on July 27 from La Rochelle, dreams of furthering commercial relations between France and America, and in particular between La Rochelle (Canada's warehouse when it was still a French possession) and Baltimore. He wants to assemble a great cargo but finds his colleagues lethargic in that respect. He has been able to gather only 96,000 *l.t.* so far and needs 80,000 more which Franklin can certainly procure through his

5. The visit may well have produced the 2 *l.* 8 *s.* BF gave on Sept. 5 to "A poor English Woman." Cash Book.

connections and influence. He will, if desired, send the best attestations about his character.

Writing from Amsterdam on July 15 in excellent English, the firm of Wernier, Hartsinck & Wernier express their wish for "connections with the Merchants of the american United Provinces." Their experience and integrity are well known and they are willing to offer favorable terms.

Business means problems in cashing bills of exchange. Pillat Delacoupe writes from Paris on July 23 that he has waited more than eight days for Franklin to accept seventeen such bills that he has deposited in the hands of banker Grand. Would Franklin please hand those letters, accepted, to the bearer or remit them directly to Grand? Were it not that he is on the eve of departure for a prolonged absence, the writer would not disturb the Doctor for such a small matter.

From Nantes, H.F. Greland sends his request on October 12. He has just received from St. Domingue six bills of exchange drawn by Hopkinson on the American Commissioners for a total value of 174 dollars. Since he does not know anybody in Paris, he is sending them directly to Franklin, with apologies for disturbing him over such a paltry sum.[6]

M. Bourgeois, *directeur de la Régie Générale,* wonders how he should proceed to cash an *effet* of December 11, 1778, for 1,500 *l.t.* by Hopkinson, Treasurer of Loans, on the commissioner or commissioners in Paris. It is countersigned by Jo. Clarke, of the Loan Office of Rhode Island, and payable at thirty days' sight to Philip Allen for interest due on money borrowed by the United States. His letter is dated October 19.

A different facet of money and its uses is brought to mind by Johann Matthias Diterich who writes in German from Berlin on July 3 in order to urge Franklin to buy a lottery ticket.

Not every favor seeker was concerned with money. Seven people asked Franklin to forward letters for them or give them news of their relatives in America.

On July 10, an Englishman, J. Hare, writes from Venice where he is visiting, to beg Franklin (in English) to send on a letter of his to a dearly beloved brother in Philadelphia from whom he has not heard in years because of the war. He gives assurances that "no one

---

6. Endorsed: "Recd the 20 Oct / Ansd 23d / The Bills were all accepted."

offensive Syllable is in the Packet" which he invites Franklin to examine.[7]

The father of one of the officers who accompanied Du Coudray writes on August 12 from Chauny in Picardy, in the hope that Franklin will forward a letter to the son he has not seen in two and a half years and who lives currently in Boston. The son's name is de Matigny. Thanks to his knowledge of English, he had become Du Coudray's aide-de-camp. After the latter's accidental death, the young man and two of his comrades remained in Boston.[8] Some day, perhaps, Franklin will enable him to send money to that cherished son. The father's name is Garde de Matigny.

The same set of circumstances serves as background to the appeal sent from Clermont-Ferrand on July 21 by M. de Fontfrede, father of another of the young engineers who accompanied Du Coudray and was allowed to remain in Boston after his death. The last he heard from his son was that, in February, 1778, he was preparing to campaign under the orders of General *Guest* (Gates). No news since then. Is his son still alive?[9]

The Captain De Frey who serves in Cremona in the Belgiojoso regiment, and appeals to Franklin on September 26, is the brother of the Captain De Frey who serves in the Pulaski Legion. Could a letter be sent from brother to brother?[1]

Another brother anxious to communicate with his sibling turns to Franklin on October 8. His name is A.C. Schüler and he serves as councillor and private secretary of the Duke Ferdinand of Brunswick-Lunebourg. He explains, with more than a little embarrassment, that his brother, desirous to see the world, enrolled in the ducal troops in spite of his parents' objections. As fate would have it, he was one of those captured along with General Burgoyne and the desolate family has been without news ever since. He knows that Franklin is generous enough to send their letter over to Amer-

7. The writer is undoubtedly the brother of Robert Hare, the Philadelphia brewer and merchant who had emigrated from London in 1773: XX, 141n. He is probably the unnamed Hare brother for whom JA wrote letters of introduction to his friends in Boston in September, 1776, assuring them that Hare had no interest in politics but was merely traveling to satisfy his curiosity: *Adams Papers,* V, 11–12.

8. They were Romanet, Gribeauval's nephew, and de Loyauté. See *JCC,* VIII, 705; IX, 877; Lasseray, *Les Français.*

9. BF inquired after Jean-Baptiste Fontfrede (or Fontfreyde) in his letter of Aug. 3 to Lafayette. Lasseray, *Les Français,* I, 218, gives a brief sketch of the young man's background.

1. De Frey's sister had also asked BF a favor: XXVIII, 48.

ica. It would be best to address it to one of the generals posted along the Virginia coast.

On August 18 J. Carÿ, who is in Paris, wishes Franklin would forward to the French consul a note informing him that the packages that he, Carÿ, was entrusted with have been duly delivered to the Doctor. Someone called Depond(?), living in Loches, encloses a *petite missive* on September 9, to be sent on, if possible, to Philadelphia.

Two men offered their services as potential consuls. The Irishman Robert O'Connell writes in English from Malaga on August 24. He has lived in Spain and Portugal since 1745, as patented officer and substitute to the Royal Academy of Sciences in Spain, and as keeper of the King's Cabinet of Physics in Portugal. He has never gone back to Ireland but hopes that a "compleat triumph over our common Enemys" will make his return a possibility. Considering that all the ports of Spain are open to the thirteen United Provinces, he believes that a person acting on behalf of the Americans would be most useful.

Another proposal is sent on September 13 by Jacob Emery. A native of the canton of Bern in Switzerland, he has lived three years in England, eighteen in Spain, and nine in Montpellier, the city from which he is writing. His letter is in French, with an English translation, and he is familiar with the Spanish language as well as with trade. He feels he could be quite helpful, especially in peace time, when North American trade "will soar up."

A number of people thought the Doctor might help them reacquire their freedom. On September 8, twenty-five-year-old Le Duc sends a little *impromptu* he did not have a chance to deliver when Franklin visited Bicêtre, the jail where he is held unjustly, a victim of calumny and of his envious family. He hopes his new protector, about whom France entertains such a high opinion, will say a kind word about him to the King.[2]

---

2. BF had visited Bicêtre and La Salpêtrière on Sept. 4 and made a donation of 24 *l.t.* 12 *s.* (Cash Book). Bicêtre was a village south of Paris where, on the grounds of the thirteenth-century castle of the bishop of Winchester (hence the name), the government established a hospice, a hospital, a jail, and an insane asylum—which is why Bicêtre eventually acquired a connotation akin to Bedlam. La Salpêtrière was, since 1648, the Paris building in which women, be they prostitutes, delinquents, or simply those who had displeased their father or husband, were detained under incredibly harsh conditions, along with abandoned children between the ages of two and seven.

The vicomte de la Potherye d'Andilly, chevalier de l'Ordre de Malte, needs twenty louis urgently in order to get out of jail, For-l'Evêque to be precise, where he has been languishing for almost three months because of some miserable *dettes judaïques*. Franklin can do no less than help him since they are fellow citizens, the vicomte being the son of the late major general of troops in Guadeloupe. His family now resides in Canada but, having come to France to look for service, he found himself involved in a series of misfortunes which led to his current deplorable situation, totally out of keeping with his birth and social rank. His letter is dated September 12.

A man called Lucy, notary in Meaux en Brie, informs Franklin on September 28 that two Bostonian sailors are languishing in his town's jail. According to their story, they were captured by the British and brought to France on a Danish vessel. They have no passport and do not know any French. A young Irish ecclesiastic who has spoken to them will soon relate their plight to Franklin and other important people, but should this take too long, the *intendant* of Paris may obtain the facts from his delegate in Meaux.

On October 24, J. Grillet, first surgeon on the privateer *Le grand zombie*, tells Franklin that after his capture while serving under the American flag, he has been kept prisoner for two years in Winchester, and is still languishing there. Now that exchanges are taking place, he wants to be included in one of them.

Finally, there are people whose requests cannot be easily categorized.

On July 13, a journalist at the *Courier de l'Europe*, named Boyer de la Croix, begs for a fifteen-minute appointment. He is appealing

---

Both the *Journal de Paris* and Bachaumont's *Mémoires secrets* provide interesting background to BF's visit. The prison administration, at the urging of police commissioner Lenoir, was trying to replace horsepower by manpower in working the well, a substitution that would keep twenty-four men busy and allow them a little extra food and money. The experiment, carried out on Aug. 12 (see the *Jour. de Paris* for Aug. 16, 1779), was declared quite successful. On the 31st the public was invited to admire the humanitarian innovations originated by Malesherbes during his brief tenure as Secretary of State for Household Affairs between 1774 and 1776: a workshop for glass polishing, an ingenious mill to produce better flour, and improvements in bread baking. Bachaumont, *Mémoires secrets*, XIV, 156–7, 158, 169–70. BF's friendship with Malesherbes and Lenoir and his interest in baking procedures were so many incentives to visit Bicêtre.

directly rather than through Dubourg and trusts that his devotion to Franklin and the United States will procure him a quick response.[3]

Reminding Franklin that he has been promised a recommendation for his razors, should they prove satisfactory on inspection, a man named Moreau announces on September 28 that he is sending the Doctor four of them, two mounted on tortoise-shell and two on whalebone. He will pay a visit within two weeks to hear Franklin's decision. His letter comes from Paris.

The name Moreau, belonging to a merchant of the rue St. Martin, reappears in another, undated, document which looks more like an advertisement than a private letter. The handwriting is somewhat different and it is not certain that we are dealing with the same Moreau. This one announces that he has discovered a new metal alloy, totally devoid of copper, and strikingly similar to silver. It is called *argiroïde*. Having experimented with it to his satisfaction, he is now selling a line of tableware for which he quotes prices and plans to expand his offerings.

A long and flowery letter was sent on September 29 from Rennes. Its author, who signs himself Commandant Brilhacq(?), *vicaire général de St. Malo,* waxes lyrical over the similarities between the French and American people and suggests that Concarneau, in Brittany, be made a free port for the Americans. He lauds its harbor, its commercial facilities, and its safety guaranteed by the vicinity of Lorient and Brest. Franklin must be aware of this, since he visited Concarneau upon landing.[4]

Charles Phelps writes in English from Philadelphia on September 23. He has seen Sarah Bache two days previously and presented her with his grand plan for raising funds in France in favor of the inhabitants of Charlestown, Massachusetts, the burned-out victims of British cruelty. What better way to bring Catholics and Protestants together? Franklin's daughter did not seem "in the least" opposed to his idea.

From Stenz, in the Unterwalden canton of Switzerland, comes a very different suggestion. On October 25, Traxler, the *statthalter* and

3. Perhaps Jacques-Vincent Delacroix (1743–1832) who edited *Le Spectateur français,* and wrote *Mémoires d'un Américain* (1771) as well as a *Tableau des constitutions des principaux etats de l'Europe et des Etats-Unis d'Amérique* (4 vols., Paris, 1791–92) and other works: *DBF; Larousse.*

4. Auray, where BF landed, is separated from Concarneau by Lorient. BF endorsed this letter, "Free Port."

banneret[5] of the city, offers to raise between four and six thousand men, both Swiss and German, to serve in America. Switzerland's oldest ally, France, employs twelve such regiments. Should Franklin be interested, he would be delighted to pursue the matter.

An eleven-page letter, unsigned, was sent on July 22.[6] Its author, obviously an elderly man, reveals that governmental organization has been the main object of his study since 1736. He is currently employed but if Franklin could procure him the title of *correspondant des Etats unis pour la partie de l'administration,* with emoluments equal to what he is presently earning, he would give his whole time to an elaboration of his proposed plan of government for the United States. The gist of it is that if freedom is indeed the key word of most revolutions, it should be preserved but circumscribed as soon as tranquillity is restored. He advocates a constitution for the new country as soon as the war is over, with Washington as governor general and Franklin as organizer of the legal, judicial, and executive systems.

Finally, as usual, there is the poet who delights simply in telling the Doctor of his admiration, without asking for anything tangible in return. He writes on July 18, his name is St. Suire, he is a pensionary of the King living in Passy, and his poem, unfortunately, seems to have disappeared.

à Montbeillard le 9.
Trés honorable, Trés Illustre,   Juillet 1779.
      et Trés Gracieux Seigneur.

Suplie en très profond respect George-Leopold Besson, domicilié à Montbeillard, et dit, Que feu ferdinand Jérémie Besson, son pére, aprés avoir servi longtems comme bas officier, dans un des Régimens Suisses attaches au service de S. M. T. C., vint se retirer à Montbeillard, ou il est mort, en laissant le trés humble supliant dans un état d'autant plus triste et déplorable, que perclus de la majeure partie de ses membres, allité depuis plus[ieurs] années et sans aucun mouvemens et Sensibilité dés la Ceinture en bas; il se voit privé des ressources qu'il auroit pu trouver dans le travail, pour se procurer les moyens de subsister dont il est absolument destitués.

5. A lord who had enough vassals to raise at least fifty armed men under his own banner. There is no indication that BF showed any interest in Traxler's project.
6. It is at the Historical Society of Pennsylvania.

Dans lintention d'alleger ses maux, il prit la liberté de faire parvenir [il] y à quelques années, sa trés humble requete à M. Le Comte de st. Germain, alors Ministre au Departement de la Guerre et une seconde requête à S. A. M. Le Prince de Montbarrey, actuellement Ministre au même Département, apres y avoir été renvoyé premierement par M. Turgot, en second lieu par M. De Malesherbes, et dernierement par M. Necker, Directeur Général des finances Du Roi, pour qu'il plut aux Ministres de la Guerre, cidessus nommés, lui accorder quelqu'assistance dans l'etat malheureux ou il se rencontre, comme il le justifie par la Lettre jointe de M. Necker; il ose joindre aussi la copie du Certificat de son Médecin pour faire conter de son etat de maladie,[7] et un Lettre en original de M. Le Garde des Sceaux.

Mais jusqu'a present ses requêtes n'ayant point produit les effets qu'il osoit s'en promettre, il vient trés humblement vous supplier, Monseigneur, de lui accorder Votre Protection, vivement persuadé, que si Vous daignés appuïer sa Demande auprés de Monseigneur Le Prince de Montbarrey, elle lui sera aussitôt accordée.

Il ose se flatter que vous lui ferés d'autant plûtot cette Grace, qu'il est connu d'un chacun que Votre Grandeur se plait â faire des heureux.

Le trés humble supliant se voit par une suite de cette déplorable maladie dans l'impossibilité de travailler pour gagner sa vie, celle de sa femme et de ses enfans, et se voyant aussi sans appui et sans protecteur dans le triste et pitoyable etat ou il se trouve réduit, ce qui fait qu'il vient, très humblement, implorer la Clémence de Votre Excellence.

Il a trop bonne opinion de Votre Pieté, pour douter de la Grace qu'il ose Vous demander; Encore qu'il n'a point l'honneur d'etre connu de Votre Excellence, l'estime que tout le monde fait de sa Générosité, lui à donné la hardiesse de la suplier trés humblement comme il fait de lui accorder Votre Protection.

Jusques-ici, Monseigneur, Les ressources que le trés humble

7. Dr. Berdot fils wrote a certificate, dated Aug. 6, specifying that Besson, a maker of stockings, was afflicted with an incurable disease.

supliant à eus pour vivre avec sa femme et ses enfans provien-
nent, de la commisération, que son état malheureux à excitée,
chez differentes Personnes de cette Ville; mais comme [ces?]
mêmes ressources ne sont pas toujours égales, et qu'il
éprouve journellement qu'elles diminuent, au point qu'à
p[eine?] peut il vivre avec le peu qu'il reçoit actuellement, il à
osé, Monseigneur, espérer que Votre Excellence, informée de
son triste sort, et qu'il est fils d'un pére qui â longtems servi
dans les Troupes au service de S. M. T. C., voudroit bien par
un Principe de Charité; contr[ibuer] pour quelque chose â son
entretient â son soulagement, et â celui de sa triste et malheureuse famille; entretient [que] le genre de sa maladie, l'em-
pêche absolument de procurer. Il ose donc se flatter aussi,
Monseigneur, que Votre Excellence, touchee de compassion à
la vue de son etat triste, daignera assister le trés humble supliant de ses charités; celui-ci l'assurant trés respectueusement
des ardentes prieres qu'il fait â Dieu, et qu'il fera jusques a sa
mort, pour sa prospérité, et celle de son Auguste Famille. Il
fait aussi journellement des voeux sincéres au Tout puissant
pour la prospérité des Armes de S. M. T. C., et celles des
Treizes États Unis, ainsi que pour la Gloire et la Durée du
Règne du Meilleur des Rois. Le trés humble supliant ose s'assurer de n'etre point éconduit en sa demande, parce qu'il sait
que Vous étes extrêmement bon, et que Votre Excellence prend
un singulier plaisir à obliger un chacun, il en conservera éter-
nellement la mémoire dans son coeur, se sera une Grace
spéciale.   GEORGE LEOPOLD BESSON

A Son Excellence Monseigneur Le Docteur Franklin Ministre
et Ambassadeur Plénipotentiaire Des Treizes Etats-Unis De
L'Amérique Septentrionale, Auprés de sa Majeste Trés-
Chrétienne, Le Trés Auguste et Trés Vertueux Roi De France
et De Navarre, &c. &c: &c:

Notation: Berdot fils à Montbeillard 6 aout 1779. Besson,
George Leopold

From John Paul Jones

ALS: American Philosophical Society; AL (draft):[8] National Archives; copy: United States Naval Academy Museum

Bon homme Richard L'Orient
Honored and dear Sir,   July 9th. 1779

I should have acknowledged sooner the receipt of Your Orders dated the 30th. Ulto. which I recd. the 7th. Curr.[9] but waited for the letter which yours alludes to from M. de Chaumont which has but this moment appeared and except the Name of a Merchant contains nothing New.

I have had another Proof this day of the communicative disposition of M de ————.[1] He has written to an Officer under my command a whole Sheet on the Subject of your letter and has even introduced more than perhaps was necessary to a person commanding in chief.— I have also strong reasons to think that this Officer is not the Only improper person here to whom he has written to the same effect.— This is surely a strange infatuation; and it is much to be lamented that one of the best of Hearts in the World should be connected with a mistaken Head whose errors can afford him neither pleasure nor profit; but may effect the Ruin and Dishonor of a Man whom he esteems and Loves. Believe me, my worthy Sir, I dread the thoughts of Seeing this Subject too soon in Print,[2] as I have done Several Others of greater importance with which he was acquainted, and which I am certain he communicated too early to improper Persons; whereby very important Services have been impeded and Set aside.

Had I received your Orders two days sooner I should not have Suffered the Alliance to be Hove Down—but, notwithstanding the very bad weather which we have had here, that

---

8. With numerous changes and interlineations. We note, below, his marginalia, written on the draft at a later date (see XXIX, 708n).

9. XXIX, 780–1.

1. In the draft Jones here inserted the name of Chaumont; see also Jones's of July 4. Chaumont was in contact with his former secretary, Lt. Peter Amiel: Bradford, *Jones Papers*, reel 3, no. 655.

2. In the margin of the draft: "I found it in Print when I reached Holland."

work is now too far Advanced to save above two or three days by giving up the design.— Besides the Kings Mast Maker has this morning reported that the Bon homme Richards Bowsprit is Sprung.— This has occasioned a work which I did not till now expect, and the Bowsprit will be Landed this Night to be well examined.— I hope it is not much hurt; but should it be found Unfit for Service, I am told that there is an Old Bowsprit now in the Yard that may be conveniently Substituted— And either way the little Squadron will not I think be detained so as to interfere with the execution of your Orders.

When we meet with the Enemies property of no great value or that cannot be conveniently sent into Port, would it not be proper to "Sink, Burn, or otherwise destroy" Such property?— I have Always had such a charge in my instructions from Congress[3] and it is therefore that I Mention it now.— I would also beg leave to ask whether I may or may not Attempt to avail myself of every opportunity that may seem to present itself to distress the Enemy.[4]

The reason why I have not yet Ordered a Court of inquiry is because the Officer principally concerned has been Sick ever since my Arrival—[5] As I am told he is now better the Court will be held and the events transmitted to you without loss of time.— I hope very soon to have the Satisfaction of informing you that I am ready to proceed with a good prospect of executing your Orders; and in the meantime it gives me pleasure to find that your Ideas on that Plan correspond exactly with mine.

In proportion as I am detained here I may be expected to arrive later at the port of my destination; unless ample Success or your Orders to attend to the letter of the Instructions which I have already received should Impel me to Steer for that Port Sooner.

3. Jones's citation, slightly misquoted, is from the Marine Committee instructions of June 18, 1777: Smith, *Letters*, VII, 216–17.

4. Marginal note: "I have ever made this my Study."

5. Lt. Robert Robinson of the *Bonhomme Richard*, presently ill in Lorient.

I am ever with Sentiments of real Affection and Esteem Dear Sir Your very Obliged Friend and most humble Servant.

JNO P JONES

N.B. M de Chaumont has written to one of my Captains[6] that it might be expedient for the Pallas & Vengeance to go out for a few days to Cruise after privateers until the Bon homme Richard & Alliance are ready for Service. I have consulted M. de Thevenard the Commandant at L'Orient on the Subject,[7] who is as well as myself of a contrary Opinion—because they would in all probability either return without having had Success, or else after being disabled either by the Seas or the Enemy which would occasion a further loss of time, as our whole force is not more than Sufficient.

His Excellency Doctor Franklin.

Notation: Capt. Jones. July 9. 79.

From James Lovell[8]

ALS: American Philosophical Society (three), University of Pennsylvania Library;[9] copy and transcript: National Archives

Honble. Sir   Philada. July 9th. 1779
I send by this Opportunity Journals & Gazettes with some Letters which were to have gone by Way of Martinique some time ago with others that I hope will reach you by that Channel. I add a Compleat Set of the Journals as far as they are

6. Probably Capt. Cottineau, who communicated directly with Chaumont; he may also be the officer discussed in the second paragraph of the present letter.

7. Antoine-Jean-Marie Thévenard (1733–1815) who served as naval minister in 1791: Didier Neuville, *Etat sommaire des archives de la marine antérieures à la Révolution* (Paris, 1908), p. 140.

8. Writing on behalf of the committee for foreign affairs of the Continental Congress, of which he was a member. With this letter Lovell enclosed a copy of his of June 13 (XXIX, 683).

9. Marked "4plicate" and "by Capt. Sapet." One of the ALS at the APS is marked "3plicate" and includes a triplicate of his July 16 letter. They contain numerous minor variations.

printed viz 1st. Vol 2d Vol and from Jany. to June 12th. this year with two spare Pamphlets of Ns. 2. 3. 11. 12 to make those already sent compleat.[1]

Perhaps I may have the honor of writing again before the Vessel[2] sails out tho she is now falling down the River.

Your most humb Servant   JAMES LOVELL

Honble. Doctor Franklin.

Notations in different hands: James Lovell Phyladelphie 9. juillet 1779. / Tripl: June 13 Dup July 9

From Samuel Wharton   ALS: American Philosophical Society

Dear Sir   Paris July 9/79

I return the american paper with many Thanks. Inclosed, you have the London packet, containing part of Mr. Galloway's extraordinary Evidence.[3] A Gentleman, a Native of the united States, writes July 2d,— That Sir Charles Hardy sailed out of the Channel with thirty One Sail of the Line, and if the Wind continued Easterly a few Days, several more Ships would follow Him.

1. For publication data about these journals of Congress see Charles Evans *et al.*, compilers, *American Bibliography* ... (14 vols., Chicago and Worcester, 1903–59), VI, 51–2.

2. The French ship *Victorieux*, carrying dispatches from Gérard: Smith, *Letters*, XIII, 182–3. Copies of the committee for foreign affairs' July 10 letters to her captain, Sapet, are at the National Archives. On Aug. 13 the ship's owners, Mercy & Lacaze & fils of Cadiz, report the ship has arrived and her captain has delivered papers for BF to the French consul there. They plan to send the ship back to Philadelphia, where they hope to found a branch of their firm under Messrs Lacaze and Mallet (who accompanied the ship on her first voyage). They ask BF's recommendations for the new firm and also for the Baltimore firm of Terrasson & Poey, in which the Cadiz partners are also interested. APS. Meanwhile, Lacaze and Mallet had become involved in a serious dispute stemming from their sale of part of the *Victorieux*'s cargo to Robert Morris: Hubertis Cummings, "Robert Morris and the Episode of the Polacre 'Victorious,'" *PMHB* LXX (1946), 240–1.

3. Wharton had moved from London to Paris around March and now received regularly newspapers and intelligence from his associates in England. See, for example, XXIX, 276n.

I am with the sincerest Respect & Esteem Dear Sir yr. Excellency's most affectionate Fnd.   SAML. WHARTON

His Excellency Benjan. Franklin Esqr.

Notation: James Wharton Paris 9e juillet. 1779.

From John Antes[4]   ALS: American Philosophical Society

Sir   Grand Cairo July 10th 1779.
You may perhaps still remember a young Man wich in the Year 1763 amussed himself with making Musicall Instruments such as Harpsichords Violins etc. whome Curiosity and Disire of Learning once led to your House at Philadelphia without anything to introduce him but a little American Cordiality. This Man am I. The noble and generous Treatment I received of you that Time, when I have been an intire Stranger to you has all this many Years left a deep Sense of Gratidute and the highest Opinion of your kind and obliging Caracter in my Heart. And this is the only Motive wich induce me to send you with the Pressent a Copy of six Quartettos wich I have lately composed in my leassure hours for my Frind the Marquis de Hauteford,[5] to make use of at the Harmonical Society of Bengal, where he had last Year an Intention to go, if the

4. A minister and son of the founder of the Moravian church, Antes (1740–1811) was by turns a clockmaker, instrument maker, composer, inventor, and missionary who was stationed in Egypt between 1770 and 1781. The six quartets he mentions in this letter have not survived, but his three trios for two violins and cello (opus 3, London, *c.* 1790) are now called the first known chamber music by an American composer. He is also known as one of the earliest American violin makers. His only surviving instrument, from 1759, is in the museum of the Moravian Historical Society at Nazareth, Pa. Stanley Sadie, ed., *The New Grove's Dictionary of Music and Musicians* (20 vols.; London, 1980); Donald M. McCorkle, "John Antes, 'American Dilettante,'" *The Musical Quarterly* XLIII (1956), 486–99.

5. Armand-Charles-Emmanuel, marquis de Hautefort (1741–1805): *Dictionnaire de la noblesse*, X, 399; *DBF.* It is not clear whether BF ever received this music. The present letter was forwarded from Marseilles by the merchant Louis Michel Ollive on March 8, 1780; in his cover letter, Ollive promised to send the packet of music by another conveyance. APS.

pressent War had not make him change his Ressolution. I am very sensible that in Paris you are not in Want of good and much supperior Music to what my poor Talents may afor'd, But poor as the may be, The Composition of a Country, man, and the Manner in wich the are given, as a mere Sign of sincere Gratidute, will perhaps make them agreeable. And if after a fair Trial, by able Performers such as play wich good Expression and Taste, the should still be So lucky to afor'd you some Amussement, I should certainly be extreemly happy. I acknowledge I don't make Profession of Music, and all I know of I picked up here and there by good Frinds, Therefore I should not be surprized if great Master, should find Faults here and there.

Since I left America wich has been in the Year 64. I employed all my Talents to Mechanic, and chiefly to the Watchmaking Branch, in wich I have been pretty lucky, so that I did something above the common Way.

Being in London in August 69. I took the Liberty to call at your Lodgings, but have not been so fortunate to see you as you had just made a Trip to Paris. Most of my Time since that I have spent here in Egypt, where the United Brethren, to wich Society I belong, have a Missionary Post, tho observe what good may be done for the Furtherance of the Gospel in this Country and Abissiny.

If I could here be of any Service to my Mother Country or to you in Particular I should allways embrace every Oppertunity with the greatest Plassure. I will not begin wich any Discription of Things concerning this Country, well knowing that Paris is not in Want of better than ever I could afor'd. But any particular question put to me I should allways answer with Pleassure according to my Abilities. One Circumstance however will perhaps not be disagreeable to mention that after a few Days southerly Wind, the Heat has been so excessive in the Night between the 6th. of June to the 7th. that the Thermomete of Reaumur rose at 11 a Clock in the Night to the 36th. Degree, wich is a very extraordinary Thing, the greatest heat in the middle of the Day is in Sommer commonly. no more but between 25 to 30. Many People died verry sudden that Night and the following Day, but thank God it did not last long.

May God grand soon Peace to the Satisfaction of all to our Mother Country, for wich I have still the greatest Regard, and wish well to evry Individual of it from the Bottom of my Heart.

But pray, give my Leave dear Sir to mention one Circumstance to you by the Pressent. You know that the United Brethren had allways some religious Scrupel of bearing arms, and as long as America has been under Great Britain, we have been exempt of that, and of swearing, by an Act of Parlement. Many Individuals would most probably not have settled in any of the Colonies without this. But since the Independency of the Colonies the have sufferd great hard ships on this Acct. I am fully convinced that nothing can be more just, As that those that can not bear Arms, should contribute to the Expences of the whole by paying their Equivalent in Money and assist in any other Occasion as much as in their Power, wich the also have never refused to do. But I leave it to you to judge if 50 £ Penalty for the Year 77 for every Person from 18 to 53 Years of Age,[6] must not fall very hard and soon be the Ruin of poor working People, wich at the very same Time had given up their large Houses and Workshop's for a Lazaretto for the Provincial Army. I need not to inform you of what Utility this Society might be to the Colonies, and that the will be as faithful Subjects to the Congress as ever the have been to the King of England, and that out of a religious Principel. You are very well aqainted with their Settlements and Constitution. I dont doubt that by your Influence a little more Indulgence may be used against them. You will excusse the Liberty I have taken to mention this, It has not been my Intention when I began this Letter, But the high Opinion I have of your good obliging

6. The Pennsylvania militia law, approved on March 17, 1777, established these steep fines for nonassociators. For a discussion of the fines, see Steven Rosswurm, *Arms, Country, and Class* (New Brunswick and London, 1987), pp. 135–7. See also James T. Mitchell and Henry Flanders, comps., *The Statutes at Large of Pennsylvania from 1682 to 1801* (Harrisburg, 1896–1915) IX, 79–80, 82, 83, 86.

Caracter made me free, and full of Hopes that you will take Notice of.

As the above mentioned Quartettos are not yet in the Hands of anybody but my Frind the Marquis the Hauteford, and one Member of the Harmonical Society at Calcutta in Bengel, wich latter is just now taking them to England to get them printed for the said Society. I think it nessesary to aqaint you, that I promissed not to make them publick myself at least in the first 8 Months. I don't mean by this that your Frinds might not have Copies of, if you chuse it.

It is far beyond my Expectations to have an Answer from you on the pressent, well knowing that all your Time must be employed with Matters of much greater Consequence. It would however be of great Satisfaction to hear that it came safe to Hand, and for this one single Line to my Frind Louis Michael Ollive at Marseille would be sure to reach me.

Pray excuse the Trouble I give you with my long Letter and bad Language. Be assured that is comes from a cordial and sincere American Heart. And give me Leave to call myself Sir Your most obedient humble Servant.   JOHN ANTES

From Arthur Lee

ALS: American Philosophical Society; AL (draft): National Archives

Sir,   Paris July 10th. 1779

I had the honor of receiving your Letter of yesterday in which you inform me, that Messrs. Bayard, Chaumont, & Montieu were the Merchants you alluded to in your Letter to my Brother, & that you understood their terms were those proposed by Virginia.

The first of these Gentlemen, who never applied to me, I understand is a Bankrupt.[7] The second you may remember declind an application made by us with Mr. King, similar to that by Mr. Lemaire, but to a much smaller amount.[8]

Mr. Lemaire brought Mr. Montieu to my House, as one who

7. For Bayard's bankruptcy see XXIX, 232n.

8. John King was a Petersburg, Va., merchant who seems to have accompanied Silas Deane to France (XXIV, 503n); he contracted with Penet,

had a Manufactory of Fusils.[9] But he made no proposals that I remember at all conformable to those of the State of Virginia. Your Nephew[1] however informs me, that he believes Mr. Montieu sent his Proposals to you in writing. If so I shall be much obligd to you for a Copy of them.

I have the honor to be with the greatest respect Sir Yr. most obedt. Humble Servt.   ARTHUR LEE

The Honble. B. Franklin

To Thomas Digges   Copy: Library of Congress

Dear Sir   Passy July 12 1779.
Your Bill on Mr. Grand[2] will be paid. I am much obliged by your kind Letters, and pray you to continue them. I find it an Endless and fruitless Business to consider and give Opinions upon Propositions of Peace, drawn up by Persons who have no authority to treat. I hope You will therefore excuse my Silence on yours.[3] I can at present only thank you.— We are in daily Expectation of important News.

With great Esteem, I am &c.

M Digges.

To David Hartley   LS,[4] copy, and transcript: Library of Congress

Dear Sir,   Passy July 12. 1779.
I am glad to hear that another Cargo of Prisoners are on the Way.[5] I will give Directions to assemble an equal Number im-

---

d'Acosta frères for various supplies for Virginia, but the contract was not fulfilled: *Jefferson Papers,* III, 91.

9. For Montieu's arms see XXII, 464n. Lee was suspicious of him: XXIX, 133, 166–7. Le Maire's relations with the Lees also were less than cordial: XXVII, 361–3 and following.

1. In the draft Lee deleted "Nephew" and interlined "grandson".

2. For supplying funds to William Peters; see Digges's letter of July 6.

3. XXIX, 583–4.

4. In WTF's hand.

5. Hartley had reported this on June 24: XXIX, 732–3.

mediately at Nantes in order to dispatch the Cartel with all Expedition: And I will direct Mr. Schweighauser to correspond more exactly with the Board, and send Returns of the Prisoners as desired. I shall endeavour to obtain Morlaix for the third & subsequent Cartels, as it seems to be so much desired.[6] I have hinted the Proposition of exchanging French Prisoners at the same Place; but am told that such an Exchange will not be consented to, till the Crews of the two Frigates seized by Admiral Keppel before the War commenced are returned.[7] I will endeavour to obtain the Lists of the Prisoners in Spain, and consider of the most convenient means, of exchanging them, on which you shall hear from me hereafter.[8]

With great & sincere Esteem, I am ever, Dear Sir, Your most obedient & most humble Servant   B FRANKLIN

D. Hartley Esq.

Endorsed: DF July 12 1779

To Richard Bennett Lloyd   Copy: Library of Congress

Dear Sir   Passy, July 12. 1779.

I received the honour of yours inclosing two Letters from Maryland.[9] I have made some enquiry, and cannot find that any Person here would be willing to purchase Bills upon Maryland; Those who want Tobacco's from thence having already more Money in that Country than they can well get away, one Cargo from hence being sufficient to purchase several of the product, and Vessels there to freight upon are so difficult to be found, and so hard to be got out of the Bay in the present situation of Affairs, that the Commerce is scarcely practicable.— If I could be of Use to you in this or any other

6. The commissioners for sick and hurt seamen had suggested in May the use of Morlaix as an exchange site: XXIX, 427n, 469.

7. For the capture of the *Licorne* and *Pallas* see XXVI, 680n; XXVII, 32n.

8. Bondfield had proposed transporting to France and including in the exchange prisoners who had been taken by American privateers and carried into Spanish ports: XXIX, 373. Hartley had also raised the issue: XXIX, 733.

9. See Lloyd to BF, July 2. Lloyd on Sept. 11 thanked WTF for sending him a copy of the present letter. APS.

affair, it would be a real Pleasure to me, being with sincere Esteem, Dear Sir Your most obedt. and most humble servant.

Please to make acceptable my Respects to Mrs. Loyd.

M. Lloyd.

To Richard Peters

Copy: Library of Congress

Dear Sir   Passy July 12. 1779.

I have at Length found your Good Father, as you will see by the inclos'd, and have given Orders to furnish him with 100 £. which you will please to remit to me in Congress Interest Bills, or in a Bill from ———.

The Bearer of this M. Vateville who goes over with a View of settling in Pensylvania and leaves some Money with our Banker. He is recommended to me, as a Gentleman of good family & excellent Character by several respectable Persons. M. Le Count De Vergennes, Minister for foreign affairs thinks he would be a valuable Acquisition to our Military, as you will see by his letter to me, wich I send inclosed.[1] I have acquainted the Count and the Gentleman himself that I could give him no promises nor even Expectations of Employment in our Armies, which were full but that there was no doubt of his meeting a hospitable favourable Reception in our Country as a stranger of Merit who desired to become our fellow Citizen.— I accordingly recommend him warmly to your Civilities and Counsels, and Those of my friends, who may with you be assured of my considering them as done to myself, and of my Readiness to pay an equal Regard to their Recommendations. My Compliments to Mrs. Peters, and believe me to be with great Esteem, Dear Sir Your most obedient and most humble Sert.[2]

Richard Peters. Esq.

1. Vergennes had recommended the Swiss military man Vatteville in May. BF could only promise to provide him with letters of introduction: XXIX, 527–8, 665.

2. Mrs. Peters was the former Sarah Robinson; they married in 1776: *DAB*. Peters apparently never received the present letter. He wrote BF on

From Jonathan Loring Austin

ALS: American Philosophical Society

Sir   July 12th. 1779

I have only now to acknowledge the foregoing to be Copy
of my last,[3] & to congratulate your Excellency upon the repulse given the British Troops the 14 may by Genl moultrie at
Charlestown South Carolina,[4] we have been impatiently waiting for particulars of this glorious Event authenticated by
Congress, but some Accident, or a Desire to compleat the Advantage by the Capture of the whole, has hindred— this Defeat will its probable frustrate the Designs of this Campaign;
their chief aim at present appears to be to distress us by burning & ravaging defenceless Towns, the Effect has & I imagine
will have a different Tendency from what they designed, it
rather exasperates than intimidates, & possibly these cruel
wanton Barbarities will so entirely disaffect, as to exclude to
Eternity all Intercourse with such Savages unless ample reper-
ation is made, should they continue their Depredations much
longer as they have lately done at Newhaven &c,[5] we must of
Consequence be ever sworn Enemies.

I beg leave to refer your Excellency to the Newspapers
I have the Honor to forward by this Opportunity, & to the
Letter directed to Mr Adams provided he should not be in
France,[6] we understand here he is coming out in the Alliance,
his Freinds however hope its only report—

I have the Honor to be, with my Compliments to Mr Frank-

March 28, 1780, that he had received only one letter from him, dated Oct.
25, 1779, during the previous two years. APS.

3. Austin opened the present letter with a copy of his previous one, dated
Boston, June 10: XXIX, 656–7. These were the first letters from Austin since
his return from Europe.

4. See our annotation of Digges to BF, July 14.

5. The British had recently raided New Haven and several other Connecticut towns; see the committee for foreign affairs to BF, July 16.

6. Austin to JA of July 7: *Adams Papers,* VIII, 96–8. JA had sailed for America aboard the French frigate *Sensible* on June 17: XXIX, 490n.

lin, with all due Respect Your Excellencys most Obedient and
very humble Servant   JON LORING AUSTIN

His Excellency Dr Franklin

Addressed: Son Excellence / Monsieur Dr. Franklin / Ministre
plenipotentiare de l'Amerique / a la Cour de France— / Passy /
pres Paris / per favor Mr Knox[7]

Notation: J.L. Austin June 10. 79

From John Paul Jones

ALS: American Philosophical Society; AL (draft): National Archives;
copy: United States Naval Academy Museum

Honored and dear Sir,   L'Orient July 12th. 1779
   The Bowsprit of the Bon homme Richard, having been
landed and examined is found not only Sprung in 2 places but
in several others much decayed and Rotten:— It is therefore
condemned as being Unfit for future Service.— The Old
Bowsprit mentioned in my last is now Undergoing a Survey
and is generally expected to answer as a good Substitute for
the one Condemned.— M. De Thevenard has shewed me a
letter from M. De Sartine expressing a desire that the Pallas,
the Cerf, and the Vengeance should go out and Cruise for a
few days in the Bay Until the Bon homme Richard and Alliance are again ready for Service and I have given them my
orders to depart in Consequence—[8] They are not yet out of

7. William Knox (1756-*c.*1795), the younger brother of Gen. Henry
Knox, who spent a year in Europe: North Callahan, *Henry Knox: George
Washington's General* (New York and Toronto, 1958), pp. 17, 166, 358. Knox
also carried Austin's letter of July 27, Jonathan Williams, Sr.'s of July 29,
and Elizabeth Temple's of July 30, all below.
8. In response to the French request Jones ordered the three ships to
cruise for ten days under Thévenard's orders: Bradford, *Jones Papers,* reel 4,
no. 680. Thévenard reported to Sartine on July 21 that the vessels had
sailed on the 13th and that he expected the *Alliance* and *Bonhomme Richard*
to be ready for service in another week: Archives de la Marine, B³DCLXV:
108. The *Pallas, Cerf,* and *Vengeance* returned to Lorient on the 23rd, having
made no prizes: *ibid.,* f. 117; Morison, *Jones,* pp. 195–6.

Sight.— We are to Rendezvous at Groa about the 20th. or 22d. and I think we shall then be ready to proceed on real Service.

I have inspected very particularly into the Situation of the Bon homme Richard and am sorry to find that it is the constructor's opinion that the Ship is too Old to admit of the necessary alteration. Thus circumstanced I wish to have an Opportunity of attempting an essential Service to render myself worthy of a better and faster Sailing Ship.— My destination from hence as there is a fair prospect of taking many Prizes makes the greater number of Men necessary; And M. de Gourlade writes this day a proposal to M. de Chaumont to Apply at Versailles for liberty to Embark an hundred to an hundred and Thirty Portuguise and other Seamen that have Arrived here in the Epervier and another Small Vessel from the Southward.— This would be a desirable thing if it could be obtained, because I could afterwards proceed with more confidence and they would be necessary towards Manning the Indien, if that Ship can at last be Obtained.— The Leveller Wherry is now nearly ready for the Sea and would be very Useful if Joined to our little force to take the Merchant Ships while we attack their Convoy.—[9]

I am ever with greatful and Sincere Affection Dear Sir Your very Obliged Friend and most humble Servant   JNO P JONES

His Excellency Doctor Franklin.

Notation: Capt. Jones July 12. 1779

From the Marquis de Lafayette

ALS: American Philosophical Society

Dear Sir   At the havre 12th july 1779
How happy I feel, when surrounded By so many preparations Against England, My respected friend doctor franklin

---

9. The *Leveller* was a captured 14-gun English cutter which Jones had requested from Chaumont: XXIX, 493n. Thévenard mistakenly told Sartine that Jones had asked BF for the corvette *Lively,* 20 (captured from the British in July, 1778 by a French frigate): Archives de la Marine, B³DCLXV: 119.

will easily conceive— There is nothing to be found in france which might offer to me so delightfull a prospect, as those ships, troops, warlike stores of all Kinds which are Getting Ready for to visit our good neighbours—Every thing will be soon provided for and we shall be able within these few days to set of at a moment's warning—so that our expedition will go on very well on the part of the Army, and we entirely depend on Mr d'orvilliers and his naval circumstances.

The Army is about thirty thousand strong, all in good spirits and will, I am sure, behave in the most Glorious manner— Besides this number we have a Van guard of light infantry and Grenadiers under a reputed General Officer—[1] Heavy pieces of artillery are embark'd with us—there is a Great proportion of engeneers. The more we shall be masters of the Channel the More I think will be undertaken— What I believe to be Certain, is that the Ministry are in Earnest, and I want if possible to give the ennemy some stroke or other before the end of the Campaign— on the other hand I hear that the British fleet is getting strong, and our future motions must as yet be very uncertain.

But if Gibraltar is Besieged, if jamaïca was attak'd, do'nt you believe, my dear doctor, that some thing must succeed, or that at least the ennemy must run the greatest dangers and support an enormous expense.

Theyr succes in Virginia[2] tho not very important I Cant however help lamenting— Suppose as it is reported fort pitt was taken and Mk intoch drove off,[3] that state would be

1. By early July some 31,000 troops had been assembled at Le Havre and St. Malo for the attack on England (for which see the intelligence reports discussed above on July 3). The vanguard, comprised of five grenadier and light infantry battalions and Lauzun's legion, was under the command of the comte de Rochambeau: Patterson, *The Other Armada,* p. 151. Lafayette was serving as a staff officer to one of the quartermaster generals of the invasion army: Louis Gottschalk, *Lafayette and the Close of the American Revolution* (Chicago, 1942), pp. 29–30.

2. News had just reached Europe of Gen. Edward Mathew's return to New York from a raid into Chesapeake Bay.

3. Gen. Lachlan McIntosh (1725–1806) commanded the western department from May, 1778, to March, 1779; his headquarters was at Ft. Pitt: *DAB.*

caught at once by the sea side and the back country, which Might good deal distress the trade by theyr cruizing off and destroying in the harbour, and distres the people by those enraged Bands of indians— The Ennemy will Carry on that low pillaging Kind of war, but I don't Believe them in situation of Carrying on a serious and Military Campaign— Any intelligence you may have from that beloved Country, and from my dearest friend gal washington I beg you would Communicate to me. Pray, My dear sir, let me know if you have any good opportunity of writing to America— how was the paper when Your last news have been dispatch'd to you? For I understand you have Receiv'd some letters.

I wish Spain would declare independency, and send of a frigatte to Boston— that will have A good effect, and I think some intelligences of that kind will be very welcome and very timely in the present instance—

For my part, my dear doctor, however pleas'd I May be with this expedition, my warmest desire is to serve again with My fellow soldiers of the American Army— Whenever my Country and yours will Believe that My going there is more useful than my staying here, I shall immediately set of with the sincerest and highest pleasure.

Let me know, my dear doctor, how far is our little Book advanc'd.[4] I like the idea extremely well, and want it to be soon Brought to the light.

Farewell, My dear friend, I hope I will ever possess a large part in your friendship, and that I deserve indeed by the affection, By all the tender sentiments and high Regard I have the honer to be with dear sir Yours   LAFAYETTE

Notation: La fayette havre 12. juillet 1779.

From Richard Speakman   ALS: American Philosophical Society

Sir   Gand [Ghent] 12 July 1779
    I am a Native of America & am now waiting at this place— with my Wife & Children for an Opportunity to Return—but

---

4. Lafayette and BF had selected topics for prints to illustrate a proposed book about atrocities committed by the British: XXIX, 590–3.

being at a loss how to find the most Eligible way—& as an American Subject—hope your Excellency will point out the most adviseable method to pursue & also to send a passport for travelling to the place your Excellency advises us to go to—

I am Yr Excellencys most Obedt Hble servt

RICHD SPEAKMAN

son of Tho Speakman formerly of Boston Carpenter

Please to Direct for me Chez Monsr Everad près la petite Bucherie Au Gand

Addressed: A—/ His Excellency Doctor Franklin / A—/ Paris

Notation: Carpenter Gand 12. july 1779.

From the Comte de Vergennes

L (draft):[5] Archives Nationales

a Versailles le 12. Juillet 1779.

J'ai L'honneur Mr. De Vous prevenir que la frégate américaine Lalliance commandee par Mr. Landais a arreté et conduit dans le port de l'orient le batiment anglois les trois amis, de Dublin. Le batiment etoit muni d'un passeport que le Roi a accordé le 30 8bre der [dernier] a des negotians de Bordeaux pour transporter des vins en angleterre. Ce passeport m'a été renvoyé par les officiers de l'amirauté, et le navire anglois est arreté jusqu'a nouvel ordre. Vous penseres sans doute, Monsieur que le capitaine amèricain ne peut insister sur la validité de cette prise, et je n'attens que votre reponse pour donner les ordre convenables afin que le navire les trois amis aie la liberté de continuer sa navigation et de se rendre en angleterre. J'ai l'honneur d'etre avec la consideration la plus distinguée

VERGENNES

5. In an unknown clerk's hand. The recipient's copy, unsigned and enclosing a memoir, was dated July 20. BF must have returned it to the sender, as requested by Gérard de Rayneval. See BF to Vergennes, July 25, and Gérard de Rayneval to BF, July 26.

a Mr. francklin Ministre plenipotenssiere des etats unis
dAmerique a Passy

From Jonathan Williams, Jr.: Three Letters

(I) LS:[6] American Philosophical Society; copy: Yale University Library; (II) ALS: American Philosophical Society; (III) ALS: American Philosophical Society; copy: Yale University Library

I.

Dear & honoured Sir,   Nantes July 13. 1779.

In answer to the two papers inclosed in your favour of the 9th. Instant,[7] the first containing a Detail of Insults offered to the Spanish Flagg by three american Vessells of War called the Resolution the Plimouth, and the little Resolution said to have sailed from Nantes, and the second containing an account of other Insults offered by other American Vessells in the west Indies to the same Flagg; I have to assure you in general, that I never heard of the Existence of any american Vessells of War of those Names, and particularly I never heard of any such that ever sailed from any Port in France. I therefore believe from these Circumstances, as well as from many others, that the English Cruisers have boarded Spanish Vessells, as well as those of other Nations, under the Flagg of the United States proffessing themselves to be americans, with a view of impressing on the minds of those Nations an Idea of our Ships of war being a set of Pirates.

I will however do all in my Power to gain Information on this Subject, and if I ever find the Smallest Instance of such Conduct in any american, I shall think it my duty, in justice to the reputation of my virtuous Countrymen, not only to expose them by giving immediate Information, but to do all I can to bring them to punishment. I am ever with the greatest respect Your dutifull & affectionate Kinsman

JONA WILLIAMS J

6. A Spanish translation of this letter is at the Archivo Historico Nacional, Estado, Madrid.

7. We publish it under the 8th, as it is dated in BF's letterbook.

The Honble. The Doctor Franklin.

Notation: Williams Jona. July 13. 1779.

II.

Dear & hond Sir   Nantes July 13. 1779.—
    The enclosed is an answer to Mr A. J. A s Letter to you[8]
which you enclosed to me in your last. I did not send it directly because I did not know whether you would approve of
my taking notice of your having communicated it to me, but I
beg you to send it to him (after perusel) as early as possible.— I am ever Yours dutifully & affectionately
                                                J WILLIAMS J

Addressed: a monsieur / Monsieur Franklin / *en particulier*

Notation: Williams Jona. July 13. 1779.

III.

Dear & hond Sir.   Nantes July 13. 1779.
    The privateer Genl Mifflin arrived here the 10th Inst. from
a Cruise in which she has taken three Prizes, The Elephant a
Kings Store ship, the Brig Betsey a merchant man in Ballast,
and the Tartar an english Privateer of 26 Guns & 160 men.
The Mifflin mounts but 20 Guns (6 pounders) finding therefor
her Enemy Superior, the Commander Capt Babcock made a
Desperate attack to board, in which the English Captain was
killed and the ship directly surrendered.— Captain Babcock
having now about two hundred Prisoners and his Provisions
being short he was under the necessity of sending one hundred & ninety of them in the Brig which he gave for the Purpose, and they have since arrived in England as appears by the
english Prints.— In order to secure an Exchange of an equal
Number of americans Capt Babcock took a Receipt for these
Prisoners from the master of the Elephant the master of the
Brig & the 1st Lieutenant of the Tartar (the Captain of the
latter being killed) promising a Release of american Prisoners
accordingly.— I have had this Instrument authenticated by the

---

8. Probably Alexander John Alexander's letter of June 17: XXIX, 689.

admiralty of the Place and inclose the Copy in due form to
serve as you may think necessary.—⁹

Capt Babcock was obliged to quit the Tartar at Sea the 23d
of June and if she is not taken we expect her hourly to arrive.— I shall deliver the prisoners who remain on board the
Mifflin into the prisons here and shall desire Mr. Schweighauser to engage for their maintenance or I shall do it myself
untill I receive your Orders: The mifflin and her Prizes if they
arrive are to my address.

I am with the greatest Respect Dear & hond Sir Your dutifull & affectionate Kinsman   JONA WILLIAMS

His Excellency Doctor Franklin.

Notation: Williams Jona. July 13 1779.

From Jacques-Donatien Le Ray de Chaumont

AL: Historical Society of Delaware

[on or before July 14, 1779]¹

M. de Chaumont suplie Son Excellence M. franklin d'ecrire a
M. Jones que M. de Sartine desire que M. Chamillard de Varville Lieutenant Colonel d'infanterie² aye Le Commandement

---

9. Capt. George W. Babcock captured the three prizes in May during the
General Mifflin's third European cruise. Among BF's papers is a certified copy
(dated Nantes, July 12, 1779) of a May 19 statement signed by Babcock and
a representative of each of the three prizes that Babcock was sending the
prisoners to England on the *Betsy* in the expectation that an equal number
of American prisoners would be released in exchange (APS). Further information on the *General Mifflin* and her prizes can be found in the *Courier de
l'Europe,* VI, no. 4 (July 13, 1779), p. 32; Allen, *Mass. Privateers,* p. 149; John
A. McManemin, *Captains of the Privateers during the Revolutionary War* (Spring
Lake, N.J., 1985), pp. 103–6.

1. The date on which BF enclosed it in a letter to Jones, immediately
below. Another request from Chaumont is not as easy to date. Addressed
to BF, it reads, "M. de Chaumont prie Monsieur franklin de faire ce matin
Les lettres pour h." APS.

2. Lt. Col. Paul de Chamillard de Varville, who subsequently served as
one of Jones's officers. Jones chose him to bring BF his account of the battle
with H.M.S. *Serapis:* Jones to BF, Oct. 3, below. A recent authority identifies
the officer in question as Charles Chamellard de Bonnemare, a former ma-

en Second des volontaires francais du Bonhomme Richard, attendu que M. Chamillard de Varville devoit S'embarquer avec M. le Marquis de la fayette dont il est Connu pour un officier Experimenté et qui a l'avantage d'avoir Commandé dans Les Colonies.³

C'est aujourdhuy La poste.

To John Paul Jones
ALS: Historical Society of Delaware

Dear Sir, Passy, July 14. 1779

In compliance with the within Recommendation of M. de Sartine, I do hereby desire you to admit M. Chamillard de Varville to the Command *en second* of the French Voluntiers on board the Bonhomme Richard. Wishing you every kind of Success and Prosperity, I have the Honour to be, Dear Sir, Your most obedient & most humble Servant B FRANKLIN

To the honourable Jno Paul Jones Esqr

From Thomas Digges
ALS: Historical Society of Pennsylvania

Dr Sir July 14. 1779—

Having the promise of getting this safe into a Post office on the other side of the water I have stept into a Coffee House to inclose to you the Satys. and yesterdays Gazettes of the Amn News. Much joy was expressd on the rect of the first wch came remarkably quick from N York, but was as most Gazettes are lookd upon as nothing the day after. There were accots of a later date via Corke, wch. mentiond that Provosts army had been defeated & routed in their attempt to possess Chas

---

jor in the regiment of Guadeloupe: Boudriot, *John Paul Jones and the Bonhomme Richard,* p. 62. On July 19 Chaumont wrote Jones directly to reinforce what he here requested for the officer: Bradford, *Jones Papers,* reel 4, no. 689.

3. Jones later thanked Lafayette for Chamillard's assistance: *ibid.,* no. 723. Lafayette subsequently supported his application for membership in the Society of the Cincinnati: Lasseray, *Les Français,* I, 152–4; Asa Bird Gardiner, *The Order of the Cincinnati in France . . .* (Providence, 1905), p. 207.

Town; The *dates* of this affair do not seem to confirm this important news, but most people here who wish to establish the falsity of it seem to beleive it true—[4] If it should prove so, the southern parts of America will be left tolerably free from similar invasions.

Our grand fleet is probably saild again from Torbay by this day with an additional three ships, & not a word has been yet heard about the Combind fleet, but there are high fears of its not being far off, and nothing now talkd of but Invasions.

I have had a letter from Peters since I drew the bill on you for £100—& seemingly pacified his fears of being again disapointed of remittances from home. My Bill on you A Monr Grands for 100£ was remittd the 9th Inst. As soon as there are accots. of its acceptance the money will be paid to Mr Peters order. I am to observe to You that the box of books did not amount *wholly* to ten pounds, but the difficiency shall be accounted for to you.[5] I have not the exact shop bill now with me, or I would inclose it. There was a mistake in the first bill which occasiond the error in me, and which I did not discover until minutely examining it some days after. I wrote You twice lately by private conveyance, & should be glad to have some name given me at Ostend to address Lettrs. to for forwardance &a—as it will be soon very difficult to forward in the usual way. I expect to have another private conveyance in

4. Conflicting accounts of Gen. Augustine Prevost's march toward Charleston, S.C., early in May (XXIX, 658n) reached London in the first part of July. British dispatches optimistically reported that Prevost would soon be in possession of Charleston. Extracts of these were printed in *The London Gazette* for July 6–10 and 10–13. American newspapers arriving in London at about the same time contained the more recent information that Prevost had failed to take the city. The American sympathizer John Almon published in *The London Evening Post* for July 10–13 both the American accounts, which predicted another "Burgoynade," and the extracted British dispatches. *The General Advertiser, and Morning Intelligencer* of July 13 did likewise. Subsequent issues of it and *The London Evening Post* continued to print conflicting accounts but gave greater credence to the American. Other newspapers rejected the American reports as the fabrications of Congress; see, for example, *The Public Advertiser,* July 16, 17, and 19.

5. BF had requested materials for William Gordon, who was writing a history of the American Revolution: XXIX, 577, 667, 701, 736.

about 10 days till wch time I do not expect any material occurence in this quarter.

I am with very Great regard Yr. mo obedt. & oblig H Sert

V. J——D

Addressed: A Monsieur / Monsieur B.F— / a Passy

Endorsed: July 14

Notations: Digges July 14. 79. / July 14. 1779.

To Richard Bache

Copy: Library of Congress

Dear sir   Passy, July 15. 1779.

The Bearer, M Vatteville, goes over with Views of establiching himself in our Country. He bears the Character here of a Valuable Man, Likely to make a good and Useful Citizen among us. I recommend him warmly to your Civilities and Counsels. Ben continues well and behaves in his College as one could wish. I am ever Your affectionate father   BF

P.S. The Chevalier Crenis has been with me lately and expresses great Satisfaction with the Civilities he received from you and others in America.[6]

Mr. Ricd. Bache.

From John Bondfield

ALS: American Philosophical Society

Sir   Bordeaux 15 July 1779

I am honord with your favor of the 4th Instant am obliged to you for the Trouble you took in the Honor done to my drafts. The Master of a Ship arrivd here yesterday taken off Bell Isl left Hampton Road the 22 May past in the Night the English Men of War that lay off Norfolk the reports were all confused of the Actions of the English[7] he threw his papers

---

6. Martial-Jean-Antoine Crozat de Crénis had carried letters from the Baches when he left America in January: XXVIII, 386, 392.

7. General Mathew's raiding party captured Norfolk and Portsmouth and burned Suffolk, Va.: XXIX, 761n.

overboard he saild in Company with 4 Sloops a schooner and a small french Ship all bound to Europe some of them may be dayly expected.

The attention paid at present by the Convoys to the Ships Under their care begins to revive the Trading Body. Two Frigates arrived with a fleet from Brest[8] imediately went on Cruizing Grounds the Frigates with Mons Dorvillier took & destroyd on the Coast of Spain four Privateers & five Merchant men from all wch. we may flatter ourselves to meet due protection I got ensured on the General Mercer for Philadelphia[9] at 30 per Ct. being 20 per Cent lower than any done at this port for twelve months past, a few more favorable Circumstances and we should be again on float. I have the Honor to be with due respect Sir your most Obedient Humble Servt

JOHN BONDFIELD

Addressed: To / His Excellency Benj Franklin / Esqr. / Plenipotenry from the American States / Paris

Notation: Jonh Bendfield Bordeaux 15 juillet 1779.

From John Brig

ALS: American Philosophical Society

Sir   Aix July 15th. 1779

I make free to trouble you with these few lines as knowing you to be a friend to my Country in hopes you will purchase my liberty & a pass to Travel to Burdeaux where I understand there is three frigats fitting out in the American Servise which would be my desire to Embrace the Oportunity if possible. I wrote to my Friend Heifield D. Coningham which knows me to be Master of a ship or Ships out of Phalladelphia this fifteen years past & likewise knows my property & Brothers in America & has Receivd no Answer from him as yet. I directed my letters to Bordeaux perhaps he is not there or I would Receivd. a Answer sooner so if my liberty & a pass could be

8. The frigates *Courageuse* and *Hermione* brought a merchant convoy to Bordeaux: Archives de la Marine B³MDCLXVII: 298–9.

9. Bondfield had announced on June 22 the impending departure of the *General Mercer*: XXIX, 714.

108

obtaind. by giving any Security Demanded I can have the Best Security in Merseilles for what sum the Parliment Demands that I will go to no other place but Burdeaux or any Other port where you Direct me to where there is an American frigate your answer to this & Instruction where to write to Mr. Coningham will much oblige your Humble Servant

JOHN BRIG

P.S. I was taken in the American Servise but was not Imprisoned. I went to Ireland where I traded to Many Voyages with passengers & Servants the Merchants gave me Comand of this Ship. I was taken in here in Merseills & is now on my paroll in Aix[1]

Rd. Doctr. Frankland

Addressed: A Monsieur / Monsieur Franklind / Ministre Plenipotentiaire des etats / unis de L'Amerique En son hotel /a Passy / *a Passy*

Notations: Brig John July 15. 1779. / John Brig. Aix July 15. 1779 / De B. D. Versailles

From the Committee for Foreign Affairs

ALS: American Philosophical Society, University of Pennsylvania Library, Harvard University Library;[2] copy and transcript: National Archives

Honble. Sir   Philada. July 16. 1779

We find from the Minister of France that your Appointment has given high Satisfaction to his Court, and we are encouraged to expect Proofs of its most confidential Reliance upon your Character.[3] We have not had a Line from you of this year's date; indeed I believe your latest is of Novr. 7th. 1778.[4] Two days ago we received several Letters from Doctor Lee

1. Having received no answer, Brig repeated his request on Aug. 4. APS.
2. That at the University of Pennsylvania is marked "4plicate" and the one at Harvard, "Copy." There are minor variations in wording among the three versions.
3. Meng, *Despatches of Gérard,* pp. 539, 771.
4. XXVIII, 55–6.

and one from Mr. Izard: the latter March 4th. the former up to April 6th. The Vessel was from Rochelle about the middle of May. It was unfortunate that we did not get the Information of Mr. Lee earlier respecting the Enemy's designs against Connecticutt: They had accomplished Part of them a few days before.—[5] Will no one under a Commission from these United States retaliate on the Coasts of England for the Burning of our beautiful Fairfield? A single Privateer might I think show, there, a striking Sample of the Species of War now carried on by Britain against America.

We are told this Evening that Genl. Lincoln has had an Advantage over Prevost in an open Field Fight in which the Militia behaved to Admiration, on the 20th. of June.[6]

We forward two Letters for "Our great faithful beloved Friend & Ally Louis sixteenth King of France & Navarre." We submit, however, the Superscription to your Judgement. You will manage the Invoices by your best Abilities.[7] The Probability of Success was held up to us by one who doubtless makes known by this Opportunity how much our present Circumstances render such Aids essential to us.[8]

A Report of the Treasury respecting the just Stipend of our late and present Ministers at foreign Courts is not quite deter-

5. Izard's March 4 letter asked leave to return to America; Arthur Lee's of April 6 warned of an attack on Wethersfield and New Haven. Wharton, *Diplomatic Correspondence*, III, 73–4, 110–11. Between July 5 and 11, in fact, the British burned Fairfield and Norwalk, and did lesser damage to New Haven and East Haven: Richard Buel, Jr., *Dear Liberty: Connecticut's Mobilization for the Revolutionary War* (Middletown, Ct., 1980), pp. 190–4; Ward, *War of the Revolution*, II, 619–20. For a list of Lee's other letters see Smith, *Letters*, XIII, 230n.

6. At the Battle of Stono Ferry, S.C., a British detachment beat back an American attack: Mark Mayo Boatner III, *Encyclopedia of the American Revolution* (New York, 1966), p. 1062; Ward, *War of the Revolution*, II, 686. Congress was told, however, that the battle had ended favorably: Smith, *Letters*, XIII, 231.

7. Enclosed were a July 10 request for military supplies from President of Congress John Jay to Louis XVI and several lists of such supplies, particularly for the American navy: Smith, *Letters*, XIII, 187–8, 229n. For further details see BF to Vergennes, Sept. 18.

8. Presumably French Minister Gérard, who did write Vergennes about the woeful state of American finances: Meng, *Despatches of Gérard*, p. 749.

mined upon. A Determination is peculiarly necessary as to Mr. W Lee & Mr. Izard after the Proceedings, here, of June 8th.[9]

We have put up for you a Set of the Journals which have been printed this Year, adding some spare Numbers to compleat what have been sent in part of the 15.

Presuming from Report and a Passage of a Letter from Doctr. Lee that Mr. Adams is on his Return hither,[1] We do not write to him now. Should he remain in France we beg he may be made acquainted with the Cause of our Omission.

Good as this Opportunity is we expect very shortly a much better when we shall renew Assurances of being Honble. Sir Your most humble Servants

JAMES LOVELL
for the Committee of for. Affairs

Honble. Doctor Franklin

P.S. The Letter & Papers respecting Mr. De Francy's Agency were only this day delivered to us from the Secretary's Office; but Mr. De Francy has had Sextuples.[2]

Addressed: Honorable / Benjamin Franklin Esqr. / Minister Plenipotentiary / of the United States of America / Paris

Notation: James Lovell Philadelphie 16. juillet 1779.

---

9. On that day Congress voted to recall Izard and William Lee as commissioners to Tuscany and to Prussia and the Holy Roman Empire respectively, but then voted they need not return to the U.S.: *JCC,* XIV, 700–5. No decision had yet been reached on compensating them: Smith, *Letters,* XIII, 240.

1. The news was in a March 6 letter to Samuel Adams; see Smith, *Letters,* XIII, 232.

2. Congress had recently ordered BF to reimburse Beaumarchais' agent Francy for the military supplies he had provided: XXVIII, 528; XXIX, 707–8.

From Samuel Wharton

ALS: American Philosophical Society

Dear Sir   Hotel de Rome Friday Evening [July 16, 1779][3]

I send inclosed the News paper, and am informed by some Friends in London, That two Transports are arrived from New York in short Passages, & bring such Accounts as incline People in general to think, That General Provost has been beaten near Charles Town, with the Loss of his Artillery &c. They don't mention any other Particulars.

I am respectfully, and affectionately y'r. Excellency's most obedt. & most humble servt.   S. WHARTON

His Excellency Mr. Franklin

Notation: S. Wharton Paris

From Antoine-Alexis Cadet de Vaux

ALS: American Philosophical Society

Monsieur,   ce 17 Juillet 1779

Dans le compte que J'ai rendu (Journal de Paris) de l'acte soutenu au college Mazarin, J'ai cru devoir parler de ce qui vous est relatif, après avoir pris l'attache de M. Barbeu du Bourg.[4]

Je me suis appercu de l'Insuffisance des Expressions pour rendre les sentiments de respect et d'admiration que votre présence inspire, sentiments que personne n'éprouve plus vive-

---

3. By which date the contradictory accounts of Prevost's march on Charleston could have reached Paris from London. See our annotation of Digges to BF, July 14.

4. Cadet is referring to an article published that very day in the *Jour. de Paris* (pp. 806–7), which he had founded in 1777. It tells of BF's presence at the Collège Mazarin on July 15 to hear a dissertation on electricity dedicated to him by Louis-Hilaire Fagnan. The Latin text of the dissertation is at the APS.

D'Alembert was there, too, and both men were warmly greeted by the students. Cadet remarked that students were now introduced to experimental science rather than abstract discussions. BF is referred to as "le prince de la Physic."

ment que moi et avec lesquels Je suis Monsieur Votre très humble et très obeissant serviteur   CADET LE J.

Notations: Cadet 17 Juillet 1779. / Mr King,[5] Hotel Vauban Rue de Richelieu

From Vergennes

L (draft):[6] Archives du Ministère des affaires étrangères; copy: Library of Congress

a Versles le 18 Juilt. 1779.

Jai lhonneur de vous envoyer ci-joint, M, copie d'une lettre de M. de Sartine; vous y verrez les ordres donnés au sujet des effets du Sr. Samüel Warthon.[7]

J'ai l'hr

M Franklin

To John Paul Jones

LS:[8] National Archives; copy: Library of Congress

Dear Sir,   Passy July 19. 1779.

I have before me your Letters of the 5th. 9th. & 12th of this Month. I received all the Papers relating to Capt. Landais Prize. That Matter is now under Consideration. I am sorry for

5. The Irishman to whom BF delivered a passport on July 22, below.
6. In the hand of Joseph-Mathias Gérard de Rayneval.
7. A month earlier BF had forwarded to Vergennes a memoir by Samuel Wharton on behalf of two would-be emigrants to America whose effects had been impounded by customs officials at Dieppe: XXIX, 574–6, 681. A copy of the enclosure, Sartine to Vergennes of July 12, is at the Library of Congress. In it Sartine expressed surprise that the effects were being held, since the ship from which they had been taken as English was actually a smuggling ship for which a Boulogne merchant had stood security. He has ordered that they be released to Wharton. Two weeks after the present letter BF issued a passport to one of the potential emigrants, Thomas Burdy: below, Aug. 2.
8. In WTF's hand.

the Communication of Plans[9] that you mention, but hope no ill Consequences will attend it.

I think the Instruction of Congress which you mention should be observed; and also that every Opportunity of Distressing the Enemy should be embraced, that is not inconsistent with the Execution of your general Orders.

The Delay of your Cruise occasioned by Accidents makes it necessary to give a longer Time for your finishing it at the Orcades, before you quit it to go to the Port of your Destination. I do therefore at the Request of M. De Sartine, lengthen it to the End of September.

With great Esteem, I have the honour to be, Dear Sir, Your most obedt. humble Servant.   B FRANKLIN

Honble Capt. Jones.

Addressed: A Monsieur / Monsieur le Capitaine Jones. / Commandant la Frégatte le / Bonhomme Richard, au / Service des Etats Unis, de L'Ameque. / à L'Orient

Endorsed: From Doctr. Franklin July 19. 1779. No. 11.

From Samuel Wharton   ALS: American Philosophical Society

Dear Sir   Monday Morning. [July 19, 1779][1]

I send the News Paper, and a short Note from a Friend.—

The packet, which was bringing the Mail of the 6th Instant, was taken by an American Privateer, and carried into Dunkirk. The News from South Carolina, in the News Paper, of the Success of General Lincoln, I think, bears strong Marks of Authenticity upon the Face of it.

I am with great Respect Dear Sir your Excellency's most obedient & most humble Servt   SAML. WHARTON

I thank you for the Perusal of the within very foolish Paper, and am persuaded, It is the performance of a Junto of Ameri-

---

9. At a later date Jones inserted a mark here, underlined the preceding three words, and in the margin wrote, "It is clear I saw my Danger and sailed with my Eyes Open rather than return to America Dishonored."

1. See our dating of his preceding letter, July 16.

can Tories,—Who are Tools in the Hands of Lord George Germaine.[2]

His Excellency Mr. Franklin &c &c &c.

Notation: Saml. Wharton

From the Marine Committee: Proposed Letter[3]

AL (draft) and copy: National Archives

Sir   [after July 19, 1779]

Inclosed you have a certified Copy of a Resolution of Congress dated July 19. 1779; By which you will perceive the Marine Committee are empowered and directed by Congress to carry into Execution their Manifesto of the 30 of Octr. 1778. In pursuance of this Authority and for the more speedy accomplishment of the Ends proposed, we authorise and most earnestly request you, to take every Measure in your power, to aid and assist us in the Execution of this Business.—

It is not our Intentions to confine the Measures to be used on this Occasion to open and hostile operations; But on the contrary it is expected and we wish and desire, that you would cause, at the Expence of the United States, any of the Towns of Great Britain or the West Indies, secretly to be set on fire. In particular London, Bristol, Liverpool, Glasgow and Edinburgh are to be considered as the first objects of national re-

---

2. In all likelihood the letter from "Daniel Thomson": XXIX, 771–6.

3. There is no evidence that this letter was ever sent. It is dated by the congressional resolution of July 19 directing the Marine Committee to execute Congress' October Manifesto (XXVIII, 359n) by burning and destroying enemy towns in Britain and the West Indies in retaliation for British depredations. The letter is in the hand of William Whipple, a New Hampshire delegate, who was one of the three members of the newly reconstituted committee. (The other members were John Dickinson of Del. and John Collins of R.I.: *JCC*, XIV, 708.) Whipple was also a member of a committee appointed on July 19 to consider Washington's recent report on the British attacks on Connecticut towns and recommendation that Congress make reprisals. Its proposed letter, John Jay to BF, is below, Aug. 2. See Smith, *Letters*, XIII, 263n, for the genesis of that letter and the present one.

taliating resentment;[4] and above all, London, the Seat of royal Residence and vindictive rage and the quarter from which have issued the orders for the conflagrations which have by the Enemy been lighted up in these United States.—

America would have the Monarch see, that when provoked she can light up fires even at his own Doors.—And in this Business it is requested, that you will use every possible Exertion. This Measure, in which so many Calamities are involved, and so contrary to the known and acknowledged Humanity with which Congress have heretofore carried on the present war, has, at length become, for the sole and direct purpose of self preservation, absolutely and indispensibly necessary, from the cruel and unprecedented Manner in which our Enemies are daily carrying on the present War. Our Villages on the Sea Coasts are numerous, most of them defenceless, and all of them, with very few Exceptions, exposed and easily accessable to a naval Force, which renders them at any Time a prey to a savage and desolating Enemy.—

The Towns of ——— here to fore laid in ashes, and the late successful attempts in burning and destroyed the Villages of Fairfield, Norwalk and Bedford in Connecticut & New-York,[5] and the unquestionable proofs Congress have received, that the Vengeance denounced against these States in the Manifesto of the British Commissioners will be executed in its fullest extent, has induced them, as the only effectual Means, to put a stop to the further destruction of our Country, to retaliate upon our Enemy by destroying, if possible, some of the most distinguished Cities in Great Britain and the West Indies.—

Our Countrymen have long complained of the slow and forbearing disposition of Congress, when every day announces to them the destruction of some part of their Country. To meet these Ideas, they have at length solemnly deter-

4. BF had previously ordered John Paul Jones to refrain from burning defenseless towns, though he would be permitted to do so if ransom was refused and if he gave sufficient notice for the sick, aged, women, and children to be first evacuated: XXIX, 387.

5. The British had burned Bedford, N.Y., as well as the Connecticut towns: Fitzpatrick, *Writings of Washington*, XV, 426, 469.

mined to revenge themselves on their Enemies, and to leave untried, no exertions for carrying into execution their Manifesto of the 30 of Octr., 1778.

A few *determined*[6] Men, under the promise of handsome rewards, and well acquainted with the Situation of the large Towns in England & Scotland, will perhaps be the best instruments that can be employed for the Accomplishment of this Work.— We do not however wish to point out any mode that shall be obligatory upon you; your own Judgment and observation will readily suggest to you such steps as are most likely to answer the Ends proposed.—

As the avowed Determination of the Enemy, as set forth by the British Commissioners, is to render us of as little use as possible to our ally, perhaps it would not be improper, if Capt. Jones should be in France, and his own force is inadequate, to request further aid, and attempt the destruction of some of their Towns by a naval surprise.—

How such a Measure will accord with the Sentiment of the Court of France, your Situation will best enable you to determine. If it should appear to you improper to communicate the Matter at all to the Minister of France, you will then forbear to do it.

We cannot conclude without once more earnestly pressing upon[7] you, the Necessity of striking some blow similar to those suggested in the resolution of Congress:— The destruction of a single village would instantly convince our Enemy of the Danger to which they are exposed, and the Necessity there will be, of desisting from the present destructive mode in carrying on the War.

Notation: Entered Page *385*

From William Bingham ALS: American Philosophical Society

Sir! St Pierre M/que July 20th 1779

As the recent Events that have arisen from the operation of the two fleets & Armies in these Seas, are of the most interest-

6. Replaces "*desperate*".
7. Replaces "requesting".

ing & important Nature, I shall enter into a regular Detail of those that have taken place Since the Date of my last Letter.[8]

The French Forces that sailed in the Expedition to Grenada arrived there the 2d Inst, when 1300 Troops were immediately disembarked, & the Country reconnoitred;[9] A Flag was sent in the next Day to the Governor, requiring him to surrender, & informing him at the same time that the Forces employed in the Reduction of the Island were So far Superior in Number to those engaged in its Defence, as to render all Resistance useless & presumptuous; Lord Macartney[1] expecting the Approach of Admiral Byron to relieve him, returned for answer, that he was ignorant of the Strength of the Enemy, but had great Confidence in his own, & was determined to make a vigorous Defence; In Consequence of which Count D'Estaing prepared for an Attack, & marched his Troops in three Columns at Midnight of the same Day, Stormed the principal Fort & Retrenchments, & carried them sword in hand;— As this Fort commanded the Citadel, the Governor too late convinced of his Temerity, Sent out a Flag & offered to capitulate, but this being now refused him, he was forced to receive the Terms imposed on him, which were to surrender at Discretion—

As no Capitulation was entered into, by the Laws of War the Troops were allowed to pillage & The Remembrance of the Sufferings of their allies might have animated them to do their Duty in that Service; This occasioned many of the Inhabitants to experience some small Retaliation for the great

8. We have found no news from Bingham, the American agent in Martinique during the preceding several months; his three most recent substantive letters were clustered in January and February: xxviii, 347–50, 475–6, 501–3.

9. The arrival of naval reinforcements gave Admiral d'Estaing the opportunity to embark 6,000 troops for an attack on Barbados; foiled by contrary winds he turned instead against the rich sugar-producing island of Grenada: Jacques Michel, *La Vie aventureuse et mouvementée de Charles-Henri, comte d'Estaing* (n.p., 1976), pp. 204–9.

1. George Macartney, Baron Macartney of Lissanoure (1737–1806), captain-general and governor of Grenada, Tobago, and the Grenadines: *DNB*.

"Le chapeau à la Grenade"

Excesses of the English Troops in America aggravating the Calamities of War by more than Savage Cruelty.

This important Conquest fell into the Hands of the French the 4th Inst, without any other Misfortune than the Loss of 35 officers & Men Killed, & 71 wounded.

Seven hundred Troops were found in the Fort, of which 168 were Regulars of the 46th Regiment, the Remainder Volunteers & Militia; the Succeeding Days were employed in establishing the civil & military Government of the Island.

1500 Troops were left to garrison it, & the Rest were embarked on an Expedition against St Christophers, when admiral Byron made his appearance; The Count D'Estaing did not hesitate a Moment to weigh Anchor, advance & give him Battle;— Admiral Byron had received an Accession of Strength of three Ships of the Line, in Addition to the Eighteen he had Sailed with from St Lucie— These two fleets that had long been opposed to each other, but had never untill now come to Action, were mutually animated with eager Resentment, with national Antipathy & with all the passions that inspire obstinate Bravery & great Exertions— The Shock of Battle was violent & corresponded to Such Sentiments;— The Sea was smooth, & the Ports of the lower Batteries of the two Fleets were all opened;— The Execution was accordingly great in a Short time;— The Engagement lasted five hours in which Seven of the British Ships were So disabled as to be towed out of the Line of Battle.— Admiral Byron had the Advantage of being to Windward, which prevented many of the Count D'Estaing's Squadron from engaging.

Night separated the Fleets;— The French were prepared in the Morning to renew it with redoubled Vigor, but no Enemy appeared;— The English had taken Advantage of the friendly Protection of the Evening & made their Retreat—

The Victory was decisive;— Count D'Estaing remained Master of the Field of Battle, & the boasted veteran fleet of the Enemy found no Security but in flight; In whatever Manner their partial Pen may gloss over the fatal Miscarriages of this memorable Day, yet, from a Consideration of the Circumstances, no Perversion of Language can impress on the Mind a different Idea than that they were compleatly beaten—

This Splendid Action, besides the Reputation it has gained, & the Encouragement it has given to the french Arms, will be attended with great & manifest Advantage as Nothing can now oppose their Progress in these Seas, except the Want of a Sufficient Number of Men to secure their Conquests; The french Fleet sustained in the Engagement the Loss of 176 Killed, & 773 wounded— After having disembarked the latter at Grenada, Count D'Estaing immediately took his Departure from thence, & arrived off this place the 18th Inst;— he continued his Route to Guadaloupe, where, his Intention was to take in a few more Troops, to form an Attack against the Island of St Kitts, whose Resistance would be more feeble than that of Grenada, if it was not for the unlucky Arrival of the English Fleet & Transports there, the former in a most Shattered Condition. Perhaps he will now alter his Destination for Barbados or Montserat;—[2] He at present reigns triumphant in these Seas, & has very little Reason to dread being molested in his Operations by another appearance of the English Squadron, who from its precipitate Retreat must have greatly suffered or been greatly dismayed—

The Island of Tobago which is an appendage to the Government of Grenada, must fall of Course, & Some Troops I hear, were dispatched to take possession of it— It is greatly to be regretted that Circumstances will not admit of an Attack upon St Kitts;— The Acquisition of that Island from its local Situation, must be an Event of the greatest Importance, it being the Rendezvous of all the English fleets from the Windward Islands to take the Benefit of Convoy. Besides its Position in the Vicinity of St Eustatia must greatly controul the Movements of the Dutch, who on the least Appearance of active Hostilities in favor of G Britain, might expect to lose that valuable Possession, the greatest Mart of Commerce in these seas—

I sincerely congratulate you on the great & immediate Advantages that will be derived to the United States from the

2. After failing to draw the British Navy from St. Christopher (St. Kitts) d'Estaing proceeded with a convoy to St. Domingue: Michel, *Vie aventureuse*, pp. 217–18.

rapid Success of the Arms of our Allies which must convince G Britain of the Folly of persevering in So ruinous & destructive a War, & of the Necessity of withdrawing her Troops from the Continent to preserve the Remnant of her antient Possessions—

Her Commerce must feel most Sensibly the Loss of these important Islands, which must occasion numberless Bankruptcies, from the immense Sums they owe to the Metropolis, they being all established on Loans, which the Planters procure by Mortgages on their Estates;— Another Solid Advantage to be derived from these Acquisitions, is the Effect that the Loss of them must have on the public Credit of G Britain, whose Resources must uniformly diminish with her Trade, which must occasion her operations to be proportionably slow & dilatory—

The infatuated Councils which have brought the British Nation to the Brink of Ruin, still prevail in the Cabinet & are Strengthened with a personal, rather than a national Animosity against the Americans, which has become implacable, & is the Cause of every Consideration of Interest or Advantage being Sacrificed for the pleasure of gratifying it.

Tis the Operation of Such Sentiments that has occasioned positive Orders to be given to the Commander in Chief of their forces at St Lucie, to embark for America all the Troops in the West Indies, after leaving a feible Garrison in that Island, credulously believing that the supposed Superiority of Admiral Byron in these Seas would be a Sufficient Protection for their Islands, & that the internal Devisions which appear to prevail in America, would give them great advantages in the Operations of the present Campaign— Three thousand Troops were accordingly embarked with all their Baggage, & were intended to make a Descent, ên passant, at St Vincent to endeavor to retake it, but the determined appearance of the Caraibs, & the imminent Danger which threatned Grenada, inclined them to lead all their Forces to the succour & assistance of that Island—[3]

3. For the naval battle of Grenada see W.M. James, *The British Navy in Adversity: a Study of the War of Independence* (London, New York, Toronto,

Unfortunately their Transports with their Troops were placed during the Engagement that ensued, Seven Leagues to Windward which prevented their being taken.— But one was captured, which had 170 Troops on board— They have arrived at St Kitts with the Fleet, & will in all probability be kept for the Defence of that Island & Antigua, which must inevitably be reduced, if these Troops Should continue their Route to America— It is generally imagined that if the Ressources of G Britain Should not be exhausted, & the War Should continue another Year, that the West Indies will be a busy Theatre of Action, & the Windward Islands in particular a Scene of the most active Hostilities, as the English will naturally endeavor to recover Such valuable Possessions—

I have the honor to be with unfeigned Respect Sir Your Excellency's most obedt & very humble Servant

WM. BINGHAM

Triplicate

Notation: Bingham July 20. 1779.

From Samuel Hill

ALS: American Philosophical Society

Sir   Gerhaix 20th July 1779

Permit me to inform your Excellency, that I was Surgeon of the British Sloop of War Drake, when She was taken by the Ranger Continental Sloop of War, off Corrickfergus on the 24th April 1778 and was confin'd on board the Patience Brig in Brest Road from the 7th May following, until the 12th Jany. 1779[4] at which time I was sent on shore to the Hospital at

---

1926), pp. 147–52, 434–5. Gen. James Grant, commander of the British army in the West Indies, had been ordered to loan most of his troops to Gen. Clinton in New York for the summer. The troops, however, were diverted to the attempt to recapture St. Vincent which was interrupted by the French capture of Grenada and subsequent naval battle. They then were returned to garrison duty: James, *British Navy in Adversity*, pp. 146–7; Mackesy, *War for America*, pp. 259–60, 272–3.

4. During which he and his fellow prisoners complained of the ill treatment they were receiving: XXVIII, 210n.

Brest for Cure of a Fever, and on my recovery was sent to this Town on my Parole of honor, on the 26th Feby. last, since which I have been inform'd that the Crew of the said Sloop Drake is return'd to England.—[5]

I beg leave to pray your Excellency to consider my Case, and to grant me permission to return to my native Country as one of the said Sloops Company. I have the honor to acquaint your Excellency that I have received an order, to leave this Province, and go to Angier [Angers], but have leave from Monsieur Laporte Intendant of Brest to remain her a month longer. I flatter myself your Excellency will honor me with an Answer, before that time is expired.[6]

I have the honor to be your Excellency's Most Obedient & Most humble Servant   SAML: HILL

Addressed: To / His Excellency / Benjamin Franklin Esqr: / Minister and Plenipotentiary / for the united States of / America / at Paris

Notation: Hill Saml. 20. July 1779.

From Jonathan Williams, Jr.

ALS: American Philosophical Society; copy: Yale University Library

Dear & hond. Sir   Nantes July 20. 1779.

Mr Lee in answer to the Gentlemen arbitraters of my accounts wrote a Letter of which the enclosed is a Copy, & this Copy I am directed to transmit to you.[7] I am ever Your dutifull & affec Kinsman   J WILLIAMS J

The Hon Doctor Franklin.

Notation: Jona. Williams July 20. 1779.

5. Sartine had already informed BF of Hill's plight: above, July 5.

6. BF did write Schweighauser on Hill's behalf: below, Sept. 17.

7. The Gentlemen had informed Lee on July 9 that the examination of JW's accounts had begun, and requested his objections by return post. Lee's response of the following day was that he first needed a copy of that letter "by which you think yourselves authorized to make this application to Me," and a copy of the accounts. APS.

From the Committee of Commerce

LS: University of Pennsylvania Library

Commercial Committee Philadelphia

Dear Sir   21st July 1779

By a Letter dated New Orleans 10th April last from Oliver Pollock Esquire Continental Agent at that place is the following Paragraph. "I have this day drawn on Messrs. Samuel and J.H. Delap sundry Bills amounting to 10,897 Dollars at 90 days sight, but as it is still uncertain whether Mr. Geronimo la Chapelle[8] will be there when they arrive, or that Messrs. Delaps may have funds of mine in their hands to do honor to those Bills, I have taken the liberty of writing the Honble. Benjamin Franklin Esqr. your Ambassador at Paris very minutely on this subject[9] in order he may see those Bills paid for the credit of the States: I have taken this precaution in consequence of your Letter of the 12th June 1777 wherein you desire me to let you know on what terms I can sell Bills on France or Spain."[1]

Now Sir, as this Gentleman in purchasing many necessaries by Orders from the Committee of Commerce is largely in advance (say about 70,000 Dollars) for the United States, and thereby greatly distressed, nor is it in our power at present to give him relief until new Flour is brought to Market, an Article much wanted there, and the only one in our power to reimburse him with. In order to prevent the evil that will inevitably ensue to him as well as to the honor of these States should those Bills be protested, induces us most earnestly to request your interference in this matter, so as to prevent the Bills being protested, and please to advise us with the result.

---

8. With whom Pollock had signed an agreement involving the exchange of pelts from Louisiana for goods from Bordeaux: Pollock to Committee of Commerce, Aug. 11, 1778 (National Archives). Pollock later spelled his name Lachiapella: Pollock to William Pickles, Jan. 20, 1780 (National Archives).

9. XXIX, 303–4.

1. The committee's letter had appointed Pollock its agent in New Orleans: National Archives; James A. James, *Oliver Pollock: the Life and Times of an Unknown Patriot* (New York and London, 1937), pp. 113–14.

We have the honor to be With the greatest respect and esteem Your Excellency's Most humble Servants

signed by order
FRA: LEWIS[2]

(Duplicate)
His Excellency Benjamin Franklin Esquire Minister Plenipotentiary from the United States of America at the Court of France.

Passport for Mr. King

ALS (draft): American Philosophical Society

Passy, July 22. 1779[3]

To all Captains & Commanders of Vessels of War, Privateers & Letters of Marque belonging to the United States of America
Gentlemen,

The Bearer of this, Mr King, an Irish Gentleman & Friend of America, being on his Return to that Kingdom with his Lady & Family; if the Packet Boat or Vessel in which they may take their Passage from Flanders to England or from England to Ireland should happen to fall into your Hands, this is to request that besides your accustomed Humanity to Prisoners, you would treat them with particular Civility & *Tenderness*,[4] and give them as soon as possible their Liberty. In so doing there is no doubt but that your Conduct will be ap-

2. Francis Lewis of New York, one of the five members of the committee. He had served with BF on the committee's predecessor, the Secret Committee: XXII, 204; *JCC*, XII, 1217.

3. A copy of a cover letter, without addressee but dated July 22, is at the Library of Congress: "Mr. Franklin having receiv'd when in Ireland great Civilities from the Gentlemen of that Country, is pleas'd with every Opportunity given him of manifesting the grateful Sense he retains of their Politeness and hospitality; He therefore Sends immediatly the passport requested: with his sincerest Wishes that the unhapy Contest which makes it necessary may be a means of producing some advantage to their kingdom."

4. Written in the margin: "[Kindness & *Respect*]".

prov'd by your Employers, and you will very much oblige Gentlemen Your most obedt & most humble Servt.

BF

Minister Plenipotentiary from the United States to the Court of France

Another for His Lordship the Bishop of Derry in Ireland, Sir Patrick Bellew, & Mr. French of the same Kingdom, Friends of America being on their Return thither[5]

Notation: Passport given to Irish Gentlemen *returning thither*

From James Thompson[6] LS: American Philosophical Society

Gentlemen,   Brest, July 22nd. 1779

I have sent to you by Capt. Carey[7] all the Letters that I brought from Boston with me[8] as I am certain they will be delivered to you with the greatest care. He is a Gentleman who came Passenger with me. I shall sail for Nantz in two or three Days where I shall take in a small Cargoe for Boston. I expect to sail from Nantz by the first of next Month. If your Honours should have any Commands, I should be glad to have the Honor to serve You.

I have the Honor to be,— Gentlemen Your most Obedt. & Huml Servt.   JAMS. THOMPSON

Addressed: For / The Honble. Benjamin Franklin / Paris / Favd. by / Cap. Carey

Notation: Thompson Brest 22. juillet 1779.

5. BF jotted this note at some later time. Their undated request for a passport is printed below, before Sept. 10.
6. Captain of the schooner *Lee:* XXIX, 656n.
7. Probably the veteran Boston ship captain John Carey: Claghorn, *Naval Officers,* p. 49.
8. Including a letter to BF from Jonathan Loring Austin (XXIX, 656–7).

From Jonathan Williams, Jr.: Four Letters

(I) and (II) ALS: American Philosophical Society; copy: Yale University Library; (III) and (IV) ALS: American Philosophical Society

I.

Dear & honoured Sir.   Nantes July 22. 1779

Since writing you on the 13th Instant in which I informed you that the Privateers complained of by the Spanish Court could not be american ones, I have made more particular Enquiry, and in order to satisfy the Ambassador in the fullest manner I return you the Paper you sent to me with a Certificate from the Brokers here declaring that such Privateers have never appeared in France.[9] I can say nothing about the one in the West Indies but I am convinced that all such Insults have been from the English & not from the americans.

I am ever with the greatest Respect your dutifull & affectionate Kinsman   JONA WILLIAMS J

His Excelly Doctor Franklin.

Notation: Williams Jona. July 22 1779.

II.

Dear & honoured Sir.   Nantes July 22. 1779

I informed on the 13th Instant, I informed you that Capt Babcock Commander of the Genl Mifflin Privateer had released one hundred & ninety Prisoners at Sea and I inclosed you a Receipt for the same properly authenticated.— On hearing that the Cartel Ship was arrived in this River I thought it my Duty to claim an Exchange of these Prisoners and accordingly wrote the enclosed to Mr Schweighauser.[1] If

9. On July 30 Spanish Ambassador to France Aranda wrote Chief Minister Floridablanca forwarding the certificate, which had been brought to him by Ferdinand Grand (Archivo Historico Nacional, Estado, Madrid).

1. This appears to be the first mention of the *Milford*'s arrival. JW's July 21 letter to Schweighauser enclosed a copy of the receipt for the 190 prisoners sent back to England on the *Betsy,* and requested that Schweighauser obtain the release of an equal number of Americans from the cartel ship. If there were fewer than that number, he was to obtain the commander's receipt for the remainder, and a promise to deliver them at his next return. APS.

you think it is just & expedient to insist on my Receipts being accepted in Exchange for 190 Americans you will no Doubt give orders accordingly.— I am with the greatest Respect Your dutifull and affectionate Kinsman   JONA WILLIAMS J

His Excellency Doctor Franklin.

Notation: Williams Jona. July 22. 1779.

III.

Dear & honoured Sir.   Nantes July 22. 1779

This is the 3d Letter I have written to you to day, I write seperate Ones in order to keep the Business of each seperate.— My arbitration goes on but slowly, the Gentn thought it was necessary to write to Mr Lee to make their proceedings perfectly impartial, and he tries by his answer to put a Stop to the Examination; I sent you by last Post a Copy of this Performance, you will see how he tries to twist himself out, and because he knows he can't support his malicious accusations he wants to impress the Gentlemen with an Idea that they have not sufficient authority, but in spight of all his endeavours I shall I hope obtain my End.— They have examined and *approvd* of my Vouchers already & from everything that I can discover their opinion is very honourably for me; they have seen that I never have made use of a Sol of public Money for a private Speculation and they have also seen that even were I to be allowed as a merchant would have been by another merchant for doing the same Business, the public would owe me a great deal of money. As soon as it is over I will bring their award to you in Person. I am impatient to do this for I find my presence only can prevent my losing ground when I want to be most firmly established. I hope you have delivered my last to Mr A and that you approve of it. Can any man be more open than I am, they may know the Worst of me with all my heart, and so they hear only truth I do not care what they hear, for I want to conceal nothing.—

I am ever with the greatest Respect Dear & hond Sir most sincerely & affectionately Yours   J WILLIAMS J

I have just received your Recommendation of Mr Watteville and I will do all I can for him, but there is no way of his going to America from this at present.—

Addressed: a monsieur / Monsieur Franklin / Ministre Plenipotentiaire / des Etats Unis en son Hotel / a Passy près Paris

Notation: Williams Jona. July 22. 1779.

IV.

Dear & honoured Sir.   Nantes July 22. 1779

This will be presented to you by Captain Foligny who commanded the Marquis de la Chalotais in her first Voyage to America early in the War.[2] He is just returned from the West Indies and being an experienced Officer will be able to give you a good Accot of the naval Operations in that part of the World.

I recommend him to your Civilities and am with the greatest Respect Your dutifull & affectionate Kinsman

JONA. WILLIAMS J

His Excellency Doctor Franklin.

Notation: Williams Jona. July 22. 1779.

From Walter Pollard[3]   AL: American Philosophical Society

Hôtel du Roi petit Carousel près de Thuilleries.

[before July 23, 1779]

The Arrival of the inclosed Letter to Mr: Pollard makes it unnecessary for Him to trouble Doctor Franklin with the Parcel intended for England. It comes from the Gentleman to whom that Parcel was directed—his respected Friend Mr: J——s,[4]

2. JW had first written a letter of introduction for François-Jérôme de Foligné-Deschalonges in August, 1777: XXIV, 391.

3. The young American sympathizer and would-be secret agent whom Dumas had introduced: XXVIII, 5, 22–8. On July 23, BF lent him ten *louis* (240 *l.t.*), describing him as, "a Sufferer in the American Cause. His Father is a Physician in Barbadoes." Cash Book (Account XVI, XXVI, 3.)

4. William Jones, the eminent scholar and mutual friend of Pollard and BF: XVIII, 201n; XXVIII, 24n.

who had undertaken to procure, if possible, what was necessary for Mr: Pollard's Return to his Family. How the Efforts of his Friend have succeded may be seen in his own Account. Amongst the several Persons to whom the Application was made, Mr: Daniel[5] is alone accountable to the Friends & Father of Mr: Pollard, for his first & last Distresses, having unfairly witholden Supplies from Him not many Months ago, & now (in the present Alarm of the British Commerce) refusing to supply with only a Part the Son of a Gentleman to whom He formerly professed a Friendship. The others if able would unquestionably have lent their Assistance, which would not have been sollicited without the Assurance of his Father's Ability & Readiness to repay them. This, Sir, is the Subject of this Letter; & the Pain & Uneasiness of being obliged to write it cannot easily be expressed. Mr: P. had requested of them 50£, half of which would serve to pay his Expenses, incurred since his Disappointment of Mr: Norton's Coming to Paris[6] & the other Half would supply Him to Eustatia. But He is perfectly sensible, that where this Letter is written there must be many others who doubtless have better & stronger Claims to Assistance:—& the Thought of this has long restrained Him from a like Application. However, Mr: Js. having fairly marked the Crisis (and advised to the best of his Knowlege, whatever may be the Merit of his Advise)—the Necessity is too obvious to Mr: Pollard of doing something—but how—He cannot venture to determine. His Duty to His Father (whose Sentiments & Sense of Things are the same with his Son's) is the first Movement of his Soul; but Necessity (the Cause of which was honourable, though the Effects of it are severely felt by him, as He now finds Himself a Burthen where He vainly wished to be of Service) obliges Him to explain his Situation. He hopes there is no Impropriety in doing it in this Manner

5. Perhaps Edward Daniel, a solicitor in Bristol for nearly 50 years before his death in 1818: *Gentleman's Magazine*, LXXXVIII, part one (1818), 471. Pollard had stayed in Bristol (where his brother was ill) before fleeing England: XXVIII, 25–8.
6. A Virginian named George Flowerdewe Norton had been a student in London. He did come to Passy in 1779, at least long enough for BF to issue him a passport: XXIX, 513.

& if any Thing is obscure, & wanting a further Explanation, Mr: P will wait upon his Excellency whenever it may be convenient to give Him Notice.

Notation: From Mr Pollard no Date 1779.[7]

From Bernard Dehez

ALS: American Philosophical Society

⟨San Sebastián, July 23, 1779, in French: I have the honor of informing Your Excellency that Capt. Gustavus Conyngham, in command of the armed privateer *La Vengeance* (*Revenge*), captured the brigantine *Le Gracieux*, whose French captain, Manuel Augustin Letournois, sailing from London, had entirely loaded his ship with British goods, supposedly destined for Coruña.[8] The prize was brought into this port and the *commandant général* of the province [Marquis de Bassecourt] allowed part of the goods to be sold at auction. During that time, I rendered essential services to Capt. Conyngham and his crew.[9] Impatient, he sailed away before the trial had taken place, without leaving any retainer to provide for its outcome.

The trial dragged on and ended surprisingly in the victory of the opposing party, whereupon the *commandant,* in his search for fairness, referred it to the War Council in Madrid. Meanwhile, Capt. Conyngham, who had left with me a power of attorney of which I include a copy,[1] never deigned to an-

---

7. To the best of our knowledge, this is the last communication from Pollard. One of his letters (we don't know which) was forwarded to BF by Joseph Brown, Jr. (XXVI, 455; XXIX, 134, 379), who sent it under cover of his friend WTF in an undated note. APS.

8. For the initial accounts of Capt. Conyngham's capture of the French merchantman *Gracieux* see XXV, 410–12; XXVI, 498–9. Dehez, a merchant in San Sebastián, had been assisting him with the litigation: XXVI, 498n.

9. His efforts had obtained the liberation of the prizemaster and four crewmen who had been arrested: Neeser, *Conyngham,* p. 130.

1. Conyngham on Jan. 10, 1778, had given Dehez a general and unlimited power of attorney to represent his interests before the War Council in Madrid. A copy is with BF's papers at the APS. He obviously was not aware that Conyngham had been a prisoner of the British since April: Digges to BF, Aug. 20, below.

swer the various letters I sent him requesting the funds necessary for the pursuit of this judicial matter.

In order to protect Conyngham's interests, and those of Congress, I entrusted a friend in Madrid with enquiring quietly into the business; he informed me on July 15 that Conyngham has no legal representative in Madrid, but that, given the new ordinance passed by the King of Spain upon his declaration of war against England, the outcome of the trial is bound to be favorable, provided legal counsel is in place.

I beg Your Excellency to give instructions to Messrs. Gardoqui in Bilbao or anybody you choose to provide me with the financial means to pursue this affair which is bound to bring a considerable amount of money to Conyngham or to Congress.

P.S. I am enclosing the text of the ordinance of July 1, to let you appreciate how much it bolsters Conyngham's claim.[2]⟩

From Joseph-Jérôme Le Français de Lalande and Jacques Barbeu-Dubourg

ALS: American Philosophical Society

Monsieur et illustre confrere

au college royal le
23 juillet 1779

Permettés moi de vous presenter m. des raggi,[3] homme de merite et de talent, qui voudroit passer dans les etats unis, non pas comme un homme embarrassé de sa personne, mais comme pouvant y former un etablissement avantageux même au pays. Il a été pendant plusieurs années dans ma province de Bresse directeur d'une belle manufacture de fayance, cet art est peu commun en amerique; vous pourrés au moins lui dire ce qu'il peut faire ou esperer dans ce genre; on a eté tres

2. The enclosure, in Dehez' hand, included a paragraph from the royal ordinance stating that ships carrying goods belonging to the enemy could be seized and carried into Spanish ports. Dehez went on to assure BF that Conyngham's prize was indeed valid. APS.

3. He may have been the director of the *manufacture de fayence* established in the 1770's by a M. de Marron in Bourg-en-Bresse. *Almanach des marchands*, p. 115.

content de sa conduite et de ses talens, ainsi je ne fais aucune difficulté de vous repondre de lui, et de vous demander votre protection pour lui. Je vous en aurai une obligation personelle.

J'ai bien du regret de ce que la Loge des neuf sœurs n'a pas pu aller cette année faire Sa fête a passy[4] pour vous voir illustrer notre assemblée, mais nous esperons que vous voudrés bien orner celle que nous preparons pour le commencement d'aout a Paris.

Je Suis avec un profond respect Monsieur et illustre confrere Votre tres humble et tres obeissant serviteur

DELALANDE
de l'academie des Sciences

The Bearer of the present letter appear very honest and intelligent, he desires transmigrate to America, and establiss there an usefull fabrick, if he can obtain a proper soil. Moreover he desires by your protection have his passage frée under the condition of defending with his person and sword te ship, which he shall be at the board of. M de la Lande the Astronomer [recommended?] him to your benevolence, and begged my adjonction to that end. Be so good as favouring him, I pray you, Dear Sir, if in your power.

You have some papers of mine, I beseech you that you remitt them to me by that, or any next occasion, and am with attachment and respect, your most obedient humble servant

DUBOURG

Addressed: A Monsieur / Monsieur franklin ministre des etats unis de l'amerique / a Passy

Notation: Dubourg 23 juillet 1779.

4. XXVI, 697.

From Samuel Wharton

ALS: American Philosophical Society

Hotel de Rome Friday Afternoon.
Dear Sir   [July 23, 1779?][5]
   I have several Letters but no News from London. Sir
Charles Hardy's Fleet was at Anchor in Plymouth Road on
the 17th Instant.
   I am with the sincerest Respect your Excellency's affection-
ate & most obt. Servt   S. WHARTON

His Excellency Mr. Franklin

Notation: S. Wharton Paris—

From John Bondfield

ALS: American Philosophical Society

Sir   Bordeaux 24 July 1779
   The following is a petition rather of a Singular Nature yet I
think I have some grounds.[6] In the private Armaments made
in this Kingdom on the Granting Commissions I embarkt in
order to engage others to the extent of a considerable Sum.
Our Vessels took many, but of Little value, of course hurt the
Enemy without indemnifying the Interested Twenty Six or
Seven prizes produced only to refit the Privateers at Forreign
Ports that by Loss's of our Ships since taken all our Capital is
absorbd this is the fortune of War and of which we were aware
but in One of the adventures I cannot help thinking myself
Agreived. The Ship La Marquise de Lafayette[7] was bought by

5. An extract of a letter from Plymouth dated July 17 reporting the an-
chorage of the grand fleet was published in *The Public Advertiser* on July 21,
making this the earliest likely date on which Wharton would have written
this letter.
   6. The petition, in French, addressed to Sartine and dated July 24, out-
lined the details of Bondfield's investment and asked the government to
restore to him his 25,000 *l.t.* APS.
   7. Quite large for a privateer, this 32-gun frigate, Capt. Loisel, carried a
crew of 335 men. She was seized by the creditors of Reculès de Basmarein
& Raimbaux, a Bordeaux merchant house which went bankrupt in February, 1779: Robert Castex, "L'Armateur de La Fayette: Pierre de Basmarein
d'après des documents inédits," *Revue des questions historiques,* CII (1925), 115.
See also XXVI, 677n; XXVII, 404n. She seems to have been acquired by the

Gouverment to Lend to Basmarin & Co. who engaged to fitt her out at their expence in being indulged with 18 Months service of the Ship on their application to me I agreed to take an Interest of 25000 Livres and paid into their hands that Sum, she was most compleatly fitted for her Cruise and a few days after she was out fell in with some outwardbound fishermen & Whalemen tho' but of Little Value to the Owners was a National benifit the number of Prisoners obliged the Captain to put into port to Land them. The Captain hearing of the Failure of the House of Basmarin sent an Express for Instructions. The Interested emediately orderd him to proceed on his Mission and laid in a fresh Supply out of the proceeds of the prizes for a four Months Cruize. Six Weeks after she put into this Port not having had any success to that day. On her arrival Monsr Le Moine Commissaire de La Marine[8] took possession of her in behalf of the King and consequently all our prospects with our Capital is become an entire Loss. As this Vessel was equipt with our Capital was to have been at our disposal eighteen Months was compleatly Mannd and having in no manner diviated from the Original Convention with Gouverment who now taking her into their possession ought to indemnify the Interested for their advances. This being an affair that your Worthy friend Mons. Le Rey de Chaumont can make light give me leave to request your Influence with him if any plan other than this can be offerd to recover my said Capital. It may not be amiss to enforce our Spirritted efforts to set on float these adventures wherin we lose by our Concerns in privateers only lost & taken upwards of 110,000 *l.t.* including the Twenty five Thousand Interest I hold in this Vessel which becomes a Loss from the Sole motion of the Loss of Possession Gouvernment stand indemnified should they reimburse our advances by the value of the effects they obtain. I do not enter into any of the transactions of the House of Basmarin with whom I have no other conections but in two of these

---

French Navy in 1780: Pierre Le Conte, *Répertoire des navires de guerre français* (Cherbourg, 1932), p. 109.

8. *Commissaire général* Le Moyne, the *ordonnateur* at Bordeaux: Sartine to BF, June 25, 1780 (Archives de la Marine).

adventures. I only humbly represent my own Griefs recommending my Interest to your protection. I am with due respect Sir Your most Obedient Humble Servant   JOHN BONDFIELD

His Excellency Benj Franklin esq

Notation: Bondfield John 24. Juillet 1779.

From Jonathan Williams, Jr.

ALS: American Philosophical Society; copy: Yale University Library

Dear & honoured Sir   Nantes July 24. 1779

I wrote you last Post relative to the Claim I had made of Prisoners from this Cartel. The Subject of this is the Reception these Prisoners have met with and their Present Situation.— I beg leave to ask your perusal of my Letter to you of the 7th of April last.—[9] I am sorry if you think me too importunate but I have some of the Milk of human kindness about me and the Situation of these poor People touches me. The Reason of my writing now is, that I am told that Mr Schweighauser has told them that he had *"positive orders from you to advance no money to any prisoners."*[1] And in consequence of this Mr White who has been 29 months in Prison & is a 2d. Lieut. in the Virginia Service, has been with me & related his Situation with the above Circumstances.— Capt Babcock who commands the Mifflin Privateer to my address has already taken about 40 of these Prisoners onboard, but he cannot engage to take a greater Number unless they are first provided with Cloathes Provisions & necessarys; if this is done, he will give Ship Room to all of them if you think proper. His Reasoning appears to me good, & his Actions hitherto generous, you will judge what allowance is proper for these poor People For their Subsistance, and 'till I receive your answer I expect to be obliged to engage from my private Purse for the Maintenance of Many of them.

9. XXIX, 276–8.
1. Schweighauser may have misinterpreted the commissioners' letter to him of Aug. 22: XXVII, 287.

I am ever with the greatest Respect Your ever dutifull & affectionate Kinsman JONA WILLIAMS J
I would have it understood that in my Reccommendations of Supplys to Prisoners I mean only *Necessarys.* Mr White has shewn me the Copy of a Letter which he says was given him in prison I enclose it to you to know if it is genuine.[2]

Notation: Williams Jona. July 24. 1779.

To Sartine

Copy: Library of Congress

Sir Passy, July 25. 1779.
Having received Copies of the Papers found in the English Vessel called les trois amis, taken by Captain Landais, I desired a Person conversant in Such Matters to examine them, and I have now the honour to send to your Excellency here with the Remark he has made upon them.[3] What Weight they may have is submitted to your Excellency's Judgement.

For my own Part, I should be for paying the most perfect Respect to the Pleasure of the king signified in his passport or

2. JW was especially concerned (as he wrote WTF on July 27) about the rumors circulating that BF was a "cruel inhuman Man who wantonly wished these People to suffer." He added that Schweighauser was now paying the escaped prisoners' landlady out of his own pocket. APS.

3. Chaumont was the person in question. After analyzing the documents (among them was the passport described by Jones in his July 2 letter and by Vergennes in his draft July 12 letter), he prepared a five-page undated memoir pointing out the numerous inconsistencies in the ship's papers. He suggested that, because of the likelihood of fraud, the case be turned over to the courts. If the French government intends to return the ship to its owners, could not both ship and cargo be sequestered at American expense until BF receives instructions from America? A notation in BF's hand reads, "Promise Capt. Landais the whole of naval Store Prizes" and another, in WTF's hand, "Mr Chaumonts Memoire relative to the 3 Friends." APS. An undated copy of this memoir in Dumas' hand is at the Archives Nationales. In response, the French naval ministry prepared a memoir for Sartine dated July 26, analyzing the case and recommending the minister bypass the controversy by turning it over to the courts; Sartine, however, endorsed it, "non, il vaut mieux retirer le passeport dont on a vraisemblablement abusé et laisser l'americain user de ses droits." Archives Nationales.

otherways. But the Captain Officers and People of the Alliance being persuaded by every body that as the Ship and Cargo is clearly english Property and the king's Commands in his Passport, are directed only to his own subjects, "a tous *nos* Officiers and Sujets" with the usual Clause et nous prions et desirons que les officiers et Ministres de touts Princes et Etats liés d'amitié avec nous laisse et permette le passage, &c. they believe they are justifiable in taking her, and they would think I did them a great Injury, if I should order them to deliver up their Prize without a legal Trial and sentence ordaining it and It might give occasion to a fresh Mutiny in that ship, very inconvenient to the present service she is engaged in. Indeed I do not think myself authorised to dispose of what they consider as their Property, without such Trial. The Congress have given Orders to all their Captains to submit their Prizes when carried into france to the Jurisdiction of the king's admiralty Courts having the greatest Confidence in the Justice of these Tribunals. I have the same Confidence and do therefore request your Excellency that a regular Trial of the Validity of this Prize may take place, in the Event of which I shall, and I think all parties ought to acquiesce. With the greatest Respect, I am your Excellency's

To Jean-Daniel Schweighauser   Copy: Library of Congress

Sir,   Passy July 25. 1780. [*i.e.,* 1779][4]
I received duly the Letters you did me the honour to write me of the 10th. Instant, and another of the 20th.[5]
The Objection I made was not to your Commission of 5. per Cent for the general Business, tho' I am informed that is higher than the Custom; but as I understand, it was settled so with you by Mr. Lee, I had no Intention to propose an Alteration, leaving that to Congress. If, as some have imagined, you have agreed to allow Mr. Wm. Lee a Part of it, as I hear was proposed to Mr. Delap, in his Behalf, and was actually given

4. A copyist's error: given the subject matter this could have been written only in 1779.
5. Both are missing.

138

by M. Lee's Collegue to the Person who did his part of the Business, to be sure it will not appear so extraordinary.⁶ What I objected to was your Charge of 5 per Cent on the mere delivery of two Cargoes of Tobacco, a Commission that amounted to more than 600£ Sterling for the Business of at most a few Days: To make this swell the higher, you valued the Tobaccos at 90 Livres, tho' we delivered them by Contract, at about 40.⁷ It is this particular Commission that I cannot approve or agree to, being informed by more than 10. Merchants of whom the Question has been asked that 1 per Cent. is the most allow'd on such Occasions. And when I spoke of not paying so much of your Drafts as amounted to that Difference in that article, it was not from any Doubt of your Credit or ability. But merely to express more strongly my Disapprobation of the Charge, and to prevent it being said hereafter, on any general Settlement, that I had already allow'd it by paying it. Your over drawing in any other Circumstance, I should have considered only as a Mistake and should have paid your Bills in full confidence of your rectifying it, and to prevent the disagreable Circumstance of protesting any Bills drawn by you, I requested you to retain as many in your hands as amounted to that Sum, which I hope you have done I have as yet refused none of your Drafts. And your Bills being usually drawn at so many Days *date* and not *Sight,* are generally due before they appear, & of Course are immediately paid, to which Manner of drawing I have made an [no] Objection, being desirous that you should never be long in Advance; tho' others draw on me at one two & some times three Usances, which might in some Circumstances be a Convenience. I am glad to hear that the Milford Transport is arrived with more

6. Upon his departure for Germany in 1778, William Lee appointed successors to assume his responsibilities from Congress as American commercial representative in France. In addition to Schweighauser these included the firm of S. & J.H. Delap, which was offered but declined the post in Bordeaux eventually taken by Bondfield: XXVI, 60, 196. Lee's earlier colleague had been the late Thomas Morris: XXIV, 451–3.

7. For more than two months BF had been objecting to the commission Schweighauser had charged for delivering tobacco to the farmers general: XXIX, 497, 556–7, 628–9, 710–11.

american Prisoners. With regard to the necessary assistance they may Want, I would have you treat them with the same kindness that was shown with the Approbation of M. Adams to those of the first Transport. I hope they will all find Births in the Alliance, the Bonhomme Richard, or the general Mifflin.— As to the English to be given in Exchange, I would have you collect all that are in all the Prisons of which I think you have already a List: if they do equal the Number received, we must then send an Acknowledgment of so many received on account of the Agreements made with the brave Captain of the General Mifflin[8] and others, of which a Copy should be sent to the Board in England that transacts this Business of the Cartel. I have not the List of Names of the Prisoners dismissed on Parole by that Captain; but as he is at Nantes, you can get it from him, I hear we have a great many Prisoners in Spain[9] but know not the Number nor Places. I wish you to write to your Correspondents there for Information, and shall be glad of your Opinion of the Measures to be taken for exchanging them.

As to the enormous Demand of the Captain of the Swedish Ship,[1] it seems to me that it should be disputed in the Courts, and nothing paid but what is adjuged to be just by a regular Sentence, I shall communicate the affair as you desire to the advocate of the Bureau des Prises, with the Reasons you give; but having sent the Papers to you, I cannot show what time the Captain acknowledges he first produced them to Capt. Landais.— You can send me an authentic Copy of that Piece I wanted.

I approve of your sparing an anchor from the arsenal to Mr. Peltier for M. Monthieu's Vessel.[2]

8. George W. Babcock. On July 21 JW sent Schweighauser a copy of Babcock's receipt for the prisoners he had ransomed; a signed copy of JW's covering letter is with BF's papers at the APS.

9. See BF to Hartley, July 12.

1. The prize *Victoria*, which Landais had captured on his way from America to France; Schweighauser had been involved from the beginning in the legal repercussions: XXVIII, 563, 632.

2. Beaumarchais' agent Jean Peltier-Dudoyer also represented Montieu (*e.g.*, XXIV, 40; XXV, 159–60n; XXVI, 206).

As to Capt. Jones's Shares, I think it a Matter settled by the Navy Board in America. With great Esteem I have the Honour to be &c.

M. Schweighauser

To Vergennes Copy: Library of Congress

Sir, Passy, July 25. 1779.

I received yesterday a Letter dated the 20th. Instand,[3] under a Cover mark'd with your Excellency's Name but the Letter not signed by you or any other Person enclosing a Memoire which is likewise not signed, relating to the taking of the English ship the three friends by Capt. Landais, who is charg'd in the Memoire as having made that Prize in Contempt of the King's Passport. Having had the Honour of conferring with your Excellency on this Subject the Same Day on which the Letter is dated, and of communicating to you the Reasons offered in the Captain's Justification, I apprehend that this anonymous Letter which expresses an Expectation that I should order an immediate Restitution of the Said ship, does not come from your Excellency, but is sent me by some other Person, or by some Mistake. I do not therefore here repeat those Reasons, nor trouble your Excellency at present with mine for thinking that a regular Trial of the validity of that Prise, would be the most satisfactory; I have however given them to M. Desartine in a Letter of this Day. With the greatest Respect, I am Your Excellency, most obed.

M. De Vergennes.

From John Paul Jones ALS: American Philosophical Society

Honored & dear Sir L'Orient July 25th. 1779.

I have had the pleasure to receive your esteemed Letters down to the 19th. and you may be sure that I will pay due Attention to your Orders.— It gives me pleasure to find my

3. Of which we print the draft: above, July 12.

Authority enlarged because it will enable me to attempt whatever enterprise may present itself and afford a prospect of Success.— And because I shall endeavour to make my Cruise a
busy one rather than a long One.— Before I depart I will send
you a Cypher for a private Correspondence, and in the meantime I would wish it may be convenient that your further Orders may be at the Port of my destination before the Middle of
September.

I beg you to read the inclosed.— I expect the Answer will
find me ready in the Road of Groa. I am ever Dear Sir Your
Obliged and Affectionate Friend & Servant,   JNO P JONES

His Excellency Doctor Franklin.

Notations: Capt. Jones. July 25. 79 / Capt. Landais

From Stephen Marchant   LS:[4] American Philosophical Society

Sr.

On board the black prince Morlaix Road
July 25th. 1779

I recd. yr Excellencies Letter of the 10th Inst.[5] which has
gave me Infinite Satisfaction to find yr Excellency Approves
of my Conduct in my last Cruize, I hope I shall Continue in yr
Esteem as I mean never to Derogate from the honour of an
American Subject having Greaved the Cutter and got every
thing Necessary for Sailing I set out from Morlaix Road thursday 15th Inst. and sailed to the Westward. And on Friday the
16th. Sunk 2 Sloops and One brig they not being worth bringing in. I not having Men that cou'd be depended upon being
obliged before I left Morlaix for Want of Men to take 12 of my
former prisoners on board my Cutter at their own Request
they being good Seamen. Ransomed a Small Sloop kept a few
Prisoners the Rest I sent in sd. sloop they signing a Duplicate
to be Answerable for as many American Prisoners in Great
Britain when a Cartel shou'd happen to pass between England
and the United States and on Saturday 17th Inst Course N.N.E

4. In the hand of Timothy Kelly, one of the *Black Prince*'s crew (XXIX, 718n).
5. Undoubtedly the letter dated July 4 in BF's letterbook.

Wind S.E Distance from Tapstow [Padstow?] 2 Leagues Sunk one Sloop Ransomed another on Sunday the 18th Inst At M. Course N.b.E Wind S.E Lundy Isle Distance 4 Leagues Sunk two Sloops Ransomed one brig set the following Men at Liberty they Signing a Duplicate as Aforesd. Viz Henry Rowe Master Brig Lucy Samuel Pickesgill Mate both from St Ives. Robert Cowling St Jearth [Portreath?] John Lewis Swansey, George Landin Owner Sloop John Kinsale Ireland, John Wellis Capt. Cornelius Fowler Mate, Henry Eastway Capt Sloop Rebecca William Gross his Boy John Trick Capt Brig Union Boscastle William Becken his Mate. Sunk one Sloop and one brig more and on Monday 19th Inst at 6 in the Morning Course S.S.E Wind S.W Lundy Isle bore S.E Distance 3 Leagues took the St Joseph Brig being a Prize taken by the Emperor Letter of Mart of Bristol examining her papers found her to be an Irish property Goods likewise Consigned to Irish Merchants took the English Prize Master and two Men out of her, and Sent her into France together with the Spanish Capt who was rejoyced to Escape an English Prison, At 4 past M. Course N.b.W, Wind S.W. Milford bore N.b.W. Distance 5 Leagues took a brig the Dublin Trader laden with Sugar Oil Copper and Tin and Bale Goods sent her to France Tuesday Wednesday and Thursday Variable Winds Cruizing in the Bristol Channell On Friday July 23d. Course S.S.W Wind Westerdly at Meridian brought an Armed Brig to she Informed me she was an American Prize taken by a Bristol privateer blew hard cou'd send no Boat out to Board her but made her keep the same Course, believes her to be the New York Packett was taken from me to my Grief by an English Frigate, which Obliged to Croud what sail the wind wou'd permit me to do to get Clear of the Frigate— At 4 past M, Saw a Large fleet of Liverpool Merchant Ships under Convoy to the Windward. I thought to pick up some of them but cou'd not they keeping Close to their Convoy Regrets the Loss of not having a Frigate in my Company as I am Sure we wd take the whole fleet which was I am Informed Very Valuable Saturday July 24th Course S. Wind N.N.W modeate Gales AM Saw an English Frigate under my lee distance 2 Leagues hauled the Wind to get Clear made the Coast of France at 6 past M, Distance 4 Leagues saw my Prize the Dublin under my lee bearing down on her(?) Night came on so I lay to all Night on Sunday 25th Inst. Course S.S.E Wind W.N.W, at 4 before M. Saw my prize the Dublin under my lee bore from us East Distance one League & a half at 10 before M My Prize and we Came to Anchor thanks providence in Morlaix Road in 3 1/2 fathom Water, she is I believe a Valuable prize the following Prisoners I have brought in Viz— Richd Lewis from Emperor Letter of Mart of Bristol on board the st Joseph Bartholomew Downey Mariner Do— Thomas Dedford do— Morgan Griffiths Capt Dublin Trader John MaCrackin passenger in Do. Arthur Millin Do. Willm. Owen Mariner Do. Joseph Minehead Do. Hugh Williams Do. John Hynes do. Richard Davis Do.

I hope yr Excellency knowing my Distress not having sufficient Men to trust to will Excuse me in not bringing more prisoners than the above. I have done the Enemy as much Damage as was possible for me to Do and hopes soon to do more be pleased to give my kind Respects to yr. Nephew and all the American Gentlemen of yr Excellency's Acquantance, I Remn. with all Duty to yr Excellency yr most Obedient Hble Sert   STEPHEN MARCHANT

Endorsed: Sail'd from Morlaix Thursday July 15 1779—

	Sunk	Ransomed	Sent to France
Friday 16.	2 Sloops 1 Brig	1 Sloop	
Saturday 17.	1 Sloop	1 Sloop	
Sunday 18.	2 Sloops	1 Brig	1 Brig St Joseph
Monday 19.			1 Brig. Dublin Trader
Friday 23—		{ Took an armed Brig retaken by a Frigate }	
	Total Sunk 6	Ransomed 3	2 sent in

Addressed: To / his Excellency Benjamin Franklin / Minister of the United States of North / America at the Court of France / at Passy / near / Paris—

Notation: Capt. Merchant July 25. 1779

From Samuel Wharton

ALS: American Philosophical Society

Dear Sir   Sunday Morning July 25th. [1779]

I send your Excellency the within Letter, and parts of the Leidger,[6] which may, perhaps, contain some News, That you have not received. The Letter is from a Gentleman of good Connexions & Information in London, and Therefore I would ask the Favor of its not being shewn.[7]

I am with great Regard your Exellency's most affectionate & obt. Servant   SAML. WHARTON

Addressed: A' Son Excellence / Monsieur / Monsieur Franklin / &c &c &c / Passy

From Joseph-Mathias Gérard de Rayneval

ALS: American Philosophical Society

A Versailles Le 26 juillet 1779

Vous avez écrit à M. le Cte de Vergennes,[8] Monsieur, au sujet d'une lettre que vous avez reçüe le 20. de ce mois, et qui est relative au navire de Dublin les trois amis. Vous mobligerez beaucoup si vous voulez bien me renvoyer cette lettre avec l'enveloppe: j'ai lieu de la croire de M. le Cte. de Vergennes, et c'est par inadvertence qu'elle a eté expédiée sans être signée:[9] elle finit par ces mots dommages et intérêts.[1]

6. *The Public Ledger, a Daily Register of Commerce and Intelligence,* founded in 1760, offered mercantile news and advertisements: H.R. Fox Bourne, *English Newspapers. Chapters in the History of Journalism* (2 vols., London, 1887), I, 196–7, 250.

7. The letter, unsigned, was from Capt. Thomas Hutchins and dated July 9. It reported that the British fleet of thirty-seven ships of the line arrived at Torbay on July 6, and was due to sail the following day. Wharton endorsed the letter, which is now at the National Archives. A notation, "Intelligence from France," indicates that BF included it among the intelligence reports he forwarded to Congress. Hutchins was arrested in late August for treasonable correspondence with BF: Digges to BF, Sept. 4, below.

8. On July 25, above.

9. Gérard de Rayneval's responsibilities as *premier commis* included the preparation of such letters for Vergennes' signature.

1. A draft of the letter to which Rayneval refers is published under July 12, above.

145

J'ai l'honneur d'être avec un parfait attachement, Monsieur, votre très-humble et très obeisst. serviteur

GERARD DE RAYNEVAL

M franklin

Notation: Gerard de Raimond 26. juillet 1779.

From John Paul Jones

ALS: American Philosophical Society; AL (draft): National Archives; copy: United States Naval Academy Museum

Honored and dear Sir,   L'Orient July 26th. 1779.
Since I wrote to you last night I have received advice that the Jamaica Fleet will sail homewards escorted by a Fifty Gun Ship and two Strong Frigates.—[2] Should we fall in with that Force we will certainly Engage and I hope Overcome it; but in all probability our Ships will be so much cut to pieces in the Action that we shall be unable to prevent the Escape of the Convoy.— As it was proposed, when I was last at Paris, to put the Frigate the Monsieur under my Command,[3] and as that Ship is now newly Careened and ready to Sail, If it could be convenient to add that force to my present Command, it would give us a Superiority over the Enemies Convoy, and might perhaps enable us to Take and Destroy their Jamaica Fleet— Or if we failed in that we might turn our Arms against other Objects which might I hope do them equal mischief.— If this reaches you before the Departure of the Express, I submit the Idea to your Superiour Wisdom. I thought it my Duty to mention it, and am with sincere and Grateful Affection Dear Sir Your Obliged Friend and very humble Servant

JNO P JONES

His Excellency Doctor Franklin
Notation: Capt. Jones July 26. 1779

2. This convoy was intercepted off Newfoundland in mid-July by the American warships *Providence, Queen of France,* and *Ranger,* which captured eleven of its merchant ships: Gardner W. Allen, *A Naval History of the American Revolution* (2 vols., Boston and New York, 1913), II, 382–5.

3. A privateer which Jones had long hoped to add to his squadron: XXIX, 494. She did eventually sail with it.

From J. Rocquette, T.A. Elsevier & P.Th. Rocquette

LS or ALS: American Philosophical Society

Sir!   Rotterdam 26 July 1779.

We begg the liberty to referr our selfs to the contents of our last respects to you of the 24 of past month,[4] and have now the honour to inclose you a parcell which we just now recd. from St. Eustatia for your Exceelÿ. we desire you to accuse us the receit of it; we make free to join to it a Letter for Mr. Arthur Lee, which, praÿ have handed to him.

We have the honour to be with the most deep respect Sir! your verÿ húmble servants   J. ROCQÚETTE T.A. ELSEVIER, & BROTHERS ROCQÚETTE

His Excelly. Benj: Franklin, Minister Plenipotentiary from the united States of North America at the Court of Versailles at Passÿ

Endorsed: Holland

From Jonathan Loring Austin

ALS: American Philosophical Society

Sir   Boston July 27th. 1779

I flatter'd myself I should have the pleasure by this Opportunity, of confirming & sending your Excellency a particular Account of the Repulse, said to have been given the British Troops at South Carolina in May last, which for some Weeks was reported & fully credited here, & led me to mention it with so much Assurance in the enclosed Letter—[5]

I now beg Leave to introduce to your Excellency Mr William Knox of this Town, Brother to Brigadier General Knox an Officer of Merit in our Army, who proposes in his way to Holland to do himself the Honor of paying his Respects to you at Passy; & to refer your Excellency to this Gentleman

---

4. This letter from the Rotterdam merchant firm is summarized in XXIX, 68on.

5. His own, dated July 12, above.

for a particular Account of our Situation at the Southward, & all other Occurrences—

I have the Honor to be with Respect Your Excellencys most Obedient & very humble Servant   JON LORING AUSTIN

His Excellency Doctor Franklin

Addressed: Son Excellence / Monsieur Dr Franklin / Ministre plenipotentiare de l'Amerique / a la Cour de France / a Passy / pres Paris / per mr Knox

Notation: J L. Austin July 27. 79

From Jane Mecom   ALS: American Philosophical Society

Dear Brother   warwick 27—July 1779

I have after a long year recved yr kind leter of nov 26—1778[6] wherin you like yr self do all for me that the most Affectionat Brother can be desiered or Expected to do,[7] & tho I feel my self full of gratitude for yr Generousity, the conclution of yr leter Affectes me more; where you say you wish we may spend our last days togather. O my Dear Brother if this could be Accomplished it would give me more Joy than any thing on this side Heaven could posably do; I feel the want of suitable conversation I have but litle hear, I think I could Asume more freedom with you now & convence you of my affection for you I have had time to Reflect & see my Error in that Respect, I Suffered my Defidence & the Awe of yr Superiority to prevent the femiliarity I might have taken with you & ought, & yr kindnes to me might have convenced me would be acceptable; but it is hard overcomeing a natural propensity, & Difedence is mine—

I was in a few months after I wrote you the leter to which yrs is the ansure[8] Relived of my Distres as I have since In-

6. Missing.

7. BF apparently proposed a "Schem of business" to Jonathan Williams, Sr., for her benefit; see Williams' July 29 and Aug. 8 letters.

8. Undoubtedly hers of Aug. 15, 1778 (XXVII, 255–8).

formed you,[9] that if any of my leters to you must be lost I wishd it might be that as I knew it must give you pain, but as you have recd that I am not out of hope the rest or at least some of them have since come to yr hand tho those I have wrote by perticular persons who have desiered to be Introdused to yr Notice I have wrot in a hurry & comonly Just after a long won containing all the perticulars I wishd. to Inform you of, that it is likely the most Insignificant have reached you & the others are lost.

I recd a Leter from mr Beach Latly he says they have had no leter from you or there son above a year the Last from Temple & that was dated in November his was June 22d they were all well then Jonathan Williams Expected but not Arived.[1]

It is a very hapy circumstance that you Injoy yr helth so perfectly[2] it is a Blesing vouchsaifed to me also Exept some trifeling Interuption & that but sildom which I a good deal atribute to my observation of yr former Admonitions respecting fresh Air & diet for whatever you may think, Every hint of yrs apeared of two much consequence to me to be neglected or forgoten as I all ways knew Everything you said had a meaning.

The few friends I have hear flock about me when I recve a leter & are much disopointed that they contain no Politicks, I tell them you Dare not trust a woman Politicks, & prehaps that is the truth but if there is any thing we could not posable misconstru or do mischief by knowing from you, it will Gratife us mightly if you add a litle to yr future kind leters.

Mr Collas met a man in the street & sent my leter I have had no line from or His wife so do not know his Inclination concerning the crown soap[3] but shall as soon as posable make

9. On Feb. 14, 1779 (xxvⅠⅠⅠ, 541–3), she reported the death of her mentally incapacitated son Peter.

1. RB's letter is apparently not extant, but her reply to him of July 21 is at the APS.

2. BF also reported himself in good health in an April 22 letter (xxⅠx, 357–8), which his sister had not yet received.

3. BF had advised Jane's son-in-law Peter Collas to leave the sea and to employ himself using the Franklin family recipe for crown soap: xxvⅠⅠⅠ, 364. His ship had been reported in March ready to return to America: xxⅠx, 28.

some to send to you but fear whether that can be till the new wax comes in for I have tryd shops & aquaintance hear & can not procure any, the country people put it in to there sumer candles, I have desiered cousen Williams to try to pick up a litle in the shops there, & shall try at provedence, I am sorry to be deprived of the pleasure of gratifieng you, but my power was allways small tho my will is good. Yr Friends Greene are well & He gives satisfaction in His Office, they have boath writen to you since the date of yrs to me.[4] They are happy to hear of your helth & suckses, My Grandson & Daughter send there Duty to you— They are a happy cople have won child calld. Sally, he is a sensable & very Industrous man & she a very good wife,[5] boath treet me very kindly, & I beleve I am as happy as it is common for a human being, what is otherways may proceed from my own Impatience.

That God may Grant what you hope for in the conclution of yr leter is the prayer of yr affectionat sister—

JANE MECOM

Addressed: For Dr Franklin

From Rudolph Erich Raspe

ALS: American Philosophical Society

Honoured Sir,   London. July. 27. 1779.

At my return from a four months Tour through the best parts of the Kingdom I have had the honour of receiving yesterday Your Excellency's favour of May 4th.[6] Your Excellency's favoured disposition towards Baron Waiz, whose worthy Grandfather You have been pleased to remember on my account,[7] and Your good opinion of some of my publications

4. William Greene and his wife Catharine had each written on Dec. 1, 1778 (missing); Greene wrote again on Dec. 10: XXVIII, 216–18.

5. Elihu and Jane Flagg Greene's daughter Sarah was now sixteen months old: I, lxi; XXIX, 724n.

6. XXIX, 430.

7. Apparently, the baron was one of the grandsons of Jacob Sigismund Waitz, freiherr von Eschen (XXIX, 375n), who delivered Raspe's March 26 letter to BF: XXIX, 214. Thomas Digges forwarded the present one on Aug. 13, below.

have convinced me, that absence, time and greater objects have not cancelled me from Your generous mind, and that some day or other You might exert Your Kindness and Your influence on my behalf, who have no reason to think myself either easy or happy in this Kingdom, whence low ambition and the pride of Kings seem to have driven useless Virtue and that prosperous support of usefull learning, which ever have caracterized and adorned nations emerging from Slavery. I am so little engaged here, that I could wish to indulge and to try any better prospect abroad; and that I desire Your interest, protection and commands in whatever may procure me that advantage and the satisfaction of proving by the most zealous services and attachment that, tried by adversity and improved by experience and years in Knowledge and conduct, I am with the highest and most dutyfull respect Your Excellency's most obedient humble Servant   R E. RASPE.

At Mr. Lockyer Davis's Bookseller Holbourn.

Addressed: His Excellency / D. Benj. Franklin / Passy / near Paris.

Notation: Holbourn July 27. 1779.

From Jonathan Williams, Jr.

ALS: American Philosophical Society; copy: Yale University Library

Dear & hond Sir.   Nantes July 27. 1779.

My Arbitration is not yet finished, but the Gentlemen have so well informed themselves that I think there is but little to do as to their Judgment. They have ordered my Accounts to be all transcribed from the Beginning and they intend to write their Opinion on the Set of accounts so transcribed, in doing this they will make some alterations in the form, but the Matter will stand as it now does. It appears to me however very odd, that the Gentlemen do not think they have power to make any alterations in my *Favour*, but if any should appear necessary they have full power to make them *against* me. For Instance In several Instances I have not taken a Commn where I ought to have done it, and my allowance for the first 4 months Business is not so much by 10,000 Livres as a half of a Commission on the Goods I shipped, and neither of them would have done it for less, but I was content at that time so it cannot be altered. They think however that I had no right to charge a Commn on the arms I repaired because it was not a merchants Business, but a Gunsmiths, so I expect that will be taken off, and leave me the Satisfaction of doing for nothing the Business of an overseer of about 60 men, and supplying the Place of a man, whose allowance, had he come & done the same Business which I was obliged to do by his not coming (I mean Mercier) would have amounted to about 6000 Livres by *Contract*.[8] I am not uneasy however, for it is not profit I seek, and my Reputation I am sure will be healed, for I will venture to say that there never was a more thorough & rigid Examination of accounts since the World began.— Lee has tried by his Letter to stagger them as to their authority, and he has had some success for in consequence of his Reasoning they do not think they have authority finaly to examine & decide unless all 3 of the Commrs had agreed to it.— If I was a Judge with them of another mans Conduct I should find no difficulty in confuting this Reasoning, but I am the Culprit on trial so must be Silent.— To wait for the 3 late Comrs to join in an agreement for my arbitration would be to wait forever, for I believe they never will exist together again as Commissioners and if they did D & L never would think alike.[9]

I shall be obliged to you if you can tell me the Cost of the Cloathes Sabatier supplied,[1] and the Cost of Goods in general that were sent down to me to Ship, so that an Estimate of the Value may be Formed—if you can also let me see all Mr Beaumarchais & Mr Montieu's Invoices it will be a guide to us in finding out what my Commission is to be, the Gentlemen have desired me to write for this.— I do not know what answer the Gentn wrote to Lee, they have not communicated it to me.—

8. The American commissioners' contract with Mercier for the repair of arms was made on May 30, 1777; he proved unreliable, and caused no end of trouble for jw. See xxviii, 497–8.

9. Deane and Lee.

1. Given in Account XV: xxv, 3.

As soon as the Business is over I will go with all possible Speed to see our Friends at St G—² and have the pleasure of seeing you directly after, but I am afraid I shall not be able to do this in less than 3 weeks for the Gentn have given me at least 10 days hard work in transcribing before they will come to a decision.

I am ever Your dutifull & affectionate kinsman

JONA WILLIAMS J

The Hon. Doctor Franklin.

Notation: Williams Jona. July 27. 1779.

From Chaumont

ALS: American Philosophical Society; copies: National Archives, Library of Congress

A Passi ce 28. Juillet 1779.

M. de Chaumont a L'honneur de prevenir S. Ex. Monsieur le Docteur franklin qu'il sera peutestre Necessaire de Retarder Le Depart du Vaisseau le Bonhomme Richard Capitaine Jones afin de luy former un meilleur Equipage,³ et en Ce Cas M. de Sartines desire que M. franklin veuille Bien donner Ses ordres au Sr. Landais Commandant la fregatte americaine L'alliance, de partir incessament de L'orient pour Croiser Jusqu'a la fin de 7bre. dans le Nord de L'ecosse.   LERAY DE CHAUMONT.

Notation: Le Ray de Chaumont 28 July 79.—

2. William Alexander and his daughters, who had recently moved to Saint-Germain-en-Laye: XXIX, 534n. JW had proposed marriage to Mariamne; see his third letter of July 22 and our headnote to Alexander's letter of Sept. 8.

3. Through the Lorient merchant Gourlade, Jones had asked Chaumont to apply to the French naval ministry for additional seamen for the *Bonhomme Richard;* see Jones to BF, July 12. Jones also wrote Chaumont directly on July 14; Chaumont's reply of five days later relayed orders from Sartine to remove all Englishmen from the crew and, if possible, to replace them with other foreigners: Bradford, *Jones Papers,* reel 4, nos. 680, 689.

To John Paul Jones

LS:[4] National Archives; copies: Library of Congress (two)

Dear Sir, Passy July 28. 1779.

I have just received yours of the 25th. I was Yesterday with M. De Sartine at Versailles who appear'd uneasy at some Accts. he had received of a mutinous Disposition in your Crew.[5] He desired me to acquaint M. De Chaumont that he wished to see him that Evening. This Morning M. De Chaumont sent me a Note, of which I enclose a Copy: I understand he goes down with a View to provide you a better set of Hands.[6] You must have heard that 119 American Prisoners are arrived in a Cartel at Nantes: Perhaps out of them you may pick some very good Seamen. But if this Affair should be likely to take Time, the Alliance will have my Orders to make a Cruise alone, agreable to the Ministers Desire. But I hope the Reports of your Crew are not founded, & that your joint Cruise will still take Place, and be successful.

I have the honour to be, with sincere Esteem, Dear Sir, Your most obedient & most humble Servant   B Franklin

Honble Capt. Jones.

Endorsed: From Doctr: Franklin inclosing One from M. de Chaumont—July 28. 1779. No. 11.

To Pierre Landais

Copies: Library of Congress; Harvard University Library

Sir Passy, July 28. 1779.

In case the Circumstances of the Bonhomme Richard, should make a Delay of her Sailing necessary of which Mr.

---

4. In WTF's hand.

5. Thévenard had reported to Sartine on Jones's problems with his crew: Morison, *Jones*, p. 196.

6. Chaumont's note is printed immediately above. He must have left soon for Lorient as he wrote BF from there on Aug. 2, below. Jones wrote a marginal note on the present letter, keyed to a sign after "View," that is too faint to reconstruct.

De Chaumont will inform you, I do hereby direct that you proceed to the North Seas by Such Route as you Shall judge most proper, and cruise there till the end of September in such Parts as are most convenient for intercepting the Northern Trade to England; after which you are to go in to the Texel, and there wait farther Orders.[7] With great Esteem and great Confidence in your Abilities, zeal and activity, I have the honour to be. &c.

Capt. Landais.

From John Diot[8]

ALS: American Philosophical Society

Sir   Morlaix the 28th. July 1779.

The Owners of the Black Prince privateer haveing intrusted me With the managment of all the business and transactions here, Concerning Said Vessell, I have the honnour to forward to your Excellency, a Journal of her proceedings at Sea, by which you'll See, that Captn. Merchant, Mr. Luke Ryan, one of the owners on board,[9] as well as all the Rest of the Crew, have behaved in this Cruize with as much Courage as Wisdom.

They Brought in here on Sunday last 25th. Instant their prize brig Call'd, the Dublin, Whereof Morgan Griffith was Master formerly, and Mr. Bennet Negus, Second Lieutenant of the Black Prince, was prize Master. She was bound from Bristol to Dublin and is Loaded with Sundry Sorts of Goods, whereof I Shall have the honnour to forward the particulars to your Excellency hereafter.

Captn. Marchant Sent ashoare on Monday last, 26th. Inst., Ten Men and Boys, going Security for Twelve Ransoms made

7. Although Landais eventually sailed in company with Jones, he subsequently claimed he had not been under Jones's orders, arguing that Jones's authority over him had ended with their previous cruise (in June) and citing the present letter as evidence: Landais, *Memorial,* pp. 23–4, 28, 52–3.

8. A clerk employed by John Torris and sent by him to meet the *Black Prince* and her prizes at Morlaix: XXIX, 783.

9. Ryan, a former Irish smuggler, was a part-owner and second captain of the *Black Prince* and exercised real control over the ship: XXIX, 571n.

at Sea, as particulars in the Journal, and they all Went this day to Carhaix under Guard of Three Marechaussés, untill the Ransoms they are bail for are payd.

We have Sent Expresses to Brest and all the harbours in the Neighbourhood, to Enquiere whether the Spanish Prize, El San Joseph Brig, which the Black Prince Retook at Sea Came Safe to port; but Our hearing no News of her, makes us beleive that She again fell in the hands of Our Ennemyes, as We shou'd Certainly have heard of her 'ere now.

There was Five English prisoners, which I got landed here and put in the Gaol of this Town, where they'll be laying at the disposall of your Excellency, and in a few posts I Shall have the honnour to forward their Names to Your Excellency, along with other particulars.[1]

The Black Prince has equally made some prisoners at Sea, which Thro' want of Room on board, Were Released, on their paroles of honnour and Obligations under handwriting drawn by M. Ryan, which obligations Captn. Marchants took on himself to forward to Your Excellency, without Acquainting the Owners of the Vessell, the Commissary, or the Admiralty-Office of it, therefore, I must beg leave to Refferr Your Excellency to said Marchant's Letter about 'em.

I Must allso beg leave to Request Your Excellency wou'd prompt the Condamnations of the prizes of the Black Prince, as the Sundry Sorts of Goods, their Cargoes are composed of, Suffer and decay beyond Expression by the long delay they are submitted to.

I Remain with Respect Sir Your most Obedient and most Humble servant   JN DIOT

To His Excellency B. Franklin Minister of the United States of North America at the Court of France Passy.

Notation: Diot. Aout 26. 1779

---

1. Diot sent such a list, but it contained only two names, Arthur Mellin and John Newland. It bears the notation "Diot. Aout 26. 1779": APS.

From Nicolas-Maurice Gellée

ALS: American Philosophical Society

The letter printed below, in which Franklin's French secretary tenders his resignation, sounds cool and formal, but the circumstances surrounding the event must have been highly emotional and have remained somewhat shrouded in mystery. Why did the young man, who had entered the Commission's service so highly recommended,[2] feel he had to quit one year later?

In a letter sent to John Adams the following fall,[3] Gellée gives a different version from the one he offers in the present letter: early in June, perceiving that since the dissolution of the Commission he was no longer "in the Confidence" and that Temple had taken the only interesting business upon himself, he asked Franklin to tell him "the true Motive of that Change." Franklin supposedly answered that, indeed, the business was less considerable than in the past and offered no scope for Gellée's talents. One secretary was now sufficient. Still, Franklin offered the young man a chance to stay at the Valentinois until he found another position "of greater Trust and Emolument." But Gellée would have none of this and left Passy, he told Adams. The tone of this letter and its warnings about rumors in France concerning supposedly treasonous activities on the part of John and Samuel Adams suggest that Gellée was on close terms with Adams.

That the parting was stormy is confirmed by Decambray's letter (after July 28, below) in which the applicant for Gellée's post refers to his predecessor's not having properly appreciated Franklin's kindness and thus deserved his disgrace.

Only thirteen years later, in the course of the French Revolution, did Gellée reveal the depth of his anger: he announced his plan to publish a work directed against Franklin, whose secretary he claimed to have been for *two* years.[4] His revelations about Vergennes' dealings with America, he said, were sure to compromise the late Foreign Minister's reputation. If it was ever composed, the work in question has left no trace.

2. See XXVI, 287–8, 401–2, 493–4.
3. Dated Oct. 11, 1779, and published in *Adams Papers*, VIII, 195–7.
4. Pierre Manuel, *La Police de Paris dévoilée* (2 vols., Paris, [1793–94]), II, 266.

Monsieur   A Paris Le 28 Juillet 1779
    Le Porteur de cette Lettre vous remettra La Clef de
l'Appartement que j'occupois chez vous. Les Reflexions que
vous me fites d'apres la Lettre que j'eus l'honneur de vous
ecrire il y a trois mois[5] et L'etat d'Inaction ou je me suis trouvé
depuis m'avoient decidé a Regret a quitter un Poste que Les
Circonstances ont rendu inutile.
    Je ne vous ennuierai pas du Detail des Moyens que plu-
sieurs Personnes ont emploiés pour hater ma Résolution; J'ai
méprisé des Propos qui n'avoient pas Le sens commun. Je
prendrois La Liberté de vous faire mes excuses du scandale
qu'un fripon de tailleur a causé chez vous, si je n'etois pas
convaincu qu'en refusant de le paier alors, et en voulant que
La Justice decidat Le Different, je ne faisois que profiter de
L'appui que Les loix accordent a La Jeunesse contre la fripon-
nerie. M. Adams s'est trouvé dans Le même Cas que moi.
    M. Didelot fermier general qui vouloit bien se charger de
moi dans l'absence de mon Pere, aura L'honneur de vous remettre, Monsieur, L'argent que vous avez preferé de lui Lacher
plutot que de disputer.[6] Comme Les fonctions de ma place

5. Possibly his letter of March 24 (XXIX, 205–6).
6. The settling of Gellée's affairs kept Didelot, a family friend from Châ-
lons-sur-Marne, busy through the summer. On Aug. 3, he sharply reminded the young man to come and see him the following day and to
return some books—which casts doubt on the proposed trip to Berlin mentioned in the letter. On Aug. 7, Didelot wrote BF or WTF that he was sending
someone to pick up Gellée's trunk, in accordance with the verbal agreement
reached the previous day. On Sept. 7, Didelot, assuming that his Sept. 2
letter about Gellée had not reached BF since he had received no answer,
wrote again. He was now sending a messenger to whom BF was requested
to entrust his reply. The disappearance of the Sept. 2 letter and of a copy
Didelot may have included on Sept. 7 suggests that this correspondence
might have been tampered with.
    Finally, a Parisian lawyer by the name of Bertinot (*avocat au Parlement*)
sent, on Sept. 22, an agitated message to BF's secretary (name left blank).
He had "obliged" Gellée on Aug. 4—further indication that the young man
was not in Berlin—and had not heard from him since then, even though he
had urged an answer on Sept. 13. Irritated, he had penned a strongly
worded letter that very morning and, as soon as he had mailed it, received
the desired answer from Gellée, now back in Châlons. Could BF's secretary
return the angry letter addressed to Passy? All the documents cited are at
the APS.

etoient devenües presque nulles, je serois humilié d'en toucher Les Appointemens.

M. Didelot paiera quelques Miseres que je dois a Passy et fera retirer de ma chambre une Malle que j'y ai Laissée et qui contient partie de mes effets.

Quoique je parte cette nuit pour Berlin je n'aurois pas manqué d'aller vous remercier de toutes vos Bontés pour moi. Mais j'ai pensé que ma Presence pourroit vous deplaire avant qu'on eût Levé Les Doutes qu'on a voulu vous insinuer sur mon Compte.

J'ai l'honneur d'etre avec Respect, Monsieur Votre tres humble et tres obeïssant serviteur   N M GELLEE

Notation: Gellée Paris 28. juillet 1779.

From John Paul Jones

ALS: American Philosophical Society; AL (draft): National Archives; copy: United States Naval Academy Museum

Bon homme Richard LOrient

Honored and dear Sir   July 28. 1779

The Court Martial that has been held on board here for the last two Days past has not yet come to a determination respecting the Bon homme Richard and Alliance being run foul of one another—and as the health of Lieutenant Robinson, who commanded the Bon homme Richard Deck, did not permit him to attend this day, the Court has gone into the consideration of other matters; particularly respecting Mutiny and Desertion.— Two Quarter Masters Named Robert Towers & John Woulton have been before the Court charged with a conspiracy at Sea, and I am informed by the Court that the Evidence is Strong against them, particularly Against the former.—[7] I have made report of this proceeding to M. de

7. According to Landais' later account Jones wished to have Towers hanged; on Aug. 2 he was convicted of sedition and instead sentenced to 250 lashes, after which he was to be put in a French prison as a prisoner of war: Landais, *Memorial,* pp. 21-2; Bradford, *Jones Papers,* reel 10, no. 1991. Towers' friend Woulton was mentioned in testimony, but not court-martialed; he was later wounded in the battle with H.M.S. *Serapis:* John S.

Thevenard—and Should any person be condemned to Death I will suspend the execution of the Sentence Until I have your Orders on the Subject.— In the meantime as I wish to give no Offence in a foreign Port—I submit to you whither it would not be proper to make this proceeding known at Versailles.— Should I depart from hence before I receive your Orders, if there be any Sentence of Death, I will leave the condemned in Prison on Shore—and you may be assured that the Court will proceed with due circumspection, and lenity as far as may be consonant with the Rules of the Service.— I have sent an Officer to Nantes in hopes that he will be able to Enlist a number of the Americans who are arrived there in the Cartel, and I expect his return within four Days.—⁸ I have the honor to be with great and sincere Affection and Esteem Dear Sir Your very Obliged Friend and very humble Servant

JNO P JONES

His Excellency Doctor Franklin.

Notation: Capt. Jones July 28. 1779.

From the Marquis de Lafayette

ALS: American Philosophical Society

My dear doctor   Au havre 28th july 1779
   With the Greatest pleasure I hear that By a frigatte just arriv'd at Brest you may have Got some news from America—how far my heart is Concern'd in any thing that may happen to My American fellow Citizens, I need not telling to You— I therefore entreat you, My good friend, to let me know Any public or private, important or insignificant intelligence you have Receiv'd—suppose there was some thing secret in them you might deliver Your letter to Mde de lafayette

---

Barnes, ed., *The Logs of the Serapis—Alliance—Ariel under the Command of John Paul Jones 1779–1780* (New York, 1911), p. 5; Augustus C. Buell, *Paul Jones, Founder of the American Navy: a History* (2 vols., New York, 1906), II, 407.

8. Jones sent Cutting Lunt, the ship's master: Bradford, *Jones Papers,* reel 4, nos. 706, 708.

who will forward it with safety— there are about charles town so various accounts that I am at a loss to fix any opinion on that part of the Continent— That Fort Lafayette is taken seems very certain—[9] adieu my dear doctor, I write in a great hurry, and most affectionately I am Yours   LAFAYETTE

There is nothing new at the havre and we are waiting for intelligences.

Addressed: A Son excellence / Monsieur le docteur franklin / Ministre plenipotentiaire des etats / unis de l'amerique en son hôtel / a passy près paris

Endorsed: Marquis de la Fayette

Notation: Lafayette au havre 28. juillet 1779.

From ——— Decambray

ALS: American Philosophical Society

Monsieur,   [after July 28, 1779][1]

J'ignore quelle idée pourra vous faire Naitre une demande que le desire du travail excite: peut-être la jugerez vous inconsequente; mais vous etes trop juste pour ne pas pardonner un être honnête (Je puis hautement m'en Glorifier) victime des Malheurs que Son pere a Supporté.

Je Sais, Monsieur, que le Nommé Gellée Votre Ancien Secrétaire n'a pas Connu Le prix de Vos bontés, et a mérité Sa disgrace. Que ne Suis-je Assez heureux pour les mériter. Mes Occupations en qualité de Surnuméraire aux Bureaux de M. Bertin Ministre, m'étantes plustôt onéreuses qu'avantageuses; Je dois recourir à des moyens plus Sûrs pour m'assurer, au moins, par un travail éxacte, le Necéssaire animal.

Dans la Vingt-quatrieme année de mon âge, Sans doute, je Suis ami du travail, où ne puis le devenir. Mais assûré de L'être

---

9. Fort Lafayette, a small fortification at Verplancks Point on the east bank of the Hudson, was captured by a British expedition on June 1, 1779. So, too, was Stony Point on the opposite shore: Mark Mayo Boatner III, *Encyclopedia of the American Revolution* (New York, 1966), pp. 1063–4.

1. See the headnote to Gellée's letter of that date.

et des dispositions necéssaires pour remplir la place que je desire près de vous, Monsieur, Je ne me flatterois pas en vain de posseder La Langue Anglaise, que J'avoue ignorer entierement, si J'étois appuié par vos bontés, pendant le tems de quatre mois, assez Suffisant pour y parvenir, pendant lequel tems je ferois suppléer pour le travail attaché à votre Secrétariat, par Le Maître que je Garderois continuellement près de moi, et que je satisferois.

Ce ne seroit qu'après L'attestation de personnes dignes de foy, notamment de M. Réz de Chaumont, de qui, mon pere a L'honneur d'être Connu; dailleurs je n'eus pas été admis au Bureau de M. Bertin, sans avoir prouvé l'honnêteté de mes moeurs, de la probité et de la discrétion Necéssaire dans ces Lieux. L'honneur de Votre Réponse que je vous supplie M'accorder, sera, Jusqu'à Ce moment attendu avec tout Le Respect que doit à Monsieur Le Docteur franklin Ministre Plénipotentiaire, son très humble et très obeissant Serviteur

> DECAMBRAY
> Au Bureau de M Bertin Ministre à Paris,
> au département de M. Parent[2]

D'après L'honneur de la Vôtre Monsieur, Jaurai Celui de me présenter, Si ma demande ne vous déplait.[3]

Endorsed: De Cambray.

To Schweighauser

Copy: Library of Congress

Sir,   Passy, July 29. 1779.

I received duly yours of the 24th. Instant[4] with regard to the American Prisoners returned, I refer you to mine of the 25th. in which I mentioned, that I wish'd them to be treated both officers & Seamen with the same kindness that was shewn,

---

2. Which dealt with agricultural affairs: *Almanach royal* for 1779, p. 225.

3. Dated only "Thursday morning," an unsigned note (unmistakably in Jean-Baptiste Le Roy's hand), asks BF whether it is true that Gellée no longer works for him and wonders whether he is looking for a replacement (APS).

4. Not found.

with the Approbation of Mr. Adams to those of the first Transport.— But as to the Payment of any Wages which they may say is due to them in America, it is a thing I cannot do, having no knowledge of the Persons of their Claims nor any orders to satisfay them. And if I were upon his Word to pay one what may in Truth be justly due to him, others might demand of me what is not due. All Nations keep their Pay office at home, where the Accounts are kept, and where only they can be settled. Nor can I exchange their Paper Money, of which I know not the present Value. If I were to give Silver for it here it would be brought over to me in Shiploads.

I have no Objection to the Shipping those things on board Cap. Green,[5] upon the Freight mentioned, if you approve of it.

With great Esteem, I have the Honour to be Sir, Your most obedient & most humble Servant.

Mr. Schweighauser.

To Jonathan Williams, Jr.
Copy: Library of Congress

Dear Jonathan   Passy, July, 29. 1779.

I received your three Letters of the 22 Inst and one of the 24th. As to the Report you mention be assured I never gave any *"orders to M. scheweighauser to advance no Money to any Prisoners."* On the Contrary, when the former Cartel arriv'd, I directed him to supply them with such Necessaries as Mr. Adams who was present should advise. And when he wrote me word that he had furnish'd each Officer with 124 Livres, and each private with 24 Livres and agreed to pay their board at Paimbeuf at 30 s. a Day I answer'd that I approv'd of it;[6] and on the 25th. Instant, I wrote to him to treat the Prisoners arriv'd in this Cartel with the same kindness that was shewn with Mr. Adam's Approbation to those of the first Transport. I shall write fully in answer to your other Letters per next

5. Perhaps Capt. John Green, who had recently escaped from Falmouth: XXIX, 737–8. Green told BF in a Nov. 18, 1779, letter (APS) that he had been appointed commander of a 14-gun brig at Nantes bound for America.

6. The letters he mentions are above, XXIX, 97–9, 353.

post, having now only time to add that I am ever, Your's
affectionately   BF
M. Williams

From Barbeu-Dubourg   ALS: American Philosophical Society

Mon cher Maitre   Paris, 29e. jt. 1779
    A la requisition de M de La Lande qui part aujourd'huy
pour la Bresse, j'implore de nouveau vos bontés et votre protection pour le sr. des Raggi qui a deja eu l'honneur de vous
voir.[7] Il a grande impatience de partir pour combattre sur la
mer les ennemis des 13 etats, et servir ensuite sur terre cette
nouvelle patrie, dès qu'il y sera adopté sous vos auspices. M
hennin 1er. Commis des affaires etrangeres[8] à qui il a eté
adressé par M de la Lande, lui a dit qu'on lui expedieroit im-
mediatement son passeport sans aucune difficulté, si vous
vouliez prendre la peine de le demander; comme le sr. de
Raggi vous en supplie, et que j'imagine que vous pouvez le
faire sans vous compromettre en rien.
    Par occasion, permettez moi de vous rappeler la petite re-
quête que j'ai pris la liberté de vous presenter deja plusieurs
fois, en faveur de M. Gregoire[9] Negociant du havre qui jouit
de beaucoup de consideration dans sa province et qui est
proche parent de mon ami Agatange Le Roy cloitre st. honoré.
Il desire ardemment ou le titre (sans emolument quelconques)
de Consul des Etats unis pour la Normandie, ou seulement
pour le havre, ou si cela ne se peut au moins une petite
marque de confiance pour etre designé aux Americains qui
pourroient aborder dans ce port, ou y avoir quelque affaire,
comme Ami de leur nation, digne de les servir et zelé a le faire

---

7. Lalande and Dubourg wrote on July 23, above.
8. Pierre-Michel Hennin (1728–1807) had permanently replaced Conrad-
Alexandre Gérard in that post on April 5. Jean-Pierre Samoyault, *Les Bureaux du secrétariat d'état des affaires étrangères sous Louis XV* (Paris, 1971), p.
291. He and Gérard de Rayneval shared the responsibility of preparing
Vergennes' correspondence: *Almanach royal* for 1779, p. 219.
9. XXVII, 326.

et surtout pouvoir se flatter que s'il arrivoit que le Congrès vous donnat par la suite des ordres pour etablir des consuls dans nos ports, vous auriez la bonté de vous souvenir de lui, et de ne pas donner cette commission a quelque autre qui surement ne s'en aquitteroit pas mieux et difficilement aussi bien que lui. Je vous prie instamment de me faire au moins sur cela une reponse honnete par ecrit, que je puisse montrer a son Cousin, ou a lui, s'il vient en cette ville, afin de lui prouver que je n'ai point negligé son affaire, parceque j'ai veritablement toutes sorte de raisons pour m'y interesser, ne fût-ce que parce qu'il m'a fait boire d'excellentes liqueurs de la Martinique, dont il ne faudroit pourtant pas faire mention dans votre lettre ostensible.

J'attens toujours la suite de vos oeuvres (y compris même la morale des echecs) et quand vous pourrez me l'envoyer sans vous gener, je tacherai d'en user à votre satisfaction, ou tacherai du moins de n'en pas abuser.

Est-il vrai que vous ayez des nouvelles sures de la defaite du gl. Prevost par le gl. Lincoln? Et n'en avez vous point d'autres?

Je suis en attendant le plaisir de vous revoir avec un tendre respect, Monsieur et cher Ami, Votre t. h. et o. serviteur

DUBOURG

Notation: Dubourg 29. Juillet 1779.

From [Philip?] Keay

AL: American Philosophical Society

Paris Thursday 29 July. [1779]

Mr. Keay presents his Respects to Mr. Franklin, & returns many thanks for the History of the Welch Poetry:[1] he should not have kept it so long, had he not flatter'd himself every day with the pleasure of accompanying Made. de Cheminot to

1. Possibly Evan Evans, *Some Specimens of the Poetry of the Antient Welsh Bards: translated into English, with Explanatory Notes on the Historical Passages* ... (London, 1764).

wait upon Mr. Franklin; But she is still so weak as not to be able to bear the motion of the Carriage.[2]

Notation: Keay

From John McCraken

ALS: American Philosophical Society

Sir   Murlox July 29 1779

I have ben on board the Conenintal Cutter Black prince since the 20th Inst. Not indeed as a prisoner but as a Gentelman and used in the best manner to the great Honour of your Captains on board. I inded was a pasanger on board the Dublin brig which they took and as such have obtained my Liberty to return to Bristol as Soon as I please the Pleasure I hav in Addersing your Excelency overbalances any disapointment I have met with in being stopt a little in my Jorney, not only as you are a publick Agent for American affairs (to which I have always ben a friend) but also for your Verry Philosiphical discourses some of which I have read with great pleasure. I have the Greatest inclination that Can be to remove my family from Bristol to Philadelphia or some part of the provence of penselvenia but as things are now situated their is some dificulty in the undertaking which however may Be greatly Alivated by your Excelencys interposition and assistance which I now make bold to request in any way that you think most Condusive to that end. A line from your Excelency I should receive with infinite pleasure. I have a brother & Sister both maried in the provence of penselvenia. I had a Cozen Named James McCraken who lived in Philadelphia with whom I have had

2. The name Charlotte de Cheminot was adopted by this former dancer—who had, in her youth, caught the eye of Louis XV—after she had become famous and wealthy thanks to her liaisons with a number of highly-placed men. At the time of BF's stay in France, she was the mistress of a "riche seigneur anglais" (probably P. Keay) who kept her in luxury at a hôtel on the rue Neuve-des-Mathurins. There she entertained, among others, Diderot, Lalande, Rulhière, Raynal, Beaumarchais, and the chevalier d'Eon. F.F.C. [Félix Feuillet de Conches], *Souvenirs de première jeunesse d'un curieux septuagénaire* (Vichy, 1877), pp. 37–55, 59–61, 74–76. Alluding to BF in her salon, the author describes him as "le dissimulé Franklin dont le bon sens allait jusqu'au génie" (p. 55).

Som dealings but he has been dead Some years he was a Cooper by trade and marchandized some, as I hope to return by a Dutch Ship that will Sail from hence in a few days I canot hope for the pleasure of your answer and shall take an equal favour if your Excelency would adress the Comisary of this place with a few lines in my behalf in Case I find my wife ready to second my disign in removing which I hope she will as she also is a good friend to the American Cause & if we should find a passage to any other part of Franc I shall make bold to address your Excelency again for your Pasport and recomendation to Some of your Good Friends in America. I have lived a good many years in Bristol but am a Native of the North of Ireland. I remain your Exelency's most Obedient Humble Sert. JOHN MCCRAKEN

P.S. As this Letter is a little confused I hope your Exelency will Excuse any defects as I was not willing to miss this oppertunity of writing to your Excelency, an oppertunity I Canot have in England — from as above J M

Addressed: To / His Excelency Benjamin / Franklin Minister for / the United States of North / America at the Court of / France at passy near / Paris

Notation: MacCraken 29 July 1779

From Joseph Miller   ALS: American Philosophical Society

my Lord   Tours July the 29 1779
   The Humble Petition of Joseph Miller Late Commander of the Brig Sampson: Sheweth that your Petitioner being Taken the 20th: August 1778 by the General Mifflin Captn: Daniel Mc:Nieel on my Passage to New found land and heave been a prisoner Ever Sence wherefore your Petitioner Most Humbly Presents him Self and distressed wife and Three Small Children at home distressed for want of Serport begs the Feavour of your Lord Ships Permition to returne to England that I might be of some help to my Poore distressed wife and Family as I Never Took up arms against Ammerica neither I never will but All ways Saild in the Merchants Servis and Shall so

167

Continue: and as I am the Only one Left out of Twelve Commanders that Captn: Mc:Nieel Took and my Ship a very rich Prize. I begs the feavour of your Lord Ships Permission to returne to England if Theay will not Exechang poore Ammericans in England it his hard for Them I knows it and Like wise for me and my Poore Family who his Greatly Wanting my Asistance it is Hard that I Should Suffer for bad Ministers at home and if it is not your Lord Ships Pleasure to Grant me Permission to returne home or if your Lord Ship will Greaously be pleased to Grant me Permission to go for Ammerica in Some Ammerican Merchant Ship unless your Lord Ship Thinks There will be an Exechange Soon and your Petitioner Shall Ever pray for your Lord Ships Prosperity

JOSEPH MILLER

Addressed: A Monsieur Monsieur Franklin / Chargé des affaires des treize / Provinces unies de La'merique / auprés de La Cour de France / En Son Hotel. / Près de Paris. A Chaillot

Notation: Miller Joseph July 29. 1779.

From Jonathan Williams, Sr.: Two Letters

(I) and (II) ALS: American Philosophical Society[i]

I.

Hond Sir   Boston July 29the 1779

Capt. Collas hand me a few days ago your favour in which you propose a Schem of business partly for the benifit of your worth Sister & her once unhapy Son who is now no more he died about 13 months ago—[3] On receiving your Letter I wrote aunt & Inclos'd your Letter & Desird her thoughts appon it, I Shall allway be happy to advance any monies that you Desire on any Acct. but Especially for the benifit of my much Esteemd aunt, its a great pity the Acct. that your Brother Left Should be Lost—[4] However this I have found

3. BF's letter, now missing, probably was dated Nov. 27, 1778; see Williams' of Aug. 8, below. The unhappy son was the late Peter Mecom.

4. Upon the death of his widow, part of John Franklin's estate had reverted to his nephew (and former apprentice) Peter Mecom: codicil to John

When I have advanced monies for persons who Depended on me for their Support & put them into business it Cost me more than maintainng of them Intirely tho' I belive aunt would have had Somthing beferehand if all that was a burden to her were Out of the way for as Long as Som people Can find assissdence they will not provid for themselves tho' they might do it if they would be as Industerous as those that maintain them tho' I Belive my Aunt Mecom is as Worty a Woman a Live & had She no better Friend then my Self She Should not want what I Could & would Spare—

The Bearer of this is Col. Watson of Plimouth[5] he desires me to mention him to you as a Stranger your Civilities to him as Such Will Oblige— Our famley are All well With Duty & Love I am yr Nephew & Most Hble Servt   JONA WILLIAMS

Addressed: His Excellency Benjamin Franklin Esqr / at Passy near Paris / France / per favour of mr Watson

Notation: Jona Williams Boston July 29. 1779

II.

Hond Sir   Boston July 29. 1779

The Bearer mr Knox Brother to our General Knox Comes to France partly on Business & partly for Improvement as he will be A Stranger your Civilities to him as Such will Oblige Your Dutyfull Nephew & Hble Servt.   JONA WILLIAMS

Addressed: His Excellency Benjamin Franklin Eqr / at Passy near Paris— / France / per Wm Knox

Notation: Jona Williams Boston July 29. 79

Franklin's Will, Jan. 22–4, 1756 (APS). Income from BF's half-sister Elizabeth Franklin Douse's estate had also been used to support the young man with Jonathan Williams handling the arrangements: v, 66–7; VI, 454; x, 354–61.

5. Elkanah Watson, Jr., son of Col. Watson (XXIX, 723n). He and Knox (recommended in letter II) traveled to France together on the packet *Mercury:* Winslow C. Watson, ed., *Men and Times of the Revolution; or, Memoirs of Elkanah Watson* . . . (New York, 1856), pp. 76–8.

To Sartine

Copy: Library of Congress

Sir   Passy, July 30. 1779.
The Bearer Capitain Foligny commanded the Marquis De
la Chalotais in her Voyage to America laden with Stores for
our Armies in which Voyage he rendered considerable service
on various occasions to the Americans with great Readiness
Zeal, Activity and Intelligence and as a Mark of their Approbation and Confidance he received a Commission from the
Congress Being convinc'd of his Merit and Abilities.[6] I beg
leave to recommend him to you Excellency's favorable Notice,
as an Officer who has an ardent desire of employing his talent
in the Service of his Sovereign with great Respect I am Your
Excellency's most Obedient and most humble serv.   BF.
M. De Sartine.

From the Eastern Navy Board[7]

LS: American Philosophical Society; copy: New York Public Library

Navy Board Eastern department Boston 30th. July
Sir   1779
In Consequence of Orders, from the Honorable Marine
Committee at Philadelphia, We have Equipped the Brigantine
Mercury Packet Boat, Simeon Samson Esquire Commander,
to Convey the dispatches sent us from Congress, to your
Excellency, & Count de Vergennes—[8]

6. jw had recommended Capt. Foligné on July 22: letter IV, above. All we
know about his supposed commission is what he says in his letter of Aug.
9, below. A French translation of the present letter is in the Archives de la
Marine.

7. As far as we know the Navy Board had last written BF in December,
1778 (XXVIII, 255–6). The other two members were James Warren and John
Deshon; see their letter of Aug. 18.

8. For the orders to the board see Smith, *Letters*, XIII, 238, 239. Simeon
Samson of Plymouth was the former captain of the Mass. State Navy brig
Hazard and brigantine *Independence: Naval Docs.*, IX, 254–5; Allen, *Mass. Privateers*, pp. 43, 171, 185. The packet *Mercury* is now best known for her
capture in September, 1780, while carrying Henry Laurens to the Netherlands: Gardner W. Allen, *A Naval History of the American Revolution* (2 vols.,

We have Ordered Capt. Samson to make sure of the first Port he Approaches on the Coast of France, immediatly to proceed with the Packages himself, to Paris, or deliver them into the hands of a known Agent, to these United States, or some Royal Officer; to be Conveyed in Safety to your hands.

We have further ordered him to Wait your Pleasure, for his return to America.

The latest News papers we have the honor of Inclosing, that we wish Safe to hand, and are with perfect esteem Your Excellencys Most Obedt humble Servts   WM VERNON. Pret.

His Excellency Benjamin Franklin Esqr. Minister Plenipotentiary for United States of America

Notation: W. Vernon Boston 30. juillet 1779.

From John Paul Jones

ALS: American Philosophical Society; AL (draft): National Archives; copy: United States Naval Academy Museum

Honored & dear Sir,   L'Orient July 30th. 1779.

Since my last the Irish Brigantine the Three Friends from Bordeaux taken by the Alliance has sunk at her Anchors in this Road. This unfortunate Accident happened about Eleven in the fore noon the Day before yesterday, and the Prize Master and People declare that the Vessel made no Water and that the Pump sucked at Nine in the Morning.— Neither Captain Landais nor myself were made acquainted with the matter till about a quarter before Eleven, and the assistance of several Boats which were immediatly sent could not then prevent the Vessel from Sinking.— The Admiralty have taken off the Seals and part of the Cargo is Landed.— The remainder will be landed as circumstances will admit, and I will endeavour to have the Leak found and stopped as soon as possible.— It is thought that the Prize has sunk by getting upon an Anchor:

Boston and New York, 1913), II, 508. On her present voyage she also brought mail for JA: Taylor, *Adams Papers*, VIII, 99–100.

But should it be found to have been the Effect of carlessness, a Court Martial shall determin what Punishment to inflict.

I mentioned in my last[9] that if the Court Martial should Sentance any Person to Death, and if I should Sail before I received your Orders respecting the matter I would leave the condemned ashore here in Prison.— But I have since on reflection concluded to carry the Condemned with me that the Sentance may be executed at Sea.— The Bon homme Richard is ready for the Sea— except only that the 100 Men *that I have been ordered to Land* must be previously[1] replaced.

I am ever with Sentiments of the heighest Esteem & Affection Dear Sir Your very obliged Friend and very Obedient humble Servant   JNO P JONES

His Excellency Doctor Franklin.

Notation: Capt. Jones July 30. 1779

From Landais

LS: American Philosophical Society

Port L'Orient July 30. 1779

I have to inform your Excellency that the brigantine three friends, our prize, has lately sunk down in this harbour, and we have obtain'd permission from the Admiralty to unload her, and we are discharging her Cargo with all expedition.

Her late Captain, his crew, my prize master & some of my men were on board her when she sunk, but we have not yet discover'd from what cause it happen'd.

Captain Jones has promised to write more at Large, to whose Letter I must beg leave to referr your Excellency.

9. Above, July 28.

1. Jones retained the draft and later added a marginal note: "they were replaced before Mr. De Chaumont returned to L'Orient." Cutting Lunt recruited thirty crewmen for the *Bonhomme Richard* at Nantes, while the *Epervier* contributed thirty-eight Portuguese, Danish, and Dutch sailors: Bradford, *Jones Papers*, reel 4, no. 713; Morison, *Jones*, p. 197. Lunt's group, now 29, reached Lorient on Aug. 7: Boudriot, *John Paul Jones and the Bonhomme Richard*, p. 59.

I remain with the greatest Respect Your Excellency's Most obedient and most humble Servant P. LANDAIS

His Excellency Doct. Franklin

Addressed: To / His Excellency Dr. Franklin / Minister Plenipotentiary / to the United States / at Passy / near Paris.

Notation: P. Landais July 30. 79

From Lavaysse & Cie.[2]   LS: American Philosophical Society

Monsieur,   L'orient Ce 30. juillet 1779./.

Nos amis & Correspondants de Bordeaux, Mr. Mrs. forsters freres[3] nous ont chargés de la réclamation du navire les trois amis de Dublin capitaine Röache[4] qui à été pris & conduit a L'orient par le Commandant de la frégate américaine L'alliance, bien que ce navire eut Ses Expéditions en bonne forme de Bordeaux, visées par le Commissaire du Roy & qu'il fut muni d'un passeport de la cour.[5]

A dieu ne plaise que nous prétendions inculper le commandant de L'alliance pour qui nous avons beaucoup d'estime, mais il est juste qu'il répare Son tort. Indépendament de ce que Sa démarche imprudente à D'odieux pour les particuliers françois, elle tend egalement a susciter des discussions entre les deux Gouvernements & nous croÿons qu'il est de la justice & de la gloire des Etats unis de rèprimer de pareils Excès. Le Commandant de L'alliance en S'emparant des trois amis cau-

2. Lavaysse, or more likely La Vaysse, apparently was an acquaintance of Gourlade. In 1785 he unsuccessfully attempted to join a firm headed by Gourlade which obtained a passport for a ship to China: Jean Tarrade, *Le commerce colonial de la France à la fin de l'Ancien Régime* . . . (2 vols., Paris, 1972), II, 682–3. He then must have gone into partnership with Schweighauser's former associate Puchelberg (XXVII, 59); their firm wrote WTF on April 7, 1786 (APS) and wrote twice thereafter to BF.

3. A comparatively new merchant house in Bordeaux: Paul Butel, *Les négociants bordelais: l'Europe et les îles au XVIIIe siècle* (Paris, 1974), p. 162. As Forsters Brothers they offered their services to BF on June 8, 1784 (APS).

4. Edward Roach, according to Landais: *Memorial,* p. 20.

5. See Jones's July 2 letter.

soit nécéssairement un retard préjudiciable au propriétaire. L'Evénement à été pire puisqu'il à causé la perte de ce Batiment qui a échoüé dans la Rade sur une ancre. Nous demandons, Monsieur, au nom de nos amis que le Commandant de L'alliance soit condamné à Restitüer le navire les Bons amis & sa cargaison en bon Etat, a payer les avaries survenües & a dédomager en un mot les propriétaires du tort qu'il leur a fait.

Mrs. forsters freres se sont adressés a Mr. De Sartine il nous paroit plus simple & plus naturel de vous adresser directement leurs plaintes; elles sont trop bien fondées, & votre justice trop connüe pour Douter que vous n'y aÿéz Egard sans le secours d'aucune protection.

Nous Sommes avec respect, Monsieur Vos très humbles & très obéissants Serviteurs   LAVAYSSE & C
                                              Negociants a Lorient

Mr. franklin Ministre Plénipotentiaire des Etats unis de L'amérique

Notation Lavaysse L'Orient 30. juillet 1779.

From Elizabeth Temple[6]   ALS: American Philosophical Society

Sir   Boston July the 30th. 1779
    Not having heard from Mr. Temple since he left this place, I am at a loss how to direct to him; and have therefore taken the Liberty to inclose a letter[7] for him to you, and shall esteem myself greatly obliged, if you will add a farther direction and forward it to him.

---

6. Elizabeth Bowdoin Temple, daughter of BF's old friend James Bowdoin, and her husband John left England in May, 1778, when he was sent to America to assist the Carlisle peace commission: XXVI, 466n. A year later he returned to Europe, without his family, determined to convince British ministers of the impracticality of continuing the war: Mass. Hist. Soc. *Coll.*, 6th Ser., IX (1897), 432–3.

7. The MS is torn and we have supplied the first three characters of "letter" and "greatly".

My Father desires me to present his best Compts. to you. And I am with great respect, Sir Your very humble Sert.

E. TEMPLE.

Addressed: To / The honble. Benjamin Franklin Esqr / Ambassador for the United States / of America to the Court of / France / favor of / Mr. Knox.

Notation: E. Temple July 30. 79

From Benjamin Vaughan   AL: American Philosophical Society

My dearest sir,   London, July 30th, 1779.

I have not been able to bring our business to a conclusion *within a sheet,* and I choose to send the whole together: It cannot now be more than a week. The Bp. of St. A.[8] has given another motto for a head that is engraved;— "*Non sordidus auctor naturæ verique.*"[9]

I hope I am not usually presumptuous or sanguine; but I guess you will not be displeased with what follows your Aurora Borealis. It will not in many respects probably be novel *to you,* but you will like to see others so well entering into your systems, even where not expressed in your writings. You will easily see that a thousand corollaries may be drawn from what is done: and indeed I have already got at a great number.— Pray did the Duc de Chaulnes ever shew you a letter I sent him out of the *Public Advertiser* signed A. B. upon the subject of Wilson's experiments?[1] There were errors in that paper, but some novelties: You may guess the author. It was about Novr. 1777.— I am sorry to tell you that Mr. Henly *very deliberately* cut his throat. He died in good circumstances.

Pray did you write a piece on Liberty & Necessity, printed for Shuckford or Shuckurgh in 1729 or 1739, with a dedication

8. The Bishop of St. Asaph is of course BF's old friend Jonathan Shipley.

9. "No common judge of nature and truth." Horace, *Odes,* I, 28, 14–15.

1. "A.B."'s letter, dated Nov. 6, appeared in the Nov. 11, 1777, issue of the *Public Advertiser.* It was a refutation of Benjamin Wilson's experiments concerning rounded lightning rods, and a defense of "Dr. Franklin's Points." For the controversy, see xxv, 5–6.

to *truth;* the burthen of the piece being that the mind was acted upon by Ideas, as body was by matter; and an analysis of the mind's operations was there given out?[22] The piece was short.

I think there is no news of a general nature, which is all that is worth sending. People are not yet frightened; history and the former discourses of ministry having taught them that invasions &c are bug-bears. They even lend money now & then to West Indians for short terms, that is, to West Indian merchants.

I am, my ever dearest sir, your most devoted &c &c.

Notation: B Vaughn July 30. 79

From Vergennes

L (draft):[3] Archives du Ministère des affaires étrangères; copy: Library of Congress

A Versailles le 30. juillet 1779

Vous trouverez ci-joint, M, copie de la réponse de M. de Sartine concernant les effets reclamés par le Sr. Samüel Warthon;[4] vous y verrez qu'il y a dèja du tems que les ordres pour la restitution de ces effets ont été expédiés.

M. franklin

2. Joseph Priestley had asked the same question on May 8. BF's answer is summarized there: XXIX, 454n.

3. In Gérard de Rayneval's hand. The copy is misdated July 3.

4. For Wharton's effects see our annotation of Vergennes to BF, July 18. The enclosure to the present letter must be Sartine's of July 26 to Vergennes, of which there is a copy at the Library of Congress. Sartine reported that the officers of the Admiralty of Dieppe had informed him that all the papers and effects had been sent on June 6 to S. Burthon, and Wharton should address himself to him. Burthon was Burton, captain of the ship: XXIX, 575.

From the Abbé Le Breton de la Loutière

ALS: American Philosophical Society

paris 31 juill. 1779 chez Mr. Le Breton imprimeur
Monseigneur   Du roy rüe hautefeuille[5]
Permettes moy De faire part à votre Excellence D'un petit
ouvrage que je viens D'imprimer Sur La guerre presente. Jattends avec Empressement La victoire Derniere Et complette
De vos ètats unis pour achever de celebrer toute Leur gloire
Et Leur indépendance. Je tascherai Si vous Le trouves Bon De
Leur témoigner Dans La personne De Leur Digne plénipotentiaire Les sentimens quils ont inspirés a Toute LEurope Et
dont je suis Le prémier pénétré. Ce Tribut Si bien Du à votre
nouvel Empire me Donnera une occasion nouvelle De vous
renouveller Les assurances du très profond respect avec Lequel jay L'honneur Destre Monseigneur De Votre Excellence
Le Tres humble Et Tres obeissant serviteur

LABBÉ LE BRETON DE LA LOUTIERE[6]

Notation: Le Breton, l'abbé le Bereton de la Lautiere 31. Juillet
1779.

From Jonathan Williams, Jr.

ALS: American Philosophical Society

Dear & honoured Sir.   Nantes July 31 1779.
Captain Thompson Commander of the Gen Lee who sent
an Express to you from Brest is arrived here by land, and on
his arrival he gave me news which I immediately made Public
supposing the particulars to be sent you from Brest; But as Mr
de Chaumont who arrived here to day tells me no mention is
made of it in your Dispatches, I set down to give it to you as I
have it, and as I have given it to the whole Change of Nantes.

---

5. André-François Le Breton (1708–79) was known especially as the first
printer of the *Encyclopédie.* He died on Oct. 4, and was succeeded by his
widow. Larousse; A.-M. Lottin, *Catalogue chronologique des libraires et des
libraires-imprimeurs de Paris* (Paris, 1789).

6. A short word or abbreviation, which we cannot decipher, follows his
signature.

"Capt Thompson sailed from Boston the 21 June and reports that on the 19th. in the Evening an Express arrived from So Carolina to Genl Heath Commander of the Troops in that Department of the Massachusetts State. The 20th the News which the Express brought was by permission of the General given out, and Capt Thompson was informed by Mr Carter aid du Camp to the General as follows.—

"That the English Troops & the Americans in Carolina had an affair the 14 May which was not decisive, but on the 17th it was renewed with great vigour on both Sides and the English finaly put to Flight leaving 1500 Dead & wounded on the Field with the Loss of about 500 on our Side. It was not known whether the English had regained their Shipping or whether they were intercepted, nor was the accot of Dead & Wounded absolutely certain as the Express came away in great haste.— The English who had been ravaging in Virginia had returned to N York, and three American Frigates the Ranger Providence & Queen of France had sailed the beginning of June to Cruize off the Entrance of the Chesapeak."

This is what I have given out, & if it is not true I will never again believe anything that is *reported* to me, but it cannot be otherwise for the accot accords exactly with what the English have already given us extracted from the New Jersey Gazette, and Capt Thompson is a man of too much Sense not to understand what he says, & of too much Probity to tell such a falsehood.—

The post hurries me so I have only time to give you Joy & wish for Confirmation if you think it needs any.

I am ever most dutifully & affectionately Yours

J WILLIAMS J

The Hon. Doctor Franklin.

Addressed: a monsieur / Monsieur Franklin / Ministre des Etats Unis / en son Hotel a Passy / prés / Paris

Notation: Williams Jona. July 31. 1779.

From Henry Lucas

ALS: American Philosophical Society

Cherbourg the   July 1779.

May it please your Excellency,

The Suppliant, Henry Lucas of the Province of Virginia, officer a board the Brigg Betsy from Baltimore in Maryland, freighted with Tobacco, takes the Liberty of representing to your Excellency, that in his passage from America to Bourdeaux the Vessel had been taken by a Jersey and two Guernsey privateers, the crew conducted to England and imprison'd, from whence your Suppliant with several of his comrades & country men have made their escape at imminent peril of their lives; in a small Boat; at our arrival in France we happily met with a mercht. named Charles Drouet of Cherbourg[7] who humanely furnish'd us with the necessary instructions for our future conduct and embark'd us a board a french privateer, that we might, at the same time, be instrumental in revenging our country and particular Losses and likewise preserve the small fund, which we fortunately concealed from the rapine of our Enemies, 'till an occasion offerd wherein we might signalize our Zeal for the cause of the Congress. The opportunity presents itself, the above mention'd Drouet offers to join me in the purchase of a Privateer, which he calls the happy Alliance,[8] nothing but your Excellency's concordance to grant me a Commission to command it under American Flag, hinders me from retaliating on the Enemies of our country the injuries they have made it suffer. May I presume that your Excellency will display its usual Bounty in granting my request— Father of America! will you leave one of its children an orphan? Permit me to act, under your influence, in concert with my countrymen, who wait but your orders to make our Enemies feel what a spirit of patriotisme, the love of liberty and indepen-

7. Who had befriended other American officers: XXIV, 173, 194, 212, 308.
8. Drouet wrote an undated letter on behalf of Lucas, describing him as a young man with a perfect knowledge of navigation, particularly of the English coast. The small privateer he wished to command would be manned by Americans presently in France and would be ready to sail immediately if BF provided a congressional commission. APS.

dancy can operate in the Breast of a true born American when his Contry's at stake.

Give me leave to subscribe myself, Your Excellency's most obedient, most devoted and most humble Servant

HENRY LUCAS.

Your Excellency will kind enough to let me have an answer.

To Becker and Saltzmann[9] Copy: Library of Congress

Gentlemen Passy, Aug. 1. 1779.

I received the Letter you did me the honour of writing to me, dated the 3d. of July past,[1] but the Pacquet you mention containing the Cloathing of a Soldier never came to hand. Coarse Cloths are always much wanted in America and would sell well if you should send them there, but I have at present no Orders to execute, either for Cloths or Clothing. When I have I Shall remember your offers and you will hear from me. I have the honour to be Gentlemen, Your m. o. and m. h. S.

Messr. Becker and Saltzman.

From Samuel Petrie[2] AL: American Philosophical Society

Rue Ste. Anne. Sunday Evening Augt. 1th. 1779.

Mr. Petrie presents his Compliments to Dr. Franklin.— He Sets out tomorrow Morning early, with two Friends, on a Tour into Flanders for a few Days;[3] & as it is not improbable but

9. Berlin merchants with surplus uniforms for sale. They had forwarded a sample via Strasbourg: XXIX, 343.

1. Described in XXIX, 343–4n.

2. This Scottish merchant had attended the recent Independence Day celebration.

3. Petrie planned to meet William Lee at Valenciennes, near the French border with the Austrian Netherlands, for an "affair of honour." (The rendezvous apparently was selected so it would not be conducted on French soil.) Petrie and the Lees had accused each other of stockjobbing and leaking information to the British: *e.g.,* Ford, *Letters of William Lee,* II, 625n, 627–8. Petrie did not arrive at the appointed time, however, and the duel did not take place: *Lee Family Papers,* reel 6, frames 268–9, 338–9; Arthur Lee to

Nous Benjamin Franklin,

Ecuyer, Miniftre Plenipotentiaire des Etats-Unis de l'Amerique, près Sa Majefté Très Chretienne,

PRIONS tous ceux qui font à prier, de vouloir bien laiffer feurement & librement paffer *Thomas Burdy, allant à Oftende pour paffer en Angleterre,* fans *lui* donner ni permettre qu'il *lui* foit donné aucun empêchement, mais au contraire de *lui* accorder toutes fortes d'aide et d'affiftance, comme nous ferions en pareil Cas, pour tous ceux qui nous feroient recommandés.

EN FOI DE QUOI nous *lui* avons délivré le préfent Paffe-port, valable pour *deux Mois,* figné de notre main, contre-figné par l'un de nos Secretaires, & au bas duquel eft le Cachet de nos Armes.

DONNÉ à Paffy, en notre Hôtel, le *2e Jour d'Aouft,* mil fept cent *foixante et dixneuf.*

GRATIS.

B. Franklin

Par Ordre de M. le Miniftre Plenipotentiaire.

W. T. Franklin fe

Passport for Thomas Burdy

they may wish to cross the Borders before their Return, he will be much obliged to the Doctor to favour him with a Pass.

Addressed: Son Excellence le Ministre / Plenipotentiare des Etats unis / de l'Amerique

Notation: M. S. Petrie August 1st. 1779.[4]

Passport for Thomas Burdy[5]

Passy, printed by Benjamin Franklin, 1779. Printed form, signed, with MS insertions in blanks: Public Record Office, London

The first official document printed on Franklin's Passy press seems to have been this passport, the first of many that would be issued throughout the war. All in French, identical in wording,[6] the Passy

---

Edmund Jenings, Aug. 14, 1779 (National Archives). Insults continued to be exchanged between the parties, with a certain Dr. William Boush (whom Arthur Lee had sent to Valenciennes with Walter Pollard to act as his brother's seconds) serving as courier. Arthur Lee threatened to have Petrie arrested: Lee to Petrie, Aug. 17, 1779 (National Archives). When the "bullying young Fellow" Boush showed up at Petrie's door on Aug. 30 to demand satisfaction of his own, the alarmed merchant wrote to Vergennes and sent a copy to WTF, along with a lengthy explanation and copies of his correspondence with the Lees: Petrie to WTF, Aug. 30 (APS). Two brief undated notes from Boush are at the APS; they indicate that he met with BF at the latter's invitation, and loaned him some newspapers and magazines.

4. This notation is in Wharton's hand. On a separate slip of paper (APS) WTF reported, "Mr Wharton told B. F. the 5. August that Mr P. was gone to meet Mr W. Lee." Arthur Lee described Petrie, Wharton, and the brothers William and Alexander John Alexander as recent additions to the "Council at Passy": to JA, Sept. 24, 1779, *Adams Papers,* VIII, 168–70.

5. At the end of May, Samuel Wharton had appealed to BF on behalf of Thomas and Robert Burdy, whose belongings had been seized in Dieppe. They had been living in that city for a year, according to Wharton's memorial, and were hoping to emigrate to Philadelphia: XXIX, 574–5. BF interceded with the French government (see Vergennes' letter of July 18), and now favored Burdy with this pass. Once in England, Burdy was immediately, but briefly, imprisoned; see Digges's letters of Sept. 4, 6, and 20. To the best of our knowledge, he does not reappear in BF's papers.

6. The language follows that which Gellée had written for the commissioners when they were first called upon to produce a formal passport. See

passports vary only in typography—but there they differ widely. Among the fourteen known examples there are no fewer than six variants. These fall into chronological clusters, suggesting that Franklin printed only a modest number of sheets at a time, and then altered the format and font according to whim when he reset the forms. This passport for Thomas Burdy is unique among the fourteen and, doubtless because of its location, has hitherto eluded American scholars.

[August 2, 1779]

Nous Benjamin Franklin, Ecuyer, Ministre Plenipotentiaire des Etats-Unis de l'Amerique, près Sa Majesté Très-Chretienne,

prions tous ceux qui sont à prier, de vouloir bien laisser seurement & librement passer *Thomas Burdy, allant à Ostende pour passer en Angleterre,* sans *lui* donner ni permettre qu'il *lui* soit donné aucun empêchement, mais au contraire de *lui* accorder toutes sortes d'aide et d'assistance, comme nous ferions en pareil Cas, pour tous ceux qui nous seroient recommandés.

en foi de quoi nous *lui* avons délivré le présent Passe-port, valable pour *deux Mois,* signé de notre main, contre-signé par l'un de nos Secretaires, & au bas duquel est le Cachet de nos Armes.

donné à Passy, en notre Hôtel, le *2e Jour d'Aoust,* mil sept cent *soixante et dix neuf.*

gratis.[7]   B Franklin
                            Par Ordre de M. le Ministre Plenipotentiaire.

                    W.T. Franklin *seca*

From Chaumont

als: American Philosophical Society

Monsieur le Docteur   L'orient ce 2 aoust 1779.

Je Rends Compte a M. de Sartines qu'au moyen de L'expulsion des anglais du Bord du Bonhomme Richard et de leur

---

xxvi, 440–1, where the handwriting of the young man, soon to become bf's French secretary, is unidentified.

7. bf's seal appears in the left margin. The ms insertions throughout the document are by wtf.

Remplacement par de Bons americains et par trente portu-
guais,[8] Ce vaisseau peut Naviguer en Sureté et Remplir Sa
mission.[9] Je Suplie V. Ex. Si elle a des ordres a Donner a M.
Jones de ne pas Les Differer pour eviter La perte du tems et
de L'argeant.

Je Suis avec Respect Monsieur Le Docteur Vostre tres
humble et tres obeissant Serviteur   LERAY DE CHAUMONT

M. Le Docteur franklin.

Notation: Le Ray De Chaumont L'Orient 2. aout 1779.

From John Jay: Proposed Letter[1]

L (draft): National Archives

Sir,   [on or before August 2, 1779][2]
The Burning of[3] Suffolk in Virginia Fairfield East Haven
Green's Farms & Norwalk in Connecticut together with the
Ravages committed in Georgia & South Carolina form a cruel
Commentary upon the Proclamation of the british Commissioners.[4] This Proclamation was defended in their Parliament
as meaning no more than that in future the War was to be
carried on agt. America as agt. other Nations. It becomes
therefore a common Cause of all Nations to punish a People

8. From the *Epervier.*

9. Sartine agreed that the anticipated crew of 380 would be adequate:
Morison, *Jones,* p. 197. Crew lists are given in John S. Barnes, ed., *The Logs
of the Serapis—Alliance—Ariel under the Command of John Paul Jones 1779–
1780* (New York, 1911), pp. 3–16 and Augustus C. Buell, *Paul Jones, Founder
of the American Navy: a History* (2 vols., New York, 1906), II, 407–13.

1. Like the proposed letter from the marine committee (after July 19,
above) this letter was probably not sent. It is in the hand of Gouverneur
Morris, who was appointed by Congress on July 19 (with William Carmichael and William Whipple) to consider a July 13 letter and enclosures
from Washington about the recent British attacks on Connecticut towns.
See our annotation to the marine committee's letter, just cited.

2. The date on which the committee submitted this letter for Congress'
consideration: *JCC,* XIV, 915.

3. Deleted: "Portsmouth and".

4. A threatening Oct. 3, 1778, proclamation by the Carlisle peace commission: XXVIII, 257.

who so daringly violate the Rights of Humanity and it is particularly incumbent upon the united States as well to check their present Barbarities as to conform to the Manifesto published in answer to the Proclamation abovementioned and to deter all others by striking Examples from a Breach of those laws which are held sacred among civilized Nations. I am therefore to instruct you that you employ Incendiaries to set fire to the Capital of the British Dominions particularly the royal Palace and to such other Towns in Great Britain as may be most expedient and that as soon as some great Object of this Sort can be accomplished You do in a proper Manifesto avow the same as having been Done by the order of Congress and declare that they are determined at all Times to meet their Enemies in whatever Kind of war they shall chuse to carry on whether it be of civilized or of Savage Nations and call upon all the Powers of Europe who may have formerly suffered by the Pride and Cruelty of Great Britain who feel a just indignation at her present Conduct to join their Efforts in vindicating the insulted Laws of Humanity.

I am, &ca.

Notation: No 39 Report of comee on letter of 13 July 1779 from genl Washington. Read Aug. 2.—Burning report. N21

The following Draft of a letter from The Presidt to The Minister Plenipotentiary of the united States at the Court of Versailles

To the Marquis de Lafayette   Copy: Library of Congress

Dear Sir   Passy, Aug. 3 1779.

I received two Letters you did me the honour of writing to me from Havre[5] but have never Since had any News worth communicating to you.— Here is indeed a little Vessel arriv'd at Brest, which brings me a great many old Letters and newspapers, but no Dispatches of Importance.— I have the Pleasure however of seeing by the address of Congress which I

5. Above, July 12 and 28.

send you inclos'd that in the great Points of determining to maintain their Independence and the french alliance there is the most perfect Unanimity.[6] Virginia was evacuated by the Ennemy in a few Days after they had entered it, the Militia beginning to gather round them.[7] The Story of fort Pit I find nothing of in the Papers. Mr. Gerard and the Spanish Agent had made a Visit to the Army and were entertain'd by General Washington with a Review &ca.[8] The Paper Money was very Low, but it was thought the tax for 45,000,000 would stop its Depreciation.— The Accounts from Charlestown are so uncertain and contradictory that one knows not what to believe. When any News of Importance arrives you Shall immediately partake of it. My best Wishes attend you wherever you are:— being ever with the highest Esteem Yours most affectionately

BF.

The Black Prince Capt. Merchant has made two Cruises in the Channel. In the first she took 8 Vessels but 6 were retaken. In the second she was out only ten Days and has taken 11. Sail. Can you give me any Intelligence of a French Officer. Mr. Jean Baptise fontfreydd. His father enquires after him.[9]

Marquis de La fayette

6. The address probably is the one Congress presented to the states at the end of May, calling on them to contribute another $45,000,000 by Jan. 1, 1780, and taking particular care to praise the conduct of France: *JCC*, XIV, 649–58.

7. Actually, Gen. Mathew's raid on Virginia met so little resistance that its naval commander wished to establish a base there: Willcox, *Portrait of a General*, p. 275.

8. Gérard praised highly the American troops in describing for Vergennes his visit to the American camp at Middlebrook, N.J.: Meng, *Despatches of Gérard*, pp. 621–2.

9. Above, 78.

From the Marquis de Lafayette

ALS: American Philosophical Society

Au havre 3d August 1779

I have done myself the honor of writing to you some days ago, my dear doctor,[1] and with a friendly impatience I waït for your answer— There are arriv'd some vessels from our Country which have certainly Brought Accounts of American affairs— By the french Consul at Boston I have Got a parcel of newspapers But no letters from My friends are yet come to hand— That french Gentleman informs me that Mr Knox Gal Knox's Brother was just setting of for france— As soon as he arrives you will Certainly hear of him, and I will think it a particular favor, my good friend, if you direct him to me at the havre where certainly he will be Glad to pay me a visit. By a letter just arriv'd from l'orient I hear that Gal washington's army is said to be very Strong, and that Gal Sullivan is gone into Canada—[2] Those news however pleasing they are, I Can't indulge myself to Credit, till some better Confirmation is Given to me.

We are now on every point Ready to embark— But mr d'orvillier's fleet is not yet to be heard of—[3] intelligences are arriv'd to the minister, and none of us in the army has Got any Account of them, which is a proof that he was not then very Near the Channel.

With the most sincere affection and Regard I have the honor to be My dear doctor Yours   LAFAYETTE

I think the jamaïca fleet a Great deal threatened.

Notation: Lafayette au havre 3. aout 1779.

1. July 28.
2. Gen. John Sullivan at this time was in northern Pennsylvania, beginning a campaign against the Iroquois: Mark Mayo Boatner III, *Encyclopedia of the American Revolution* (New York, 1966), pp. 1072–6.
3. On Aug. 2 d'Orvilliers' fleet was 51 leagues southwest of Cape Ushant: Patterson, *The Other Armada,* p. 167.

From Joseph Palmer[4]   ALS: American Philosophical Society

Dear Sir   Germantown, August 3d. 1779.

This moment I hear that Mr Adams arrived at Boston last Night—& that our Fleet & Army, sent to Penobscutt to dislodge the Enemy, who had taken possession with 7 or 800 Land Forces, 6 or 8 Men of War & other arm'd Vessels, had driven the enemies Ships up the river, taken all their outworks, & obliged them to retire to their center Fort, so that they must Surrender, if not reinforced immediately; but of this you will have a better account from Mr Adams &c.[5]

This will be handed to you by my Nephew, Joseph Palmer, who having finished his Studies at Harvard College, was to have returned to his Father (near Plymouth) in England, by way of New-York, but being disappointed in his Passage on board the Cartel for that place, & the Mercury being order'd to sail for France tomorrow Morning, we have concluded to send him in her, 'tho' only a few hours notice.[6] I beg your friendship to him, so far as to advise him in all things neces-

---

4. Gen. Joseph Palmer (1716–88) came to America from England in 1746. He was one of several people, including BF, who between 1750 and 1756 acquired property in Germantown, a section of Braintree, Mass., where a glassworks had been established (whose management Palmer took over): V, 119n. Palmer was involved in numerous manufacturing ventures and served in the war in various capacities. *DAB*. His wife Mary Cranch was the sister of Richard Cranch, Palmer's partner in the glassworks and Abigail Adams' brother-in-law: *Adams Papers*, I, 155n.

5. This implies that JA had already arrived in Braintree and Palmer expected he would write BF; for his return home on Aug. 2 or 3 see Butterfield, *John Adams Diary*, II, 400n. A detailed account of the expedition did reach Passy. Among BF's papers at the Library of Congress is a four-page description of the events in WTF's hand and headed, "Extract of a Letter from Boston dated July 30. 1779." We surmise that the extract was intended for Dumas and was designed for insertion in the Dutch press. Its favorable news, however, was overtaken by events. On Sept. 24 the *Courier de l'Europe* reported that the British had surprised the expedition, destroyed its naval escort, and inflicted heavy losses on the American troops: VI (1779), 196–7. See also the *Gaz. de Leyde* of Oct. 1 and, for the events themselves, *Adams Papers*, VIII, 31n.

6. Upon his return home to Plymouth, England, the young Palmer was suddenly taken ill with a fever and died: Butterfield, *Adams Correspondence*, III, 381.

187

sary for his passage to Plymouth: It is not likely that he will want any Money, but if he Should, & you will please to supply him, you may rely upon being repaid by himself or Father, in such a way as you shall point out. His Father is a Farmer, of between 2 and 300 £ Stg per Anm. a friend to our American Cause of Liberty, & an honest Man. Joseph is as amiable, & worthy a young Man, as I ever knew; & your favour will be gratefully acknowledged by him, & will lay an additional obligation upon, Dear Sir, Your Sincere Friend, & Most Humle. Servt.   J: PALMER

His Excellency Benjamin Franklin Esqr at Passy near Paris

Notation: J Palmer Augt: 3. 79

To Francis Coffyn   Copy: Library of Congress

Dear Sir   Passy, Aug. 4 1779.

Sixteen French Sailors who belonged to Cap. Cunningham having been exhanged by the Last Cartel as Americans after an Imprisonnement of near two years, are now on their Way to Dunkirk.[7] As I am quite unacquainted with the affairs of that Ship which were managed between Mr. Deane and M. Hodge,[8] I can say nothing to any Claims made by the People on her Account. Whatever they are, they must be adjusted in

---

7. They had been part of the crew of Gustavus Conyngham's privateer *Revenge*, fitted out at Dunkirk in June, 1777. A list of the sixteen, captured aboard one of Conyngham's prizes, is given in Stevens, *Facsimiles*, XVI, no. 1589. WTF had written John Ross on Aug. 3 about two of them—Jean Ricard and Pierre Joseph "Manjot" (Mangonet), who had arrived at Nantes being owed all their back wages. WTF's notation on the letter reads "My Grandfather has given them 12 Livres each, to assist them in returning to Dunkirque. If their Wages are paid them this ought to be deducted. W.T.F." Haverford College Library. Their names appear in the Alphabetical List of Escaped Prisoners. BF also helped several more of them: to Sartine, Oct. 19, below.

8. Deane drafted Conyngham's orders: XXIV, 243–4. His associate, the merchant William Hodge (XXII, 619n), had helped fit out the ship, raise her crew, and arrange a fictitious sale to cover her departure: Neeser, *Conyngham*, pp. xxxiii-xxxv, 96–7. Arthur Lee claimed he and BF had been neither consulted nor informed: Stevens, *Facsimiles*, III, no. 269, p. 6.

America, neither of those Gentlemen being now in Europe. But Justice as well as humanity, will induce us to assist the poor men in recovering what may be due to them. If you are acquainted with the Terms upon which they engaged, you can assist them in stating and authenticating their Demands which I will then transmit to America in order to obtain the Payment.

With great Esteem, &ca.

M. Coffin.

From Deacon M. Auer

ALS and translation:[9] American Philosophical Society

Grace & Paix
M.

Ebingen près de Bahlingen, au Duché de Wurtemberg, 4 Août 1779.

La renommée a fait connoître la noblesse de votre grande ame dans nos contrées; & cest elle qui nous enhardit à vous adresser une humble requête, dans l'espérance que le coeur de V.E., à l'exemple de celui de Dieu, que vous aimez, et qui daigne du haut de son trône jetter ses yeux paternels sur le petit comme sur le grand, m'écoutera favorablement.

Une digne femme ici, Anne Catherine, Veuve de feu *Sigismond Hoklins* marchd. de cette ville, avoit envoyé un fils en Pensylvanie chez son Beaufrere *Christian Schneider* à Gérmantown, où exerçant sa profession de corroyeur, il avoit épargné la somme de 1650 fl., lorsqu'il mourut il y a 3 ans. La Mere, avec 5 enfans, & pauvre, desire avec autant d'ardeur que de justice de recueillir ce petit héritage pour subvenir à sa détresse.

Elle m'a ouvert son coeur, & je l'ouvre avec le mien à V.E. ne doutant point que vous ne voudrez partager avec moi la satisfaction de soulager la Veuve & les orphelins, en leur facilitant les moyens de recouvrer ce qui leur appartient: ce dont je vous prie au nom de notre Dieu & Sauveur miséricordieux.

Sur votre premier ordre, on vous enverra de la part de notre

9. The ALS is in German. We print from a translation made for BF by Dumas, who was visiting Passy at the time.

Regence les pouvoirs necessaires pour faire recevoir ces deniers.[1] Nous avons d'ailleurs reçu par des Marchds. d'Amsterdam, voie de St. Eustache & Curaçao, avis, que Christian Schneider desire ardemment, dans les présents troubles de la guerre, une occasion sure pour faire tenir cet argent à sa Belle-Soeur, dont il connoit les tristes circonstances. L'avis est de Germantown en date du 22 fevr. de cette année.

Ainsi Dieu benira les Etats Unis de l'Amérique, & toute votre famille & postérité. Je suis avec une profonde veneration, &c. M. AUER, Diacre

Notation: Dumas 14 August 79

From Julien-Pierre de La Faye

ALS: American Philosophical Society

Monsieur   a Paris le 4 aoust 1779.

Ne pouvant accompagner Mad. du Lin, comme je l'aurois désiré, je vous prie de Vouloir bien écouter la proposition qu'elle est chargée de vous faire et que je crois qui pourroit vous être agréable dans les circonstances présentes.

Je proffite avec empressement de cette occasion pour vous

1. While no reply to Auer's letter is extant, a letter written by the minister plenipotentiary for the Duke of Würtemberg to the Court of France on the deacon's behalf nearly two years later indicates that BF wrote on Aug. 17, 1779, instructing Auer how to obtain from Germantown the money due the widow: Baron de Thun to BF, July 6, 1781. On Sept. 7, 1779, Auer thanked BF for agreeing to act as mediator for the widow and enclosed a "writing" in quadruplicate with the request that BF forward the same to Germantown. The following year Auer wrote again and, referring to the letter sent to BF in September with the latter's full permission, said that they had received nothing and that the good widow still suffered in poverty: Auer to BF, June 20, 1780. All three letters are at the APS; Auer's are in German.

In response to de Thun's letter cited above, BF wrote to Auer on July 17, 1781, acknowledging his letter of the year before. BF advised him to have Mr. Schneider pay the money from the inheritance to RB and promised to remit the same to the widow when he obtained a receipt from RB. Both letters are at the Library of Congress. Correspondence on this matter continues through the end of 1782.

réiterer les assûrances du très respectueux attachement avec lequel J'ay l honneur d'etre, Monsieur votre très humble et très obeissant serviteur[2]   DE LA FAYE

Permettés que je presente icy mil compliments a Monsieur votre fils.

Notation: De La faye Paris, 4 aout 1779.

From Cradock Taylor   ALS: American Philosophical Society

Sir,   Aix in Provance Augst. 4th 1779

This is the second time I have made bold to trouble your Excellency with my misfortunes for I cannot help thinking it exceeding hard to be kept a Prisonier in this Country as I am (& can prove my Self to be) a Native of Virginia & Subject to the United States of America.[3] I amagine your Excellency may think me an Imposture by my being in the British Navy but I can assure you I was Betrayed on board the Zephyr Sloop of War by her shewing American Colours & the Lieutenant Declaring himself to be an American now Sir I embrace this oppertunity of getting my Liberty & Returning to my Native Country which I hope Your Excellency will assist me in I hope Sir you will be so good & Condesending as to send me an answr. by the Return post that I may know the worst of my Unhappy fate for I am now in the greatest Distress; I beg your Excellency's pardon for so troubling you but to serve my Country is the greatest desire of Sir Your Most Obedient Humble Servant—   CRADOCK TAYLOR

Addressed: To / His Excellency Benjmm. Franklin / Esqr. Plenopatery. to the Eunited / States of America / now at / Parris

Notation: Cradock Tailor Aix en Provence 4. aout 1779.

2. Ten days after writing this La Faye sold his splendid château of Rocquencourt, from which place he had previously written BF (XXVII, 55–6) and where he had entertained the American more than once. He sold it to no less than Monsieur, the King's brother: the Minutier Central, LXXIX, 218, kindly communicated by David Smith.

3. His first letter is dated June 29: XXIX, 770–1.

To Chaumont

LS:[4] American Philosophical Society; copy: Library of Congress

Dear Sir,   Passy August 5th. 1779.
I received your Favour of the 2d Instant. I have no farther Orders to give Capt. Jones: My best Wishes attend him & his little Fleet; and I hope soon to have the Pleasure of seeing you and my young Friend[5] well at home. Being ever with the sincerest Esteem & Affection Dear Sir, Your most obedient humble Servant   B FRANKLIN
M. Le Ray De Chaumont.

From Pierre-Jean-Georges Cabanis[6]

AL: American Philosophical Society

[c. August 5, 1779][7]
Mr. L'Abbé Morellet se Rendra chez mr. franklin avant midy et ne Lui donnera pas La peine de venir Le prendre. Voici La nouvelle heloïse. Mr L'abbé de La Roche va à paris. Tout auteuil salue messrs. franklin.

---

4. In WTF's hand.
5. Probably Chaumont's son Jacques-Donatien, who we assume accompanied his father to Lorient as he had done during a trip in May: XXIX, 491.
6. Identified by the handwriting. He was acting as secretary for the abbé Morellet.
7. In an undated, unsigned note sent to WTF apparently on the previous day, Cabanis, once again in his capacity as secretary for Morellet, had asked the Franklins to give him and the abbé a ride "to the party" since there was so much mud. APS. That note can be dated through its allusion to the imminent death of Mme Helvétius's brother-in-law. He was the farmer-general François Baudon, husband of her sister Charlotte-Anne de Ligniville, and died on Aug. 5, 1779. Information kindly provided by Dorothy Medlin. Baudon's funeral was announced in the *Jour. de Paris,* Aug. 7.

From Richard Bache

ALS and copy:[8] American Philosophical Society

Dr. & Hond. Sir Philadelphia August 6, 1779

A few days ago I recd: two packets indorsed & forwarded by Mr. Williams of Nantes the 25th. February last, inclosing french Memoirs & papers of Inquiry after a number of french Gentlemen on this side the Atlantick, without a single line from you, Temple or Ben.[9] Within two or three weeks last past, there has been several arrivals from france, into this port, Boston, & Virginia, but we have not recd: a word from you by any of these Vessels, nor did our friend Mr. Wharton bring us a single Letter;[1] I am the more astonished at not hearing from you, as I wrote you very fully and particularly by the Marquis de la Fayette, whose arrival in France we have long since heard of;—by him I sent you the first Bills of several Setts for the amount of your Interest in the loan office;[2] the 2d & 3d Bills I sent by the Brig Saratoga & the Snow Proteus, both of which were taken—[3] I have wrote you repeatedly by the way of the West Indies, & by way of Holland, but it is now up-wards of twelve Months since we have heard from you— I must beg leave to trouble you with a few more circular Letters from Bache & Shee,[4] & intreat you to interrest yourself on our behalf, please to let me have the names of the houses you give or send our Letters to, that we may establish a correspon-dence with them— I congratulate you on Count De Estaing's

8. The copy is in RB's hand and was enclosed with his Aug. 9 letter, below.

9. Before his recent letters to his son-in-law and daughter, written in June (XXIX, 597–600, 612–15), BF's last extant letter to them was in March, 1778: XXVI, 202–3.

1. Joseph Wharton, Jr., the brother of Samuel Wharton; for his return to America see XXIX, 261–2.

2. The loan office certificates in which RB had invested on BF's behalf: XXIII, 280–1; XXVII, 601.

3. The Maryland brig *Saratoga* had been used to carry dispatches to France in 1778: XXVII, 34; Charles Henry Lincoln, ed., *Naval Records of the American Revolution 1775–1788* (Washington, 1906), p. 454.

4. RB on April 7 had sent BF a number of circular letters on behalf of his new firm: XXIX, 273–4.

successes in the West Indies, a particular account of which you will doubtless have recd: before this reaches you, we were rejoicing on the occasion here yesterday by ringing of Bells, bonefires in the eveng. &ca. &ca.[5]

I have the pleasure to inform you that Sally and the Children are well, we expect an addition to our family in a few weeks. With joint Love & Duty I remain Dr. Sir Your ever affect. Son   RICH BACHE

Dr. Franklin

From James Lovell

ALS: American Philosophical Society, Harvard University Library, University of Pennsylvania Library[6]

Honble. Sir   Philadelphia Aug. 6. 1779

Your favor of July 22d 1778, forwarded from Nantes by Mr. Williams the 25th of February this Year, arrived not here till the 31st. of July.[7] I wonder the more that so very few of yr. letters reach Philada. in the Course of a Year as Mr. Dumas finds means to convey a series above the Numbers of the Alphabet in the same term of time, and is also in continual Correspondence wth. you.

It is needless at this Season to take up the different Parts of your long letter, for which I feel myself, however, obliged to you: But, I cannot omit to notice that you are totally mistaken as to "partial Objections" having been before Congress at the

5. Philadelphia Quaker Elizabeth Drinker recorded on Aug. 5 the "ringing of Bells, and other demonstrations of Joy" over the taking of Grenada: Elaine Forman Crane et al., eds., *The Diary of Elizabeth Drinker* (3 vols., Boston, 1991), I, 357. Gérard reported the celebrations to Vergennes, observing that "on sent toute l'importance de cet evenement." Meng, *Despatches of Gérard*, p. 827.

6. The Harvard University MS is marked "(Copy) private" and is signed with Lovell's initials. That at the University of Pennsylvania is marked "/3plicate/private" and lacks either notation or endorsement. We use it to supply several words missing because of a tear in the APS MS.

7. For BF's letter see XXVII, 135–42. He and JW share responsibility for the long delay in its reaching Congress: XXVII, 142n.

time of their dissent to the 11th. & 12th. articles.[8] It is true that, since that Period, much has been read from the Persons you suppose to have written on that subject.

You will long e'er now have seen the use which has been made of my letter to you respecting Mr. Deane's Recall.[9] I at least made a Show of a Disposition to befriend him. I really had such a Disposition; and, early on his arrival, let him know what had grounded that Proceeding of Congress, in hope that he would not be driven by a false Jealousy, which he discovered, so as to suffer Wreck upon the Quick sands of Indiscretion. All my Aim was in vain; He has been borne headlong. His Publication of Decr. 5th[1] has, in my opinion, totally ruined his claims to any public trust on the ground of his Hability in Affairs. And, however you may not discover the great Malignity of his Innuendoes, you cannot but see & own that his Peice contains dowright Lies which must be pointed out to the Public, who have not yet your good Grounds for Conviction.

There is not a single Circumstance which is mentioned against Mr. Lee that is supported, except his not having the Confidence of the french Court. The Ministers must have been Angels of Light not to have conceived Prejudices in Consequence of the indefatigable Arts of one who thought himself saddled, when a Colleague of Sense Honor and Integrity was given to him by Congress.[2] The Ministry were misled but, the

8. Of the Treaty of Amity and Commerce: XXV, 605. These articles were dropped at the request of Congress: XXVI, 448–9, 462; XXVII, 138–9.

9. In a letter of May 15, 1778, Lovell discussed Deane's recall as a consequence of the agreements he had made with foreign commission seekers: XXVI, 470. This letter was printed in the Dec. 21 *Pennsylvania Packet* as part of a defense of Deane by Matthew Clarkson, who said Deane had communicated it to him: *Deane Papers,* III, 111–12; Smith, *Letters,* XI, 369n.

1. Deane's "To the Free and Virtuous Citizens of America," printed in the Dec. 5 issue of the *Pennsylvania Packet (Deane Papers,* III, 66–76) questioned the conduct of Arthur and William Lee; for the former's reaction see XXVIII, 470–1.

2. Deane had said he was "honoured with one colleague and saddled with another": *Deane Papers,* III, 67. The word "saddled" is underlined in the other two ALS.

Consequence does not follow that, therefore, Congress should destroy an able & faithful Servant. What slippery Ground would this make for our Ministers abroad?[3] Will there not probably be ambitious Men always in Congress to trip them? But I drop the disagreable Subject and go to the pleasing Office of assuring you of the Attachment with which I am Honorable Sir Your most humble Servant   JAMES LOVELL

Honble. Doctr. Franklin.

Addressed: Honorable / Doctor Franklin / Minister Plenipotentiary / of the United States of America / at the Court of France / Passy

Notation: James Lovell Phyladelphie 6e. aout 1779.

From ———— Aycard[4]   ALS: American Philosophical Society

                              Marseille le 7ême aoust 1779 hors la porte
Excellence,   du Paradis

J'avois employé mon ciseau à sculpter la statüe de mon Roi, dont je voulois me faire un monument à la publication du traité d'alliance conclu entre Sa Majesté très chrétienne, et les très honnorables et intimes seigneuries des treize provinces

3. On Aug. 6 Congress gave evidence of support for the commissioners by retroactively voting them a salary of 11,428 *l.t.* per annum, payable from the date they left their place of abode to take up their duties until three months after the notice of their recall: *JCC,* XIV, 928. A copy of the resolution among BF's papers at the APS bears Lovell's signed notation, "It is requested, that Doctr. Franklin wd. furnish Copies to such Gentlemen whom it concerns to have them and who are not furnished by this opportunity, thro haste. James Lovell." Three other copies of this resolution (all bearing Lovell's notation) are at the Harvard University Library as well as partial copies at the APS (two), the Harvard University Library, and the University of Pa. Library.

4. Aycard's *oeuvre* has left no trace. All that is known about him is that he moved from Paris to Marseilles in 1777 and was still alive in 1790. E. Bénézit, *Dictionnaire critique et documentaire des Peintres, Sculpteurs, Dessinateurs et Graveurs* (10 vols., Paris, 1976). He wrote Congress on Oct. 21, 1783, inquiring once again about the fate of his statue. The secretary of the Committee of the States was instructed to answer him that his letter contained the only advice Congress had ever had of said statue: *JCC,* XXVII, 598.

des colonies unies. Je résolus de faire hommage de cette statüe de mon Roi aux illustres Etats, dont vous êtes le digne ministre en France. Elle fut embarquée sur la Frégate L'Adélaïde commandée par le capitaine Hubaq, le dix d'avril 1778; et sur la caisse je mis pour adresse, *aux très honnorables et intimes Seigneurs des treize provinces des colonies unies:* J'accompagnai cet envoi d'une Lettre d'avis aux mêmes très honnorables et intimes seigneurs. Je ne sais, Excellence, si le vaisseau est arrivé, si ma caisse et mon hommage ont été acceptés. Dans l'incertitude, j'ai osé vous en écrire, espérant que par votre moyen, je saurai quelle en a été la destination. J'attends des bontés de Votre Excellence, qu'elle daignera me faire instruire de l'heureuse arrivée de la Frégate et De la Remise de l'image. Puissai-je Recevoir bientôt la nouvelle agréable, que, cette image de mon souverain agréée par leurs très honnorables et intimes seigneuries, est un monument de mon parfait dévouement pour mon Roi, et pour les etats-unis ses alliés. Je suis avec le plus profond Respect De Votre Excellence Le très humble et très Respectueux serviteur   AYCARD
                                                                                      sculpteur

Notation: Aycard 7. Aout 1779.

Certificate for John Ross[5]

Copies: American Philosophical Society,[6] Harvard University Library, Library of Congress (two)

[August 8, 1779]
I the underwritten do hereby certify whom it may concern, that Messrs. Wharton and Bancroft Merchants, Citizens of the United States of America, at present in France, have at my Request examined with Care the Accts. of Mr. Ross with the

5. Who had been pressing BF for the money Congress owed him for supplies he had purchased: XXIX, 378. On July 10, at BF's request, Samuel Wharton and Edward Bancroft certified after examining Ross's accounts that a balance of £18,077.8.2 sterling was owed him as of July 1. A copy of their certificate, in WTF's hand, accompanies the present document at the APS.
6. In WTF's hand.

197

said States, and I knowing them to be Men of Integrity, skilled in such Affairs, and being therefore perfectly satisfied with the report they have made as above, do recommend it to the Committee of Commerce to make immediate Provision for the Payment of the Ballance which appears due to him on the first of July 1779. And in Case of my receiving Funds from them for that purpose I will discharge the same in France in compliance with an Order of Congress dated 11. Augt. 1778.—[7]

Given at Passy near Paris this 8th. Day of August 1779.—

(signed) B. FRANKLIN
Minister Plenipo: &ca.

Copy of a Certificate given to Mr. Jn. Ross.—

From Samuel Wharton   ALS: American Philosophical Society

Dear Sir   Hotel de Rome August 8 1779.

Messrs. Neave desire me to acquaint your Excellency, That They return to Diepe on Tuesday Morning early, and That They intend to wait upon you To Morrow Morning, In Order to take the Oath of Allegiance to the United States. They would be particularly obliged to Mr. William Franklin, if He would be so kind, as to prepare two sets of the usual Deposition.[8]

I am your Excellency's most obt. & most humble Servant

SAML. WHARTON

His Excellency Mr. Franklin Minister Plenepotentiary &c &c &c—

7. The Congressional orders were actually approved on Aug. 1: *JCC,* XI, 738–40. The cargoes which were to provide the funds failed to arrive, however, and BF continued to resist Ross's appeals for payment: to John Jay, Oct. 4, and to Schweighauser, Sept. 9, below.

8. The merchants Richard Neave and his son Richard, Jr., were in Dieppe, waiting for Wharton to make good his promise of a passage to America for them: XXIX, 574–6. They signed oaths of allegiance at Passy on Aug. 9, pledging to abjure allegiance to George III and to support, maintain, and defend the U.S. The father's oath is in WTF's hand, and the son's is in Gellée's. BF attested both documents. APS.

198

Addressed: A' Son Excellence / Monsieur / Monsieur Franklin / &c &c &c/ Paris.

Notation: Jam. Wharton Paris—

From Jonathan Williams, Sr.

ALS: American Philosophical Society

Hond sr.   Boston Augt. 8. 1779
I am honour'd with your favours of novr. 27 by Capt Collas,
& of Apl. 22. 1779[9] in boath your pleas'd to place a Confidence in me, that I will answer your Intentions in Supplying
your Worthy Sister if nead in this you do me Great honours
as well as aford me one of the Greatest pleasures, in Life.
I wish for every Opportunity to Express my Greatitude for
the many Obligation you have lay'd me under by your kind
Care & notice of my Childred I hope Jona will Continue to
Desarve your Esteem & Friendship then I know he will not
want your partonage & advise.
Now that aunts unhappy Son is no more[1] that Truble is
over, tho' I have allways endeavr'd to Liten the burden &
make it as easy as Possible & your Bounty has been as Sufficient as I Desired—
Monr. de la Luzerne Ambassador from the Court of France
to the United States ariv'd here in fine helth & Spirits[2] his
High Character will Command the respect and attention of all
True Friends to this Country & its generous Allies, he is

9. Both letters are missing. Williams discusses them in his first letter of
July 29, above.
1. Peter Mecom.
2. The new French minister plenipotentiary had come to Boston on the
Sensible: XXIX, 345–6. When he stepped ashore at about 5 P.M. on Aug. 3 he
was met by a delegation from the Mass. Council and saluted by thirteen
canon: Butterfield, *John Adams Diary,* II, 400n. From Aug. 3 to Sept. 4 he
was in Boston conferring with members of the Massachusetts Council and
other leading citizens before proceeding to Philadelphia to replace the ailing Conrad-Alexandre Gérard: William E. O'Donnell, *The Chevalier de La
Luzerne, French Minister to the United States, 1779–1784* (Bruges and Louvain,
Belgium, 1938), pp. 43–4.

pleasd to honour me with trust & Confidence; he has Dined at my house & Calls in a frendly Way to See us & I Doubt not he will have all that publick & private respect Due to his Character & Merrit. My Sons Ship the three Friends & Capt Young & a Tendor is arivd Likewise but Capt Cowzins is missing I am Sorry as I understand Monr. La Chaumont has Large Interest On Board however Shee may yet arive tho' She was Left in a Bad Condition with her Pumps Going Continuly—[3]

Inclos'd you have a Letter from your Sister[4] we are all Well Belive me Ever Your Dutifull Nephew & Hble Servt

JONA WILLIAMS

My Love to your Familay

Addressed: His Excellency Benjamin Franklin / Passy / France

Notation: Jona Williams. Boston 8 Augt. 79

From Richard Bache

ALS: American Philosophical Society

Dr. & Hond. Sir   Philadelphia August 9th. 1779.

The preceding is Copy of what I had the pleasure to write you a few days ago per Brig retaliation.[5] When I sent you your Bills, I sent Bills to Mr. Jonathan Williams for 210 Dollars, being Interest on some Money I put into the loan office for my Brother, and requested him to lay it out in Shirting Linen, Sheeting Linen, Stocking Gauze, Ribbons, & sundry other things for Sallys & the family's use,[6] their not coming has been a real disapointmt to us, and my not hearing from

3. jw's ship (XXIX, 501n) on this trip carried La Luzerne's baggage: *ibid.*, 778–9. John Young was captain of the *General Washington:* XXIX, 85. These ships were given convoy escort by the *Sensible* and arrived in Boston a day later than her: *The Boston Gazette, and the Country Journal,* Aug. 9. "Capt. Cowzins" is Capt. Cazneau, whose ship also traveled with the *Sensible:* Butterfield, *John Adams Diary,* II, 381.

4. Presumably her letter of July 27, above.

5. On Aug. 6, above.

6. As Sally had reported in January: XXVIII, 390. jw sent the goods (worth almost 1500 *l.t.* or roughly $280 in specie) aboard the *Squirrel,* Capt. Jones, which did not arrive until the beginning of November; he also sent Sally a

Mr. Williams on the subject seems still more strange; We fully expected these things in, by the begining of Summer, & expecting them every day since, we have rubed on, 'till we have rubed almost every thing out— As I cannot conceive that my Letters by the Marquis could miscarry, I do not think it necessary at present to send the fourth Bills, if it should be found necessary I must get them recorded here, and will send them, in the mean time I could wish Mr. Williams would ship to the amount of 210 Dollars or thereabouts agreeable to the within list, which is duplicate of what I sent him before. I remain as ever Dr. Sir Your affectionate Son   RICH BACHE.

Dr. Franklin

From François-Jérôme de Foligné-Deschalonges

ALS: American Philosophical Society

Monsieur   à passy Le 9e. Aoust 1779.
Le sieur de foligné officier Dupoïnt d'honneur aû tribunal de M.M. Les Marechaux de françe à L'honneur d'observer á Vôtre Excellençe, que Dans Le Mois de Janvier 1777. M.M. Le Ray de Chaumont, de Montieu & de Baumarchaÿs Le Choisirent[7] & lui confiérent Le Commandement de la frégate Le Marquis de la Chaltolais Arméé De 24. Canons et En guerre, Chargéé d'une Cargaison Riche & Intéressante. pour Compte Des états Unis de l'amerique, il fut assé heureux de faire Cette Mission en 4. Mois Et de rendre pendant Le Cour de Cette Expedition Des services distingué Aux Amériquains, a son rétour à paris il Eut L'honneur Dans rendre Compte à Vôtre Excellançe,[8] qui En Réconnoissançe d'une Mission

---

few articles on his brig the *Three Friends:* JW to RB, May 27 and Dec. 26, and to Sarah Bache, June 13 (Yale University Library).

7. Jean-Joseph Carié de Montieu chartered ships to Beaumarchais' trading company, Roderigue Hortalez & Cie., and had extensive dealings with Chaumont. Chaumont had furnished part of the cargo of the *Marquis de la Chalotais:* information kindly provided by Professor Thomas Schaeper.

8. For the meeting with BF after the return of Foligné's ship, see XXIV, 402–3. In our annotation of that document we failed to cite Foligné's "Jour-

Aussi Délicatte & Importante où il avoit Courûs Les plus gros Risques, Eut La bonté de lui prométre quelle demandéroit pour lui, à L'honorable Congress, Un Brevet D'honneur de Capitaine De frégate Au service des états Unis de l'amérique, Se Brevet à ète demande *par Vôtre Excellance,* Expedié par L'honorable Congress, Et pris par nos Ennemis sur les Batiments Amériquains qui Le portais, il En à été Informé par M. Le Chr. Rocher[9] & Le Ray de Chaumont.

Le sieur de foligné qui Arrive de saint Domaingue apres Avoir servi sa patrie & la Cause Amériquaine Avec distinction et Le plus grand désintéressement, Désireroit porter L'huniforme de la Marine du Congress, Comme il n'a d'autre titre dévers lui qui Constatte C'est serviçes, Au service des états Unis de l'amérique, qu'une Commission En guerre du Congress qui lui á été délivréé à Charlestonw par le parlement de Cette provinçe pour Le Mêtre plus à Même de protéger les Bastiment Amériquains, il suplie *Vôtre Excellance,* de lui Donner Une permission par Ecrit qui puisse l'hotoriser à porter Lhuniforme Amériquains, Autant De foi que Cela lui fera plaisir, Et Ce En Consideration de ses serviçes et de son attachement à la Cause Amériquaine, et il fera des Voeüx Au Ciel pour la Santé & prospérité de Vôtre Excellançe.[1]

DE FOLIGNÉ

---

nal de Navigation dans l'Amérique Septentrionale," Archives de la Marine, B⁴CXXXII: 81–106.

9. Perhaps Joseph du Rocher, a lieutenant in the dragoons de La Rochefoucauld, made a chevalier in 1773 but no longer listed among the regiment's officers in 1779: Mazas, *Ordre de Saint-Louis,* I, 629; *Etat militaire* for 1779, pp. 389–90.

1. On June 21, 1781, Foligné sent BF still another memoir, recapitulating his previous services and outlining the new ones he had rendered American shipping after the Ministry had sent him once again on a mission to St. Domingue. APS. Thanks to the recommendation BF had sent to Sartine on his behalf on July 30, 1779, Foligné was now a *lieutenant de frégate,* with a promise of being made *capitaine de brûlot* or *lieutenant de vaisseau* as soon as his mission was accomplished. But on his return he discovered, to his chagrin, that Sartine had been replaced by the marquis de Castries as minister of the navy. Since Castries was totally unaware of his accomplishments, Foligné begged BF to send to the new minister a copy of his letter to Sartine. We do not know whether BF obliged but Foligné was made *capitaine de*

À Son Excellançe Monsieur franklin Ministre plénipotançier des états Unis De la Mérique a la Cour de françe

Notation: Memoire de Mr. De foligné à Mr. franklin.

From John Torris   ALS and copy: American Philosophical Society

Sir   Dunkerque 9th. Augt. 1779

I am Informed that Mr. John Diot our Chargé of Procuration, we sent to Morlaix to Transact the affairs of our Black Prince Privateer, has wrote your Excellency the Particulars relative to her second Cruise.[2]

I do myself the honnour to write you the great uneasiness I crave under, for the fate of the Poor 21. men of her Crew, Taken the 22d. June, off Morlaix, by the Quebec Frigate, on Board of her 6. Prises, & who were Landed in Guernsey; your Excellency has had their Names; Several are Born Americains, others Irish, but they are all Sworn Subjects to the United States.[3] I read in the Kentish Gazette that these People were Sent to Penzance to be there Tried by the high Court of Admiralty for Piracy, Because, they were Irish men, or Subjets to Great Britain. Messrs. Jno. & Thos. Kirwan of London,[4] to whom I sent a Ransom Bill for recovery, a Prise to this american Privateer, answerd me that the Black Prince is Looked upon there, as a Pirate Ship, because she is maned by their own Subjects, & if taken, 'Twou'd go hard with them. Humanity & Friendship make me Shake for these Poor People, & I haste to Communicate your Excellency these advices, that

---

brûlot, albeit only for the campaign of 1782 and, four years later, *sous-lieutenant de vaisseau.* Feeling that Castries was treating him unfairly, he applied for retirement in 1787. From information kindly sent us by Commandant Gilbert Bodinier.

2. On 28 July, above.

3. See Torris' letter of July 2. The *Black Prince* was formerly an Irish smuggler. Many of her crew had passed themselves off as Americans in order to obtain an American commission which was meant to have protected them from charges of piracy in case of capture. Clark, *Ben Franklin's Privateers,* pp. 7–8, 24–5, 27–9.

4. Merchants: *Kent's Directory for the Year 1779* (London, 1779), p. 101.

you might Take quickly, the measures your Prudence & Wisdom will direct, to put these Prisonners of war, Sworn subjects to the united States out of the reach of malice & furour of the British Court— The 25. a 30. English Prisonners Taken by the Black Prince & landed at Morlaix, will doubtless, be awfull to the Ennemy, as they might Justly be made fearfull of reprisails on them.

I shou'd be very gratefull, to your Excellency to be favourd with a few Lines removing my fear, & Letting me know your Success in your Promised Exchange of these 21. men of the Crew of the Black Prince americain Privateer.

I have the honnour to be with great respect Sir Your most obedient most humble servant   J. TORRIS

Notation: Mr. Torris Augt. 9. 1779

From Samuel Wharton   ALS: American Philosophical Society

Dear Sir   Paris Augt. 9/79

Mr. Craig (of Philadelphia)[5] left London about the 2d. of this Month, and writes as follows.— A Vessel was arrived from North Carolina at Amsterdam; left it the 4th of June, and the Captain says, That just as He sailed, It was currently reported,— General Provost was totaly defeated near Charles Town. On what Day this happened, Is not mentioned. A Vessel was arrived in a short passage at London from New York, and brought Advice, That a few Days before She sailed There were great Illuminations, and firing of Guns in Elizabeth Town, and Newark—; and That it was generaly believed,— General Provost was vanquished.— And this was the more credited, as another Vessel arrived from New Providence at New York and the Captain said,— Advice was received there of that Event. St. Vincent, I suppose, you know was taken about the Middle of June by Count D'Estaign;— That Byron with his whole Fleet was gone to St. Christophers, and the

5. Probably John Craig, the Philadelphia merchant: XXVI, 260n.

English West India Fleet of 240 Sail was arrived, without losing a single Ship of the Convoy.[6]
I am y'r. Excellency's yr. most obedt. humble Servt.

S WHARTON

His Excellency Dr. Franklin

Addressed: A' Son Excellence / Monsieur / Monsieur Franklin / &c &c &c / Passy

Notation: S. Wharton Paris 9e. aout 1779.

To Gérard de Rayneval

LS:[7] Archives du Ministère des affaires étrangères; copy:
Library of Congress

Sir,   Passy Augt. 10. 1779.
The foregoing are the Articles requested by the States of Maryland & Virginia.[8] If to these could be added Cloth, Linnen, Stockings, Shoes, & Hats for clothing 20.000 Men, and also ten thousand more Fusils, the whole addressed to the Congress,[9] I am certain it would be a very seasonable & necessary Supply, as private Merchants have been lately discouraged from adventuring to send Cargoes of such Goods, by the numerous Losses of their Effects in going & returning, and I am not able to fulfil the Orders of Congress for want of Money. I have the honour to be, sir; Your most obedt. & most humble Sert.   B FRANKLIN

M. Gerard de Raynevalle.

6. *The Public Advertiser* of Aug. 2 declared that the arrival of the West Indian fleet had provided the additional sailors Adm. Hardy would need "to seek our perfidious Enemies and convince them that British Valour has not yet seen its Meridian."

7. In WTF's hand.

8. The foregoing virtually duplicated the list BF had sent Vergennes three months earlier and consolidated the Virginia and Maryland requests: XXIX, 416–17. For the background to them see BF's covering letter: XXIX, 415–16.

9. BF had strongly criticized the requests of individual states to France for "great Quantities of Arms, Ammunition & Clothing" and recommended that such requests be chaneled through Congress: XXIX, 557.

From Barbeu-Dubourg

ALS: American Philosophical Society

Mon cher Maître,   A Paris ce 10e. aout 1779

Entre nous cecy, s'il vous plait; c'est a dire le secret, et prompte reponse. Il paroit que votre projet d'emprunt (par le moyen de M Grand et de M Le Pot d'Auteuil)[1] n'a pas reüssi. Quelquun de ma connoissance croit qu'il est possible de le faire reussir en s'y prenant d'une certaine façon qu'il vous communiqueroit, et qu'il pense qui ne sauroit vous deplaire mais il desire etre prealablement informé avec la franchise qu'il vous connoit, des propositions que vous aviez a faire aux préteurs, et du benefice que vous auriez accordé a ces Messieurs vos notaire et Banquier, pour leurs soins, peines et entremise.

1.° quelle somme auriez vous reçue de châque particulier, pour le moins? mil ecus, cent ecus? plus, moins? afin de donner à chacun toute la facilité possible, et de tirer d'une multitude de petites bourses.

2.° quel interêt auriez vous assuré? Etoit ce plus ou moins de six pour cent du capital?

3.° le tems du remboursement etoit-il determiné? Etoit-ce à la fin de la guerre? ou une, ou plusieurs années apres?

4.° n'étoit-ce pas au nom, et sous l'autorité du Congrès continental que cet emprunt se seroit fait?

5.° les interets ne devoient ils pas en etre payés annuellement par vous en Europe, en votre qualité de Ministre des Etats unis?

6.° Le remboursement ne devoit il pas aussi en etre fait dans son tems en Europe, par vous, ou par vos Successeurs?

7.° N'accorderiez vous pas un ou deux pour cent, plus ou moins de benefice (de remise, de courtage, ou comm'on voudra l'appeler) a celui ou ceux qui vous procureroient de l'argent à emprunter ainsi?

8.° Pour faciliter les moyens de vous faire préter, n'adopteriez vous point la methode souvent employée en france de recevoir la somme qui vous seroit pretée partie en argent comptant, et

---

1. See Dubourg's letter of June 1 (xxix, 595–6) where the topic of bf's meeting with Grand and Le Pot is broached.

partie en papier monnoye provenant du Congrès general, ou de quelquun des etats particulliers aujourd'huy unis? Et en quelle proportion les admettriez vous? Par exemple moitié argent et moitié papier-monnoye, ou trois quarts en argent et un quart en papier monnoye, ou neuf dixiemes en argent, et seulement un dixieme en papier monnoye?

9.° Ne Promettriez vous pas de n'employer aucunes autres persones à des emprunts de la même nature, si vous etiez bien servi à cet egard par le canal que j'ai l'honneur de vous proposer, et si cela suffisoit à peu près à vos besoins?

Telles sont les questions de mon Commettant auxquelles je ne crois pas que vous soyez embarrassé comment repondre, parce qu'elles me paroissent assez simples. Ainsi je vous prie de satisfaire le plustôt que vous pourrez sa vivacité françoise.

Je suis avec un tendre et respectueux attachement Dear friend your most obedient, humble servant   DUBOURG

Permettez moi d'ajouter icy une question pour mon propre compte. J'ai deux differens titres de creances sur quelquun a Boston. J'en distrairois volontiers 25 Louis, si les Etats unis, ou quelquun d'eux vouloit les recevoir sur le pied de leur valeur primitive (ce que nous appellons *au pair*) et me donner pour cette somme des terres à defricher dans une ou plusieurs colonies, ou tout ensemble pour former un seul corps de ferme ou par cent acres pour le moins en chaque partition. Le Congrés n'auroit rien a debourser pour retirer cette petite portion des papiers qu'il est de son honneur d'aquitter tôt ou [tard]. Je sçais bien que par toute autre voye je ne pourrois m'en defaire qu'a grande perte; mais par cellecy, ce ne seroit pas non plus un avantage present pour moi; et quand j'y gagn[erois] au lieu d'y perdre, qu'importe au Congrès pourvu que ce [ne] soit pas à son prejudice, et que cela ne soit meme onereux a personne, soit en particulier soit en general?

Notation: Dubourg Paris 10 aout 1779.

From Thomas Digges

ALS: Historical Society of Pennsylvania

Dr Sir   Lond 10 Augt 1779

The last mail brought the needful for your Friend Mr. W.
P——rs's remittance, & I immediately placd it to His credit in
the Bank he requested, taking the proper rects. &c. The Excha. being rather unfavorable he lost seven shillings by the
Bill; but, from his late letters, I make no doubt the remittance
will be highly acceptable to Him. From there being a mistake
in the original shop bill for the books, I am something in your
debt, which shall be settled hereafter or discounted in some
future accot. when you may find it convenient to command
me.[2] I dare say I need not repeat my offer of services or give
any fresh assurances of my readiness to do any thing you may
command me.

We have had many ups and downs of joy lately. The arrival
of the whole Leeward Island fleet, 270 sail, not a ship missing,
gave us great satisfaction on the saturday week last,[3] and on
the tuesday following, we were as much depressd on the news
of the loss of St Vincents and the probability of Granada falling a day or two after; as well as that DEstaign has been considerably rienforcd as to give a decided majority of *French ships
only* in the West Indies, and that Byron in his folly of quitting
St Lucia to conduct the Leeward Island fleet a small part of the
voyage (they say to the Island of St Thomas) had thereby fell
so much to Leeward as to make it a worke of some weeks to
get back to the protection of St Lucia, St Kitts Antigua &c.
They begin to talk very freely of him here, & like *all the rest,* I
dare say he will return to England a disgracd officer. We got
accots on the 8th. that the Jama Fleet was also arrivd safe 106
sail; but again comes a black tuesday, & we are told that a
certain Mr Hopkins picked up three of them on the banks, &
that He has probably taken the twelve that are missing.[4] Also

2. The remittance for William Peters and the bill for BF's books are discussed in Digges's letter of July 14, above.

3. The arrival of the Leeward Island fleet in Bristol and Portsmouth was
reported on July 31: *The General Advertiser, and Morning Intelligencer,* Aug. 2,
1779.

4. John B. Hopkins of the *Warren* was not involved; he had been suspended for disregarding instructions during the capture of the *Jason* in

208

that *certain* accots are come thro France that Prevost had been beaten in two battles on the 11th & 14th June, & that He surrenderd the 26th. This is rather a sad affair, and more than usual Credit given to it from its probability, and that it is no ways contradicted by the generals which arrivd in Town the 7th at night from N York which place they left on the 6th July. Gen Jones, Sr W Erskine, *some say* Sr. J. Baird, Col. West & two or three others were landed out of an armed transport which put into Milford.[5] Altho they are three nights & two days in Town, nothing has been given out to raise our spirits—probably the Gazette of this Evening may do it. When asked the news at New York, these Gentlemn are remarkably silent—nothing material has been done—the army is in good health & spirits plentifully supplyd &c.—but not a word as to any intended active expeditions or opperations; and it would seem that the game there is nearly up. We however do not quite despair, as we continue still to get assurances from Ministry that all is well & in a fairer way than ever. You would be astonishd to see how uniformly our leaders pursue the old game of deceiving the People, & how admirably the bait takes. Our friend H has been some weeks out of Town, & has I believe lost all patience with them. We are dayly amusd with their wranglings & dessention but no apparent good comes out of it. I am promisd to have this put safe into a foreign Post Office and mean to keep it open as long as possible to add any thing that I may pick up this evening. Wishing you every success and happiness I remain very truly yrs.   V. J Drouillard

(after noon Tuesdy)
The news of Prevosts repulse before Chas. Town is confirmd by a vessel to Glasgow wth official accots from N York of the

---

April: XXIX, 762; Mark Mayo Boatner III, *Encyclopedia of the American Revolution* (New York, 1966), p. 512.

5. Maj. Gen. Daniel Jones had wanted to return to England since the end of 1778: Willcox, *Portrait of a General*, p. 236. Maj. Gen. Sir William Erskine was coming home for reasons of health: K.G. Davies, *Documents of the American Revolution 1779–1780*, Colonial Office Series (21 vols., Shannon and Dublin, 1972–81), XVI, 131–2. Lt. Col. Sir James Gardiner Baird, 6th Bt., continued to serve in the war: *Burke's Peerage*, p. 202.

4th July. I suppose it will be kept snug from the public as long as possible. The late arrivd Generals must have known it, & had political prudence enough not to let so great a national calamity come forth to the public sooner than was absolutely necessary. It is however, like all other disagreeable news, much molifyd. "Prevost got very near to Chs Town, & was about to summon the town to terms, when Pulaski arrivd with succour & assiste., finding this, Prevost thought proper to take better ground on St Johns Island 16 miles from Chs Town, where he now waits for rienforcements.—" If He was not Burgoind before the 26th June I think He will have had very good luck.

Addressed: Monsieur— B. F——, Passy

Endorsed: Augt 10

Notations in different hands: Digges Augt. 10th. 79. / Mr Digges.—1779 / August 10. 1779

From Richard Harrison[6] ALS: American Philosophical Society

Sir   Amsterdam Augt. 10. 1779.

When the inclosed was put under my care I promised myself the Honor of conveying it to you long before this. But an accident which obliged me to take a circuitous Voyage by the West-Indies,[7] prevented, & will, I trust, be a sufficient Excuse for the length of time it has been on it's way.

I have the Honor to be most respectfully Sir Yr Excellency's obt. & very hble. servt.   RD. HARRISON

Notation: Rd. harrison 10. aout 1779.

6. A Maryland merchant, who formerly had been agent in Martinique for both Virginia and Maryland.

7. While in Martinique he obtained a letter of introduction from his former business partner, William Bingham: XXIX, 640–1. He was in Passy on Nov. 26, when he took an oath of allegiance, attested by BF. APS. He subsequently became American agent, and later consul, at Cadiz: Richard B. Morris, ed., *John Jay, the Winning of the Peace: Unpublished Papers 1780–1784* (New York, Cambridge, London, 1980), p. 41 and *passim; Jefferson Papers,* XVII, 246.

From William Moody and John Crawford

ALS: American Philosophical Society

Honoured Sir   august the 11 1779

These Lines Comes With our Humble petition to you Hoping you Will Have Sum compasion upon us poor amarican prisoners Here in prison and We Do Humbly Beg that you Will try to Get us out of Here and We Will Go in any of our Continentall Ships or any Ship you pleas to put us on Board. I William Moody Was Born in Newbury port Was Taken By The English in The year 1776 and Have Ben There Ever Since till This Sumer and Came from There and Was Taken By The Generall Miflin privater from Boston Capt George Babcock Comander and after He took us We Entered on Board and after We Had Done all the Hard Work He Sent us Here to prison and Wat He Sent us Here for i cannot tell and i John Crawford Belonging to philidelphia Was Take By the Same Ship and We Do Humbly Beg Sir you Will Do the Best you can for us. This is from your Humble Servants and We Do Humbly Beg you Will Send us an answer as Soon as you Can and Here is Sum more Seamen Will Go With us if you can Get us clear from prison   WILLIAM MOODY
                                                                        JOHN CRAWFORD

May pleas your Honour to Bestow Sum Cloes upon me for When Capt Babcok Sent me Here Naked for He took every thing from me When He Sent me Heare this from your Humble Servant and Every one the Same   WILLIAM MOODY

The Honourable Mr amable Hardy Marchant at Nantes Was So kind as to Give us Clothes as to civer our Nakednes Sinc We Came Here and We Do Humbly Beg that you Will not Send us to an Enimys Country[8]

---

8. Amable Hardy forwarded this letter with one of his own on Aug. 12. Writing in French, he reported that these two Americans were among the English prisoners taken by the *General Mifflin* and currently held in the château of Nantes. In addition to furnishing them with clothes, he had also given them wine and tobacco. Although a "simple Negociant," he hoped he could be of service to the American cause. APS.

Addressed: To The / HonoraBell Mr / Franklin The amarican / Ajant Living in / Paris

Notation: Moody William John Craford 11. Augt. 1779.

To Gérard de Rayneval   Copy: Library of Congress

Sir,   Passy, Augt. 12. 1779.
I send you here with the best Copy I have of the address I mentioned to you.[9] It was worn in the Carriage, but the Difficiency is supply'd from another. I request you would show it to M. le Comte de Vergennes and remark particularly the Sentiments express'd by the Congress, of the Alliance, and the absolute Unanimity with which the address passed.

With great Esteem I have the honour to be, sir, Your most obedient and most humble servant.   BF.

M. Gerald De Raynevall

To John Harris[1]   Copy: Library of Congress

Sir   Passy, Aug. 12. 1779.
I received your Letters of the 7th. Instant.[2] I wish it was in my Power to Accommodate the exchang'd Prisoners with every thing they desire. But the Number is so great, and my Means so Small by the Loss of Several Cargoes sent by the Congress, that it is with difficulty I can provide them with mere Necessaries. I have directed M. Sheweighauser to furnish the Officers and Men that came in this Cartel in the same manner and Proportion that was advis'd and approv'd by Mr.

9. Presumably the one BF had sent Lafayette on Aug. 3, above.
1. A captain in the Va. navy, who had been captured in June, 1777: XXV, 415–16n; XXVII, 92–4. Among BF's papers is a July 26, 1779, inquiry about him by one Blittenberg, whose friend Lewis Dupré had just returned to Paris after three months' captivity in Gosport (near Portsmouth). Dupré had left his trunk with Harris, who was expecting to be exchanged. Had Harris arrived yet in Nantes? APS.
2. These letters (missing) were written some two weeks after the arrival of the *Milford*'s group of prisoners.

Adams a Member of Congress late Commissioner here then at Nantes. I cannot exceed this nor do for one what I am not able to do for all. As to any Money that may be due to particular Persons for Shares of Prizes or Wages, it is a Matter I cannot meddle with, being totally improvided with the Means of ascertaining and adjusting Such Claims, or any Orders to authorise me in paying them. They can only be settled in the proper Offices at home; whither I wish you all a safe and happy Return. I have the honour to be Sir Your most obedient and most humble Servant.

Capt. John Harris Nantes.

To ———— Perret

LS: Bibliothèque municipale de Nantes; copy: Library of Congress

Sir,   Passy Aug 12. 1779

I received duely the Letter you did me the honour of writing to me of the 6th. Instant, together with the Pacquet of Papers therein mentioned relating to the English Vessel called the Betsey, agreable to the Inventory that accompanied them.

I have the honour to be with great Regard Sir, Your most obedient and most humble Servant   B FRANKLIN

M. Perret

To Cradock Taylor[3]

Copy: Library of Congress

Sir.   Passy, Augt. 12. 1779

If you were engaged in the English service, and taken fighting against the United states or their Allies, I cannot obtain your Liberty. The king of france will justly claim the Return of a french Prisoner in exchange for you, and you must therefore wait the Establishment of a Cartel. You have not sent me any of the Proofs you say you can produce in your favour, and as we have already been impos'd upon by some Englishmen pretending to be Americans, and may be more so if we take

3. In answer to his of Aug. 4, above.

every Man's Word who is pleas'd to Say he was born there, you cannot wonder at my Diffidence. I am Sir Your most obedient humble Servt.

Mr. Cradock Taylor Prisoner among the English at Aix in Provence.

From Francis Coffyn   ALS: American Philosophical Society

Hond. Sir.   Dunkerque Augst. 12th. 1779.

I had the honour of writing to your Excellency on the 2d. inst, Since which I have been favour'd with your Excellency's letter of the 4th.[4] As nothing can aford me greater pleasure then to be instrumental in helping your Excellencys charitable & humane vews in favour of the French Sailors who belonged to Capn. Cunningham & who have been Exchanged by the last Cartel as Americans, I will gladly render these poor men the service that lays in me, on their arrival here, but as they were ship'd clandestinely by Capn. Cunningham, I am intirely unacquainted with the terms upon which they were engaged, and therefore it is not in my power to certiffy their demands; however I shall advise them to make their deposition under oath before a Notary publick, an authentick Copy of which with their procuration, I shall take the liberty to address your Excellency, to be transmitted to America in order to obtain payment. One of said Sailors arrived here last monday, he inform'd me that his agreement was for 6 months, to receive 3. Guineas per month, besides a Share in the prizes agreable to the American laws; if so, I dare Say that either M. Deane or Mr. Hodge, will adjust their demands according to Justice.

Several other french Seamen who ship'd on board Said vessell, and who have been taken in the prizes, made their Escape out of prison, Some of 'em are now here, and the rest are dispersed; I shall gather as many as possible, to join in one deposition & procuration, to avoid the trouble of making different applications, my next will inform your Excellency of the result; interim I make free to advise your Excellency, that the

---

4. Coffyn's letter is missing; BF's is above.

man who arrived here, has made a Sort of complaint to Mr. Quesnel Commissary of the navy at this place, who in consequence of the orders formerly given him to make a Strict inquiry into the particulars of said ship, Seems to make himself rether busy about these men. He apply'd to me, and tol'd me that he would write to the Minister about their demands, this induced me to shew him your Excellencys letter, which must have convinced him, that your Excellency are favourably disposed to see them Justice done, and therefor tol'd him that it was needless to trouble the Minister about these matters.[5]

Mr. Torris owner of the black prince privateer shew'd me a few days ago, a letter he received from his friend in London to whom he had sent the ransom bills for the vessells taken and ransom'd by sd. privateer, to procure the payment; the Gentleman Expresses some apprehensions in his letter, that the discharging of these bonds will Suffer difficultys, because (says he) in England they look upon that vessell to be a sort of a pirat, navigated by a parcell of Irishmen and that those who were found on board the Six prizes which have been retaken, will be tryed by the high Court of Admiralty in England, as pirats. This letter I observe, has struck a terror amongst a number of Irish Sailors who (encouraged by the Success of the black prince has had) have flock'd to this place, with an intend of shipping on board other privateers. I take the liberty at the request of Mr. Torris to ask your Excellency's opinion upon this Subject, and to claim your Excellency's protection, and advise on the steps that may be taken to save the poor men (who have had the misfortune of faling into the hands of the Ennemy) from an ignominious punishment. The English I think ought to be the last to punish the crimes of that nature, for no power has been So forward in forcing the subjects of the nations with which they are at war, to enter into their service.

I have the honour to remain with due respect Your Excellencys Most obedient & most devoted humble Servant

FRANS. COFFYN

5. Some of the *Revenge*'s former crewmen pursued their demands; see Sartine's first letter of Oct. 14.

Addressed: To his Excellency / Dr. B. Franklin, / Minister plenipotentiary for the united / States of America, at the Court of /
Versailles / at Passi.

Notations in different hands: Francois Coffin Dunkerque Aug. 12.
1779. / Copy

From Robert Montgomery

ALS: American Philosophical Society

Sir   Madrid 12th August 1779
I had the Honour of writing your Excely. the 29th June[6]
Advising that the Governour of Alicante had on the Declaration of the war Against England, Embargoed my house and
put me under an Arrest until he Should know his Majesty's
Pleasure Concerning the Americans, and I Shortly after wrote
you that the Minester of State el Conde de Florida Blanca on
hearing this, Immediate dispatched a post Extraordinary to
that Govert: Severely Censuring his Conduct, with Orders to
Give me Every Liberty and Protection, on which Requested
you would take no farther Trouble on my Acct: Supposing
myself then in full Security;[7] but unfortunately being in Company with the Governour's Assesor Shortley after this Affair, I
was So Imprudant as to Ralley him tho' in Good Nature, on
his not better understanding his Majestys Order of the 21st
June, which Was to Seaze all British Ships then found in any
of the Ports of those Dominions. This Creature who Could
Not Bear to See his own Weakness, has to Be Revenged Informed the Minester that I have Never been in America, and
that the passport and Certificate I Produced Signed by your
Eccely. Mr Lee and Mr Adams, are no more than Counterfits
and ware never Given by you. On this false Information I am

6. Actually, the 26th; see his letter of July 6.
7. From France Spanish Ambassador Aranda sent Foreign Minister Floridablanca a copy of Montgomery's June 26 letter (which BF provided him,
as he told Montgomery on Oct. 28, below); on Aug. 2 Floridablanca replied
that he had ordered the situation rectified: Purificación Medina Encina, *et
al.*, eds., *Documentos relativos a la independencia de Norteamérica existentes en
archivos españoles* (11 vols., Madrid, 1977–1985), VI, 153, 283–4.

Ordred to Retire 20 Lagues from the Coast, till I Can Prove the Authenticity of those Papers. This (I may Say Vile[?]) Insinuation of the Assesor of Alicante Is So Injurious to My Honour, as well as to My Credit as A Merchant, that I hope you Sir, will not Hisitate a Moment to Repair it as you are the only Person who has Power to do it. I Reley on your Justice and Honour for this Redress. On being Ordred to Retire from Alicante I Came directly here and Expect to Morrow to be Introduced to the Minester, but fear I May meet many Deficultys, till I am Honour'd by a Letter from you Ratefying the Certifycate and Passeport Given Me the 8th Sepr. 78 at your Hotel in Passy,[8] this would fully Satisfy all douts with the Minester by Shewing it to him, and hope you will not be Silent on this Occation, as that would Perfectly Confirm this falce Assertion, which must be Attended with the worst Consequences, I am with True Respect. Sir Your Eccelly's. Most Obedt Most Humble Servent   ROBT MONTGOMERY

Please Direct A Los Srs: Don Pedro Casamayor & Co⁹ Para Entregar A Don Roberto Montgomery Madrid

Benn: Franklin Esqr—

Addressed: à Son Excc. Monsieur / Monsieur Ben: Franklin / Plenipotentiare des Etates Unie de l'Amerique / En Passy / Paris

Notation: Robt. Montgomery

From William Peters   ALS: American Philosophical Society

Sr.   Nottingham 12th: August 1779.
Thro' the kind good Offices of Mr: [*deleted*] Virginia Gentn.[1] who has been resident in London for sometime, I received

8. His oath of allegiance of that date (APS) is attested by JA and Arthur Lee, but not by BF. See also XXVII, 414.

9. Montgomery's banker: *Adams Papers,* VIII, 314. This may be the Pierre Casamajor of Malaga mentioned in Lüthy, *Banque protestante,* II, 189n, or a descendant of his.

1. Thomas Digges, actually a native of Maryland. His name has been deleted at each occurrence.

(under Cover of one from him of the 15th. May last) a Letter of the 27th. Novr: last, addressed to you from my Son Richard at Philada.[2] wherein he writes you that "he had troubled you frequently to gain some Information respecting me, whether living or dead, and if living entreating you to convey me something for my Support and to advise me either to go over to Philada. or to reside in France. And by an Indorsment on that Letter of my Son's, you were so kind to request Mr: [*deleted*] to endeavour to find me out & if he succeeded to acquaint me that you were ready to do any thing in your power for me agreeable to my Son's request & that you had written twice to me to that purpose, but supposed your Letters had miscarry'd as you had received no Answer from me." Your Supposition that your Letters miscarry'd is right as I never received either of them, or knew any thing of your having wrote to me till informed of it by Mr: [*deleted*] sd. letter of 15th. May, in wch. he proposed also to assist in procuring me the Supply you were so good to offer me, and having since got the Bill negotiated he has agreeable to my Directions, paid into the hands of Messrs. Fullers & Co: Bankers, in London One Hundred Pounds Sterling for my Account; Wch. has been so great & seasonable a Relief to me that I am at a loss for words sufficiently to express my Gratitude to you for it.

The inclosed, wch. you will please to forward to my Son,[3] is to advise him of my having received the £100, and I cannot doubt his Care to acknowledge your Favour to us and to reimburse you. He is very urgent with me in several Letters that I have received from him, to go over to my dear Family at Philada., than wch. tho' surely nothing cou'd give me greater pleasure yet in my advanced Age & this perilous State of things between this Country & France &c and the horrid Dread I have of being made a Prisoner in the Voyage, I cannot now prevail on myself to undertake it, and I must entreat you will be so kind to give my Son your Sentiments by what

2. Both letters are missing. Richard Peters' last extant request for help in finding his father was Nov. 4, 1778: XXVIII, 33.

3. BF sent it with his letter of Oct. 25, below.

Channel it will be best for him to make me any future remittances towards my Support till better times and you will much
oblige Good Sr. Your already greatly obliged obedient
Servant   WM. PETERS

If you favour me with any letter please to direct it to [*deleted*]
to forward to me.

Dr. Franklyn

Addressed: Monsieur Le Docteur / Franklin / Dr: F——n.

Notation: Mr Wm Peter's. Letter. 100£ Sterlg.

To Barbeu-Dubourg[4]   Copy: Library of Congress

Dear Sir   Passy, Aug. 13. 1779.
    Having begun the affair of our Loan by the Means of our
friend M. Ferdinand Grand Banker Rue Monmartre, he is in
possession of all the Particulars relating to it, and can fully
satisfy the Curiosity of the Person who enquires thro' you. I
need only mention in Answer to your 8th Query, that the
Money borrow'd being to be laid out in France for Arms Am-
munitions Soldiers Cloathing, &c. it will not answer our purpose to take Any Money but such as is current in France, and
the American Paper has no Business here.— Those who have
brought any of it into France (except Bills of Exchange) have
committed a folly, in exposing their property to two Risques
for nothing, as it must go back again to find its Value.
    With regard to your proposition concerning your Property
in America: I should be glad to assist you in it, but I do not
conceive it practicable.— First because the Congress has no
Lands in its Disposition; The vacant Lands are all in some or
other of the Particular states, they dispose of them by general
Rules; and an Application to them for a Deviation from those
general Rules in favour of a particular Person, will hardly be
attended to; for they will probably apprehend, that having

4. In answer to his of Aug. 10.

done it in favour of one; they will be urged to do it for Many which would be attended with great public Inconvenience. I am ever my Dear Friend Your most affectionately   BF

M. Dubourg.

From Thomas Digges   ALS: Historical Society of Pennsylvania

Dr Sir   Londo. 13. July [*i.e.,* August] 1779[5]

I wrote you the 1st Int. by common conveyance of post a Ostend, and also by the last packet the 10th, which I had a promise should be put into the post office at Ostend, the bearer of it being bound to Brussels. In my last I acquainted you that the needful had been properly done as to Mr. P——rs Remittance— His money has been placd in the bank he requested me to pay it into & I have the necessary rects. I am in your debt something, on accot of the first shop bill for the Books being erroniously made out. The house to whom you desird me to forward them, have informd me by letter they got safe out.

Having now a safe oppertunity to Ostend I inclose you a letter from Raspe.[6] It has been some days in my possession, but a late journey to Birmingham & my not always having my papers about me, put it out of my power to forward it so soon after Mr Raspes delivery of it as I could wish.

I write you in great haste, having accidently met at an Inn the friend who bears this abroad, & who is on his way to the Packet. I wrote you in my last *doubtfully* about Prevost. We have now our doubts cleard up by arrivals from N York to Glasgow, St Augustine to London, & a vessel quicker than either from Bermudas to the River. By this last it appears He was attackd by Lincoln at his post on St Johns Island 18 miles from Chas Town, & with the loss of about 100 Men obligd to get southward into a warmer climate; & it is beleivd here he got to Beaufort with his army & is there waiting reenforce-

5. The letter of the 10th that Digges mentions in the first sentence is clearly his of Aug. 10, above. The one of the 1st is missing.
6. His of July 27, above.

ments. It does not appear He has capitulated or surrenderd, but this must be soon the case.

The grand fleets have yet done nothing. Our Commander is very unpopular in the Navy as is his Employers on shore, & the talk of the day is, that Lord Howe is to have the command. It would take more than his skill to save this Country, and the people begin now to think so. The accots. from N York by the lately arrivd Generals are that Washingtons army had been strongly reenforcd by the neighbouring militia—that he had crossd the Hudson River with 10,000 Men & got nearer to New York. This was a movement *after* Genl Clinton had returnd from his Expedn. up the No River. There was an expedition about to depart from N York on the 6th July—two small ships of war, several transports, and abot. 1500 Men among them a Corps of respectable Refugees. It was said to be meant for New London. The accots. from Canada by the only vessel come home this year & wch saild the 18 June are very bad a universal disposition in the native Canadians to revolt & provision flour & bread remarkably scarce. They had particular accots there that the Govr. of Detroit (Capt Hammilton who used Mr. Jno Dodge so remarkably ill as stated in the last No of the Remembrancer) having venturd too far into the habitable parts of America in one of his Indian Scalping Expeditions, had been made prisoner with abot 200 Indians & English, and that the americans soon after got the Fort.[7] I see many of yr. friends often, and you have their best wishes among numberless complaints that the communication is so obstructed & that letter writing is so dangerous in these times of alarm from immediate invasion &c.

---

7. The account to which Digges refers can be found in *The General Advertiser, and Morning Intelligencer* for July 31. Lt. Col. George Rogers Clark had captured Lt. Gov. Sir Henry Hamilton, commander of the British forces at Vincennes, in a surprise attack in February: Frederic L. Paxson, *History of the American Frontier 1763–1893* (Boston and New York, 1924), p. 39. The narrative of John Dodge's capture and cruel treatment by Hamilton is published in *The Remembrancer; or, Impartial Repository of Public Events.* (17 vols., London, 1775–84), VIII (1779), 73–81. Hamilton was transported to Virginia and remained in captivity there until his exchange in March, 1781: *Jefferson Papers*, II, 287n; IV, 566–7.

I have been made a little uneasy of late by some secret insinuating whispers from *two Brothers*[8] whom you have some reason to know—implying that I was cool & backward to a certain cause, had rejected offers of employ to serve those I wish best, & similar tittle tattle calumny; which I feel the less from knowing my own feelings & inability to serve more than I have done. It is true, from private, rather secret offers of their own I might have found bed & board in their habitations; & however irksome such a situation might be to me, would willingly have submitted, even to the prejudice of my private views or interests, provided I had been properly desird to do so. But why need I trouble you, who have had enough from that quarter already. I shall write whenever an oppertunity offers, & always be made happy by hearing of your welfare & success. I am very respectfully Yr obligd & Ob Sert

A McPHERSON

There is a small fleet arrd. at Corke from N York which saild the 10th. July & before their sailing an express had arriv'd there with the accot. of Prevosts being *retreating*. I am sorry to find by the returns from Sweighauser that there were only 92 Engl. Prisors. in France so that the American Cartel will stop on the return of the Transport to England. Now about 140 at Portsmo & 160 at Plymo. and in other places about sixty—

Addressed: A Monsieur / Monsieur B. F—— / A—Passey

Endorsed: July 13

Notations: Digges July 13. 79. / July 13. 1779

From John Paul Jones   LS: American Philosophical Society

Ship Bonhomme Richard at Anchor in the Road of
Honored and Dear Sir   Groa August 13th. 1779

It is but this moment that the Court martial has finished the affairs of the Bonhomme Richard and the Alliance being run foul of Each other. I inclose you the Whole proceedings of that Court, Which being the only one of Consequence, it is

---

8. Arthur and William Lee; see Digges's letter of July 6.

unnecessary to trouble you With bundles of papers Where the Conclusions have only Amounted to Whipping Which has been Executed.[9]

The Within paper respecting the prise money of this Little Squadron is Submitted to your regulation, and from the Inclosed paper addressed to me by the Captain and officers of the Vengeance I am persuaded that you Will think it unreasonable that he (the Captain) Should Share *Equally* With the Captain Landais or the Captain of the Pallace and Rather that Each Ship and Vessel Should first Share in proportion to the Number and Calibre of her Guns and the number of her Men; and that they Should afterwards divide their respective Shares by the Law of their flag, or otherwise to their mutual Satisfaction. The Within State of the force of Each Ship and Vessel Will be useful in forming your decision.[1]

Mr. De Chaumont has made an useless Journey here as I had taken all the necessary measures to Engage the Men that Were Wanting before his appearance even at Nantes. I am however much obliged to him and to the Minister for that attention as well as all former favors.

I Shall Certainly Sail to morrow at Day break and I hope Shortly to find opportunities to testify my gratitude to our great and good Ally for the honor Which he has Confered on the American flag and on my Self.

The inclosed dictionary[2] will be useful When I Write to you on particulars Subjects.

9. Lt. Robert Robinson of the *Bonhomme Richard* was cashiered for the collision between his ship and the *Alliance*. The enclosed minutes of his trial are now at the University of Pa. Library. Other information relating to the trial can be found in Landais, *Memorial*, pp. 21–3, and Bradford, *Jones Papers*, reel 4, nos. 714–16; reel 10, no. 1998.

1. The enclosures mentioned in this paragraph presumably are the Aug. 13 agreement or "concordat" among the captains of Jones's squadron governing the succession to command should Jones be killed or resign, the management of prizes, and the distribution of prize money; an Aug. 12 letter from Capt. Taillot *et al.*; and an Aug. 13 list of the ships in the squadron with their armament and number of crewmen: Bradford, *Jones Papers*, reel 4, nos. 722, 721; reel 9, no. 1954.

2. Probably a cipher with numbers used to represent words or syllables. There are several of these among BF's papers at the APS and Library of Congress.

This Little Squadron appears to be unanimous; and if that good understanding Continues, We are able to perform Essential Service.

I Look forwards With pleasing Expectation and an ardent desire to merit your friendship and that of America.

Being ever With the heigest Esteem and Respect Dear Sir the most obliged of your obedient Servants   JNO P JONES

His Excellency Doctor Franklin

From Landais

LS: American Philosophical Society

Ship Alliance, under Isle of Groa,
May it please your Excellency   August 13. 1779

I could not answer your favour of the 28 July before, having had no occasion for an express, & not being willing to trust the Letter to the post: and I could not comply with your orders to go out upon a cruise, not being ready before this time, by reason of our Prize Brigg's sinking,[3] which happen'd the 27th. Instant; having employ'd our crew to save her Cargo. The said prize, according to the direction of Capt. Jones & Mr. de Chaumont, I leave in the hands of Messrs. Gourlade & Moylan, with a midshipman & a seaman to take care of her.

Having heard that Capt. Gust Berg of the Sweedish ship Victoria, has presented a request to the admiralty at Morlaix, to have extraordinary charges paid to him,[4] & he having asserted that he had not time allow'd him to shew his papers when I met him at Sea; I have sent to Mr. Pitot a Certificate from Mr. Blodget, (a copy of which is inclosed,) that he had time enough to take his papers & to have produced them all at first, had he been inclined; they were all demanded & he shewed only a part, for he never produced the Register 'till he got to Morlaix. The Charges he has made for the maintenance of himself & crew are also very unjust, his people lived on board this Ship in Brest, & himself lived on board as long as

3. As was reported by both Jones and Landais on July 30.

4. Berg had been in contact with the Morlaix Admiralty for several months: XXIX, 368n. BF had asked Schweighauser to handle Berg's claims for damages: XXIX, 496–7.

he pleased; neither did it cost him any thing for boat hire, another considerable charge he has made, for my boats were used to transport himself & Crew.

This is favour'd by M. de Chaumont, who will inform you, we are all under the Isle of Groa & ready for Sea. I am with the greatest respect, Your Excellencies most obedient & most humble Servt. P: LANDAIS

His Excellency Dr. Benjn. Franklin

Addressed: His Excellency Dr. B. Franklin / Minister plenipotentiary to the / United States / at Passy / near Paris / favd. by M. / de Chaumont

Notation: P. Landais Augt. 13 79

To Sartine
Copy: Library of Congress

Sir. Passy, Aug. 14. 1779.
I received the Procedures of the admiralty of Morlaix Which your Excellency did me honour to send me, relating to the prises and Ransoms taken by the black Prince. With Great respect I am Your Excellency most Obedient and most humble Servant.

M. De Sartine.

From Barbeu-Dubourg
ALS: American Philosophical Society

Dear Sir Paris 14e. août 1779
I tank you heartily for your gracious answer. I will address the person to our friend M Grand, and am in some hope the can easily concord together. In the meantime I recommand to your favour and benevolence M Gregoire, who desire to be if not Consul at less reputed friend, correspondent, and in howsoever degree intrusted by the Americans.

I am with the utmost attachment and respect Dear friend Your most obedient humble servant DUBOURG

Notation: Dubourg Paris 14. aout 1779.

From the Continental Congress: Instructions

Copies: Library of Congress (two),[5] Massachusetts Historical Society (two), New-York Historical Society; AL (draft): National Archives

Much of Congress' time in 1779 was spent drafting peace ultimata, a task imposed on it by Spain's offer in April to mediate Britain's conflicts with the Americans and French. France, which conveyed the offer, used Conrad-Alexandre Gérard, her minister in Philadelphia, to lobby Congress to demand terms which would not prolong the war, should Britain prove willing to recognize American independence and end hostilities.[6] France's basic interest was American political and commercial independence from Britain, so as to weaken Britain's position in the European balance of power.[7] She had no desire to fight further for specifically American goals and moreover she had to mediate between the wishes of the United States and those of her new ally Spain. She was also concerned that the American desire to retain her traditional fishing rights off Newfoundland and in the Gulf of St. Lawrence might lead Britain to further restrictions on France's own fishing rights in the area. The New England delegates to Congress led by Samuel Adams, among others, fought hard to present demands for such rights as an ultimatum to Britain for entering any peace negotiations; against them Gérard successfully ranged a coalition in which were found many

5. One of the copies is incomplete. We print from the complete one in BF's letterbook. The draft is in the hand of Gouverneur Morris (N.Y.), member of a congressional committee appointed on June 17, 1779, to draft instructions for a peace commissioner (*JCC*, XIV, 744). The other members of the committee were John Dickinson (Del.) and Henry Marchant (R.I.); on Aug. 4 the committee was expanded to include Henry Laurens (S.C.), Samuel Huntington (Conn.), and Thomas McKean (Del.), while Marchant was dropped: *JCC*, XIV, 922. The draft is printed in *JCC*, XIV, 963–6. The copy at the N.-Y. Hist. Soc. is with the papers of John Jay, later elected minister plenipotentiary to the court of Spain, and the copies at the Mass. Hist. Soc. are in the papers of peace commissioner-designate John Adams. There are numerous differences in capitalization and punctuation among the various versions of the letter.

6. The Spanish mediation attempt is discussed in XXIX, 559n. Two good summaries of Gérard's efforts are in Meng, *Despatches of Gérard*, pp. 99–116, and William C. Stinchcombe, *The American Revolution and the French Alliance* (Syracuse, 1969), pp. 62–76.

7. Jonathan R. Dull, *A Diplomatic History of the American Revolution* (New Haven and London, 1985), p. 59.

southern delegates anxious for French military assistance. After months of debate Congress finally decided to present such demands as an ultimatum not for a peace treaty, but for any subsequent commercial treaty with Britain; on August 14 it approved instructions for a peace commissioner and for a commissioner to negotiate a British-American commercial treaty which incorporated this decision.[8] At the same session it approved these related instructions to Franklin. It then put the instructions aside while it turned to the equally contentious problems of electing the peace commissioner/ minister to Britain and also a separate minister to the court of Spain. Not until October 16 were the instructions finally signed by the new president of Congress, Samuel Huntington.

Sir,   [August 14–October 16, 1779]
  Having determined in order to put a period to the present War conformably to the humane dispositions, which sway the allied Powers, that we would not insist on a direct acknowledgement by Great Britain of our right in the fisheries this important matter is liable to an incertitude, which may be dangerous to the Political and commercial interests of the United States, we have therefore agreed and resolved, That our right should in no case be given up. That we would not form any Treaty of Commerce with Great Britain, nor carry on any trade or Commerce whatsoever with her, unless she shall make an Express Stipulation on that subject—And[9] that if she shall after a Treaty of Peace, disturb the Inhabitants of these States in the Exercise of it we will make it a common Cause to obtain redress for the Parties injured. But notwithstanding these Precautions as Great Britain may again light up the flames of War and use our exercise of the Fisheries as her pretext; and since some doubts may arise, whether this object is so effectually guarded by the treaty of alliance with his most Christian Majesty, that any Molestation therein on the part of Great Britain is to be considered as a *casus fœderis*[1] you are to

  8. *JCC,* xiv, 955–62. The approval of the latter set of instructions was by the margin of five states to four with two others divided and two not voting.
  9. Deleted from the draft: "we have pledged our Faith".
  1. A case of the treaty, *i.e.,* that Britain by so doing would break the peace and hence reactivate the defensive alliance between the United States and France (for which see xxv, 585–95).

endeavour to obtain of his Majesty an explanation on that Subject, upon the principle that notwithstanding the high Confidence reposed in his wisdom and Justice, yet considering the uncertainty of human affairs & how doubts may be afterwards raised in the breasts of his royal successors the great Importance of the fisheries renders the Citizens of these States very solicitous to obtain his Majesty's sense with relation to them as the best security against the Ambition and rapacity of the British court. For this purpose you shall propose the following Article, in which nevertheless such alterations may be made as the Circumstances and situation of Affairs shall render convenient and proper. Should the same be agreed to, and executed, you are immediately to transmit a Copy thereof to our minister at the Court of Spain.— "Whereas by the treaty of Alliance between the most Christian King and the United States of North America the two parties guaranty mutually from that time and forever against all other Powers, to wit, the United States to his most Christian Majesty the possessions then appertaining to the Crown of France in America as well as those which it may acquire by the Future Treaty of Peace; And his most Christian Majesty guaranties on his Part to the United States their Liberty sovereignty and Independence— absolute and unlimited as well in matters of Government as Commerce and also their Possessions and the additions or Conquests that their Confederation might obtain during the War according to the said Treaty;[2] and the said parties did further agree and declare that in case of a rupture between France and England, the said reciprocal guaranty should have its full force and effect the moment such War should break out:[3] And whereas doubts may hereafter arise how far the said guaranty extends to this, to wit, that Great Britain should molest or disturb the subjects and Inhabitants of France or of the said States in taking fish on the Banks of Newfoundland and other the fishing banks and seas of North America formerly and usually frequented by the subjects and inhabitants respectively: And whereas the said King and the united States have

2. A paraphrase of article 11 of the treaty: xxv, 590–1.
3. A paraphrase of article 12: xxv, 591–2.

thought proper to determine with precision the true intent and meaning of the said guaranty in this respect; Now therefore as a farther demonstration of their mutual good will and affection it is hereby agreed concluded and determined as follows, to wit, That if after the Conclusion of the Treaty or Treaties, which shall terminate the present War, great Britain shall molest or disturb the subjects or Inhabitants of the said United States in taking fish on the Banks, seas and places formerly used and frequented by them so as not to encroach on the territorial rights, which may remain to him after the termination of the present War as aforesaid and war should thereupon break out between the said United States and Great Britain; or if Great Britain shall molest or disturb the subjects & Inhabitants of France in taking fish on the Banks seas and Places formerly used and frequented by them, so as not to encroach on the territorial rights of Great Britain as aforesaid, and war should thereupon break out between France and Great Britain;[4] in either of those Cases of war as aforesaid, his most Christian Majesty and the said United States shall make it a common cause and aid each other mutually with their good offices, their counsels and their forces according to the exigence of conjunctures as becomes good and faithful Allies:[5] Provided always that nothing herein contained shall be taken or understood as contrary to or inconsistent with the true intent & meaning of the treaties already subsisting between his most Christian Majesty and the said States but the same shall be taken and understood as explanatory of and conformable to those treaties."

Done at Philadelphia this sixteenth day of Octr. in the year of our Lord one thousand seven hundred and seventy nine and in the fourth year of our Independence.

4. At this point an entire passage has been lined out in the draft: "Or if such War should break out in Consequence of any Molestation or Disturbance by Great Britain to either of the said Allies with Respect to any particular Right or Privilege in the Fisheries formerly secured or which may hereafter be secured to them respectively by the Treaty or Treaties which shall terminate the Present War."

5. Congress voted on the preceding clause, only Virginia and North Carolina voting no: *JCC,* XIV, 965n, 966.

By the Congress of the United States of America

SAML. HUNTINGTON
President

Attest CHAS. THOMSON secy.

The Honble. B: Franklin Esqr.

From Arthur Lee

ALS: Archives du Ministère des affaires étrangères;[6] copy: National Archives

Sir,   Paris August 14th. 1779

A decent time having now elaps'd, since the declaration of his Catholic Majesty against the King of great Britain; it seems proper to apply to the spanish Court, to know whether they are inclind to enter into the Alliance, which Congress have agreed to.[7] At the same time it appears to me, that to ask Count de Vergennes's opinion of such a step, before I take it,[8] woud be an agreable & useful mark of confidence in this Court.

But as I think, such an application cannot with propriety be made to his Excellency by any one but you as Minister here, I must beg you, Sir, to take the trouble of consulting Count Vergennes, both upon the propriety & manner of my applying upon this subject to the Court of Spain; & that you will have the goodness to communicate to me his opinion. I woud very

6. BF forwarded this letter to Vergennes on Aug. 17; see his letter of that date.

7. The Franco-American Treaty of Alliance was accompanied by a secret act by which Spain could join it: xxv, 593–5.

8. Lee had undertaken a journey to Spain on behalf of the commissioners in 1777 to obtain funds. Subsequently he was selected by Congress to conclude a commercial treaty with King Charles III: *JCC*, VIII, 420, 522–3n. His mission had remained dormant, however, due to Spanish unwillingness to receive him. At the end of May, 1779, he expressed to Congress his desire to resign his commission but the following month wrote Floridablanca hinting that he wished to return to Spain. The Spanish foreign minister, responding on Aug. 6, ignored the hint: Wharton, *Diplomatic Correspondence*, III, 196, 234, 290. No longer accredited to France and unwelcome in Spain, Lee was reduced to pursuing diplomacy through BF as an intermediary.

willingly apply myself, were I not persuaded that it woud be a trespass against the deference due to your situation; and that an observance of this order in our proceedings, will contribute to the attainment of the public object I have in view.

I have the honor to be, with great respect, Sir, Yr. most Obedt. Humb Servt. ARTHUR LEE

The Honble. Dr. B. Franklin Minister Plenipotentiary of the U.S. of America

From the Abbé Thomas du Rouzeau[9]

LS: American Philosophical Society

[August 16, 1779]

L ∴ R ∴ L ∴ D ∴ N ∴ S ∴[1]

Extraordinairement convoqué ce jourdhuy 16. du Courant a arreté

1°. que Le Venerable F franklin Lui ayant fait present de Son Buste,[2] L'inauguration S'en fera dans Son assemblée academique du Dix huit.

2°. que Comme cette Ceremonie ne Sauroit être trop Solemnelle il est de La dignité de L.L. que Chacun de Ses Membres y Vienne et y Contribue.

3°. que Le prix de La Souscription de 9 *l.t.* sera exigible même des freres absents Comme La Cotisation annuelle.

Par Mandement de L ∴ R ∴ L ∴   L'AB. DU ROUZEAU Secret.

9. The abbé's post as secretary lasted exactly one year, from late May, 1779, to late May, 1780. The allusion to the *assemblée académique* of the eighteenth makes it certain that this convocation was sent on Aug. 16, 1779. See our annotation of the *fête académique* under Aug. 18. Of the forty-odd invitations to masonic convocations preserved at the APS (their dates run from April 9, 1779, through July 4, 1785), a fair number, including this one, have duplicates addressed to WTF. The tone of these communications is both urgent ("very important deliberation") and stern ("send *excuse motivée* if you cannot attend"). Fines are sometimes threatened, and the brothers are advised as to the wearing of ornaments.

1. La Royale Loge des Neuf Soeurs.

2. Sellers, *Franklin in Portraiture,* pp. 306–7, describes the Houdon bust, but misdates the invitations to the inauguration. The bust is reproduced as the frontispiece to this volume.

Addressed: A Monsieur / Monsieur franklin / A Passy / N.S

Notation: L'Ab. Du Rouzeau

From Samuel Tabor ALS: American Philosophical Society

Rotterdam 16th Augt. 1779

I beg pardon for troubling your Excy. with the inclos'd but the loss of my valud friend the *Revd. Mr Sowden* of this place[3] has obligd me for this time at least to take this liberty which is the only & the best apology I can make for it, to convince you that no disagreable correspondence subsists between Mr Gordon & myself.[4] I send the Lr. unseald for your perusal if you choose it, if not, I request to seal & forward it per first conveyance & wherein I can return this liberty or render you any kind of service in these parts I shall cheerfully do it with which offer I have the honr. to subscribe myself Your Excellys. Most obedt. Hble Servt   SAML. TABOR

N.B. The droll circumstance of *Jonathan* for *Samuel* had occasiond my Lrs. to go to England & were opend & copyd there which not a little provokd me, as sometimes Mr. G sent them under cover & put my name without my place of abode, wh: will accot. to you for the reprehension given.

Dr. B: Franklin a Paris!

Addressed: A Son Excellence / Docter B: Franklin / á / Paris

Notation: S. Tabor Augt. 6. 79

3. Benjamin Sowden died June 22, 1778: XXVII, 203.
4. Tabor had been a correspondent of the historian William Gordon for at least two and a half years: XXIII, 600; XXV, 39.

From John Welsh   ALS: American Philosophical Society

Gentn   Cadiz 16 augt 1779
I presumed that my late partnership of Duff & Welsh has been
known to you,[5] as it has been for 16 years to most of the
trading places on that Continent, it is now dissolved by the
present change in publick affairs, as James Duff has retired
home via Lisbon above a month ago, by wch means the liqui-
dation of their accounts & business will be carried on hence
forwd under my sole signature & shall be provd to render you
or your friends any service in my power.

I have had several late consignments from america & such
as have had the good luck to get home have made good
bills(?) with salt wine &ca.

Yesterday I recd by the French Polacre Victorieux the in-
closed letter under cover from our friends Messrs. Sam Ingles
& Co. of Philadelphia[6] wch affords me the pleasure of paying
you my respects & to assure you I am Gentm Your most Hum
Servt   JOHN WELSH
The honourable Commissioner or Commissioners of the
United States of america Paris

Addressed: To / The Honourable The Commissioner or / Commissioners of the United States of / America / at / Paris

Notation: J. Welsh 16 Augt. 79

To the Marquis de Lafayette   Copy: Library of Congress

Dear sir   Passy, Aug. 17. 1779.
   I received duly your much esteemed favours of july 12. and
Aug. 3.— You have found out by this time that I am a very

---

5. BF doubtless knew of the merchant firm although this is the only mention of their name in his extant correspondence. James Duff was a particular
friend of Robert Morris; see, for example, *Deane Papers,* 1, 475, and for the
firm, Smith, *Letters,* IV, 656.

6. Samuel Inglis (1745–83) was associated with Willing, Morris & Co.:
Ferguson, *Morris Papers,* III, 121–2n.

bad Correspondent. As I grow old I perceive my aversion to writing increases, and is become almost insurmountable.

The Expedition of the Enemy into Virginia has done us some harm, but not considerable, and it has done them no good. They have only more exasperated the People by their Barbarities; and they have shown their Weakness, by not being able to maintain their Post but a few Days. The Reports about Fort Pitt are Newyork News, and not confirmed.[7]

I inclose a Letter I have just received for you from America; but I believe it is a very old one as it comes far about.— I send you also a Copy of a note just come to hand from Holland relating to the affair at Charlestown.[8] It is strange that we have no direct Authentic Advices of it.— But the Rumour comes so many different Ways, that one can scarcely forbear giving some credit to it. With the Sincerest Esteem and affection, and my best Wishes for your success in your present expedition, and safe return to your friends and amiable family crown'd with fresh Laurels, I am ever Your most obedient and most humble servant   BF.

Marquis De La Fayette.

To Arthur Lee   Copy: Library of Congress

Sir   Passy Sept. [i.e., August] 17. 1779.[9]

I this day communicated to Mr. Le Comte de Vergenes the Letter you did me the honour of writing to me, relating to the

7. BF had already responded on Aug. 3 to Lafayette's July 12 comments about the British expedition to Virginia and the rumored American evacuation of Ft. Pitt. By "Newyork News" BF undoubtedly means the gossip retailed by the Loyalist press of New York; in fact the story about Ft. Pitt did appear in the May 17 issue of the *New-York Gazette and the Weekly Mercury.*

8. The note is dated "Rotterdam 11th. August 1779" and bears WTF's notation "News from America by the Way of Rotterdam" (University of Pa. Library). It reports the arrival of a Philadelphia paper confirming the defeat of the British Army near Charleston on May 11. American losses in the lines were fewer than 40, and Pulaski's cavalry took 180 prisoners. The British left 563 dead.

9. We are confident that this letter was actually written on Aug. 17. The one BF forwarded to Vergennes is Arthur Lee's of Aug. 14, above. On Aug.

Accession of Spain to The Treaty. His Excellency was pleased to say that he would Speak about it to Mr Le Count d'aranda, who would probably write to his Court for Instructions concerning it. With great Regard. I have the honour to be, Sir, Your most obedient and most humble servant   BF

To the honble. Arthur Lee Esqe.

From John Bondfield   ALS: American Philosophical Society

Sir   Bordeaux 17 Aug 1779
The want of Subject say no intelligence from the American States in any of the ports on this Coast keeps me from giving more frequent advices. It cannot be many Days before some arrives. Many Sail were preparing at Philadelphia for Europe and particularly the Deane Frigate—[1] the difficulty to procure Seamen I apprehend the principal obstacle to their departure.

We may expect dayly to receive advice of the arrival of the Ships under Convoy of Mr. La Motte Piquet[2] and by the first packet from Philadelphia I hope you will be advised of the safe arrival of our Ships with the Stores for the States, it is probable you will receive the inteligence first when at hand I shall esteem the favor of your advices our Interest stands deeply concernd in them adventures—

Pray can you flatter me with the hopes of receiving any indemnification from Gouvernment for the Loss of my prop-

18 Lee wrote BF that he had received his "favor of yesterday, in which you inform me of your having communicated to his Excellency Count Vergennes my Letter of the 14th, with his Excellency's determination upon it." APS. The recipient's copy was also misdated Sept. 17; see Lee to BF, Oct. 8.

1. Although the American navy was at the peak of its wartime activity in July, 1779, none of its frigates had orders for Europe; the *Deane* made cruises out of Philadelphia and Chesapeake Bay over the summer and finally arrived in Boston at the beginning of September: Jonathan R. Dull, "Was the Continental Navy a Mistake?", *American Neptune*, XLIV (1984), 167; Gardner W. Allen, *A Naval History of the American Revolution* (2 vols., Boston and New York, 1913), II, 381–2, 398, 401–2.

2. The convoy was accompanied by a number of American merchant ships: XXIX, 371n.

erty in the Marquise de la fayette in Virtue of my petition.[3] I have the Honor to be with due respect Sr., your very hhb Servant JOHN BONDFIELD

Passi His Excely. B Franklin Esq

Addressed: His Excellency B Franklin / Esq / á / Paris

Notation: Bondfield John 17. Aout 1779.

From the Abbés Chalut and Arnoux

AL:[4] American Philosophical Society

passy mardi 17 aout. [1779]
Les abbés de Chalut et Arnoux ont l'honneur de faire leurs compliments respectueux à Monsieur franklin et de faire leurs amitiés à Monsieur son petit fils et de leur proposer d'aller diner demain mercredi à St. Cloud chez M. de Chalut fermier general qui est très empressé de recevoir le pere et le fils, on ne dinera qu'à quatre heures.[5]

Addressed: A Monsieur / Monsieur franklin Ministre / plenipotentiaire des Etats / unis d'Amerique / à Passy

From the Marquis de Lafayette

ALS: American Philosophical Society

Dear Sir   Au havre 17th August 1779
I wish it was in My power to Give you any intelligences, But however Great are our preparations, however superior we find our fleet Nothing is as yet in Motion, and we are impatiently waïting for orders— do you think, my dear Doctor, our British friends will let the Blow fall so heavily upon them, and don't you Rather Believe they'll try to set up a Negotia-

3. Which he enclosed with his July 24 letter.
4. In Arnoux's hand.
5. The farmer general, a very wealthy man, had bought his first house in St. Cloud in 1749. He kept buying more, as well as land and vineyards: Yves Durand, *Les Fermiers généraux au XVIIIe siècle* (Paris, 1971), p. 147.

tion, and will if necessary Consent to A peace—[6] Be so kind as to Give me your opinion which I have the Greatest Regard for, and in the same time tell me what may have happen'd in the political way, since I had the pleasure of seeing you— How are you satisfied with the ministry? How do Your Monney affairs? What do you think Might be spoken of in the present situation of affairs for the Advantage and wellfare of the United States.

So many efforts and preparations, the whole end of which is towards american independency, cannot But fill My heart with joy.— I am Glad my Country is doing so much for the Noble Cause in which I am so far engag'd— What I hear from America, is so uncertain, that I don't know what to depend upon— Do you know, my Good friend, any tolerable opportunity of writing to General Washington and my acquaintances in that part of the world.

Farewell, dear doctor, very affectionately I am Yours

LAFAYETTE

Lafayette au havre 17. aout 1779.

From Rouzeau

Printed announcement: American Philosophical Society

[before August 18, 1779]

FÊTE

ACADÉMIQUE,

POUR LA CLÔTURE

DE LA LOGE DES NEUF-SŒURS,

Au Wauxhal de la Foire Saint-Germain,

le Mercredi 18 Août 1779.[7]

---

6. In which case Lafayette hoped to carry the treaty to America: Idzerda, *Lafayette Papers,* II, 300–1.

7. This *fête académique* had initially been planned for Aug. 11 but was postponed until Aug. 18 because of the illness of a number of members.

L'Ouverture de cette Fête se fera par un Discours, que prononcera le Président.

Ce Discours sera suivi d'une Symphonie à Grand-Chœur.

Un Fr. . . . prononcera ensuite l'Eloge de Montagne.

La Musique reprendra.

Plusieurs autres Morceaux de Littérature, soit en Vers, soit en Prose, tels qu'un Poëme *sur Voltaire;* le *Repentir de Pigmalion;* le *Mois de Novembre,* &c. seront également entremêlés de Musique instrumentale & vocale.[8]

La Fête sera terminée par un Banquet.[9]

Cette Assemblée sera composée de deux cent cinquante Personnes seulement, tant FF . . . que Dames.

On entrera depuis quatre heures jusqu'à cinq. On commencera à cinq heures précises; & alors personne ne sera plus admis.

(The initial invitation and the notice of postponement are both at the APS.) The ceremony is recounted in detail, with its political implications, by L. Amiable, *Une loge maçonnique d'avant 1789: la R. L. les neuf soeurs* (Paris, 1897), pp. 146–50. That account, in turn, is based on Bachaumont, *Mémoires secrets,* XIV, pp. 161–4. In both cases the date is erroneously given as Aug. 16. BF did not attend. The memorialist of Bachaumont explains that the American minister had specified, before accepting the *Vénéralat,* that he would do so only if allowed some leeway in its obligations and that such a latitude had been granted since the lodge was primarily interested in his name. In his absence, the comte de Milly presided over the festivities.

After the lectures, music, and poems making up the first part of the program, the audience went up one floor to admire the artistic and scientific masterpieces exhibited in a gallery, notably some Houdon sculptures (including BF's bust), paintings by Greuze, and a kind of barometer never shown before.

8. Among the literary pieces was the preface of Michel-René Hilliard d'Auberteuil's *Essais historiques et politiques sur les Anglo-Américains,* eventually to be published in Brussels in 1781–82; this publication generated an abundant correspondence in the spring of 1782 since BF helped the author correct the proofs. The passage on BF appears in *Tome* II, pp. 60–65. The *Mois de Novembre,* which turned out to be the high point of the proceedings, was by the poet Jean-Antoine Roucher, whose work had been much applauded during Voltaire's commemoration (see XXVIII, 287).

9. The banquet, "simple et spirituel," lasted well into the night. Amiable, *Une loge maçonnique,* p. 150.

La Souscription est de neuf livres pour les FF. Elle sera de quinze livres pour ceux qui désireront amener une Dame.

Cette Fête étant uniquement consacrée aux Arts, les FF . . . qui ameneront des Dames sont priés de les prévenir que la Danse en sera exclue.

On ne sera plus admis à souscrire passé le 17 de ce Mois; & l'on souscrira chez le F . . . VIEL, Architecte, rue Poissonniere, la porte cochere vis-à-vis les Gardes-Suisses. Ce F . . . déli-vrera les Billets d'Entrée des FF . . . & des Dames.

Des Artistes célèbres, Membres de la Loge, ont promis d'envoyer quelques-uns de leurs Ouvrages, pour en décorer le local.

La Loge se tiendra le matin à dix heures, au local ordinaire, rue Pot-de-Fer. Les seuls FF. . . . des Neuf-Sœurs y seront ad-mis, attendu qu'on y traitera d'affaires.

Par Mandement de la Loge   L'ABBÉ DU ROUZEAU
                                         Secrétaire.
                                         Rue de la Bucherie.

Nota. *Tous les FF ∴ tant ceux de la Loge que les Visiteurs, seront décorés à cette Fête de leurs Cordons seuls, sans Tablier & sans aucun attribut.*[1]

Addressed: A Monsieur / Monsieur franklin / a Passy / N ∴ S ∴

From the Eastern Navy Board

LS: American Philosophical Society; copy: New York Public Library

Navy Board Eastern department
Sir   Boston August 18th. 1779
We were honored with your favor of the 2d of June, but not till several days after the Arrival of the French Frigate,[2] which

---

1. Because of the presence of women.
2. BF's letter by the *Sensible* does not seem to be extant but he wrote the marine committee on June 3 about Landais' misunderstandings with the officers of the *Alliance:* XXIX, 616.

prevented us the pleasure of acknowledging it by the Mercury Packet which sailed for France about a fortnight agoe.[3]

We are Sorry that any differences have subsisted among the Officers on board the Alliance, there may in this case as you observe in most others be blame on both Sides, but from the knowledge we have of Capt. Landais Temper & discretion,[4] & other circumstances, Joined to the Intelligence we have Collected of this Matter, We Incline to think it wholly the fault of the other Officers.

As it is our duty to send Ships to France when ordered by Congress, & not having it in our power to furnish any thing that will command the Necessary Supplies there: We have Transmitted the Marine Comtee. a Copy of Your Excellencys Letter that proper regard may in future be had with regard to that matter.

We wish all Immaginable Success to the Expedition you mention. We Inclose the papers to this day with the Journals of Congress & several Letters received from Mr Lovell the Papers contain all the News of Importance, they go by French Cutter. We only add that it seems necessary that we should be furnished with an Account of the Advances made to the Officers against the Ship returns to this Port.

We are with great respect Your most Obedt humble Servts.

J. WARREN
WM. VERNON
JNO. DESHON[5]

Excellency Benjamin Franklin Esqr.

Addressed: His Excellency / Benjamen Franklin Esquire / Minister Plenipotentiary / from the United States of America / at the Court of France / Paris

Notation: W. Vernon Boston 18. aout 1779.

3. Carrying their letter of July 30, above.
4. The board had supervised Landais' preparations for departure from Boston: XXVIII, 255–6.
5. Each of the three members of the board represented a different New England state: James Warren of Massachusetts, William Vernon of Rhode Island, and John Deshon, a sea captain from New London, Conn.: William

To Benjamin Franklin Bache

ALS (draft): University of Pennsylvania Library

My dear Child,   Passy, Augt. 19. 1779

Do not think that I have forgotten you, because I have been so long without writing to you. I think of you every day, and there is nothing I desire more than to see you furnish'd with good Learning, that I may return you to your Father and Mother so accomplish'd, with such Knowledge & Virtue as to give them Pleasure, and enable you to become an honourable Man in your own Country. I am therefore very willing you should have a Dictionary, and all such other Books as M. du Marignac or M. Cramer shall judge proper for you. Those Gentlemen are very good to you, and you are I hope very thankful to them, and do every thing chearfully that they advise you to do; by so doing you will recommend yourself to me, and all good People as well as me will love & esteem you for your dutiful Behaviour. Your Friends Cochran and Deane are well. Cochran gave me a Letter for you a long time since, which I mislaid, but having now found it, I send it inclos'd. The Small Pox is in that Pension, and 4 of the Scholars are dead of it. I will speak to Cochran to send you their Names.[6] He has not yet had it. How happy it is for you that your Parents took care to have you inoculated when you were an Infant! which puts you out of that Danger. Your Cousin is well, and will write to you and send you the Portrait you desire. Present my Respects to M. Cramer & M. Marignac. I heard lately from your Father & Mother who were well, as is your Brother Will & little Sister. I continue very well, Thanks to God; and I shall always love you very much if you continue to be a good Boy; being ever Your affectionate Grandfather

BF.

M. Fowler, Jr., *Rebels under Sail: the American Navy during the Revolution* (New York, 1976), p. 74.

6. Jesse Deane and Charles Cochran were BFB's schoolmates in Passy (XXIX, 413n) and in fact Cochran had been ill in June (XXIX, 733). In an undated note to WTF, BFB wrote that he was glad Cochran was better and asked for the names of his friends who had died of smallpox. APS.

Let me know what you are learning, & whether you begin to draw.

B.F. Bache

To Philibert Cramer

AL (draft): University of Pennsylvania Library

Passy, Augt. 19. 1779

I have deferred too long acknowledging the Receipt of your obliging Letter relating to my Grandson.[7] Your favourable Account of him gave me a great deal of Pleasure. I hope he will not fall much short of your kind Expectations.— Please to accept my Thanks for your friendly & fatherly care of him, and for the Permission you are so good as to grant him of visiting in your Family, which I am sure will be a great Advantage to him. Tho' at such a Distance from me, I feel myself perfectly satisfied respecting him, esteeming it a most happy Circumstance for him & me, that you are so good as to take him under your Protection, and to inspect his Education. Bills drawn upon me from time to time for the Expence of that Education, will be punctually paid. But I can never fully discharge the Obligation I am under to your Goodness. With great Esteem & Respect, I am, Sir, Your most obedt. & most humble Servt.

Mr. Cramer

From the Marquise de Lafayette[8]

AL: American Philosophical Society

ce 19 aouts 1779

Mr. De La fayette a envoyé par une occasion, la lettre ci-jointe, a Mde. De la fayette, pour monsieur franklin.[9] Elle a lhonneur

7. Missing.

8. She had been a correspondent of BF's for the last year: XXVII, 204–5.

9. The marquis' letter of the 17th. We presume BF's reply, immediately below, was sent that afternoon, as the marquise suggests.

de la lui envoyer; et de le prevenir en meme tems, que sil a quelque reponse a faire, il part cette nuit pour le havre une occasion très sure. Le Commissionaire repassera s'il le veut cet après midy pour prendre ses lettres. Mde. De la fayette prie seulement monsieur franklin de vouloir bien lui donner ses ordres a ce sujet. Elle a lhonneur de lui faire mille complimens.

Notation: M. De Lafayette ce 19 Aout 1779.

To the Marquis de Lafayette

ALS (draft) and copy: Library of Congress

Dear Sir,   Passy, Aug. 19. 1779

I have just now received your Favour of the 17th. I wrote to you a Day or two ago, and have little to add. You ask my Opinion what Conduct the English[1] will probably hold on this Occasion, & whether they will not rather propose a Negotiation for a Peace: I have but one Rule to go by in devining of those People, which is, that whatever is prudent for them to do, they will omit; and what is most imprudent to be done, they will do it. This like other general Rules, may sometimes have its Exceptions; but I think it will hold good for the most part at least[2] while the present Ministry continues, or rather while the present Madman has the Choice of Ministers.— You desire[3] to know whether I am satisfy'd with the Ministers here? It is impossible for any body to be more so. I see they exert themselves greatly in the common Cause; and do every thing for us that they can. We can wish for nothing more, unless our great Want of Money should make us wish for a Subsidy, to enable us to act more vigorously, in expelling the Enemy from their remaining Posts, & reducing Canada. But their own Expences are so great, that I cannot press such an Addition to it. I hope however that we shall get some Supplies

1. BF first wrote and then deleted "our British friends", the ironic expression Lafayette had used.
2. "At least" has been added above the line.
3. Originally, "You ask me".

of Arms and Ammunition; and perhaps when they can be spar'd some Ships to aid in reducing New-York & Rhode island. At present I know of no good Opportunity of Writing to America. There are Merchant Ships continually going, but they are very uncertain Conveyances.— I long to hear of your safe Arrival in England: but the Winds are adverse, and we must have Patience.— With the sincerest Esteem & Respect, I am ever, Dear Sir, Your most obedient & most hu— S—

BF—

Notation: M. La Fayette.

To Gabriel-Louis Galissard de Marignac

AL (draft): Historical Society of Delaware

Sir,   Passy Aug. 19. 1779.
My Grandson writes to me that he has Occasion for a Dictionary. I beg the favour of you to furnish him from time to time with such Books as you may judge proper and necessary for him, and I shall chearfully pay for them with your Account. I hope he will under your Care make a good Use of them. I shall be glad to hear sometimes how he proceeds in his Studies; and whether he continues to behave himself to your Satisfaction. I have the Honour to be Sir, Your most obedient & most humble Servt   BF

M. de Marignac

From Richard Nairne[4]   ALS: American Philosophical Society

Sir   Aix. Provence August 19. 1779—
Knowing the intimacy, & friendship subsisting between your Excellency, & my Brother,[5] I presume to solicit your interest in my unhappy situation, nothing but the disstresses of my family, & the cruel advantages, the owners of the Ship I

4. Captain of the merchant ship *Generous Friends,* captured in March by a French frigate: XXIX, 716–17.
5. The scientist and fellow of the Royal Society, Edward Nairne.

command'd, are taken, can excuse this liberty, & the certainty of being inevitably ruin'd, If I remain here much longer.

If you honour me with assistance, I may get my Parole to England, Mahon, or Gibralter, where I am certain, I can get, persons, of equal rank with myself, & Son exchanged. Your friendship on this head with lay me under such an Obligation, which I shall remember as long as I live, with pleasure, & gratitude.

Any letter your Excellency may favour me with, I shall receive safe, If directed to Messr. Gregoire, at this place.[6] I am your Excellency's Most Obt. & most Humble Servt.

RICHARD NAIRNE

To His Excellency Benjamin Franklin

Addressed: A Son Excellence / Monsieur Benjamin Franklin / Ministre Plenipotentiaire des Etats / Unis de L'Amerique, auprez de la Cour / de France / A / Paris

Notation: Nairne Richard August 19. 1779.

To Thomas Digges

Copy: Library of Congress

Dear Sir   Passy Augt. 20. 1779.

I hear Capt. Cunningham is confined in England a Prisoner. I desire you would take care to supply him with Necessaries that a brave Man may not suffer for want of assistance in his Distress.—[7] I ordered Payment of your Bill but it has not yet appear'd.— I am ever Your affectionate   BF.

M. Digges.

6. A cloth and silk merchant in Aix (*Almanach des marchands,* p. 11), Gregoire had assisted Nairne the previous month: XXIX, 717.

7. For Gustavus Conyngham's capture near New York in April see XXIX, 670n. He arrived in Falmouth on July 7, and was imprisoned at Pendennis Castle and then at Mill Prison, Plymouth: Neeser, *Conyngham,* pp. 160–73.

To David Hartley
Copy and transcript: Library of Congress

Dear Sir   Passy Augt. 20. 1779.

It is a long time Since I have had the Pleasure of hearing from you. Your last favours received were two of the 24th of June, and one of july 5. The second Cargo of Prisoners you mentioned is since safely arrived. M. Schweighauser wrote to me that the Captain of the Cartel was impatient to return, and as Capt. Babcock of the general Mifflin, and others of our Cruizers, had set at liberty a much greater Number of English Prisoners on a written parole or Contract that as many Americans in England should be released on that Account, he desired to know, (as the Collecting your People would take some time) whether he should send the Cartel back empty with those Contracts as some of our Merchants at Nantes advis'd, they fearing that when you had got all your People back you would not regard such Engagements. But I ordered him to collect and send as many as he had received; and If he could not in time collect the whole Number, that he should only Send a Discharge on Account of those Contracts, for a Number equal to the Deficiency. I chose this Method, partly in Compassion, to so many poor Men who have been long confin'd here partly from gratitude for the Charities our People have receiv'd in England and farther to show my Confidence in the honour of your board of Commissioners, who by what they have already done, have convinced me of their humanity, and persuaded me, that this Mode of dismissing Prisoners almost as soon as taken, will as it tends to diminish so far the Calamities of War, receive Encouragement from them by their ordering Compliance with the Terms Stipulated. I send you enclos'd a Copy of one of those Agreements and by the next post will send you a Number of others.

I see in your News papers, that Capt. Cunningham one of our Cruizers is at length taken, and carried Prisoner into England, where it is proposed to try him as a Pirate on the Pretence that he had no Commission. As I am well acquainted with the fact, I can assure you that he really had a Congress Commission. And I cannot believe that mere Resentment, occasioned by this uncommon success, will attempt to sacrifice a

246

brave Man, who has always behaved as a generous Enemy, witness his Treatment of his Prisoners taken in the Harwich Pacquet, and all that afterwards fell in to his hands. I know I shall not offend you recommending him warmly to your Protection.

They write me too from Dunkirk, that twenty one Men lately belonging to one of our American Privateers, Captain Merchant, and put on board some Prizes which were afterwards retaken and carried into your Ports, are also threatned with Hanging, as being most of them born in England or Ireland.[8] We have here in The french Prisons a considerable Number of Americans who have been taken in your service; and in America a much greater Number, perhaps more than a Thousand. If we are to put to death on each side all that are in these Circumstances, we shall have a good deal of Butchery in cold Blood, to no manner of purpose but to make us still more odious to one another, and create an eternal Enmity between our Posterities.

Let you and I, my dear friend, oppose all such mad Proceedings. We may do some Good. We shall at least enjoy the Pleasure of reflecting that we meant well, and that we strove to promote the Happiness of our fellow Creatures and lessen the Miseries attendant on a state of War. Adieu, yours most aff.

BF.

P.S. I wrote you before that I should endeavour to obtain Morlaix in which I now hope to succed. It is undoubtedly much more convenient.— If you can Send me any Proposals relating to french Prisoners, and wish me to negociate that Matter, I will readily undertake it. I told you the Preliminary expected. I have not yet a perfect Acct. of the Prisoners in Spain: but hope soon to receive it— I have ordered Mr. Schweighauser to keep a regular Correspondence with the Commissioners.

M. Hartly.

8. See John Torris' letter of Aug. 9.

From Claire Delon-Cramer[9]

ALS: American Philosophical Society

Geneve vendredi 20e aoust [1779]
Votre fils Monsieur est si interessant que la famille de Monsieur Cramer a qui vous l'aviez confié partageoit la tendre amitié qu'il avoit pour cet enfant. Nous venons de perdre ce protecteur que vous aviez choisi a votre enfant, cette innocente créature a marqué la plus tendre sensibilité, il m'a montré une douleur si vive et si vrai que des ce moment Monsieur je prend votre enfant sous ma direction jusqu'au moment que mon mari revenus de la douleur affreuse que lui donne la mort de son frere pourra s'en charger lui meme.[1] Si votre confiance accordée a l'un vous fait juger que son frere puisse le remplacer il se fera un devoir de faire tout ce qui dépandra de lui, pour cultiver les heureuse disposition que Monsieur votre fils manisfaite depuis qu'il est ici, ma belle Soeur[2] dont le desespoir ne se peut exprimer la prié de venir tous les soir coucher chez elle pour distraire la douleur de son fils, voilà Monsieur la position de cette malheureuse famille je vous écrit dans le premier moment ce coup inopiné répand un désordre dans mon esprit qui se communique dans mes expressions mais vous y verrez l'envie de vous etre utile. Je Suis Monsieur Votre très humble et très obeissante Servante

DELON-CRAMER

---

9. A high-spirited, witty woman from southern France, Claire Delon (who had married Gabriel Cramer in 1751) was a particular favorite of Voltaire, in whose plays she often acted—to the disapproval of a segment of staid Geneva. See Lucien Cramer, *Une famille genevoise: Les Cramer* (Geneva, 1952), p. 18.

1. At the time of his death, Philibert Cramer had become so involved in public life that the family printing business had devolved entirely to his brother. *Ibid.*, p. 42.

2. Catherine Wesselowsky Cramer, daughter of Peter the Great's ambassador to Vienna, would soon take charge of BFB. Her son Gabriel was to be Benny's life-long friend. *Ibid.*, pp. 60–1.

From H. Sykes[3]

ALS: American Philosophical Society

Sir, Place du Palais Royall, August the 20th. 1779

In Consequence of Your Permission, I take the Liberty to Acquaint You that my Large Electricall Machine is quite Compleated. It was to have been deliverd on Monday next, but I shall keep it till Wednesday or Thursday, in hopes that you will do me the Honnour to Comme and see it, and favor me with Your Opinion on its Construction.

I have the Honnour of being Sir, Your Most Obedient humble Servant H SYKES

Addressed: A Monsieur / Monsieur Franklin, / Deputé des Etats Uniees de L'Amerique / en Son Hotel / à Passy

Notation: h. Sykes Paris 20. 1779.

From Cradock Taylor

ALS: American Philosophical Society

Sir, Aix in Provance Augst. 20th. 1779

Your favour of the 12th Instant I Recd. by yesterdays post & have no Reason to complain of your Excellencyes good conduct in not being too hasty in procureing me my liberty as you inform me you have already been Deceivd. by more than one or two; as to my being taking out of a Portaguese Vessel & Compelled to Serve his Britanick Majesty against my Inclination it is well known to all the English Officers in this place I have Endeavoured to get a Certifycate from them but the Acquaint me it is what they cant do for me as it is assisting an Enemy; but as to my being a Native of Virginia I hope when it comes from Mr. Frazer who has the Honr. to Bear a Commission in the Army belonging to the United States who knows me perfectly well I hope your Excellency will be so kind as to pay some attention to it & if Possable Obtain me my Liberty.

3. This is the last extant letter from or to the English optician who had settled in Paris and had a shop in the Palais Royal (XXVIII, 430–1n). BF had bought a barometer from Sykes for which he paid 36 *l.t.* on July 23: Cash Book, Account XVI, XXVI, 3.

Inclosed is a letter I Recd. from the Commandant of Merreen at Toulon as I have applied to him also.[4] I am Sir with the greatest Respect Your Excellencies most obbligd. Hbl. Servt.

CRADOCK TAYLOR

Addressed: To / His Excellency Benjn. Franklin / Esqr. Plenapotentiary to the / United States of America / Parris

Notation: Cradock Taylor Augt. 20 1779.

From Chaumont

AL: American Philosophical Society

Passi ce 21. aout 1779.
M de Chaumont a l'honneur de prévenir Monsieur franklin qu'il a fait Venir de Bordeaux par M Grignon une petite Caisse de quina à l'adresse de M de Chalut fermier général pour être remise à Monsieur franklin cette caisse a été apportée par le Nommé Lemaille Courier de Bordeaux.[5] Monsieur franklin voudra bien la faire demander à M de Chalut le fermier général par M L'abbé de Chalut.[6]

4. The commandant at Toulon was Paul-Hippolyte de Beauvillier, marquis de Saint-Aignan: Didier Neuville, ed., *Etat Sommaire des archives de la Marine antérieures à la Révolution* (Paris, 1898), p. 133n. The enclosure, dated Aug. 17, notes that Taylor is considered a British prisoner of war because he was taken in the King of England's service, and therefore the Navy cannot give him a passport for Bordeaux where two American ships are about to leave. The English may trade him for a Frenchman of the same rank or if a well-known person posts a bond of 2400 *l.t.* guaranteeing that a French prisoner will be returned to France, the commandant can accede to Taylor's request. Otherwise the Americans will have to claim him. APS.

5. Discovered in Peru in the 17th century, quinquina or quina (cinchona bark, also known as Peruvian or Jesuit's bark) was popularized in France under the reign of Louis XIV and widely used to combat fever. *Poor Richard* for 1758 prints a remedy for the "Fever and Ague" containing the bark, and JA used it while in Paris: VII, 350; XXIX, 3.

6. Indeed, the abbés Chalut and Arnoux had already told BF on Aug. 12 that a crate had arrived for him at the Paris residence, Place Vendôme, of Farmer General Geoffroy Chalut de Vérin, in whose house they lived. APS. BF paid 46 *l.t.* 16 *s.* for its delivery: Account XXIII (XXIX, 3).

From Sartine

Copy: Library of Congress

A Versailles le 21. Aout 1779

Votre recommandation, Monsieur, en faveur du S. Foligny ci devant Capitaine du Navire le Mis. de la Chalotais a fixé mon attention, sur le Compte que j'ai rendu au Roi des Services de ce Capitaine et particulierement de ceux qu'il a rendus aux Ameriquains; Sa Majesté pour lui en marquer Sa Satisfaction l'a admis dans sa Marine en qualité de lieutenant de fregate et je m'empresse de vous l'annoncer.

J'ai l'honneur d'etre tres parfaitement, Monsieur, votre tres humble et très obeissant Serviteur. (signé) DE SARTINE.

M. Franklin.

From Félix Vicq d'Azyr

ALS: American Philosophical Society

Monsieur ce 21 aoust 1779.

J'ai l'honneur de Vous envoier le Volume que la societé Royale de Médecine Vient de Publier. Vous y trouverez, dans l'histoire, l'extrait d'un mémoire que Vous avez bien Voulu nous faire parvenir et dont l'auteur est M Perkins Médecin Resident à Boston.[7]

Je suis aussi chargé de Vous faire remettre un Certain Nombre de Billets dont Vous disposerez Comme Vous le Jugerez à propos, pour la séance publique de la société R. de Médecine.

Cette assemblée aura lieu le mardi 31 de Ce mois à 4 heures et demie très précises non pas au collège Royal comme cydevant, mais au Louvre, pavillon de l infante place du Louvre. La société R. de médecine Vous y invite et Elle desire bien Vivement que Vous assistiez à Cette seance.[8] J'ai été Chargé de Vous faire parvenir Son Vœu à Ce sujet.

---

7. John Perkins had sent to BF a paper on epidemic catarrhal fevers: IV, 267.

8. Vicq d'Azyr, *secrétaire perpétuel,* presided over the meeting. A full description is in the *Jour. de Paris,* Sept. 1 and 2, 1779.

J'ai L'honneur d'etre avec Respect Monsieur Votre trés humble et très obeissant serviteur. VICQ D'AZYR

M franklin.

Notation: Vic D'azir Paris 21. aout 1779.

From Mademoiselle ——— Juppin[9]

ALS: American Philosophical Society

mon cher papa   a st germain en laye ce 22 aoust [1779]

Je ne puis resiter au doux plaisir de me rappeller dans votre souvenir, depuis quelque tems je suis a la campagne, je pense a vous, je parle de vous, jentens parlér de vous, japplaudis aux éloges que lon vous donne en ne fesant que vous rendre justice; les ameriquains viennent de remporter un grand avantage, je partage tout ce qui leur arrive dheureux, vous etes leur pere, et je me met au nombre de vos enfans, par le sentiment que vous m'avez inspirer. Je nose mon papa vous priere de me donner de vos nouvelles, votre tems est precieux, mais si Monsieur votre petit fils a qui je dis mille choses honêtes, et agreables, vouloit vous servire de secretaire, et me donner de vos nouvelles, et des siennes, je les receverois avec reconnoissance.

Je suis mon cher papa avec lestime, la considération, et le sentiment tendre de la bonne amitié, votre tres humble tres obeissant servante   JUPPIN

mon adresse est, chez Mr de Rochefort a st germain en laye.[1]

9. When last heard from, the governess of the Brillon girls (whose name, following Mme Brillon's example, we wrongly spelled "Jupin") had been expelled from the household for having had an affair with Madame's husband: XXVIII, 215n, 452n, 599n; XXIX, 450–2. The name of the month in this document could also be read as "avril," in which case Mme Brillon's emotional outburst of May 8 would have been a reaction to Mlle Juppin's attempt to keep herself in BF's good graces. If the letter belongs to August, it might be linked to La Faye's of Aug. 4, above, the presumption being that BF was looking for a housekeeper, as he had already mentioned to Polly Hewson in late 1778 (XXVIII, 164).

1. In a brief note sent from Chaillot on an otherwise unspecified "mecredy matin," Mlle Juppin—assuming that she was still on the best of terms

Addressed: A Monsieur / Monsieur frankuelin / a passi pres paris / a passi

Notation: Juppin st. Germain en Laye 22. aout.—

From Jean-Paul Marat

AL: The Philip H. and A.S.W. Rosenbach Foundation
(Philadelphia, 1955)

Ce 22 Août 79.

Le D. Marat a l'honneur de faire ses complimens à Monsieur le Docteur Franklin, et le prévient qu'il rassemble, mardi 24 du courant, Messieurs Les Commissaires qui se rendront sur les neuf heures et demi du matin, et dineront chez lui. [2]

M. Marat seroit très aise que Monsieur Franklin voulût augmenter le nombre de la bonne compagnie. Il se flatte de lui faire voir de nouvelles Expériences intérressantes et curieuses.[3]

Notation: Le D. Marat 22. aout 1779.

---

with BF—invited herself for dinner on any day he wished and proposed a game of chess. APS.

2. On June 19, acting through one of its members, Marat presented the Académie des sciences with a copy of his *Découvertes sur le feu . . . (Procès-verbaux,* XCVIII, 200). The *Jour. de Paris* on July 17 announced the publication of that 38-page brochure. Marat also wrote a letter to the *Académie* announcing that he was pursuing his research. The commission that had reported on his first series of experiments (see XXIX, 105–6) was re-appointed for the new ones which dealt with light and were meant to invalidate Newton's optical theories on color; see Roger Hahn, *The Anatomy of a Scientific Institution: The Paris Academy of Sciences, 1666–1803* (Berkeley, Los Angeles, London, 1971), pp. 150–1. A very laudatory comment on Marat's 116 experiments appeared in the Aug. 4 issue of the *Jour. de Paris* and the Oct. 25 issue praised his *microscope solaire.*

3. Marat sent BF a note on Aug. 23 to tell him that the meeting had been postponed to Thursday [Aug. 26]. APS.

From Stephen Marchant LS:[4] American Philosophical Society

Sr/   Brest Augt. 23d 1779

I am now arrived Safe in this harbour after a Short Cruze which however has proved pretty Successfull, on the 15th Inst being clear pleasant Weather we weighed Anchor at 5 past Noon from Bass [Batz] road and Set Sail to the Westward and on Tuesday the 17th. Inst. fell in with a Danish Ship from St. Thomas West Indies bound to Amsterdam laden with Sugar Tobacco and other dry Goods. Examined her found her to have been two Years detained in Ireland on Suspition of Smugling her Cargoe there but was cleared with Great Cost to the Revenue of Ireland, having no proof I let her prosecute her Voyage to Amsterdam, took out of her two English Subjects as prisoners whom I brought to France their Names is John Newlan and John Nicholson both revenue officers from Dingle Ireland, on the 18th. near the English Shore took a Brig Called Reward came from Fishing near the Western Island [Azores], bound to London, took Brig Diligence laden with Mines [Wines] from Bassiscove [Bassett's Cove] to Swansey, took Sloop Friends Adventure from Bassiscove to Burry, in Ballast, on the 19th. took Brig Blessing with Coals from Minehead to Cork took Brig Matthew and Sally with Coals from Minehead to Cork took the Sloop Resolution with Coals from Minehead to Cork took Sloop Betty with Bark from Bideford to Youghall, at Noon Distance from Waterford Ireland 3 Leagues, fell in with the Spy Armed Tender was Informed by a Fisherman that she had two hundred Men on board. We fought her for an hour untill shee sheered of and we chased her untill we Run her Ashore at Waterford blew hard Gales of Wind, on the 19th took Ship Sauthom from Whitehaven to Waterford laden with Coals, at 4 in the Evening blowing Very hard Broke our Boltsprit was obliged to Set the Treasail foresail and Storn Jyb and Steered for the Coast of France—we passed on the 21st. thro a fleet of Men of War unobserved thro favour of Hazy Weather. I Wrote after my last Cruze, from the Town of Morlaix to yr. Exellency giv-

4. In the hand of Timothy Kelly.

ing you a Minute Account of our Transactions but has Recd. only one letter from yr. Excellency since I left Dunkerque[5] which has given me great Trouble for fear of Miscarriage of Letters as I Recd. no Answer from yr. Excellency makes me Suspitious you have not Recd. my letters So I hereunder give yr. Excellency a Brief Acct. of my last Cruze, on the 15th. of last Month July weighed Anchor from Bass Road and Stood for the English Shore Clear pleasant Weather on the 16th July lost one Man in Boarding a Dutch Man, on the 17th July took Brig Ann with Cullom from Bideford to Plymouth, Distance from Landsend ten Leagues on the 18th took Brig Lucy with Coals from Swansey to St Ives took Sloop John with Copper Ore from Bassiscove to Bristol took Sloop Rebecca from IlfordCoome in Coals to Bassiscove took Sloop 2 Brothers with Coals from Swansey to patstow took Sloop Speedwell with Coals from Swansey to Patstow, on the 19th took Brig Union with Oats from patstow to Bristol on the 20th. took brig St Joseph with Wine being a Prize to the Emperor Letter of Mart of Bristol found Sufficient proof that she was an Irish Propperty and Good Consigned to Irish Merchants sent her to France Took Brig Dublin Trader from Bristol to Dublin laden with oil Copper Tin and Bale Goods on the 21st took Sloop Charlotte from Cork to Bristol laden with Tallow and dry skins, on 22d. took brig Monmouth from Lancaster to Chapstow with Coals—on the 25th. Came to Anchor in Morlaix Road on the 26th sent our prisoners on Shore was Informed our Prize the St Joseph was retaken and four of my Men in her was Obliged in this Cruze to Set the following Men at Liberty they signing a Duplicate to be Answerable for as many American Subjects prisoners in Great Britain, Viz Henry Rowe Capt Brig Lucy, St Ives Robert Cowling St Jearth John Lewis Swansey, John Kneebones St Ives, George Landin Owner Sloop John Kinsale, Cornelius Fowler Mate Kinsale, Eastway Capt Sloop Rebecca Ilsfordcoome [Ilfracombe] William Gross Ilsfordcoome John Trick Capt. Brig Union of Boscastle, William Berkin Mate, Boscastle we are almost Ready

5. Marchant's letter is above, July 25, while BF's must be the one of July 4, also above.

255

for Sea has got a New Boltsprit hopes thro the providence of God, to make our next Cruze Successful all hands behaves Well with true Courage. I have no more to add at present but gives my Respect to yr. Excellency's Nephew and the American Gentlemen in Paris of yr Excellency's Acquaintance. I Remn. with all Duty Yr. Excellency's most Obedient Hhble. Servt.   STEPHEN MARCHANT

Addressed: To / His Excellency Benjamin / Franklin Minister of the United / States of North America at the / Court of France, at Passy / near / Paris

Notation: Capt. Merchant Augt. 23. 1779

From Isabella Strange[6]   AL: American Philosophical Society

August 23d 1779 paris

Mrs Strange presents Her most respectful compliments to Dr Frankland she presumes to give Him the trouble of the Inclos'd to Her Friend Mr Livingston who she supposes to be with His Namesake but where she knows not. He and His Family left St Johns Several years agoe. He was a Carpenter and Builder and if not a Soldier now will be in the same way. All Mrs Strange wishes to know is that He and His Family are well— adieu—

Mr Strange is at Versails otherwise He would have had the Honour of delivering this.[7]

Addressed: A Monsieur / Monsr Frankland / passy

6. Wife of the engraver Sir Robert Strange. The couple had been living in Paris since 1775; see XXIII, 226n; *DNB.*

7. A number of the Stranges' requests to forward mail are among BF's papers, most of them dated and from a later period. An undated note in the husband's hand, in French, and directed to a "Monsieur Guillaume," asks for a letter to be forwarded to Mr. Alexander. APS. WTF was most likely the recipient.

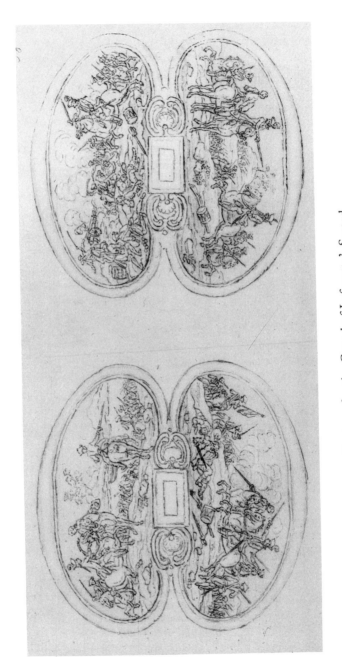

Designs for the Guard of Lafayette's Sword

From Samuel Wharton

ALS: American Philosophical Society

Dear Sir   Hotel de Rome August 23d. 1779

I inclose three News papers just received by way of Amsterdam. The postage cost Fourteen Livres.— All Papers are intercepted, which come by Way of Ostend; And I could wish your Direction, as to my Friend's continuing to Send Them, Via Amsterdam.

I am with the utmost Respect & Esteem Dear Sir Your Excellency's most obt. & most humble Servant   S. WHARTON

His Excellency Benjamin Franklin Esqr.

Addressed: A' son Excellence / Monsieur / Monsieur Franklin / &c &c &c / Passy

Notation: S. wharton 23. aout 1779 Paris.

A Sword for the Marquis de Lafayette: Four Documents

(I) D: American Philosophical Society; (II) ADS: American Philosophical Society; (III) AL: American Philosophical Society; (IV) D:[8] National Archives; D (draft): American Philosophical Society

On October 21, 1778, Congress granted Lafayette leave to return to France. They thanked him for the "disinterested zeal" that had brought him to America and directed Franklin to present him "an elegant sword, with proper devices."[9] It was suggested that this ceremonial sword represent the military actions in which Lafayette had most distinguished himself. The Marquis desired that his own cutler in Paris, Liger,[1] make the item, and the craftsman consulted Franklin about it (I).[2] The sword was ready by August 24, on which

---

8. In WTF's hand, and enclosed in BF to Jay, Oct. 4, below, along with the illustrations of the sword. The draft is also in WTF's hand, with revisions and interlineations by BF that have been incorporated into the fair copy. An outline of the opening paragraph, in BF's hand, is at the APS.

9. *JCC,* XII, 1035. For our first discussion of the sword see XXVII, 619n.

1. XXVII, 666; *Almanach des marchands,* p. 383.

2. This is one of two brief notes probably left when Liger or his assistant came to call in BF's absence. The second one, a simple calling card from "Liger fourbisseur &c jeweller" and in the same hand, is at the APS.

day Liger signed a receipt for payment in full (II). In a brief note to Temple, Franklin requested that the sword be shown to Madame Brillon (III). And it was Temple who was entrusted with bearing the sword to Le Havre to present to Lafayette personally.

Before sending the sword to Lafayette, Franklin composed a description of the splendid object (IV), probably for the purpose of publicizing Congress' gift. This piece appeared in the French press, the *Gazette de Leyde*, and English newspapers.[3] At least one French writer mocked the lavish manner in which the sword was described, comparing it to Homer's rendering of Achilles' shield. The marquis' grandfather-in-law, the duc de Noailles, is said to have called it "plus poétique que ruineux." Franklin apparently responded: "cela prouve que chacun a sa façon de voir."[4]

On August 29, below, Lafayette thanked Franklin for the "Noble present." While the marquis was in Austrian captivity during the French Revolution, his wife buried the sword for safekeeping. Although the blade rusted, the handle and mounting survived and were smuggled to him by his son.[5]

I.

[before August 24, 1779]

Liger fourbisseur bijoutier De Mr Le Marquis De Lafayette rue Coquillerre au coin De celle Des vieux augustins pour la legende wich you was to send him for the sword of the Marquis.

II.

a paris ce 24. aoust 1779

Je reconois avoir Receu de Monsieur De franclin La Somme de quatre mil huit cent livres pour payement Dune Epéé Dor a Bataille en Bas Relief Dont quittance   LIGER

3. A French translation by Dumas is at the Library of Congress, and a partial translation, in an unknown hand, at the APS. Dumas' appeared in the Sept. 3 issue of the *Gaz. de Leyde* along with his translation of BF's Aug. 24 letter to Lafayette. Both items also appeared (retranslated into English from the French) in the Sept. 13 supplement of the *General Advertiser, and Morning Intelligencer.* A detailed description and sketches of the sword are in Jules Cloquet, *Souvenirs sur la vie privée du Général Lafayette* (Paris, 1836), pp. 214–23.

4. Métra, *Correspondance secrète*, VIII, 335–6.

5. Cloquet, *Souvenirs*, pp. 213–14.

Bon pour quittance de: 4800 *l.t.*

Endorsed: Liger, Sword Cutler, Receipt. Aug 24 1779 £4800 *l.t.*

III.

[*c.* August 24, 1779]

Madame Brillon is desirous to see the Sword. Be so good as to send it by my Servant.

Addressed: A Monsr Mons Franklin

IV.

[*c.* August 24, 1779]

Description of the Sword given by Congress to the Marquis de la Fayette.

On one Side of the Pommel are the Marquis's Arms, and on the other the Device of a new Moon reflecting Rays of Light on a Country partly cover'd with wood & partly cultivated. Symbol of the Republick of the United States; with this Motto, *Crescam ut prosim.*[6] By this it was intended modestly to express 1. Her present Mediocrity of Strength, as the Light of the Moon tho' considerable, is weaker than that of the Sun.
2. Her Expectation of becoming more Powerful as she increases, and thereby rendering herself more useful to Mankind[7]
3. The Gratitude with which she remembers, that the Light she spreads is principally owing to the kind Aid of a greater Luminary[8] in another Hemisphere.

On the *Bow,* is this Legend: *From the American Congress to the Marquis de la Fayette 1779.*

The Handle is ornamented with two Medallions. In One America represented by a Woman, presenting a Branch of Laurel to a Frenchman. In the Other a Frenchman is treading on a Lyon.

6. "May I grow in order to be useful."
7. Two separate articles in the draft: "2. Her expectation of becoming More Powerful as she increases 3. Her desire of becoming more useful to Mankind."
8. Footnote in text: "The king of France; whose Symbol is the Sun."

On the Guard are Seperately represented, in fine Relieve,
The affair at Gloucester
The Retreat off Rhode Island
The Battle of Monmouth
And the Retreat at Barren Hill.[9]
The Hilt is of Massive Gold. & the Blade two edged.—
Cost 200 Louis.[1]
Made by Liger, Sword Cutler, Rue Coquillierre

Notation: Description of the sword given by Congress to the Marqs de la Fayette

To the Marquis de Lafayette

AL (draft): American Philosophical Society; copies:[2] National Archives, Library of Congress (three); transcript: National Archives

Sir,   Passy, Augt. 24. 1779
    The Congress sensible of your Merit towards the United States, but unable adequately to reward it, determined to present you with a Sword, as a small Mark of their grateful Acknowledgement.—[3] They directed it to be ornamented with suitable Devices. Some of the principal Actions of the War, in which you distinguished yourself by your Bravery & Conduct, are therefore represented upon it. These with a few emblematic Figures all admirably well executed, make its principal Value. By the help of the exquisite Artists France[4] affords I

9. Lafayette's role in these actions is detailed in Louis Gottschalk, *Lafayette Joins the American Army* (Chicago, 1937), pp. 80–2, 186–93, 218–28, 265–6.
    1. Or, 4,800 *l.t.* A critic of the French government claimed it had secretly reimbursed BF 1,000 *l.t.* for the sword: Métra, *Correspondance secrète,* VIII, 413. On Oct. 13 BF paid Liger 216 *l.t.* for two drawings of the sword: Accounts VI and XXIII (XXIII, 21, and XXIX, 3).
    2. The copy at the National Archives and one of those at the Library of Congress is in WTF's hand. One of the other Library of Congress copies is by Dumas, who composed a French translation, the draft of which is at the Library of Congress and a fair copy at the APS.
    3. BF wrote in the margin "See vote," probably referring to the congressional resolution directing him to have the sword made; see *JCC,* XII, 1035.
    4. Replaces "Paris".

find it easy to express every thing, but the Sense we[5] have of your Worth & of our Obligations to you. For this, Figures & even Words are found insufficient.— I therefore only add, that with the most perfect[6] Esteem & Respect, I have the honour to be, Sir,

P.S. My Grandson goes down to Havre with the Sword, and will have the Honour of delivering it unto your Hands.[7]

Marquis de La Fayette.

From Robert Montgomery

ALS: American Philosophical Society

Dear Sir   Alicante 24th August 1779
    I had the honour of writing Your Eccelly. from Madrid advising that I had by the Malicious asertation of a wretch in this place been ordered to return 20 Leagues inland and that I expected to have an Interview next day with the Minester of State,[8] in which I succeeded so well on account of a letter you ware already pleased to write in my favour[9] that he ordered me to return Back to my house Saying he would give the Necessary order to this Governour Respecting my Residence here But on my return yesterday was Surprised to find not only the order promised me by the Count De Florida Blanca, Secretary of State that I should remain peaceably in my Establishment But allso one from the Count De Ricla Secretary of war that I should not only retire inland but not be permited to

5. Originally drafted as "all the world".
6. Replaces "greatest".
7. WTF advanced himself 600 *l.t.* for the trip, which cost 320 *l.t.:* Account XXIII (XXIX, 3); Account VI (XXIII, 21). He was accompanied by Jacques Brillon, who wrote him on Aug. 22 to inquire about the carriage or carriages they would take and indicated they planned to leave on the 24th. APS. On Oct. 28 WTF paid 30 *l.t.* to Maugé for six days' hire of a cabriolet for the journey to Le Havre: Account XXIII.
8. This letter is above, Aug. 12.
9. BF assured Montgomery on Oct. 28, below, that he had requested Ambassador Aranda's interposition on his behalf, but we have no further record of the communication.

Carry on Business during the War. These Extreams has oblidged the Governour to Suspend attending to either orders
till farther Information I find that the order from De Ricla is
in Consequence of the falce Informations given him by the
asesor here mentioned in my Last Respects, And therefore
must again request that your Eccelly: will do me the honour
to write this Minester in my favour, or else the Count de Aranda Embasador at Paris on this Matter that thro' your means
I may be permited to Live quietly with my Family and no
Sacrifice to the Malice of an Irreted bad man. I need not mention to Your Eccelly that even the honour is Concerned in my
being mintained in our rights and Previliges at this Juncture
and as I have always Suported th highest Reputation here as a
Merchant and allso been honoured with an Intimacy with the
Governour, Lieutenant General Dn George Dunant with
General Mace,[1] and the first Spanish Familys in this City, I do
not fear giving a very good account should either of the
Minesters Require a General Information of My Conduct
Since my Establishment in this place, But Very Justly fear that
as they have already made a party Master of it I shall fall a
sacrifice to their Reconciliations if not suported by Your Eccellys Interpassing warmly in my favour, Should you please to
give me any order to Execute I think it will Effectualy secure
my Residence and should it be for any suplys of this Produce
for America shall Execute it at my own Expence and acct if
you think proper and should it be in any other Line either
here or at Madrid you may Depend on my utmost Abilitys
being Exerted in obeying any of your Commands.

Being with the Most Profound Respect Dear Sir Your Eccellys: most obedt. humble Servt   ROBT MONTGOMERY

We have Just Learned but without Circumstances that the
United fleets have gained a Compleat Victory over the English
which if true will Certainly bring us a Peace with Independancy—

Notation: Robt Montgomery

1. Gen. Claudio Mace (1722–1805) had been made a brigadier in
1771: *Enciclopedia Universal Illustrada Europeo-Americana* (80 vols., Madrid,
n.d.–1933).

Certification of Jonathan Williams, Jr.'s Accounts[2]

DS:[3] Yale University Library; copy: Historical Society of Pennsylvania

[August 26, 1779]

I hereby certify that Jonathan Williams junior, late Agent to the Commissioners of the United States at the Court of France, has exhibited before me his Accounts as settled up to the twenty fifth of July 1778, by Joshua Johnson, James Cuming John Nesbitt, and Joseph Gridly Esqrs: Arbitrators appointed for that purpose, the Ballance of which then was nine thousand one hundred and ten Livres, nineteen Sols, and six deniers, and is regularly carried forward to the Credit of the said Commissioners in the said Williams's subsequent Account, he being then under further Engagements. I also certify that the said Williams has exhibited before me his said subsequent Account, with Vouchers for every Charge, which I have carefully examined and do approve. I further Certify, that I have received from the said Williams, the Sum of two thousand and sixty Livres, one Sol, and seven Deniers, being the Ballance of his Account in full of all Demands.

IN TESTIMONY whereof, I have signed four Certificates, all of this Tenor and Date.

At Passy, near Paris, this 26th Day of August 1779.

B FRANKLIN
Minister Plenipotentiary, from the United States at the Court of France./.

---

2. The Gentlemen appointed to examine jw's accounts had approved and signed them on Aug. 17. On that same day, jw thanked them as a group for their "Justice and Impartiality," and wrote a separate letter to Cuming and Nesbitt saying that he had asked BF to see to reimbursing their expenses in coming from Lorient. Both letters, and a copy of jw's approved accounts, are in the Yale University Library.

jw himself was in Lorient on Aug. 21 (the last day of the summer on which his letterbook records any activity) and from there proceeded to Passy. Once he had laid his accounts before BF, he presumably turned his attention to preparations for his marriage on Sept. 12. After the wedding he lived at the Alexander's estate in St.-Germain until mid-October, when the couple returned to Nantes.

3. In WTF's hand.

Notation: Certificate from Dr Franklin relative to settlement of my Accounts.

List of Articles Purchased by Fizeaux, Grand & Cie. on Franklin's Orders

D: Library of Congress[4]

⟨Amsterdam, August 26, 1779: The articles in question, to be purchased in Holland and delivered to Nantes by *La Ville de Bordeaux,* Capt. Claas, are thirteen in number. Eleven of them call for pharmaceuticals, two for textiles. The pharmaceuticals comprise large quantities of hipoquana root and jalap (both purgatives), sublimated sulphur (*fleur de soufre*), *pannacea mere,* opium, two kinds of rhubarb, two kinds of quinine, and re-fined camphor. The textiles are divided between Osnabrück linen and sail cloth. The total cost, including the extras, amounts to 2810 *banco florins.*⟩

To Charles Epp[5]

Copy: Library of Congress

Sir   Passy Augt. 27. 1779

I received the Letter you did me the honour to write to me concerning your Inclination to remove to America. In so great a Country as is at present possess'd by the thriteen United States extending through Such different Climates, and having such a variety of soils and Situations there is no doubt but you might if you were there, find one to your Mind. Lands in gen-eral are cheap there, compared with the Prices in Europe. The air is good, there are good Governments, good Laws, and good People to live with. And as you would probably make a good Citizen, there is no doubt of your meeting with a Wel-come among them. But since you are in easy Circumstances

---

4. The document, in the Silas Deane Papers, consists of two slightly variant copies of the same account.

5. In answer to his of July 12, discussed in our headnote to the would-be emigrants: from ———— Vigneron, July 4. BF enclosed the present letter in his reply to Gresslang (quoted in our annotation of Vigneron's letter), Epp's countryman who had several times written on his behalf.

where you are, and there is no immediate Necessity for your Removing, I cannot advise ycur making Such a Voyage with a family in this time, when if taken by the Enemy, you might be Subject to Many Inconveniences. I have the honour to be Sir Your most obedient & humble servant   BF

Mr. Charles Epp, Procureur at Altdorff in Swisserland

From William Bingham   ALS: American Philosophical Society

Sir!   St Pierre M/que August 28th 1779
    The Departure of the Troops that were embarked at St Lu-cie & intended for Georgia, is now postponed, & they are retained at St Christophers & Antigua for the Defence of those valuable Islands—[6]
    There have been no Accounts received from Mons D'Esta-ing for upwards of a Month past, which convinces me that he is engaged on an Expedition to Georgia, where he will have an Opportunity of rendering most essential Services to the common Cause.[7]
    I am the more inclined to think that he has undertaken this Enterprize, as the prospect of succeeding is almost certain, & as during the Hurricane Months the Danger of cruizing in these Seas is so great, that he would be compelled to lay up his Ships in Fort Royal Bay & remain inactive.
    In the Course of a Correspondence that I have had the honor of holding with him on the Subject of affording us As-sistance, with some Ships of the Line, to cooperate with our Army in Georgia, he always expressed an eager Desire of ren-

6. The garrison at St. Christopher's was shielded there by Byron's fleet when d'Estaing appeared off the island on July 21. After failing to lure Byron to sea, d'Estaing sailed to Cap-Français on the north coast of St. Domingue: W.M. James, *The British Navy in Adversity: a Study of the War of American Independence* (London, 1926), p. 154; Jacques Michel, *La Vie aventureuse et mouvementée de Charles-Henri, comte d'Estaing* (n.p., 1976), pp. 217–18.

7. D'Estaing sailed for Georgia on Aug. 16 with some twenty ships of the line and some 4,000 troops in response to appeals from Gov. Rutledge of South Carolina, Gen. Lincoln, Minister Gérard, and others: Dull, *French Navy,* p. 161; Michel, *Vie aventureuse,* pp. 222–3.

dering us that Service, as soon as any favorable opportunity might present, or a Change of Circumstances make it prudent;—for he had at that time a force far inferior to that of the English & he knew that Admiral Byron had received positive orders not to lose Sight of him— Several fortunate Occurrences have Since happened, which have brought about a Junction; the most favorable we could wish, for the Execution of Such a Design— Admiral Byron finding that the french Fleet had taken its Departure, has gone in quest of it, having lately received a Reinforcement of three Ships of the Line—[8] Perhaps he may steer his Course towards New York, imagining that Count D'Estaing may have taken that Route in order to intercept the Reinforcements that are expected to arrive there under the Convoy of Admiral Arbuthnot—[9]

If he once gets Possesion of Port Royal, [South Carolina] he may take or destroy all the British Fleet that is there collected, & bid defiance to the whole British Navy, as it is a very safe Harbor, & as no Ships can cruize in the Neighbourhood of it, from the Impetuosity of the Gulf Stream, which is there very violent— He has 3000 Regular Troops on board; which, united with the American Forces, will be able to compel the British Army to Surrender, especially when they find all hopes of a Retreat cut off—

They made an Attack upon Charlestown, but were repulsed with considerable Loss, & intended to remain inactive untill the Arrival of fresh Reinforcements—

I hope the recent & Splendid Success of our allies, joined to the Declaration of Spain, & the favorable Disposition of the other Powers of Europe, may raise the drooping Spirits of the Americans, & unite them Steadily & inseparably to use all their Efforts to take Advantage of the present critical Moment, & put a finishing Stroke to the War.—

I am sorry to find by the last Letters from America, that a Discussion & a Party Spirit have entered into the great Coun-

8. Byron sailed for England with four ships of the line on Aug. 23: James, *British Navy in Adversity*, p. 154; Dull, *French Navy*, p. 162n.

9. Adm. Marriott Arbuthnot's convoy with its 3,800 troops (XXIX, 476n) reached New York only on Aug. 24; John A. Tilley, *The British Navy and the American Revolution* (Columbia, S.C., 1987), pp. 165–6.

cil of the Nation, which retards the Decision of the most important Business, & when decided on, opposes its Execution—

Our Enemies derive greater Advantages from our internal Decisions, & are more encouraged by them in the Continuation of the War, than by any Success they can expect from their military Efforts & Enterprizes—

The Depreciation of the Currency is another Circumstance of a most alarming Nature, which Seems to be progressive, & to increase in proportion to the Duration of the War, & the Consequent Necessity of uttering new Emissions of Paper Money—

Besides the Ruin it has involved thousands in, whose fortunes were made off of that precarious Article, it encourages Monopolies, throws a damp upon the Spirit of foreign Speculations, & occasions general Murmurs & Discontents; Many Adventurers have found from dear bought Experience, that notwithstanding the flattering Appearances of an immense Gain on the sales of Merchandize received in America, their Profits were merely nominal;— for the Proceeds of Sales laying a twelvemonth exposed to the unfavorable vecissitudes that have hitherto attended the declining State of our Paper Currency, have so decreased in Value, that they would not, if realized in Solid Coin, or good Bills of Exchange, nett the Amount of their first Cost— Altho there cannot be a Shadow of a Doubt in regard to the favorable Issue of this War, yet it is greatly to be lamented, that America will have to struggle under various Difficulties, that might perhaps have been obviated by a Continuation of the same public Spirit & disinterested Patriotism that distinguished the Infancy of this Contest.

I shall do myself the honor of continuing to communicate to you from time to time the various & interesting Occurrences that may take place in this Quarter—

I have the Honor to be with perfect Respect Your Excellency's most obedient & very humble servant   Wᴍ Bɪɴɢʜᴀᴍ

Septr. 6th
ᴘ.s. From Some late Accounts received from St Eustatia, there is Some reason to doubt that Admiral has left these Seas— A

Captain of a Dutch Ship that has arrived there having deposed that he met with the English fleet on the 17 Ulto: eight Leagues to Windward of Antigua

Notation: Bingham 28. Augt. 1779.

From the Marquis d'Amezaga

AL: American Philosophical Society

Paris ce 29 aoust. [1779]

Mr. D'amezaga fait ses très humble compliment a Monsieur de franklin, et luy fait demander sil dinne chés luy aujourd'huy dimanche, et au cas qu'il n'y dinne Pas S'il vouloit venir dinner demain lundi chés Mr. amelot á Paris.

From John Bondfield

ALS: American Philosophical Society

Sir   Bordeaux 29 Aug 1779

By Letters from Lisbon of the 3 Instt. we are advised of the Capture of one of our Ships (that went with La Motte Piquet) with Military Stores and sent into New York.[1] The fate of the other two is not yet come to hand. A continued chain of Miscarriages have attended every Operation in which I have stood Interested. Could predestinarism Exist I should be tempted to place faith or had I been an object sufficient to attract as in past days the resentment of some Deity there would be latitude to invoke the oposing power [*torn: word or words missing*]. We are without any American advices by Letters from Cadiz they confirm the report of Provosts defeat and say Packets are arrived at that Port from Congress for you[2] if

1. Bondfield and two business associates had chartered the *Chasseur* (*Hunter*), *Governor Livingston,* and *Mary Fearon* to Arthur Lee to carry military supplies to Virginia: XXIX, 330n. The *Chasseur* was captured on the way to America by a British letter of marque (*Courier de L'Europe,* VI [1779], no. XXXIV, Oct. 26, 1779) but the other two arrived safely.

2. Congress had recently sent at least one letter to France through Cadiz. On June 13, Lovell wrote Arthur Lee via Cadiz (with a copy going via Martinique): Smith, *Letters,* XIII, 62–3. On the same day, however, he sent a packet to BF via Martinique only: XXIX, 683.

real you are 'ere this in Posession of them. I have the Honor to be with due respect Sir Your very hhb Servant

JOHN BONDFIELD

His Excellency B. Franklin Esq

Addressed: His Excellency B. Franklin / Minist Plenip. des Etats Unies / a Paris

Notation: John Bondfield Bordeaux 29. aout 1779.

From the Marquis de Lafayette: Two Letters

(I) ALS: American Philosophical Society; copies: Library of Congress, National Archives;[3] transcript: National Archives; (II) ALS: American Philosophical Society

I.

Sir   At the havre 29th August 1779
Whatever Expectations Might have been Rais'd from the Sense of past favors, the Goodness of the United States for me has ever been such, that on every occasion it far surpasses any idea I could have conceiv'd— A new proof of that flattering truth, I find in the Noble present which Congress have been pleas'd to honor me with, and which is offered in such A Manner By Your excellency, as will exceed Any thing, But the feelings of My unbounded Gratitude— Some of the devices I Can't help finding too honorable A Reward for those slight services which in Concert with My fellow soldiers, and under the God like American hero's orders, I had the Good luck to Render— The sight of those Actions where I was a witness of American Bravery and patriotic spirit, I will ever enjoy with that pleasure which Becomes a heart glowing with love for the Nation, and the Most ardent zeal for theyr Glory and happiness.[4]

Assurances of Gratitude which I Beg leave to present to

3. The copy at the Library of Congress is in Dumas' hand, that at the National Archives in WTF's.

4. Lafayette expressed similar pride in a letter to Arthur Lee: *Lee Family Papers,* reel 6, frames 328–30.

Your excellency are much unadequate to My feelings, and nothing But those sentiments May properly acknowledge Your kindness towards me— The polite Manner in which Mr. Franklin was pleas'd to deliver that inestimable sword, lays me under Great obligations to him, and demands my particular thanks.

With the most perfect Respect I have the honor to Be Your excellency's Most obedient humble servant   LAFAYETTE

his excellency Mr. Benjamin franklin Esq.

Notation: Marqs. la Fayette 29. Augt. 79.

II.

My dear sir   At the havre 29th August 1779

After I have pay'd to the Minister from the United States that düe tribute of my Gratitude, which I have the honor to offer him on this occasion, Give me leave to present My friend doctor franklin, with particular and private thanks, for which no expression may adequate the sense I have of Your Goodness— The noble present I have the Honor of Receiving from Congress has been adorned By you with so many flattering attributes, that I have no idea of such a glorious Reward being ever conferr'd By A Nation upon Any soldier, and that Nothing may be added to it, But a much Greater share of Merit on My part, which Might Render Me a More proper objet for so Great an honor— I waïted for Mr. franklin's departure that I Might send Back my answer By that Gentleman, to whose politness I am particularly indebted— There is a great matter, My dear sir, for which I am to Confer with you, and in which your Grandson's feelings are deeply interested— So many preparations have fill'd his heart with a desire of seeing them exerted against the Common Enemy, and he most ardently wish to obtain Your leave for Going to England with us— In Case You are dispos'd to Grant that liberty, I will feel very happy to Render him this Campaign as agreable As May be in My power— You might then, My dear Sir, apply to M de vergennes, and tell him that as an american General officer you would intrust me with an aid de Camp, whose fate is extremely dear to You— The Minister will most Certainly write to Me on the occasion, and also to the count de vaux, or duke of harcourt who Commands at the havre—[5] And if[6] you approuve of mr. franklin's being with me I will Carry him along on any occasion, and he will see as much of the service as myself— Be Certain, My dear sir, that Nothing might please me more than such a mark of your Confidence, and that I will feel very happy in Giving you one of my tender and sincere sentiments.

From the time when Count d'estaing left Martinico I would be Rather induc'd to Believe that he Might have gone to North America— Suppose it was the case, and I had time to go there nothing Could Make me happier than your asking me from the Ministry for to join again American colour.

With the Most sincere affection and perfect Regard I have the honor to be Dear sir Your most obedient humble servant

LAFAYETTE

I leave to mr. franklin the Care of speaking to you of our present situation, and on any other point Relating to amer-ica— He will also tell you what immense effect the Noble present from Congress has made in the army.

Notation: Lafayette Au havre 29. Aout 1779.

From Francis Coffyn   ALS: American Philosophical Society

Hond. Sir   Dunkerque 30th. Augt.[7] 1779.

Since the last letter I had the honour to write Your Excellency, on the 12th. inst, I am deprived of your Excellency's favours.

In the instructions delivered to Capn. Marchant of the black Prince privateer (for which your Excellency was pleased to

5. The comte de Vaux commanded the entire expeditionary force, the duc d'Harcourt one of its four divisions: Patterson, *The Other Armada,* pp. 151–2.

6. BF added above the line, "M. de Vergennes &". WTF prepared an extract of the part of the letter, including his grandfather's addition, that concerned him. BF sent it to Vergennes on Aug. 31, below.

7. Coffyn had written "July"; BF corrected it to "Augt".

grant a Commission,) is mentioned arte. 3d.—that the trial of the prizes made on the Ennemy by the American Ships of war, which may be carry'd into the ports of France or Spain, shall be Submitted to the Courts there instituted to determine Such causes.[8]

On the 23d. June Said privateer carry'd into Morlaix an English brig call'd the good will, and landed the hostage of a vessell he ransomed. On the 24th. of July the Same privateer conducted into the Same port another brig call'd the Dublin, and landed 12 hostages for the Same number of vessells he ransomed, the particulars of which I had the honour to send to your Excellency by my letter of 2d. inst.[9] The prisoners on board Said prizes, & the hostages have been Examined by the officers of the Admiralty at Morlaix and the process's have been instructed in the Same manner & form as is practised with the prizes taken by the French ships of war, and the papers respecting Sd. prizes have been Sent to Mr. De Grandbourg Secretary general of the marine Department in order that the *Conseil des prises* should pronounce their condemnation, to the forwarding of which Mr. Torris owner of said privateer wrote to Mr. Bigot, Greffier or Clark of said Court, in order that he might be enabled to sell the prizes & recover the ransoms; but by the answer he received from this Gentleman, it appears that Sd. Tribunal has no orders to Judge the American prizes, and that the papers have been Sent to M. De Sartine. This induced M. Torris to write to the Minister on the 11th. of this month, but as he has not yet received any answer, and the officers of the Admiralty at Morlaix refusing to sell the prizes before they receive the condemnation, Mr. Torris desired me by a letter he wrote me the 27th. inst. (which I take the liberty to inclose with a copy of that he address'd to M. De Sartine) to represent to Your Excellency that there are Several perishable articles on board said prizes, which may be Exposed to a total loss if the sale suffers a longer delay, & to request your Excellency to pronounce the condemnation of said prizes, or to mention what steps may be taken to obtain

8. For Marchant's instructions see XXIX, 496n, 687.
9. Missing.

leave to Sell them.[1] I further understand that the owners in England of the vessells which have been ransomed by said privateer, are unwilling to discharge the bonds & redeem the hostages, before a regular condemnation is pass'd over them as lawfull prizes. Its the more necessary that this matter should be brought into its proper channell, as it seems that this adventurer causes great interruption to the Ennemys Trade, by letters the owners received last night from Brest, they are advised that he put again into that port, after a weeks cruize, with Eight Hostages on board, for the Same number of English vessells he ransomed, the particulars of which are not mentioned. These Successes have determined the proprietors to fitt out an other Cutter of 60 feet keel, & 20 feet beam mounting 16. three pounders 24 Swivels & small arms with 65 men, all Americans & Irish under the command of Capn. Edward Macarter of Boston; this Cutter will be call'd the black Princess, and is intended to cruize in Company with the black Prince.[2] The owners have again apply'd to me, to request Your Excellency to grant them a Commission. If Your Excellency thinks proper to comply with their request, I shall conform to Your Excellencys orders and intentions, respecting the instructions, and oath of allegiance to the united States to be taken by Capn. Macarter his officers & Crew, a formula of which I beg Your Excellency to send me, as I did not keep a copy of that taken by Capn. Marchant. Interim I here inclose an acknowledgement Sign'd by three prisonners he Set at liberty under their promise of obtaining the Exchange of the same number of Americains.[3] If these two privateers cruize

1. Torris' Aug. 27 letter to Coffyn and his Aug. 11 letter to Sartine are at the APS; the latter is quoted in Clark, *Ben Franklin's Privateers,* pp. 58–9. Sartine promptly communicated with BF on the subject; see BF's Aug. 14 reply. BF had already been warned that the cargoes would spoil if the prizes were not condemned: Diot to BF, July 28.

2. The prospective captain was Edward Macatter, Luke Ryan's fellow Irish smuggler: Clark, *Ben Franklin's Privateers,* pp. 5, 61.

3. Four such certificates, signed within a few days of one another, are now at the APS. One, dated July 18 and endorsed, "No 1.," was signed by John Trick, captain of the *Union,* and two other men. The second, endorsed, "No 2.," was signed on July 16 by Nicholas Randle and two fellow residents of Clovelly, Devonshire. The third and fourth were signed on July 17, one

together as intended, I hope they'll be able to keep all their prisonners on board, which the former could not do on account of the Smalness of his vessell. I beg the favour of your Excellency's answer as Soon as convenient, interim I have the honour to remain with due respect. Your Excellency's Most obedient & most devoted humble Servant   FRANS. COFFYN

The papers concerning Capn Cunningham's people, will be Sent to your Excellency by my next.

Mr. Torris also requested me to send the Copy of a letter he wrote your Excellency on the 9th. inst. which he apprehends miscarry'd.

To his Excellency Dr. Bn. Franklin at Passy.

Notation: Mr. Coffin Augt. 30.1779

From ——— Rattier with Chaumont's Draft of a Reply

ALS: American Philosophical Society

Monsieur   a Tours le 30 Août 1779

Quatre Prisoniers de Guerre Anglois, qui sont a Tours sur leur Parole m'engagent de Vous faire part du desir qu'ils ont de passer au Service des Etats unis de l'Amerique, Deux en qualité de Capitaines de Prises, et les Deux autres en qualité de Volontaires.

Si cette affaire peut avoir lieu, je Vous prie Monsieur de me faire connoitre la marche que je dois tenir.

Ces Prisoniers etoient cy devant Sur des Vaisseaux Anglois Corsaires ou Marchands.

Je suis bien flatté de trouver cette occasion de Vous assurer des sentiments d'estime dont je Suis penetré pour Vous, Monsieur; Sentiments que je partage avec toute la France.

J'ay l'honneur d'être connu de M Le Ray De Chaumont, et d'être lié intimement avec Mrs Montaudc in freres de Nantes.

---

by George Lowder, owner of the sloop *John,* along with the sloop's captain and master; the other by Henry Eastaway, captain of the *Rebecca,* and his "boy."

274

Je suis avec un profond Respect Monsieur Votre tres humble et tres obeissant Serviteur

RATTIER
Receveur de la Ville et Commissaire des Prisoniers de Guerre Anglois

Notation in Chaumont's hand:

Monsieur

Je ne peux accepter la proposition que quatre prisonniers anglais vous ont Chargés de me faire de leur services pour les Etats unis d'amerique afin d'estre Employés a Commander des prises,[4] il est prudent de Se Mefier de pareils offres de la part des anglais.

J'ay l'honneur d'estre très parfaittement Monsieur[5]

Notation: Rattier Tours 30. aout 1779.

To Gérard de Rayneval

LS:[6] Archives du Ministère des affaires étrangères; copy: Library of Congress

Sir,   Passy Augt 31. 1779.

I received Yesterday Evening, in good Order the Packet you were so obliging as to send me, & which had been missing.[7] I am sorry you have had any Uneasiness about it. I received

---

4. Here he crossed out, "ayant deja fait la triste Experience", a possible allusion to the Job Prince episode related in vol. 28.

5. Chaumont penned a fair copy of this reply which is now at the APS. Dated Aug. 5 (by which he must have meant Sept. 5), it is unsigned and bears WTF's notation: "Not certain whether the Letter was sent."

A letter among BF's papers at the APS makes it clear that these prisoners were not Englishmen at all. H. Touzel, writing from Tours in fluent French to "Monsieur frankling" on Sept. 10, begs BF to allow him and his three companions to join a friend who sails with Capt. Thompson on the *Drake*. They are ready to die for the American cause; a reply should be directed to Mr. Rattier.

6. In WTF's hand.

7. BF apparently had used Ferdinand Grand to tell Rayneval a certain packet had not arrived; an Aug. 29 apology from Rayneval to Grand is among BF's papers at the APS.

also by the Hands of M. De Chaumont the Packet directed to Mr. Adams.

With great Esteem, I have the honour to be Sir, Your most obedient & most humble Servant B Franklin

M. Gerard de Raynevalle.

To Vergennes

ʟs:[8] Archives du Ministère des affaires étrangères; copy: Library of Congress

Sir,   Passy August 31. 1779.
I have just received from M. De la Fayette a Letter, containing the Paragraph, a Copy of which I enclose[9] praying your Excellency to cast an Eye on it. If you should not disapprove the Proposition it contains in favour of my Grandson, I am willing he should embrace this Opportunity of improving himself, in seeing the excellent Discipline of the Armies of France, hoping he will thereby be render'd more capable of serving his Country & our Common Cause.[1] With the greatest Respect, I am ever, Your Excellency's most obedient & most humble Servant.   B. Franklin

M. le Comte de Vergennes.

8. In WTF's hand.

9. An extract from the second of Lafayette's Aug. 29 letters.

1. On Sept. 1 Vergennes forwarded BF's request to the war minister, the prince de Montbarey, asking him to send the necessary orders as soon as possible, provided he agreed (AAE). The next day Montbarey personally wrote WTF that the king had approved his embarkation at Le Havre with the expeditionary force and given him permission to wear the uniform of an aide-de-camp (APS). Lafayette sent congratulations on the 7th and agreed that WTF could wait to report until after JW's marriage (for which see our headnote to William Alexander's letter of Sept. 8). By mid-month, however, d'Orvilliers' fleet had returned to Brest and Lafayette had to inform WTF that the invasion had been postponed: Idzerda, *Lafayette Papers*, II, 306–9, 310–11.

Certificate for a Georgia Lieutenant

AD (draft): American Philosophical Society

[August 31, 1779]

I do hereby certify whom it may concern, that to my Knowledge M. —— was a Lieutenant in the —— Regiment of Georgia in the Service of the United States of America, and had a regular Commission of the Congress appointing him to that Office, which I understand he lost when he was unfortunately taken by the English. Esteeming him a young Gentleman of Merit, I willingly give him this Certificate, to serve as there may be Occasion. At Passy, this thirty first Day of August, 1779.

From Jean-Baptiste Le Roy

AL: American Philosophical Society

Dear Doctor   Tuesday morning [August 31, 1779][2]

I hope you wille excuse me if I do not accept of your good offer and go along with you to the Société de Médecine but I have so many things to do before to morrow that I go to the academy that I have thought it best to stay here the afternoon but I hope nevertheless you will do us the honour to come and take a dish of tea with us at your return and we shall have

2. Dated by a number of clues. The Société royale de médecine met on Tuesday, Aug. 31; see Vicq d'Azyr's letter of Aug. 21. The Académie des sciences met bi-weekly, on Wednesdays and Saturdays. In this letter Le Roy implies that he will be making a presentation at the next day's meeting. The presentation may have been postponed one session; the following Saturday, Sept. 4, he reported to the Académie on his dispute with the abbé Rochon over the lightning rods at the château de la Muette, in Passy, where the abbé was *garde du cabinet de physique et d'optique du roi*. It was decided that a committee of five, BF among them, would make an on-site inspection and settle the dispute. *Procès-verbaux*, XCVIII, 276. The third clue, which argues for the summer of 1779, is the word "circonspection," a reference to "The Morals of Chess" which BF had written for his Passy friends at the end of June.

a game or two at chess and I will endeavour if possible not to play so fast and with so little *circonspection*.[3]

Addressed: M Le Dr Franklin

Franklin and Madame Helvétius: An Exchange through Cabanis

(I) Reprinted from *Curious and Facetious Letters of Benjamin Franklin Hitherto Unpublished* (privately printed, 1898), 15–16; (II) L: American Philosophical Society

Since the following two letters are undated, we can do no more than guess that they might answer each other and belong to the early stage of friendship during which the Doctor and the widow corresponded rather coyly through her permanent house guest and secretary, Pierre-Jean-Georges Cabanis. Franklin's message is addressed to him; the lady's answer, if such it is, is in his hand. This could place both documents in 1779, more precisely in the summer because of the "nuits claires" mentioned in II. The allusion in I to the "4 Mesdames Helvétius" must be an inside joke; Mme Helvétius had two married daughters, and her granddaughters were in their infancy.

I.

A Passy, Dimanche matin. [August or September, 1779?]

M. Franklin étant levé, lavé, rasé, peigné, beautifié à son mieux, tout habillé & sur le point de sortir, avec sa tête pleine des 4 Mesdames Helvétius, & des doux Baisers qu'il propose de leur dérober, est bien mortifié de trouver la Possibilité de cette Félicité remise à Dimanche prochain. Il prendra autant qu'il peut de Patience, espérant de voir une de ces Dames chez

3. Another Le Roy letter, dated simply "mardy matin," may well belong to the summer of 1779. The writer expresses his regrets for having spent so little time in Passy and having enjoyed BF's *voisinage* so little this summer, but he has been kept in Paris by a variety of circumstances. He has not yet located the paper that BF requested but will keep searching through his files. He thanks BF for having returned a number (but not quite all) of his books. APS.

M. de Chaumont le Mercredi. Il sera là à bonne heure, pour la voir entrer avec cette Grace & cette Dignité qui l'ont tant charmé il y a sept Semaines dans le même lieu. Il projette même de l'arrêter là & de la retenir chez lui pour la vie. Les trois autres restantes à l'Auteuil peuvent suffire pour les Serins & les Abbés.

Addressed: A [*deleted:* Madame] Monsieur / Monsieur Cabbanis / chez Made Helvétius / à Auteuil

II.

[August or September, 1779?]

L'aimable lettre que vous mavez Ecrite, mon cher ami, m'a fait sentir encor plus vivement le Regret de n'avoir pu Dîner avec vous mercredy. J'esperais qu'après m'avoir dit de si jolies choses sur le papier, vous viendrez m'en dire de vive voix: je suis bien piquée d'avoir trop esperé; car je vous avoue que j'aime beaucoup les jolies choses, et surtout celles qui me viennent de vous. J'aurai aujourdhuy de vos nouvelles, et je compte qu'on ne m'en donnera que de bonnes de votre douleur D'Epaule. Mais à propos qu'avez-vous fait à cette Epaule? Si C'était par hazard un Rhumatisme gagné sous Les fénétres de quelqu'une de mes Rivales, où vous êtes bien assès jeune pour aller passer Les belles nuits Claires à jouer de La guittare & à soufler dans vos doigts! Songez y bien,[4] je ne vous plaindrais gueres. En tout Cas Ce sera une bonne Leçon pour vous; et je vois mieux tous Les jours combien la jeunesse Legere et inconsidérée en a besoin. Ce qui me Rassure, c'est que Mr. votre fils veille sur vôtre Conduite: et je vous recommande de suivre ses avis.

Adieu, Mon ami, je vous embrasse tendrement, et je vous desire beaucoup.

4. Deleted: "je ne vous pardonnerais pas de souffrir et même".

From David Hartley

Two copies:[5] American Philosophical Society; transcript: Library of Congress

To Dr F   Sept 1. 1779

Yours of August 20th recd. I entirely agree with you in all the Sentiments of humanity wch you express & shall always most heartily concur with you in every endeavour to lessen the Miseries attending the State of war. I will to the best of my power recommend your propositions respecting the most facile & expeditious method of releasing prisoners of war, & when I get any final answer from government here I will transmitt it to you.— I had heard the report wch you mention of Capt. Cunningham but as I now find that he is sent to Plymouth in the common state with the other prisoners I conclude that the report has no real foundation. I will take care to make known the circumstance of his having acted under a Commission together with his conduct towards the prisoners wch he has taken himself.[6] In general I can only say that from the Conversations that I have had with the Commissioners of Sick & Hurt, that I see no reason to expect any thing like butchery in Cold blood.— There is an officer whom I do not personally know Capt Joseph Tathwell of his My's sloop the Swift.[7] I am desired by the board of Sick & Hurt to apply to you upon his account. I understand that he entered into a Parole at Philadelphia to negotiate the exchange of himself & his Crew against Capt. Harris & his Crew. When he came to England he found Capt. Harris exchanged & the Crew taking their turns in Exchange so as to defeat all possible completion of the intended specific bargain viz Capt Tathwell & Crew against Capt Harris & Crew. The request therefore wch I have to transmitt to you is that Captain Tathwell under these circumstances may be considered by you as discharged from his

---

5. We print from the one in Hartley's hand, which he included (along with his of Sept. 18 and Oct. 11) in his second letter of Oct. 26. Digges also made a copy of the three September letters when he copied Hartley's of Oct. 26, below.

6. Here Hartley added in parentheses "I have done this".

7. Tathwell and his crew were captured in late 1778: XXIX, 367n.

Parole. I have nothing farther yet in commission respecting the English & french prisoners.

I am &c   DH:

From the Chevalier de La Luzerne

LS:[8] American Philosophical Society; copy: Archives du Ministère des affaires étrangères

Monsieur   A Boston le I. 7bre I779.

Les connoissances que Vous m'avés procurées à Boston et les directions que j'avois reçues de Vous avant mon depart m'ont été trop utiles pour que je n'aie pas le plus grand empressement de Vous en marquer ma reconnoissance.[9] Les paquets que Vous m'aviés confiés pour cette ville ont été exactement remis à leurs addresses, et j'ai fait parvenir par des voyes sûres à Philadelphie ceux qui y etoient destinés. J'ai trouvé Votre famille Monsieur en très bonne santé et j'en ai reçu toutes sortes de politesses:[1] Vos amis, et ils sont nombreux se sont empressés d'avoir de Vos nouvelles, tout ce qui Vous regarde les interesse et j'ai observé que ceux qui ne Vous connoissent pas personnellement ont encore plus de desir de savoir toutes les particularités relatives à un citoyen qui a aussi bien merité de son pays et je puis ajouter du monde entier. Il m'est bien agreable de les satisfaire et j'ai autant de plaisir à raconter ce qui Vous interesse, qu'on en prend à l'entendre.

Les troupes Americaines continuent à deffendre leur pays avec un zele bien respectable et avec des succès dont Vous avés été sans doute informé. Mr. Clinton retire en ce moment tous ses postes avancés et paroit craindre que Mr. le Cte. d'Estaing ne profite de ses avantages pour detacher quelques vaisseaux

8. The complimentary close is in La Luzerne's hand.

9. BF had written a number of letters introducing the new French minister plenipotentiary, now traveling to Philadelphia via Boston: XXIX, 601–2, 606, 609–10, 621, 623, 624. We have no record, however, of his directions to La Luzerne.

1. Presumably a reference to BF's nephew Jonathan Williams, Sr., as no closer member of BF's family was in Boston; the Baches were in Philadelphia, his estranged son in N.Y., and his sister in Warwick, R.I.

de Sa Flotte contre Newyork.[2] Ce Général Anglois a perdu 1200. hommes que les Americains ont fait prisonniers en differentes affaires, qui se sont passées depuis mon arrivée ici. Les Americains ne peuvent ressentir plus de joye que moi de ces succès. Le desavantage de Penobscut se trouve amplement compensé par la prise de 10. Vaisseaux de la Flotte de la Jamaique.[3] J'ai eu le plaisir de les voir entrer dans votre port et ce n'est qu'une continuation de l'ascendant des armateurs americains sur les Anglois. On evalue à 3. millions Sterling les prises qu'ils ont faites depuis 3. ans.

Donnés moi de Vos nouvelles, Monsieur, je les desire pour moi même; mais il ne me sera pas moins agreable de pouvoir en donner à Vos compatriotes; c'est un moyen de leur plaire que de pouvoir leur dire que Vous jouissés d'une bonne santé et que Vous serés en etat de servir Votre patrie pendant de longues années./.

M. de Marbois[4] vous prie d'aggréer les assurances de son respect: nous avons resisté l'un et l'autre à une traversée qu'on peut apeller malheureuse eu egard au nombre de malades et de morts que nous avons eus.[5] Voulés vous bien aussi, Monsieur, faire nos complimens à M. votre petit fils. Jai l'honneur detre avec un tres sincere et parfait attachement Monsieur votre tres humble et tres obeissant serviteur

LE CHR DE LA LUZERNE

Notation: Chev. de la Luzerne

2. On Aug. 25 Gen. Clinton had learned that the fleet was en route to America, but he did not know its destination: John A. Tilley, *The British Navy and the American Revolution* (Columbia, S.C., 1987), p. 170; Willcox, *Portrait of a General,* pp. 289–92.

3. Taken by the *Providence, Queen of France,* and *Ranger.*

4. François Barbé de Marbois, La Luzerne's secretary of legation.

5. Accounts of the *Sensible's* voyage to America are provided in Butterfield, *John Adams Diary,* II, 381–400, and Eugene P. Chase, ed., *Our Revolutionary Forefathers: The Letters of François, Marquis de Barbé-Marbois* . . . (New York, 1929), pp. 39–64.

From William Lee

ALS: American Philosophical Society; copy:[6] Virginia Historical Society

Sir.   Frankfort Sept. 1st. 1779.

I have not had the Honor of receiving any Letter from you for some time past, & as by your last Letter in June[7] you seem'd desirous of declining to make any farther application to the Ministers of his Most Christian Majesty for the Arms, Artillery & Ammunition on account of the State of Virginia, as I requested the favor of you to do in March last; I presume those articles have not been obtain'd:[8] I am now therefore to desire that you will decline taking any farther steps in that business in consequence of my application.[9]

I have the Honor to be with the highest Respect and Consideration Sir Your most Obedient and Most Humble Servant

W: LEE

Honorable Benjamin Franklin Esqr.

6. In Lee's hand with a note, "N.B. The above inclosed with a note to Mr. Grand at Paris desirg. him to have it safely deliver'd."

7. XXIX, 688–9.

8. BF in fact had recently renewed his request for arms for Virginia and Maryland: to Gérard de Rayneval, above, Aug. 10. For Lee's request see XXIX, 231, 249–50.

9. Lee had learned from private correspondence that Congress had revoked his commission to Prussia and the Holy Roman Empire. He informed Gov. Thomas Jefferson that he expected to return to Virginia and summarized his services to his native state: *Jefferson Papers,* III, 90–3. He did not return to America, however, until September, 1783: *DAB.*

Franklin and Chaumont to Dumas[1]

ALS: Pierpont Morgan Library; copy:[2] National Archives

Passi ce 2 7bre. 1779.

Du 2. 7bre. 1779

Notte pour Monsieur Dumas agent du Congres des etats unis d'amerique et pour Luy Seul:

Je prie Monsieur Dumas de Se Rendre incessament a amsterdam pour Rendre tous les Services qui pouront dependre de luy a unne Escadre Sous Le Commandement de M. Jones portant pavillon americain qui doit Se Rendre au texel.

Les Vx. qui Composent Cette Escadre Sont[3]

Il est essentiel que M. Dumas Exige des Commandans de Ces vaisseaux La plus grande Circonspection pour ne pas offenser Les hollandois et ne donner Sujet a aucune plainte.

Si Cette Escadre a Bezoing de quelques Rafraichissemens ou Secours, M. Dumas voudra bien S'adresser a M. Jean de Neuville pour les procurer.

Aussitost L'arrivée de la ditte Escadre Je prie M. Dumas de m'en prevenir pour que Je prenne Les Mezures Necessaires pour envoyer aux américains Les Secours dont ils peuvent

1. As Chaumont was the liaison between Sartine and Jones, the French naval minister was probably involved in preparing these orders. On the following day BF and Vergennes furnished passports for Dumas; certified copies of them in Dumas' hand are at the National Archives. BF's, in French, was good for six months and was countersigned by JW on behalf of WTF.

2. In Dumas' hand and attested by him to be a true copy. He made a paraphrase of this letter and sent it to Jones on Oct. 9: Bradford, *Jones Papers*, reel 4, no. 763.

3. Here he made a table of the vessels of the squadron: the *Bonhomme Richard* (Capt. Jones), 42; the *Alliance* (Capt. Landais), 36; the *Pallas* (Capt. Cottineau), 30; the *Cerf* (Capt. Varage), 18; the *Vengeance* (Capt. Ricot), 12; the *Monsieur*, 40; the *Grandville*, 12; and the *Mifflin*, 22. For the first five vessels and their captains see XXIX, 493n. The American privateer *General Mifflin* did not accompany the squadron even though according to a July 21 letter from JW to Schweighauser (APS) she was nearby at Paimboeuf, downriver from Nantes. By the beginning of September the French privateers *Monsieur* and *Grandville* had parted company from the squadron and the cutter *Cerf* had inadvertently become separated from it: Jones to BF, Oct. 3, below.

284

avoir Bezoing; Sans quil puisse estre question d'aucun objet qui puisse mettre les hollandois en Contradiction avec les Menagements qu'ils Croyent devoir observer avec les anglais.

LERAY DE CHAUMONT.

Approuvé, B FRANKLIN

From the Abbé Nolin[4]

ALS: American Philosophical Society

Monsieur   A Versailles le 2 7bre. [1779]

J'ai reçu il y à trois semaines une Lettre de Mr. Gérard avec un cathalogue de Plants quil m'envoyoit. La datte de sa Lettre est du 3 décembre 1778. Le 26 Juillet dernier J'ai recu une autre Lettre avec des cathalogues d'arbres et graines, la datte de cette derniere Lettre est de Philadelphie le 28 mars 1779.

Ces deux Lettres m'ont été Envoyées des Bureaux de Mr. le Cte. de Vergennes. Comme il n'est point fait mention dans les Lettres de M. Gérard du nom des Vaisseaux par lesquels il ma fait les envois, je n'ai fait que des démarches Inutiles pour en avoir des nouvelles, on na pu me dire chez M. de Vergennes par quels Vaisseaux sont arrivées ces deux Lettres.

Je recois dans le moment une autre Lettre de M. Gérard dattée de Philadelphie le 6 Juillet 1779 par laquelle il me marque quil a fait charger sur le navire le Victorieux Capitaine Sapet, des caisses de Plants. C'est la premiere fois quil m'a annoncé le nom du capitaine chargé de ses Envois. M. de Renneval ma assuré que personne ne pouvoit mieux que vous me faire Instruire par vos Bureaux dans quels Ports les Navires americains arrivent.

Si ce n'est pas abuser de votre complaisance Je Vous serois Infiniment obligé de Vouloir bien en faire donner la notte à la Personne qui aura l'honneur de vous remettre ma Lettre. Il y a tout à Craindre que les Plants annoncés ne soyent perdus si on tarde à les reclamer.

J'ai déja payé 2168 *l.t.* pour les Envois qu'on ma fait d'Amérique et Je n'en ai reçu que deux fort médiocres que le

---

4. An agricultural specialist, the abbé was particularly interested in exotic plants and ran a royal nursery specializing in foreign trees and shrubs. He had published in 1755 an *Essai sur l'agriculture moderne*. Larousse.

hazard m'a procuré. Dans des temps plus tranquiles nous serons plus heureux.

J'ai L'honneur d'Etre avec Respect de Votre Excellence Le
trés humble & trés obéissant serviteur

> L'ABBÉ NOLIN
> Directeur gal des pepinieres du Roy
> au Roule. fg st. honoré

Notation: L'abbé Nolin Versailles 2. 7bre.

From Samuel Smith

ALS: American Philosophical Society

Sir,   Nantes Sepre: 2nd: 1779

I take the Liberty to trouble you with a few Lines, which
hope you'll excuse, on seeing the immediate Necessity of my
writing—

I embark'd from Philada: for France & was unfortunately
taken, haveing at the same Time with me a Sum, in Loan
Interest Bills drawn on the Commissioners for the Thirteen
United States of America at Paris, which was oblidg'd to destroy, they being the first Bills of the setts—[5]

Since my Arrival here I'm inform'd of a Ship from Philada:
called the Mary & Elizabeth[6] being taken with her Mail and
carried to Lisbon, have great Reason to believe that I had Letters with either the 2nd, 3rd: or 4th: Bills inclosed to me on
board the said Vessell—

Should those People be so dishonest as to present any of
these Bills, it must be under a false signature, as I do here
declare to you, that I have not as yet, receiv'd any of the remaining setts, & must beg of you if any of said Bills have been
already presented & accepted, to stop the payment, but if
none of them have yet appear'd, not to accept them when they

5. Smith, captain of the brig *Kensington,* was carrying packets for James
Lovell: XXIX, 398n.

6. A 14-gun ship commanded by Benjamin Weeks or Wickes of Baltimore: Charles Henry Lincoln, comp., *Naval Records of the American Revolution 1775–1788* (Washington, D.C., 1906), p. 387; Claghorn, *Naval Officers,*
p. 330.

do without advice from me, as those Bills are made payable to me by indorsement from Messrs: Wikoff, Turnbull & Compy. & when I shall receive any of the setts of the said Bills, shall send them forward for your acceptance with a Letter of advice—

If you would please to favour me with an Answer to this Letter by the next Post, it will greatly contribute to the releif of a distress'd mind, & am Sir, with the utmost Respect your most Obedt: & very humb servt   SAML SMITH

The Honourabl: Benjamin Franklin

Notation: Ansd 8 Sept

From Anne-Louise Boivin d'Hardancourt Brillon de Jouy

AL: American Philosophical Society

Mon bon papa,   ce vendredi matin [September 3, 1779][7]

J'ai appris hiér au soir que mr votre fils alloit bientost partir et qu'il étoit aide de camp de mr de la fayétte; ils sont faits l'un et l'autre pour se distinguér et il est juste que votre enfant aille déffendre la libérté que votre sagésse a procuré a l'amérique; mais je vous plains mon bon papa, il en couttera a votre áme d'estre séparé de votre aimable fils dont les soins vous sont utils, et dont l'ésprit vous amuse;[8] si la quallité de votre fille que vous m'avés accordée avéc tant de grace peut me donnér quelques droits pour vous distraire et vous consollér; vous sçavés que mon coeur est tout a vous:/:

Si je ne partois de trés bonne heure pour allér voir ma mére, et réstér avéc elle jusqu'a mardi au soir; j'aurois été prendre le thé aujourd'hui avéc vous; j'espere que vous viendrés mércredi de bonne heure le prendre chés moi; c'est toujours un

7. The first Friday after BF had forwarded to Vergennes Lafayette's proposal to take WTF as an aide-de-camp on his expedition: BF to Vergennes, Aug. 31.

8. Those sentiments were echoed in a letter her husband (just returned from Le Havre) wrote BF on a Monday at 5 P.M., praising him for his "genereuse façon de penser" and assuring him that Lafayette would be delighted. APS.

nouveau plaisir pour moi de passér quelques instants avéc vous:/:

Recevés les respécts de vos petites filles:/:[9]

Addressed: A Monsieur / Monsieur Franklin / [*In another hand:*] A Passy

From Ferdinand Grand: Receipt

DS: American Philosophical Society

Paris le 3 septembre 1779.

J'ai recu de Monsieur Franklin ministre plenipotentiaire des Etats unis de l'amerique Deux mille soixante Livres un sols sept deniers[1]   GRAND

L 2060.1.7 *l.t.*

Endorsed: Mr. Grand's Receipt

From Roger Luscombe

ALS: American Philosophical Society

Honour'd Sir/   Angers September 3d. 1779

I hope you will excuse the Liberty I have taken in sending you those few unpolish'd lines, but as you are the only Person, of Power in France that is appointed by the Independant States of North America, it prompts me to apply to you for your Assistance in getting to America, for I am at present a Prisoner in France, and know of no other method of getting there without applying to you, as I beleive it is in your Power to have me releasd and get me a Passage to America; My reasons for going there are this, My only Friend that I have any Dependance on is a Commander in the Independant Army, which is Major General Horatio Gates my own Cousin[2] he allways

9. Her daughters Cunégonde and Aldegonde.

1. Corroborated by a Sept. 3 entry in BF's private account with Grand (Account XVII: XXVI, 3): "La Remise sur J. Cottin fils & Jauge ... 2060.1.7."

2. Gates's family background and even place of birth are obscure: Paul David Nelson, *General Horatio Gates: a Biography* (Baton Rouge, 1976) pp.

promised to get me a Surgeons Birth in the Army, but since the Disturbances betwixt America and England I have never heard from him, but am Confident if I were in America that he would do every thing in his Power for me; I should have been with him long before this time but it was not in my power so hope for the honour he has done the Independant States that you will give me your Assistance in geting to America with him, and your Petitioner will ever pray for you and take it as the greatest favour that can be conferd on your most Humble Servt. at Command.   ROGER LUSCOMBE

at Angers in the Province of Anjou

Addressed: For / Alexander Frankling Esqr. / Plenipotentary / for the Independant States / of North America / at Passy near Paris

Notation: Roger Luscombe Angers Sept. 3. 79

From Cradock Taylor   ALS: American Philosophical Society

Sir   Aix in Provance Septr. 3th. 1779
    I hope your Excellency will excuse my troubling you with this letter as I think it a favourable Oppertunity of Convincing you that I am no Imposture. Mr. Gregoire (a Merchant of this City who I am perfectly well acquainted with) will do me the Service to acquaint your Excellency that he has always Understood me to be an American & that he has likewise been Informd by the Officers of the Ship I was taken that I was betraed into the British Service. I hope by this time Mr. Frazer has Informed you who I am & that your Excellency will procure me my Liberty which Shall ever be Acknowledged as an Obbligation confered on your Excellencies Most Obbligd. & Obedient Humbl. Sert.   CRADOCK TAYLOR

P.S. Mr. Gregoire has favoured me with the cariage of this letter as he has Businiss at Parris

---

6–8. All we can say of Luscombe is that he appears to be, like Gates, English by birth.

Addressed: To / His Excellency Benjmn. Franklin / Esqr. Plenipotentiary to the / United States of America / Parris

Notation: Cradock Taylor

From François Bordot[3]   ALS: American Philosophical Society

Honorable Sir,   Rochelle, septr: 4. 1779.
    Yesterday evening the frigate Diligente, belonging to Count
DEstaing's fleet, arriv'd in St. Martins Roads, with Express
Dispatches from that Admiral. The Captain, Mr. Duchilo,
came a Shore at 6 o'clock, told the Governor and Commissary
he brought material and welcome News,[4] Recommended to
them an English Prisoner of great Distinction he had on
board, and took Post immediately for Versailles.[5]
    I have the honor to be with all due Respect, Honorable Sir,
Your most obedient and humble servt.   F BORDOT

Notation: Bordot La Rochelle 4e. 7bre. 1779.

From Thomas Digges   ALS: American Philosophical Society

Dr. Sir   Saty. morng 4 Septr. 1779
    I have risqued two letters to you very lately, and having an
oppertunity by private conveyance I repeat to you the substance of them.[6] Mr. Peters's affair has been settled to His wish
as you will see by his inclosd Letter.[7] I am rather surprisd that
my bill forwarded the 9th July had not appeard on the 20th

---

3. Bordot, a former admiralty clerk, had been sending occasional intelligence from La Rochelle since February: XXVIII, 625; XXIX, 611.
    4. D'Estaing selected *capitaine de vaisseau* the comte du Chilleau to bring
the news of the capture of Grenada and the subsequent naval battle:
Amblard-Marie-Raymond-Amédée, vicomte de Noailles, *Marins et soldats
français en Amérique pendant la guerre de l'indépendance des Etats-Unis (1778–
1783)* (Paris, 1903), pp. 82–3.
    5. The prisoner was Lord Macartney, the former governor of Grenada:
ibid., pp. 86–8.
    6. Both are apparently missing. One may be that of the "3d Int." which
he mentions in his letter of Sept. 20, below.
    7. Of Aug. 12, above.

Augt.— but suppose it is at the Bankers unknown to you. There was every care and attention paid to Capt Cu——m immediately on its being known He was in England; He was wrote to three or four times with offers of service but by means of his being shifted about, I fear some of the letters did not reach him, & he might think himself neglected. He was movd from F——th by strong solicitation to P——h among the rest, but during the late alarm, I heard they were movd inland— I hourly expect a line in anr. to mine pointing out what necessarys he may want, & you may be assurd they shall be freely & carefully given him.

You will by this time have read that Capt Hutchins was taken up last Sunday at a frds. house nr. Leatherhead, his papers all seizd, has had three or four close examinations as to accomplices, & himself a close prisoner in New Prison Clerkenwell. His accusation is treasonable correspondencies with Dr. Franklin Mr S. Wharton & other Americans— A Mr. Beasley & a Mr Bundy are said to be his accomplices— it appears the former has been a carrier for him, & it looks as if he had betrayd H——s.[8]

Since these examinations others have been taken up & their papers seizd & examind, particularly a Miss Stafford, and a Clerk of Mr Neaves who it is said lately came from Paris; all Neaves books and papers have been searchd, & they seem to be going onto the seizure of all papers of Persons who appear

8. Digges offers a garbled version of a story that appeared in the London newspapers on Sept. 1. Capt. Thomas Hutchins (x, 210n; xix, 72n), a native of New Jersey and now a captain and engineer in the British army, was arrested in Leatherhead, Surrey. He was apprehended as a consequence of a government investigation of one James Peisley, former keeper of a lottery office in the Strand, who was overheard en route to Ostend boasting of his intimate knowledge of state secrets. Also implicated was Thomas Burdy, identified in the news account as "clerk to a merchant on the French coast." Richard Neave is not mentioned. For additional information see K.G. Davies, ed., *Documents of the American Revolution 1770–1783* (Colonial Office Series, 21 vols., Shannon and Dublin, 1972–81), xvi, 167–8, 243.

On Feb. 27, 1780, Hutchins provided BF with details of his arrest and confinement and requested permission to join the American army. BF forwarded the memorial to Samuel Huntington on March 16. The memorial is at the Yale University Library and BF's covering letter is at the National Archives.

by the above correspondencies to have any connexion or intercourse with the partys, so that every person may suffer whose names have been imprudently used. Two friends of S W in Wimpole and Marybon street[9] may have their papers searchd, from meerly having their names (I mean the former) imprudently mentiond in these correspondencies; which I suppose will turn out to be a meer friendly correspondence between Cap H and Mr W as Countrymen; for in these times I cannot suppose any person imprudent enough to enter into politics, or by mentioning the sailing of fleets, movements of armys, or panickes given at the apprehension of invasion, thereby be supposd to be given information.

I understand Capt H. gives himself up as a lost man & desponds very much of being acquitted, He being in the service & in all likelyhood to be tryd by Court martial. It is said He has confessd to every thing that gives the least appearance upon paper against him—not unlikely from his little acquaintance in these matters and a natural timidity he may have acknowleged too much, & thereby helped his own condemnation. By every accot his examination & papers have not led to that depth of information & the convicting others, that His prosecutors seem to be aiming to obtain. A little blood may be wanting to stop the popular clamour against our Leaders and turn the public conversation from the present gloomy state of affairs in this once great & flourishing Country. It may be necessary for you to give immediate information of this to W, to whom a letter directed in the usual way has no chance whatever of reaching him. I should be very glad to know a proper person at ostend to direct to, and it woud be useful to have your proper address when I inclose to Monr. Grand. From the situation of the two grand fleets (wch. are now said to be both within sight of St. Helens) a grand naval combat may be hourly expected, & the Empire of the Sea decided in favor of one or the other. It is a critical hour for us English-

9. Samuel Wharton's friend and fellow stockjobber Robert Ellison (xxvii, 377n) was a merchant in Marylebone Street: *The London Directory for the Year 1779*, printed by T. Lowndes (London, 1779), p. 53.

men. If there is not a material rumpus or convulsion to prevent it, I will write you by a friend via Holland in a very few
days. I am very truly & sincerely Yours   V.J. BERTRAND

Endorsed: Sept. 4

Notations in different hands: V.J. Bertrand Ostende 4. 7bre. 1779. /
Messieurs fr. Romberg & Comp. a Ostende[1]

From Rudolph Erich Raspe

ALS: American Philosophical Society

Honourd Sir   London. Sept. 4. 1779.
   Since my last of July 27. which I hope came to Your Excellency's hands I have been ever more convinced that the publick as well as my own privat affairs grow worse and worse
from day to day and as I am to speak only of my own concerns
I beg leave to tell Your Excellency that a foreign Nobleman
has almost accomplished my ruin.[2] He engaged me by the fair-
est promises and words to be very liberal with my time to him
ever since November last, nay he prevailed on me even so far
as to go with him on a five months Tour through the King-.
dom. His external appearance and recommendations gave
weight to the fairness of his professions, when I told him I
was accountable to myself for my time and that I had Scarce
any thing to depend upon in this Kingdom but the well earned
fruits of my honest industry. But alas! I have trusted to his

1. Frédéric Romberg & fils, bankers (Lüthy, *Banque protestante,* I, 617), in
care of whom BF instructed Digges to direct letters to Grand: Oct. 7, below.
   2. Baron von Offenburg, Chamberlain to the Duke of Courland in Lith-
uania, employed Raspe as a guide, apparently hoping to use his letters of
recommendation to gain admission to Cambridge society and the art and
manuscript collections of numerous aristocrats. Offenburg claimed to have
paid him fifty guineas as well as travelling expenses. Raspe nevertheless
attempted to press charges against Offenburg. Robert L. Kahn, "Some Unpublished Raspe-Franklin Letters," APS *Proc.,* XCIX (1955), 130n; John
Carswell, *The Prospector. Being the Life and Times of Rudolf Erich Raspe (1737–
1794)* (London, 1950), pp. 123–7; Timothy L.S. Sprigge *et al.,* eds., *The
Correspondence of Jeremy Bentham* (9 vols. to date, 1968-), II, 272n, 389–90.

honour with too much facility, since at our return to Town he has so much underrated and so illiberally taxed my time, my labour and my losses, that I am reduced to the utmost difficulties and that to recover my losses I have no prospect but the visionary hopes of a Law Suit.

Therefore I most humbly beseech Your Excellency to save me from utter ruin and to grant me Your influence and protection on any side of the Sea it may be in Your power usefully to employ my Literary abilities.

I could wish to have some support in France for a couple of months in order to make some enquiries at the Royal Library that bid fair to prove acceptable to the learned; and thence to pass over to America under Your auspices to be employed there in the education of young Gentlemen or in any other branch of business my abilities and circumstances will point out to me or to those, who will please to be my Protectors and Benefactors on Your account; and in consequence of my faithfull attachment, which in particular is Sacred and devoted to Your Virtues by Your Excellency's most obedient humble distressed Servt.[3] R E RASPE.

Addressed: Monsieur / Monsieur B F——— / Passy

From Vergennes

L (draft):[4] Archives du Ministère des affaires étrangères; copy: Library of Congress

A Vlles. le 4. 7br. 1779.

M. l'ambassadeur de Suède,[5] M, vient de m'addresser le mémoire ci-joint; le seul usage que je puisse faire de cette piéce, c'est de vous la renvoyer, afin que vous puissiez prendre sur

3. Digges forwarded the present on Sept. 6, below.
4. In the hand of Gérard de Rayneval.
5. Ambassador Creutz had lodged a protest in 1778 about Conyngham's capture of a Swedish ship: XXVII, 552. BF knew him well enough to loan him a book: XXVIII, 179.

son contenu le parti que la justice et la prudence vous suggé-reront.[6]

M Franklin

From Clément Noguères[7] and Geneviève-Elisabeth Belamy Le Veillard

Printed form with MS insertions in blanks: American Philosophical Society

M   [before September 5, 1779][8]
Vous étes prié, de la part de Monsieur le CURÉ & de Ma-dame *Le Veillard,* Trésoriere des Pauvres, de vous trouver à l'Assemblée de Charité qui se tiendra dans l'Eglise Royale & Paroissiale de Notre-Dame-de-Graces[9] de Passy, à l'issue des Vépres, Dimanche prochain *5 7bre 1779*

6. With the Library of Congress copy of this forwarding letter is a copy of the Aug. 31 memoradum Creutz sent Vergennes. It asked the French minister's good offices with BF in regard to the claims of the owners of the Swedish ships *Victoire* and *Anne Louise,* which Landais had captured while en route from England to Italy. According to Creutz, Landais "maltraita, frappa, et pilla presqu'a nud les Equipages, et transfera la meilleur partie à son bord pour ensuite les conduire a Brest." Subsequently the latter ship had been recaptured by a British privateer and taken to Falmouth, while the former and her crew had been released. The owners of the ships never-theless sought compensation for damages and for the "traitement barbare" suffered by the crews. Creutz wished BF to resolve the matter by satisfying the claim or by making a formal refusal in order that the owners could proceed further with their case. Landais had given a brief account of the captures: XXVIII, 488.

7. The parish priest of Passy since 1773: *Almanach royal,* 1779, p. 100. On another occasion the *curé* wrote to BF, forwarding a message from two prisoners who were seeking protection: XXVIII, 50. For Mme Le Veillard see XXIII, 542.

8. While the year and the day are difficult to read, BF did give 24 *l.t.* "to the Parish Poor at the Sermon" on Sept. 5, 1779: Cash Book (Account XVI, XXVI, 3). The date might also be read as Sept. 6, 1778, a Sunday, but BF was visiting Mme Brillon in Anet on Sept. 6 and 7: XXVII, 332.

9. The parish church of Passy, located just east of the Hôtel de Valenti-nois: Hillairet, *Rues de Paris,* I, 92.

Il y aura Prédication, par *mr L'abbé gautier vicaire général*[1] *du diocèse de gap.*
Ceux qui ne pourront point s'y trouver, sont priés d'envoyer leurs Aumônes à M. le Curé.[2]

Date eleemosinam. Luc. 12. 33.

Beatus qui intelligit super egenum, & pauperem; in die malâ liberabit eum Dominus. Ps. 40. 1.[3]

Addressed: Mr franklin

To Sartine   LS:[4] Archives de la Marine; copy: Library of Congress

Monsieur,   Passy ce 5 Sept. 1779.
J'ay l'honneur d'informer votre Excellence, que le Commodore Jones a prie le vingt du Mois d'Aoust, par les 50 Degrés 20 Minutes Latitude, un Brig Anglois nommé le May Flower, de soixante dix Tonneaux, Chargé de Beuf et de Beurre Salés, de Biere et de quelques Balles de Plumes, destiné pour Londres.[5] Le Capitaine de cette Prise arrivé a L'Orient, a rapporté que le dix neuf du dit Mois le Corsaire le Monsieur qui

1. A *vicaire général,* one of several, was a priest who assisted the bishop in his ecclesiastical duties: Marcel Marion, *Dictionnaire des Institutions de la France aux XVIIe et XVIIIe siècles* (Paris, 1923, reprinted, New York, 1968), p. 553.
2. In France public assistance was generally the responsibility of each parish. Alms were collected at the annual *Assemblée de charité* where a sermon was delivered by a prominent preacher. Invitations for Sept. 3, 1780, Sept. 9, 1781, Sept. 1, 1782, and Aug. 24, 1783 are among BF's papers at the APS.
3. Both Latin quotations encourage charity: Give alms (Luke 12:33); Happy is he who cares for the poor and the weak: if disaster strikes, the Lord will come to his help (Psalms 40:1).
4. In WTF's hand.
5. Jones's squadron had sailed on Aug. 14. The prizes mentioned in the present letter were the first it took. The *Mayflower* had sailed from Limerick, Ireland: Jones to BF, below, Oct. 3. She was provided with a midshipman and four sailors as a prize crew and sent to Gourlade & Moylan at Lorient: Bradford, *Jones Papers,* reel 4, no. 730; Morison, *Jones,* pp. 207–8. Apparently BF's information about her was provided by Chaumont; see Gourlade & Moylan to BF, Sept. 6.

s'etoit joint au dit Commodore avait fait une Prise chargé de Vin d'Espagne et de Soye d'assez grande Importance pour que le dit Corsaire se separat de l'Escadre pour la conserver.[6]

Je suis avec Respect, Monsieur, Votre très humble très obeissant Serviteur   B FRANKLIN

M. De Sartine, Ministre & sece. D'Etat.

From Robert Henderson and John Smith

ALS: Historical Society of Pennsylvania

Revd Sir   Vandome Sepr the 5th 1779

I hope you well excues me for making So Bold as to troub-ale you with thes feaw lines: in the meantime it is the humbl Petition of a Prisinor of war that is willing to enter in the America Serves as I hear that there is two Cutters fitting out at St Malos and I know how to Manage a Cutter on the Cost of England for I formley Belonged to a Smuggling Cutter of Dover and I am aquanted with all the Banks about the Downs and elswhere: Sir if you Could Per Coure lave for us two to Go whear the Cutters is and a Pas Port to travel to them: Sir I hope your honor will Be So obliging as Send an answer to this and Derect for me at Vandome and in So Dowing you will oblige your most Humble Servants &c   ROBERT HENDERSON
                                                        JOHN SMITH

Addressed: To / the Reverand Dr / francklin ameriacan / eagent in Paris

Notation: Prisoners Requests Vandoine Sept. 5. 79

6. The prize was a large Dutch ship carrying brandy and wine from Bar-celona. The subsequent parting of the *Monsieur* was acrimonious: Jones to BF, Oct. 3.

From Francis Hopkinson

ALS: American Philosophical Society

My dear Friend   Philada. Septr. 5th. 1779—

Your very obliging Favour of the 4th. June came to hand within these few Days. My Friendship & Pride were both highly gratified by this Indulgence. I hope I shall always endeavour to merit your Esteem & the Esteem of all good Men. The Trust you have been pleased to repose in me does me Honour, & I doubt not but you may depend on the Exertion of my best services in every thing that respects you or your Affairs.

I thank you for the little Piece of Oxford Wit—[7] I have just made your Pig squeak in Dunlap's Packet. *Kill pig* has brought his Pigs to a fine Market truly—& as 'tis Pity his knife & steel should be unemploy'd; the best he can do is to cut his own Throat.— In Return for your Rocket I send you a few of my political Squibbs.[8] Ammunition of this kind hath been rather scarce with us. Most of our Writers have left the great Field of general politics, wherein they might have been of considerable Service, to skirmish & bush-fight in the Furs and Thickets of Party Dispute—for which I blame them much.—

I am greatly obliged by the Use of your electric apparatus, of which I shall take particular Care. You will perhaps repent of your Kindness when I tell you that I am preparing a long Letter to you on the Subject of Electricity. It would have been forwarded to you before now, but the Summer Season being unfavourable for Electrical Experiments & my Time much engaged in the Duties of my office, I have not been able to compleat my System.— Should you find Time to write to me again, I would just hint that you cannot oblige me more than by communicating any new philosophical Discoveries, or Systems, new Improvements in Mathematical or philosophical Machinery—new Phenomena—new Doctrines Gim-Cracks &ca for all which I have an insatiable Avidity— When I was

7. For the poem about a pig escaping the knife of his butcher see XXIX, 622n.

8. Two of his political ballads: "The Battle of the Kegs," and "Date Obolum Belisario." APS.

in London I never ventur'd into Nairne's or Adams's Shops, 'till I was just ready to sail for America & had spent all my Money not caring to expose myself to irrisistable Temptation.[9]

I have been honoured with the Post of Judge of the Court of Admiralty for this State & have Reason to believe that I have hitherto given Satisfaction in that Department. As this office does not interfere with my Business as Treasurer of Loans, I retain both & have Occasion to use much Industry and Attention.—[1] Such is the unhappy State of our Currency that I am but just enabled to support my Family with the two offices but my Hope is, in future Prospects.

Monsr. Luzerne not yet arrived in this City but soon expected. I shall think myself honour'd in his Acquaintance. We have been extreamly happy with Mr. Gerard who has made himself beloved by every Body here (except the Tories) & will be universally regretted when he leaves us—by him I send this Letter.

Mrs. Bache tells me you have sent a Bust of yourself by Mr. Luzerne— She has promised to send for me when it is to be unpack'd— I hope she won't forget her Promise— She has been so good as to give me one of the Profiles in Clay you sent over.[2]

A good Likeness of General Washington goes over with Mr. Gerard— I doubt not but there will soon be capital Engravings done at Paris from this Picture— I shall expect one from

9. He was ready to spend money now, however. On Oct. 15, Hopkinson gave William Carmichael (who would sail to Europe within a fortnight) a bill for 60 *l.t.* with which to purchase two sets of premium quality crayons. With the remainder, Carmichael was to buy "some Knick-Knack, Gim-Crack, Rattle-trap or whim-wham at the joint discretion of the said Mr. Carmichael & Dr. Franklin. Any little Phylosophical Machine of a new Construction & Use within the Compass of the Sum in Hand, would be acceptable." The note, now in the APS, is endorsed by BF: "Mr Hopkinsons Note, to M. Carmichael."

1. On Sept. 8 Hopkinson sent a list of the bills of exchange he had issued to the state loan offices since the date of his previous letter (XXIX, 49n): to N.H., $10,860; to Mass., $76,500; to R.I., $14,400; to Conn., $24,600; to N.Y., $18,600; to N.J., $12,720; to Penn., $112,440; to Del., $4,632; to Md., $6,630; to Va., $4,800; and, to S.C., $4,200. APS.

2. One of the Nini medallions: XXVII, 603. For the medallion and bust see XXIX, 613.

some Body or other—some Friend at Paris or Passey will doubtless remember me.—

But I detain too long with Chit Chat from more important Objects;— I will therefore take my leave of you for the present with most hearty Assurances that I am as I ever have been Your sincerely affectionate Friend & humble servt

FRAS HOPKINSON

P.S. We buried a very worthy Member of Congress yesterday— Mr. W: H— Drayton from So. Carolina—[3]

My Mother & Sisters desire to be respectfully remembered to you.—

Dr. Franklin

Notation: Fra: Hopkinson Sept 15 79

From Sartine   Copies:[4] Library of Congress, National Archives

A Versailles le 5. Sept. 1779.

Je m'occupe, Monsieur, de l'éxecution du projet que j'a eu l'honneur de vous communiquer et qui, S'il a le Succès qu'il y a lieu d'en esperer, fera entrer dans nos ports des Munitions très interessantes, vous avez bien voulu donner ordre à M. Jones de relacher à la fin de sa Croisiere au Texel avec tous les Bâtimens qui composent la Division dont il a le commandement.[5] Le terme de cette croisiere devant expirer dans les derniers jours du mois courant, vous jugerez sans doute a propos

---

3. William Henry Drayton died of typhus on Sept. 3: *DAB;* Smith, *Letters,* XIII, 451.

4. The copy at the National Archives is in WTF's hand and was enclosed in BF's Sept. 7 letter to Jones.

5. On Sept. 5 Sartine also wrote Ambassador La Vauguyon in the Netherlands that after completing his cruise Jones would come to the Texel to provide escort to France for ships carrying naval stores. Sartine doubted, however, that the *Indien* could be brought out as well, although that would be desirable (AAE). Although the French navy needed the timber and naval stores which had been accumulating at Amsterdam it could not provide such an escort itself and the Dutch had proven reluctant to run the risk: Dull, *French Navy,* pp. 174–5.

d'arranger les choses de maniere que M. Jones trouve, à son arrivée au Texel, des Instructions par les quelles il lui sera prescrit de prendre sous son Escorte les navires Hollandois et autres neutres chargés pour le Compte du Roi et de les conduire dans les ports de leur Destination. Je donne de mon Côté des ordres pour qu'ils soient tenus prêts et je suis persuadé que leur Expedition ne causera pas le moindre retardement. Au surplus je n'ai pas laissé ignorer au Roi, la maniere dont vous vous étes prêté à ce que je vous ai proposé à cet égard; Sa Majesté m'en a paru très satisfaite.

J'ai l'honneur d'être avec une parfaite consideration, Monsieur, votre très humble et très obeissant Serviteur.

(signé) DE SARTINE

M. Franklin.

From Thomas Digges   ALS: Historical Society of Pennsylvania

Dr. Sir   Sept. 6. 1779

I ventured to try the fate of two letters to you very lately by common post, cheifly to give information to you & others of a late publick arrest; as also that Mr. Peters's remittance has been settled to His wish, and that every necessary step has been taken to give Capn. C——n——m information that I was ready to help Him to money or any other necessarys he might want: on accot of his removal from Pendennis to Mill Prison, and from thence (on accot of the late alarm at Plymouth) to an inland Prison of Devonshire, I have not yet been able to get an ansr. to any one of four letters conveyd by different modes to Him, but am in hourly expectation of one. I had taken these steps before yr. letter of the 20th Augt. came to my hands, and by the help of a common friend who forwarded that letter to me. We had obtain his removal from Pendennis & got him among his friends in Mill Prison, in order to take his rotine of Exche.; and altho there is at present no promising aspect from the Cartel, I am in hopes He will soon get out.

I wrote you on the 4th. by the Chaplain to your Russian Embassy, and put my letter under the usual cover. I could wish

You would give me a *proper name* for the direction of those
Letters put under cover to Monr. G. for their may be less risque in so doing. My last was principally to recite the former
parts of this letter, and to give further information of Captain
Hutchins being apprehended for supposd treasonable correspondence with You and Mr. S. W——n. He has since his
commitment undergone three or four close Examinations before Sr. Jno. Feilding, Lord G. G. Mr. DeGrey Mr. Knox;[6] is
committd a close prisoner to N Prison Clerkenwell & will
likely be tryed for his life at the old Baily in 10 or 12 days.
Some say, as an Officer, He will have a Court Martial; but I
hope not. Mr. Peisley (who is generally suspected to have
turnd informer) has been dischargd on condition of appearing
an Evidence agt. him, and Mr. Bundy yet remains a prisoner.
As the papers of these three mentiond other names, some
other people have been taken up, their papers seizd and examind. &c. Mr. Neaves books & papers have undergone this
fate; and *it is said* a Clerk of his just returnd from France has
been apprehended & committed. There was a Miss Stafford
also examind and Her papers taken; She was releasd but her
papers held. It appears but too clearly that these worthy Examinants are bent upon all the mischief they can towards
American People and their abettors, & most likely with an aim
to get some publick Execution and raise a clamour against the
friends of America, in order to turn the minds & conversation
of the populace from the present very gloomy situation of
publick affairs. As I obtaind a communication with Capt H and
the Lady, I find the principal aim & bent of the Examinants
were to pin crimes upon others; and there were particular
questions asked about Mr. E——s, Mr. D——s, Mr. E——n
and others. Mr. S. W[7] (whom it may be essentially necessary

6. Sir John Fielding, Henry Fielding's half-brother, was also a magistrate:
XXIII, 326n. William Knox served as under-secretary of state for the American Department: xv, 94n. Thomas de Grey (1748–1818) was also under-
secretary to Lord George Germain: Namier and Brooke, *House of Commons*,
II, 307.

7. Elias and Finch, *Letters of Digges*, p. 82, render E——s as Ellis, who
eludes identification. The others mentioned are Digges himself, Robert Ellison, and Samuel Wharton.

to inform of these particulars in order to prevent his further writing) can inform You who these people are. It is more serious against the former than any of the rest; but if I can judge right, it is not mischeviously so, & the others are not afraid. Poor Capt. H—— disponds exceedingly, says he is a marked victim, is sure no mercy will be shewn him, and hopes his friends will not forsake Him. Every thing will be done for Him that can; and I am strongly of opinion He desponds too much; for I well know His Enemies have been much disapointed that 'more has not come out.'

The *good* Mr. Knox has been closer upon Him than any of the rest. He said "You now see Capt H——, by *your own confession* your life is in our power, but it may be spar'd by your openly delaring every thing & discovering Yr. accomplices and the other secret traitors who are ruining this Country." I fear very much that Capt. H, being a timid man, has answerd questions put to Him, which He was in no ways obligd to reply to.

I come now to the principal point for which I write You this letter & indeed for which the Bearer purposely takes a trip to Paris: He is a little known to You, but the person who is principally engagd with Him is not. Mr. C——y Sterry is from R Island, & I beg leave to recommend Him to You.[8] The other Gentn (who is ill at present or would also wait on You) is Mr. W Smith of Baltimore Brother to my friend Collo S. Smith who defended mud Fort.[9] These two Gentn have a consider-

8. Cyprian Sterry had been a major in the Rhode Island brigade raised in December, 1776. By October, 1778, he had escaped from an English prison and received aid from the American commissioners: XXVIII, 57n; Samuel Greene Arnold, *History of the State of Rhode Island and Providence Plantations* (4th ed., 2 vols., Providence, 1894), II, 391. Sterry also carried a letter of introduction dated Sept. 6 from Edward Bridgen, who called him "an honest tryed Citizen." APS.

9. Lt. Col. Samuel Smith (1752–1839) had been honored by Congress for his role in the defense of Fort Mifflin on Mud Island in the Delaware which had delayed Howe's Philadelphia campaign in late 1777. *DAB;* John W. Jackson, *The Pennsylvania Navy 1775–1781: the Defense of the Delaware* (New Brunswick, 1974), pp. 156, 225–66, 281 and *passim*. His brother was John Smith, Jr.; BF issued a passport in his name and in Sterry's on Sept. 24, below.

able quantity of Blankets, and Coarse Cloths, and other articles much wanted in a certain Army; and for which Mr. S principally came from Maryland to supply. There is *one* risque, much lighter than the usual one to Holland St. Eustatia & so on to the Continent; by purchasing a vessel here, getting a crew of their own, & clearing for N Y and taking an oppertunity to slip into the Delaware or some other port. But a cover is wanted to shew that the vessel & Cargoe is orriginally meant for the use of the States, for fear She may be taken & claimd by Amn. Privateers or cruisers going in. As I know the extreem want our people are in for winter Cloathing, and that these two Gentlemen can throw in several thousand pounds worth at a critical season of the year, I have encouragd their trying to get a certificate from You, that the Ship was orriginally meant for some port of the Northern Colonies, & the Cargoe meant to be offerd to the States at the current price. I have no doubt it will be of great public good should they succeed; and as to the propriety of the measure You are the best judge of. I think I can justify my strong recommendation of them & their scheme to You. Mr. Sterry will talk further upon it.

There has been a man here, & who left London abot 8 days ago to return to Paris, that I think worth mentioning to You, tho among the race of Sad Dogs. I suspect as He loung'd pretty much about Almons & tryd to put himself into Company of our friends, & for some other reasons, that He is rather a spy upon Your friends. It is Sr. H. Ecklyn, who has resided many years at Paris, rather a fugitive from this Country.[1] He passd here by the name of Loyd; & when he went away gave out to his intimates He should return from Paris in 10 or 12 days, in order to publish some secrets, relative

---

1. Henry Echlin, an Irish baronet engaged in squandering his family's fortune, had sought BF's aid in early 1777: XXIII, 209n. He was recently bailed out of a debtor's prison by his friends, Horace Walpole among them: Lewis, *Walpole Correspondence,* XLI, 398–9. John Almon, the pro-American publisher and bookseller, was known to receive inside information on the American situation from his numerous contacts: Deborah D. Rogers, *Bookseller as Rogue: John Almon and the Politics of Eighteenth-Century Publishing* (New York, Bern, and Frankfort, 1986), p. 80.

to underhand offers made to the Court of France by Lord M——s——d and other great men here, if they woud give up America.[2] He is a thin genteel dark man abot 45. There is also another person here from France whom I have reason to believe has been with the Minister. Passes by the name of Monr Belson, is from Britany, lives in a stile, & keeps a Carriage, a genteel dark man, & like most Frenchmen, apt to brag of his importance and being in the secrets of the French ministry.

Poor Raspe has been often with me lately and is much down in the mouth at the treatment He has lately recd from a Russian nobleman by whom He is likely to loose some money. I forwarded a letter from him some weeks ago & by this post send You another.[3]

I shall keep this open until I go into the City to hear the news of this Evening for we are all in such consternation & tremor that every hour may bring some alarming account from Portsmo in which port it is now reported our grand fleet is blockd up by a far superior one of the Enemy. I am with the greatest truth & sincerity Dr. Sir Yr. very obedt. Servant

V.J. DROUILLARD

Endorsed: Sept. 6

Notation: Digges Sept 7.79

2. Mansfield, a warm advocate of the policy of coercion, was suspected of having made a secret mission to France in 1774 when he traveled incognito and stayed with his nephew David Murray, sixth Viscount Stormont, then British ambassador to France. Walpole speculated, possibly incorrectly, that Mansfield had sought to prevent France's intervention in American affairs. *DNB,* XIII, 1310; A. Francis Stuart, ed., *The Last Journals of Horace Walpole* ... (2 vols., London and New York, 1910), I, 373; H.M. Scott, *British Foreign Policy in the Age of the American Revolution* (Oxford, 1990), p. 248n.

3. Raspe's letters are July 27, and Sept. 4, above.

From Gourlade & Moylan

ALS:[4] American Philosophical Society

Honord Sir   L'Orient 6th. September 1779

The Schooner Grand Tyger Cap: Blackwell[5] arrived here yesterday from Fredericksbourg in Virginia with a Cargo of Tobacco. She left them Capes the 5th. of last month.

The following few lines is extract of a letter to us from thence, dated 25th. July last and annexed, you will find another extract of a letter to us dated the 20th. of the same month. "We have just now accts. from Charles Town of a Capital Action between our Troops & the Enemy. Our noted General Lincoln, gave them a severe beating, drove them from their entrenchments & took possession of their ground.— Our noble General & Commander in Chief is Idle, Sir Henry Clinton not yet presuming to get out of his Den, tho' the season is far advanced, I apprehend it must grow warm, but he knows the Country to be still more so, as he woud meet with incessant fire from all quarters."

The few arrivals from America make us imagine that this intelligence will not be disagreeable to you.— This Vessel we mean to dispatch in fifteen days, she sails remarkably fast for your government.

We have the honor to be respectfully Hond. sir Your most obt. hbl. sts.   GOURLADE & MOYLAN

P.S. Our friend M. Le Ray de Chaumont, no doubt advised you the arrival here of a prize taken by the poor Richard.[6] She arrived too late the last post day for us to have given you advice ther of and to comply with Cap: Jones's message to us of acquainting yo., he & his fleet were well and that he had not leasure to write you as he was then in pursuit of a cannonade wch. he heard.   G & M

---

4. In James Moylan's hand.

5. Capt. George Blackwell of Northumberland County made several successful voyages to the West Indies and France: *Jefferson Papers*, v, 295.

6. The *Mayflower*.

Extract of a Letter from Frederick'sbourg Virginia Dated 20th. of July 1779[7]

We have nothing in the political Line worthy communicating but that some plans have very lately been adopted by some of the states to give some permanency to our Courrency, by reducing the prices of Imported Goods regularly each month, in the same proportion as they have rose. They have also Limited the prices of the produce of our Country & the Committee of Philadelphia have addressed the Honnble the Congress that they would not emit any more Money for the service of the public but that the people generally should subscribe sums of money, as their Ability wd. admit wch. sums should be Carried to their Cte. in payment of their annuel Taxes;[8] how far these Plans may answer so desirable purpose as the appreciating our Currency time alone must Discover.

Our Latest Accts. from the soward, where the principal scene of Action has been this Campaign, say the ennemy have abandoned the Design of taking Charles-town, nor do they appear very formidable on any part of the Continent, their Want of Reinforcements must soon Compel them to Relinquish every hope of effecting what they have so long aimed at, the subjugating America.

7. This extract is in another hand.
8. For a discussion of popular efforts in several states to stabilize currency by regulating escalating prices of commodities see Richard Buel, Jr., "The Committee Movement of 1779 and the Formation of Public Authority in Revolutionary America," in *The Transformation of Early American History: Society, Authority, and Ideology,* James A. Henretta, Michael Kammen, and Stanley N. Katz, eds. (New York, 1991), pp. 151–69. For the Philadelphia committee specifically see *ibid.,* pp. 159–66; Douglas M. Arnold, *A Republican Revolution: Ideology and Politics in Pennsylvania, 1776–1790* (New York and London, 1989), pp. 124–47; and Steven Rosswurm, *Arms, Country, and Class: the Philadelphia Militia and "Lower Sort" during the American Revolution, 1775–1783* (New Brunswick and London, 1987), pp. 166–71, 184–99. The address to Congress by the Philadelphia committee refers to the committee's plan to raise money by subscription for the war effort. It was published as a broadside on July 14, 1779: *Evans' American Bibliography* (14 vols., Chicago and Worcester, 1903–59), VI, 38, no. 16470.

Since writing the foregoing another prize loaded with fish oyl arrived from Cap. Jones's fleet./.⁹

Notation: Gourlade et Moylan L'Orient 6. 7bre. 1779.

To Dumas

LS:¹ University of Pennsylvania Library; copy: Library of Congress

Sir,   Passy Sept. 7. 1779
Inclosed is a Letter for Capt. Jones, which you are desired to deliver him yourself as soon as possible, after his Arrival.— It will be well to keep secret that you expect him there.²
I hope you had a good Journey home.³ I am with great Esteem Sir, Your most obedient & most humble Servant.
                                                    B FRANKLIN
M. Dumas.

To John Paul Jones

LS:⁴ National Archives; copy: Library of Congress

Sir,   Passy Sept. 7. 1779.
This will be delivered to you by M. Dumas, Agent of the United States of America residing at the Hague, who has Instructions to render you any Services in his Power.
Inclosed I send you a Copy of a Letter I have just received from M. De Sartine.⁵ You will do your utmost to render the Service therein mentioned effectual, which will in the present Circumstances be very advantageous to the common Cause,

9. Probably the brigantine *Fortune,* carrying "Oil Blubber & Staves from Newfoundland": Jones to BF, Oct. 3, below.
1. In WTF's hand.
2. See Chaumont to Dumas, above, Sept. 2, for Dumas' rendezvous with Jones.
3. Dumas must have left Passy soon after receiving the passports which BF and Vergennes wrote for him on Sept. 3; his first letter after his return was not written until the 14th.
4. In WTF's hand.
5. Above, Sept. 5.

and very acceptable to his Majesty. It will be well to keep your Intention of convoying those Vessels as secret[6] as possible, lest Notice should be sent of it to England, & Ships placed to intercept you.

Your Irish Prize is arrived, that under Convoy of the Monsieur not yet heard of.[7]

I congratulate you on the Taking of Grenada & the Beating of Byron by Count D'Estaing.

I wish you all sorts of Success being ever with great Esteem, Sir, Your most obedient & most humble Servant.

B Franklin

Commodore Jones.

Endorsed: From Doctr. Franklin of the 7th September inclosg. One from M. de Sartine of Septr: 7th: 1779 No. 12.

To Sartine   Copy: Library of Congress

Sir   Passy, Sept. 7. 1779.

Agreable to the Letter your Excelly. did me the honour to write me of the 5th. Instant I Sent the orders desired to Capt. Jones, under Cover to Mr. Dumas who will take Care to deliver them.

I have to thank your Excellency for your favour to Capt. foligny, in giving him a Lieutenancy. I flatter myself that he will do honour to your Appointment.

Please to accept my hearty Congratulations on taking of Grenada and the Beating of Byron. With the great Respect, I am Your Excellency's most ob. and M. h. Servant   BF

Mr. De Sartine.

6. Here Jones later inserted a mark and wrote in the margin, "I found our Object in the Publick Papers when I arrived in Holland and Sir Jos. York had sent an Express to England, informing also that part of my business there would be to take out the Indien. I was then under a necessity to represent the Want of secrecy of Mr. Chaumont to Court & to complain of his conduct towards me in the Affair of the Concordat." As soon as he arrived at the Texel Jones began to complain of Chaumont's indiscretion. For the "concordat" see Jones to BF, Aug. 13.

7. See BF to Sartine, Sept. 5.

From Cadet de Vaux

ALS: American Philosophical Society

Monsieur   ce 7 7bre 1779

Ma belle Soeur doit bien regretter dans ce moment-cy de n'avoir pas fait inoculer ses enfants, car ils ont la petite Vérole et comme cette maladie s'est déclarée à sa maison de Montmartre, Elle est privée de l'honneur de vous y recevoir Lundi 13 Jour que vous avés bien voulu donner à mon frere.[8] Je vous demanderai la permission de vous la présenter un jour, pour la dédomager en partie d'une privation qu'elle ressent, on ne peut pas plus Vivement.

J'ai Eté hier aux Invalides juger une Expérience dont les résultats vous intéresseront. Il s'agit de la conservation des blés et farines. Nous avons Vu 25 sacs de blé dans lesquels il n'y avait pas de *charançons* et le meme ble conservé en tas dans des Greniers en est infesté, ce qui prouve la nécessité de ne les conserver qu'enfermés dans des sacs.[9] Aussi l'administration de l'hotel Royal des Invalides se décide a prendre ce parti.

Je suis avec le plus profond respect Monsieur, Votre très humble et très obeissant serviteur   CADET

Notation: Cadet Paris 7e. 7bre. 1779

From John G. Frazer

ALS: American Philosophical Society

Honoured Sir,   Bordeaux 7th. Septr. 1779.

I received a Letter from Mr. Cradock Taylor by the last post, who has been detained as a prisioner at Aix in Provence this Twelve Months, he informs me that you want proof of his being a Native, and Subject, of the United States of America, before he can obtain his liberty— I have known him ever since he was a child, and am exceeding well acquainted with

---

8. Marie-Thérèse-Françoise Boisselet became the wife of his brother Louis-Claude Cadet de Gassicourt (1731–99), a distinguished chemist and pharmacist, and member of the *Académie des sciences.* She was a beautiful woman and rumor had it that Louis XV had fathered Charles-Louis (1769–1821), one of the children now ill with smallpox. He survived it and had a brilliant career in science, politics, and literature. *DBF.*

9. Cadet de Gassicourt held the post of *apothicaire-major* at the Invalides.

his Family, and Friends, some of which live in the same Neighbourhood I do in King William County upon York River in
Virginia, this Young Man was born in Caroline County which
joins King William, altho he was taken in an English Ship
which service I am well convinced he was forced into, as many
of our Countrymen and good subjects have been this War,
much against their inclination that this unfortunate young
Man is as good a Friend to his Country & any man in it, and
only wishes to get his liberty to go home where he immediately purposes entering in the Service of his Country or if any
Armed Ship belonging to the United States is now in this
Country he will go on board in any capacity whatever, he is
without any Friend, or acquaintance in this country except
myself— I have supplyed with a little money otherways he
wou'd have suffered much, and it is out of my power to supply
him with any more, which hurts me exceedingly—as I know
his Friends are able and wou'd reimburse me any sum I wou'd,
or cou'd, advance for him here, I will swear to the above relation, I have given of Mr. Taylor at any time, if necessary, I
have the Honour to be with the greatest respect, Sir, Your
Most Obt. Hbl. Servt.   JOHN G. FRAZER

Addressed: His Excellency / Benjamin Franklin / Plenipotentiary to the / United States of America / at Passy / near Paris

Notation: J.G. Frazer Sept 7. 1779

To Francis Coffyn   Copy: Library of Congress

Sir,   Passy. sept. 8. 1779.
    I duly received yours of the 30th. past, which I Should have
answered sooner, but that I have been and still am at a Loss
what to do as to the Condemnation of the Prizes you mention.
In the Commission given to our armed Vessels, they are directed to submit The prizes they may carry into any foreign
Port, to the judgment of the Courts of admiralty there establish'd and I expected all along that the admiralty Courts of
france would try, and condemn or acquit our Prizes. And I do
not yet find that I have any authority to try any Causes of The

kind or to pronounce the Condemnation you desire.[1] But I Shall endeavour to inform myself more particularly by consulting Some Lawyers. &c. and will write you the Result. However, to avoid all Such Difficulties for the future, would it not be best for the black Prince, and also the Princess, to take french Commissions?[2] Especially as I have no blank Commission left except one which I would keep, as I may have occasion to produce it to Show what they are. Explain to me, if you please, why those of America are desired— I am glad to hear of The farther Successes of the Black Prince, and have the honour to be, &c

M. Coffyn. Dunkirk.

To Samuel Smith

Copy: Library of Congress

Sir   Passy, 8 sept. 1779
   I received yours of the 2d. Instant, and am very sorry for your Misfortune: the Loan office Bills you destroyed to prevent their falling into the hands of the Enemy, you do not sufficiently describe; it is necessary for me to know before I can find out whether they have not been already presented the following particulars of each Bill, viz Number, Quantity of Dollars, Date, In whose favour drawn, and by whom Countersigned.[3] If they Should be presented hereafter some of these Particulars may enable me to Stop them. As soon as you favour me with this Description I Shall take the earliest Opportunity of complying with your Request. I have the honour to be, Sir &c. &c.

M. Saml. Smith. Nantes.

   1. As American representative in France BF did hold such authority under article XI of the 1778 French prize regulations: Wharton, *Diplomatic Correspondence*, II, 686. He soon must have discovered this, as ten days later he began exercising his powers; see the condemnations he issued on Sept. 18, below.
   2. A question BF had posed several months earlier: XXIX, 120–1.
   3. Smith replied on Sept. 23 that he had destroyed the paper containing the information, but that happily a second set of bills had now arrived at

To John Torris

Copy: Library of Congress

Sir   Passy, Sept. 8. 1779.

I duly received yours of The 9th. past and wrote immediately to England relating to The Prisoners you mention.[4] I do not apprehend there is any more Danger of Their Lives than of any others taken in this War by the English: for if Those Men having formerly been English Subjects is a reason for having [hanging] Them, it is the Same for hanging other American Prisoners, who have all been English Subjects. But on The contrary the Britich Government has agreed to a Cartel for exchanging them. If those Men Should be prosecuted, of which I think there is no Probability, my Correspondent in England will furnish Money for their Defence.— But we have so many American Tories among our Prisoners, both in france & America that the Apprehension of Reprisals, would be Sufficient to prevent the Enemy's taking So wrong a step. And I am persuaded the 21. Men will be exchanged in ther Turn: those who have been longest in Prison claiming with some Justice to be first discharg'd.— I congratulate you on the Success of your Vessel, & have the honour to be Sir Your m. o. & m. h. S.   BF.

M. Torres Mercht. Dunkirk.

From William Alexander

ALS: American Philosophical Society

In the spring of 1779, Franklin had taught Jonathan Williams, Jr., the principles of "moral algebra" to help him resolve one of his most troublesome dilemmas—whether or not to return to America. "By the Way," Franklin added, "if you do not learn it, I apprehend you will never be married." Williams protested that where marriage was concerned, his negative column seemed always to outweigh the

---

Lorient. This set was endorsed to Penet, d'Acosta frères, and Smith asked BF to honor the bills. APS.

4. To Hartley, Aug. 20.

positive one. Besides, he observed, falling in love was rather like falling into a well, which takes more than algebra to get out of.[5]

The weightiest elements in Williams' "negative column" seem not to have had to do with the women themselves, but rather with their formidable fathers, and the probabilities of the match increasing his fortunes. He had first met sixteen-year-old Mariamne Alexander while he, at the age of twenty-four, was in England with Franklin in 1774. Smitten, but timid, he periodically consulted with his great-uncle (even after Franklin had returned to Philadelphia) on the course of their affections and the likelihood that her father might be willing to offer a "reasonable assistance." The Doctor thought she was a "sweet Girl" and encouraged the romance.[6] William Alexander, however, when finally approached by the anxious suitor in 1776, set what seemed to be an insurmountable condition to marriage: that Williams be in possession of two thousand pounds, which Alexander would augment with three thousand more in dowry.[7]

Within a few weeks of arriving at Nantes in January, 1777, Williams gave up hope of marrying Mariamne (citing the hostilities between their countries) and set his sights on a new alliance: he would enter a business partnership with Jean-Daniel Schweighauser and wed his beautiful second daughter.[8] The courtship with Miss Schweighauser (her first name is not known) progressed quickly. By August, Williams, encouraged anew by Franklin, spoke to her father. Once again, the suitor's "present uncertain situation" led to a chilly reception.[9]

The following spring Williams, abruptly replaced as American agent at Nantes by his would-be father-in-law, found himself enmeshed in the auditing problems occasioned by Arthur Lee's trumped-up accusations against his business practices. Disheartened, he considered returning to America.[1] Although his relationship with Schweighauser was permanently soured, his romance with the merchant's daughter survived at least through the end of

5. BF to JW, April 8, and JW's reply of April 13: XXIX, 283–4, 318–19.

6. XXII, 269, 394–5.

7. XXII, 588. JW later wrote his parents that it was BF who at that time had "recommended my first obtaining some settlement in Life": to Jonathan and Grace Williams, Nov. 4, 1779, Yale University Library.

8. XXIII, 352–3.

9. XXIV, 220, 477.

1. He first broached this idea to BF on Nov. 5, 1778: XXVIII, 40.

Franklin's Wedding Gift to Mariamne Alexander

April, 1779, a month when he also received a visit from his English-born illegitimate son Josiah.[2]

By late July, when Williams was assured of a favorable judgment in the audit of his accounts, his thoughts returned to Mariamne Alexander. He penned a proposal to her father, to be forwarded by Franklin.[3] In mid-August, he left Nantes and journeyed to the Alexanders' home in St.-Germain, stopping along the way and writing his parents of his matrimonial intentions.[4] For reasons which remain unclear, William Alexander was now receptive to the proposal. And so—it seems—was his daughter.

The wedding, to which Alexander alludes in his letter below, was held on September 12 in the Protestant chapel in the *Hôtel des Ambassadeurs de Hollande,* 47 rue Vieille-du-Temple in Paris. The chapel's records show that one of Franklin's relatives was married there to a Scottish girl.[5] The family reception seems to have taken place the following day at the Alexanders' residence at St.-Germain. One of the guests, a visiting American who accompanied Franklin's carriage, later recalled the journey from Passy. They traversed the Bois de Boulogne, passed by the Château de Madrid and Bagatelle, crossed the Seine via the beautiful stone Pont de Neuilly, rode through the magnificent grounds of Marly, and climbed the steep road to St.-Germain, with its commanding view of the countryside. When they reached the Alexander estate, they dined with a host of "distinguished guests," including the mayor of Nantes.[6]

2. JW confided in code to John Paul Jones about the romance on April 29, 1779: Bradford, *Jones Papers,* reel 3, no. 582. For Josiah's visit earlier that month see XXIX, 380, 563–4.

3. See his letter of July 27, above.

4. That letter, now missing, is mentioned in JW's Nov. 4 letter to his parents, cited above.

5. BF had visited the "Dutch Chapel" on Sept. 5, the preceding Sunday, and made a donation of 3 *l.t.*: Cash Book. The information about the chapel and wedding is cited in Hillairet, *Rues de Paris,* II, 637. We have not been able to verify the event in L. A. van Langeraad, *De Nederlandsche Ambassade-Kapel te Parijs* ('s Gravenhage, 1893). This famous *hôtel,* still in existence, had been rented by Beaumarchais in 1776 and it was there that he ran Roderigue, Hortalez & Cie. and wrote, in 1778, *The Marriage of Figaro.*

6. Elkanah Watson, who traveled on horseback, provided the only eyewitness account: Winslow C. Watson, ed., *Men and Times of the Revolution; or, Memoirs of Elkanah Watson . . .* (New York, 1856), p. 92. For an illustrated description of the road to St.-Germain see Howard C. Rice, Jr., *Thomas Jefferson's Paris* (Princeton, 1976), pp. 103–12.

All we know about the ceremony itself is what Williams reported to his parents: that Franklin, having given his blessing, acted in the role of surrogate father.[7] As to his bride, Williams admitted that since their first meeting, "Our History . . . has been on both Sides full of Changes in point of Situation," but "our Affections have uniformly been the same, and we are now as happy a Couple as exists." Indeed, he continued,

> Were I to describe my Wife to you as appears to me, you would suppose the picture to be drawn by a young Lover. I will therefore only tell you what the World says of her, & in a few Words all who know her at all, know her to be Sensible, accomplished good natured prudent, and, what to me crowns all, the tenderest of Wives,—in short, nobody that ever saw her says anything but her Praises.

As a wedding gift, Franklin obliged the bride by presenting her with a miniature of himself. Painted by an unknown artist after Duplessis, the portrait is opaque water color on ivory. On the back of the miniature was affixed a small oval, in which were placed intertwining locks of the bride and groom's hair.[8]

The newlyweds remained at St.-Germain until mid-October, but Williams' honeymoon lasted only a day. On September 13, he was already submitting bills to his great-uncle and conducting business for his father-in-law.[9]

My Dear Sir   St. Germain 8 sept 1779

We have agreed to dine wt you on Sunday after our Ceremony— I think I mentioned to Mr Williams That we woud Expect you here to spend Monday wt us as the distance is great we can mannage quarters for you & your Son that night when you will be at hand to proceed to Versailles Tuesday—

7. The letter of Nov. 4, cited above.

8. See the illustration on the facing page, and Sellers, *Franklin in Portraiture*, pp. 269–71, pl. 25.

9. Alexander's concerns about property in Grenada, mentioned in jw's letter of Sept. 13, below, were now of immediate interest to jw himself. His wife's fortune, tied up in mortgages on Grenada, was worth £4,000. jw to Jonathan Williams, Sr., Nov. 4, and to Alexander Scott, Nov. 10: Yale University Library.

but whether this Suits or not we shall Relye on your Company Monday to dinner— That you may see whether our young Couple are as well pleased after as They Seem before They are united— all here join in assuring you of their warmest attachment & I am ever Yours   W ALEXANDER

Addressed: Monsieur / Monsieur Franklin / Passy

Notation: W. Alexander St. Germain 8. 7bre. 1779

From George Blackwell   ALS: American Philosophical Society

Hond. sir   L'Orient Septr., 8ht. 1779
  The Hurry I was obliged to leave Virginia in preventd my Application to Congress for a letter of Marque for the Schooner Grand Tyger of Virginia which I now Command, my principal Owner Mr. Henry Armistead of Fredericksburg[1] desird I Should apply on my Arrival heare to you for one which I request you will do me the favour to furnish me with as soon as you possibly can if requisite. Messrs. Gorlade & Moylan of this place will be guarantees for the faithfull performance of Any instructions contained therein and they will inform you that my Said Schooner is the built & property of America[2] I Shall Sail in the Course of twelve days if you Should have Any Commands for America I Shall encharge my Self with their with pleasure,
  I have the honour to be with Respect Hond. sir Your Most Obt. Humbl. Servt.   GEO. BLACKWELL
The Honorable Benj: Franklin Esqr.

1. Armistead (d. 1787) became clerk of the court organized at Fredericksburg in 1782: S.J. Quinn, *The History of the City of Fredericksburg, Virginia* (Richmond, 1908), pp. 124, 130.
2. Gourlade and Moylan forwarded Blackwell's letter with one of their own of the same date. In it they offered to act as sureties for Blackwell's performance. APS. On the verso of Blackwell's letter is the notation, "Gourlade et Moilan L'orient 8. 7 bre. 1779."

From Chaumont AL: American Philosophical Society

[September 8, 1779]
Chaumont aura L'honneur de Mener M. franklin Diner chez Madame helvetius aujourdhuy 8. 7bre. 1779.

Addressed: S. Ex / M. Le Docteur / franklin

From Vergennes Copy: Library of Congress

à Versailles ce 8. 7bre. 1779.
Le Comte de Vergennes a l'honneur de renouveller à Monsieur Franklin l'assurance de ses sentimens et de lui envoyer des Paquets à son adresse arrivant d'Espagne.[3] Il en est resté un a Madrid que M. Le Cte. de Montmorin croit ne contenir que des Journaux.

To Schweighauser Copy: Library of Congress

Sir   Passy Sept. 9. 1779.
It appearing on the Examination of Mr. Ross's Accompts, that the Committee are very considerably indebted to him, I conceive you may Safely Settle with him the accts. you have with the Committee agreable to Orders received by him from Robert Morris Esq.[4] I have the honour to be &c.

M. Schweighauser.

3. The packet was probably the one carried by the *Victorieux* which arrived in Cadiz on Aug. 13; see our annotation to Lovell's letter of July 9.

4. Ross had represented in Nantes Morris' firm of Willing & Morris, and the orders mentioned presumably were those governing Ross's dealings with Schweighauser; see XXVI, 281. Ross continued the association. When he returned to America in 1780 still claiming from the Secret Committee (now the Committee of Commerce) money owed him for his services in France, he turned to Morris for help: E. James Ferguson *et al.*, eds., *The Papers of Robert Morris, 1781–1784* (7 vols. to date, Pittsburgh, 1973—), I, 168, 169n, 191–2.

Arthur Lee to [William Temple Franklin]

AL (draft): National Archives

Paris Sepr. 9th. 1779

Mr. L. thanks Mr. Franklin for the Pacquets he was so good as to forward to him. They contain only the Journals of Congress & old Newspapers without any Letter. Mr. L. will be obligd to Mr. F. for letting him know if he can have it, by what vessel they came, to what Port & when She saild.

From Frederick Augustus Hervey, Sir Patrick Bellew, and ——— French

AL: American Philosophical Society

Franklin did not often grant passports to British citizens, least of all to those who were spying on him. But in this case, the self-appointed spy was so innocuous, and the intelligence he communicated to the British government so patently outrageous, that he was neither suspected by Franklin nor valued as a source by his own government. In short, despite his attempts to create an air of intrigue, no one seems to have taken him very seriously.

The author of this passport request was Frederick Augustus Hervey, fourth Earl of Bristol and Bishop of Derry (1730–1803), the colorful scion of a family famous for eccentricity.[5] He arrived in Paris sometime in late July, 1779, on his way back to England after two years' residence in Italy, and immediately reported to Lord North on the French plans to invade Ireland.[6] By August 4, when William Temple Franklin had arranged for his lodgings in a house which, according to English rumor, was across from Franklin's,[7]

5. For a detailed biography see William S. Childe-Pemberton, *The Earl Bishop* . . . (2 vols., New York, 1925). For the Herveys of Ickworth see the *DNB*.

6. North, who forwarded Hervey's letters to George III, thought the invasion scheme plausible but Hervey's claims of its scale exaggerated. The King also found the accounts "highly exagerated," and his proposal for preventing the operation so dangerous that "no man in his Senses could suggest it." Fortescue, *Correspondence of George III,* IV, 402–3.

7. A letter from Hervey to WTF of Aug. 4 thanked him for the trouble he had taken over finding him lodgings. Hervey would rent them at the price

Hervey was reporting to Lord Germain that he had seen the American ambassador four times. Franklin, he maintained, was "dissatisfied" with Congress and Versailles, and "would gladly contribute to a reunion of the Empire."[8]

Hervey's subsequent letters laid claim to his having penetrated Parisian society. Alongside allusions to dinner parties and high-ranking informants—whose names would be revealed in time—he spoke of the French navy's devastation, of the government's growing ambivalence towards the American cause, and of Franklin's plummeting reputation among the French.[9]

Hervey seems to have stayed in the environs of Paris through August. He must have secured his passport sometime before September 10, the day on which he wrote Lord Germain from Ostend. Two days later he was in Dover, and the course of the war remained unaltered.[1]

au Parc Royal a Paris [before September 10, 1779]
The Bishop of Derry Sr. Patrick Bellew & Mr. French[2] beg the favor of Mr. Franklin to allow them a passport to secure their passage from Ostend to Dover.

Notation in William Temple Franklin's hand: The Bishop of Derry & Mr French Application for a Pass —[3]

---

named if linen were provided by the proprietor. He requested WTF to meet him there at eight the next morning. APS. The location of those lodgings was reported by Horace Walpole: Lewis, *Walpole Correspondence,* XXV, 454.

8. *Report on the Manuscripts of Mrs. Stopford-Sackville . . . prepared by the Historical Manuscripts Commission Great Britain* (2 vols., London, 1904–10; reprinted, Boston, 1972), II, 135–6.

9. BF's party was the "object of public scurrility," while the Lees were gaining "ascendency": *Report on the Manuscripts of Mrs. Stopford-Sackville . . . ,* II, 139–40.

1. His letters from Ostend and Dover are quoted in *ibid.*

2. Sir Patrick Bellew was an old schoolfriend of Hervey's who became a leader of disaffected Irish Catholics: William S. Childe-Pemberton, *The Earl Bishop . . .* (2 vols., New York, 1925), I, 19. French may be Sir Thomas French, Bart., another agitator for Irish Catholic rights: T.W. Moody *et al.,* eds., *A New History of Ireland* (5 vols. to date, Oxford, 1976—), IV, 306, 317.

3. The passport BF issued resembled the one he had given to Mr. King on July 22, above. See BF's notation on that draft.

To Becker & Saltzmann

Gentlemen, Passy, Sept. 10. 1779.

Since Mine of the 1st. of last Month, of which the above is a Copy, I have received the honour of yours of The 23d. of July;[4] and The Packages containing the Sample of a Soldiers uniform mention'd in yours of april 20. is also Since come to hand. I cannot at present give any orders for such cloathing but I am of opinion that if you were to send those uniforms to Virginia, Maryland or Carolina They would sell there to great advantage.[5] The other Goods mentioned in your last, would sell well in Pensilvania, and the more Northern States; the Prices appearing reasonable, execpt of the fusils, which Seem Dear;[6] but perhaps, they may be so good as to merit Such Price.— In Order to open your Commerce with America, my advice to you would be to begin by Sending a Small Vessel with an assorted Cargo to Philadelphia, under the Care of a discrete observing Person who being on the Spot would find what kind of Goods were most in demand, what Commodities were best to take in Return, with The Characters of Persons fittest to correspond with for the future. After receiving the Information he could give, you would walk in Day light. And I am persuaded a very great Demand would Soon be found there for your Commodities, & a growing commerce established between the two Countries. Your Vessel might go from Hambourg or Embden under Prussian Colours; and I would furnish your Supercargo with Letters of Recommendation.— That written in your favour by Prince ferdinand[7] has great weight with me, & you may depend on my doing you every Service in my Power. I am, Gentlemen, Y. m. o. b. h. S. &.

Messrs. Becher & Saltzman.

4. Described in our annotation of their April 20 letter: XXIX, 343–4n.
5. For uniforms needed by Maryland see XXIX, 416.
6. The firm had offered fusils at 32 *l.t.*, 36 *l.t.*, and 40 *l.t.*
7. Probably Prince Ferdinand of Brunswick, who had commanded the British army in Germany during the Seven Years' War, although conceivably BF might mean his nephew, Charles William Ferdinand of Brunswick-Wolffenbüttel (X, 329n).

From Marie-Elisabeth De Lamoignon[8]

ALS: American Philosophical Society

de la visitation rüe st jaques de paris 10 sept 1779

✝

vive jesus

Permette moi monsieur d'avoir l'honneur de madresser directement a vous pour s'avoir s'il est possible des nouvelles de Mr le chevalier Delaluzerne mon neveu a qui je suis tendrement attachée je pense que son arrivée chez vous peut estre süe a present dans ce paiis cy et vous avez surement les nouvelles les plus sures.[9] Je desire encore lui faire parvenir une lettre aurié vous monsieur la complaisance de la faire passer dans vos depeches, je vous en aurez la plus grande obligation j'en dois beaucoup a loccasion qui me procurera de vous assurer combien j'ai l'honneur d'estre monsieur votre tres humble et tres obeissante servante

PE [PRIEURE?] MARIE ELISABETH DELAMOIGNON

Dieu soit beni

Notations: Eliz. de la Moignon. 10 Sept. 79 to enquire after the Chevalier Dela Luzerne / Ansd

To Vergennes

AL: Archives du Ministère des affaires étrangères

Passy, Sept. 11. 1779—
Mr Franklin presents his Respects to M. le Comte de Vergennes, with Thanks for his kind Care in sending him the Packets that came by the Way of Spain.[1]

8. Born in 1723, Agathe-Françoise de Lamoignon adopted the name Marie-Elisabeth when she took orders. It happened to be the name of her deceased older sister, mother of the chevalier Anne-César de La Luzerne. *Dictionnaire de la noblesse,* XI, p. 387.

9. La Luzerne had sailed on the *Sensible* on June 17 and arrived in Boston on Aug. 3.

1. See Vergennes' letter of Sept. 8. On a Sept. 12, possibly in 1779, BF was sent another packet, this one by Sartine and containing dispatches from Martinique. APS.

Mr Franklin sends herewith some Packets he has just Receiv'd from America in a Vessel arrived at Nantes, a swift Sailer, which is soon to return.[2]

From Louis-Casimir, Baron de Holtzendorff[3]

AL: American Philosophical Society

à paris Ruë du faubourg St. Denis
le 11e. Septembre 1779./.

Le Baron de Holtzendorff s'etant rendû hier à Passy, pour avoir l'honneur de conférer avec Monsieur Franklin sur un objet important, et n'ayant pas eû celui de trouver ce Ministre, il Le prie, afin de ne pas risquer inutilement un autre voyage, de vouloir bien lui indiquer un jour de la semaine prochaine et l'heure de sa commodité pour être seur de le trouver: le Baron attendra avec une vive impatience la reponse de Monsieur Franklin.

To Arthur Lee

AL: Harvard University Library

Passy, Sept. 12. 79

Mr Franklin presents his Compliments to Mr Lee, and sends all the Journals he has; but, as he has not yet had time to read them, he prays Mr Lee to return them when he has perus'd them.—[4]

Addressed: The honble A Lee Esqr / Paris.

Notation: Sepr. 12. 1779

2. The *Mercury.*
3. A former colonel in the Continental Army. He had been pressing BF to expedite his reimbursement from Congress for travel expenses: XXVIII, 296–7; XXIX, 569–70.
4. Lee did so later that day with a note saying, "Mr. Lee presents his Compts. to Dr. Franklin & returns the Journals, with his thanks." APS.

To Schweighauser

Copy: Library of Congress

Sir, Passy. Sept. 12. 1779.

I yesterday received your favour by Mr. Schorndorff[5] with the Packets for Mr. De Vergennes and myself. I have acquainted the Minister with The Opportunity of writing by the return of the Mercury, and shall not unless he desires it, keep her here Longer than may be necessary on her own Account.

I have a Letter also from The Navy Board of Boston; but as they make no mention to me of the Stores wanted, nor have furnished me with any means of purchasing them, and I am totally unacquainted with such Business, I can give you no directions about them.[6] There is I believe Some Sheet Copper in your hands belonging to the States,[7] and some Anchors which may Serve in Ballasting the Mercury. And If you are disposed to answer any other Part of the order of the Board, by advancing upon their Credit, you can add such articles as you think proper and I doubt not but they will take care to make you due Remittances. Or you can add such Part of The other stores, Arms, &c. from the Magazins as you may judge most useful. The funds in my hands are all appropriated, and I Cannot engage upon new subjects without having where with to pay. Please to present my Compts. to Captain Sampson who I hope is recovered from his indisposition.

I wish to know whether the Cartel is return'd, and with what Number of Prisoners.— You mention your not furnishing the American Prisoners with Money in consequence of an express order from me. I do not remember Such an Order, nor can I find any trace of it. I apprehend there is some Mistake in it, and wish you to examine it, and send me a Copy of the

---

5. Apparently one of Schweighauser's clerks: BF to Schweighauser, Sept. 24, below. He may have been related to the Paris merchant Jean-Rodolphe Schorndorff, for whom see Lüthy, *Banque protestante,* II, 446n.

6. Presumably he is referring to the Eastern Navy Board's letter of July 30, above.

7. BF had recommended to Landais six months previously that he seek copper from Schweighauser: XXIX, 41.

order If such there be. I hope the Salpetre not disposed of, as I believe I shall Send it to America.[8]

I find by your late Letters that you have abated the Commissions on the delivery of one of the Cargoes of tobaco. I suppose you mean to do the same on the other. I have the honour to be with much esteem Sir, Your most obedient and most humble servant   BF.

Dr. franklin not being at home,[9] I send this Letter without being signed by him, but you may depend on its being an exact Copy from his Rough Drafts.

(Signed) W. T. FRANKLIN

M. Schweighauser.

From Mademoiselle Juppin

AL: American Philosophical Society

a chaillot ce dimanche matin, 12 septembre [1779][1]

mon papa

je suis arrivée hier de la campagne, il y a deux mois que je ne vous ai vue, jai le plus grand désir de vous voir, voulez me donner a dinér aujourdhuy, jyrai savoir par moi meme de vos nouvelles, et vous embrasser de tout mon coeur.

Addressed: A Monsieur / Monsieur franklin / a passy

From Jane Mecom

ALS: American Philosophical Society

Dear Brother   Warwick Sept 12—1779

I have now before me yrs of Nov 26 1778 Brought me by my unfortunate son Collas & won of Apr 22 79.[2] The first I

---

8. Schweighauser had been ordered to sell locally the saltpetre in his possession: XXVII, 287; XXVIII, 153, 458, 558–9, 632.

9. It was the day of JW and Mariamne Alexander's wedding.

1. The only Sunday, Sept. 12, during BF's stay.

2. The first of these letters is missing, but its contents are described in Jane Mecom's reply of July 27, above. The second is published in XXIX, 357–8.

ansuered some time ago but as you may not recve it I now Renew my thanks for it & the Benifits there bestowed & confermed in the other, mr Williams writs me He is redy to comply with your Desier, but as mr. Collas does not See any other way to settle on shore it does not Apear to me it will in any measure do to soport a famely, it would be a grat help when we could convinc people they have been decved by a miserable Imitation, & that no won Els can make the trew soap,[3] but that would be a work of time, & there will be no wax to be had till affter Frost comes, I did by laying out Every way procure a small cake & made a litle but not of the very best Posable as you desiered owing to some unavoidable Impedements, but sent it notwithstanding as it will Ansir for your own Use, & Temples, but would wish you not to make any presents of it; as I had not convenancy to make but half the meterals I procured I hope the other will ansure your wish & shall make it & send it by the first opertunity, I desiered Collas to mark it No 1—that you might know which it is if boath come to hand.

Your very affectionat & tender care of me all along in life Exites my warmest gratitude which I cannot Even think on without Tears, what manyfold blessings I injoy beyond many of my worthy Acquantance who have ben driven from there home, Lost there Intrest, & some have the Adion of Lost health, & won the Grevous torment of a Cancer & no kind Brother to soport her[4] while I am kindly treeted by all about me & ample provition made for me when Ever I have ocation.

You could not have recd. Information of the Death of my son peter when you wrot the last I have recd as I had it not

3. Not surprisingly, given the crown soap's ingredients and the complexity of the instructions for making it: Van Doren, *Franklin-Mecom*, pp. 129–32.

4. A note marked with an asterisk identifies her: "Sally Hatch cornl Hatchs sister who went of with the British." She was the sister of Nathaniel Hatch, a former colonel of militia and now a Loyalist: Butterfield, *Adams Correspondence*, I, 257n; *Sibley's Harvard Graduates*, XI, 150–2. A contemporary described her as an "amiable maiden": Winthrop Sargent, ed., "Letters of John Andrews, Esq., of Boston. 1772–1776," Mass. Hist. Soc. *Proceedings*, VIII (1864–5), 335.

my self till 20 days after the date of myne which you then recved,[5] I hope some others I wrot afterwards are come to yr hand, I cannot but take grat pleasure in hearing you Injoy so much Helth & could wish you had no ocation for the Remedy of thos fitts of the Gout you are sometimes Exercised with, I fear you feel Pane anouf when under them to consider it as a disease, or as we some times say wors— The Respect & Friendship of all sensable people where Ever you go I am shure you can not fale of but it is a grat satisfaction to have a number of them so near you that you may take your own time to go to them. I have not the privilige of won Neibour near than two miles but we have many agreable people come to viset us & I am allways contented at home, & pleasd. to go abroad when sent for, otherways I cannot go for our people[6] have no carrage & I hant courage to ride a hors.

You say Temple is still with you & I hope the same Dutyfull & Affectionat child & agreable companyon remember my love to him, but poor Ben how will he soport the Lose of you boath, was he willing to go.[7] I Lately had a Leter from mrs Bache she maks no mention of it but I sopose they will Chearfuly Acquese in what you think for the best. Our friends hear are well & desier to be Dutyfully Remembred to you, I heard the Governers wife say she would write.[8] When shall I have any foundation for the hope that we shall again meet & spend our last Days to gather, America knows yr consequence two well to premit yr Return if thay Can posable prevent it, & yr care for the Publick good will not suffer you to Desert them till Peace is Established, & the Dismal sound of fiveteen year from the comencment of the war Dwells on my mind which I

5. BF's April 22 letter acknowledged receipt of his sister's letter of Jan. 4, but not of hers of Feb. 14 reporting the death of Peter Mecom; they are printed in XXVIII, 344–5, 541–3.

6. Mecom resided with her granddaughter Jane Flagg Greene and the latter's husband Elihu, who lived in Potowomut, Warwick township, R.I.: Van Doren, *Franklin-Mecom,* pp. 176–7.

7. In his latest letter to her, BF had mentioned BFB's recent departure for Geneva.

8. Catharine Ray Greene did so on Sept. 19, below.

327

wonce heard you say it might Last, if it does it is not Likely I shall Last that long, but that you may contineu in Health & Usefullnes is the constant Prayer or yr Affectionat sister

JANE MECOM

[*torn:* I] have no Instruments [*torn:* to stamp] the soap but hope that will not Depretiate is valeu⁹

Addressed: Dr Franklin

From John Torris

ALS: American Philosophical Society

Sir   Dunkerque 12th. Sepr. 1779.

I have Received with all gratitude the Letter your Excellency did me the honnour to write me the 8th. Instant.

The expressions of your Excellency are the expressions of Humanity; they will give all Comfort & quietude to the Prisonners & to the Crew of the Black Prince Privateer; they will encourrage the People already Listed for my New fine Vessell the Black Princess Capt. Edward Macatter of Boston, which will be ready for sea soon & intended to go in Company with the former. Mr. Coffyn the agent here of your Excellency, has Sollicited a Commission for the Brave Macatter,¹ & we all hope your goodness will grant it directley.

The most oblidging Compliment your Excellency is pleased to address me, on the Success of our Black Prince, is a proof of your respectable disposition in favour of the Concerns; But the aim of your Excellency is far yet, as we are rather very great Sufferers, for want of haveing obtained the Righteous Condamnation of the Prises, which we in Vain have Sollicited to this moment, from your Excellency & from M. De Sartine, the Ministers who, we are Told, are appointed for the Condamnation of all the Prises brought in France by the americans. The Cargoes are deperishing & Spoiling, & a great part thereof already Lost. We are forced to advance daily fresh

---

9. We follow Van Doren's guesses at the missing words: *Franklin-Mecom,* p. 197. The Franklin family's soap derived its name from the crown with which it was stamped: I, 348n.

1. Above, Aug. 30.

Sums for the use of our Privateer, & all the Concerns are recriminating on me for the armement, Let the appearances be what they will. Justice & Humanity, nay, the honnour & Interest of Both the American & French Government, requiere Immediate satisfaction shou'd be given, according to the Terms expressed in the Commission deliverd by Your Excellency.

I do appeal to your Justice, Sir, & all my hopes & the relief of my havey Misfortunes, are now Intierely Confined in it & in your Humanity.

I have the Honnour to be with great respect Sir your most obedient, Most Humble & oblidged servant   J. TORRIS

Notation: Mr. Torris Sept 12. 1779

From Vergennes

Copy: Library of Congress

12. Sept. 7bre. 1779.

Le Comte de Vergennes fait tous ses remercimens à Monsieur Franklin des paquets qu'il lui a envoyés hier. Ils lui ont apris l'arrivé a Boston de M. Le Chr. de la Luzerne, et des differens Evenemens avantageuses aux Etats unis dont le Cte. de Vergennes desiré que M. Franklin puisse lui donner la Confirmation mardi prochain.[2]

To Schweighauser

Copy: Library of Congress

Sir   Passy. 13. sept. 1779.

The Bearer M. De Guio[3] having been an officier in The American Service and brought Prisoner into England, I request you would procure him a Passage to Boston if convenient in the Mercury Packet. He will pay the Captain for his passage on his arrival there; having considerable arrearages of pay due to him. I have the honour to be, Sir &c.

M. Schweighauser.

2. At the King's weekly audience for foreign diplomats.
3. Jean de Guio, a Canadian to whom BF loaned ten louis (240 *l.t.*) on the same day as he wrote the present letter: XXIX, 541n; Account XVI (XXVI, 3). BF described him to Vergennes on Sept. 16, below.

From Bartholomew Raredon

ALS: American Philosophical Society

Sir   Fougeres Sept: 13: 1779

May it Please your Excelencys Goodness: Whereas your Petticioner Is a Native american and has Now A Wife and Family in the Province of Pensilvenia in Lancester County, Left I Fear in great distress as By Reason of The War, i Came to Sea in the Swallow Slope Belonging to Rhoad Island Commanded By Capt: Murphy and Was taken And Carried into Portsmouth Where I Rmaind A prisoner 2 Years almost[4] But Have Got Out and in hopes of Escapeing Safe to France to Claim your Protection And Return to my Country in duty I was Retaken and Brought Back to Prison Again and Sent un Board of the Princis Amilia, and When the Carteel arived I was Not Suffrered to Come in my turn With My Shipmates But When the Ardent Which is Now Taken[5] Was Fitted for Sea I was Sent un Board of her against my Will, When i Wrote to Mr: Wren of Portsmouth Who answerd me and Bid me Comfort my Self As Well as i Could that he Would Endeavour To Get me oaf again But the Ship Sailing Before i Could be Releasd: i Came to Sea in her And Was Taken and Brought to this Place at My Arival at Brest i Wrote your goodness A Letter But Not thinking Sircumstances Clarely laid down and Being Sent hither I here Present your Exelency With the Reality of my Cause as i am Ready to Prove upon Oath My Name is Bartholemew, Raredon, and as you are appointed for the Relief of your Distresd Country hope your Godness will endeavour for my Speedy Release I add No more But Rest, Most Excelent Sir, yours in duty To my Country

BARTHOLEMEW RAREDON

Addressed: To His Excelency / Benjaman Frankland / Esqr: Ambasador for the / States of America / Resident at Paris

Notation: Faredon Bartholomeu 7bre. 13. 1779.

---

4. He was committed to Forton on Jan. 23, 1778: Kaminkow, *Mariners.*
5. By d'Orvillier's fleet on Aug. 17: Patterson, *The Other Armada,* p. 182.

From Jonathan Williams, Jr.

ALS: American Philosophical Society

Dear & Hond Sir   St Germain Sept. 13. 1779

I send herewith a number of Bills which when Billy has examined please to accept.—[6]

Mr Alexander is desirous of knowing from Lord MCartney the particular Situation of his Estates and affairs when he left the Island and for this Purpose wishes to know whether he is to remain at Rochelle, or to have liberty to come to Paris that he may apply accordingly. This you will probably know tomorrow at Versailles and if you can without giving yourself too much trouble, at the same time learn, what arrangements have been made with Respect to the Inhabitants & moveable property in consequence of the Conquest, it will be an additional obligation.—[7] We all expect to see you tomorrow.— My dear mariamne joins me in dutifull & affectionate Respects.—

I am ever Your   J WILLIAMS J

Please to enquire whether any Persons of Note fell in the Attack on the Fort & who they are.—

Addressed: Doctor Franklin.

Notation: Jon. Williams St. Germain 13. 7bre. 1779.

To George Blackwell

Copy: Library of Congress

Sir   Passy. Sept 14. 1779

I am Sorry I cannot give you the Commission you desire[8] having none Left.— But I see nothing amiss in your taking what you can, and carrying it in tho' without a Commission for since the Congress, in reprisal, have immitated the Gov-

---

6. JW's letter to WTF of Sept. 13, sending a list of the bills and covering the same points mentioned in this letter, is at the APS.

7. For Alexander's interest in the captured island of Grenada see our annotation of BF to Vergennes, Oct. 24.

8. Which he had requested on the 8th, above.

ernement of England, and encouraged Sailors employ'd in Ships to Seize and bring them in giving them the whole as a Reward for their breach of Trust,[9] I Should think there is stronger Reason for allowing an honest Man the Prize he has openly taken from the Enemy and that resolution of Congress Seems to me to be of The Nature of a General Commission. However, the taking particular Commissions is certainly the best and most regular and ought not to be dispenc'd with, unless in such Cases as yours, where Circumstances have made it at Present impracticable.

I am, Sir, Your most obedient and most humble Servant

BF

Capt George Black well, of the Swoner Grand tyger, L'Orient.

To Gourlade & Moylan
Copy: Library of Congress

Gentn.   Passy Sept. 14. 1779.
I should with great Pleasure comply with Capt. Blackwell's Request on your Recommendation if it were in my Power; But I have now no blank Commissions left. I am much obliged by the Intelligence you have so often so kindly Sent me, and am with great Esteem Gent Your m. o. & m. humble Servant.

(signed) BF

Messrs. Gourlade and Moylan.

From Sarah Bache

ALS and AL (draft): American Philosophical Society

Dear & Honoured Sir   Philadelphia Septr. 14. 1779
Every body seems to be sorry that Mr Gerard is going to leave Philada. but particularly this Family whose esteem he has entirely gain'd, he is kind enough to take charge of a Box

---

9. *JCC,* IX, 802. BF is recapitulating a point he had made with Vergennes several months earlier: XXIX, 388–9.

of Squirril skins for Temple[1] in which is a parcel of news papers for you, and a peice of homespun Silk which I have long wish'd to send you for the Queen whose character I admire, and spoke to M Gerard last winter about it, but never had an opportunity that I chose to trust it by, I could not presume to ask her acceptance of it from myself, but from you it may be agreable, it will shew what can be sent from America to the Looms of France— We are well satisfied with your sending Benjamin to Geneva knowing well that you would do every thing by him for the best, but I cannot help feeling very sensibly when I consider the distance he is removed from you, I wish with all my heart that his Brother Will was with you, but much more so that you were with us—

I am indeed much obliged to you for your very kind present it never could have come at a more seasonable time, and particularly so as they are all necessary,[2] and the Bills Mr Bache sent to Mr Williams with a list has never been heard of,[3] the Ministers Secretary[4] Cousin Williams writes has taken charge of them from Boston, and he is now expected every hour, but how could my dear Papa give me so severe a reprimand for wishing for a little finery, he would not I am sure if he knew how much I have felt it, last Winter was a Season of Triumph to the Wigs and they spent it gaily, you would not have had me I am sure, stay away from the Ambassadors, or the Generals entertainments, nor when I was invited to Spend the day with General Washington and his Lady,[5] and you would have been the last person I am sure to have wished to see me dress'd with singularity, tho I never loved dress so much as to wish to be particularly fine yet I never will go out when I cannot apear so as to do credit to my Family and Husband, the Assembly we went to as Mr B: was particularly chose to

1. She discusses the skins further in her Sept. 16 letter to WTF, below.
2. BF had enclosed some "useful and necessary" articles with his June 3 letter to her: XXIX, 615.
3. See RB to BF, Aug. 9.
4. François Barbé de Marbois. "Cousin Williams" is Jonathan Williams, Sr.
5. For her prior contacts with Washington see XXVIII, 391.

regulate them, the subcribtion was 15 pound, but to a Subcribtion Ball of which there was numbers, we never went to one tho always ask'd, I can asure my dear Papa that industry in this house is by no Means lay'd aside, but as to spinning linnen cannot think of that till I have got that wove which we spun three years ago, Mr Dufeild[6] has bribed a Weaver that lives on his Farm to weave me eighteen yards, by making him three or four shutles for nothing and keeping it a secret from the Country people who will not suffer them to weave for those in town, this is the third weavers it has been at, and many fair promises I have had about it, tis now done and whitening, but forty yards of the best remains at Ledietz yet, that I was to have had home a twelvemonth last month, Mrs Keply who is gone to Lancaster is to try to get it done there for me,[7] but not a thread will they weave but for hard money, my Maid is now spinning Wool for winter stockins for the whole Family, which will be no dificulty in the Manufactering as I knit them myself, I only mention these things that you may see the Ball is not the only reason that the wheel is lay'd aside, I did not mention the Feathers and pins as necessarys of life, as my Papa seems to think, I meant that as common necessarys were so dear, I could not aford to get any thing that was not, and beg'd he would send me a few of the others, nor should I have had such wishes, but being in constant hope that things would soon return to their former channel, I kept up my spirrits and wished to mix with the world, but that hope with me is now intirely over, and this winter aproaches with so many horrors that I shall not want any thing to go abroad in, if I can be comfortable at home, my spirrits which I have kept up during my being drove about from place to place, much better than most peoples I mett with, has been lowered by nothing but the depreciation of the money which has been amaizing lately, so that home will be the place for me this winter, as I cannot get a common winter cloak and hat but just decent under two hundred pounds, as to gauze now its fifty

6. Edward Duffield (VII, 211n).

7. Most probably Catharine Gross Keppele, daughter-in-law of the Baches' neighbor Henry Keppele, who was from Lancaster: XII, 318n.

dollars a yard tis beyond my wish and I should think it not only a shame but a sin to buy it, if I had Millions.[8] I should be contented with muslin Caps if I could procure them in the winter, in the Summer I went without, and as to cambrick I have none to make lace of, it is indeed as you say that money is too cheap for there is so many people that are not used to have it, nor know the proper use of it, that get so much that they care not wether they give one dollar or a hundred for any thing they want, but to those whose every dollar is the same as a silver one, which is our case, it is particularly hard, for Mr B: could not bear to do business in the manner it has been done in this place, which has been almost all by Monopolizing and forestalling, however if he gets business from France all may yet be well again— Aunt Mecom was very well lately, I had a letter from her, my little Girl has just return'd from Mr Dufeilds, she has gone through the Summer charmingly and got all her teeth,[9] I think myself very lucky to have had such a Friend, it has been very unhealthy this Summer in town, and the houses for many miles round so much distroy'd that there was no getting a place to take the Children to; all Mr D: family were fond of Betsy and very good to her, she loves them quite as well as she does us, I wish with all my heart you could see her and hear her talk, I think she is the favorite of her Papa, indeed she is one of the best behaved little things I ever saw, and quite as grave as Benjamin—

The first time I see General Washington I shall deliver your message to him,[1] he talk'd to me several times about you last Winter— There has so many people desired me to remember them to you that I know not were to begin, but Mr Dufeild's Family and the Miss Cliftons[2] I must not forget as they were

8. For the sharp decline in the value of the Continental currency in 1779 see Charles W. Calomiris, "Institutional Failure, Monetary Scarcity, and the Depreciation of the Continental," *The Jour. of Economic Hist.*, XLVII (1988), 57–9.

9. Sally had been worried about her two-year-old daughter Elizabeth's teething for over a year: XXVIII, 32.

1. That old generals in France studied his operations and highly approved his conduct: XXIX, 615.

2. XXIX, 612.

among those who desir'd to be particularly rememberd to you— I am my dear Papa with the greatest afection your Dutifull Daughter S BACHE

Addressed: Dr. Franklin

From Jean-Etienne de Chezaulx[3]

Press copy:[4] Library of Congress

Monsieur à Berghen en Norvege le 14. 7bre 1779

J'ai l'honneur de vous remettre ci jointes les lettres de deux officiers de la fregate l'Alliance commandée par le Capne. Landais,[5] qui ont conduit en ce port deux prises considérables faites sur les ennemis par la dite frégate le 29 Aoust & 1er de ce mois. Je ne puis entrer aujourdhui Monsieur dans aucun detail relativement à ces prises. Je me bornerai quant à present à vous faire mon sincére & respectueux compliment sur les bons & heureux succés de cette frégate & à vous remettre ci jointe copie de la lettre que j'ai ecrite à M. Caillard chargé des affaires du Roi à la cour de Danemarck.[6] J'ecris aussi à Mgne. de Sartine Ministre de la marine relativement à cet objét.

Je me propose Monsieur, de vous ecrire plus amplement par le courier prochain & de vous informer de mes demarches auprés des gouverneurs Danois ici, comme aussi de mes opérations ulterieures relativement à vos prises.[7]

3. The French consul at Bergen: Halkild Nilsen, "Frigivelsen av tre amerikanske priseskip i Bergen 1779, og amerikanernes krav om erstatning," *Historisk tidsskrift,* 12th series, 1 (1963), 70.

4. In the hand of Jefferson's secretary William Short (*DAB*). Jefferson was involved in the settling of the accounts of John Paul Jones and the members of his squadron, for which see Morison, *Jones,* pp. 340–1.

5. They were Thomas FitzGerald and Thomas White: FitzGerald to BF, Sept. 14, below.

6. Norway was a part of the Danish monarchy to which Antoine-Bernard Caillard was accredited as French *chargé d'affaires* from 1777 to the end of 1779: *Repertorium der diplomatischen Vertreter,* III, 112. The enclosure is missing, but Jones later sent to Jefferson an extract of it describing the prizes *Union* and *Betsy* and their cargoes, which were worth at least 1,000,000 *l.t.: Jefferson Papers,* X, 208.

7. The Danish government would prove unreceptive; for a summary of the diplomatic effects produced by the arrival of the prizes see Soren J.M.P.

J'ai accordé à vos officiers, Monsieur tous les sécours dont ils ont pû avoir besoin, & je vous suplie de vouloir être bien persuadé que j'en agirai de même à l'égard des batiments de votre nation, soit marchand soit armé en course avec leurs captures, qui pourront entrer, aborder ou relâcher dans les ports de mon departement; & je donnerai toute mon attention pour qu'il ne leur soit fait aucune injustice. J'ai l'honneur &c.

From Dumas

ALS: American Philosophical Society; AL (draft):[8] Algemeen Rijksar-chief; extract:[9] National Archives

Monsieur,   La Haie 14e. 7bre. 1779.

Une course faite à Amsterdam, pour les objets que vous savez, a seule pu m'empêcher de prendre la plume, dès mon arrivée ici, pour vous remercier de toutes les bontés que vous m'avez témoignées. Je n'entreprendrai pas de vous peindre par des paroles la reconnoissance que j'en ressens; je ne ferois qu'affoiblir l'idée d'un sentiment très-vif & profond. Je vous dirai seulement, que dans ma solitude ici j'éprouve que l'on ne

---

Fogdall, "Danish-American Diplomacy 1776–1920," *University of Iowa Studies in the Social Sciences,* VIII, no. 2 (1922), 11–21.

8. Instead of the final two paragraphs of the ALS, the draft has a paragraph in which Dumas criticizes La Vauguyon: the French ambassador wishes Amsterdam were less opposed to the augmentation of the Dutch army, as that would be compensated by the adoption of unlimited convoys. Dumas feels that augmentation of the army would place a dangerous weapon in the hands of the pro-British party and that the instituting of convoys would still be eluded and the republican party led by the nose. He praises van Berckel, who believes the Netherlands should restrict itself to being a commercial power. Since even the pro-British admit the only war to be feared is with Britain it is naval forces which should be expanded.

9. Enclosed with Dumas' Sept. 20 letter to the committee for foreign affairs (Wharton, *Diplomatic Correspondence,* III, 333), it consists of the third paragraph of the ALS, the final paragraph of the draft (with some differences in wording) and another sentence predicting that opposition to taxes would prevent the augmentation of the army or navy. It also includes a new paragraph dated Sept. 20 reporting that France had prohibited the importation of cheese from northern Holland until unlimited convoys were approved.

se sépare pas de vous impunément, & qu'il faut de la force pour se consoler de ne pas être près de Vous.

L'équipage du Vaisseau de guerre Hollandois au Texel reste toujours soulevé. Ces gens, au nombre de 60 (car ils ne forcent personne de rester), se comportent d'ailleurs avec un calme singulier, font le service, tant pour leur sûreté, que pour celle du Vaisseau & de son contenu, & laissent aborder tous les jours un canot parlementaire. Mais ils sont déterminés à se faire sauter avec le navire, si l'on veut leur faire violence, préférant de périr en braves gens, plutôt que sur l'échafaut. Ils prétendent qu'on veut violer leur capitulation; la voix publique leur donne raison. Il y a Conseil de guerre à ce sujet au Texel.

Les affaires politiques sont toujours ici sur le même pied. Les Convois ne se donnent point, pas même pour les Vaisseaux & cargaisons dont on ne dispute point, parce qu'on ne veut pas que les vaisseaux chargés de bois profitent de l'occasion, en se joignant aux flottes convoyées. La Ville de Leide a enfin dû accéder au parti d'Amsterdam, qui est actuellement de 8 à 9 villes:[1] autrement tous les trafiquants en Laine, qui font un grand commerce de cet Article, qu'ils envoient entre autres en Flandres, alloient se retirer à Amsterdam.

L'Etat actuel de la question, ou l'objet des délibérations de la province est, si elle prendra ses mesures séparément pour la protection de son commerce. On vous communiquera, Monsieur, d'une autre part, un petit supplément à ces nouvelles politiques, que je n'ai pu mettre ici tout cru, sans exposer mon chiffre avec l'ami à la comparaison qu'en pourroient faire des curieux indiscrets ici ou en chemin, si par hazard on s'avisoit d'ouvrir les Lettres.

Je suppose Mr. votre fils absent.[2] Je fais bien des voeux pour son heureux retour, & pour qu'il vous rapporte une bonne

1. Recently Amsterdam, Delft, Dordrecht, Haarlem, Rotterdam, Schiedam, Leiden, Gouda (Turgau), and Gorkum had opposed a proposal by the stadholder for augmenting the Dutch army; the States of Holland resolved to support such an augmentation only if unlimited convoys were established by the end of the year: Fauchille, *Diplomatie française,* pp. 161–3.

2. Dumas must have expected WTF to have participated in the attack on England.

cargaison de Lauriers. En attendant, je prends part à la joie que doivent vous avoir causé les bonnes nouvelles de l'Ouest, & suis avec le respectueux attachement qui vous est voué pour la vie, Monsieur, Votre très-humble & très-obéissant serviteur

DUMAS

Paris à Son Exc. M. Franklin M. P. des E. U. d'A.

Addressed: à Son Excellence / Monsieur Franklin, Esqr. / Ministre Plenipe. des Etats- / Unis en France / à Passy./.

Notation: Dumas Lahaie 14. 7bre. 1779.

From Thomas FitzGerald[3]

Two ALS:[4] National Archives; press copy:[5] Library of Congress

Bergen (Norway)

May it please your Excellency   Septr 14th 1779

I arrived here yesterday after a passage of fourteen days in the Ship Betsy, John Fisher Commander bound from Liverpool to New York & Jamaica mounting 22 Guns and 84 Men a Letter of Marque captured by the Alliance Peter Landais, Commander.[6] We left L'orient the 15th of August in Company with the Bonne homme Richard, Pallas, Monsieur Grand Ville Vengeance & Cerf, but parted the Monsieur in four days having taken one prize and she choosing to Cruize alone. We stood for Ireland & off Limerick took two Brigs, one from Newfoundland bound to Bristol with Oil, the other from Ireland to London with Provisions which were ordered for France.[7] When on board the Alliance we parted the Fleet of the Skillocks to Westward of Cape Clear, in a heavy gale of wind, the 26th of August but fell in again with the Richard,

3. A master's mate of the *Alliance:* XXIX, 38.
4. The second ALS, slightly abbreviated, is dated Sept. 15. Both were forwarded by de Chezaulx.
5. Made by William Short; see our annotation of de Chezaulx's Sept. 14 letter.
6. The *Betsy* was captured on Aug. 29 after a brief skirmish: Landais, *Memorial,* p. 30.
7. The prizes taken off Limerick were the *Fortune* and the *Mayflower.*

Pallas & Vengeance off the North of Scotland where we cruized and took another Ship called Union from London bound to Quebec, which has likewise arrived safe in this port according to Orders.[8] I kept Company with the Alliance as long as possible and after parting with her in the best of my way for this place, where we are politely received by the French Consul and Gentlemen belonging to the town. I now wait your Excellency's advice, and shall execute any orders from you with pleasure I am Sir your most Obedient humble Servant   THOS FITZ-GERALD

His Excellency Benjn. Franklin Esqr Paris

Addressed: His Excellency / Benjamin Franklin Esqr / Minister for the United States / of America / Paris

From Barbeu-Dubourg   ALS: American Philosophical Society

My dear Master   Paris 7ber. 15th. 1779
  I am appointed by Mr. Cochin,[9] an old friend of mine, to invït your Excellency at his garden, that is renowned for the most curious and uncommon plants, at Châtillon distant about four miles from that city, to dine with him, the wednesday 22th, or thursday 23th. of this month; or any other same day of the following weeks, at your pleasure. It should be needfull to go very early in morning, not only for visiting the plants at leisure, and walkink around, but also because the house's

8. FitzGerald and Midshipman Thomas White, commanding the prize crew of the *Union,* were ordered to accompany the *Alliance* as long as possible; if separated, they were to take their ships to the French consul at Bergen: Landais, *Memorial,* pp. 30–1. Bergen was one of three ports to which Jones had been ordered to direct his prizes: XXIX, 780. White wrote the same day to report the arrival of the *Union* on Sept. 12; he asked BF's advice and said that he had been received "very kindly" by the French consul and "the best Gentlemen in Town." National Archives.

9. Denis-Claude Cochin (1698–1786) was a celebrated botanist. The marvels of his Châtillon garden were described in the *Jardin des curieux ou Catalogue raisonné des plantes les plus rares et les plus belles* (Paris, 1771). Larousse.

master usually dine at twelve aclock, when anothers usually breakfast.

He desire an answer from you, and I one from M. Williams. And am with the softest respect, Dear Sir, Your very obedient, humble servant   DUBOURG

Addressed: A / Monsieur franklin / A Passy

Notation: Dubourg. Paris 15. 7bre. 1779.

From Henry Coder

ALS: American Philosophical Society

paris ce 15e 7bre 1779 hotel dangleterre
Monsieur,   rue de seine

La bonté que vous avez eu de faire parvenir à Mr. de Sartine l'intéret que vous prenez à mon Sort a determiné plus que tout ce ministre a renvoyer mon frere à St. Domingue avec un Conseil de Guerre qui a eu le courage de s'opposer à la volonté injuste et oppressive du Gouverneur qui avoit mandé au ministre que mon frere ne pouvoit plus retourner à son regiment ni même dans la Colonie.[1]

Si vous daigniez, homme juste et vertueux faire dire encore un mot en ma faveur à Mr. de Sartine, je ne doute point qu'instruit que vous connoissez toute l'innocence de mon frere et la persecution odieuse qu'il éprouve, il ne s'empresse enfin à lui rendre justice et a remplir ainsi le voeu de toute la Colonie qui a en horreur Mr. D'argout son eternel et injuste Persecuteur.[2] Mon intention dimanche dernier en passant à Passy étoit de vous communiquer la lettre cy jointe que je viendrai retirer au 1er. jour.[3] Je ne vous ai jamais demandé de nouvelles de votre

1. The background to the dispute between Gabriel-Aphrodise de Coderc and the comte Robert d'Argout, governor of St. Domingue, has appeared in XXVII, 406–7n.

2. In his next letter (Oct. 17, below) Coder communicated the text of the memo he wished sent to Sartine.

3. This must be the undated "Note pour Monsieur le Docteur franklin," with the notation "Coder," now at the APS. The author relates a proposal he has just presented to Maréchal Charles de Soubise about sending to America an expeditionary corps of two thousand Frenchmen to be put at

pays que dans la vue de trouver quelque moyen de vous servir utilement, fidelement et sans intérêt ce que je ferai tant que je respirerai malgré le grand nombre d'ennemis que ma conduite à votre egard m'a fait.

Je suis avec Veneration, Monsieur, Votre tres humble et tres obeissant serviteur
CODERC

Monsieur le docteur frankelein

Notation: Codere—15 Novre. 1779.

From De Chezaulx
Press Copy:[4] Library of Congress

Monsieur,   à Berghen en Norvege ce 15. 7bre. 1779

Ci-dessus et de l'autre part est copie de la lettre que j'ai eu l'honneur de vous ecrire hier par la poste. Je profite aujourd-hui de l'occasion d'un batiment qui part pour Amsterdam pour vous remettre, Monsieur, deux autres lettres des officiers commandant les deux prises dont je vous ai annoncé l'arrivée en ce port & qui sont le duplicata de celles que j'ai eu l'honneur de vous remettre hier.[5] Je vous préviens, Monsieur, que j'ai pris des arrangements avec un banquier de cette ville M. Danckert D. Krohn,[6] qui est la maison la plus opulente & la

---

the disposal of Congress. Officered by experienced men and reinforced by four warships under the command of John Paul Jones, such an elite corps could expel the British from the continent and eliminate the undesirable French who are giving their country a bad name in America. Needless to say, Coder and his brother, brilliant officers both, wish to take part in such an expedition. This scheme, including his recommendation to send junior rather than senior officers, goes back to February, 1777; see XXIII, 362–65.

Beginning in 1779, Coder's signature took on a final letter which was often read as an "e," and we followed suit (see XXIII, 362–3). We now believe it was a "c," corresponding to his brother's name. Their mother, however, continued to sign as "Coder."

4. In the hand of William Short, who had also copied de Chezaulx's letter of the preceding day.

5. A copy of one of these letters, that from Thomas FitzGerald, is at the National Archives, but we have found only one letter from Thomas White; see our annotation of FitzGerald's Sept. 14 letter.

6. Danckert Danckertsen Krohn (1726–95), for whom see the *Norsk Biografisk Leksikon* (19 vols. to date, Oslo, 1923—).

plus solide de toute la Norvege, dans la caisse duquel seront versés les fonds provenants des ventes de vos prises, si Elle est permise, pour que la remise en soit faite promptement. Quoique ce negociant soit d'une probité à toute épreuve & digne de vôtre confiance tout se passera sous mes yeux & mes auspices. Je vous suplie de vous reposer sur mon zéle & mes attentions à cet égard. Vous pouvez lui ecrire & vous informer à Amsterdam, Londres, Hambourg & toute autre grande ville de commerce de la maison de Mr. *Danckert D. Krohn* à Berghen. C'est le banquier dont je me sers ici pour les affaires de commerce & de change de ma nation. Il est à tous égards recommandable. Je vous rendrai compte, Monsieur, successivement de mes démarches & operations ulterieures relativement à vos prises. Je ne pourrai rien vous marquer d'intéressant qu'après que nous aurons reçu la reponse de Copenhague. J'ai l'honneur d'etre &c.   (signé) DE CHEZAULX
(Copy W short secy)

From Vergennes

Copy: Library of Congress

A Versailles le 15. 7bre. 1779.

Je suis informé, Monsieur, que le Lundi 6. du présent mois, un particulier qui a dit se nommer Jean Deguio, Lieutenant au Regiment Anglois du Colonel Jemi d'Invistony,[7] S'est presenté à M. Le Comte de Chabôt,[8] Lieutenant Général des Armées du Roi Commandant le Camp de St. Omer[9] pour obtenir des Secours et se rendre près de vous; Il a declaré être parti de Winchester le 25. Août dernier et être hors d'Etat de marcher a Cause de ses Blessures. Mais L'officier chargé d'examiner cet Etranger a crû appercevoir quelques contradictions dans ses Responses, l'a regardé comme Suspect, et lui a refusé les Secours qu'il sollicitoit. Il a pris place dans le 1er. Carosse public pour se rendre a Paris où il doit être actuellement arrivé. J'ai

7. Col. James Livingston; see the following document.
8. Louis-Antoine-Auguste de Rohan-Chabot, comte and later duc de Chabot (1733–1807): XXIV, 141n; *Dictionnaire de la noblesse,* IV, 994.
9. Near Dunkirk, a favorite entry point into France for prisoners who had escaped from England.

cru devoir, Monsieur, vous communiquer ces Details en attendant les Eclaircissemens ulterieurs qui pourront m'arriver sur le Compte de ces particuliers et dont je vous ferai part.

J'ai l'honneur d'être très parfaitement, Monsieur, votre tres humble et tres obeissant serviteur   (signé) DE VERGENNES

To Vergennes
Copy: Library of Congress

Sir   Passy, sept. 16. 1779.

The Person mentioned in your Excellency's Letter of yesterday, has been with me, and by the Papers he show'd me I was Satisfy'd of his having been a Lieutenant in our Canadian Regiment, commanded by Col. Livingston.[1] I gave him Money, as he had none Left, to bear his Expenses to Nantes, where he hop'd to find a Passage to America. He proposed to set out directly for the place on foot, as he Said he could not bear the Motion of The Common Cariages and I gave him a Pass whether he has really taken that Road, may easily be known by enquiry as he wore a blue Uniforme turn'd up with red, is very meagre, and limps a little in Walking.—[2] I look'd upon him as an honest man, but I may have been impos'd on. I Shall write to morrow to Nantes, to know if he arriv'd there. It was on ———— that he came here, and it was the Day following that he propos'd to proced to Nantes, With The most perfect Respect I am Your Excell'ys Most obedient and most humble servant

M. Le Comte de Vergennes.

1. The First Canadian Regiment of the Continental Army, formed of Canadian refugees and commanded by Col. James Livingston (*DAB*): Fred Anderson Berg, *Encyclopedia of Continental Army Units: Battalions, Regiments and Independent Corps* (Harrisburg, Pa., 1972), p. 16.

2. De Guio's signatures on the promissory notes for the loan granted by BF (for which see our annotation of BF to Schweighauser, Sept. 13) are in a hand which appears either unsteady or unpracticed.

French Loan Certificate[3]

Passy, printed by Benjamin Franklin, [after May 30, 1780]. Form with
MS insertions in blanks, signed: American Philosophical Society; form
with blanks partially filled:[4] Yale University Library

[September 16, 1779]

N° 2.   Pour 250,000 livres.

Nous *Benjamin Franklin* Ministre Plenipotentiaire des ETATS-
UNIS de l'Amerique Septentrionale, en vertu du pouvoir dont
nous sommes revetus par le CONGRES desdits Etats, promet-
tons en son nom et solidairement pour lesdits Treize ETATS-
UNIS, faire payer *& rembourser au Tresor royal de sa Majesté tres
chretienne* le premier Janvier mil sept cent quatre-vingt *huit* au
domicile de M. Grand, Banquier a Paris, la somme de *deux cent*

3. Promising repayment for the second installment of a 1,000,000 *l.t.* loan
from the French government, for which see XXIX, 594n. Appearances to the
contrary, this elegant form does not date from Sept. 16. It was printed on
the marbled wove paper that BF had ordered from London stationer James
Woodmason in June, 1779, and would not receive until May 30, 1780. (BF
to Ferdinand Grand, May 30, 1780, Dibner Library of the History of Science and Technology, Smithsonian Institution. See also our headnote to
BF's letter to Fizeaux, Grand &. Cie., Oct. 29, below.) BF gave Vergennes
hand-written receipts for the first loan installments, and then replaced them
with back-dated forms when the English paper arrived.

Dozens of similar certificates, for installments of successive French loans
that would continue through 1782, were produced at Passy. They were
typeset in duplicate: identical forms printed side by side on a single sheet,
separated by a wide strip of marbling. When a set of certificates was filled
in, it was cut irregularly down the center of the marbled strip, creating a
unique pair. One half was submitted to the French government, the other
half was retained. The combination of the English wove paper, manufactured according to a technique that was as yet unknown in France, and the
interlocking marbled borders, insured that the documents could not be
counterfeited.

BF received the third installment of the present loan on Oct. 4, and the
fourth on Dec. 21. One half of certificate no. 3 is at the APS, and the other
is owned by Perc S. Brown, Orinda, Cal. (1956). Certificate No. 4 has not
survived. For a list of the loan installments see *JCC*, XXIV, 52–3.

4. This form, which does not have a marbled border, appears to be either
a proof sheet or a blundered copy. All the blanks are filled except the payee,
and BF misdated it twice; he originally wrote "4 Octobre," then changed it
to "6 Septembre."

cinquante mille livres, argent de France, avec les interets a raison de cinq pour cent, l'an, valeur reçu comptant, a Paris, ce *16 Septembre 1779*   B FRANKLIN

From Simon-Pierre Fournier le Jeune

ALS: American Philosophical Society

This letter is the earliest known reference to the script type that was cut especially for Franklin by the premier typefounder of Paris. It is proof that Franklin and Fournier had designed the type—which was not used at Passy until 1782—far earlier than has been generally suspected.[5]

Simon-Pierre Fournier le jeune, eldest son of the famous Pierre-Simon Fournier le jeune, had inherited his father's foundry in 1775, at the age of twenty-five.[6] His introduction to Franklin came three years later, when the American ordered a font of type to be shipped to the United States.[7] When the font was delivered and purchased, at the end of February, 1779, the newly appointed Minister Plenipotentiary had printing very much on his mind: he was at that moment negotiating with the man who would soon set up his Passy foundry.[8]

At what point Franklin hit upon the idea to have a unique type cut for his own official use is not clear. The suggestion may have come from Fournier, whose interest in cutting script led him to develop two other script character sets in 1780 and 1781.[9] If Fournier

5. As far as we know, BF used this type exclusively for passports; the earliest surviving example is dated May 8, 1782 (Hist. Soc. of Pa.). For the most thorough discussion of this type to date, which places its manufacture in 1781, see Luther S. Livingston, *Franklin and his Press at Passy* (New York, 1914), pp. 108–9, 116–17, 196.

6. The elder Fournier had died in 1768, leaving the typefoundry to his widow, who managed it with the assistance of Simon-Pierre. At her death in 1775, the son added "le jeune" to his name. See Jeanne Veyrin-Forrer, *La lettre et le texte* (Paris, 1987), pp. 110–11; A.M. Lottin, *Catalog chronologique des Libraires et des Libraires-Imprimeurs de Paris* ... (Paris, 1789), second pagination, pp. 238, 241–2.

7. XXVII, 92, 392–3; XXVIII, 505; XXIX, 347n. BF had previously purchased type from Fournier's cousin, Jean-François Fournier fils (XXVII, 618), and from Jacques-Louis Joannis (XXVII, 3).

8. See XXVIII, 586n; XXIX, lxiii–lxiv.

9. Veyrin-Forrer, *La lettre et le texte,* pp. 112–15.

346

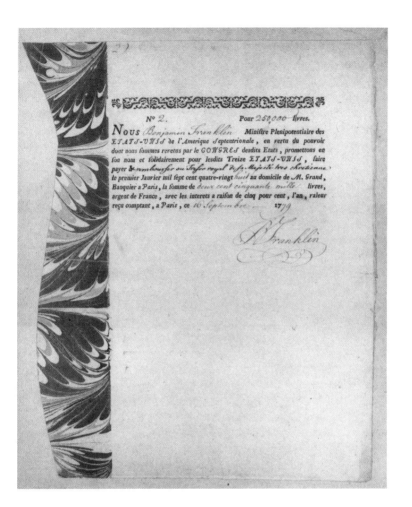

French Loan Certificate

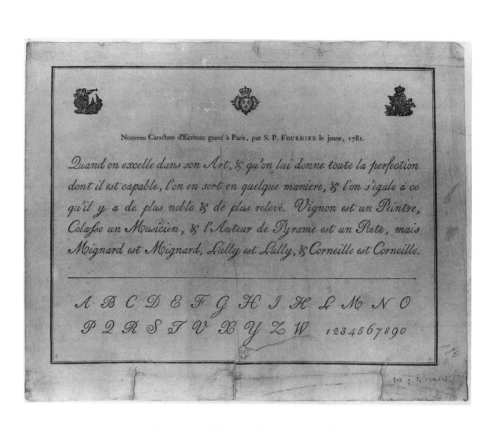

Specimen Sheet of "Le Franklin"

had already made the preliminary engravings and was beginning to cut punches by September, as he says here, then discussions between the two men must have substantially predated this letter.

Franklin and Fournier continued to confer about the type throughout 1780. Around June of that year, preliminary proofs of "le Franklin" were printed. By early 1781, the font was completed and a full specimen sheet printed. The matrices, along with the type, were delivered to the Passy press, and were eventually inherited by Benny Bache for use in his Philadelphia print shop.[1]

Monsieur! Paris Le 16 7bre. 1779.

J'ai L'honneur de vous envoyer Lucien Serrurier Pour vous prier de vouloir Bien lui expliquer Les 2. moules qu'il vous faut Pour Le Caractere que Je vous Grave.[2] Je Compte vous faire voir incessament plusieur Poinçon que j'ai Gravé dont vous serai Surement Satisfait. Si Je n'eu point été malade J'aurais eu L'honneur de vous en porter, mais Cela ne tardera Pas. J'y travaille a force, Je tache d'imiter La finesse des traits qui Sont Sur l'epreuve. Je Crains qu'a Limpression cela ne Grossit; J'en approcherai du Plus Pret qu'il me sera Possible. Si vous voulez lui expliquer Vos intentions il les fera supérieurement ayant Beaucoup de talent Pour Cette Partie C'est La son Genre.

J'ay l'honneur d'être très sincerement Monsieur Votre très humble et très obéissant serviteur FOURNIER LE JEUNE

Addressed: a Monsieur / Monsieur francklin / a Passy

Notation: fournier Le Jeune Paris 16. 7bre. 1779.

---

1. The 1780 proof is at the Columbia University Library. One of the 1781 specimen sheets, reproduced on the facing page, is at the Bibliothèque Nationale, Paris. Another, reproduced in Livingston, *Franklin and his Press at Passy,* facing p. 196, is at the APS.

2. Among BF's papers at the APS is the calling card of "Lucien Serrurier a la Place Cambray dans St Jean de Lateran." The smith had already received 24 *l.t.* from BF on Aug. 23: Cash Book (XXVI, 3). Letter-moulds, immensely complicated to construct, varied from font to font. BF had to specify the precise dimensions of the type he wanted. The process of typefounding was first detailed by Pierre-Simon Fournier le jeune in his *Manuel Typographique.* For an English translation, with reproductions of the original engravings, see Harry Carter, *Fournier on Typefounding* ... (London, 1930); the letter-mould is explained on pp. 192–8. See also John Dreyfus,

From James Lovell

ALS: University of Pennsylvania Library

Honble: Sir   Philada. Septr. 16th. 1779

On the 30th. of Augst. I received yr. favr. of June 2d. with the ministerial Paper containing Mauduit's Speculations[3] and, since that, several Pamplets wch. came under the care of Chevalr. de la Luzerne and, I think, under a Superscription in yr. Grandson's handwriting, have reached me. I am sure Hartley is stumbling only over a Mistake about the eventual alliance.[4] It is now in Vigor. It is defunct of course upon a Peace,[5] except so far as a Guarantee of the articles of that Peace and there can be no Sincerity in any pacific compact of Britain if she is not willing to have it guaranteed to us. He is more mistaken in his Idea of a distinction being *yet* in Vigor here, between the Ministry & People of Britain.[6] A short Space of Time will probably produce for his Perusal a solemn Vow & Compact not only of the Delegates in Congress but of the

---

Aspects of French Eighteenth Century Typography (Cambridge, England, 1982), pp. 2–5.

3. XXIX, 607–9.

4. Hartley argued that since the Treaty of Alliance was eventual (*i.e.,* did not come into effect automatically upon ratification) it was contingent on the British ministry's continued "hostile measures and designs" against America: *Letters on the American War* . . . (2nd ed., London, 1778), p. 85. This must be one of the pamphlets BF sent Lovell. BF had already attempted to disabuse Hartley of his hope that the United States would abandon the French alliance: XXVIII, 417–18, 461–4.

5. In a private letter BF professed to hope the alliance would be eternal and even after the signing of a provisional peace agreement with Britain in 1782 he argued that America's "true political interest" lay in continued exact fulfillment of the alliance: XXVIII, 369; Wharton, *Diplomatic Correspondence,* VI, 169. The French also argued that the alliance was perpetual; it was they who drafted Article XI of the Treaty of Alliance, which provided that the alliance's guarantees were to last "forever" and they continued to insist on this position after the war's conclusion: XXV, 521, 590–1; Lawrence S. Kaplan, "Toward Isolationism: the Rise and Fall of the Franco-American Alliance, 1775–1801," in Lawrence S. Kaplan, *Entangling Alliances with None: American Foreign Policy in the Age of Jefferson* (Kent, Ohio, and London, 1987), p. 83; "Correspondence of the Comte de Moustier with the Comte de Montmorin, 1787–1789," *American Hist. Rev.* VIII (1902–3), 728.

6. Hartley, *Letters on the American War,* p. 71. BF had expressed his disagreement on the point: XXVIII, 420.

348

whole Legislatures of the Union, never, *never* to form even a commercial Treaty with Great Britain. It was indeed once held out here, for political Purposes in the days of our Irresolution, that this was not a popular War in England. But it is not now at all necessary to disguise the Certainty that from the Tyrant George down to the Shoe and Soot Boy there is a proud desire to be yet able to say "*our* Colonies."

I have sent you so many Setts of the Journals of this year that I now only convey additional Numbers to compleat those Setts. I send you also 1777. I shall particularly press what you say to me of Pacquet Boats.[7] The Navy Board at Boston write to me in the same manner. I am, Sir, your most humb. Servt.

JAMES LOVELL

Honble. Doctr. Franklin

private

Endorsed: Mr. Lovell's Letters between April 29 & Sept. 6 1779. Recd. June 12. 1780

From Jonathan Williams, Jr.

ALS: American Philosophical Society

Dear & honoured Sir.   St Germain Sept: 16 1779

Notwithstanding my Industry, which I believe is equal to that of any new married Man, I have not been able to finish the Paper you left me. I am however far advanced & think I can promise it to you tomorrow morning at farthest.— I send my Servant to give you this Information least you should expect it to day, please to return my Bills by him if they are accepted.—

I likewise send by him the Copies of my Accounts which please to leave in your Bureau 'till I can come & compare them with the original.—

My Wife joins me in dutifull & affectionate Respects. I am ever your   J WILLIAMS J

---

7. BF had suggested that Congress establish a monthly packet boat service to France: XXIX, 609.

Addressed: His Excellency / Doctor Franklin.

Notation: Jonathan Williams Sept. 16. 79—

Sarah Bache to William Temple Franklin

ALS: American Philosophical Society

Dear Temple   Philadelphia September. 16 1779

There is nothing you could have sent me that would have been half so acceptable as the Bust of my dear Father, I am in hourly expectation of seeing it, and long as anxiously for its coming as if I could converse with it,[8] Mr Hopkinson has made me promise to send for him when it comes, and I promise you every ceremony shall be performed on the opening of the Box that you desire.

I have had two or three letters from your Father this Summer, who is perfectly well, always inquires afectionately about Papa's health and yours, he sent Betty a present of a Bonnet lately, whenever I hear from you I always write to him, by the great fire in N. York when the Kings stores were burnt, he writes me he lost four thousand pound's, Thomas is still with him—

Mr Bache writes to you by this opportunity, the Children are quite well Willy often speaks of you and asks when he is to go to Paris to his Grandpapa—

Mr Gerard will take care of a little Box of Squirril Skins for you, which is all I could get at present I think there is eighty four, as soon as I can collect more you may depend on my sending them to you, ever since you have been gone I have been looking out for some and tho I have been most of the time in the country could never procure any tho I have had a thousand promises, I have been lucky enough to find out two little Boys who live near Mr Dufeilds that have traind a house

8. WTF had written on June 1 that he was sending the bust with the chevalier de la Luzerne. In answer to the present letter, he explained that the chevalier could not find room on the frigate for the crate, and it has been lying at Lorient ever since. See XXIX, 613n; WTF to Sarah Bache, March 18, 1780, APS.

Cat up to hunt ground squirrils and they will let me have all they take—[9]
The house at Bethlehem is at present so unsetled cotton so scarce, and the people so much taken up in Manufacturing for their own Family that there is no such thing as getting any thing done by them, at Ledietz the second Moravian setlement, where there is plenty of their best spinners, and the Lady Abbess an acquaintance of mine (who Papa will know by the name of Polly Pennery she inquired much about him and desired her best respects when I wrote) who promiss'd to use her interest to get me two pound of Cotton spun for Stockings and a piece of Linnen of forty yards wove, I took it some months before I left Manheim myself, and was to have had it home last month was a year, the other day I had a letter telling me that if I would wait with patience another year I might depend on having it, but I have sent for it away, as my patience like my linnen is quite wore out, however you may depend on me that if things on this side the water should be in any degree as they used to be the cotton shall be sent to you or any thing else that its in my power to oblige you in, for their is few people for whom I have more afection, you desire me to name what I want on your side the Water, I shall take the liberty of mentioning a few things which I cannot procure here for money and which I shall be much obliged to you for, a small trunk with writing materials from paper down to sand, this bad as it is we were obliged to a Freind for, a small pocket book a good pen knife and scissors, and some paris needles with some of the darning kind, the last three articles I hear are better made at Paris, than any other part of the world, the thead you ordered me was the best I ever worked with I wish you could procure me some more of the same, and some of different colours, and a small quantity of Muslin, or any other

9. WTF had wanted the skins to line a winter coat. He did not receive the box until February, 1781, at which time he complained to his aunt that they had been destroyed by worms. The next shipment, he directed, should be packed in tobacco dust and placed in a tin case. WTF to Sarah Bache, Feb. 19, 1781, Library of Congress. See also Lopez and Herbert, *The Private Franklin*, p. 224.

materials for Caps as I now am grown too old to go without, and I cannot give forty pound a yard for Muslin and ten dollars a yard for ribon to fasten it on, the things may be sent in something that will serve me for a work trunk or Basket as all mine have been worn out with traveling about, perhaps you may have it in your power to send them by the return of this ship which would greatly add to the obligation— when my Father is at leasure I wish you would mention to him that our beds are much worn out with moving about and no ticking to be had here the pillows too in the same way, I am obliged to borrow dishes and plates whenever we ask a Friend which is very disagreable tho but seldom, and knifes and forks, I should be glad to have some common hankerchiefs, with coarse check for Bed cases, these things I hope my dear Papa will not think unnessary, and I shall be obliged to your Friendship to take a proper time to mention it to him—

Willy and our little Black ey'd parrot[1] who I am sure you would be fond of if you knew her, (she is just the age Will was when you came from england, and goes down stairs just like him) both join in love to you, she desires you would send her a doll not a fine one, but one that will bear to be pul'd about with a great deal of Nursing, there is no such things to be had here as toys for Children— the plates I mentioned above I do not wish to have of China any thing in the Queens Ware way will do every bit as well, a common sett of what is called breakfast China would be very acceptable, tho Mr B. and I drink milk of a morning yet I want the other when a Friend comes here in the afternoon as I dont like to use my best in common, this will be a troublesome letter but I trust you will excuse it—

The Dufeild Family, and the Miss Cliftons I delivered your compliments too, and they desire to be remembered to you in a particular manner, the latter have just made a Vandue and are going in lodgings almost as far as Pools bridge, Mr & Mrs Peters I have not seen since I receiv'd yours, she now lays in the Country with her second Son,[2] I shall deliver your Com-

1. Elizabeth.
2. He was Richard Peters (Aug. 4, 1779–1848), who became a prolific legal scholar: *DNB* under his father Richard Peters.

pliments as soon as she comes to town— I am with great Sincerity your very Afectionate Aunt   S BACHE

Endorsed: Ansd 19 Mar 80— / Mrs Bache Sep. 16. 1779

To Schweighauser   Copy: Library of Congress

Sir   Passy, Sept. 17. 1779
    I have now before me your favours of july 31. & Aug. 19.[3] Your testimony with Regard to Mr. Wam. Lee, is fully Sufficient to remove the Suspicion of his Sharing in your Commission. I mention'd it not as a Charge against him, but as an Excuse for you; 5 per Cent being, as I understood more then double of what is usual.[4] I could wish I had nothing to do with mercantile Business, as I am not vers'd in it. I perceive that you have abated the Commission on the Delivery of The Tobacco to one per Cent. but then that is 1 per Ct. paid to your Correspondent, and another 1 Per Ct. for your self. To me it Seems that your Commission should be not on the whole sum, but on what you paid your Correspondent for doing the Business; otherwise we pay twice for The Same service. I must submit however to the Custom of Merchants. It may be against me, and if it is I suppose it is founded in some Reason that at Present I am unacquainted with. But if these Two Commissions are right, the Article for travelling Charges 1024 livres wants Explanation.
    Notwistanding what I Said relating to Such of your Drafts as are founded on the part of your Account, I have refused none, but honoured them all.
    I am Satisfy'd with your Reason about the Date of your Bills. If I Should at any time be so Straitned for Money when in your Debt, as that a Sudden Demand from you would be inconvenient to me, I will mention it to you, and request your Bills may be drawn at one or two Usances.
    The Swedish Ambassador has presented a Memorial to Mr.

3. Both letters are missing.
4. See BF to Schweighauser, July 25. Schweighauser finally did reduce his commission to 2½ percent: *Adams Papers*, VIII, 73n.

De Vergennes relating to The Prize[5] and the demanded Damages. He mentioned that the Swedish People were beaten and cruelly treated by ours. This is so contrary to our Custom, that I can hardly believe it. I must answer his memorial, and therefore wish to see again the Papers, that I may examine them. I think I sent them down to you, when I desired you to get some of the Letters Translated. Please to return them to me, and you Shall have them again when wanted for the Trial. If you have received the Opinion of The advocate of The Bureau of Prizes, which you expected, please to Send me a Copy of it.

The two Sick Persons who came over among the Prisoners from England, Should undoubtedly be taken care of till they are able to go home. I wish to know their Names and the Parts of America they come from. I have no Objection to continuing the allowance to Capt. Harris, Supposing that he intends going by the first Opportunity.—[6] Please to present my Compliments to him, and request him to inform me about a Trunk belonging to Mr. Louis Dupré, which was intrusted to his Care, and which is enquired after.

I thought to have had the Dispatches ready to send by Capt. Samson this Day; but there are some Points on which I must wait an answer from the Court, in order to send that answer in my Letters; This may yet require some days: but I think it will not exceed another Week.

I approve of your assisting the American Prisoners that are arrived from Lisbon, in the manner that Mr. Adams ordered for those come from England. They were I believe generally pretty well cloathed by Charities collected there if any of These should be apparently in great want of cloathing it will be well to assist them with what may be absolutely necessary in that Article.

I should think it would be right to discharge M. Hill the Surgeon.[7] I am Sorry he has been kept so long. In my Opinion Surgeons Should never be detain'd as Prisoners, as it is their

5. The *Victoria.*

6. Capt. John Harris, to whom BF had written on Aug. 12, above.

7. Samuel Hill had written BF on July 20, above, to appeal for his freedom.

Duty and their Practice to help the Sick and wounded of either side when they happen to have an Opportunity— They Should therefore be considered not as Parties in any War, but as friends to Humanity.

I request you to make enquiry by your Correspondents in the Different Ports of Spain, what English Prisoners brought in by the Americans, were confined There. When you receive Answers, please to communicate them to me.

I inclose you a Copy of what I write to Mr. Williams relating to my Orders about the Prisoners.[8] We must not regard Reports.

I have the honour to be with great Esteem. Sir &c

I will transmit to Congress the memoire relating to The Barron d'Autroche.

M. Schweighauser.

From Edward Bridgen[9]   ALS: American Philosophical Society

Dear Sir   Sepr 17 1779

I have sent to the care of our good Monsieur Genet 2 Samples of Metal intended for the Current Coin,[1] where they are doubtless much wanted and yield an immense profit to the Govermt.

I hereby engage to deliver at the port of London as fine in quality and of the Same Size and weight as those samples any quantity at 14 d Sterling per pound weight—Package, Cartage and other Incidental expences to be paid by the purchaser. Peices of half the weight or double the weight may be had on the same Terms and all of the best Copper. These peices are

8. Missing.

9. This is the first mention of Bridgen's plan to supply Congress with blank copper rounds, to be stamped and used for coinage. BF was enthusiastic but lacked the authorization to contract for the copper; see his answer of Oct. 2. When Bridgen wrote a formal proposal to Congress in 1782 BF forwarded it with his endorsement (to Livingston, Dec. 24, 1782, National Archives) but the plan was never adopted.

1. Edme-Jacques Genet forwarded the samples with a cover letter dated Sept. 29, which asked BF for confirmation of their receipt. APS.

1/3 of an Ounce and may well pass for the Same value as half pence do in England. I beg to know your sentiments as soon as possible otherways the proprietor *must* make his offer to another quarter here.

If a Die is wanting that may also be procured here with the necessary implements for working the Same. In that case proper drawings must be furnished but I think it would not be so prudent to have the execution here.

As it will be a ready Money Article upon the delivery of the Metal the Cash or good Bills at 2 Usa should be provided and if the proposal be accepted I wish to know your opinion how much may be wanted.

May your most valuable life be preserv'd to Nestorian age[2] or as long as you can be happy in yourself and can contribute to the felicity of Mankind is the sincere wish of my Dr Sir Yr: faithful & affect. EDWD: BRIDGEN

Notation: Edw Bridgen 17 7bre 1779.[3]

From Girardot, Haller & Cie.[4]

AL: American Philosophical Society

Paris 7bre 17. 1779

Messieurs Girardot, Haller & Co. most respectful Compliments to the Honourable Doctr. Franklin And send him the inClos'd letter, should it require An Answer, please to send it to us, and they will take care to forward it, to its addres.

To The Honble Doctr. FrankLin at Passy

Notation: Girardot haller Paris 17. 7bre. 1779.

2. BF had reached it: Nestor was in his seventies while dispensing sage advice in the *Iliad.*

3. Elsewhere on the same sheet as the notation are the following jottings in BF's hand: "1000 lt   48000 Pieces   Cost £58.6.8".

4. As far as we know, these bankers had last written BF in November, 1778: XXVIII, 32–3. The present letter is in the hand of Rodolphe-Emmanuel Haller.

From the Marine Committee

Gentlemen   September 17th 1779
   We have received the honor of yours of the 3d. June last to
which we shall now reply.[5] We are sorry for the trouble which
you have had with the Conspirators belonging to the Alliance,
and at this time can think of no better method of disposing of
them than Sending them out to this Continent by different
Vessels proportioning the number to each Vessel, so as not to
render it dangerous or inconvenient; and upon their Arrival if
Sufficient evidence can be had it is our intention to bring them
to trial by Court Martial. We are perfectly satisfied with the
manner in which you have disposed of the Alliance, and have
strong expectations that the little Squadron under Captain
Jones will by their Success furnish Ample funds to repay All
the Disbursments that have been made for that ship.
   Although we are fully sensible of the perplexity which you
have already had in transacting our Maritime business & of
the impropriety of taking up your time from affairs of more
general importance, when Consuls should be appointed at the
several seaports & provided with funds for that purpose, yet
the necessity we are now under of furnishing the sr Gerard
with a suitable ship to carry himself & family to France
obliges us once more to trouble you by committing the direction of that ship to your care having at present no alterna-
tive—assuring you that we shall use our endeavours to make
it the last of the kind. This Ship is called the Confederacy
mounts 36 Guns, commanded by Seth Harding Esqr who we
have Ordered, on his arrival, to transmit you a state of his
Ship, and to be governed in all things by your orders as you
will perceive by the enclosure.[6] We have in view that this Ship

   5. XXIX, 615–18. This letter reported on BF's problems in outfitting the
Alliance and asked the Marine Committee to outfit no more ships in France.
   6. The frigate Confederacy was launched at Norwich, Conn., in November,
1778, and placed under the command of Seth Harding (1734–1814), a longtime resident of the city: DAB; William James Morgan, Captains to the Northward: the New England Captains in the Continental Navy (Barre, Mass., 1959),
pp. 144–5. The Marine Committee's Sept. 17 instructions to him (a copy of
which presumably was enclosed with the present letter) are given in Smith,

on her return should bring back as much Military Stores for the use of our Army as can be provided in time so as not to detain her or incommode her as a Ship of war which we request you will order Accordingly and dispatch her as soon as possible. As it is probable that the Captain, Officers and Crew will stand in need of some Supplies of Cloathing (and as they have wages due to them) a little money, we request that you will Order them advances to be made but with a sparing hand. We have the honor to be Your Excellencys very Hble servants

P.S. We have the pleasure to inform you that our frigates have lately had very great Success, having among many other Captures, taken ten homeward bound Jamaica Men fully ladened and two packets One Outward and the Other homeward bound—[7] For particulars beg leave to refer you to the Papers.—

His Excellency Dr. Benjamin Franklin Minister Esqr Plenipotentiary at the Court of Versailles

To Sartine
Copy: Library of Congress

Sir   Passy, Sept. 18. 1779.
I have examined the Papers which your Excellency did me the honour to Send me the 11th. of last Month relative to the Prizes and Ransoms taken by the american Privateer the Black Prince, and am of Opinion that the Same are good being taken from the Enemies of the United States.[8] I therefore pray your

---

Letters, XIII, 510–11. The *Confederacy* finally sailed from downriver of Chester, Pa., on Oct. 26, carrying both Gérard and John Jay, minister designate to the court of Spain: Meng, *Despatches of Gérard,* pp. 901–2n; Morgan, *Captains to the Northward,* pp. 181–2.

7. See our annotation of Jones's July 26 letter.

8. The enclosed papers probably were from the Admiralty of Morlaix; see BF to Sartine, Aug. 14, and Coffyn to BF, Aug. 30. On Sept. 8, above, BF expressed to Coffyn his doubts that he had the authority to judge prizes. He must have learned in the interim that according to French prize law he did have such authority; see also his Sept. 18 condemnations of the *Bonhomme Richard*'s and the *Black Prince*'s prizes and his Sept. 19 letter to John

Excellency to give such Directions relating thereto, to the admiralty of Morlaix, as may be necessary for the advantage of the Owners of that Privateer. With the greatest Respect, I am, Your Excellency's most obedient.

M. De Sartine.

To Vergennes

LS:[9] Archives du Ministère des affaires étrangères; copy: Library of Congress

Sir   Passy, Sept. 18. 1779.

I send herewith to your Excellency a Translation of the Invoices of the Goods desired, with the Original.[10] The Packet Boat which brought our Dispatches will be ready to depart for America next Week, but shall wait your Orders. She is a fast Sailer being built expressly for the Business; and the Captain[11] is a trusty Person who will take good Care of any Letters you may think fit to charge him with.

It will be of great Importance that I should inform the Congress by this Opportunity what Success is like to attend their Application.

I am, with the utmost Respect, Your Excellencys, most obedient & most humble Servant.   B FRANKLIN

M. Le Cte. de Vergennes.

Torris. Meanwhile Torris had pleaded to BF for an immediate decision: above, Sept. 12.

9. In WTF's hand.

10. The invoices were those which the committee for foreign affairs had sent BF on July 16, above. They included a list of materials for a 74-gun ship of the line building at Portsmouth, N.H. (the *America:* XXVIII, 623n), a similar list for a 36-gun frigate (a copy of which is at the Hist. Soc. of Pa.), a list of clothing desired for the navy (a copy of which is at the APS), and a list of items to be imported for the board of war and ordnance (a copy and French translation of which are at the Hist. Soc. of Pa.). All of these are at the AAE. For a more detailed description of them see Smith, *Letters,* XIII, 229n.

11. Simeon Samson of the *Mercury.*

Certificate Condemning a Prize

Printed by Benjamin Franklin, Passy, 1779. Printed form with MS insertions in blanks: Archives Départementales du Morbihan

By the time Franklin received Francis Coffyn's letter of September 18, below, enclosing a copy of the French government's regulations concerning American prizes, he had already seen those regulations and had finally understood that he bore responsibility for judging the prizes' legality. On September 18 he issued his first two certificates of condemnation. The one immediately below, printed at Passy in Fournier's *gros romain*, is a form designed for the case of a single prize ship and was obviously composed with the help of a French hand. The document that follows, handwritten and in English, is a certificate judging the legality of multiple captures, including ships ransomed rather than being brought into port. It would serve as a model for all subsequent certificates covering multiple prizes or ransoms, which Franklin would continue to draft on an individual basis in English.

Four days after sending this printed form to the Admiralty of Vannes, Franklin submitted to them an identical certificate made out for another of Jones's prizes, the *Fortune*.[1] He filled out both forms himself, and in his perennial battle with French genders, wrote "Bonne" in the feminine even though it preceded "homme." He also corrected by hand a number of typographical errors, adding the final "e" to "Capitaine" and drawing in cedillas, where needed, on the letter "c." At some point thereafter he corrected the type, this time using the character "ç" and also deleting the "e" in the word "reçeu." Only five examples of the second printing are known; one is dated December 21, 1779, and four are blank.[2]

1. The second condemnation, dated Sept. 22, is also at the Archives Départementales du Morbihan and is printed in J.-L. Debauve, "Un Américain en Bretagne: séjours dans l'Ouest de John Paul Jones (1778–1780)," *Annales de Bretagne et des Pays de l'Ouest (Anjou, Maine, Touraine)*, LXXXIV (1977), 221. For Jones's prizes see BF to Sartine, Sept. 5, and our annotation of Gourlade & Moylan's letter of Sept. 6. The *Fortune* and *May Flower* were sold on Oct. 4 and 12, respectively: Debauve, "Un Américain en Bretagne," p. 213.

2. The certificate of Dec. 21, made out for the *Betsey*, is at the Bibliothèque municipale de Nantes. One of the blank forms is at the Library of

MESSIEURS,   Passy, ce *18. septembre* 1779

J'ai reçeu les Procés verbaux, & les autres Papiers, que vous m'avez fait l'honneur de m'addresser, en conformité de l'Article onze du Reglement du 27 Septembre 1778. Ces Pieces concernent la Prise du Navire nommé le *Fleur de May* dont étoit Captaine le Sieur *Thomas Molony,* parti du Port de *Limerick en Ireland,* & qui étoit destiné pour le Port de *Londres,* & arrivée dans le Port françois *de l'Orient* aprés avoir été pris le *21* du mois de *Août,* par le Capitaine *John Paul Jones* commandant le Navire Americain le *Bonne homme Richard,* & muni d'une Commission du Congrés des Etats-Unis de l'Amerique. Par l'examen, Messieurs, que j'ai fait du susdittes pieces, il me parait que le dit Navire le *Fleur de May* est de bonne Prise, étant fait sur les ennemis des Etats-Unis; Et je vous prie, lorsque vous en serez requis par le Capitaine on Armateur du dit Navire le *Bonne homme Richard* ou par leur Representant, de proceder à la vente de la susditte Prise, en conformité du Reglement du 27 Septembre 1778.

J'ai l'honneur d'étre, MESSIEURS, Vôtre trés humble, & trés obeissant Serviteur,   B FRANKLIN

A Messieurs les Juges de l'Amirauté de Vannes—

Notation: Engregistré au greffe de lamirauté a vannes le 22 8bre 1779. LEMAREC

Certificate Condemning Prizes[3]

ADS (draft): Historical Society of Delaware

[September 18, 1779]

I the underwritten, Minister Plenipotentiary from the United States of America to the Court of France, have perused the

---

Congress, one is at the Yale University Library, and two are at the APS. The blank form is reproduced in Luther S. Livingston, *Franklin and His Press at Passy* (New York, 1914), facing p. 80.

3. Which BF sent to Torris with a covering letter of Sept. 19, below. See also BF to Sartine, Sept. 18.

Procès verbaux, or Examinations taken before the Judges of the Admiralty at Morlaix and communicated to Me by M. de Sartine Minister of the Marine, relating to the Capture of the Brigantine Dublin of Bristol, Thomas Griffiths, Commander, made by the Black Prince, Capt. Merchant, an American Privateer, on the 19th of July last, and brought into Morlaix, and relating to sundry Ransoms for a Number of Vessels, taken by the said Privateer,[4] the Ransomers for which were all examined on Oath; viz.

John Martin, For the Sloop two Brothers, John Guy Master ransomed for 150£ Sterling, and also the same

John Martin, For the Sloop Diligence, or Speedwell, William Sleman Master ransomed for 100£ Sterling.

John Williams, for the Brigantine Anne, James Evans Master, ransomed for 100£ Sterling.

Thomas Row, for the Brigantine Lucy, Henry Row, Master, ransomed for 300£ Sterling.

Richard Hodgson for the Brigantine Monmouth, Thomas Hodgson, Master, ransomed for 315£ Sterling.

William Trich for the Brigantine Union, of Bortcastle John Trich, Master, ransomed for 200£ Sterling

Philip Peak or Peack for The Brigantine Sea Nymph, Philip Peak or Peack, Master, ransomed for 120£ Sterling

Thomas Codd, for the Sloop Charlotte, Thomas Codd Master ransomed for 515£ Sterling—

Robert Lander, for the Sloop John, George Lander Master, ransomed for 105£ Sterling—

George Sharp, for the Sloop Rebecca; Nicholas Randel, Master, ransomed for £73.10. Sterling

Stephen Brown, for the Sloop Rebecca, Henry Eastaway Master, ransomed for 120£ Sterling.

All which Captures appear to me from the said Examinations & *Procès verbaux* had before the said Court of Admiralty, to be good and lawful Prizes, being taken from the Enemies of the United States of America, by Virtue of a Commission from

---

4. The prizes mentioned were made during the *Black Prince*'s second cruise; see Marchant's July 25 letter and Clark, *Ben Franklin's Privateers,* pp. 45–52.

the Congress of the said States. And I do therefore pray the Judges of the said Court, that when they shall be requested so to do by the said Captain or his Owners, or their Representative, they will proceed to the Sale of the said Prize the Dublin in Conformity to the Royal Ordinance of the 27th of September 1778.   B FRANKLIN

At Passy this 18 Day of Sept. 1779.

From Richard Bache   ALS: American Philosophical Society

Dear & Hond: sir   Philadelphia Sepr. 18, 1779.

I have yours of 2d. June via Boston— I have also since received a few Lines from you of 10th. Jany., covering Letters for some French Gentlemen in our Army, which I have forwarded to them—[5] I am glad to find you got mine of the 22d. October last, as I am now certain you have received the loan Office bills for Interest of your Money—[6] You do not mention the receipt of them, but I suppose it was thro' the multiplicity of your business that you forgot it.

I now send you first Bills of four sets for another years Interest, amounting to 486 Dollars, which I wish safe to your hands; these Bills now sell here Sixteen for one. I have sold some that I received for Interest of my Brother's Money, at that rate, which in nominal value is almost equal to the original sum deposited in the Loan Office—

I find I was not so particular in my Letter of 22 Octr. last respecting the Types sold to the State of Virginia as I had been in some of my preceding Letters, but I now beg leave to mention to you, as I still find myself at a loss how to make out the account, that the state of Virginia took all the Types, except the Six cases of Types which the Congress have, all the Letters, flowers, cases, Iron chasis &c. &c.—[7] The Mahogany

---

5. BF's letter of June 2 is in XXIX, 597–600. The Jan. 10 letter is missing; requests of that period for BF to forward mail are summarized in XXVIII, 46–7.

6. XXVII, 599–602.

7. For background on the types sold to Virginia see XXIX, 598–9. BF there explains that in order to set a value on the type he needed a precise ac-

Presses, they did not take, they fell into worse hands; for one Robinson a Printer, when the Enemy were here and who now lives in Newyork,[8] got some intelligence of them, & procured an order from one of the General Officers to take them, & convert them to his own use— When the Types were delivered to the State of Virginia, I concluded you had an account of their weight & cost, I therefore did not weigh them, nor did I know the different sorts they consisted of; and as they were sold & delivered but a short time before the Enemy came here, I was glad to get them off my hands, without being so particular in the delivery, as otherwise I should have been, seeing that it was impossible for me to have them sent out of Town to a place of Safety— Being totally ignorant of the weight it is impossible for me to make out the account as you direct— I could wish therefore, that you would put down what you think is the Stirling cost of the whole or as near it as you can come; I see no other way now of setling it, and the State of Virginia have left it to yourself to fix the price— The weight of the Six Cases taken by Congress I cannot now come at, as undoubtedly many are lost and broken, you will therefore be pleased to mention what you think the value of them may be.

I am obliged to you for your recommendation to the Merchants of France as a Correspondent; my last Letters will inform you, that I have formed a Connection with Mr. Shee, & established a house for the purpose of doing Commission business— I now send you a number of our circular Letters, with a request that you will disperse them, & return me a list

---

counting of what was sold; he seems not to have repeated this explanation to his son-in-law, who inquired again about the type's value on Sept. 9, 1783 (APS). After BF returned to Philadelphia he wrote to Patrick Henry asking for an account of the type from whoever had received it, and assistance in procuring payment (Oct. 8, 1785, APS.) He eventually received an account, and submitted a claim to the state of Virginia, through William Alexander, on Nov. 26, 1789 (Alexander to Edmund Randolph, Va. State Library). BF died without having received payment, and left the sum due him to RB: Smyth, *Writings*, x, 495.

8. Probably James Robertson, the New York Loyalist printer: xxix, 598n.

of the Merchants you send them to—[9] Our exports for Flour & other Staples will, I believe, soon take place, and as Congress have come to a Resolution, to emit no more than a certain sum & pledged their Faith to the United States that it shall be so, I trust our Money will appreciate by just degrees— As the prices of imported Articles bear a proportion with the Exports, & leave a considerable profit, I can't see that the Adventurer can be affected by the depreciation, and tho' he may not understand the depreciation, if he finds a profit accrue from the Voyage, equivalent to the risque, his purpose is answered— If from the experiments the Merchants of France have made, they have had reason to judge unfavorably of their American connections, and some of them have been induced to think they have been cheated, I am sorry for it— We wish for an opportunity of evincing to them, that such connections may be formed with this Country in the trading line, as will well answer the Adventurer's purpose, and reflect honor on the Trade & Connection—

You make me happy by telling me that you have had a great deal of pleasure in Ben, as well as by the character you give me of him— I am confident you sending him to Geneva is meant for his benefit, therefore I feel perfectly satisfied with the measure, tho' he is removed at such a distance from under your immediate Eye— His Mama & I have wrote to him by this opportunity— We shall be glad to see the Letters he writes you, as his correspondence with you will be more frequent probably than with us— We wish you may have leisure to go and see him, the Journey may conduce to your health, & prolong a Life that we affectionately respect & love—

Among the many Memoirs you have sent me, I find there is an Inquiry after Colonel Fleury[1] you may acquaint his Friends that he is in good health & that he has gained immortal honor this summer, at the attack on Stoney point up the North River;

9. For the list of merchants, and RB's earlier request for it, see XXIX, 273.

1. Several people had inquired after Lt. Col. François-Louis Teissèdre de Fleury: XXVI, 329; XXVII, 320–1. For Fleury's part in Gen. Anthony Wayne's July 15/16 capture of the British fort at Stony Point see Mark Mayo Boatner III, *Encyclopedia of the American Revolution* (New York, 1966), pp. 1062–7.

being acquainted with him, I will endeavour to prevail on him to write to his friends, but he possesses so much military Genius, that he cannot pay attention to any thing but the Art of War— We are sensibly affected at the speedy departure of Mr. Gerard; he has gained the affections of the people in this place most exceedingly—[2] He has been remarkably civil to your Daughter Sally and myself, and we are both much attached to him— We have often wished to have had it in our power, to make suitable returns, not only from pride, but from the real affection we bear him, & the pleasure it would have given us to have paid every attention to his merit; but as circumstances would not admit of it, he must take the will for the deed— He is kind enough to take charge of our packets— In the box which contains the Squirrel Skins, you will find the late Philadelphia papers, those that have come in since the Box was packt up, I send herewith; also a few more Skins which Mrs. Duffield & Miss Sally[3] brought to Town this day— They beg to be remembered to you affectionately.

Not knowing what port Mr. Gerard may put into, I send to your care a Letter for Jonathan Williams, which I beg of you to forward to him— Sally and the Children join me in Love & Duty— I am ever Dear Sir Your affectionate Son

RICH. BACHE

Dr. Franklin

2. On Sept. 13 RB wrote WTF, praising Gérard as he does here (APS). Gérard's popularity has been a subject of debate among historians. John J. Meng felt that he had made a favorable impression on Americans and that "Even those who had differed with him politically admitted his abilities as a diplomat and his qualities as an individual." (Meng, *Despatches of Gérard,* p. 119.) William Stinchcombe argued that he lacked the personality and political understanding to overcome American suspicions and that his mission was a disappointment to Vergennes: William C. Stinchcombe, *The American Revolution and the French Alliance* (Syracuse, 1969), pp. 45–6.

3. Mary Parry Duffield was an old friend of DF and the Baches and the wife of Edward Duffield; for her background see Edward Duffield Neill, "Rev. Jacob Duché, the First Chaplain of Congress," *PMHB,* II (1878), 61n. The Duffields' daughter Sarah was born Jan. 1, 1756: *ibid.,* p. 62n.

From William Bett

ALS: American Philosophical Society

May it please your Excellency Brest Sept. 18th 1779

We hope you will not be offended at the liberty taken by Three Distress'd young Men Natives of America who are at preasent on board the Gentlle Frigate[4] hear and are Very disireous of getting home as the have very responcible Freinds in America. Therefore most Earnestly Requests youll Demand us that we may return home as we Are sure our assistance is wanted on Board some of Our Vessels. If your Excellency is kind Enough to Favour us with An Answer Please to Dirict to Sir your most Obedt. Humb Servt. WM. BETT

Addressed: His Excellency / John Franklin Esqr. / Paris

Notations: W. Bett. Brest 18. 7bre. 1779. / paye a nantes

From Francis Coffyn

ALS: American Philosophical Society

Hond. Sir Dunkirk Sepber. 18th. 1779

I duly received your Excellencys much respected favour of 8 inst, in answer to which I have the honnour to inform your Excellency that on a farther inquiry about the condemnation of the prizes brought into the ports of this kingdom by the American ships of war & privateers, I found that there has been a regulation made by the french Court, & publish'd on the 27 Sepber 1778, it consists of 15. articles concerning the formalities to be observed respecting the prizes carried into the ports of the united States by the french ships of war & those brought into the ports of this kingdom by the Americans, a Copy of which regulation, I take the liberty to inclose. By the 11th. article your Excellency will observe that the same formalities are prescribed to the masters of the American prizes, as those mention'd in the 42d article of another regulation of the 24th June 1778. concerning the captures made by the french privateers, and that the officers of the Admiralty in the port where the prizes arrive, are order'd to instruct the

---

4. The French Navy frigate *Gentille,* 26: Dull, *French Navy,* p. 357.

process, and to send the Copys with the original papers to the Deputees of the united States at Paris.[5]

As your Excellency is pleased to mention that you do not find that you have any authority to try any causes of the kind, I am apt to think that the condemnation is refer'd to the Judgement of the Courts Establish'd for that purpose in America, and that your Excellency is to forward to such Courts the papers which the officers of the Admiralty are directed to send to your Excellency. But as the sending of these papers to America, would naturaly be attended with delays, it Seems that the Legislator of this law, in order to avoid the prejudices which a long lapse of time might occasion, before the condemnation is received, has permitted the Sale by the 10th & 12th. articles.[6] The officers of the Admiralty at Morlaix refusing to sell the prizes of the black prince before the condemnation is produced, makes me think that they are not acquainted with the said regulations, I therefor advised the owners of said privateer to send a Copy of it to their Correspondent at Morlaix, and in consequence present a petition to that Court to demand the Sale and if they still persist in their refusal, I will inform your Excellency of it, and I dont doubt but on applying to the Minister of the marine Department, he will immediately give orders to the said officers to conform to the said regulations. I am Sorry that I have been under the necessity to trouble your Excellency on this matter, but Justice as well as the frequent applications made to me by the owners of said privateer, has embolden'd me to transmit their representations to your Excellency. In order to avoid the same trouble & difficulties in future, I advised them to take french Commissions for the black prince & princess, but they objected that it was not practicable for the following reasons. The french privateers are only allowed to have one third part

5. Article 11 of the regulations instructed the French admiralty officers to receive reports from the captors and to send the results of their proceedings to the American deputies at Paris: Sir Francis Piggott and G.W.T. Omond, eds., *Documentary History of the Armed Neutralities 1780 and 1800* (London, 1919), p. 102.

6. Expressing particular concern about perishable merchandise aboard prizes, articles 10 and 12 authorized such sales: *ibid.*

of the crew foreigners, and the above two vessells are intended to be navigated by American & Irish Seamen only; the black prince is now recruiting on the coast of Ireland as many hands as will be necessary to man the princess, they speaking the same language, they may Easely pass for americans in case they should be taken and thereby avoid the punishment they would be Exposed to suffer, if they were taken with a french Commission; and I may venture to add, that if they could not obtain one from Congress, for the black princess which is now fitting out here, they would prefer to go back to Ireland notwithstanding the danger of being impress'd and sent on board an English man of war. Besides their conditions on board the American ships are more advantageous as they share one half of the prizes, whilst they have but one third in those taken by the french Ships, more over they shew the greatest reluctance to serve on board the latter, the difference of the language & customs are obstacles they can not get over.

On the other hand the successes of the black prince and the interruption he causes to the English navigation in the Irish Channell where in the course of three months he has taken upwards of thirty vessells, which has not been paralell'd by any other before, shews the advantage the publick may reap from these armements, they deprive the Ennemy of a number of resolute fellows, who instead of being usefull, to them, turn their arms against them, and I dont doubt if they meet encouragement here, they will be followed by a great many of their Countrymen; an other object which merits some consideration, is that if the above two privateers can cruize together, they will be able to bring a number of prisonners which will serve to Exchange against the Americans now labouring under a desagreable captivity in England.

I submit all these considerations to your Excellency, they are not dictated by any personnal advantage as I have not the value of a shilling interest in these privateers, the only object I aim at, is the publick good, and I leave to your Excellencys wisdom to decide wether there is, or is no inconveniency to comply with the request of the owners of said privateers; they have all along flatter'd themselves that they would obtain a Commission for the black princess, and I Supose it was in that

Expectation that they have run themselves into an Expence of about 100,000 livers for her outfitts which they would be exposed to lose if it is not granted.

I hope your Excellency has received my letter of the 9th inst. covering a memoir of the farmers general, and another in answer to the same from the Chambre de Commerce.[7] For a farther proof that the pretentions of the farmers are ill grounded, I take the liberty to inclose the Copys of Sundry arrests, which are the basis of the priviledges the town of Dunkirk enjoy'd as a free port since the year 1662.

I have the honour to remain with due respect your Excellencys Most obedient & most devoted humble Servant

FRANS. COFFYN

P.S. As the black prince is Expected to arrive here soon, and probably will bring some prisoners, I request your Excellency would mention wether I am to provide for their maintainance, in that case how much they are to be allow'd per day. The french Gouvernment allows the English prisoners 14 s. per day, which I think is sufficient.

Notation: Mr. Coffin Sept. 9. 1779

From David Hartley

Copy:[8] American Philosophical Society; transcript: Library of Congress

To Dr F——   Sept 18 1779

I think it very probable that the Exchange of prisoners upon acct. by certificates at Sea may take some time in considering & arranging if consented to by the British Ministry.[9] In the mean time as I hear that the second Cartel ship is come back,

7. Coffyn's covering letters are missing but the memoir to the farmers general is at the University of Pa. Library. This lengthy document, dated "Août 1779," protests the farmers restricting Dunkirk's tobacco dealings; it bears BF's notation "Privileges of Dunkerque." For Dunkirk's role in the tobacco trade see Price, *France and the Chesapeake,* II, 720–1.

8. In Hartley's hand, and included in his second letter of Oct. 26, below.

9. In fact, not until March 1, 1780, did Hartley reply that the proposal for parole exchanges by certificates at sea had been refused. APS.

I write one line to you just to suggest that if you can succeed in obtaining Morlaix for the port of Exchange & will send me a passport for Morlaix, I think a third Exchange may take place while this new proposition is under Consideration. I do not know that it will take much time for discussion but I have already experienced Ministerial delays. In the mean time I wish to hasten another cargo. If the next cargo shd still be for Nantes, pray signify this to me by the return of the Mail.

I have now a favour to ask of you upon my own account. Some friends of mine at Hull viz the Corporation of the Trinity house have writ to me to desire that I wd endeavour to obtain the release of Mr John Stephenson Master & owner of the ship Sally & a younger Brother of the Trinity house & a Burgess of Hull.[1] They do not specify to me when taken or where he is or whether captured by french or American. When I obtain farther particulars I will transmitt them to you. In the mean time if you can hear where this Mr Stephenson is, & cd assist me in procuring his release I shall be much obliged to you. I shall probably write to you again soon. I am &c

DH

From Robert Morris

ALS and two LS: American Philosophical Society

Dear Sir   Philada. septr. 18th. 1779

I have never rec'd a line from you in reply to the letters I wrote you & Mr. Deane in Decemr. 1777 and confess it surprized me a little, but the matter is entirely cleared up by the

1. The Trinity House, a charitable guild and corporation, regulated conditions of service of seamen and provided for the relief of retired seamen and their families: Gordon Jackson, *The Trade and Shipping of Eighteenth-Century Hull,* East Yorkshire Local Hist. Ser., no. XXXI (1975), p. 7. Stephenson (1738?–1805) had been admitted as a younger brother of the House in 1761 and appears on the muster rolls as commander of the *Sally* from 1775 through August, 1778: Hull Trinity House, BRN/YB, 1738–1805; Muster Rolls, vols. 20–22. On Sept. 13, 1779, the corporation requested Hartley to determine what steps were necessary to have Stephenson, now a prisoner in France, exchanged for a Frenchman of equal rank: HTH Outletters, 1777–86. Information kindly provided by the HTH archivist.

receipt of your favour of the 19th Feby last as in a P.S: thereto you mention having answered my said letters which had been entirely satisfactory,[2] desirous of retaining your good opinion you may be sure I was well pleased at the expressions in this postscript; the business recommended in the body of that letter falls under the management of my Friend Mons Holker but you may depend on my attention to all Your recommendations.[3] The Chevr Luzerne has not yet reached this City, but he sent me your Letter of the 2d June last,[4] the Character you give him is very agreable & I hope he may compensate for the loss of Mr Gerard who carries with him the perfect esteem of all Men not biassed by Selfish or Party Views. I shall pay the attentions in my power to the Chevr Luzerne both on account of your recommendation his own Merits & Public Station—

Mr Gerard will no doubt give you every information respecting our situation here he knows it well & I dare say will do it impartially. My opposition to the Constitution of this State & opposition to Parties in Congress has procured me abundance of unmerited abuse, but supported by conscious innocence & unshaken Integrity I have never failed to get the better of my Enemies on the day of tryal—[5]

With the best wishes for your health & happiness I remain Dear Sir Your most Obedt & very hble servt.   ROBT MORRIS

His Excy Benjn Franklin Esqr Minister Plenipotentiary from the United States of America at the Court of Versailles

2. XXVIII, 572.

3. BF had recommended that his friend Jean-Jacques de Lafreté contact Morris for help in obtaining satisfaction from the bankrupt Bordeaux merchant firm of Reculès de Basmarein & Raimbaux. Lafreté had already drawn up a power of attorney for French consul Jean Holker in the matter: XXVIII, 566, 572.

4. XXIX, 609–10.

5. Although not a member of Congress at the time, Morris was a chief supporter of Deane during the bitter congressional debates of 1779: Edmund S. Morgan, "The Puritan Ethic and the American Revolution," *W&MQ* 3rd ser., XXIV (1967), 30. Morris was the prime target of the Pennsylvania Radical party, currently preparing for the forthcoming election for the Pa. Assembly: Robert L. Brunhouse, *The Counter-Revolution in Pennsylvania, 1776–1790* (Harrisburg, 1942), pp. 71, 76.

Addressed: To / His Excelly. / Benjamin Franklin Esqr. / Minister Plenipotentiary / of the United States of / America at the Court of / Versailles / per The Ship Confederacy

Notation: Robt. Morris Sept 18. 79

To Cabanis

Reprinted from *Curious and Facetious Letters of Benjamin Franklin Hitherto Unpublished* (Privately printed, 1898), pp. 13–14.

à Passy, ce 19 7bre '79.

Mr. Franklin est fâché d'avoir causé le moindre tort à ces beaux cheveux, qu'il regarde toujours avec Plaisir. Si cette Dame[6] aime à passer ses Jours avec lui, il aimerait autant à passer ses Nuits avec elle; & comme il lui a déjà donné beaucoup de ses jours, quoique il en avait si peu de reste à donner, elle paraît ingrate de ne lui avoir jamais donné une seule de ses nuits, qui coulent continuellement en pure perte, sans faire le bonheur de personne, à l'exception de Poupon. Il l'embrasse neantmoins bien serrement, parce qu'il l'aime infiniment malgré tous ses défauts.

Addressed: A Monsieur / Monsieur Cabbanis, pour être / montrée à notre Dame / d'Auteuil.

To John Torris

Copy: Library of Congress

Sir   Passy, Sept. 19. 1779.

I received yours of the 12th. Instant. I have all along expected the Courts of Admiralty in france would judge of the Prizes without any Intervention of mine. But Since I find it otherwise I have written to Mr. De Sartine on the Subject,[7] and hope your affair will soon be ended to your Satisfaction. I send you here with my judgment of the Prizes and ransoms,[8] to be of use to you as far as it Shall be found valid. I desired

6. Mme Helvétius.
7. Above, Sept. 18.
8. BF enclosed his condemnation of prizes, printed above, Sept. 18.

373

Mr. Coffin to acqnt. me why our Commissions were desired by your Cruizers rather than the french?[9] but have not yet his Answer: If any Circumstances make it absolutely necessary for you, I will endeavour to oblige you, being much pleased with the Activity of Capt. Merchant. As long Nights are coming on, and a Night Glass may be very useful to a Cruiser, in order to keep sight of his Chase, I would present him with an Excellent one I have if I knew to send it to him.[1] I have the honour to be, Sir

M. Torris Dunkirqe.

From Catharine Greene   ALS: American Philosophical Society

My Very Dear Friend   Warwick Septr the 19th 1779

The first time I wrote you Since you have been in France was in the greatest hurry with my Bunnet on Just going a Journey.[2] Which is the only one I Can ever hear you have Received[3] which incorages me to imbrace a nother moment in allmost as great a hurry Just to tell you we are well Spoues and Family and Friends. Except our Dear mrs Mecom Who for a fortnight has been worried a good deal with the Assme[4] and her old Cough She is now with Jenny. When we have the Emtyest house We Send for her to Stay with us She Cant Bear Company as She used to do We love her and She loves us. Capt Colás and Spoues has been up which gave her a good deal of Pleasure. He gave us an agreeable history of Doctr Franklin Which is Pleasing to us as we love to hear of your health and yr Releaving us from the Brittish Yoke &c &c Mr Greene has Receivd your favor and the Dittoes from mr Wil-

---

9. See his letter of Sept. 8.

1. On Aug. 2 BF had purchased two telescopes at a cost of 240 *l.t.:* Cash Book (Account XVI, xxvi, 3). The Cash Book states that one of the telescopes was given to Marchant and the other to Luke Ryan.

2. xxv, 118–19.

3. See xxv, 732–3.

4. Jane's asthma appears to have been a recurring problem: Van Doren, *Franklin-Mecom*, p. 166, mentions an earlier attack.

liams that is they are at Providence the State the Books from you[5] Mr Greene writes you as Soon as an hours Leisure he has Company Now he Joyns me in love and Regard as does My Children Samey Ward[6] Ray Continues at Schoo Near Newbury and they Say makes good Improvement[7] Pleas to Remember us to Your Grandson with you and Benny when you write. Mrs Mecem had a letter from Mrs Bache this Summer[8] which gave a Pritty Particuliar account of the family which I Seamd to be interested in I am Calld upon God Bless you My Dear Friend and Permit me to Subscribe my Self yr Very affectionate friend   CATY GREENE

Doctr Franklin

Notation: Caty Greene. Warwick Sept. 19. 1779.—

From Thomas Digges   ALS: Historical Society of Pennsylvania

Dr. Sir   Sepr. 20. 1779

I have written you the 3d. Int by Post,[9] the 4th. by the Chaplain of the Russian ambassador at Paris, & the 6th. Int. by a person who purposely went to you on some business, & whom I am now in hourly expectation of hearing from. Since writing these sundry letters, I have found means to communicate with Capt C. whom You desire in Yr. last letter of the 10 Augt.[1] I may give some help and assistance to. I have had three letters from him & the treatment He speaks of & describes is realy shocking. He was brot. over all the way in Irons, & put into the first Prison (amidst the scoffs hisses threats & insults of a Mob, at which he *cryd* with rage & indignation) with only a common sailors thin jacket, one

5. The books were a history of Geneva; see Gov. Greene's Oct. 5 letter.

6. Samuel Ward Greene, now age eight.

7. The fourteen-year-old was at Dummer Academy: xxix, 724n; *Sibley's Harvard Graduates,* xii, 50.

8. Probably the one Jane Mecom mentions briefly in her Sept. 12 letter, above.

9. Missing.

1. *I.e.,* Aug. 20.

check shirt Trowsers, & pr. of Shoes. As soon as I heard he
was at F——h, I got a frd to petition for his removal to Mill
Prison[2] which was granted, & where he has recd my two last
letters, after having verbally describd his wants to a friend of
mine who supplyd him with some Cloaths when he was
shippd from Falo. I have informd Him of your request to give
him help, & he is extreemly thankful for it. He writes me that
the Cloaths he stands in need of, his common maintainance,
(for our subscripn fund has now got very low), and a few
guineas to serve as occasion may offer, will make the sum he
may want forty pounds or upwards, of which He has sufficient
to repay in the hands of people in Nantes & Cadiz. I have
given orders to a very worthy man of Plymo.[3] to look towards
the proper supply to him of Cloaths and a little money, & he
is now well off for the present. I shall draw as I last did on you
for that sum, & remit his order on me for so doing when He
forwards it; which I expect He will by next post. You will
please to give orders to Mr Grand to be attentive to the bill,
which will be drawn by me on Him without mentioning your
name, for the more safe negotiation of it here.

The last Cartel arrivd at Plyo. some days ago, & Interest is
now making to let the whole 190 Prisors. now there go in the
next trip, in order to save a second voyage to that port; but I
am fearful it will not do; as they say at the Office, there are no
more prisoners for this Excha. in France. There is 140 odd at
Forton, and about 30 at Pembroke.

I have left Mr Wh——ns direction, with my papers in a safe
& distant quarter, or I would write to Him by this Conveyance
about his friend Capt. Hutchins. It is too dangerous to do it by
post, or I would have wrote to both of you more frequently &
explicit. Since my last of the 6th. Int. the junto who set as
Examiners Judges &c &c. ie Sr. J. F, Lord G. G. Mr De Grey,
& Mr Knox, have found means, thro the assistance of a person
who lodgd in the same house with Capt H——, and Capt

2. The friend was David Hartley.
3. The Rev. Robert Heath, a dissenting minister who aided escapees
from Mill Prison. William Bell Clark, "In Defense of Thomas Digges,"
PMHB, LXXVII (1953), 400n, 405.

Grant & Peisley who betrayd Him,[4] to get at an Iron Chest which Mr. W——n left under care of Hutchins, and wch. was broke open before the junto & the papers strictly Examind. Wherever those papers or Capn. H——s's had references to other names, the papers of those other persons have been examind or the holders of them strictly enquird about. The papers & books of Mr Neave have been taken; two young men I beleive formerly his Clerks were taken up; also a Mr. Bundy who was confind a night or two & is releasd. Mrs. Carr a Milliner in Covent Garden was before the junto & dischargd after many questions about Mr. W——n, Mr. E——s, Capt H Miss Stafford &c &c. Miss Stafford (who had time to secret *some* papers) was in prison *one* night; her house strictly searched, & very scrutinous enquirys of what she knew? of Mr. W——n, Mr E——s, Mr. Ell——n, Mr D——s, & others. Mr W—— to whom I beg you will communicate this, can inform you of these connexions. The Evidence has turnd out much to the disapointment of the junto; for they fully expected to criminate some others, & get a publick Execution of some *Miscreants* as they are pleasd to call all those who are averse to their measures. I do beleive the proofs against Capt H are not sufficient to authorise his being tried, *for the key to the Cypher in which he wrote,* has been destroyd. There is no knowing what degree of mischief may attend him if brought to a Court martial. Mr. E——s and Mr. E——n are naturally uneasy & if they were ever wrote to by Mr. W——n, he should now be cautious how he writes.

I wish to have some name given me to direct to you under, for tho I always inclose to Monr G——d, I am obligd to express to him for whom the letter is, and this may be a risque in the Post Office. I requested this favr. in my last letter of the 6th. by Mr S——y, and if he bears not the ansr. to me, it may be done by common post in a single letter, wrote in any hand, for I shall know from whence it comes, and directd a monr. monsr. Wm. Singleton Church Nandos Coffee House

4. For Hutchins' arrest see Digges's letters of Sept. 4 and 6. Grant, of the Prince of Wales's American regiment, had turned Peisley in: *The Public Advertiser,* Sept. 1, 1779.

Londn.— A careful hand at Ostend to put letters under cover to, may also be very useful. At Amsterdam I use the Gentlemen whom I forwarded the box of books to.[5] If you know of any means by which I can be useful, I hope you will not spare me, & you may depend upon my attention to any thing you may request.

We have not a word of news from the West Indies since the late Gazette. Since the two grand fleets in Europe have got into their respective ports, there is nothing talkd of but the miserable situation of our affairs in the West Indies; and Amea. is now of too trifling consequence even to be ever mentiond. I beleive the prospect from the Continent is full as gloomy as that from the Islands, but nothing authentic is given to us from authority altho ships arrive frequently at Corke from N York. It is said ministry have accots from thence to the 17th. Augt. and that the Garrison was inactive, had done nothing, & were anxiously expecting the arrival of Adl Arbuthnot with his 4 ships of the line and 3180 Recruits. This fleet was spoke with in the neighbourhood of Bermudas the 6th Augt. & they were in extreem want of water. Notwithstanding this miserable picture in the West, bad accots from the East, and a still more gloomy prospect at home, the Stocks are getting up, on accot of a general Report that has got abroad of a serious mediation in your quarter from Russia & Holland for Peace, on the terms of American Independence.[6]

It was in every ones mouth last week that the Cabinet had determind to withdraw the army from N York & Rhode Island, & send them to the Wt Indies. It is now said the army from R Island *only* is to be sent: a Frigate was dispatchd a day or two ago to that quarter, not improbably (I think) with an

---

5. Georges Grand and his business partners: XXIX, 701.

6. *The Public Advertiser* declared on this day, "It is believed by many People in the City, that some Movements have been made towards a Negotiation for a Peace. The Funds seem to bespeak as much." The report went on to say that a year's truce had been suggested. Sir James Harris, British ambassador to Russia, at the time was trying to persuade Catherine the Great to allow Russia to act as an armed mediator: Isabel de Madariaga, *Britain, Russia, and the Armed Neutrality of 1780* . . . (New Haven, 1962), pp. 105–11.

order for its evacuation. It has been long the language of ministerialists that this post was of no consequence, & that 3,000 men have been kept there doing nothing for these two or three years.

Our homeward fleet seems to be snugg in harbour for at least some weeks, if not the winter, that under Adml Ross[7] may be soon heard of on the coasts of France, or probably in Ireland, to conduct safe home the Eight India men & a rich manilla ship carryd into Ireland. It consists of 3 of the Line, 3 fiftys & Eight frigates. Paul Jones has given much alarm to the Coasts of that Country, but as yet has done no mischeif; *here* he is lookd upon as already taken by Ross's Squadn.

I am yr. very obt. & obligd Servt.   V.J. DROUILLARD

I expect this will be put safe into a foreign Post office by a young Genn. who having finishd His Education here is pushing to his native home via Holland & St. Eustatia— He bears a paper parcel (from a friend in Mincing Lane) for you & which He will contrive to forward by some private hand from Amsterdam to Paris, in case he finds none, it will be left with Messrs. Grand & Co of Amsm. to be forwarded to You.[8]

Since writing the Inclosd, I have got a letter from Mr W——n[9] which informs me that the Cartel Ship has been at Portso above a fortnight & that there has been no step taken

7. Sir John Lockhart Ross (1721–90) had been appointed rear-admiral on March 19, and in the summer was fourth in command of the Channel fleet aboard the *Royal George*. He had been sent to cruise in the North Sea with a small squadron on the lookout for Jones. *DNB.*

8. In his letter of Nov. 15, 1779 (Hist. Soc. of Pa.), Digges mentions having "some time ago" forwarded to Grand at Amsterdam a "parcel from Mr V——n, by Mr. Manigault of So. Caroa." The parcel contained sections of Benjamin Vaughan's edition of BF's writings. Samuel Vaughan & Son, his father's merchant firm, was located in Dunster's Court, Mincing Lane: *Kent's Directory for the Year 1779* (London, 1779), p. 172. Gabriel Manigault (1758–1809) was from a prominent Charleston family. He studied law at Lincoln's Inn and returned to Charleston shortly before the British occupation of the city. He eventually overcame his reputation as a loyalist, and married Ralph and Alice Izard's daughter Margaret. He served in the state House of Representatives and as a delegate to the ratifying convention for the Constitution. Maurice A. Crouse, "Papers of Gabriel Manigault, 1771–1784," *S.C. Hist. Mag.,* LXIV (1963), 1, 7–8.

9. Rev. Thomas Wren.

towards her resailing with another Cargoe of Prisoners. The Capt. of this vessel says there are *no more* American-capturd Prisoners in France in or near the Ports of the Ocean, but that there are several in St. Maloes Havre, & Dunkirk. The Agent at Nantes says there are no more in any Ports of France, but that there are considerable numbers at Bilbao St Andero and Corunna, but there Exchange would require a Spanish passport.

If your multiplicity of business will allow you to look towards procuring such a passport I wish most cordially Sir you would do it; for I am certain it would have a most happy effect. You can scarcely immagine the distress another winters confinement may bring on these unhappy people, for our subscription is very nearly expended, & in the present state of things it is hardly to be expected we can get more money by opening the subscription. The money raisd, never extended, & consequently could not be applyd, to any but those in actual confinement; the consequence of this is, that any American sailors in distress, hiding from the press gangs, or who have found means to liberate themselves, generally fly to me, and drain me exceedingly of Cash: I should not think this a hardship, could I possibly get money from home or borrow it here on easy terms. I have spent larger sums on them & other purposes than may be strictly prudent, and the fear of being still further distressd by them, & to try to get them releasd by Cartel, is my principal motive for now troubling you. There shall be nothing wanted on this side to expedite the Exchange or to help them.

Endorsed: Sept. 20—79

Notation: Digges Sept 20. 1779

From Rocquette, Elsevier & Rocquette

ALS: American Philosophical Society

Sir!   Rotterdam 20 September 1779

Inclosed a parcell which we recd. for you by way of St. Eustatia, by which conveyance we also recd. one for A: Lee,

Esqr. which you'll also find Inclosed, we desire you to deliver it to that Gentn. if with you, or to forward it to him where he may be.

We have the honour to be with the most respectfull regard Sir! Your very humble Servants

J. ROCQÚETTE T.A. ELSEVIER, & BROTHERS ROCQÚETTE

Benjn. Franklin Esqr. at Paris

Notation: J. Roquette A. Elsevier and Brothers Roquette Rotterdam 20. 7bre. 1779.

From Benjamin Vaughan   AL: American Philosophical Society

My dearest sir,   London, Septr. 20th: 1779.

There was some little tumult when I sent you the last printed pacquet, (which however missed two opportunities of going) and therefore you had no letter.—[1] By the present opportunity I wish to inquire your opinion as to the *time of appearance. I* am for the present moment; the bookseller for deferring: But as my opinion will rule, I wish without giving reasons, you would express a hint which way I ought to give that opinion.— As to a neat bound-up copy, you shall shortly have one; but at present the time is too short.

We are in the state here of none acting, but many wishing, and more permitting change, were it to appear; but John Bull, as to *act & deed,* is still asleep; spreading out his lubber length for any to tread on that choose, whether acquaintances or not.— In winter we shall see whether the great are more inclined to good sense than formerly, but I know them well enough to do more than doubt them. I am quite tired with them; but I am, as ever, my dearest sir *yours* most everlastingly & devotedly.

P.S. I shall, after looking at another Aurora or two, send you a farther conjecture on that subject.— Mr: Crawford's book on

---

1. Perhaps a reference to the sighting of the combined fleet in the English Channel on Aug. 15, and the resultant invasion scare which had subsided by mid-September: Patterson, *The Other Armada,* pp. 180–3, 216–17.

heat is most admirable.[2] I shall put his system on a sheet of paper & send it, with remarks; and as it will save you prodigious trouble I wish you to wait for it, a fortnight or so. I read anew last night Newton's *Optical queries,* which are indeed very powerfully written;[3] but I hope Mr. Crawford as he grows older, will be one of *you.*— Mr: Henly certainly cut his throat most deliberately. His family endeavored to talk him into quiet, but in vain: He cut the veins with a pen-knife, and at last lay in a posture to drain into the chamber-pot.

I shall thank you for the immediate return of my *three* manuscripts on Jamaica, vapor, & the vis inertiæ.[4] If you think any *passages* worth your farther attention, they shall be copied & sent you, if you will mark them out: But I ask for those MSS, because being my own amanuensis, I really felt it too much trouble to take other copies for myself and was moreover in haste at the time of sending to you asually.

Notation: B Vaughn Sept. 20. 1779

From Dumas   ALS: American Philosophical Society

Dear & honoured Sir   Sept. 21st. 1779

I have received the same day, being the 18th., first your favour of the 10th. Inst. by Mr. Ross, & then that of the 7th. Inst. by the g. Factor, who was at Amsterdam, from whence he has sent it me.[5]

2. Adair Crawford, *Experiments and Observations on Animal Heat, and the Inflammation of Combustible Bodies* (London, 1779). The work seems to have been issued at the beginning of August: Robert E. Schofield, *A Scientific Biography of Joseph Priestley (1733–1804)* (Cambridge, Mass., and London, 1966), p. 175. At some point BF got his own copy and lent it to Le Roy: XXVIII, 178.

3. The queries are printed in Sir Isaac Newton, *Opticks: or a Treatise of the Reflexions, Refractions, Influxions and Colours of Light* ... (4th ed., London, 1730, reprinted N.Y., 1952), pp. 339–406.

4. We have found no trace of any of these papers, or their cover letter. Vaughan had summarized the arguments of his *vis inertiae* paper in his letter of April 30: XXIX, 401–2. See also XXIX, 293–4, 588.

5. The letter of the 7th is above. We have not found the letter brought by John Ross and have learned little about the Nantes merchant's trip to the

382

I am to see our friend this Evening, & to set out to morrow morning very early, for the place where the person, to whom you write, is expected, & there to stay till he arrives.[6] This is the best & shortest manner to deliver him your Letter & former instructions, without loosing time, & to prevent all inconveniencies. For nobody know's me there, & nobody shall know what I expect there.

I should be glad (as well as our Friend), to receive as soon as possible our sketch of the future Treaty with yr. Excies. remarks on it.[7]

Proper care Shall be taken of the circular Letters of Mrs. Bache & Shee, at the first oportunity, & then Mr. F—— shall know the names of the houses.[8]

I am with the most respectfull attachment Dear & honoured Sir, your most obedient & most humble Servant

DUMAS

Be pleased Sir, to acquaint Mr. De Cht. [Chaumont] with where I am going to morrow.

Passy, His Exc. B. Franklin

Notation: Du Mas 21. 7bre. 1779.

From Benjamin Vaughan

ALS: American Philosophical Society

My dearest sir,   London Septr. 21. 1779.

I beg the favor very particularly of you to give a letter of recommendation for Langford Lovell Esqr. (who gives the in-

---

Netherlands. We do know he was at a Paris hotel on Sept. 1, from where he wrote a brief note to WTF (APS), and that he was still in the Netherlands on Oct. 11; Dumas, then at The Hague, told Jean de Neufville that he hoped to see him again (National Archives).

6. *I.e.,* Dumas was preparing to leave for the Texel to meet John Paul Jones. His friend was Pensionary van Berckel.

7. Presumably the American-Dutch commercial treaty on which Dumas was working: XXIX, 100–1n, 195n.

8. RB had first enclosed circular letters about his new business firm with his April 7 letter: XXIX, 273. BF sent copies to Dumas via WTF: Dumas to BF, below, Oct. 2.

closed account of himself)[9] addressed to the Govr. of Dominica. I should esteem it an addition to the favor, if you would *yourself* inclose a duplicate of such letter to Mr Lovel in Dominica, by some safe conveyance; as in such case, by means of the copy you convey & I convey, he will be in bad luck if he does not receive his recommendation safe. The family connections of this gentleman in the West Indies are considerable & respectable, and his friends here very amiable and such as I wish to oblige very much. He is a relation of Mr Richard Oliver.[1] I am as ever, my dearest sir, yours most devotedly

BENJN. VAUGHAN

I beg the favor of the inclosed request being granted by the first opportunity.

I am very much distressed by not having M. Dupont's table or map of the System of the Œconomistes, which you had the goodness to promise to procure for me. I could not get it myself, nor by any of the very various people I have made use of. I therefore again have recourse to you.[2]

Addressed: A Monsr. / Monsr. F.

Notation: Vaughn Sept: 21. 1779

9. Lovell (1732–95) came from a Quaker merchant family of Philadelphia and Antigua: Vere Langford Oliver, *The History of the Island of Antigua* ... (3 vols., London, 1894–99), II, 196. The enclosure was probably a letter of Lovell's dated Antigua, June 11, 1779. He requests a recommendation for occasional travel to Dominica. Since the French conquest he has acted as a neutral, engaging in neither privateering nor military duties. APS.

1. Lovell and the former alderman (XXII, 13n) were cousins. Lovell's elder brother, Michael, was in partnership in a London merchant firm with another of their cousins, Thomas Oliver (to BF, Oct. 8, below): Oliver, *The History of the Island* ... , II, 196; *Kent's Directory* (London, 1779), p. 126. Vaughan had recommended the firm to JW on Dec. 5, 1778, as "a most solid house as a West Indian house." In a letter to WTF of Feb. 2, 1779, he again pronounced it worthy of favor. Both letters are at the APS.

2. Vaughan was referring to Pierre Samuel Du Pont de Nemours, *Table raisonnée des principes de l'économie politique,* a broadside originally published in Baden in 1775, and reissued in Paris in the spring of 1778. It was an expansion of Quesnay's *Tableau Œconomique* (Versailles, 1758), which attempted to convey the physiocrats' economic theory in tabular form. See Ambrose Saricks, *Pierre Samuel Du Pont de Nemours* (Lawrence, Kansas,

From Ann Conyngham[3]

Two ALS: American Philosophical Society

Honoured Sir   Philadelphia September the 22th 1779

In what manner shall I apologize for the liberty I now take, but sertain I am you will excuse me when you now that I am the Wife of the unfortunate Capt. Conyngham, one who I beleve you are not unacquanted with. In what language shall I address you Sir to endeavour to save the life of the best and tenderest of Husbands. To you Sir, I look up for redress in hopes it may be in your power in sum measure to appeas the wrath of his enimies. If thay would one moment think of the distress of an afflicted wife, if they had not lost every feeling of that humanity, which once characterized Britons: thay seartainly could not be so cruell as to part us for ever: Oh! what must be his feelings at this moment, to be confined in a strange place, where he has not one friend, to whom he can realy on, waisting his health and spirits in hopeless grief— and at last Compleating the measure of his sufferings, by an ignominious Death— Good God my hart shudders at the thought— Forbid it Heaven— Is it posable no means can be procured for his safty, am I never more to behold the man I love, my only comfort, and my only hope, my only support, under every affliction and distress—

Pardon me Sir, if I request the favour, of your forwarding the inclosed as directed: as they will be the means of affording some relief to my dear Gusty— Your distingushed character for benevolence and humanity has imbolden'd me to take this liberty—

I must inform you Sir, that Capt Conyngham was Commander of the Cutter, Revenge, who was taken in April, car-

---

1965), pp. 29–30, 72, 366, 379. BF sent the *Table* to Vaughan on Nov. 9, recommending it as "an excellent thing." APS.

3. Ann Hockley Conyngham (1756–1811) had married Gustavus in 1773: Charles R. Hildeburn, ed., *The Inscriptions in St. Peter's Church Yard Philadelphia* (Camden, 1879), p. 136; *DAB*. On July 17 she wrote to the President of Congress describing Conyngham's distress and asking Congress' immediate attention to his case: Neeser, *Conyngham*, pp. 179–80.

ried into New York, from thence sent to England, to have his tryal—

This, I presume, will be a sufficient motive with you, to procure justice for him, and to afford some consolation, to Hond Sir, your most obedient and most devoted—

ANN CONYNGHAM

Addressed: A Ms. / Ms. Docr. franclain / Ministre Plenipotenteri / a La Court / De france

Notation: Ann Conynham 21 Sept 79

From Jonathan Nesbitt

ALS: American Philosophical Society

Sir   L'Orient Septr: 22d: 1779

By the Brig Retalliation Captn: Kollock which left Philada: the 10th: August,[4] I have receiv'd Letters informing me that Captn: G: Conyngham late Commander of the Cutter Revenge, had the misfortune to be taken last Spring by the Galatea & sent into New York, from whence he has been sent to England with a design to have him try'd for Piracy.— They pretend to say that he took the Harwich Packet without having any Commission which your Excellency must know to be false, as I believe you were in Paris at the time that his Commission & orders were deliver'd him.— The Commission under which he Acted as Captn: of the Revenge is dated, I apprehend, after the taking of the Harwich Packet. It is on this Circumstance without doubt, that the Charge of Piracy is founded. His first Commission was taken from in Dunkirk after he was put in Gaol, & sent up to Paris, and I think was lodg'd in the hands of Monsr: le Comte de Virgennes.[5] I have to request that your Excellency will do every thing in your

4. The *Retaliation* and Philipps Kollock are listed in Charles H. Lincoln, comp., *Naval Records of the American Revolution* (Washington, D.C., 1906), p. 438.

5. For Conyngham's cruise on the *Surprize* and capture of the Harwich packet on May 3, 1777, see XXIV, 6n, and *passim*. His first commission, dated March 1, 1777, was taken away from him upon his arrest and his second was antedated May 2, 1777, by the American Commissioners to precede the confiscation of the first: XXIV, 243n.

power to prevent this poor fellow from suffering. Considering the smallness of his Vessell, & the difficulty he labour'd under when he first left France, he has done a great deal for the service of his Country. He has done so much harm to the Enemy that he can expect no mercy at their hands, & if they can find any pretence whatever, they will certainly destroy him. Captn: Kollock informs me that he was sent home in Irons. I should certainly have heard from him was he not closely confined.— I once more take the liberty to recommend this unhappy Mans case to your Excellencys particular attention.

I have the honor to be, wth: great respect. Your Excellencys most Obedt: most hble Servt: JONATN: NESBITT

Addressed: Son Excellence B: Franklyn Esqr / a son Hotel / a Passÿ

Endorsed: Ansd—[6]

Notation: Jona. Nesbitt Sept. 22. 79 rele. to Cunningham

From Jean-Sylvain Bailly[7]

AL: American Philosophical Society

a chaillot ce jeudi 23 7bre. [1779]
Mr Bailly presente ses respects a Monsieur Franklin. Il envoie savoir s'il sera demain après midi chez lui, et s'il peut recevoir Mad la comtesse de Beauharnois qui desire infiniment de le voir.[8] Mr Bailly se fait un grand plaisir d'accompagner Mad.

6. On Sept. 29, below.

7. This is the first extant letter from a man whom BF met as a colleague (in astronomy) at the Académie des sciences, and with whom he would collaborate, in 1784, in the investigation into Mesmer's theories and practices. Appointed the first mayor of Paris at the beginning of the Revolution, Bailly (1736–93) perished during the Terror. *DBF.*

8. Marie-Anne-Françoise Mouchard (1737–1813), better known as Fanny, married comte Claude de Beauharnais, whose niece Josephine was to become empress. Separated from her husband, she held, on rue Montmartre, a salon frequented by several of BF's friends, and had just published *Lettres de Stéphanie,* an historical romance. *DBF.*

de Beauharnois chez Mr Franklin et de lui renouveller l'assurance de sa respectueuse amitié.

Mr le cher de Cubieres,[9] frere du marquis de Cubieres ecuier du Roy, a demandé aussi detre admis a rendre hommage a Mr Franklin et Mr Bailly a cru pouvoir l'assurer que sa visite ne deplairait pas. Mr. le cher de Cubieres est homme de lettres et connu par des ouvrages agréables en prose et en vers.

Addressed: A Monsieur / Monsieur Franklin ministre / plenipotentiaire des etats unis de / lamerique / a passy

Notation: Bailly.

From John Bondfield

ALS: American Philosophical Society

Sir   Bordeaux 23 Sep 1779

I have the Honor to forward by the Express going with the dispatches receivd by the same Conveyance the Inclosed packets arrived last Evening by Cap Benin(?) from Boston he saild from that port the 25 August, he reports that by a considerable reinforcement arrivd at Ponobscot our People were oblidged to destroy their Shiping and abandon the attempt against that establishment to the Enemy.[1]

Our Ships the Governer Livingston & Mary Fearon are arrived in Virginia the Chasseur as advised in my former is taken and sent into New York.

I have the Honor to be with due respect Sir Your most Obedient Humble Servant   JOHN BONDFIELD

To His Excellency Benj Franklin Esq

Notation: Bondfield John 13. Sept. 1779.

9. Michel, chevalier de Cubières (1752–1820), was a prolific writer who had a knack for embracing every new regime France was to experience. He is credited with saving Fanny's life during the Revolution. *DBF.*

1. The Sept. 24 issue of the *Courier de l'Europe* (VI [1779], 196–7) carried a British account of their recent victory and a list of seventeen burned, captured, or sunk American ships (including the number and weight of their cannon). A similar list in WTF's hand (with one addition and two deletions) bears BF's notation, "Marine of America" (APS).

From John Torris

LS: American Philosophical Society

Honnd: Sir   Dunkerque 23d. September 1779

I have received with due respect & gratitude your Excellency's most Esteemed favour 19th Inst.

We apprehend that your Excellency's Judgement there in Joined, for the Brig Dublin Thomas Griffitths, & for the 11. Ransoms taken by the Black Prince, will Suffice, & the request there in made to the admiralty, will, I hope, determine them without hesitation to Sell, because, previous, a few posts past, by the advice of the Worthy Mr. Coffyn, we Ordered our Correspondant at Morlaix,[2] to petition the Admiralty to Sell both Prises, in Virtue of The *Reglement* of the 27th. Sept. 1778., & in Case of a refusal to protest against them for all dammages &ca.— I have Sent This Judgement & demand of your Excellency, per yesterday post; & If the process of the Admiralty was Contrary to our Expectations, I shall have The Honnour to Inform your Excellency thereof.

Your Excellency has omitted in the Judgement, to relate The first prise of the Black Prince. Capt. Marchant Carried into Morlaix The 22d. June Being The Sloop the *Good Will* from London to Cork, *William Power Master;* & also the Ransom of the brig Three Sisters for £73 Stgn. *Geo: Crooker master Geo: Hooper Ransomer* now at Carhaix.[3]

This Omission Might make Some alteration, & I beg of your Excellency to Send me an other Judgement for them, per the return of Post, According to the *procés Verbal* of the admiralty at Morlaix Here Inclosed & to Include the 8. new Ransoms, The Ransomers for which are in Carhaix & were Landed at Brest the 22d. of august, & there Examined by the admiralty, as per List of them Subjoined.[4]

Mr. Coffyn has promised me, to address to your Excellency the Strong Motives that Induced me to Sollicit american Commissions for my Vessells; & Indeed, my Brave Irish Friends wou'd not fight under french Colours, & the Consequences

---

2. John Diot.
3. The *Good Will* and the *Three Sisters* had been captured on June 21, during Marchant's first cruise: xxix, 719–20.
4. The list is missing.

attending Same, wou'd no ways allow my principles of Humanity, to prompt them to Cruize otherwise. Thus, I hope your Excellency's Human & generous disposition, have allready determined the Sending to the Generous Mr. Coffyn, the waited for Commission from Congress.[5] I may give all assurances to your Excellency, you will have as much Satisfaction from the honest & brave Macatter, as you are Now pleased to Express with The Hero Luke Ryan, a part owner & my particular & worthy friend, who is the Real Capt. of the Black Prince, Stephen Marchant is but the Ostensible one, & by all the accounts from Board, every time She Comes to Harbour, he is proved to be but an advanturer, neither Sea man Nor Soldier: Everybody is So much tired of him, that the whole Crew are resolved at the Expiration of the 3. months Cruise they are engaged for, to desarm, & to beg of your Excellency to grant the deserving Mr Ryan a Commission in his own Name, for the new armement of The Same Cutter, which, being Joined by the Black Princess, will Certainly perform Wonders & prove a Terror to their Ennemys.

The Night Glass your Excellency's Generosity intend sending to the Commander of the Black Prince, Shou'd be directed to Mr. Luke Ryan, to my Care, as I Expect the Vessell here daily. A Letter of Apology from your Excellency Joined to the Present, will flatter Mr. Ryan more than any thing in the World & raise his Spirits to the Highest pitch.

I am with Veneration & respect Honnd. Sir Your most oblidged, most obedient & most Humble Servant.   J: TORRIS

P.S. The only French privateer from this port that Ventured to the West, which is Commanded by Mr Royer has retaken the Brig Orange tree & Carried her Into Morlaix.[6] The People on board Informed Mr. John Diot that our 21 men Brave prisonners, taken from the Black Prince's Prises, had been put in Guernsey Jail, where they attempted their Scape, which prompted their removal to plymouth or to portsmouth, where

5. Coffyn had written BF on Sept. 18, above, asking for a commission for Capt. Edward Macatter of the *Black Princess.*

6. Jean-Baptiste-Charles Royer (1746–80) was captain of the *Commandant-de-Dunkerque;* his exploits are recounted in Henri Malo, *Les derniers corsaires. Dunkerque (1715–1815)* (Paris, 1925), 134–9.

They are most Cruelly used. They are the best of the Men, & thro' ill usage & Strong Sollicitations, am afraid they might be induced to Serve on Board The English men of War. If we had them here for the Black Princess, 'twou'd do Immense Good to us all & to america. Let me humbly Petition your Excellency, to have them Exchanged first of all, & Sent to Dunkirk as Soon as possible. T'wou'd be doing an act of Justice & Good Policy, to preffer these Brave men in a Circumstance where They Can be So Very usefull to the power They Swore allegeance to. We have all reason to Believe false & without any foundation the report of the Black Prince Being taken./.

Notation: Mr. Torris Sept 23. 1779

To John Dawe *et al.* Copy: Library of Congress

Gentlemen   Passy Sept. 24. [1779]
I received your Request, dated the 24th Inst.[7] and have by this Oportunity desired M. Schweighauser to furnish Such of you as absolutely want with Shoes stockings, Shirts, &c. and to take care of you till you can find Opportunities of getting home. Wishing you a happy Sight of your own Country, after your long unfortunate Captivity, I, am, Gentlemen, Your Most obedient and most humble servant   BF

To Mr. John Dawe Prize master and others.

To Schweighauser Copy: Library of Congress

Sir   Passy, Sept. 24. 1779.
I duly received your favour of the 18th. the Letter addressed to Mr. De sartine which I Omitted mentioning before was also deliver'd.[8] The extracts you send me[9] are of Letters, which

---

7. BF forwarded their petition to Schweighauser; see the following document.

8. Schweighauser's letters to BF and Sartine are missing.

9. Also missing, but from the subsequent description they seem to have been copied from the various admonitions the commissioners had sent about unnecessary expenditures, *e.g.,* XXVI, 525, 594; XXVII, 287.

were written, to check the Extravagant Demands of Officers, Such as that of Wm. Morris,[1] and Others; money having been taken upon our account at divers Ports of france by Americans and others pretending to be such without Any authority from us, and also the Demands of escaped Prisoners after their arrival at Nantes from Paris, where we had reliev'd them and furnish'd them with Sufficient to pay their Expences thither, with something to spare which Several of Them spent foolishly in Paris before they set out and others extravagantly on the Road, on the Supposition that they might call for as much more as they pleased on Acct. of Wages, which they Said was due to him.— It was not I believe intended by either of us, I am sure it was not by me when I Sign'd these Letters drawn up by my Colleagues, to refuse necessary Charity and Relief to our Countrymen when Sick or otherwise in Distress. Accordingly I approv'd of what you furnish'd to the Prisoners of the first Cartel,[2] and desired that those of The Second might be treated with the same kindness,[3] and I now recommend to you the Case of the Persons who send me the enclos'd Petition,[4] requesting that you would furnish them with what is absolutely necessary for them which I make no doubt you will do in the most frugal Manner, and that you would subsist them as you did their fellow Prisoners, till they can find a Passage home.

I have detain'd Mr. Schondorff from Day to Day hoping for a Definitive Answer from Court to some Propositions, So as to be able to close my Dispatches. But as they are Still under consideration and I am now told it will be Towards the End of next Week before I can receive that Answer, I have concluded not to detain your Clerk any longer, as you may want his service and I Shall have another good Oportunity in about 8 Days. I send by him however most of my Packets; but the Mercury must not Sail til the rest arrive.

1. An escaped prisoner whom Schweighauser had refused to pay: XXV, 171, 262–3; XXVI, 606.
2. XXIX, 353.
3. Above, July 25.
4. See BF's letter to John Dawe et al., immediately above.

I have the honour to be with great Esteem Sir &c.

M. Schweighauser.

Passport for Cyprian Sterry and John Smith[5]

AD (draft): American Philosophical Society; ADS (fragment):[6]
Boston Public Library

[September 24, 1779]

To all Captains & Commanders of Vessels of War, Privateers, & Letters of Marque, belonging to the United States of America, or to any of their Allies.

It being represented to me, and appearing by good Testimony that Cyprian Sterry, & John Smith Junior, Natives of America & Subjects of the United States, having recovered Debts due to them in England to a considerable Amount, which Property they are desirous of transfering to their own Country, by vesting it in such Merchandise as may be most useful to the Publick Service there, as coarse Woolens, Linnens, & other Clothing fit for the Army; &c. and proposing to purchase in London the Brigantine Hope of about 120 Tons, to transport the said Goods; And the Congress having by a special Resolution for that purpose permitted the Importation from the English Domins. of the Property of the Inhabitants of America, or of Persons who are about to become Inhabitants in any of the said States; I do therefore request that if the said Brigantine Hope commanded by Thomas Holland, manned by about Eight Seamen, and having on board the said Messieurs Sterry & Smith, should in the Course of her said Voyage from London to America be met with by you, you would let her pass freely, with her Company, Passengers, Goods & Merchandize, without any Let, Hindrance, Seizure or Molestation

---

5. Sterry was introduced by Bridgen and Digges in letters of Sept. 6, above, where he is identified.

6. Consisting only of BF's signature, seal, and dateline, neatly cut off from a passport, presumably this one.

whatsoever. Given at Passy, this 24th Day of September One Thousand Seven hundred and seventy nine.

Notations: Pass-port given to C. Sterry— & nearly the same to W. Johnston & Walter Belt / On the 25th of Sept Mr Sterry took the Oath of Allegiance to the U. S.[7]

From Thomas Bond[8]   ALS: American Philosophical Society

Dear Sir   Philadelphia Septemr. 24. 1779

The Departure of your very worthy & very Sensible Friend, the Sieur Gerard affords me an Opportunity of telling you, that your Thursday Night Associates had the Pleasure of hearing from Mr. Joseph Wharton of your Health & affectionate Remembrance of them, who also told us we might Expect to See You again amongst Us, an event which would give us the highest Satisfaction.[9] Luke Morris Says we cannot do without You & that you must Come. Hugh Roberts desires me to tell you he is become Old, or he would Write to you, he does not concern himself with Public Affairs, he is So much Engaged in Monthly Meeting, Committees & Setting Negroes free, he Scarcely goes to the Point twice a Year, and is become a real Philosopher.[1] Phil Syng[2] is well. S. Roads[3] is a good

7. That oath, written by WTF and attested by BF, is at the APS. William Johnston and Walter Belt would apply for passports in November, 1779, and February, 1780, respectively.

8. Bond, an old associate of BF's, was an original member of the APS, a trustee of the College of Philadelphia, and a principal founder of the Pennsylvania Hospital.

9. The "Thursday Night Associates" might be an informal continuation of the Junto. That club initially had met on Fridays: *Autobiog.*, p. 116.

1. Luke Morris and Hugh Roberts were early members of BF's Union Fire Company. Roberts had a country place at "the Point" (or Point-No-Point) near where Frankford Creek joins the Delaware. Information kindly supplied by Whitfield J. Bell, Jr.

2. A former member of the Junto and Union Fire Company, as well as ex-treasurer of the APS.

3. The builder who had supervised construction of BF's house.

Whig & Sends his love to You. Poor Israel[4] is no more; his loss to the Quakers is Great; there is a great Revolution among us, the Great are become little, & little Great; The Poor are the happiest People Among us.[5] Our Poor house & Hospitals are almost untenanted. I can Scarce Support my Clinical Lectures in the latter, without hiring the Sick to go into it: And shall be Obliged to give up my Demonstrations of MidWifery, for Want of Subjects in the lying in Wards. Mr. Gerard was elected a fellow of the American Philosophical Society. We presented him with an elegant Certificate, & a Volume of the Transactions neatly & emblematically bound with which he Seemed Pleased.[6] From Seeing the many Objections yet made to Inoculation especially in France, a Country I love, I wrote an Essay in Defence of it, & presented it to my Kind Friend the Minister, who will Shew it to You,[7] I am Certain the Contents of it are important; but I fear it is incorrect, being wrote in haste under perpetual Interruptions of Business, I therefore beg you to give it a friendly reading &ca.

When General Howe came to the Banks of the Delaware I Sent my Family with good Mrs. Venables[8] to Allentown near

4. Israel Pemberton, Jr., a charter member of the Library Company, manager of the Pennsylvania Hospital, and member of the APS, died on April 22, 1779: *DAB*.

5. The "great Revolution" was the seizure of political control over the city by the Radical Party. By an almost ten to one margin they won an Aug. 2 general election of a 120-member committee on price regulations and set about limiting the amount of money in circulation. Meanwhile the radicals laid plans to ship to New York the wives and children of Loyalists in exile: Robert L. Brunhouse, *The Counter-Revolution in Pennsylvania 1776–1790* (Harrisburg, 1942), pp. 72–5.

6. He was elected on April 16, 1779. The certificate and bound volume of the APS *Transactions* with which he was subsequently presented cost the society $36 (undoubtedly specie dollars): Meng, *Despatches of Gérard*, p. 645n.

7. A translation was published as *Défense de l'inoculation, et relation des progrès qu'elle a fait à Philadelphie en 1758* (Strasbourg, 1784). It was also translated into German: Elizabeth H. Thomson, "Thomas Bond, 1713–84: First Professor of Clinical Medicine in the American Colonies," *Journal of Medical Education*, XXXIII (1958), 614–24.

8. A relative of Thomas and Sarah Bond; see XXVI, 590n.

Bethlehem, where they remained very Conveniently for two Years. I am now happy with Mrs. Bond & my Grand Children about me. Mrs. Martin & her two Children[9] are in Burlington; they all present their Love to You. I hope the Prospect of a more frequent literary Correspondence betwixt us & Europe brightens, & that we shall be Soon again furnished with the Improvements & Publications of the learned World, Which we Should be extremely Obliged to them & You, for I am dear Sir Your very affectionate humble Servt.   TH BOND.

Notation: Th: Bond 24 Sept 79

From Francis Coffyn   ALS: American Philosophical Society

Hond. Sir.   Dunkerque 24. Sepber 1779.

I beg leave to refer your Excellency to my last letter of 18 inst, and have now the pleasure to inform your Excellency That the Cutter Black prince Capt. Merchant arrived this afternoon in this road: one of his officers is comed on shore, who told me that Since their last departure from Brest, they have had but indifferent success,[1] they took only two prizes in the Irish channell, the one a large vessell loaded with Iron Tarr, & timber bound from Gotthenbourg to Dublin, which they sent for a port in France, the other was a light vessell which they ransom'd for 300 Guineas, the hostage with 18 prisoners are on board; I requested M. De Chaulieu the Commander at this place[2] to have them committed to the common Jail where the English prisoners are, which he promised to grant the moment they should be Sent on shore, and to allow a guard to conduct them. I shall now Expect your Excellencys orders respecting said prisoners maintainance; interim I here enclose an acknowledgement of the Commissary at Brest for

9. Elizabeth Bond Martin (b. 1736) was Bond's daughter by his first wife. She married Dr. John Martin of Maryland in 1765 and had two children, Susan and William Bond Martin. Information kindly supplied by Dr. Bell.

1. The *Black Prince*'s fourth cruise, which began on Sept. 4, is described in Clark, *Ben Franklin's Privateers*, pp. 81–7.

2. De Chaulieu was a *maréchal de camp* who had served as a staff officer during the Seven Years' War: *Etat militaire* for 1779, pp. 23, 88.

two prisoners Capn Merchant delivered to the keeper of the Bagne prison at said place. Per my next I shall forward to your excellency a Copy of Capn. Merchants Journal, by which appears that he has attack'd an English Schooner of 18 guns which only escaped by outsailing the black prince.

I have the honour to remain with profound respect Your Excellency's Most obedient and most devoted humble servant

FRANS. COFFYN

His Excellency Dr. Bn Franklin

Notation: Mr. Coffin Sept 24. 1779

From Sarah Bache

ALS: American Philosophical Society

Dear & Honoured Sir   Philada. Sepr: 25. 1779

We wrote to you fully some days ago,[3] but Mr Gerard staying longer than he expected[4] gives me an opportunity of telling you we still continue well, and of sending you some more Newspapers, it has been my earnest wish that Mr G: might be detaind a few days longer still, as I wanted him to stand Godfather to a little stranger that is hourly expected, and is to be named after one of their most Christian Majesty's. I must beg you my dear Papa to make the request to him and desire he will name some body to stand proxy, in my present situation I could not have it mentioned to him before he left Philad:—[5] The Queen has so many names, one of them will be honour enough, I must beg you to say which will be the most pleasing to you—

The enclosed Petition, and which I could not get off sending, is wrote by a person that came down to Congress, from the people of Vermont about their Land and has always been

3. She last wrote on Sept. 14, her husband on Sept. 18; both are above.

4. La Luzerne asked him to remain until Congress selected a minister to conduct eventual peace negotiations with Britain and another to go to Spain: Meng, *Despatches of Gérard,* pp. 896–7. This did not occur until Sept. 27; see our annotation of Huntington to BF, Oct. 16.

5. We have no record of BF's involvement, but as Gérard brought him RB's announcement of the birth (below, Oct. 17) the Baches may have discussed the subject with him themselves.

employ'd to represent them, and tho he does not want understanding, is one of the greatest oddities in the world, Mr B:
told him it was an improper time when France was doing so
much for us, and that all the other towns that were burnt
would think their claim's to Charity equal, that the United
States would take the matter up, but he will not be said nay, I
would have given a good deal if Temple who used to delight
in Originals, had heard him converse and read his petition—[6]
Mr Bache has been to wait on the new Minister, who told
him my things were coming on with his baggage,[7] I wish they
would arrive before Mr G: goes, as he spared me eight yards
of fine white flannel last winter when it was not to be bought,
and I wish'd to return it, but as there is no chance of my
having that in my power now, shall I beg the favor of you to
return it to him with my best thanks—
Mr Wharton[8] gives us very pleasing accounts of your
Health and Spirrits, that they may long continue is the constant prayer of your Dutiful and Afectionate Daughter
S BACHE

From Vincenzio Martinelli[9]

ALS: American Philosophical Society

Monsieur　　　　　　a Florence ce 25me. septembre 1779
Monsieur Jan Batiste la Bordet natif de Pau en Bearne a
l'occasion de retourner a la Patrie a eu la complaisence de se
charger d'une petite brochure sur les Colonies Angloises

6. Probably the flamboyant Ethan Allen, who with his friend Jonas Fay
(*DAB*) had come to Congress to lobby for Vermont's admission as an independent state and to explain his suppression of anti-Vermont agitation in
Cumberland County: Charles A. Jellison, *Ethan Allen: Frontier Rebel* (Syracuse, 1969), pp. 227–9.
7. Aboard jw's brig, the *Trois Amis*.
8. Joseph Wharton, Jr.
9. The *Enciclopedia Italiana* (36 vols., Rome, 1929–39) describes Vincenzo
Martinelli (1702–85) as both a historian and an adventurer. In trouble in
his native Tuscany, he settled in London in 1748 and published various
books, notably an edition of Boccacio's *Decameron* and the first history of
England written in the Italian language. Back home in 1776, he brought
out *Storia del governo d'Inghilterra e delle sue colonie d'India e nell'America Setten-*

Americanes que j'ai dernierement publièe pour instruire mes Compatriots des motives qui ont cause leur presente dispute avec l'Angleterre. Comme j ai compilé dernierement l'Istoire d'Angleterre que j'ai dediè a monsr. Thomas Walpole chez qui vous m'aurè rencontrè quelque fois a dinner. J'ay crus de mon devoir de vous en offrir une Copie comme a l'heroique liberatoeur des ces honorables Nations. Je finiray en recamandant a votre protection l'honnete et ingenieus porteur que j'ay connu fort bien digne dêtre encouragè et protegè par les Personages de votre merite.

J'ay l'honneur d'etre de votre excelence le tres humble et tres obeissant ser. VINCENZIO MARTINELLI

From ———— Rabŷ du Moreau

ALS: American Philosophical Society

Monsieur Le Docteur,   à Bordx. 25. 7bre. 1779.

Les papiers publics nous laissent floter dans une incertitude cruelle sur les Evenemens arrivés dans la Caroline Méridionale: il y a ici, rélativement à Eux, des paris considerables qui restent indécis, un mot de la part de votre Excellence peut les terminer. "Prevost at-il attaqué Charles-Twn? Y at-il Eu une affaire devant cette ville du 10. au 20. may dernier où Prévôt ait Eté batu et repoussé par les Amériquains?"

S'il n'y a pas d'indiscrétion, Monsieur le Docteur, à vous demander une réponse positive Sur ces faits *Et Sur la date*, je prie vôtre Excellence de me la faire Et d'agréer L'hommage du sincère Et respectueux attachement avec le quel j'ai L'honneur d'Etre, Monsieur le Docteur, vôtre très humble Et très obéissant Serviteur.   RABŶ DU MOREAU
cher. de St. Louis.

Notations: Raby de Moreau 25. sept. 79 / ansd [1]

---

trionale, in which he foresaw the American Revolution. BF once mentioned the Florentine in a letter to Philip Mazzei on Dec. 27, 1775 (XXII, 308–9). As will appear from a later letter from Martinelli (April 10, 1781, Hist. Soc. of Pa.), BF sent him a book and conveyed Walpole's greetings.

1. BF's letterbook (Library of Congress) records the following response, dated Passy, Oct. 1,1779: "I have not had for a long time any direct Intelli-

From Vergennes: Two Letters

(I) and (II) L (draft):[2] Archives du Ministère des affaires étrangères; copy:[3] Library of Congress

I.

A Velles. [Versailles] le 25 7bre. 1779.

J'ai l'honneur de vous envoyer, M, un paquet pour M. le cher. de la Luzerne; je vous prie de vouloir bien en charger le cape. du bâtiment amèricain qui se trouve dans le port de Nantes, et qui est au moment de Son dèpart pour l'amerique.[4]

Je ne suis pas encore en état, M, de vous informer de la resolution du Roi relativement aux diverses demandes du Congrès,[5] parceque[6] les cahiers qui les renferment doivent être examinés, et que ce n'est qu'après cet Examen, qu'il pourra en etre rendu compte à S. M. Dès qu'Elle aura prononcé, elle repondra au Congrès pour lui faire part de Sa determination.

J'ai l'honneur d'etre &

M Franklin

II.

à Versailles le 25. 7bre. 1779.

J'ai l'honneur de vous envoyer, M, copie d'un mémoire qui m'a été adressé par M. Le Pr. de Montbarey; vous y verrez que

---

gence from South Carolina, and know nothing more of the State of Affairs there than what you see in the News papers, otherwise I should comply with your Request with Pleasure."

2. Both in the hand of Gérard de Rayneval.

3. The copy of II mistakenly attributes Sartine as the sender.

4. On Sept. 18, above, BF had volunteered the use of the *Mercury* to carry Vergennes' dispatches.

5. The lists forwarded by BF with his letter of the 18th.

6. The remainder of the letter has been inserted in the margin, replacing the following passage, which has been lined through: "S. Mté. n'a rien encore statüé à cet égard; mais je crois pouvoir vous assurer d'avance que ses dispositions sur l'objet dont il est question sont analogues à son affection pour les Etats-unis, et qu'elles dirigeront la détermination qu'il ne tardera pas de prendre; des qu'elle me sera connüe, je serai exact à vous en

deux caporaux d'une compagnie d'ouvriers du Corps-royal d'artillerie reclament leur part dans la prise du bâtiment anglais *le Fox,* faite par la frégate américaine *la Boston;* comme cette demande me paroit on ne peut pas plus juste, le Roi m'a ordonné de vous la communiquer, afin que vous puissiez la transmettre au Congrès,[7] qui certainement s'empressera de faire rendre justice aux deux Caporaux qu'elle interesse: M. le cher. de La Luzerne reçoit l'ordre de leur accorder ses bons offices.

To Vergennes

ʟs:[8] American Philosophical Society; copy: Library of Congress

Sir,   Passy Sept. 26. 1779.

I received Yesterday Evening the Letter your Excellency did me the honour of writing to me,[9] together with the Pacquet for M. De la Luzerne, which I shall take Care to forward with my Dispatches. I could have wished it had been possible to have written something positive to the Congress by this Opportunity on the Subject of the Supplies they have asked, because I apprehend great Inconveniences may arise from their being left in a State of Uncertainty on that Account, not only as the Hope or Expectation of obtaining those Supplies may prevent their taking other Measures, if possible, to obtain them, but as the Disappointment will give great Advantage to their Enemies external and internal. Your Excellency will be so good as to excuse my making this Observation, which is forced from me by my great Anxiety on the Occasion.

---

prévenir en même tems que le Roi en informera le Congrès en rèpondant à la lettre qu'il luy a addressée." The copy incorporates the revision.

7. In his Oct. 4–28 letter to John Jay, below, ʙғ said he was enclosing it, but we have found no further trace of it. H.M.S. *Fox* was captured on June 7, 1777, by the Continental Navy frigates *Boston* and *Hancock: Naval Docs.,* ɪx, 47.

8. In ᴡᴛғ's hand.

9. Letter I of Sept. 25. ʙғ's Cash Book for Sept. 25 (Account XVI, xxvɪ, 3) records a payment of 12 *l.t.* to Vergennes' messenger. ʙғ did not answer the other letter until Oct. 1, below.

With the greatest Respect, I am, Your Excellency's, most obedient & most humble Servant.   B FRANKLIN

M. Le Cte. De Vergennes.

From John Jay[1]   AL (draft): Columbia University Library

Dear Sir   Pha. 26 Sep 1779

I have had the Pleasure of recg. your favor of the 2d. June last.[2] The act of Congress respecting Col Diricks alluded to in it; mentioned no public Business comd. to his Care, but in Compliance with his Request supported by Govr. Trumbul simply recommended him to your notice—[3]

As this will be delivered to you by Monsr. Gerard It will be unnecessary to enlarge on american Politics or Intelligence. This Gentleman has done essential service to the Alliance, and by the wisdom of his Conduct done much towards binding the two nations to each other by Affection whose union at first resulted from motives of Interest. I am happy to assure you that similar Ideas of You prevail & extend in this Country as well as the one you are in—

The Chevalier de LaLuzerne has brought with him many recommendatory Letters. Few will be more useful to him than yours— If he treads in the Steps of his Predecessor, they will

1. Written by Jay in his capacity of president of Congress, and acknowledged by BF (Wharton, *Diplomatic Correspondence*, III, 597) although we have not located the recipient's copy. On the following day Jay was elected minister plenipotentiary to the court of Spain and thereupon resigned the presidency: *JCC*, XV, 1113, 1114.

2. XXIX, 605–6.

3. BF had told Jay that he had met Lt. Col. Jacob Gerhard Dircks in Passy, but had learned nothing of his business in the Netherlands. Dircks's business there was procuring a loan; he was unsuccessful but his optimism about the prospects of America's obtaining a Dutch loan prompted Congress to send ex-President Henry Laurens there. Laurens was selected for the mission on Oct. 21: Richard B. Morris, ed., *John Jay, the Making of a Revolutionary: Unpublished Papers 1745–1780* (New York, 1975), pp. 644–5n.

lead him to the Hearts of the Americans— My Endeavours shall not be wanting to render this Country agreable to him.

You will oblige me by continuing this Correspondence and by believing that I am with great Esteem & Regard your most obt. & hbl Servt

Docr Franklin

Notation: To Doctr. Franklin 26 Sep 1779

From Arthur Lee: Two Letters

(I) AL: American Philosophical Society; copy: National Archives; (II) ALS: American Philosophical Society; copy: National Archives

I.

Paris Sepr. 26th. 1779

Mr Lee has the honor of presenting his Compts. to Dr. Franklin; & of forwarding the enclosd, which came in Mr Lovell's letter to him.[4]

II.

Sir/   Paris Sepr. 26th. 1779

It has pleasd Congress to continue me as their Commissioner to the Court of Spain,[5] without making any alteration, that has come to my knowlege, in their former Resolve relative to the manner in which the Expences of their Commissioners are

---

4. Lovell wrote Lee on June 13 and on July 17, informing him that the attempt in Congress to recall him had failed: Smith, *Letters*, XIII, 62–3, 251–3. We assume Lee had just received one or both of the letters and that the enclosure was related to the May 3 congressional decision: *JCC,* XIV, 542–3; H. James Henderson, *Party Politics in the Continental Congress* (New York, 1974), pp. 202–6.

5. A mission long dormant which Lee had recently been attempting to revive; see his letter of Aug. 14. Lee was nominated in Congress on Sept. 26 to be minister plenipotentiary to Spain, but on the following day Jay was elected: *JCC,* XV, 1110, 1113.

to be supplied.[6] The spanish funds[7] which were in my hands are not only exhausted, but I am considerably in debt upon them. I shall therefore be obligd to you for informing me, whether you can supply me with money for my Expences; that if you cannot; I may return forthwith to America, & deliver up a Commission for the execution of which the means are not provided.

I have the honor to be with great respect, Sir yr. most obedt. Humbe. Servt ARTHUR LEE

Endorsed: Recd the 29th at 9 a Clock A.M.

From ——— Maussallé[8]   ALS: American Philosophical Society

Monsieur   a Paris ce 26. 7bre. 1779.

Je suis chargé d'avoir L'honneur de vous voir pour une affaire qui interresse un Negociant de Dunkerque dont j'ay la confiance, et qui vous a été renvoyée par M. De sartine. Je vous prie de m'indiquer le jour et l'heure de votre commodité auxquels je pouray me rendre chez vous a cet effet.

6. The resolve, of May 7, 1778, was that the commissioners to the courts of Spain, Tuscany, Vienna, and Berlin "should live in such style and manner, at their respective courts, as they may find suitable and necessary to support the dignity of their public character," for which purpose they were empowered to draw bills of exchange on the American mission in France: *JCC,* XI, 473. The present letter may have been prompted, however, by Lee's having seen a more recent resolution on reimbursements for the commissioners which Lovell had asked BF to communicate to his former colleagues and which BF had shown to Izard; see our annotation of Lovell to BF, Aug. 6, and BF to Izard, Sept. 27.

7. The 187,500 *l.t.* obtained during Lee's 1777 mission to Spain: XXIV, 557.

8. A Paris lawyer. The *Almanach royal* for 1779 (p. 251) lists him among the "avocats aux conseils du roi" at the address given below. The "négociant de Dunkerque" he represents here is probably John Torris and the "affaire" most likely concerns the judgments that Torris had requested of BF for the *Goodwill* and the ransomed *Three Sisters* (above, Sept. 23). For an account of the steps taken by Torris and his representatives to obtain judgments for these prizes and ransoms see Clark, *Ben Franklin's Privateers,* pp. 57–9.

Torris continued to have Maussallé represent him and in later correspondence with BF mentions him by name: Torris to BF, May 13, 1780 (APS).

Je suis avec Respect Monsieur Votre tres humble et tres obeissant serviteur MAUSSALLÉ

avocat aux Conseils

Rue Montmartre vis avis la Jussienne

Notations in different hands: Maussalé 26. 7bre. 1779. / Ans'd[9]

To Dumas

Copy: Library of Congress

Dear Sir   Passy, Sept 27. 1779

I received your favour of the 21th. and one before[1] acquainting me with your Safe arrival, which gave me great Pleasure. You Shall have the Treaty and my few Remarks very soon. I inclose four of our latest Newspapers, which contain some Intelligence from Carolina, the Particulars of the taking of the fort at Stony Point, and the Devastations made by the Enemy in Connecticut. I am ever. Your affectionate friend And most obedient servant   BF

M Dumas.

To Ralph Izard[2]

Copy: Library of Congress

Sir   Passy sept. 27. 1779.

As Soon as I knew you were in Paris I Sent you a Copy of the Congress Resolution of the 6th. of august respecting their

9. BF answered on the 27th saying that he had received Maussallé's letter and would see him the next day at noon. The LS, in WTF's hand and in French, is at the Yale University Library; a copy, also in French, is at the Library of Congress.

1. Above, Sept. 14.

2. Formerly the commissioner designate to the Grand Duchy of Tuscany, Izard was recalled by Congress on June 8. Congress also voted, however, that he "need not repair to America": *JCC*, XIV, 700–3. On Aug. 6 Congress took up the question of salaries for Izard and the other former commissioners, resolving an allowance be paid them for past services, but requesting them to transmit accounts and vouchers for the public money they had spent: *ibid.*, p. 928. When Izard learned of this latter resolution from BF, he asked if the American minister had received directions from Congress to pay him or whether he thought himself authorized by the resolution to do

Commissioners in Europe being desired so to do by the Committee of Correspondance from whom I had just received the Original.[3] But I received with it no "Orders from Congress to pay you any Money," nor can I think myself authorised by that resoluton to make any Such payment, their being not a word in it to that purpose; and if it did authorise me; it does not enable me.— But on the other [*hand*] there is a Part of it which directs that every "commissioner who has been entrusted with public money Shall transmit without Delay his Accounts and Vouchers to the Board of Treasury in order for settlement."[4] Till Such settlement is made I conceive it cannot be known what or whether anything is due to you.

I recollect upon this Occasion a Promise I made you of complying with your Request in giving you a Copy of the Drafts of a Letter I proposed to the Commissioners to send you last January, in answer to a fresh Demand you then made of more Money.[5] I now fulfill that promise by inclosing it and have the honour to be Sir, &c &c

Honble. M. Izard.

From Barbeu-Dubourg
ALS: American Philosophical Society

Mon cher Maitre,   [September 27, 1779][6]

Vous etes prié de vous souvenir que vous avez promis d'aller apresdemain (29e. 7bre.) chez M Cochin a Chatillon, et meme de tres bonne heure pour raison. Neuf heures n'est pas trop matin. Si vous avez la bonté de me prendre en passant, je me tiendrai prêt pour cette heure.

Autre chose. Un jeune homme de 16 ans, fils d'une des

SO: Wharton, *Diplomatic Correspondence*, III, 351. Note that Arthur Lee in requesting money from BF had cited instead a 1778 congressional resolution: above, Sept. 26.

3. See our annotation of Lovell's Aug. 6 letter to BF.

4. BF here condenses a long passage of the resolution which, applying to all the commissioners, originally was written in the plural.

5. XXVIII, 381–3, 401–2.

6. Our dating is based on his mention of Sept. 29 as "the day after tomorrow."

bonnes amies de Madame de Cheminot part jeudi pour faire une promenade en Amerique, et specialement aux Antilles. Comme quelque aventure pourroit le pousser vers le Continent, on souhaiteroit qu'il pût se reclamer de vous, et qu'a cet effet vous vouliez bien lui en donner quelque espece de permission, en le chargeant d'une lettre ouverte adressée a qui il vous plairoit, et qu'il pût montrer dans telle ville des Etats unis où il aborderoit. Il n'est question que d'etre annoncé comme un jeune homme honnete et bien né. Il n'a d'ailleurs ni pretentions ni besoins. Il part assez bien muni d'argent et de lettres de change.

Il s'appelle Jean Baptiste Charles Pinon Duclos de Vulmer, et il est fils du Directeur des vingtiemes de la province de Champagne.[7]

Me. de Cheminot qui vous prie de cela est une de vos amoureuses les plus passionnées; et espere que vous ne l'oublierez pas. Si elle n'etoit enrhumée, elle auroit saisi cette occasion pour aller vous voir. Je suis avec le plus tendre respect, Cher Ami, votre tres humble, tres fidele et tres zelé serviteur   DUBOURG

From Joseph Priestley

ALS: American Philosophical Society

Dear Sir   Calne Sep. 27. 1779

Though you are so much engaged in affairs of more consequence, I know it will give you some pleasure to be informed that I have been exceedingly successful in the prosecution of my experiments since the publication of my last volume.[8]

I have confirmed, explained, and extended my former observations on the purification of the atmosphere by means of vegetation; having first discovered that the *green matter* I treat of in my last volume is a vegetable substance, and then that

---

7. In what would turn out to be his last extant letter to BF, Dubourg (who died in December) repeated this request on Sept. 30, stressing that the young man was about to leave. APS. BF obliged in his letter to RB, Oct. 1, below. Duclos' father is listed in the *Almanach royal* for 1779, p. 501.

8. He had completed *Experiments and Observations Relating to Various Branches of Natural Philosophy* . . . in March: XXIX, 99–100.

other plants that grow wholly in water have the same property, all of them without exception imbibing impure air, and emitting it, as *excrementations* to them, in a dephlogisticated state. That the source of this pure air is the impure air in the water is evident from all the plants giving only a certain quantity of air, in proportion to the water in which they are confined, and then giving more air in fresh water. I also find that the water before the plants have been confined in it yields impure air, and afterwards pure air.

From these observations I conclude that the reason why my sprigs of mint &c sometimes failed to purify air, was their not being always *healthy* in a confined state; whereas these water-plants are as much at their ease in my jars as in the open pond.

I have made many other new observations, but they are chiefly of a chymical nature, and not worth while making the subject of a letter; tho, when you see an account of them in my next publication, I flatter myself you will think some of them curious and important.

As the expence of my experiments is necessarily considerable, Dr Fothergill (who, in a very obliging manner, interests himself much in them) has, of his own motion, engaged a few of his friends to contribute about 40£ per Ann to assist me in defraying the expence.[9] Indeed, without this assistance I must have desisted altogether. While I had but a small family I suffered myself to be drawn by my success into expences that now appear to have been rather imprudent.

I have been made very happy by the communication of your very ingenious paper on the *Aurora Borealis*,[1] and by several accounts of the good state of your health and spirits. May this long continue— Yours most sincerely   J Priestley

9. Fothergill had first offered £100 per year but Priestley declined, fearing the reaction of Lord Shelburne, his employer: *Memoirs of Dr. Joseph Priestley, to the Year 1795* . . . (London, 1806), p. 91.

1. XXVIII, 190–200.

From Sartine

Copy: Library of Congress

Versailles le 27. 7bre. 1779.

J'ai l'honneur, Monsieur, de vous envoyer les procedures in-struites par les Officiers de l'Amirauté de Brest concernant la prise le jeune Domnique, et huit rançons faites par le Cor-saire Americain le Prince Noir.[2] Vous savez, Monsieur, que le Conseil des Prises n'a pas jugé convenable de prendre connoissance de ces Sortes de procedures; et je vous prie de m'accuser la reception de ces Differentes pieces.

J'ai l'honneur d'etre, avec la consideration la plus distin-guée, Monsieur, Votre tres humble et tres obeissant serviteur.

signé DE SARTINE/.

M. Franklin

To Francis Coffyn

Copy: Library of Congress

Sir   Passy, Sept. 28. 1779.

I received your several favours containing the Claims of Capt. Cunningham's french Sailors,[3] and The Memoirs rela-tive to the Privileges of your Port.[4] With regard to these Claims, I Shall Send them to Congress, but I observe that they are Simply the Declarations of the People themselves, that an Agreement was made with them for such high Wages with Shares of Prizes and are not confirmed by any testimony of Persons concern'd in that Equipment, which methinks they ought to be. The just Privileges of your Port I hope you will be able to maintain. I am fully Satisfied by your former Memoir[5] of its Conveniency for the American Commerce, and

---

2. The eight ransoms are from the *Black Prince*'s third cruise. On Sept. 23 Torris had requested BF to send a judgment of them.

3. The sailors in question had been exchanged in the recent cartel; see BF's Aug. 4 letter to Coffyn. On Aug. 12 Coffyn told BF that he would forward their depositions and on Aug. 30 promised to send the papers with his next letter: above. His next letter seems to have been the now-missing one of Sept. 9 (for which see Coffyn to BF, Sept. 18), so the sailors' claims are also missing.

4. See our annotation of Coffyn's letter of Sept. 18.

5. Described in XXVI, 522n.

I make no doubt but you will in time have a large Share of it. I thank you for the Copy of the regulation relating to Prizes.[6] By this Post Mr. Torris will receive all that he desires, except for the last 8 Ransomers, I having been little instructed as to the Part I am to act in such Business; he will here after meet with no delay in his business from me.

In compliance with your Recommendation I Shall also Send commission for the Black Princess. As to the Maintenance of Prisoners these Privateers may bring in to your Port, you will find that Matter arranged in the same regulation of sept. 27. 1778. Article 15.—[7] With great Esteem I have the honour to be Sir Your most obedient and most humble servant   BF

M. Coffin, Dunkirque.

To Sartine   LS:[8] Yale University Library; copy: Library of Congress

Sir,   Passy Sept. 28. 1779.

As our Prisoners now exchanging are chiefly at Portsmouth and Plymouth and the Distance between those Places & Nantes is double of that between them and Morlaix, and a great Part of the Voyage to Nantes, being in the Bay of Biscay, which will be very inconvenient to the Cartel Ship and other Poor Passengers, in the Winter Season, I am desired to request of your Excellency, if it may be granted without inconveniency, a Passport for the next Cartel, permitting her to land the Prisoners at Morlaix. This Favour will the more oblige me, as I find the English make a difficulty of continuing the Exchange on that Account.

With the greatest Respect, I am Your Excellency's, most obedient and most humble Servant.   B Franklin

His Exy. M. De Sartine.[9]

6. Enclosed with the letter of the 18th.
7. Wharton, *Diplomatic Correspondence*, II, 687.
8. In WTF's hand.
9. Apparently this letter was referred to a subordinate official at the naval ministry, who made a French translation for Sartine (Archives Nationales). On the bottom in Sartine's hand is written "accordé"; at the top in a clerk's

To John Torris

Copy: Library of Congress

Sir   Passy Sept. 28. 1779.

I received yours of the 23 Instant, and having examined the Procès verbaux Sent me from Morlaix relative to the Sloop Goodwill, and being of Opinion that she is a good Prize, I Send you herewith my Letter to the Judges of the admiralty, at Morlaix,[1] Expressing that Opinion tho' I must acquaint you that the Circumstance of your firing at her under English Colours created some Difficulty with me and you should caution your Captains not to be guilty of the like Error again; for it is Said that in such cases tho' the Ship taken Should be adjudged a good Prize the Share of the Captain and Owners would be legally confiscated.

As to the Ransoms you mention I Send you herewith my Judgmt on that of the three Sisters;[2] But for the 8 New ones, I do not find that the Proces Verbaux relating to them have yet been Communicated to me, and therefore I cannot at present give any Judgment concerning them.[3]

The Papers are preparing for the Black Princess and will be sent in a few Days: as well as the Night Glass.

Your 21. Men will be exchanged as soon as possible. The more Prisoners you bring in, the Sooner that Exchange will be effected.— Wishing you continued Success, I have the honour to be Sir &c. &c.

Mr. Torris Negociant a Dunkirque.

---

hand is recorded "accordé le 14 8 1779." This date may be that of the King's approval; see Sartine's Oct. 17 letter to BF.

1. Missing.

2. BF enclosed a certificate condemning the *Three Sisters,* Capt. George Hooper of Bideford, England, which had been taken by the *Black Prince* in June (see our annotation of Torris' Sept. 23 letter). Its language is almost identical to the certificate of Sept. 18, above. It states that Richard Hooper, taken hostage in the capture, was examined by the judges of the Morlaix Admiralty on July 24. An autograph draft of the certificate is at the Hist. Soc. of Del.

3. BF had not yet received the papers Sartine had sent him the previous day.

From Charles Thomson

ALS: University of Pennsylvania Library

Sir,   In Congress Septr. 28. 1779
I have the honor to inform you that Congress have this day elected his excellency Samuel Huntington esqr. their president. I am Sr Your humble Servant   CHA THOMSON secy.

Honble Benj Franklin Esqr.

Endorsed: Cha Thompson Sept. 28. 1780 notifying the election of Mr Huntington as President of Congress.

From the Baron von Steuben[4]

Copy: New-York Historical Society

Dear Sir   Head Quarters West Point, Sept. 28th. 1779
I take the Liberty of transmitting you a few Copies of the Regulations published last Winter for the service of the Infantry.[5] As this Work has been made under my Direction, I must let you know that Circumstances have obliged me to deviate from the Principles adopted in the European Armies, Such as the formation in Two Ranks, the Weakness of our Battalions &c. Young as We are, We have already our prejudices as the most ancient Nations, the prepossession in favor of the British service, has obliged me to comply with many Things, which are against my Principles. However, We have now fixed Regulations, which will at least produce an Uniformity in the Service, & our System, tho' imperfect, is far preferable to having none.
I leave it to your other Correspondents to give you an Account of the present State of our Army; If they tell you that

4. BF two years earlier had provided Steuben with a letter of introduction to Washington: XXIV, 499–500.
5. *Regulations for the Order and Discipline of the Troops of the United States* (Philadelphia, 1779), popularly known as "the blue book"; for its composition and publication see John McAuley Palmer, *General von Steuben* (New Haven, 1937), 140–1, 200, 202–4.

our Order & Discipline Equals that of the French and Prussian Armies, do not believe them, but do not believe them neither, if they compare our Troops to those of the Pope, & take a just medium between those two Extremes. Tho' we are so young that we scarce begin to walk, we can already take Stoney Points, & Powle's [Paulus] Hooks with the point of the Bayonet, without firing a Single Shot. This is very premature, yet we have still many Weaknesses which bespeak our Infancy. We want, above all, the true meaning of the Words *Liberty, Independence* &c that the Child may not make use of them against his Father, or the Soldier against his Officer.

I will say nothing of our Political Affairs. These do not fall within the verge of my District. All I can assure you of, is that the English will not beat us, if we do not beat ourselves.[6]

As I receive no Letters from Europe which pains me Very much, I have taken the Liberty to direct my friends & Correspondents to address my Letters to you. I rely on your goodness for transmitting them.

I am with great respect & Esteem Dear Sir Your most obedient & most humble Servant

His Excellency B. Franklin, Esq; Minr Plenipoy: &c &c.

Notation: Doctr Franklin Sept 1779

To the Gentlemen at Nantes

Copy: Library of Congress

Gentlemen

Passy, Sept 29. 1779.

I received your Report.[7] I am much obliged to you for the Great Pains and Care which you have taken in examining and adjusting the Accounts of Mr. Williams and beg you to accept my thankful acknowledgments. I shal not fail to acquaint the

6. Originally written (but then lined through), "as long as we do not quarrel together."

7. That report, now missing, must have accompanied jw's accounts; see bf's certificate of Aug. 26. jw sent the accounts to Congress in early November. His letter to Jay, dated Nov. 9, mentions the additional enclosure of his own memorial on the background of the audit, dated Nov. 6. Copies of the letter and the memorial are in the Yale University Library.

413

Congress, with your services being with much Esteem and respect Gentlemen

Messieurs Joshua Johnson, &c.

To Elisha Hart[8]

Copy: Library of Congress

Sir   Passy, Sept 29. 1779.

I received yours,[9] and I do by this Post request M. Schweighauser to furnish you with the Same Supply that has been received by other officers in your Situation. It is not much, but the great Number we have to relieve from time to time obliges us to be more Sparing than we Should otherwise be. I wish you safe home to you friends and Country, and I have the honour to be Sir,

Capt Eisha at Mr. Schweighauser, Nantes

To Jonathan Nesbitt[1]

Copy: Library of Congress

Sir   Passy, Sept 29. 1779.

Capt. Conyngham has not been neglected. As soon as I heard of his arrival in England, I wrote to a friend to furnish him with money he might want, and to assure that he had never acted without a Commission. I have been made to understand in answer that there is not intention to prosecute him, and that he was accordingly removed from Pendennes Castle and put among the common Prisoners at Plimouth to take his Turn for Exchange the Congress hearing of the Threats to sacrifice him put 3 Officers in close Confinement to abide his fate, and acquainted Sir George Collier with their

8. BF's letter to Schweighauser of the same date, below, implies that Hart had arrived with the second cartel. We assume he is the Capt. Elisha Hart of Saybrook, Conn., who returned to command the sloops *Retaliation* and *Restoration* in 1780 and 1781: Claghorn, *Naval Officers,* p. 142; Louis F. Middlebrook, *History of Maritime Connecticut during the American Revolution 1775–1783* (2 vols., Salem, 1925), II, 204–6.

9. Missing.

1. In answer to his of Sept. 22, above.

Determination, who probably wrote to the British Ministers.—² I thank you for informing me what became of his first Commission. I Suppose I can now easily recover it, to produce on Occasion.— Probably the Date of that Taken with him being posterior to his Capture of The pacquet, made The Enemy think they had an advantage Against him.— But when the English Governement have encouraged our Sailors intrusted with our Vessels to betray that Trust, run away with the Vessels, and bring them into English Ports, giving such Traitors the Value as if good and lawful Prizes, it was foolish Imprudence in the British Commodore to talk of hanging one of our Captains for taking a Prize without Commission. I have the honour to be, with Great Esteem Sir

Mr. Nesbit.

To Sartine

Copy: Library of Congress

Sir   Passy, Sept. 29. 1779.

I have received the Proceedings of the admiralty at Brest concerning the young Dominique Prize, and eight Ransoms made by the Black Prince Privateer which your Excellency did me the honour of Sending to me the 27th. Instant. With the greatest Respect I am, Your Excellency's most

M. De Sartine.

To Schweighauser

Copy: Library of Congress

Sir   Passy Sept. 29. 1779.

Please to furnish Capt. Elisha Hart with the Same sum you advanced to the Officers Prisoners, who came over in the first

2. On July 17, in response to a plea from Ann Conyngham (see our annotation of her letter of Sept. 22) and a petition from the inhabitants of Philadelphia, Congress dispatched a letter to the commanding officer of the British fleet at New York, Sir George Collier (*DNB*). The resolution demanded that Conyngham be released or that an explanation be given for his ill-treatment. If no satisfactory answer was received by Aug. 1, the Marine Committee was empowered to take into custody as many persons as

Cartel with the approbation of Mr. Adams, taking his Promissory Notes for the Same per triplicate, payable to the President of Congress, or his Order. I have the honour to be, Sir

Mr. Schweighauser

From the Board of Treasury

LS: American Philosophical Society

Philadelphia, Treasury-Office, September 29th.
Sir,   1779
   The inclosed Resolutions were referred by Congress to the Board of Treasury with Direction to take Order thereon.[3]
   The impractibility of executing the Work in this part of the World obliges the Board to forward them to you with an earnest request to have the Medals voted struck as soon as possible with such Devices as may be judged emblematical of the Occasions which excited the Notice and obtained the Thanks

---

they thought proper to retaliate: *JCC*, xiv, 849–50. Collier's curt reply (made through his secretary) declining to answer their "uncivil" demands is printed in Neeser, *Conyngham*, pp. 182–3. Congress responded by taking a British naval officer hostage (although BF claimed it took three hostages): Neeser, *Conyngham*, p. 184; *JCC*, xv, 1373; BF to Conyngham, Nov. 22, 1779 (Library of Congress).

   3. Although the enclosed resolutions have become separated from the letter, it is obvious they concerned Congressional decisions to reward the leaders of two recent military exploits. On Sept. 24 Congress, recognizing Maj. Harry Lee's "prudence, address and bravery" in a surprise attack on the British post at Paulus Hook, N.J., resolved "That a medal of gold, emblematical of this affair, be struck, under the direction of the Board of Treasury, and presented to Major Lee": *JCC*, xv, 1099–1100. Lee was the only officer during the war below the rank of general to receive such a medal: Charles Royster, *Light-Horse Harry Lee and the Legacy of the American Revolution* (New York, 1981), p. 21. The Board of Treasury also must have forwarded a July 26 resolution of Congress to present a gold medal to Brig. Gen. Anthony Wayne and silver medals to Lt. Col. François-Louis Teissèdre de Fleury and Maj. John Stewart for their roles in the capture of Stony Point, N.Y. (*JCC*, xiv, 890). BF gave the commission to the royal medallist, Pierre-Simon-Benjamin Duvivier, in the spring of 1780; their correspondence (APS) will appear in vol. 32. On Aug. 10, 1780, BF reported back to Troup on his progress (National Archives).

of Congress. They are also desirous that the Dies of the different Medals, should be sent by the first Opportunity to America, in Order to be lodged with this Board.

Colonel Fleury will have the Honor of delivering you a Duplicate of this Letter and should he arrive in France previous to the Execution of this Order his Assistance may be of Use to the Medallist as he hath been either a Gallant Actor on the Spot, or an Attentive Observer of the Scenes of the Events and their important Consequences.[4]

I have the Honor to be, Sir, With the greatest Respect, Your most obedient and Humble Servant   ROB. TROUP.[5]
Secretary

By Order of the Board

Honorable Benjamin Franklin Esqr. Minister Plenipotentiary of the United-States of America at the Court of France—

From Stephen Marchant   L:[6] American Philosophical Society

Sr/   Dunkirk Sepr. 29th. 1779

I take the Earliest Opportunity of Acquainting your Excellency of my Safe Arrival at Dunkirk in the Black prince. After Dangers both from the Enemy and bad weather, we are Safe Arrived and hath ten prisoners in Dunkirk Goal. I am just setting off to Ostend to take the Command of a Frigate of 26 Guns called the Countess of Berigin, but expects in a few Days to have the pleasure of Waiting upon yr. Honoure. Excellency at Passy with the Journal of my whole Cruize along with me we burnt in the Last Cruize Some of the Enemy's Ships, run others ashore the whole Account of which I shall

4. On Sept. 27 Fleury was granted a nine-month leave of absence by Congress: *JCC*, xv, 1111. For a description of the medal he received see Glenn Tucker, *Mad Anthony Wayne and the New Nation: the Story of Washington's Front-Line General* (Harrisburg, 1973), p. 158.

5. Troup (1757–1832), formerly secretary to the Board of War, became secretary to the Board of Treasury on May 29, 1779: *DAB*. The dateline, complimentary close, and everything below his signature are in his hand.

6. In the hand of Timothy Kelly. It is reproduced opposite p. 116 of Clark, *Ben Franklin's Privateers*.

with all Expedition Carry with me to Paris as soon as I return from Ostend, my kind Compts. to yr Excellencies Nephew and the rest of the American Gentlemen at Paris I remn. with all Duty yr. Excellencies most Obedient Hhble. Sert.

STEPHEN MARCHANT

Addressed: To / His Excellency / Benjamin Franklin, Minister / for the United States of North America / at the Court of France / at Passy / near Paris

Notation: Capt. Marchant Sept 29. 1779

From Samuel Wharton   AL: American Philosophical Society

Paris Wednesday Sepr. 29/79

Mr. Wharton presents his Compliments to Dr. Franklin, and returns the Journals of Congress, and News papers with Thanks. He does not find any Paper upon the Subject of back Lands. Upon Enquiry, and looking over his Invoice Book, He finds, That Copper in Sheets, was in the year 1770, from 87/6 to 90/ Sterling per hundred;— of 112 pds. to the hundred.[7] Mr. Wharton thinks there has been little Alteration in price, if any, since that Time.

Addressed: A Son Excellenc / Monsieur / Monsieur Franklin / Passy

Notation: Wharton Paris 29. 7bre. 1779.

To James Cuming   Copy: Library of Congress

Sir   Passy, Sept. 30. 1779.

I received the Letter you did me the honour of writing to me the 22d. Inst.[8] Several Parcels or Packets have lately come

---

7. According to information kindly supplied by Eric P. Newman, this was equivalent to roughly 9.5 pence per hundred weight. Newman has suggested that BF must have been inquiring about whether the cost of making copper planchets for coins could be reduced if they were produced from copper sheets; see Bridgen's letter of Sept. 17, above.

8. Missing.

418

to my hands from Mr. Lovel Sent by different Vessels and I make no doubt but those you mention were among them.

If the Bills you write about were originally drawn in favour of Mr. Thorp, his Letter to you relating to them may perhaps be nearly equivalent to an Indorsement, and be Sufficient to justify my accepting them without an Indorsement. It may not be quite regular, but I am desirous of accommodating you. I therefore wish you would attach that Letter to The Bills when you present them.—

I inclose a Letter for Mr. Lovel,[9] of which I pray your care, I have the honour to be Sir, &c &c.   BF.

Mr. James Cuming Negociant a L'Orient.

To Arthur Lee

LS:[1] University of Virginia Library; copy: Library of Congress

Sir   Passy Sept. 30. 1779.

I received but Yesterday Morning just as I was going out of Town; the Letter you did me the honour of writing to me dated the 26 Inst. respecting my supplying you with Money for your Support in Spain. As I cannot furnish that Expence, and there is not, in my Opinion, any likelihood at present of your being received at that Court, I think your Resolution of returning forthwith to America, is both wise & honest.

With great Respect, I have the honour to be Sir Your most obedient and most humble Servant   B FRANKLIN

Honble. Arthur Lee Esqr—

Notations in different hands: B. Franklin to A. Lee Sep 30th. 1779. / Sepr. 30th. 1779

9. Of this same date, below.
1. In WTF's hand.

To James Lovell

LS:[2] National Archives; copies: National Archives,[3] Library of Congress; transcript: National Archives

Sir   Passy, Sept. 30. 1779. 2 PM.

I have within these few Days received a Number of Dispatches from you which have arrived by the Mercury and other Vessels. Hearing but this Instant of an Opportunity from Bordeaux, and that the Courier Sets out from Versailles at 5 this Evening, I embrace it just to let you know that I have delivered the Letters from Congress to the King, and have laid the Invoices of Supplies desired, (with a translation) before the Ministers.[4] And tho' I have not yet received a positive Answer I have good reason to believe I shall obtain most of them, if not all.— But as this Demand will cost the Court a Vast Sum, and their Expences in the War are prodigious, I beg I may not be put under the Necessity by occasional Drafts on me of asking for more money than is requir'd to pay our bills for interest. I must protest those I have advice of from Martinique and New Orleans[5] (even if they were drawn by Permission of Congress) for want of Money; and I wish the Committee of Commerce would caution their Correspondents not to embarras me with their Bills.— I put into my Pocket nothing of the Allowance Congress has been pleas'd to make me, I shall pay it all in honouring their Drafts, and Supporting their Credit, but do not let me be burthen'd with Supporting the

2. In the hand of L'Air de Lamotte, whom BF would hire as a secretary in February, 1780. One of Lamotte's early duties was to prepare duplicates of the correspondence BF had last sent to America, to be carried by Lafayette when he sailed in March. (The *Mercury*, which had taken those letters in November, 1779, ran into treacherous weather; BF only learned of her safe arrival in May, 1780.) BF corrected the duplicates, signed them, and frequently marked them "Copy" at the top of the first page. The present letter is the earliest of these duplicates.

3. Made by WTF (who signed for BF), marked "Duplicate," and identifying Lovell as the recipient.

4. See the committee for foreign affairs to BF, July 16; BF to Vergennes, Sept. 18; and Vergennes' first letter of Sept. 25.

5. *I.e.*, from William Bingham and Oliver Pollock; see BF to Bingham, Oct. 4, and XXIX, 303–4.

Credit of everyone who has claims on the Boards of Commerce or the Navy. I shall write fully by the mercury. I send you some of the latest newpapers, & have the honour to be with much Esteem, Sir Your most obedient and most humble Servant   B Franklin.

Copy

From Cyrus Griffin[6]   ALS:[7] American Philosophical Society

Sir   Philadelphia September. 1779.

I do myself the honor to enclose a packet of letters which being carried by your Servant to the place directed will greatly oblige me. We thank you for the trouble of attesting a Bond executed by the late Earl of Traquair.[8] This Letter will be conveyed by Mon. Gerard, a most valuable and most amiable man indeed! and who has given all the satisfaction possible in his public and private Character.[9] No doubt you were astonished how any part of Congress should wish that all the Commissioners might be recalled to Philadelphia: it was for the purpose of explaining those unhappy dissentions and animosities which have arisen among them; and tho yourself would have left Europe at a most critical period, yet returning to France with accumulated honors after receiving the blessings of America and convincing Congress in what path to walk upon this unhappy and most disgraceful business, perhaps the

6. A Virginia lawyer, Cyrus Griffin (1748–1810) was a legislator and congressional delegate. In 1788 he was elected the last president of the Continental Congress. *DAB*.

7. Marked "Copy."

8. John Stewart, sixth earl of Traquair (b. 1698/9) had died in Paris in March: G.E. Cokayne *et al.*, eds., *The Complete Peerage* ... (13 vols. in 14, London, 1910–40), XII, part II, 13. While studying law at the University of Edinburgh, Griffin had eloped with the earl's eldest daughter, Lady Christiana: *DAB*.

9. Griffin was part of a bloc of southern delegates who were favorably inclined toward Gérard and supported Silas Deane against the allies of Arthur Lee: Meng, *Despatches of Gérard*, p. 574n; H. James Henderson, *Party Politics in the Continental Congress* (New York, St. Louis, San Francisco, 1974), pp. 203–4.

421

whole matter impartially considered the united States would have found great benefit if such a plan had taken place.[1] The French are a gay people and *entertain* a good deal; I am afraid Mon. Gerard has thought the Delegates in Congress were rather deficient in that respect; but really the expence of every article is so very enormous, and the allowance from the different States so very trifling, that a person of a handsome *American* fortune could not entertain frequently without absolute ruin in the period of two or three years—and especially since some of the states think it best for their delegates to live in seperate houses. In the course of conversation you would do some of us a singular favor to hint this matter to Mon. Gerard—since it has the appearance of not paying proper Civilities to a man of his worth and elevated station.

I have the honor to be, Sir, Your most obedient Sert.

C. GRIFFIN

Copy.

From Henri-Maximilien (Henry) Grand

AL: American Philosophical Society

[before October, 1779][2]

Mr. Hy. Grand a lhonneur d'assurer Monsieur le Docteur Franklin de son Respect, & de le prier de vouloir bien le mettre a même de faire reponse a une Dame Angloise qui est venu passer cet Eté a Paris, & qui etant a la Veille de son depart pour Londres desire obtenir un Passeport de Monsieur Le Docteur Franklin. Elle se nomme Le Beillard, & est de la Connoissance de Mr & Mme. Grand.

Monsieur Wm. T. Franklin a mis une petite Notte a 2 traittes du Loan office de 1500 *l.t.* $\overset{150^+}{\}$ en 2des. du 26 avril 1779. Mr. hy.

---

1. The inclusion of BF among those whose recall was to be considered by Congress seems to have been a tactical move by the southern supporters of Deane: Henderson, *Party Politics,* p. 200.

2. The enclosed loan office certificates can be expected to have arrived within five months.

Grand ne la pas bien comprise. Elles sont neanmoins accep-
tées.

Addressed: Grand / a Monsieur / Monsieur Le Docteur / Franklin / Passy.

Notation: Grand.—

To Richard Bache

Copy: Library of Congress

Dear son   Passy, Oct. 1. 1779.
    The Bearer, M. Jean Babtiste Charles Pinon Duclos Vulmer,
is a young Gentleman of Good family and good Character,
who goes to America for the Sake of Seeing that part of the
World as a traveller, Your Civilities to him as a stranger of
merit will much oblige. Your affectionate father

B FRANKLIN.

Mr. R. Bache

To the Marquis de Lafayette

Copy: Library of Congress

Dear Sir,   Passy, Oct. 1. 1779.
    It is a long time since I did myself the honour of writing to
you:[3] But I have frequently had the Pleasure of hearing of
your Welfare.
    Your kindness to my Grandson in offering to take him
under your Wing in the Expedition is exceedingly obliging to
me.[4] Had the Expedition gone on it would have been an infinite advantage to him to have been present with you so early
in Life at Transactions of Such vast Importance to great Nations. I flattered myself too, that he might possibly catch from
you Some Tincture of those engaging Manners that make you
so much the Delight of all that know you.— Accept hower my
warmest and most grateful Acknowledgements.—
    I Send you enclos'd a Newspaper containing the Particulars

3. BF's most recent extant letter is dated Aug. 24, above.
4. See Lafayette's second Aug. 29 letter and our annotation of BF's Aug.
31 letter to Vergennes.

of Waynes gallant attack of Stoney Point. This is good News. But it is follow'd by some bad the Loss of our little Squadron from Boston at Penobscot, which it is said our People were obliged to blow up.— I hope Count d'Estaign's Arrival in America will give us our Revenge.[5] Six thousand Troops are ordered to the West Indies to secure your Conquests, and I hope make more. But I do not hear of any Intention to send any to our Country.[6] I have no Orders to request Troops, but large ones for supplies. And I dare not take any farther Steps than I have done in such a Proposition without orders.—[7] Accept in Beehelf of the Congress my Thankful Acknowledgements for your Zeal to serve America. Occasions may offer which at Present do not appear, wherein your Bravery & conduct may be highly useful to her. May every felicity attend you is the wish of dear Sir, Your. A. and m. o. servt.   BF.

Mr. Le Marquis De Lafayette.

To Vergennes   LS:[8] Archives du Ministère des affaires étrangères; copy: Library of Congress

Sir,   Passy Oct. 1. 1779

I received the Letter your Exy did me the honour of writing to me of the 25th past, inclosing a Memorial relating to the Claim of two Corporals of the Artillery to Shares of the Prize Ship the Fox, taken by the Boston Frigate, on board of which they were, and assisting in the Action. Nothing appears to me more just than that Claim, if the Facts are as stated in their Memorial; and I shall therefore transmit it to Congress, who will, I doubt not, take Care that Justice be done them. But I

5. D'Estaing sailed for Georgia on Aug. 16. Presumably BF learned of his destination from either Sartine or Vergennes, as the French government itself had just learned it; see our annotation of Lafayette to BF, Oct. 8.

6. On Oct. 1 Vergennes told the comte de Montmorin, his ambassador in Spain, that France planned to send 4,000 reinforcements to the West Indies (AAE). Details are given in Dull, *French Navy,* pp. 166, 187, 377.

7. Possibly a tacit admission he had exceeded his orders the previous February in asking for troops (XXVIII, 603–4); his orders to request supplies are those enclosed by the committee for foreign affairs, July 16, above.

8. In WTF's hand.

have always understood that the Fox was retaken before she got into Port;[9] and I never heard of any Money or other Things of Value taken out of her, which I think Mr. Adams would have mentioned to me if it had been true. Indeed it was never usual for Merchant Ships to carry Money from England to America so much more Profit was to be made by carrying Merchandize. However the Matter will be duly inquired into.

With the greatest Respect I am, Your Excellency's most obedient and most humble Servant   B FRANKLIN

M le Comte de Vergennes.

To the Duc de Villequier   Copy: Library of Congress

Sir   Passy, Oct. 1. 1779.
I return herewith the Queries you did me the honour to send me, having written the Answers in the Margin.[1] If they are satisfactory to you it will be a pleasure to me, being with great Respect Sir, Your most obedient and most humble servant

M. Le Duc De Villequier.

9. BF is correct. While still cruising with the *Boston* and *Hancock,* the *Fox* was recaptured on July 7 by H.M.S. *Flora: Naval Docs.,* IX, 228–30.

1. Louis-Alexandre-Céleste d'Aumont, duc de Villequier (1736–1814), had sent a four-page letter on Sept. 23. He wrote that he was planning to install lightning rods on his castle in Picardy and his Parisian residence—not that he was afraid of lightning but to reassure his female relatives—and wished to be brought up to date as to the latest findings in the field, so that no untoward incident would deter others from following his example. APS. The duke was the son-in-law of BF's colleague at the Académie des sciences, the marquis de Courtanvaux. *DBF,* IV, 636, and *Dictionnaire de la noblesse,* XVIII, 825.

From Robert Montgomery

ALS: American Philosophical Society

Sir   [between October 1 and October 12, 1779][2]

Presuming on the aquaintance I had the Honour of having with your good Self as well as with Mr Adams at Passy in Sept 78 I Without Invitation Addressed your Eccellancy the 26th of June last Advising that I had been Confounded amongst the English houses here and put under Arrest with them having My Effects Embargoed by the Governour on the first Notice of a War with England, but on Making a Representation to the Minister of State that I had been always Registerd here in the list of Foraign Merchents as an American and also Producing your Certifycate of My being Such he Immediately dispathed a Courier Extraordenary with Orders for My Relacemente, of which I also had the Honour of Advising you, I again wrote from Madrid the 12th Augt. that I had been Ordred by the Count de Ricla to Retire inland 20 Lagues in Consequence of a General Order Given by his Majesty against the English and Irish Catholicks Naturalized in this Countrey amongst Whome I again found My Self Confounded, I then Apleyed in Person being well introduced to the Count de Florida Blanca to Whome I Shewed My Certifycate from the Plenipotentiarys of the united States on which he withdrew De Ricla's Order and desired me to Return to Alicante, of which I had the Pleasure of Advising you also Each time Requesting you would Condesend to Confirm my Certifycate of Allegiance, but to my Great Mortifycation I have yet had No kind of Answer to any of my Letters, It is with the utmost distress I find my Self Abandond by the Onley Gentleman in Europe from Whome I would Either Ask or Expect Protection as I Cannot Suppose that a Gentleman of Mr Franklins Knowledg in the world tho in the Most Exalted Station Could think it beneath

2. BF answered Montgomery on Oct. 28, without indicating when he received the merchant's latest appeal. As a previous one had taken 15 days to reach Passy (*Adams Papers,* VII, 232), we assume this was written sometime during the first dozen days of the month. At the very latest it must have been written before Montgomery's Nov. 3 acknowledgement of BF's assistance. APS.

him to Write a Merchant of the first Credit and Reputation, I fear he May have Some Motive for his Silance of which I am Intirely Ignorant. Tis True Spain does Not yet Acknowledge Publickly the Independancy of America but Tacitly they do by Tolerating their Vessels in all their Ports and Harbours, and puting them on the footing of those of any other freindly Nation. As well as any other Subject I find I am Entitled to all the Protection the Government I belonge to Can Give Me, and in Europe have None to Ask it from but your Excellency which I hope will Not Onley Pardon My Inportunitys but also afford me all the Releif in your Power, I Pointed out in My last Respects that a Letter from the Count de Aranda to Count de Ricla in My favour would Certainly have the desired Effect, but Should you find that Improper to be Asked and not think Me Impertinent for Presuming to Dictate farther I would Request you will Give Me a fwe Lines to the French Embasador at this Court who I beleive has Orders to Assist and Protect the Subjects of the united States as Much as in his Power.

I am here to fore Since my Interview with Count Floridablanca Living Quietly and My Business Regular, but as the Irish and English Catholicks here are in a fwe days to Retire 20 Lagues from the Coast I am Certain I Shall be Oblidged to March Same time they do if I am Not favoured with Some timeous Releif from you, I beg Sir for Gods Sake that you will diegn to Give Me your Protection as I have No Other Suport It being Impossible I Can have any Releif from the Congress before I May be Ruined here, please Consider also that I am the first American House Established in this Countrey which I hope will be Some Inducement to your taking Notice of Me Which Shall Ever be Remember'd with True Affection by Sir Your Eccellencys Most Obedt Humble Servant

ROBT MONTGOMERY

His Eccelly Benjamin Franklin Esqr.

Notation: Robt Montgomery.

From William Scot

ALS: American Philosophical Society

Ser   Leorient 1st Octr. 1779—

I Am at this time Necessiated to apply to your honnour for protection in my preasent Condition and I hope Ser you will excuse the freedom I has taken. I am Ser, a subject to the states of Ammerica and has Been since the Commencment of the war. I Came to Nance in the General washington where I Contracted a Disorder and Before I was Recoverd the Vessle saild and left on shore I heard from there that there was some Ammerican Vessels in leorent. I Gote from the Commisonarey a pass and Came to this place and as there was no Ammerican Vessels when I Came I was Obligd to goe on Board a french privateer where I served my Cruise wich was for six months and on applyin for my freedom to ship on Board some of our Vessels in this port the turnd me over to a french man of War and on my Refuseing to serve, the has Committed me to prison as an english prisoner, where I has Been 5 Days with out aney thing to eat or Drink.

I has not aney thing to eat or Drink onless what the english prisoners Gives me out of there allowance to Keep one from starving, wich is not much Beetter with them. I have made my application to the Commisonarey how tells me he has nothing to Do with it. I hope your honnour will Consider my Circumstance wich is Moste wretched at preasent and what adds more to my Missery is my wife and three small Childern I left Behinde me in Baltemore fellspoint. There is two more with me In my preasent Condittion wich enterd on Board the Cruiser with me one the mate of a Brig belongin to Boston the Other has Been two years six months prisoner In england and was exchangd—the first Carteel. We Ser lays our Cause at your Honour Discreetion and Hope you will Consider our preasent Condittion and Release us from this wretched place wich is the prayers of your most Obednt Huble Servant

WILLIAM SCOT

p.s. we expects Orders every Day to Be Marchd with the Other prisoners to some other prison

Addressed: To / the Right Hounerable Dr / Franklin Ambasedor of / the United States of / Ammerica / Paris

Notation: William Scot Oct 1. 79

From Anna Maria Shipley

ALS: American Philosophical Society

St. James's Place Ocb. 1st. 1779

As I have this Moment heard of a conveyance for a letter I cannot omit intruding a few lines on you to say how much & gratefully I felt your goodness in writing to me by Mr Jones.[3] & at the same time to tell you of the welfare of a Family that esteems your friendship amongst their most valuable blessing & wishes & prays with the greatest sincerty for yr peace & happiness. I left all well in Hampshire last week. I am now going with this family into Northamptonshire 'till the meeting of Parliment.[4] Adieu my dear Sir with more esteem & admiration than I can express. Believe me affetly. Yrs.   A M S

Addressed: Doctor Franklin

To Edward Bridgen

LS:[5] National Archives; three copies: Library of Congress

Dear Sir,   Passy, Oct. 2. 1779.

I received your Favour of the 17th. past, and the 2 Samples of Copper are since come to hand. The metal seems to be very good, and the Price reasonable, but I have not yet receiv'd the orders necessary to justify my making the Purchase proposed. There has indeed been an Intention to strike Copper Coin that

3. On May 28 William Jones informed BF that he was leaving Paris shortly and would carry any letters for London: XXIX, 570. He must have delivered BF's of May 25 to her: XXIX, 537–8.

4. They were probably leaving for Lord and Lady Spencer's in Althorp: XXIX, 275n.

5. In the hand of L'Air de Lamotte and marked "Copy" by BF.

may not only be useful as small Change, but serve other Purposes. Instead of repeating continually upon every Halfpenny the dull Story that everybody knows, and what it would have been no Loss to mankind if nobody had ever known, that Geo. III. is King of Great Britain, France & Ireland &c. &c. to put on one Side some important Proverb of Solomon, some pious moral, prudential or œconomical Precept, the frequent Inculcation of which by seeing it every time one receives a Piece of Money, might make an Impression upon the Mind, especially of young Persons, and tend to regulate the Conduct; such as on some, *The Fear of the Lord is the Beginning of Wisdom;* on others, *Honesty is the best Policy;* on others, *He that by the Plow would thrive; himself must either lead or drive.* On others, *keep thy Shop & thy Shop will keep thee.* On others, a *Penny sav'd is a Penny got.* On others, *He that buys what he has no need of, will soon be forced to sell his Necessaries,* on others, *Early to bed & early to rise, will make a man healthy, wealthy & wise,* and so on to a great Variety. The other side it was proposed to fill with good Designs drawn and engraved by the best Artists in France of all the different Species of Barbarity with which the English have carry'd on the War in America, expressing every abominable Circumstance of their Cruelty & Inhumanity, that Figures can express, to make an Impression on the Minds of Posterity as strong and durable as that on the Copper.[6] This Resolution has been a long time forborn, but the late Burning of defenceless Towns in Connecticut, on the flimsey Pretence that the People fired from behind their Houses, when it is known to have been premeditated and ordered from England, will probably give the finishing Provocation, and may occasion a vast Demand for your Metal.

I thank you for your kind Wishes respecting my Health. I

6. As far as we know, Congress had asked that the engravings of English barbarities be made for use in a children's book; see XXIX, 590–3.

BF's interest in mottos was far from casual. He had been a member of a congressional committee to provide forms for continental currency and a book from his library was used to provide the mottos used on the various denominations: Eric P. Newman, "Continental Currency & Fugio Cent: Sources of Emblems & Mottoes," *The Numismatist,* LXXIX (1966), 1587–98. See also XXII, 357–8.

return them most cordially fourfold into your own Bosom.
Adieu, B FRANKLIN

Mr. Bridgen.

Copy

To Edme-Jacques Genet ⟨ls[7] and copy: Library of Congress⟩

Dear Sir, Passy Oct. 2. 1779

I received last Night, the two Pieces of Metal sent me by
our good Friend Mr Bridgen, and handed to me by your Care.
Please to accept my Thanks. If you can easily forward to him
the enclosed Answer to his Letter,[8] you will much oblige me.

With great Esteem, I am Dear Sir, Your most obedient &
most humble servant. B FRANKLIN

M. Genet.

To Luke Ryan ⟨Copy: Library of Congress⟩

Sir, Passy, Oct. 2. 1779.

Being much pleased with your Auctivity and Bravery, in
distressing the Enemy's Trade, and beating their Vessels of
superior force by which you have done honour to the American flag I beg you to accept my thankful Acknowledgments to
gether with the present of a Night Glass, as a Small Mark of
the Esteem with which I have the honour to be. Sir Your &c.

Capt. Luke Ryan.

7. In the hand of WTF.
8. The preceding document.

To John Torris

Copy: Library of Congress

Sir   Passy, Oct. 2. 1779.

Enclosed I Send you the Judgment I have made on the eight
Ransomers, the Proces Verbaux being come to hand since my
last.[9]

I have also received the Proces verbal relating to
taken by the black Prince of Salem   Captain.[1] I suppose
this to be another Vessel. Please to let me know if you have
any Concern in it.

Mr. Torris.

From Sarah Bache

ALS: American Philosophical Society

Dr and Honoured Sir   Philadelphia October 2d: 1779

This Letter will be handed you by Coll Fluery, who is not
only a Hero but a man of merrit, the same which took the
Standard at Stony point, he is a favorite of General Washingtons, and Baron Stuben's the latter of which Gentlemen introduced him to Mr B: and me, one of the papers you sent over
was to enquire him out, he says he has wrote often to his
Freinds, Mr Bache was to have given him a letter to you but is
now out on business that will detain him near the whole day,
he desired I would introduce Coll Fluery to you who is to call
this morning for the Letter— The publisher of the American
Magazine[2] wrote to you some time ago, to desire you would

---

9. BF drafted, in language almost identical to the one of Sept. 18, above,
a certificate condemning the *Reward, Diligence, Friends Adventure, New Bless-*
ing, Matthew & Sally, Resolution, Betty, and *Salton,* giving in each case the
captain of the ship, the ransomer, and the amount of the ransom. Hist. Soc.
of Del. The vessels were actually taken on the *Black Prince's* third cruise
between August 17 and 20; see Marchant's letter of Aug. 23.

1. Possibly a 14-gun brigantine: Allen, *Mass. Privateers,* p. 84. The preceding day's issue of the *Courier de l'Europe,* VI (1779), 215, reported the capture
and ransom of the *Almond* of Liverpool by the *Black Prince,* undoubtedly the
same ship.

2. Actually *The United States Magazine: a Repository of History, Politics and*
Literature, for which see Frank Luther Mott, *A History of American Magazines,*
1741–1850 (New York and London, 1930), pp. 27, 45–6, 49. Founded by

432

send him some news papers, and sent you some of his first numbers, I suppose you have never receiv'd them, I now send six, not that I think you will find much entertainment in them but you may have heard there was such a performance and may like to see what it is, besides its want of entertainment may induce you to send something that may make the poor mans Magazine more usefull and pleasing, tell Temple the Cave of Vanhest[3] is a very romantic decription of Mr and Mrs Blair's House[4] and Family, the young ladies that the traveler decribes and is in love with are Children one seven months younger than our Benjamin and the Venus just turnd of five, Mrs Blair was in town last Week enquired very kindly after you both, and beg'd when I wrote to remember her afectionatly both to you and Temple, as I have mention'd her living in the Country you may think it some other Mrs Blair, tis necessary to tell you tis my old Friend Suky Shippen, who has never return'd to town since they were driven out by the Enemy but has rented a farm on the Raiton—as Mr. Gerard is still detain'd I shall have it in my power to write to you again in a few days— I am my dear Papa your Dutifull and affectionate Daughter   S BACHE

Addressed: His Excellency / Dr: Benjamin Franklin / Minister Plenepotentiary from the / United States of No. America at the / Court of Versailles / Favord / by Colle. Fleury

---

the patriotic writer Hugh Henry Brackenridge (1748–1816: *DAB*) and the printer Francis Bailey, the *U.S. Magazine* published its first issue in January, 1779, and survived only through December. Even though French Foreign Minister Gérard provided the magazine's founders with 1,000 *l.t.* to write pro-French propaganda they could not sustain publication. James McLaughlan, *et al.,* eds., *Princetonians: a Biographical Dictionary* (5 vols., Princeton, 1976–91), II, 140–1.

3. A story that was serialized over the first six issues, which she enclosed: *United States Magazine* I (1779), 14–15, 61–3, 106–110, 149–50, 213–16, 253–5.

4. Now called the Blair-Shippen house, this was the mansion in Germantown in which lived the clergyman Samuel Blair, his wife, Susannah Shippen Blair, and their children: McLaughlan, *Princetonians*, I, 302–6. Roberdeau Buchanan, *Genealogy of the Descendants of Dr. William Shippen, the Elder* ... (Washington, D.C., 1877), p. 8, identifies two daughters: Susan (b.

From Chalut and Arnoux

AL:[5] American Philosophical Society

passy samedi 2 8bre [1779]

Les abbés de Chalut et Arnoux ont l'honneur de faire Leurs Compliments respectueux à Monsieur franklin et de le prier de leur donner des nouvelles de sa santé à laquelle ils prennent le plus grand interest.

Si Monsieur franklin a reçu le Courier de l'europe Les deux abbés Le prient de leur en procurer la lecture ils seront fort exacts à le lui renvoyer.[6]

pour *Monsieur franklin*

From Dumas

ALS: American Philosophical Society

at the Helder near the road of Texel

Dear & honoured Sir   Oct. 2. 1779

Here I am since several days, like Robinson Crusoe, confined in an obscure Corner of this Country, without any body to converse with, but bare Downs, Rabbits, stubborn men, ugly & peevish women, looking out every moment & praying for northerly winds, which only can bring me your friend; at present they are still contrary, blowing from the south parts.— My Instruction ordered me to wait at Amsterdam. But then our friend could have been here 2 or 3 days before I could have reached him; & now the very moment he comes, I will be able, with a boat that is ready for the purpose, to go and deliver him your Letter[7] &c. as wel as to inform you of his arrival & circumstances, without loosing time. I think therefore I may confide, that this measure of mine will have your approbation, & that of your friends; considering more-

---

March 2, 1771) and Frances Van Hook (b. March 21, 1777). The ages he gives do not correspond to Sally's description.

5. In Arnoux's hand.

6. They returned the newspaper with an undated note of thanks. APS.

7. To Jones, above, Sept. 7; BF sent a covering letter to Dumas the same day, also above.

over, that it costs no more than if I was staying at Amsterdam. However, if the wind should become favorable in a few days, & notwithstanding it none of our friends appear 7 or 8 days after it, then I would think that they had taken another course; & in that case I would leave this station & return to Amst. &c. after having left here good orders to be exactly informed of what should generally happen afterwards.

The following is an Intelligence given me a few days ago. I transcribe it in the proper terms it was delivered to me

"La livrance des fusils, bayonnetes, bandoulieres &c. faite par Mrs. Fiz—& Gd.[8] il y a environ 2 ans, leur a coûté flor. 7. 5s. & ils les ont vendus aux Américains flor. 13. 10s., piece. Ils y ont gagné très-gros; car la Livrance a été considérable. On offre de me produire le compte du fabriquant, qui, dit-on, est de Liege."

One of the circular Letters of Mr. Bache sent me by Mr. Wm. Franklin I have given to *Mrs. Jean De Neufville & Son, at Amsterdam.*

I am with great respect, for ever, Dear & honoured Sir, Your most obedient & humble Servant   DUMAS

P.S. This was written yesterday 1st in the evening. This morning, being the 2d. I have the pleasure to find the wind turned Nord-West, which is the most favorable we can wish. Now if nothing material happens, till this evening, this Letter will go so as it is hitherto. To morrow, if things require it, I can write another; for the post goes but Monday from Amst. to France.

His Exc. B. Franklin &c.

Addressed: His Excellency/ B. Franklin, Esqr. Minister/ Plenipotentiary of the United/ States,/ *Passy./*.

Notation: Dumas. Octr. 2. 1779

8. Fizeaux, Grand & Cie. Dumas had been casting suspicion on Georges Grand for months: XXIX, 192–3. Grand had been involved with the purchase of arms in the Netherlands by the merchant John Philip Merckle: XXV, 52–3. Henri Fizeaux was his business partner; their firm, then called Horneca, Fizeaux & Cie., had been involved in 1777 in building the frigate *Indien* for the commissioners but not, so far as we know, in supplying arms: *Deane Papers,* III, 31.

From John Holker

ALS: American Philosophical Society

Dear Sir   Montigny[9] 2 of Octobr 1779

Mr. Garvey an Intemet friend of mine[1] sends me the Inclosed, beging I woud write you and Solesit your Goodness for one Mrs Butler who has been tooke by the *Black Prince* and lost som Bonds and affects, the Vallou of which she asteems at 50, pounds, and offers that same to have them back.[2]

Youl oblige me very much my Good friend If youl Intrest your Self in this affeare, as M. Garvey is a perticular friend of mine, and in caise it does not depend upon you, to send me back the leter, and let me know to whom I may apploy. My wife begs I wood Present you her Respects, as I doe, & wishing you every one happeness you can wish or desire being. My Dr. Sir your Most Obed & very humble Sevt   J HOLKER

P.S. Allthoug I am very angree with your Grand Son, I beg mine to him, and tell him Il pardon him on conditions when he passeis at Reuen he will call upon me

To his Excellency Dr. franklant

Notation: J Holker Oct 2. 79

---

9. Where Holker, the father of French Consul in America Jean Holker, and his second wife, the widow of a Rouen judge and consul, spent part of each year: André Rémond, *John Holker, manufacturier et grand fonctionnaire en France au XVIIIme siècle, 1719–1786* (Paris, 1946), p. 125n.

1. Probably a fellow Rouen businessman. When WTF was arranging his and BF's return to America in 1785 he corresponded with the Rouen firm of R. & A. Garvey about the transport of 129 unspecified articles. Their representative, a Plowden Garvey, in writing WTF on July 2, 1785 (APS), described Holker as "Our Good Friend."

2. Mrs. Butler had been bound from Bristol to Dublin along with sixteen other passengers when their ship was captured by Marchant's privateer: Clark, *Ben Franklin's Privateers,* p. 50.

From James Turing and Son

ALS: American Philosophical Society

Sir   Middelburg[3] 2d. Octobr 1779

Your Excellency will we trust pardon Our boldness in addressing you on the present Occasion, And we therefore without further apology for the intrusion, beg leave to acquant you that Our Vessel De Brunetta Cap'n Thomas Griffiey with a cargo of Wine & Fruit from Oporto was Seized upon, on the nineteenth of August in Lat: 49"11 Long: 7"3 from Teneriffe by the General Mifflin Privateer of Boston Capt Badcock, who after taking Out the Captain & Crew, as well as Some boat loads of the Cargo, Saying they were in want of those Articles, Sent the Brunetta with the remainder & a Ship's Crew of the Privateer Men, to Boston; And meeting afterwards with a Portuguese Vessel, they put the Captain and two Passengers on board her and detained the Papers & Documents belonging to the Vessel; Of all which, with the further occurrences of their Voyage, the Captain on his Arrival here took a Protest, of which we now beg leave to hand your Excellency the Authentic Copy, as well as a Duplicate of the Bill of Sale[4] which together with the other Papers, the Captain was told, were found to be in rule, notwithstanding which, the Vessel & Cargo was made a Prize of.— We purchased this Vessel from Some Friends in Bordeaux Septembr. 1778. for the purpose of Conveying Beef from Ireland to this place, from whence it was Sent to Bordeaux, as we did above 6000 barrels last Season, doubtless destin'd for the American Markett or the French West India Islands: We had a Similar project formed, on a Still larger Scale this year, & had in the mean while Employ'd Our Vessels in other lines & among the rest, the Brunetta, a couple of Voyages to Oporto; The Captain of which is a Dutchman born, & has Papers in the utmost rule, So that we cannot Conceive, what motive could have induced Capt. Badcock to make a Prize of her.

We in consequence of this Illegal Capture, now beg leave to

---

3. On the island of Walcheren in the Netherlands.
4. The enclosures, in Dutch, are at the APS.

lay Our Serious Complaints before your Excellency, requesting your Excellency's Interest & protection, to procure from Captain Badcock a Satisfaction adequate to the injury he has done us, and to the infringement of Neutral property by a quick and prompt restitution; And we need but Advert to the public Opinion to Assure Ourselves, that we Shall receive from your Excellency's Patronage, the justice we now demand.

We make bold at Same time, to Offer your Excelly. Our best Services in this Country, & have the honor to Remain, with profound respect Sir Your Excellency's most Obedient humble Servants   JAMES TURING & SON

P.S. We beg leave also to inclose the bill of Lading.

Notation: Samuel Turing & Son. Midelburg. 2. Oct. 1780.

From Vergennes

Copy: Library of Congress

à Versailles le 2. 8bre. 1779.
M. Le Comte de Vergennes prie, Monsieur Franklin de vouloir bien se charger de faire passer à M. Le Chevalier de La Luzerne le paquet ci joint par la premiere Occasion.

From Francis Coffyn

ALS: American Philosophical Society

Hond. Sir   Dunkerque Octor. 3d 1779.

I received the honour of your Excellency's letter of 28. ultmo. as the Equipment of Capn. Conningham's vessell required the greatest circomspection at that time, the only person employed in Shipping the French Sailors, who coul'd have confirm'd their claims, was obliged to abscond himself on account of the perquisitions made after him, and he has never been hear'd off since; but I dare say that Mr. Hodge who had the manegement of said vessell, will do these people justice.[5]

5. William Hodge, her part-owner, had outfitted Conyngham's privateer, the *Revenge:* Neeser, *Conyngham,* pp. xxx-xxxviii. His latest extant letter, written more than a year previously (XXVII, 70–2), had discussed postpon-

438

I was informed at the time that they was promised the wages and shares of prizes stated by their declaration, but as their engagement was not made in my presence, I can not certiffy it myself.

What your Excellency is pleased to Express respecting the just priviledges of this port, is very pleasing, and makes me hope that your Excellency conscious of the advantages the American Commerce may reap from them, will help to maintain the Same.

I have communicated to the Commissary of the Marine the copy of the 15th. article of the regulation of the 27. Sepber 1778, respecting the English prisonners brought in by the American Ships, to which he promised to conform. The Said Gentleman tol'd me that a person of this place has made an application to him to obtain the enlargement on parole of a Captain and officers of a vessell taken by the black prince, on giving the same Security of one hundred guineas, for a Captain, and Seventy five guineas for an officer, to be forfeited in case they should break their parole, as is practised with the prisoners taken by the French ships of war; I promised him that I should write to your Excellency about this matter to request your excellency's oppinion, and in case this favour should be granted wether the Commissary or I must receive the Security.

Mr. Torris Seems to be well pleased with the manner your Excellency has Settled the business of the prizes & ransomers of his privateer Black prince;[6] he has received advise last night that two of the prizes call'd the San Joseph a Spanish vessell which had been captured by a Bristol privateer, and the brig Hopewell from Norway, have been retaken and carry'd to England.

Inclosed your Excellency will find an acknowledgement sign'd by five prisoners Capt. Marchant set at liberty on condition that an equal number of Americans shall be exchanged

---

ing his return to America, but he subsequently did return; *JCC,* xv, 1199, mentions an October, 1779, letter from him to Congress about the *Revenge,* which must have been written from Philadelphia or nearby.

6. See BF's Sept. 28 letter to Torris.

for them,[7] Capn Merchant tol'd me that the receipts of the other prisonners he Sett at liberty have been Sent to your Excellency from Brest & Morlaix. Annex'd is a list of the 10. which were landed here, & committed to the care of the Commissary,[8] the other have enter'd with him at Sea. I also inclose a copy of the report Capn. Marchant made at the Admiralty, on perusal your Excellency will find that considering the Smallness of this privateer, she has caused a great deal of arm to the Ennemy's trade, which makes me hope that her next cruize in company with the Black Princess for which your Excellency is pleased to promise a Commission, will still be more Successfull. Your Excellencys compliance to my recommendation[9] in this occasion, requires my gratefull acknowledgement, I shall endeavour to merit this additional favour, by my Zeal & Sanguine wish to be usefull to the States Your Excellency so worthily represents in this kingdom.

I beg leave to refer your Excellency to the letter I wrote yesterday to M. De Chaumont respecting the Intelligence received of the Successes of the American Squadron in the German Ocean, the capture of the Two Frigats the Seraphis of 44 guns, and the Countess of Scarborough of 20, with the destruction of the greatest part of the Fleet from the Baltick under their convoy, gains Credit, and I hope will be confirm'd by next post; as the wind has for some time blown from the South west quarter, I hope Commodore Paul Jones will have reached the Coast of Norway to repair the dammages his ships & prizes receiv'd in the engagement before the English Squadron of the Edgar of 74 guns, the Dromadary & Diamont frigats with the Speedy packett, sail'd from the Downs

7. The acknowledgement, now missing, probably was from five members of the crew of the sloop *Limont,* captured by the *Black Prince* on Sept. 10: Clark, *Ben Franklin's Privateers,* p. 85.

8. The list, dated Oct. 5, was entitled "Prisoners names of the black Prince privateer landed at Dunkerque, and committed to the care of Mr. Devillers Commissary of the marine at said place." It provided the names, ranks, and ages of eight prisoners from the *Hopewell* and another two from the brig *Peggy.* APS. Another list, in French, containing the same names but without their ages, is also at the APS.

9. In his Aug. 30 letter.

in quest of him.[1] Any further intelligence I may receive about these ships, shall be immediately communicated to your Excellency; interim I have made the needfull dispositions to give them every necessary assistance, if they should make their appearance on this Coast.

I have the honour to remain with profound respect Your Excellencys Most obedient & most devoted humble Servant

FRANS. COFFYN

His Excellency D. B. Franklin at Passi.

Notation: Frans Coffin Dunkeque 5. 8bre. 1779.

From Dumas

ALS: American Philosophical Society

Oct. 3d. 1779.

Copy from New-Lloyd's List, No. 1097,[2] receiv'd this morning from Amsterdam, Tuesday 28 Sept. 1779

Hull, Sept. 25. The Seraphis frigate, & Countess of Scarborough armed Ship, having the Fleet from the Baltic under Convoy, were attacked, between Flamborough-head & Scarborough by Paul Jones's Squadron,[3] when after a severe engagement, in which the Seraphis lost her Main-Mast, Bowsprit, Mizen Topmast, & otherwise much scattered,[4] as was also the Countess of Scarborough, they were both taken; the Merchant-Ships separated during the action. Part took Shelter

1. After its recent battle with H.M.S. *Serapis* and H.M.S. *Countess of Scarborough* Jones's squadron was unsuccessfully pursued by a number of British warships: Morison, *Jones,* p. 245.

2. A weekly compendium of shipping news provided by the marine underwriting firm: Godfrey Hodgson, *Lloyds of London* (New York, 1984), pp. 52–3, 65.

3. Most accounts follow Jones and attribute the action to Sept. 23rd; Schaeper, *Battle off Flamborough Head,* pp. 7–16, compares the evidence for that date and the 24th. For a defense of the traditionally assigned date see Ira Dyer's review of Schaeper's book in the North American Society for Oceanic History *Newsletter,* XVI (1991–92), 5–6. News of the battle was sent to London by the Admiralty at Hull, which dispatched a messenger at 3:00 A.M. on the 25th: *ibid.,* p. 15.

4. Dumas here miscopied the word "shattered"; see the extract from this letter in the Sept. 28 issue of the *Public Advertiser.*

on the Coast near Scarborough, & two are arrived at Hull.—
A valuable Ship, bound to Quebec, was taken on the North
of Scotland; also a Letter of Marque of Leverpool; & several other prizes were taken & sunk off Whitby by Jones's
Squadron.[5]

Dear & honoured Sir
from the Helder, Road of Texel 3d. Oct. 1779. at 6 a
Clock in the Evening.

I congratulate you with all my heart with the above Intelligence; & I think I can congratulate you also with the very
apparent arrival to morrow morning of the victorious squadron on this Road; for there are at least 5, if not 7 men of war,
at anchor, at the very entrance of this road,[6] the greatest of
which has his colours flying, of which, at Such a distance, we
can only distinguish here, that they are not the colours of this
country, & I think I may guess that they are American colours; for my telescope, if not my imagination gives me red &
white lines, & a blue Square in the head corner. The Nordern
wind, that has favoured them hitherto, is not so good for them
to come quite within the capes. This night I shall hear more
of them; & if the post is not then gone, you shall have it. To
morrow very early in the morning, if the wind should still
hinder them to come near us, I shall hire a sailing sloop, & go
to them, provided I am sure that they are our friends.

I have your last favour of the 27th. past, with the pensylvania papers, & another written Extract, for which you have
my hearthy thanks. They are a very welcome entertainment
for me in those Desarts.

I am in a hurry, with great respect, for ever Dear & honoured Sir yr. most obedient & humble servant   DUMAS

I guess the two prizes to be with them; for I see one them
without his Main mast.

His Exc. B. Franklin

5. The ship bound for Quebec was the letter of marque *Union,* the Liverpool letter of marque, the *Betsy.* For the ships taken off Whitby see Jones's
letter immediately below.

6. Jones's squadron now consisted of the *Serapis, Alliance, Countess of Scarborough, Pallas,* and *Vengeance:* Morison, *Jones,* p. 251.

Addressed: His Excellency/ B. Franklin, Esqr. Min. Plenipo:/ of the united States &c./ *Passy.*

Notation: Dumas. Oct. 3d. 1779

From John Paul Jones

LS:[7] National Archives; copies:[8] Algemeen Rijksarchief, Library of Congress, National Archives

This letter is of considerable historiographical interest because it forms the basis for most subsequent accounts of Jones's cruise and his battle with H.M.S. *Serapis.*[9] Central to these accounts is the premise here expounded by Jones that the *Bonhomme Richard* had to overcome the fire not only of his British opponent, but also that of the American frigate *Alliance.* Captain Pierre Landais of the *Alliance* argued in contrast that the *Alliance* came to the aid of the *Bonhomme Richard* and played a major role in the capture of the *Serapis.*[1] Landais' account of the battle is generally corroborated by the captain of the third ship participating in the battle, Denis-Nicolas Cottineau de Kerloguen, of the frigate *Pallas.*[2] To give Landais a chance to rebut Jones's charges Franklin held a hearing at Passy on November 15 and 24, but adjourned it because no other participant in the battle could be present to cross-examine him.

7. Marked "Copy." Thomas Schaeper discusses the composition of the letter in *Battle off Flamborough Head,* pp. 57–8.

8. The copy at the Library of Congress (Jones Papers) and the one at the Algemeen Rijksarchief are in the same hand and contain an inside address and signature by Jones. The Library of Congress copy has corrections and interlineations in Jones's hand. The one at the Algemeen Rijksarchief has a notation by Dumas. An extract did appear in the Nov. 5 issue of the *Courier de l'Europe,* VI (1779), 292–4.

9. *E.g.,* Morison, *Jones,* pp. 200–42. According to Landais, WTF, with BF's permission, had the present letter printed in 1779: Landais, *Memorial,* p. 68.

1. Landais, *Memorial,* pp. 35–84, gives his account of the battle and responds to the charges against him. It was not until Dec. 15 that BF sent extracts from the present letter to Landais; Landais' response is given in his *Memorial,* pp. 72–9. For a summary and analysis of Landais' defense see Schaeper, *Battle off Flamborough Head,* pp. 35–54.

2. Schaeper has rediscovered and published a letter and memoir by Cottineau: *Battle off Flamborough Head,* pp. 81–5. Extracts of both were given to Landais by Chaumont: Landais, *Memorial,* pp. 83–4.

On board the Ship of War
Serapis at Anchor without the Texel
Honoured and dear Sir   Octr. 3d. 1779.

When I had the honour of writing to you on the 11th.
August[3] Previous to my departure from the Road of Groa I
had before me the most flattering prospect of rendering essential service to the common Cause of France & America. I had
a full confidence in the Voluntary inclination & ability of
every Captain under my Command to assist and support me
in my duty with Cheerful Unremitting Emulation—and I was
persuaded that every one of them would persue Glory in preference to Interest. Whether I was or was not deceived will
best appear by a simple relation of circumstances.— The little
Squadron under my command consisting of the Bon home
Richard of 40 Guns the Alliance of 36 Guns the Pallas of 32
Guns the Serf of 18 Guns & the Vengeance of 12 Guns Join'd
by two Privateers the Monsieur & the Grandvelle Sailed from
the Isle of Groa at Day Break on the 14th. of August the same
day we spoke with a large Convoy bound from the Southward
to Brest on the 18th. we took a large Ship belonging to Holland laden chiefly with Brandy and Wine that had been destined from Barcelona for Dunkirk and taken eight days before
by an English Privateer— The Captain of the Privateer Monsieur took out of this Prize such Articles as he pleased in the
Night and the next day being astern of the Squadron & to
windward he actually wrote Orders in his proper Name and
sent away the Prize under one of his own Officers— This
however I superceeded by sending her for L'Orient under my
Orders in the character of Commander in Chief— The evening of the Day following the Monsieur Seperated from the
Squadron—[4] On the 20th. we saw and Chased a large Ship
but could not come up with her She being to Windward— On
the 21st we saw and Chased another Ship that was also to
Windward and thereby Eluded our pursuit the Same afternoon we took a Brigantine Called the May Flower laden with

3. In fact the 13th, above.
4. Landais blamed Jones for driving away the *Monsieur* by unfairly attempting to take goods from the prize: Landais, *Memorial,* p. 26.

Butter & Salt Provision bound from Limerick in Ireland for London; this Vessel I Immediately expedited for L'Orient.[5] On the 23 we saw Cape Clear and the S. West Part of Ireland that Afternoon it being Calm I sent some Armed Boats to take a Brigantine that appeared in the N.W. Quarter—soon after in the evening it became necessary to have a Boat a Head of the Ship to Tow as the Helm could not prevent her from laying across the Tide of Flood which would have driven us into a deep and dangerous Bay Situated between the Rocks on the south called the Skillicks [Skelligs] and on the North called the Blaskets— The Ships Boats being absent I sent my own Barge a head to tow the Ship— The Boats took the Brigantine She being called the Fortune and Bound with a Cargo of Oil Blubber & Staves from Newfoundland for Bristol— This Vessel I Ordered to proceed immediately for Nants or St. Malo.— Soon after Sunset the Villains who Towed the Ship cut the tow Rope and Decamped with my Barge.— Sundry Shot were fir'd to bring them too without effect— In the mean time the Master of the Bon homme Richard without Orders Manned one of the Ships Boats & with 4 Soldiers pursued the Barge in Order to stop the deserters— The Evening was then Clear & Serene—but the Zeal of that Officer Mr. Cutting Lunt induc'd him to pursue too far, and a Fog which came on soon afterwards Prevented the Boat from Rejoyning the Ship altho I caused Signal Guns to be frequently fired— the Fog & Calm continued the next day till towards the Evening— In the Afternoon Captain Landais came on board the Bonhomme Richard and behaved towards me with great disrespect Affirming in the most indelicate language and manner that I had lost my Boats and People thro' imprudence in sending Boats to take a Prize—[6] He persisted in his reproaches tho' he was assured by Messieurs De Wybert & Chamillard[7] that the

5. Landais claimed Jones prematurely abandoned pursuit of the larger vessel to capture the *Mayflower: ibid.,* pp. 26–7.

6. The disagreement, according to Landais, ended in his shoving Jones and then demanding satisfaction for Jones's behavior (*i.e.,* a duel), when the two captains returned to port: *ibid.,* pp. 28–9.

7. Chamillard and Wuybert were lieutenant colonels of the *Bonhomme Richard's* French marines. On Oct. 10 Wuybert wrote Jones asking leave to

Barge was actually Towing the Ship at the time of the Elopement and had not been sent in pursuit of the Prize— He was affronted because I would not the Day before Suffer him to Chase without my Orders and to approach the dangerous Shore I have already mentioned, where he was an entire Stranger and where there was not a Sufficient wind to govern a Ship— He told me that he was the only American in the Squadron and was determined to follow his own Opinion in Chasing when and where he thought proper and in every other matter that concerned the Service—[8] and that if I continued in that Situation three days longer the Squadron would be Taken &c, By the advice of Captain Cottineau and with the free consent and Approbation of M. De Verage[9] I sent the Serf in to Reconnoitre the Coast and endeavour to take up the Boats and People the next day while the Squadron stood off and on in the S.W. Quarter in the best Possible Situation to intercept the Enemies Merchant Ships whether outward or Homeward Bound.— The Cerf had on board a Pilot well acquainted with the Coast and was Ordered to Join me again before Night,— I approached the Shore in the Afternoon but the Serf did not appear— This induced me to stand off again in the Night in order to return and be rejoyned by the Serf the Next Day—but to my great concern and disappointment tho' I ranged the Coast along and hoisted our private Signal neither the Boats nor the Serf Joined me—[1] The evening of that

---

return to America (University of Pa. Library). Jones forwarded the letter to BF with a brief covering note on the final page to the effect that having suffered from being imprisoned in England, Wuybert needed a little time in the country to reestablish his health. The letter is reproduced in Bradford, *Jones Papers*, reel 4, no. 765.

8. Landais' defiance of Jones was based on his belief that BF's July 28 orders had superseded the earlier orders which had placed him under Jones's command.

9. *Enseigne de Vaisseau* Joseph Varage commanded the cutter *Cerf:* XXIX, 494.

1. The *Cerf* returned to France, Varage blaming the weather for his ship's having become separated. The crewmen pursuing the fugitives were captured and the countryside alerted: Morison, *Jones*, pp. 209–10; Varage to BF, below, Oct. 29; Chamillard to Jones, Oct. 9, Bradford, *Jones Papers*, reel 4, no. 764.

day the 26th. brought with it Stormy Weather with an appearance of a Severe Gale from the South West Yet I must declare I did not follow my own Judgment but was led by the assertion which had fallen from Captain Landais when I in the evening made a Signal for to steer to the Northward and leave that Station, which I wished to have Occupied at least a Week longer— The Gale increased in the Night with the thick Weather— To prevent seperation I carried a Toplight and fired a Gun every Quarter of an hour; I carried also a Very moderate Sail and the Course had been clearly Pointed out by a Signal before Night. Yet with all this precaution I found myself accompanied only by the Brigantine Vengeance in the Morning—the Grand Velle having remained astern with a Prize as I have since understood the Tiller of the Pallas broke after MidNight in which disenabled her from keeping up— but no apology has yet been made in behalf of the Alliance.— On the 31st we saw the Flannin Islands Situated near the Lewises on the N.W. Coast of Scotland and the next morning off Cape Wrath we gave Chase to a Ship to Windward at the same time two Ships appearing in the N.W. Quarter which proved to be the Alliance and a Prize Ship which She had taken bound as I Understood from Liverpool for Jamaica.— The Ship which I chased brought too at Noon— She proved to be the Union Letter of Mark bound from London for Quebec with a Cargo of Naval Stores on Account of Government, Adapted for the Service of the British Armed Vessels on the Lakes.[2] The Public dispatches were lost as the Alliance very imprudently hoisted American Colours tho' English Colours were then Flying on board the Bon homme Richard.— Captain Landais sent a small Boat to ask whither I would Man the Ship or he should—as in the latter Case he would suffer no Boat nor Person from the Bon homme Richard to go near the Prize.— Ridiculous as this appeared to me I yielded to it for the sake of Peace and received the Prisoners on board the Bon homme Richard while the Prize was manned from the Alliance.—[3] In the Afternoon another Sail appeared and I imme-

2. The *Union* was captured by the *Alliance:* Landais, *Memorial,* p. 30.

3. Landais claimed that the prisoners from the *Union* were accepted by the *Pallas:* Landais, *Memorial,* p. 31.

diately made the Signal for the Alliance to Chase—but instead of Obeying He wore and laid the Ships Head the other way; The next morning I made a Signal to speak with the Alliance to which no attention was shewn— I then made Sail with the Ships in Company for the second Rendezvous which was not far distant and where I fully expected to be Join'd by the Pallas and the Serf— The 2d. of Sepr. we saw a Sail at Day break and gave Chase— That Ship proved to be the Pallas and had met with no Success while seperated from the Bon homme Richard— On the 3d. the Vengeance brought too a small Irish Brigantine bound homewards from Norway.

The same evening I sent the Vengeance in the N.E. Quarter to bring up the two Prize Ships that appeared to me to bee too near the Islands of Schetland— while with the Alliance & Pallas I endeavoured to Weather Fair Isle and to get into my second Rendezvous where I directed the Vengeance to Join me with the three Prizes. The Next Morning having weathered Fair Isle and not seeing the Vengeance nor the Prizes—I spoke the Alliance and ordered her to Steer to the Northward and bring them up to the Rendezvous. On the morning the 5th the Alliance appeared again and had brought too 2 very Small Coasting Sloops in Ballast but without having Attended properly to My Orders of Yesterday.— The Vengeance Joined me soon after And informed me that in consequence of Captain Landais Orders to the Commanders of the two Prize Ships they had refused to follow him to the Rendezvous. I am to this moment Ignorant what Orders these Men received from Capt. Landais—[4] nor Know I by Virture of what Authority he ventured to give his Orders to Prizes in my Presence and without either my Knowledge or Approbation. Captain Ricot further informed me that he had Burnt the Prize Brigantine because that Vessel Proved leaky and I was sorry to understand afterwards that the Vessel was Irish Property the Cargo was the Property of the Subjects of Norway—

In the evening I sent for all the Captains to come on board the Bon homme Richard to consult on future Plans of Opper-

4. They were ordered to steer for Bergen should they become separated from the *Alliance: ibid.*, pp. 30–1.

ation. Captains Cottineau & Ricot Obeyed me, but Captain Landais Obstinately refused and after sending me Various uncivil Messages wrote me a very extraordinary letter in Answer to a written Order which I had sent him on finding that he had trifled with my Verbal Orders—[5]

The next day a Pilot Boat came on board from Shetland by which Means I received such advices as induced me to change a Plan which I otherwise meant to have Pursued, And as the Serf did not appear at my second Rendezvous I determined to steer towards the 3d. in hopes of meeting her there— In the Afternoon a Gale of Wind came on which continued four Days without intermission. In the 2d. Night of that Gale the Alliance with her 2 little Prizes Again seperated from the Bon homme Richard—

I had now with me only the Pallas and Vengeance Yet I did not abandon the hopes of performing some Essential service— The Winds continued contrary so that we did not see the Land 'till the Evening of the 13th when the Hills of Chevot [Cheviot] in the S.E. of Scotland appeared— The Next day We Chased Sundry Vessels and took a Ship & a Brigantine both from the Firth of Edinborough laden with Coal Knowing that there lay at Anchor in leith Roads an Armed Ship of 20 Guns with two or three fine Cutters— I formed an Expedition against Leith which I purposed to lay under a large Contribution or otherwise to reduce it to Ashes— Had I been alone the Wind being favourable I would have proceeded directly up the Firth and must have Succeeded as they lay there in a State of perfect indolence and security which would have Prov'd their Ruin. Unfortunately for me the Pallas and Vengeance were both at a considerable Distance in the Offing they having Chased to the Southward— This Obliged me to Steer out of the Firth again to meet them— The Captains of the Pallas and Vengeance being come on board the Bon homme Richard I communicated to them my Project—to which many difficulties and Objections were made by them— at last however they appeared to think better of the design after I had assured

5. The notes exchanged between Jones and Landais are quoted in Landais, *Memorial*, pp. 31–3.

them that I hoped to raise a Contribution of 200,000 Pounds Sterling on Leith, and that there was no Battery of Cannon there to oppose our landing.—[6] So much time however was unavoidably spent in Pointed Remarks and Sage Deliberation that Night that the Wind became contrary in the Morning— We continued Working to windward up the Firth without being able to reach the Road of Leith till on the Morning of the 17th. when being almost within Cannon Shot of the Town having every thing in readiness for a Descent; a very severe Gale of Wind came on and being directly contrary Obliged us to bear away after having in Vain endeavoured for some time to withstand Its Violence the Gale was so severe that one of the Prizes that had been taken the 14th. sunk to the Bottom the Crew being with difficulty saved— As the alarm had by this time reached Leith by means of a Cutter that had watched our motions that Morning,— & as the Wind continued contrary (tho' more moderate in the evening) I thought it impossible to pursue the Enterprize with a good prospect of success especially as Edinborough where there is always a Number of Troops is only a Mile distant from Leith; therefore I gave up the Project— on the 19th. having taken a Sloop and a Brigantine in Ballast with a Sloop laden with Building Timber— I Proposed another Project[7] to Mr. Cottineau which would have been highly Honorable tho' not Profitable many difficulties were made and our Situation was represented as being the most Perulous the Enemy he said would send against us a superiour Force and that if I Obstinately continued on the Coast of England two days longer we should all be Taken.

The Vengeance having Chased Along Shore to the Southward Capt. Cottineau said he would follow her with the Prizes as I was unable to make much Sail having that day been Obliged to strike the Main Topmast to repair its damages and as I afterwards Understood he told M. De Chamillard that

6. Chamillard, who was to command the 130-man landing force, was ordered to demand at least £50,000, half to be paid within the hour, the remainder to be secured by the taking of hostages. Should the demand be refused, Leith was to be burned: Bradford, *Jones Papers*, reel 4, nos. 740–3.

7. To raid Newcastle-on-Tyne, which provided coal to London and elsewhere: Morison, *Jones*, pp. 221–2.

unless I Joined them the next Day both the Pallas & the Vengeance would leave that Coast.— I had thoughts of attempting the Enterprize alone after the Pallas had made Sail to Join the Vengeance— I am persuaded even now that I should have succeeded And to the honour of my Young Officers I found them as ardently disposed to the Business as I could desire. Nothing prevented me from pursuing my design but the reproach that would have been cast upon my Character as a Man of prudence had the Enterprize miscarried— It would have been said was he not forewarned by Captain Cottineau & Others—

I made Sail along Shore to the Southward and next Morning took a Coasting Sloop in Ballast which with another that I had taken the Night before I Ordered to be sunk.— In the Evening I again met with the Pallas and the Vengeance off Whitby— Captain Cottineau told me he had sunk the Brigantine and ransomed the Sloop Laden with Building Timber that had been Taken the Day before— I had told Captain Cottineau the day before that I had no Authority to Ransom Prizes— On the 21st. We saw and Chased Two Sail off Flambrough Head— The Pallas Chased in the N E Quarter while the Bon home Richard followed by the Vengeance Chased in the S.W.— The one I Chased a Brigantine Collier in Ballast belonging to Scarborough was soon Taken and sunk immediately Afterwards— As a Fleet then appeared to the Southward this was so late in the Day that I could not come up with the Fleet before night at length however I got so near one of them as to force her to run ashore between Flamborough Head and the Spurn— soon after I Took another a Brigantine from Holland belonging to Sunderland and at Day light the Next Morning seeing a Fleet Steering towards me from the Spurn I immagined them to be a Convoy bound from London for Leith which had been for some time expected—one of them had a Pendant Hoisted and appeared to be a Ship of Force— They had not however Courage to come on but kept back all except the one which seemed to be Armed and that one Also kept to Windward very near the Land and on the Edge of Dangerous Shoals where I could not with safety Approach— This induced me to make a Signal for a Pilot and soon afterwards

451

two Pilot Boats came off— They informed me that the Ship that wore a Pendant was an Armed Merchantman And that a Kings Frigate lay there in sight at Anchor within the Humber waiting to take under Convoy a number of Merchant Ships bound to the Northward. The Pilots imagined the Bon homme Richard to be an English Ship of War and consequently communicated to me the Private Signal which they had been required to make— I endeavoured by this means to decoy the Ships out of the Port, but the wind then changing and with the Tide becoming Unfavourable for them; the deception had not the desired Effect; and they wisely put back.— The entrance of the Humber is exceedingly difficult and Dangerous— And as the Pallas was not in sight I thought it imprudent to remain off the Entrance—therefore Steered out again to Join the Pallas off Flamborough Head. In the Night We saw and Chased two Ships untill 3 OClock in the Morning When being at a very small distance from them I made the Private Signal of Reconnoisance which I had given to each Captain before I Sailed from Groa— One half of the Answer only was returned— In this Position both sides lay too till day light When the Ships proved to be the Alliance & the Pallas— On the Morning of that day the 23d. the Brig from Holland not being in sight We Chased a Brigantine that appeared Laying too to Windward— About Noon We saw and Chased a large Ship that appeared coming round Flamborough head from the Northward and at the same time I Manned and Armed one of the Pilots Boats to send in Pursuit of the Brigantine which now appeared to be the Vessel that I had forced ashore—[8] Soon after this a Fleet of 41 Sail[9] appeared off Flamborough Head bearing NNE. This induced me to Abandon the Single

8. The pilot boat, commanded by Henry Lunt, second lieutenant of the *Bonhomme Richard*, went in pursuit of the brigantine *Crow Isle*; when recalled, it was unable to catch Jones's ships: Peter Reaveley, "The Battle," in Boudriot, *John Paul Jones and the Bonhomme Richard*, p. 69.

9. There were forty-four sail in the convoy, which was bringing naval stores from the Baltic: Morison, *Jones*, p. 226. Captain Cottineau argued later that Jones should have pursued the convoy rather than concentrating on its escorts: Schaeper, *Battle off Flamborough Head*, p. 84. The convoy took refuge under the guns of Scarborough Castle, thereby escaping capture: Reaveley, "Battle," pp. 65, 68–9.

Ship which had then Anchored in Burlington Bay; I also called back the Pilot Boat and hoisted a Signal for a general Chase.

When the Fleet discovered us bearing down all the Merchant Ships Crowded Sail towards the Shore. The Two Ships of War that Protected the Fleet at the same time Steered from the Land and made the disposition for Battle— In approaching the Enemy I crowded every Possible Sail and made the Signal for the line of Battle to which the Alliance shewed no Attention.[1] Earnest as I was for the Action I could not reach the Commodores Ship untill Seven in the Evening being then within Pistol Shot when He hailed the Bon homme Richard. We answered him by Firing a Whole Broadside—[2] The Battle being thus begun was continued with Unremitting Fury— Every method was Practiced on both sides to gain an Advantage and Rake each other— And I must confess that the Enemies Ship being much more Manageable than the Bon homme Richard gained thereby several times an advantagious Situation in spite of my best endeavours to prevent it—[3] As I had to deal with an Enemy of greatly Superiour Force I was under the necessity of closing with him to Prevent the Advantage Which he had over me in Point of Manoeuvre— It was my intention to lay the Bon homme Richard athwart the Enemies Bow but as that Opperation required great dexterity in the Management of both Sails and Helm And some of our Braces being Shot away it did not exactly succeed to my wish.

The Enemies Bowsprit however came over the Bon homme Richards Poop by— the Mizen Mast and I made both Ships fast together in that Situation which by the Action the Wind on the Enemies Sails forced her Stern close to the Bon homme

1. In contrast, Landais subsequently claimed that Jones ignored *his* hail: Landais, *Memorial*, p. 35.

2. Before raising American colors and opening fire, Jones engaged in a futile attempt to deceive Capt. Pearson of the *Serapis* about the *Bonhomme Richard*'s identity: Reaveley, "Battle," p. 73.

3. According to Cottineau the *Serapis* raked the *Bonhomme Richard* three or four times (*i.e.,* she fired on the *Bonhomme Richard* while perpendicular to the American ship's bow or stern, thereby placing herself out of reach of a return broadside): Schaeper, *Battle off Flamborough Head*, p. 84. As the *Pallas* was engaged in combat with H.M.S. *Countess of Scarborough* at the time, Cottineau may have been reporting second-hand information.

Richards Bow so that the Ships lay square alongside of each Other the Yards being all entangled and the Cannon of each Ship touching the Opponents Side when this Position took Place it was Eight OClock Previous to which the Bonhomme Richard had received sundry Eighteen Pound Shot below the Water and leaked very much.

My Battery of 12 Pounders on which I had Placed my Chief dependance being Commanded by Lieut. Dale and Col. Wybert and Manned Principally with American Seamen & French Volunteers; was entirely Silenced and Abandoned—as to the Six old 18 Pounders that formed the Battery of the lower Gun Deck they did no service whatever except firing Eight Shot in all— Two out of them Burst at the first Fire and Killed almost all the Men who were stationed to Manage them.

Before this time too Col. Chamillard who Commanded a Party of 20 Soldiers on the Poop had Abandoned that Station after having lost some of his Men.

I had now only two Pieces of Cannon (9 Pounders) on the Quarter Deck that were not Silenced and not one of the heavier Cannon was fired during the remainder of the Action— The Purser Mr. Mease who Commanded the Guns on the Quarter Deck being dangerously Wounded in the head I was Obliged to fill his Place & with great difficulty Rallied a few Men and shifted to get over one of the lee Quarter Deck Guns so that We afterwards played three Pieces of Nine pounders upon the Enemy The Tops alone seconded the Fire of this little Battery and held out Bravely during the Whole Action especially the Main Top where Lieutenant Stack Commanded. I directed the Fire of one of the three Cannon against the Main Mast with double Headed Shot while the other two were Exceedingly well served with Grape & Canister Shot to Silence the Enemies Musquetry and Clear her Decks which was at last effected the Enemy were as I have since Understood on the Instant of Calling out for Quarters—When the Cowardice or Treachery of three of my Under Officers[4] induced them to

4. They were warrant officers rather than commissioned officers. John Gunnison, the ship's carpenter, and Henry Gardiner or Gardner, the ship's gunner, mistakenly believed that all the officers on the quarterdeck had been killed and that the ship was sinking. Their colleague, Master-at-Arms

call to the Enemy— The English Commodore Asked me if I Demanded Quarters And I having Answered him in the most determined Negative[5] They renewed the Battle with redoubled Fury— They were unable to stand the Deck but the Fire of their Cannon especially the lower Battery which was entirely form'd of 18 Pounders was incessant.— Both Ships were set on Fire in Various Places And the scene was dreadful beyond the reach of Language— To account for the Timidity of my Three under Officers, I mean the Gunner the Carpenter and the Master at Arms—I must observe that the two First were slightly Wounded And as the Ship had received Various Shot under Water And one of the Pumps being shot away the Carpenter expressed his Fears that she would Sink and the other two concluded that she was Sinking which Occasioned the Gunner to run aft on the Poop without my Knowledge to strike the Colours— Fortunately for me a Cannon ball had done that before by carrying away the Ensign Staff— He was therefore reduced to the Necessity of sinking, as he Supposed, or of Calling for Quarters and he prefered the Latter—[6] All this time the Bon homme Richard had sustained the Action alone And the Enemy tho' much Superior in Force would have been very glad to have got Clear as Appears by their own Acknowledgments and by their having let go an Anchor the Instant that I laid them on Board by which means they would have escaped had I not made them well fast to the Bonhomme Richard;[7] at last, at half past Nine O'Clock the Alliance appeared & I now thought the Battle at an End but to my Utter

---

John Burbank, discussed the situation with them but did not accompany them topside: Reaveley, "Battle," pp. 80–2.

5. Reaveley, "Battle," p. 82, indicates that Jones's words were "No; I'll sink, but I'm damned if I'll strike!" The well-known "I have not yet begun to fight" dates from the 1825 recollections of one of the *Bonhomme Richard's* officers. See also Morison, *Jones*, pp. 241–2.

6. Jones does not report that he had rushed at them, shouting "shoot them, kill them" and that he had knocked Gardiner unconscious by throwing his pistols at his head: Reaveley, "Battle," p. 82.

7. Pearson let go the anchor so the tide would break him clear of the *Bonhomme Richard*, thereby avoiding the risk of his being boarded. Once clear, the *Serapis*, still possessing a number of serviceable cannon, could

Astonishment he discharged a Broadside full into the Stern of the Bon homme Richard—[8] We Called to him for Gods sake to forbear Firing into the Bon homme Richard— Yet he passed along the Off Side of the Ship and Continued Firing— There was no Possibility of his Mistaking the Enemy's Ship for the Bon homme Richard there being the most essential difference in their appearance & construction—besides it was then full Moon light, And the Sides of the Bon homme Richard were all Black while the Side of the Prize were Yellow— Yet for the greater security I shewed the Signal of our Reconnoissance by putting out Three Lanthorns, One at the head Another at the Stern and the third in the Middle in a Horrizontal line— Every Tongue cried that He was Firing into the wrong Ship but nothing availed. He passed round firing into the Bon homme Richard's Head, Stern, & Broadside and by one of his Vollies Killed Agreeable to Report several[9] of my best Men and Mortally Wounded an Officer on The Fore Castle only. My Situation was really deplorable the Bon homme Richard received Various Shots under Water from the Alliance the leak gained on the Pumps and the Fire increased Much on board both Ships— Some Officers Persuaded me to Strike of whose Courage and good sense I entertain an High Opinion.— My Treacherous Master at Arms let loose all my Prisoners without my Knowledge and my Prospect became Gloomy Indeed— I would not however give up the Point— The Enemy's Main Mast began to shake, Their Firing decreased Fast Our's rather increased And the British Colours

---

have sunk her opponent and would have hardly needed to flee. See *ibid.*, p. 78.

8. According to Cottineau, the *Alliance* raked the *Serapis* twice, putting thirty-five of her men out of action: Schaeper, *Battle off Flamborough Head,* p. 83. From a variety of sources Schaeper has reconstructed the *Alliance's* movements during the battle. He concludes that the *Alliance* made three attacks on the *Serapis,* inadvertently hitting the *Bonhomme Richard* in the process. The grapeshot she fired was particularly hard to aim precisely and it inflicted casualties aboard Jones's ship. (Many casualties, says Reaveley.) See Schaeper, *Battle off Flamborough Head,* pp. 32, 44, and diagram facing p. 35; Reaveley, "Battle," p. 80.

9. This word replaces "Eleven", which is used in the other copies.

were Struck at half an hour Past Ten O'Clock— This Prize proved to be the British Ship of War the Serapis a New Ship of 44 Guns built on their most approved Construction with two Compleat Batteries one of them of 18 Pounders and Commanded by the Brave Commodore Richard Pearson.— I had yet two Enemies to encounter with far more formidable than the Britons I mean fire and Water. The Serapis was attacked only by the first but the Bon homme Richard was Assailed by both— There was five Feet of Water in the Hold and tho' it was Moderate from the Explosion of so Much Gun Powder Yet three Pumps that remained could with difficulty only Keep the Water from gaining— The Fire broke out in Various Parts of the Ship in spite of all the Water that could be thrown in to quench it and at length broke out as low as the Powder Magazine and within a few Inches of the Powder— In that Dilema I took out the Powder upon Deck ready to be thrown overboard at the last extremity and it was Ten O'Clock the next Day the 24th before the Fire was entirely Extinguished. With respect to the Situation of the Bonhomme Richard The Rudder was cut almost entirely off; the Stern Frame & Transoms Were almost entirely Cut away And the Timbers by the lower Deck especially from the Main Mast towards the Stern being greatly decayed with Age were Mangled beyond my Power of description and A Person must have been an Eye Witness to form a Just Idea of the tremendous Scenes of Carnage Wreck and Ruin which every where appeared— Humanity cannot but recoil from the Prospect of such finished Horror and lament that War should be capable of producing Such fatal Consequences.

After the Carpenters as well as Captain Cottineau and other Men of sense had well examined & Surveyed[1] the Ship which was not Finished before five in Evening I found every Person to be convinced that it was Impossible to Keep the Bon homme Richard Afloat So as to reach a Port if the Wind should increase it being then only a very Moderate Breeze— I had but little time to remove My Wounded[2] which now be-

1. This word, missing in the LS, is supplied from the copies.
2. Cottineau claimed that it was he who removed them: Schaeper, *Battle off Flamborough Head,* p. 82. Jones's concern for the wounded among his

came Unavoidable and which was effected in the Course of the Night and Next Morning— I was determined to Keep the Bon homme Richard Afloat and if possible to bring her into Port For that purpose the first Lieutenant of the Pallas[3] continued on board with a Party of Men to Attend the Pumps with Boats in waiting ready to take them on board in Case the Water Should gain on them too Fast; The Wind Augmented in the Night and the next Day on the 25th. So that it was impossible to prevent the Good Old Ship from Sinking— They did not abandon her 'till after Nine OClock— The Water was then up to the lower Deck and a little after Ten I saw with inexpressible Grief the last Glimpse of the Bonhomme Richard— No lives were lost with the Ship—but it was impossible to save the Stores of any Sort Whatever— I lost even the best Part of my Cloaths Books and Papers and several of my Officers lost all their Cloaths and Effects.

Having thus endeavoured to give a Clear and Simple relation of the Circumstances and events that have attended the little Armament Under my Command I shall freely submit My Conduct therein to the Cencure of my Superiors and the impartial Public— I beg leave however to Observe that the Force that was put under my Command Was far from being well Composed And as the great Majority of the Actors in it have appeared bent on the pursuit of Interest only; I am exceedingly Sorry that they and I have at all been concerned.

I am in the Highest degree sensible of the Singular Attentions which I have experienced from the Court of France; which I shall remember with Perfect Gratitude Untill the end of my Life— And will always endeavour to Merit while I can consistent with my Honor continue in the Public Service.— I must speak plainly; as I have always been honored with the full confidence of Congress, And as I had also Flattered myself

---

own crew and among his prisoners evokes contradictory testimony. Cottineau told Chaumont that Jones paid no more attention to the wounded among his crew than if they had been strangers: *ibid.*, p. 85. British Ambassador Yorke, on the other hand, later paid tribute to Jones's humanity: Morison, *Jones,* p. 258.

3. Lt. Mischateau: Reaveley, "Battle," p. 87.

with enjoying in some Measure the Confidence of the Court of France; I could not but be Astonished at the Conduct of M. De Chaumont When in the Moment of my departure from Groa he produced a Paper (a Concordat) for me to Sign in common with Officers Whom I had Commissioned but a few days before.—[4] Had that Paper or even a less dishonourable one been proposed to me at the begining I would have rejected it with Just Contempt, and the Word "Deplacement" Among Others should have been Unnecessary— I cannot however even now suppose that he was Authorized by the Court to make such a bargin with me— Nor can I suppose that the Minister of the Marine Meant that M. De Chaumont should consider me merely as a Colleague with the Commanders of the other Ships And communicated to them not only all he Knew but all he thought respecting our desination and opperations— M. De Chaumont has made me Various Reproaches on account of the Expence of the Bon homme Richard[5] wherewith I cannot think I have been Justly chargeable— M. De Chamillard can attest that the Bon homme Richard was at last far from being well fitted or Armed for War— If any Person or Persons who have been charged with the Expence of that Armament have Acted Wrong the fault must not be laid to my Charge.

I had not the Authority to Superintend that Armament and the Persons who had authority were so far from giving me what I thought necessary that M. De Chaumont even refused among other things to allow me Irons to secure Prisoners of War.

In short while my Life remains If I have any Capacity to render good & Acceptible Services to the Common Cause no Man will step forth with greater Cheerfulness and Alacrity than myself— But I am not made to be dishonoured nor can I accept of the half Confidence of any Man living; of Course I cannot consistent with my Honour and a Prospect of success Undertake Future Expeditions Unless when the Object and

---

4. For the concordat between the captains of the squadron see our annotation of Jones to BF, August 13.

5. For example, in his July 19 letter: Bradford, *Jones Papers,* reel 4, no. 689.

distination is communicated to me alone and to no other Person in the Marine line.— In cases where Troops are Embarked a like confidence is due alone to their Commander in Chief— On no other condition will I even under take the Chief Command of a Private Expedition and where I do not command in Chief I have no desire to be in the Secret.

Captain Cottineau Engaged the Countess of Scarborough and took her after an Hours Action While the Bon homme Richard engaged the Serapis— The Countess of Scarborough is an Armed Ship of 20 Six Pounders and was Commanded by a King's Officer—

In the Action the Countess of Scarborough and the Serapis were at a considerable distance asunder and the Alliance as I am Informed Fired into the Pallas & Killed some Men.[6] If it should be asked why the Convoy was Suffered to escape I must answer that I was myself in no Condition to pursue; And that none of the rest shewed any inclination not even M. Ricot who had held off at a distance to Windward during the whole Action; and withheld by Force[7] the Pilot Boat with my Lieutenant and Fifteen Men.— The Alliance too was in a State to pursue the Fleet not having had a Single Man Wounded or a Single Shot fired at her from the Serapis and only three that did Execution from the Countess of Scarborough at such a distance that One Stuck in the Side and the other two Just touched and then dropped into the Water— The Alliance Killed one Man Only on board the Serapis— As Captain Cottineau charged himself with Manning and Securing the Prisoners of the Countess of Scarborough— I think the Escape of the Baltic Fleet cannot so well be charged to his account.

I should have mentioned that the Main Mast and Mizen Top

6. According to the ship's captain, one man was killed aboard the *Pallas:* Schaeper, *Battle off Flamborough Head,* p. 83.

7. Jones here added the following marginal note: "This is founded on a report that has proved to be False for it now appears that Captain Ricot expressly ordered the Pilot Boat to board the Bon homme Richard, which order was disobeyed." Cottineau defended Ricot's zeal: Schaeper, *Battle off Flamborough Head,* p. 83. Schaeper feels the *Vengeance* was wise to stay clear of the battle where she would have been of little assistance; *ibid.,* p. 17.

Mast of the Serapis fell Over Board soon after the Captain had come onboard the Bonhomme Richard.

Uppon the whole the Captain of the Alliance has behaved so very ill in every respect that I must Complain loudly of his Conduct— He pretends that he is authorized to act independant of my Command— I have been taught the contrary; but supposing it to be so his Conduct has been base and unpardonable. M. De Chamillard will explain the Particulars.— Either Captain Landais or myself is highly Criminal and one or the other must be Punished.

I forbear to take any steps with him Untill I have the advice and Approbation of your Excellency. I have been advised by all the Officers of the Squadron to put Landais under Arest but as I have postponed it so long I will bear with him a little longer Untill the return of my Express.

We this Day Anchored here having since the Action been tossed to and fro by contrary Winds— I wished to have gained the Road of Dunkirk on account of our Prisoners but was over Ruled by the Majority of my Colleagues.

I shall hasten up to Amsterdam and there If I meet with no Orders for my Goverment I will take the Advice of the French Ambassador. It is my present intention to have the Countess of Scarborough ready to Transport the Prisoners from hence to Dunkirk Unless it should be found more Expedient to deliver them to the English Ambassador taking his Obligation to send to Dunkirk &c. Immediately an equal Number of Americans. I am under Strong apprehensions that our Object here will fail and that thro' the Imprudence of M. De Chaumont Who has communicated every thing he Knew or thought on the Matter to Persons who cannot help talking of it at a full Table— This is the way he Keeps State secrets. Tho' he never mentioned the Affair to me. I am ever with the Highest Sentiments of grateful Esteem and Respect. Honoured and dear Sir Your very Obliged Friend & very Humble Servant

JNO P JONES

(Copy)

Excellency Benj. Franklin Esq. &c. &c. &c.

Addressed: For His Excellency / The President of the Congress / in / Congress.

Notation: Copy Capt J P. Jones letter to Doctr Franklin Octr 3. 1779 Accot. of his cruize & capture of Seraphis

To William Bingham

LS:[8] Stanley R. Becker, East Hampton, N.Y. (1966); copy: Library of Congress

Sir,   Passy, Oct. 4. 1779.

I thank you for your frequent Communications of News Papers from North America, for tho' they are generally old before they come to hand, they always contain some Information that I am glad to receive.

I have not yet seen the Bills you mention your being about to draw on me.[9] I wish it were in my Power to accomodate every one in the Service of the Congress. But there are Limits of possibility to every thing, and I am obliged now to refuse all Drafts, but those drawn by the Congress itself. It is my Duty and a Matter of the utmost Consequence to keep up their Credit here, but it is too much to be charged with the support of the Credit of their Agents in all other Countries. With much Esteem, I have the honour to be, Sir,

Your most obedient & most humble Servant.   B FRANKLIN

Mr. Bingham.

To Dumas

LS[1] and copy: Library of Congress

Dear Sir,   Passy Oct. 4. 1779.

I received yours of the 14 & 21. past. I communicated to M. De Chaumont what you say in your last relating to your attending the Arrival of our Friend. Inform him as soon as you see him, *that he is in Holland to follow the Orders he will receive*

8. In WTF's hand.
9. XXIX, 29–30.
1. In WTF's hand.

from the g. Factor. We have just heard something of him that gives every body here abundant Satisfaction.[2]

As I have not seen in any of your Prints the Regulations made by the new Government in Grenada I enclose a Copy.[3]

We are all well and chearful in this Neighbourhood, where every Body remembers you with Respect and Affection; and none with more than Your most obedient humble Servant

B FRANKLIN

M. Dumas

Endorsed: Passy. 4e. Oct. 1779. S.E. Mr. Franklin.

To John Jay

Two LS:[4] National Archives; AL (draft):[5] Library of Congress; copies: Library of Congress, Sheffield City Library, South Carolina Historical Society; transcript: National Archives

Sir,   Passy, Oct. 4.[-28] 1779:
I received the Letter your Excellency did me the honour to

2. The Oct. 1 issue of the *Courier de l'Europe,* VI (1779), 211, carried a Sept. 26 letter from England giving news of the capture of H.M.S. *Serapis* (for which the writer gave some of the credit to the *Alliance*).

3. The Oct. 19 issue of the *Gaz. de Leyde* (no. LXXXIV) published a set of regulations promulgated by the comte de Durat, the new French governor of the recently captured island; we suspect these were the documents which BF here encloses and which Dumas provided the Dutch journal (as he so often did). For details see Oliver's letter of Oct. 8.

4. We print from the one in WTF's hand. The other, in the hand of L'Air de Lamotte, was marked "Copy" by BF, and was received by Congress on May 15, 1780.

5. There are numerous revisions, interlineations, and deletions in the draft, all of which are incorporated into the LS. We take note, below, of those of substance. Two other documents relate to the drafting of this letter: a full-page list in BF's hand of the topics to be covered in the present letter (undated, APS), and a list of enclosures sent with it (Library of Congress). Entitled, "Papers promised," it reads:

Copies of Letters to & from M. de la Fayette
Description of the Sword
Cruise of black Prince
Copy of Count Maillebois' Memoire

write to me of the   of June last[6] inclosing Acts of Congress respecting Bills of Exchange for 2,400,000 Livres tournois, drawn on me in favour of M. De Beaumarchais. The Bills have not yet appear'd, but I shall accept them when they do, relying on the Care of Congress to enable me to pay them. As to the Accounts of that Gentn., neither the Commissioners when we were all together, nor myself since, have ever been able to obtain a Sight of them, tho' repeatedly promised; and I begin to give over all Expectation of them.[7] Indeed if I had them, I should not be able to do much with them, or to controvert anything I might doubt in them, being unacquainted with the Transactions and Agreements on which they must be founded, and having small Skill in Accounts. Mr Ross and Mr Williams pressing me to examine and settle theirs, I have been obliged to request indifferent Persons expert in such Business, to do it for me, subject to the Revision of Congress; and I could wish that my Time and Attention were not taken up by any Concerns in Mercantile Affairs, and thereby diverted from others more important.

The Letters of Congress to the King were very graciously received; I have earnestly pressed the Supplies desired, and the Ministers (who are extreamly well disposed towards us) are now actually studying the Means of furnishing them.[8] The Assistance of Spain is hoped for. We expect to hear from

---

Claim of French Sailors
Claim of two Gunners
Engraving of Montgomery's Mont.

On the verso of the page is a reminder to himself "To write Mr. Bingham that I cannot answer his Draughts." (BF did so on the same day; see above.)

6. The date was also left blank in the draft and all the copies. The letter from then-president of Congress Jay was written on June 18: XXIX, 707–8.

7. In his last lengthy letter to Congress (XXIX, 552), BF had complained of Beaumarchais' failure to provide his accounts.

8. Vergennes' latest letter on the subject is above, Sept. 25. Presumably the letter graciously received by the King was Congress' of June 15 requesting portraits of him and his consort: JCC, XIV, 736–7. See also XXVIII, 91.

thence in a few Days. The Quantity is great and will cost a vast Sum. I have this Day accepted three of your Drafts, part of the 360,000 Livres drawn for on the 9th. of June:[9] but when I ask for Money to pay them, I must mention that as they were drawn to purchase Military Stores, an Abatement equal to the Value may be made of the Quantity demanded from hence. For I am really ashamed to be always worrying the Ministers for more Money. And as to the private Loans expected, I wrote in a former Letter that our public Credit was not yet sufficiently established, and that the Loan in Holland had not exceeded 80,000 Florins, to which there has since been no Addition.[1] A Mr Neufville came from thence to me last Spring, proposing to procure great Sums if he might be employed for that purpose, and the Business taken away from the House that had commenced it.[2] His Terms at first were very extravagant, such as that all the Estates real and personal in the 13. Provinces should be mortgaged to him; that a fifth Part of the Capital Sum borrowed should every Year for 5 Years be laid out in Commodities and sent to Holland consigned to him, to remain in his Hands 'till the Term (10 Years) stipulated for final Payment was compleated, as a Security for the Punctuality of it; when he was to draw the usual Commissions: that all Vessels or Merchandize coming from America to Europe, should be consigned to him or his Correspondents, &c. &c.[3] As I rejected these with some Indignation he came down to the more reasonable Ones of doing the Business as it was done by the other House, who he said could do no more being destitute of the Interest which he possess'd. I did not care abruptly to change a House that had in other Respects been very friendly and serviceable to us, and thereby throw a Slur upon their Credit without a Certainty of mending our Affairs by it; and therefore told Mr Neufville that if he could procure and show me a List of Subscribers amounting to the Sum he

9. XXIX, 652–3.
1. XXIX, 552.
2. Horneca, Fizeaux & Cie.: XXVI, 338–9n; XXVII, 322.
3. XXVIII, 629–31.

465

mentioned or near it, I would comply with his Proposition. This he readily and confidently undertook to do. But after three Months, during which he acquainted me from time to time, that the favourable Moment was not yet come, I received instead of the Subscription a new Set of Propositions, among the Terms of which were an additional *One Per Cent,* and a Patent from Congress appointing him and his Sons "*Commissioners for Trade and Navigation, and Treasurers of the General Congress, and of every private State of the thirteen United States of North America, through the seven United Provinces,*" with other Extravagances,[4] which I mention, that it may be understood, why I have dropt Correspondence on this Subject, with a Man who seemed to me a vain Promiser, extreamly self-interested, and aiming chiefly to make an Appearance without Solidity; and who I understand intends applying directly to Congress,[5] some of his Friends censuring me as neglecting the Public Interest in not coming into his Measures. The Truth is that I have no Expectations from Holland, while Interest received there from other Nations is so high, and our Credit there so low; while particular American States, offer higher Interest than the Congress; and even our offering to raise our Interest tends to sink our Credit.[6] My sole Dependence now is upon this Court: I think reasonable Assistance may be obtained here, but I wish I may not be obliged to fatigue it too much with my Applications, lest it should grow tired of the Connection. Mr. Ross has lately demanded of me near 20, thousand Pounds Sterling, due to him from the Committee of Commerce, but I have been obliged to refuse him,[7] as well as an Application made last Week by Mr Izard for more Money, tho' he has already had 2500 Guineas; and another from Mr Arthur Lee, tho' he has had 500. Guineas since the News of his being out of this Commission. He writes me that he will return to America forthwith if I do not undertake to supply his Ex-

4. xxix, 692–5.

5. xxix, 693n.

6. Alexander Gillon proposed offering higher interest for a loan for South Carolina, drawing BF's rebuke in a July 5 letter, above.

7. On Sept. 9, above, BF had told Schweighauser to settle the commerce committee's accounts with Ross.

pences. As I see no likelihood of his being received at Madrid, I could not but approve his Resolution.[8]

We had Reason to expect some great Events from the Action of the Fleets this Summer in the Channel, but they are all now in Port without having effected any thing.[9] The Junction was late, and the length of time the Brest Squadron was at Sea equal to an East India Voyage, partly on the hot Spanish Coast, occasioned a Sickness among the People that made their Return necessary: They had chas'd the English Fleet which refused the Combat. The Sick Men are recovering fast since they were landed: And the proposed Descent on England does not yet seem to be quite given up, as the Troops are not withdrawn from the Ports.[1]

Holland has not yet granted the Succours required by the English, nor even given an Answer to the Requisition presented by Sir Joseph York.[2] The Aids will be refused, and as the Refusal must be disagreable it is postponed from time to time. The Expectations of Assistance from Russia and Prussia seem also to have failed the English, and they are as much at a Loss to find effective Friends in Europe as they have been in America. Portugal seems to have a better Disposition towards us than heretofore. About 30. of our People taken and set ashore on one of her Islands by the English, were maintained comfortably by the Governor during their Stay there, furnished with every Necessary, and sent to Lisbon, where on Enquiry to whom Payment was to be made for the Expence

8. In his draft BF first crossed out and then reinstated (by writing "Stet" in the margin) the final part of this paragraph, beginning with "as well as an Application." The exchange with Arthur Lee is above, Sept. 26 and 30.

9. The ships of the fleet, both Spanish and French, arrived in Brest between Sept. 10 and Sept. 15. The French ships alone had more than 8,000 ill: Patterson, *The Other Armada*, p. 210.

1. On Oct. 4 a committee of senior military officers ordered the invasion attempt abandoned for the year, partly because mortality from the illness was increasing: Dull, *French Navy*, pp. 164–5.

2. Presumably this is a reference to Ambassador Yorke's memorial of July 22, demanding the military assistance from the Netherlands specified by the Anglo-Dutch treaty of 1678: Sir Francis Piggott and G.W.T. Omond, eds., *Documentary History of the Armed Neutralities 1780 and 1800* (London, 1919), pp. 141–2.

they had occasioned; they were told that no Reimbursement was expected, that it was the Queen's Bounty who had a Pleasure in showing Hospitality to Strangers in Distress. I have presented Thanks by the Portuguese Ambassador here in Behalf of the Congress.[3] And I am given to understand, that probably in a little Time the Ports of that Nation will be open to us as those of Spain. What relates to Spain I suppose Mr. Lee informs you of.

The Sword ordered by Congress for the Marquis de la Fayette, being at length finished, I sent it down to him at Havre, where he was with the Troops intended for the Invasion. I wrote a Letter with it, and received an Answer, Copies of both which I inclose, together with a Description of the Sword and Drawings of the Work upon it, which was executed by the best Artists in Paris, and cost alltogether 200 Guineas. The Present has given him great Pleasure, and some of the Circumstances have been agreable to the Nation.

Our Cartel goes on, a second Cargo of American Prisoners 119 in Number being arrived and exchanged.[4] Our Privateers have dismissed a great Number at Sea, taking their written Paroles to be given up in Exchange for so many of our People in their Goals. This is not yet quite agreed to on the other Side, but some Expectations are given me that it may take place.[5] Certainly Humanity would find its Account in the Practice of Exchanging upon Parole, as all the Horrors of Imprisonment, with the Loss of Time & Health might be prevented by it.

We continue to insult the Coasts of these Lords of the Ocean with our little Cruizers. A small Cutter which was fitted out as a Privateer at Dunkirk called the Black Prince, has taken ransomed, burnt and destroyed above 30 Sail of their

3. The Americans were from the privateer *Comte d'Estaing:* XXIX, 681–2. BF's expression of gratitude to the Portuguese ambassador, the conde de Sousa Coutinho, may have been delivered in person as we have no record of it.

4. Here in the draft BF wrote and then lined out, "They make some difficulty about".

5. See Hartley's Sept. 18 letter.

Vessels within these three Months. The Owners are about to give her a Consort called the Black Princess, for whom they ask a Commission. The Prisoners brought in serve to exchange our Countrymen, which makes me more willing to encourage such Armaments, tho' they occasion a good deal of Trouble.

Captain, now Commodore Jones, put to Sea this Summer with a little Squadron consisting of a Ship of 40 Guns, the Alliance, another Frigate of 20, with some armed Cutters; all under American Colours with Congress Commissions. He has sent in several Prizes, has greatly alarmed the Coast of Ireland and Scotland; and we just now hear that going North about he fell in with a Number of Ships from the Baltic, convoy'd by a Fifty Gun Ship & a 24 Gun Frigate, both of which he took after an obstinate Engagement, and forced several of the others ashore. This News is believed, but we wait the Confirmation and the Particulars.

The blank Commissions remaining of those sent to us here, are all signed by Mr Hancock, which occasions some Difficulty. If Congress approves of my continuing to issue such Commissions, I wish to have a fresh Supply, with the other necessary Papers, Instructions, Rules, Bonds, &ca. of which none are now left.

M. le Comte de Maillebois esteemed one of the best Generals in this Country, and who loves our Cause, has given me a Memorial, containing a Project for raising a Corps here for your Service,[6] which I promised to lay before Congress, and accordingly enclose a Copy: I know nothing of the Sentiments[7] of Congress on the Subject of introducing foreign Troops among us, and therefore could give no Expectation that the Plan would be adopted. It will however be a Pleasure to him to know that his good Will to serve them has been acceptable to the Congress.

A Major Borre, who has been in America, and some other

6. Maillebois had sent a memoir to the commissioners soon after their arrival in France: XXIII, 287. We have not located the present one.

7. BF first wrote "Disposition", then "Inclina", and finally "Sentiments".

Officers who have quitted our Service in Disgust, endeavour to give an Idea here that our Nation does not love the French.[8] I take all Occasions to place in View the Regard[9] shown by Congress to good French Officers, as a Proof that the Slight these Gentlemen complain of is particular to themselves, and probably the Effect of their own Misbehaviour. I wish for the future, when any of these sort of People leave our Armies to come home, some little Sketch of their Conduct or Character may be sent me, with the real Causes of their Resigning or Departure, that I may be more able to justify our Country.

Here are returned in the last Cartel a Number of French Sailors who had engaged with Capt. Cunningham, were taken in coming home with one of his Prizes, and have been near two Years in English Prisons. They demand their Wages & Share of Prize Money.[1] I send their Claim as taken before the Officers of the Classes at Dunkerque. I know nothing of the Agreement they alledge was made with them. Mr. Hodge perhaps can settle the Affair so that they may have Justice done them. These Sort of things give me a great deal of Trouble. Several of those Men have made personal Applications to me, and I must hear all their Stories tho' I cannot redress them. I inclose also the Claim of two Gunners upon a Prize made by the Boston Capt Tucker.—[2] I am persuaded the Congress wish to see Justice done to the meanest Stranger that has served them: It is Justice that establisheth a Nation.

The Spanish Ambassador here delivered me several Complaints against our Cruizers.[3] I imagine that all the Injuries

8. Philippe-Hubert Preudhomme de Borre was a former brigadier general in the Continental Army who resigned soon after the Battle of Brandywine, when his advice was spurned: Bodinier, *Dictionnaire.*

9. Replaces "Respect".

1. BF had promised Coffyn he would send the sailors' claims to Congress: above, Sept. 28.

2. See Vergennes' second letter of Sept. 25 and BF's Oct. 1 response.

3. Among BF's papers at the APS are three memoranda in French which Spanish Ambassador Aranda gave BF. They protest the American capture of the ships *Santander, San Francisco de Paula,* and *Nuestra Señora de la Merced.* The Spaniards also complained to Congress: Meng, *Despatches of Gérard,* pp. 646–7; Juan F. Yela Utrilla, *España ante la independencia de los Estados Unidos* (rev. ed., 2 vols., Lérida, 1925), I, 408–9; II, 262–6.

complained of are not justly chargeable to us, some of the smaller English Cruizers having pillaged Spanish Vessels under American Colours, of which we have Proof upon Oath. And also that no such American Privateers as are said to have committed these Robberies after coming out of Nantes, have ever been known there or in any other Port of France, or even to have existed. But if any of the Complaints are well founded, I have assured the Ambassador, that the Guilty will be punished & Reparation made.

The Swedish Ambassador also complains of the Taking of a Ship of his Nation by Capt. Landais, the Master of which lays his Damages at 60,000 Livres.[4] I understand it was his own Fault that he was stopt as he did not shew his Papers. Perhaps this if proved may enable us to avoid the Damages.

Since writing the above I have received the following farther Particulars of the Action between Commodore Jones & the English Men of War. The 44 Gun Ship is new[5] having been but 6 Months off the Stocks: she is called the Serapis; the other of 20 Guns is the Countess of Scarborough. He had before taken a number of valuable Prizes particularly a rich Ship bound to Quebec, which we suppose he may have sent to America. The English from mistaken Intelligence, imagining he had a Body of Troops with him to make Descents, have had all their Northern Coasts alarmed, and been put to very expensive Movements of Troops &c.[6]

The extravagant Luxury of our Country in the midst of all its Distresses, is to me amazing. When the Difficulties are so great to find Remittances to pay for the Arms and Ammunition necessary for our Defence, I am astonished and vexed to find upon Enquiry, that much the greatest Part of the Congress Interest Bills come to pay for Tea, and a great Part of the Remainder is order'd to be laid out in Gewgaws & Superfluities. It makes me grudge the trouble of examining, entering and accepting them, which indeed takes a great deal of time.

4. See Vergennes to BF, Sept. 4 and BF to Schweighauser, Sept. 17.

5. In the draft BF stated and then deleted that the *Serapis* was sheathed with copper. She was not: Schaeper, *Battle off Flamborough Head,* p. 71.

6. The next paragraph originally began, "The unconquerable Attack", but this was deleted.

I yesterday learnt from M. De Monthieu that every thing necessary for equipping two Frigates of 36 Guns, such as Sail Cloth, Cordage Anchors &c &c which we sent to the Congress from hence two Years since, remain stored in the Warehouses of his Correspondent M. Carrabass at Cape François, having never been called for.[7] Probably by the Miscarriage of Letters the Navy-Board never heard of those Goods being there. I shall nevertheless leave the Application I have lately made for Materials for a Frigate of 36 Guns to take its Course.[8] But I send you herewith Copies of two Invoices of the Cargo of the Therese, one of which is what was sent by us, the other by M. Beaumarchais; to the End that Enquiry may be made after the whole.[9] On this Occasion give me leave to remark, that of all the vast Quantities of Goods we have sent you by many different Vessels since my being in France, we never were happy enough to receive the least Scrip of Acknowledgement that they had ever come to hand, except from Mr Langdon of a Cargo arrived at Portsmouth, and I think of one more. This is doubtless owing to the Interruption Correspondence has met with, and not altogether to Neglect. But as such Advices of Receipt may be made in Short Letters, it would be well to send more Copies. The following is a Matter of less Importance. It is two Years, I believe, since I sent the Monument of Genl. Montgomery.[1] I have heard that the Vessel arrived in N. Carolina, but nothing more. I should be glad to know of its coming to hand, and whether it is approv'd. Here it was admired for the Goodness and Beauty of the Marble and the elegant Simplicity of the Design. The Sculptor has

7. xxv, 294–5, discusses some of the ships Montieu dispatched to America. The supplies were still unclaimed in June, 1780: *JCC,* XVII, 555–6.

8. One of the memoirs BF sent to Vergennes on Sept. 18; see our annotation of his covering letter of that date.

9. At the National Archives is an April 22, 1777, account of the goods the *Thérèse* carried to America. When she came back to France the commissioners disputed with Beaumarchais the ownership of her return cargo: XXVII, 358–9n.

1. Jean-Jacques Caffiéri's monument to Gen. Richard Montgomery eventually was mounted in St. Paul's church in New York: Sellers, *Franklin in Portraiture,* p. 117. For its sculpting and passage to America see XXII, 376n; XXIII, 522n; XXIV, 60–1, 491n; XXV, 213; XXVI, 674n.

had an Engraving made of it of which I inclose a Copy.[2] It was contrived to be affixed to the Wall within some Church, or in the great Room where the Congress meet. Directions for putting it up went with it. All the Parts were well packed in strong Cases.—

With the greatest Respect, I have the honour to be, Sir, Your most obedient & most humble Servant.   B FRANKLIN

P.S. Oct. 28. I kept the Packet in hopes of sending a more explicit Account of what might be expected in regard to the Supplies. The Express which was daily looked for from Spain when I began this Letter arrived but a few Days since. I am now informed that Court is understood to be in Treaty with the Congress in America, to furnish a Sum of hard Money there and on that Account excuses itself from sharing in the Expence of furnishing these Supplies.[3] This has a little deranged the Measures intended to be taken here, and I am now told, that the whole Quantity of Goods demanded can hardly be furnished; but that as soon as the Court returns from Marly, the Ministers will consult and do the best they can for us. The Arms I hear are in hand at Charleville. I am unwilling to keep the Packet any longer, lest she should arrive on our Coasts too far in the Winter, and be blown off:[4] I therefore send away the Dispatches. But if I have the Result of the Council in time to reach her by the Post, I will send it in a separate Letter. The hearty Good Will of the Ministry may be depended on; but it must be remembred that their present Expences are enormous./.   BF

His Exy. John Jay Esq.

Notations in different hands: Letter from B Franklin Minister plenipotentiary of the United States at Court of France Octr.

2. St.-Aubin's engraving of the monument is reproduced in Charles Henry Hart and Edward Biddle, *Memoirs of the Life and Works of Jean Antoine Houdon* . . . (Philadelphia, 1911), facing p. 62.

3. Spanish help failed to materialize. Vergennes also demanded Spanish financial assistance if an invasion of England were to be again attempted and the Spaniards were unable to provide it: Dull, *French Navy,* pp. 166–7.

4. The *Mercury* took 89 days to cross the Atlantic, reaching Martha's Vineyard on Feb. 16, 1780: Clark, *Ben Franklin's Privateers,* p. 92n.

4. & 28. 1779.— Reced March 3. 1780 Referred to the Comee. of Intelligence / Mr. Beaumarchais' Accts.—wishes to have no mercantile affairs to conduct. Letters of Congss: to the King were recd. & the Invoice De Nieuville & Sons fails in the promised Loan

To Rocquette, Elsevier & Rocquette

Copy: Library of Congress

Gentlemen,   Passy, Oct. 4. 1779.

I have receiv'd lately two Pacquets thro' your hands, the last with your favour of the 20th. Past. I am much oblig'd by your Care of them, and have the honour to be, Gentlemen Your most obedient and most humble servt.

Messrs. J Rocquette and Elzevier and Brothers Roquettes Rotterdam.

From Landais

LS: American Philosophical Society

Ship Alliance off Texel

May it please your Excellency   4 October. 1779

I now embrace the First Oppertunity to transmitt the material parts of my Journal of our late Cruize which ended Yesterday.[5]

On Saturday the 14 August we were the Ships Bon homme Richard, Alliance, Monsieur & Pallas, arm'd briggs Vengeance & Grandville & the Cerf Cutter in Company under Groa. We all weyed Anchor & put to Sea early in the Morning.[6]

the 19th. A Ship was taken by the Monsieur, laden with Canvas, bound to Spain, she was dutch but had been taken by a privateer from Liverpool.

5. See, for comparison, Jones's Oct. 3 letter, above. An expanded account of the cruise prior to the battle off Flamborough Head is in Landais, *Memorial,* pp. 26–35.

6. Here Landais began a double column format, with his journal entries on the left-hand side and on the right, a "Column for Observations" which was left entirely blank.

474

21st. Gave chace to a Ship windward she appears like an east indiaman, Capt. Jones at about 4 Miles Leeward of us at 2 oClock made Signal for forming the Line of Battle. The Chace is 5 miles windward of me. Having it in my power to take my Station at any time, being in this situation, I continued the Chace till 5. At 6 bore down & at 9 Spoke with Capt. Jones, who inform'd me he had Sent the dutch Ship to L'Orient & that the Monsieur was going to leave us.

22d. Saw the same ship we took Yesterday for an eastindiaman, but by her present conduct she is a man of War. Capt. Jones would not give chace to her, but put away after a brig, which he came up with in the evening. She is from Limerick bound to London, laden with Beef & butter.

23d. Made the Coast of Ireland, saw a sail bearing NNW. made signal & sat all sail. At 1 came up with the Bon homme Richard, she made signal for us to drop astern; took in our light sails & haul'd up our Courses. As we still kept way with her under our topsails, Capt. Jones spoke & order'd this Ship to drop a stern; bore away to let him get a head. The chace now alter'd her course to SW. The Bon homme Richard is under all Sail, but the winds are very light. At 3 saw another sail, westward of the chace. ½ past 3 a signal on board the B.H. Richard for boats. A Calm came on & several Boats were dispatch'd by Capt. Jones, after the Vessells in chace. Saw them board the nearest, a Brig. At 10 she pass'd us & inform'd they were from Newfoundland bound to Bristol, laden with oyl & blubber. At 10 Next morning spoke Capt. Jones, am inform'd that 7 of his men have run away with one of His boats, & that he has sent another boat to look after them. That the other vessell in chace Yesterday is a Sloop from Norway bound to Bordeaux. He asked if I had a Crew ready to put on board the Brig. I told him I did not choose to man any Prize that had been boarded, for my prizemaster could not be answerable for what might be done by others who had taken possession before him.

26th. The Vengeance took a brig. under portugese Colours, laden with Salt, bound to Ireland. Capt. Jones sent the Cerf in Shore to look for his boats.

27 We had a very hard Gale of wind last night, & this morning we have not one of our fleet in Sight.

29 Captured a Letter of Marque of 22 Guns, from Liverpoole bound to Grenada & on a Cruize laden with Provisions.[7] None of our fleet in sight since the night of the 26th.

31 Saw Lewis Islands bearing S½.E. Saw a Ship & brig. gave chace, when got within a few Leagues of them, they tack'd & stood towards us. Found them to be the B.H. Richard & Vengeance.

Septem. 1. In company with these Vessells captured a Letter of Marque bound from London to Quebeck, Mountg. 22 Guns, laden with Naval Stores.[8]

2d. The Pallas join'd us, having been seperated by the gale of the 26 at Night. No account of the grandville & Cerf, the former of which was also seperated by the Same gale.

5 I took a Sloop in Ballast from Leith & another laden with Coals from Greenock, both bound to Shetland. Sent them S E of fair Island where I knew they would find the B.H. Richard & Pallas.

September 6. The Vengeance rejoin'd us, having been absent & burnt a brig from Norway, laden with deals.[9] The B H Richard & Pallas took the 2 Sloops in tow that I captured Yesterday.

7th. Bent Cables & prepared to go into one of the Isles of Shetland, on condition that Capt. Jones should take the risque of this Ship upon himself, & make himself accountable for what might happen to her, having no pilot on board. Your orders to me 28 July Mention'd nothing but a Cruize. At Night a hard gale came on & parted us.

8th. I waited all day, but seeing nothing of our Ships, the 9th. proceeded to our Rendezvous at Flamborough head. In Cruizing hereabouts, we saw nothing of Consequence but a Sloop of War & a Cutter, these we chaced but could not come up with them.

13th. I took a Brig laden with Coals. After this we frequently saw numbers of Colliers, keeping close to the Land, some of which I might perhaps have taken, but hearing there were two

7. The *Betsy.*
8. The *Union.*
9. *I.e.,* boards (timber).

24 Gun Ships upon the Coast, I did not chuse to part with my Crew to man prizes of so little Note; but keep myself in force to be able to engage them, & after to intercept some of the Northern fleet.

22d. Saw a Ship & brig. chaced and reconnoitred the former to be the Pallas, two other Vessells being in sight at the Same time, I made Signal and chaced one, she chaced the other & took her, finding her to be empty, the Pallas left her, & also abandon'd the 1st. brig we saw with her. We spoke together in the evening, am inform'd they parted from the B.H. Richard 2 or 3 days before. They can give no account of what became of the two Sloops I left with them the 7 Instant.

23 Early this morning saw the Bon H Richard & Vengeance. At 2 in the Afternoon saw two Ships leewards of us, lying-to, off the Land. They appear'd to be men of war. Saw also a fleet standing for Scarboro' made Signal & gave chace to the two former, & came down to them in the Evening. They proved to be the Serapis of 44 Guns, Capt. Pearson, & the Countess of Scarborough of 22 Guns, Capt. Piercy. An engagement immediately ensued. I have inclosed a draft to which I referr you for a discription of our Manoeuvres in the course of it. The Serapis I afterwards tow'd off the Land as she was disabled & had drifted within 4 Miles of Flamborough head, while 3 of our boats wth. part of our Crew were assisting on board the B.H. Richard. All that I suffer'd in the engagement was in my Sails & Rigging, with a few Shots in our hull, & this was of but very little damage.

25 The B.H. Richard being evacuated, Sunk. After this we made the best of our way to this Place, & received a pilot on board Yesterday & got up today. We are now the Ships Alliance & Pallas & brig. Vengeance in company with the Serapis & Countess of Cumberland prizes.

The Grandville has been absent since the Gale of the 26 August, & the Cerf ever since Capt. Jones sent her after his boats, on the Coast of Ireland.

To Recapitulate our prizes I have captured when by myself
A Letter of Marque of 22 Guns
A Sloop—empty
A Sloop—with Coals

A Brig—with Coals
In Company with the Pallas
A Brig—empty which we abandon'd
In Company with the B.H. Richard &c
A Ship—with Canvas
A Brig—with provisions
A Brig—Oyl & blubber
A Brig—Salt
A Ship—22 Guns—Naval Stores
A Ship—deals—burnt by the Vengeance
Serapis Man of War 44 Guns
C of Scarboro'. Kings Ship 22 Guns
Besides these I am inform'd that there has been taken by our fleet while I was Seperated, 6 Sail of Colliers which they distroyed, being of very little Consequence. I have now on board this Ship 226 prisoners, in Officers & Men. I find I have not time to inclose the draft to elucidate our engagement the 23 Instant, I shall write you again soon & inclose it. Mr. Du Mas being on board I & the post going away I have only time to Subscribe myself With the Greatest esteem Your Excellencys Most Obedient humble Servant   P: LANDAIS

N.B. the Prizes I dispatch'd[1] were sent to Bergen According to Your Orders.

Notation: Capt Landais Journal of his Cruise in the North Seas. Oct 4. 1779.

From William Greene   ALS: American Philosophical Society

Honoured sir
Warwick State Rhode Island
&c. October 5th. 1779

I with much Pleasure received your very Friendly letter of the 4th. of last June,[2] by which I am informed of The Perticular care you took to employ your Nephew to transact my business, since which I have also received his letter enclosing the

1. The *Betsy* and *Union.*
2. XXIX, 620–1.

478

invoice of the articles I wrote you for, which have also come safe to hand.

Am much Obliged to you for the Tenderness you discover Towards my Son in law, and Ray both of whom I think are likely to be beneficial to their distress'd Country.[3]

The Chevalier, Dela, Luzern Since his arrival in Boston went by the way of Worcester on his way to Congress, His taking his Tour that way depriv'd me of the Pleasure of waiting on him.[4]

The General Assembly of this State received a letter from Mr. Williams in your behalf of March 10th. with a Package of books containing the History of Geneva by M. Berenger in Six Volums, as a Present to and for their use and benefit, for which they have requested me to return you their Sincere Thanks, and to inform you that they shall ever acknowledge The favour with gratitude as it greatly tends to discover your good Intentions to Promote the Publick welfare.[5]

I am much Pleased to hear of the Prospect you have in your Grand Son as I hope he may hereafter be instrumental in supplying his Grand Fathers Place in the great business of his Country; as by that means you may be relieved from the same in some future Period, and once more return to your Native land, and enjoy that comfort and Satisfaction which must be very agreeable, when you reflect that you have been bless'd by Heaven to continue to an advanced age, as by far the greater Part of your time has been devoted for the well being of the Publick, as I dare say the Inhabitants of this vast Continant are thorily Convinc'd, as also of the advantages they are now enjoying in consequence of it which I doubt not will

3. His son-in-law was Samuel Ward, Jr., husband of Phebe Greene; Ray is Ray Greene.

4. La Luzerne traveled via Worcester in order to meet with Washington at West Point. He left Boston on Sept. 4, saw the general on the 16th, and arrived in Philadelphia on the 21st: William Emmett O'Donnell, *The Chevalier de La Luzerne, French Minister to the United States, 1779–1784* (Bruges and Louvain, Belgium, 1938), p. 44.

5. BF had planned to send sets of Jean-Pierre Bérenger's *Histoire de Genève* to each of the states: XXVI, 5n; XXVII, 28on.

be by them handed forward to Posterity, and scarcely ever be forgotten.

Your agreeable Sister desires me to inform you that she has lately wrote to you two letters,[6] and that she has sent you two Dozen cakes of Soap, which went from here about a Month Past,[7] That she is about making a small quantety more which she Purposes to forward to you by the first convenient oppertunity together with another letter for which Reason she omits writing now. My Wife makes the same excuse as to writing, but both say they Sincerely love you, as really does your Sincere and much Obliged Friend. and most Humble Servant.

W. GREENE

Docter Franklin

Addressed: (Publick Service) / Docter Fraklin / at Paris / France / (W Greene)

Notations in different hands: Boston 10th. Octr. 1779—Received under cover & forwarded—by your Obedt Hble. servt. WM VERNON / William Greene. Warwick State of R. Island Oct. 5. 1779

From Marignac: Bill for Benjamin Franklin Bache's Schooling[8]

ADS: American Philosophical Society

[October 5, 1779–January 5, 1780]

Compte pour le Jeune Franklin

Pension depuis le 5e. 8bre. 79. au 5e.
  Janvier 80.   £130—14—6—
Papier, encre & plumes . . .   1—10—" —

---

6. July 27 and Sept. 12, above.

7. They were sent via the *Sensible;* see Peter Collas' of Oct. 12, below.

8. Marignac's previous bill had covered just one month's expenses (Sept. 5–Oct. 5). Apart from the usual charges for schooling, stationery, mail, laundry, stocking repair, drawing lessons, a hair ribbon, and weekly allowance, it included a payment of 7 *l.t.* 5*s.* 3*d.* for the swimming master and one of 43 *l.t.* 8*s.* 6*d.* for merchandise purchased from V. Griot et Pinon. APS.

Raquettes & Volans . . .	1—17—6—
Comédie . . .	1—12—″—
Dictionnaire Anglois en 2. Volumes . . .	10— 8—″—
⅓ Kalmouk . . .	1— 7—″—
Cahiers . . .	″—18—″—
pr. quatre pres. [paires] bas de laine . . .	7— ″—″—
Port de Lettres . . .	″—11—″—
écritoire . . .	″— 7—″—
Compte au cordonnier . . .	16— ″—″—
ruban de queuë . . .	″— 6—″—
Compte & étrennes à Mr. Aval, à sa servante,	″— ″—″—
& à Mr. Moliére . . .	15— 5—″—
Etrennes pr. lui & pr. Les Domestiques des personnes où il a mangé pendant l'année . . .	7— 5—3—
Etrennes pr. le perruquier . . .	1—10—″—
3. Mois blanchissage . . .	4—10—″—
3. Mois dessin . . .	11— ″—″—
1. Mois danse . . .	3—13—″—
pr. ses Dimanches . . .	3—17—″—
pr. le Maitre d'anglois . . .	7—15—3—

£227— 6—6—

227 *l.t. 6s. 6d.* argt: court: le louis à 14 *l.t.* 10*s. 6d.* pr. 24 *l.t.* argt. de france font 375 *l.t.:* 12 *s:* argt: de france.

Pr. acquit MARIGNAC

Notation: 24 *l.t.* pr Etrennes au dit sr. Marignac. £399:12

From Dumas

ALS: American Philosophical Society

at the Helder, road of Texel
Dear, honoured Sir   Oct. 6th. 1779
    Mr. Le Ray de Chaumont, will by this time, have heard, at my request, from Mrs J. De Neufville & fils, that the Vessels

are all safe on this road,[9] which I am happy to confirm to yr. Excellency; & that they entered viz. the 4th. in the Evening 1.° te Vengeance, Ricot; 2.° the Scarborough prize Ship of 20 or 22 pds., 3.° the Alliance, Landais; & the 6th. 4.° the Serapis, of 22 eighteen pounders, & 22 nine pounders, Comodore Jones (his own the B.h. Richard having sunk a few hours after the battle) my self being on board the last when coming up; & 5.° the Pallas, Cap. Cotineau. I have delivered yr. Letter[1] myself to the Commodore, & saved them all a great deal of trouble, & done my best to serve them. And now having left them here with good adresses, I am going to Amsterdam, & to the Hague with the Commodore, & present him to the Ambassador. Capt. Landais has given me the inclosed paper,[2] with request to send it you. Will your Exc. have the goodness to let Mr. De Chaumont know, that I have permitted Mr. De Chamillard, an Officer aboard the Comodore's Ship, who was in great haste to go to Paris with the Comodore's dispatches, to make use of the Cabriolet I had left at Antwerp, & to come back again with it & leave it at the same House at Antwerp, being there in good hands, if Mr. De Chaumont approves of it.

Your Excellency will have the relation of the whole Campaign, by the Commodore. Therefore I need not to enter on this Subject. I am in very great haste, with great respect Dear, honoured Sir, yr. Exc. Most obedient & humble servant

DUMAS

Notation: Dumas Octr. 6. 1779

9. Jones himself wrote Chaumont on Oct. 3: Bradford, *Jones Papers,* reel 4, no. 748.

1. Of Sept. 7, to Jones, above.

2. Presumably his letter, above, of Oct. 4.

From the Marquis de Lafayette

ALS: American Philosophical Society

Dear Sir   havre 6th October 1779

The happy intelligence which you had the kindness of forwarding to me,[3] is the more pleasing to My heart, that I am
Glad to have Given to our scoth friends, A little But full view
of the American flag— Captain Jones has ever inspir'd me
with a great Regard for his talents and patriotic Spirit, and I
am Proud to find that Both these Qualities have been display'd
to so Great an advantage as the taking of the Baltic fleet, at
the head of the little Squadron in which you know I have been
Greatly Concern'd— Sir George Collier's expedition had left
me an impression of sorrow which Could Not be alleviated
But By successes obtain'd Under American Colours— Count
destaing's arrival on our Coasts will I hope Give us a full
Revenge, and tho his Expeditions will be plann'd and executed
upon a More Generous footing than those of the Ennemy,
they will Cut a better figure in the Gazettes than the heroïc
Burning of defenceless towns— Had I thought that his operations would turn that way, Nothing Could have hindered Me
from joining Gal Washington's Army—[4] But, you know, that
was not to be expected, and you had Certainly Yourself a firm
idea that My services would be more actively employ'd or in
the expedition Against England, or in executing plans where I
Could have Brought More than My person to the American
shores— I hope Congress will be sensible of it, and approve
the Reasons I had of leaving them on this side of the Atlantic— News from Count destaing will Give Room to New projects, and if he has Not finish'd the work, Be Certain, My dear
sir, that Nothing will please me so much as fighting Again
with My American fellow soldiers.

As our first interest is By this time to Get the ask'd for

3. On Oct. 1.
4. On the following day Lafayette wrote both the president of Congress
and Washington expressing his desire to return to America: Idzerda, *Lafayette Papers,* II, 320–7.

supply,[5] that operation has My Best wishes, and I hope clothes, arms, Ammunition will be soon sent to a Country where they are I Believe much wanted.

The pacquet which is to sail for america will, I understand, be dispatch'd By the Beginning of Next week— from that intelligence I see that My letters will be timely arriv'd if they Come into your hands By Sunday Next— I shall therefore trouble you with some which I Recommend to your friendly Care.

As there is nothing material to be writen from the havre, But what you know of the Combin'd fleet, and the state of the intended expedition I will only add a few words about ireland.

Do you, My dear sir, from the new dispute happen'd at dublin,[6] aprehend that the presbiterian Counties would suffer themselves to be aided By a small french force, which might add some strength to theyr Representations in parliament? Suppose you would Conceive some new hopes of the Revolution being a little Riper than last spring, we Could advise together of some propositions to be made to the Ministry.

With the highest Regard I am My Respected sir, Your affectionate   LAFAYETTE

his excellency Benjamin franklin esq.

Notation: La Fayette 6 Oct. 1779.

---

5. *I.e.,* the military supplies that BF had requested from the French government.

6. The Sept. 17 issue of the *Courier de l'Europe,* VI (1779), no. XXIII, p. 179, carried an item dated Dublin, Sept. 7, about a mob which had saved a prisoner en route to his execution. Public disturbances in Dublin were not uncommon, however, so we cannot be sure this was the "new disturbance." A riot had taken place on June 1 directed against importers of British goods and another would occur in November: Maurice R. O'Connell, *Irish Politics and Social Conflict in the Age of the American Revolution* (Philadelphia, 1965), pp. 139, 182.

To Thomas Digges

Copy: Library of Congress

Dear sir   Oct. 7. 1779.

I received yours of Sept. 4. & 6. and am glad to hear that Mr. Peters's affair is settled to his Mind.— I have received the Letter he wrote me and have forwarded that to his son.[7]

I am Sorry to hear that any innocent Men Should suffer on suspicion of holding a criminal Correspondence with me. The Truth is, that I do not know *that* Capt. Hutchins, and never had a Correspondence with him of any kind, directly nor indirectly. Nor have I ever understood that Mr. Warton received any Intelligence from England but what the Newspapers afforded. In respect to your Recommendation I comply'd with the request of your friend.[8] Please to Let Mr. Raspe know, that if he comes here he will be welcome to live with me the two Months he mentions, and that I Shall be glad of his Company. When you have occasion to write to Mr. Grand he tells me you may direct your Letters to the Care of Messrs. fr. Romberg and Comp. at ostende. With great Esteem, I am, Dear Sir your m. o. and m. h. S.

M. Digges.

From Louis-Pierre Dufourny de Villiers[9]

ALS: American Philosophical Society

Votre Excellence   a Paris le 7. octobre 1779

Monsieur le Comte du Chillau,[1] Commandant la Frégatte la Diligente, chargé des Dépeches de Monsieur le Comte d'Estaing, des nouvelles de la prise de la Grenade et de la déffaitte de Biron, et de conduire en France les drappeaux et Lord M'cartney; connu d'ailleurs tres avantageusement de vos

---

7. See BF to Richard Peters, July 12.

8. On Sept. 6 Digges had requested a passport for Cyprian Sterry and John Smith, Jr., and on Sept. 24 BF drafted it. Both documents are above.

9. The first man to execute a bust of BF after his arrival in France, Dufourny maintained an active interest in American affairs: xxv, 516–17.

1. According to French naval records, Chilleau; see our annotation of Bordot's letter of Sept. 4.

chers compatriottes, par les services qu'il leur a rendus de son propre mouvement, surtout en les convoyant, m'a fait l'honneur de me charger de vous demander la permission de vous aller voir; pour vous faire part de plusieurs choses qui peuvent vous intérresser, pour vous offrir ses services lors de son retour aupres de Monsieur le Comte d'Estaing, et pour satisfaire l'empressement qu'il m'a toujours témoigné, de connoitre un homme d'une aussy grande réputation dans les sciences et la Politique, le principal mobile enfin d'une aussy grande révolution. Trop honoré de l'opinion qu'il a de vos bontes pour moy, je vous prie de m'indiquer le jour ou je pourrai l'accompagner chez vous, et vous assurer du profond respect avec lequel je suis de Votre Excellence Le tres humble et tres obeissant serviteur   DUFOURNY DE VILLIERS

P.S. J'observe que Mr. le Comte du Chillau n'a pas un moment de libre jusqu'a lundy exclusivement.

Je vous prie de me faire parvenir votre réponse Rue des Fosses de Monsieur le Prince vis à vis la rue de Touraine.

Notation: Dufourny De Villiers Paris 7e. 8bre. 1777.

From Jean de Neufville & fils

ALS: American Philosophical Society

High Honourable Sir.   Amsterdam the 7th. October 1779.

We have the honoúr to mention to yoúr Excellency the Arrivall of John Paul Jones Esqr. Commander of the Continentall Squadron; he did ús the favoúr of writing ús a very polite Letter from board of the Serapis;[2] and we execúted already part of his orders, as múch as Circúmstance and time would permitt; we continúe to attend to them with all Care and exactness.

From what the Said Commander in chief wrote ús and Mr. Dúmas Agent for Congress, we may flatter oúr selfs to see

---

2. Jones's letter to the firm, dated Oct. 5, asked for masts, spars, rigging, sails, boats, and provisions: Bradford, *Jones Papers,* reel 4, no. 755.

them both soon,[3] in this event, we long very múch to be personally Acqúainted with this great Heroe for the American
caúse, which long ago, we are proud to say, we endeavourd to
promote; and so we See oúr Selfs highly rewarded by the favoúr your Excellency bestowed on ús in honouring ús with
this first Publicq Commission, for the United States;[4] we begg
leave to thank yoúr Excellency most sincerely for this preference and nothing will be wanted on oúr Side to deserve further favoúrs; and, though America owes already her Libertÿ
and Independence to the Unfatigued Cares and spirit of Your
Excellency, we most sincerely wish her long to enjoy again, of
seeing this Independence very shortly reverenced and acknowledged by all the Powers on earth.

We have the honoúr to remain with all respectfull veneration High Honourable Sir! Yoúr Excellencys most devoted and
most humble Servants　　　JOHN DE NEUFVILLE & SON

Notation: Neufville & fils Oct 7. 1779

To David Hartley　　LS,[5] copy,[6] and transcript: Library of Congress

Passy Oct. 8[–10]. 1779.

My Dear Friends late Letters have been long in coming, having met some Delay on the Way. I am told the Communication is now more open.

As Captain Tattwell cannot now perform his Engagement
specifically by procuring the Release of Captain Harris and

3. Dumas had reported to BF the previous day that he and Jones were
leaving for Amsterdam.

4. Jones had told them that his squadron had orders to apply to them for
"Public wants of every Kind": Bradford, *Jones Papers,* reel 4, no. 755. With
BF's approval, Chaumont had ordered Dumas to ask de Neufville for assistance for the squadron: above, Sept. 2. Apparently he had given similar
orders to Jones.

5. In WTF's hand.

6. In addition to this one there is also a partial copy, consisting of the
second and fifth paragraphs and the final sentence of the postscript, that
Hartley made and sent to John Bell, Commissioner for Sick and Hurt Seamen, on Oct. 27. Public Record Office.

his Crew, I think he may be discharged of his Parole by obtaining the Release of some other Captain with a Number of Men equal to that with Capt. Harris: If this is done, I will send him a Discharge of his Parole accordingly. On this Occasion I would name a Captain Robertson of Philadelphia, who was Master of the Brigantine Pomona which sailed in June last from Amsterdam, and is now with his Son a Prisoner at Forton.[7] The Men to be released with him and his Son should be of those who have been longest Confined.

The Number of Places in France, in which the English are confined is so great and so remote from me, that it will not be easy for me to find Capt. Stephenson; but I will endeavour it, and will solicit his Release. The sooner you send me such further Particulars about him as you can learn, the better.

I send you inclosed Copies of the Engagements of a Number of Prisoners we have discharged at Sea. The Originals shall be sent when required.[8] One of Commodore Jones's little Squadron, which parted with him on the Coast of Ireland, is returned I hear with a Number of Prizes, & some hundreds of Prisoners. If the Commodore himself gets safe into France with his Prizes there will be another very considerable Number. I have not yet received the Accounts I have wrote for from Spain; but expect them daily.

M. De Sartine seems disposed to grant a Pass port to the Cartel for Morlaix but desired me to make the Proposition to him in writing that he might lay it before the King. I did so a few Days since but have not received an Answer.

With the sincerest Esteem I am ever, my Dear Friend, Yours most affectionately   B FRANKLIN

P.S. Oct. 10.— We have just received Advice of the safe Arrival of Comr. Jones in the Texel, with 400 Prisoners. If therefore the Board would send their Cartels thither with an equal

7. A John Robertson signed on March 22, 1779, a bond (where his name is given as Robinson) for a letter of marque for the *Pomona:* National Archives; Claghorn, *Naval Officers,* p. 260. He eventually escaped from prison and in January, 1780, was furnished 120 *l.t.:* Alphabetical List of Escaped Prisoners.

8. On Oct. 28 Hartley forwarded the contracts to Bell and asked what to answer BF. Public Record Office.

Number, it would save a great deal of Misery to your poor People which their Confinement in the Ships till they can be lodg'd in French Prisons must occasion.

D. Hartley Esqr.

Endorsed: D F Oct. 8 1779

From Amelia Barry

ALS: American Philosophical Society

Sir,   Leghorn 8th Octr. 1779

As I too well know the enlarged mind which informs my revered Friend, to imagine that all private considerations are sunk in public duties, I am persuaded that you will be pleased to hear that my long and painful residence in Barbary is brought to a close,[9] and that this place is fixed on for our abode, for some time at least.

As your Excellency was deaf to my most earnest, and repeated supplications, in favor of Mr. Barry,[1] I have little hope of this letter being honored with notice; yet as my circumstances are less eligible than I could wish, justice to my little helpless family calls upon me to entreat your Excelly. to inform me how it will be most proper for me to act, in regard to a Proprietary Grant for a Lot of Ground in the Province of Pensilvania; The papers relating to it, were lodged in the hands of Mr. Israel Pemberton.[2] I am informed that by the Laws enacted by Congress, the Property of such persons as left America before the commencement of hostilities, is not

9. She first went to Tunis in 1766 as governess to the family of the British consul and returned there in 1774 with her husband and children: XIII, 163n; XXI, 205.

1. David Barry, a ship captain whom she married in Africa: XII, 64n. She had written BF several letters about the difficulty he encountered after leaving the sea to establish a mercantile business: XXIV, 353–4; XXVI, 585–9; XXVII, 436–7.

2. Apparently part of the estate of her father, the cartographer Lewis Evans (III, 48n). Most of the estate had been willed to her: Lawrence Henry Gipson, *Lewis Evans* (Philadelphia, 1939), p. 79. The great merchant Israel Pemberton, Jr. (V, 424n) had shared his interest in the Pennsylvania frontier; we know nothing of the lot.

anhiliated: Will you then Dear Sir, cause one of your Secretaries to put me in a way to have the above mentioned Lot (which remains unlocated,) secured, or in what manner I may have it taken up.

I should be inexpressibly happy to hear how my revered God-mama[3] & Mrs. Beache do;— Perhaps that endulgence may be granted to Sir, Your Excellency's most obliged & faithful Humble Servant   A. BARRY

His Excelly B. Franklin Esqr.

Be pleased to direct to me to the care of Messrs. Gentil & Orr Mercts. at this place.[4]

Notation: A Barry Oct. 8. 79

From Thomas Digges   ALS: Historical Society of Pennsylvania

Dear Sir   8th Octor. 1779

I have taken the liberty to give the Bearer hereof, Mr Luard, an introductory line to you;[5] and to get him to bear a few of the latest news papers, as well as a packet from from Mr. V——n[6] which I expect to deliver Him with this letter. He is

3. Deborah Franklin: III, 48n. Amelia Barry did not learn of her death in 1774 until the following December: to BF, Dec. 31, 1779 (APS).

4. This Leghorn firm had been forwarding her mail since at least 1769: XVI, 135; XXVII, 436–7n. BF's answer (now missing) was dated Nov. 28, according to her reply of Dec. 31.

5. Peter Robert Luard (1727–1812) was a London merchant who went bankrupt in 1777: *The New Complete Guide to All Persons who have Trade or Concern with the City of London* ... (15th ed., London, 1777), p. 243; *Gent. Mag.* XLVII (1777), 352. By 1779 he had established a new business: *Kent's Directory for the Year 1779* ... (London, 1779), p. 110. Through his marriage in 1754 to the former Jane Bourryau, he had inherited substantial estates in Grenada and St. Kitts. *Burke's Genealogical and Heraldic History of the Landed Gentry* ... (15th ed., London, 1937), p. 1427.

In a separate letter of this date Digges introduces the merchant, who is going to Paris on important business resulting from the capture of Grenada. Although not intimately acquainted with the traveler, Digges hopes BF will extend him his usual civility and attention. Hist. Soc. of Pa.

6. See Vaughan to BF, Oct. 10.

among the capital sufferers at Grenada & goes to Paris to secure if possible his property on that Island.

Mr. Sterry having taken the route of Amsterdam & not yet returnd, I have not got the Ansr. to my last letter on the subject for which He went to Paris, but by a letter frm Him to the party concernd here (Mr. Smith) I have some reason to beleive it will do, & Mr S is preparing a large cargoe of woolens & Linins for our friends; among his articles there will be 1600£s worth of Blankets & a great quantity of the right colour Cloathing— He is to push for head quarters. Altho I am totally unconnected wth this or any similar adventures, I cannot help wishing they were more frequent, for by such means I am certain our friends can be very much releivd, & the unfair monopolys now practicing in Ama. may be very much broken.

I have done every thing in my power for Capt C——me & he is very grateful to You. He has been cloathd (for he went in nearly naked to Prison) & takes a regular small supply of money from a friend of mine near Him, He drawing on me for the amot. and for which I shall have my riembursement in the bill forwarded to Monr. G—— £50 dated Sept 24 & paye at ten days sight which by a line to Mr. G—— by post I desird might be presented to you.[7] There is also in the prison with him & who deserves some little help for His services, *James Adams* Master of the Providence sloop of war in the service of the States of Ama.[8] & who was taken some months ago & put equally naked into Prison, & probably for a like reason to that of C——m—because He behavd well. You will see in one of the papers sent you, the St Jas. Chronicle, the Letter from the Secretary of Congress to Sr. Geo Collier about Capn. C——m, together with Colliers impertinent answer.[9] There are also in another paper some resolves of Congress relative to the recall

7. Digges to BF, above, Sept. 20.

8. From Boston, Adams had been committed to Mill on May 10: Kaminkow, *Mariners*, p. 2. Hearing nothing from Digges, he wrote BF on Nov. 3 the first of several letters seeking aid. APS.

9. *The London Chronicle* and *The St. James's Chronicle* printed these letters in their issues of Oct. 5–7. We describe the testy exchange in our annotation of BF to Jonathan Nesbitt, Sept. 29.

of Mr Izard and Mr W. Lee.[1] We are so far behind hand here in American news papers or intelligence, & there are things in them so deserving of publication here that I am led to ask you for any of the Papers since May, which you may have thrown by; & which Mr. Luard will take the trouble of bringing on his return a few weeks hence.

Captn. H——ns has now got over all fears as to punishment that can effect his life. There being not a tittle of *proof* against him, He might get out by insisting on bail being taken for him, claiming the habeas corpus &ca. but we are unwilling to give the least offense *for the present,* hoping by his remaining quiet a little longer, that a promise made him of being allowd to sell his commn will be complyd with, & which will make 1500 Guins difference to Him. He will not be many days in England after he gets out of Prison.[2]

Mr. D—— H——y has done the necessary as to laying the Rect taken for the 190 men capturd at Sea by the Miflin before the board of sick & hurt; no answer could be given to it there, & it will be before the Admy & perhaps the Ministry before it will be grantd. The Cartel is now waiting for your answer and the proper passport for going to some other port with the next Cargoe. I did expect before this to get a letter from Mr. H——y to forward to you, which is meant to contain a copy of one to you dated the 29 June, which I forwarded & we have some reason to think by your late letters has never got to hand— It related to the finishing a certain business with the minister which I communicated with you upon.[3] As I am obligd to keep my papers distant from myself, I cannot at present tell how or by whom that letter was sent.

I begin to get fearful the cartel will stop, & God knows what latitude of sufferings our prisoners may experience in

1. An extract of Congress' resolves of June 8 (*JCC,* xiv, 700–5) was published on Oct. 6 in *The General Advertiser, and Morning Intelligencer.*

2. Thomas Hutchins spent seven weeks in prison. After his release he resigned his captaincy in the British army (which since the beginning of the war he had been seeking permission to sell) and fled to France. From there he sought BF's assistance: Hutchins to BF, Feb. 27, 1780, for which see our annotation of Digges to BF, Sept. 4.

3. Hartley's secret peace negotiations with Lord North: xxix, 767–70.

another winters imprisonment, as the money is very near expended & no hopes of raising more. There seems a strange detention of the Ship in every voyage; and Mr. H——y being in the Country & not sticking close to the agents here, I fear helps on this detention. There is not above 135 in Forton and 190 at Plyo. & we are endeavouring that the ship may instead of the exact *one hundd* be orderd to take the whole from each prison when she sails next; which will make a difference of two voyages. On the return of the Ship to port last voyage, it was universally given out that there were no more prisoners in France American-Captured. But this cannot well be an argument now, for Mr. Paul Jones has, in the two men of war got 350 Seamen besides the Crews of thirty odd vessels which He took & destroyd on his late cruise. Above twenty ships of war was dispatched after Him; but after throwing the northern parts of England into full as much panick as the combined Fleets did the western, He has apparently got away with much booty & no little credit to himself.

Whenever you want any thing done here I hope you will make no ceremony in commanding me I find my letters from Nantes, Spain, & Holland, come regularly safe to me under the common direction & without cover thus *Mr. Wm. Singleton Church Nandos Coffee Ho London.* Yours need not be dated from any place but simply the day of the month, and without signature.

There has been much dispondance since the arrival of Genl Vaughan & the publication of the last Gazettes people here begin to fear the Americans have alterd their mode of defensive war into an offensive one. The Genl like all other returning officers from that quarter comes home discontented, and keeps his mouth shut; when He ventures to open it, He does not speak very favourably of the British prospects in America.[4] I find that there will be a push made to get to Chas Town this winter; the burning of that Town & distressing the Colony more, are matters of great object, and there will be a de-

4. Gen. John Vaughan (1747?–95) had commanded during the British capture of Stony Point and Verplancks Point in early June. *DNB.* He brought to London dispatches from Clinton detailing British losses from Gen. Wayne's storming of Stony Point: *The London Gazette,* Oct. 2–5, 1779.

tatchment from N York to effect this purpose, and most probably such a force sent as will insure it. Twelve thousand Hessians are confidently talkd of for the American service in the Spring,[5] but this Country seems to forget that She has lost the bridge over wch. these troops must be sent. The conversation about Invasion is again revivd, & this together with the gloomy appearances from the West Indies & the improbability of doing any thing in Ama. causes a universal depression & a more than usual abuse of our wise Rulers.

I wish you health & success and am with great truth & sincerity Yr obligd & obt. Servt   T.D.

Addressed: His Excelly. Docr. Franklin

Endorsed: Oct. 8. 79

Notation: Digges Oct. 8. 79

From John Paul Jones   ALS: American Philosophical Society

Honored & dear Sir,   Amsterdam Octr. 8th. 1779.

With respect to the reception which I meet with here I beg leave to refer you to the Accounts which I know you will receive from Mr ———[6] by whose hands I had the honour to receive your esteemed favor of the 7th. of September.— His Excellency ——— I understand makes propositions respecting certain Commissions.—[7] Whatever you may find Consonant with the good of the Common Cause and with the high

---

5. *The St. James's Chronicle* of Sept. 30-Oct. 2 reported that the Hessian minister had presented a treaty arranging to send 12,000 troops under the command of George III's brother-in-law, Prince Ernest of Mecklenburgh, to open the following summer's campaign.

6. Dumas, who describes in his Oct. 12 letter Jones's reception in Amsterdam.

7. Ambassador La Vauguyon hoped to provide the commanding officers of Jones's squadron with French commissions so as to avoid embroilment with the Dutch government. He wrote Sartine on Oct. 5 and 8 requesting such commissions (AAE). Jones went along with the plan to the extent of telling a Dutch captain that he had a French commission which he had misplaced or had lost aboard the *Bonhomme Richard:* Schulte Nordholt, *Dutch Republic,* p. 86.

Respect which I shall ever entertain for Freedoms Flag, will always meet with my earnest and full attention— And especially while in pursuit of the Object for which the Congress thought proper to Send me to France; but I can accept of no honor that can call in question my Ardent Attachement to the American Cause and to the dignity of its Flag, or that can give the least offence to America.— I have not here a Sufficient number of Officers to form a Court Martal. Unless Captain Virage of the Cerf is returned to France it will be difficult for me to get through the Enquiry into Captain Landais' conduct.— I hold myself Always ready to Observe your Orders, and therefore will wait the return of M. De Chamillard before I take any measures with Landais.— In case of his deplacement, it will be necessary to put the Alliance in the meantime Under the Command of a Lieutenant, Unless some Continental Captain of Merit should be at this time in France— And if there should be at this time any deserving Lieutenant in France Whose Seniority may entitle him to a preference, I presume that you will give him directions to Repair here.— I have besides Occasion for Sundry other Officers as Some of my late Compliment have been Sent away in Prizes and others have been killed—[8] We are beginning to refit the Serapis.— The Countess of Scarborough & Vengeance are Also preparing Agreeable to my letter of the 3d.— Yet with respect to the Prisoners I am afraid I shall not be Able to Settle that matter before the return of the Express.— I am far from desiring to Quarrel with M. De Chaumont. I wish to know him long as a Friend tho not as a Master,— for it is not his Heart but his Head that has made me Unhappy.

As I left the Texel immediatly After the Ships were Moored,— And from the dispersed Situation of my Crew and Prisoners Not having previously Obtained a return of killed and Wounded, I am Sorry that I have it not yet in my Power to Satisfy you in that respect.— I will forward the list as soon

8. Of the thirteen commissioned naval and marine officers of the *Bonhomme Richard* serving under Jones, two had been killed, five wounded, including Chamillard, and two were absent from the ship on the day of battle: Augustus C. Buell, *Paul Jones Founder of the American Navy: a History* (2 vols., New York, 1906), II, 407–13.

as possible; Meantime I have the honor to be with Sentiments of the Highest Esteem and Respect Honored & dear Sir Your most Obliged & faithful Servant   JNO P JONES

His Excellency B. Franklin Esqr.

Addressed: His Excellency / Benjamin Franklin Esqr. / American Ambassador / at the Court of France / at his Hôtel in Passy / near Paris.

Notation: Capt. Jones Oct 8. 1779.

From the Marquis de Lafayette

ALS: American Philosophical Society

Dear Sir   havre 8th october [1779]
The fear of detaining your dispatches has induc'd me not to send my express of yesterday, so that the paquets which my last promises for sunday, will together with yesterday's letter, Be delivered into your hand By to morrow's evening.

Inclos'd you will find 1st a letter to Congress whom for any Minuted intelligence I Refer to your dispatches, But whom I wanted to assure of My zeal love and gratitude 2dly a paquet for My Respected friend General washington whom I also intrust with some letters for officers in the Army 3dly an other paquet privately directed to the president of Congress wherein I have inclos'd letters for several Members of Congress.[9]

There you will also find some letters which a Merchant of this City desir'd me to join to my dispatches.

As I understand a frigatte from Count destaing's is lately arriv'd,[1] I Beg you would desire your Grand son to Give me such particularities, and send such dates as will enable me to

9. For the first two letters see our annotation of Lafayette's of Oct. 6. The others undoubtedly included those catalogued in Idzerda, *Lafayette Papers,* II, 494.

1. The frigate *Minerve* arrived at Brest in late September with d'Estaing's letters to Maurepas and Sartine announcing his intention to attack Savannah: Jacques Michel, *La vie aventureuse et mouvementée de Charles-Henri, comte d'Estaing* (n.p., 1976), p. 224.

know what My friend the Admiral will have time to do Before the season Calls a part of his 27 schips Back to the west indias. I'd be very happy to know your opinion on this matter.

I Beg you to present My Compliments to Mr. franklin and thank him for the printing he had the kindness of sending to Me,[2] which of all other General washington's pictures, But mine, has the best likeness I have seen in europe.

With the most sincere affection and high Regard, I have the honor to be My dear sir Your devoted servant   LAFAYETTE

In case of a misfortune I hope your dispatches will be thrown over Board, and I have writen in Consequence of that supposition.

Notation: La Fayette 8 Oct 79

From Arthur Lee   ALS: American Philosophical Society

Sir,   Paris Octr. 8th. 1779
You had the goodness to inform me on the 17th. ult.[3] that Count de Vergennes had chargd himself with enquiring

---

2. The engraving of Washington designed as a companion to BF's "fur hat" portrait, and produced by the same artists: Charles-Nicolas Cochin and Augustin de St.-Aubin. It is reproduced in Idzerda, *Lafayette Papers,* II, 328; the "fur hat" engraving is the frontispiece of vol. 24. The artists had worked from the painting of Washington belonging to Lafayette, displayed at BF's Independence Day dinner. St.-Aubin was anxious for Lafayette to approve the likeness before the engraving was released to the public, and he asked WTF to be his intermediary.

On Oct. 1 St.-Aubin reminded WTF of his promise to show the engraving to Lafayette. The matter was of some urgency, since he was hoping to send a packet of the engravings to America, and BF had told him that a ship carrying dispatches would be leaving within the fortnight. BF and WTF had also promised to talk to JW about a possible conveyance. In an undated follow-up letter, St.-Aubin urged WTF to confer with JW about the matter soon, as JW would be returning to Nantes shortly. Both letters are at the APS.

On Oct. 11 Lafayette thanked WTF for sending the engraving, praising it (as in the present letter) as the best likeness in Europe: Idzerda, *Lafayette Papers,* II, 327. It was announced for sale in the *Jour. de Paris* of Oct. 28. BF paid St.-Aubin 36 *l.t.* on Nov. 19 for this and other engravings: Account XXIII (XXIX, 3).

3. Printed under Aug. 17, above.

whether it woud be agreable to the spanish Court that I shoud propose concluding the Treaty with them.[4]

I beg the favor of you now, to let me know whether you have receivd any & what answer to this enquiry.

I have the honor to be with much respect Sir yr. most Obedt. Servt. ARTHUR LEE

Notation: A. Lee 8 Oct. 79. ansd—

From Thomas Oliver[5]

ALS: American Philosophical Society

Dear Sir/ London 8th Octr. 1779

Notwithstanding I have not the honor of a personal acquaintance with you. I am no stranger to the Rank you hold in Europe.

I pray the favor to introduce myself to you by this Letter. You are acquainted with the Capture of the Island of Grenada, & its Dependencies: and with the Terms that Monsieur Le Compte de Durat has been pleased to lay the Inhabitants and Absentees under.[6] It does not become me to remark now upon them. But such is the situation of Proprietors of Estates there, *absolutely paid for;* that if the Court of Versailles, will not relax

4. Spain was unready to recognize American independence, let alone join the alliance; Floridablanca declared King Charles III would do so only when certain of dictating the law to England: Richard B. Morris, *The Peacemakers: the Great Powers and American Independence* (New York, Evanston, and London, 1965), p. 44.

5. A West Indian merchant born in Antigua, Oliver (1740–1803) lived in London and Leyton, Essex. He was the cousin, brother-in-law, and business partner of Richard Oliver, M.P., who was married to his sister, Mary. Vere Langford Oliver, *The History of the Island of Antigua . . .* (3 vols., London, 1894–99), II, 318–19. This letter was probably enclosed in Benjamin Vaughan's of Oct. 10.

6. Jean-François, comte de Durat (1736–c.1824) was made major-general and head of the division by d'Estaing for the attack on Grenada; he was then appointed governor of the island. *DBF.* In retaliation for having inflicted injury on the island's residents, the British were enjoined by the Regulations of July 7 from receiving any further payments on mortgages or other debts due them from the inhabitants. *Gaz. de Leyde,* no. LXXIV (Oct. 19, 1779); see George Brizan, *Grenada Island of Conflict . . .* (London, 1984), pp. 43–6.

the proclamations of Monsieur Le Compte, the concerned must materially suffer. My Brother Mr Richd Oliver, and my particular Friends Mr Wm. Smith & Mr. Tooke[7] are very much interested in that Island. But the property They hold there, is totally unincumber'd with any Debts in the Island, or to any, to Subjects of the King of France, or united States of Holland. This being their case, I take the liberty to write to you in their behalf; & to solicit (if not repugnant to yr. other great concerns) your Interest in their favor. As I am so nearly connected with the late Alderman Oliver,[8] I trust that may be my apology for this Letter. I am Dr Sir Your most obed. humb Serv.

THOS. OLIVER

Addressed: A Monsr. / Mons. F / a Passy, / pres de Paris.

Notation: Thomas Oliver 8 Oct 79

From Luke Ryan

ALS: American Philosophical Society

Honoured sir   Dunkirkque October the 8th. 1779

The Letter your Excellency did me the honnour to wright me, with the present, of the Nightglass, Expressing your Satisfaction of my Conduct, in my Cruse with the Blackprince, fills me with Gratitude, and Secures for Ever my Subjection, and attachments, to the Goverment of the united States of America, and your Exellency—[9]

My Good frind Mr. John Torris will Order Immediatly, on the Stocks, at Bouloyne, for me, a Large Cutter to Mount 22. Guns 6 and 9 pounders which is Contracted for to be Compleated in four Months,[1] and I hope that, with Such, a Cutter

7. Richard Oliver's cousin, William Smith, owned estates and still resided in Grenada; Smith became his co-heir in 1784: Oliver, *History of the Island . . .*, III, 94. John Horne Tooke (XXIII, 332) and Richard Oliver were old political allies, both having fallen out with John Wilkes in 1771: *DNB* under Tooke.

8. Richard Oliver resigned from office on Nov. 24, 1778: Namier and Brooke, *House of Commons,* III, 225.

9. BF's letter is above, Oct. 2.

1. A plan subsequently abandoned. Instead, Torris bought another cutter, the *Fearnot,* for Ryan to command: Torris to BF, Jan. 15, 1780 (APS).

as this, I Shall be able to hurt greatly the Ennemy, which is my Real Ennemy, and take or beat off aney frigate—

If my abillities and Courage Deserves the portection of your Excellency, I would beseech you would obtain me a Rank in the Navy of your united Goverment which I will allways uphould As My Owne Natural Goverment, and Loose the last Drop of My blod to Gain honnour to the American flag, and I hope your Excellency will always have Cause to Rejoyce for the honnour your Excellency has Confered on me,—

I have the honnour to be with Respect Honnoured sir your most abedient And most abliged humble Servant,

LUKE RYAN

P.S. I beg leave to Recommend to your Excellency my first Liftennant Mr. Patrick Dowling[2] as Deserving the Notis of your Excellency, and best Calculated in Every Respect to Reimplace me on board of the Blackprince, and mr. Torris will Give her to him to Reward his Services.

Notation: Ryan Oct 8. 1779

From John Torris

ALS: American Philosophical Society

Honnd. Sir   Dunkerque 8th. Octor. 1779.

I have recd. with gratitude the Two Letters your Excellency did me the Honnour to write me the 28th. ulto. & 2d. Inst.

I shou'd have had the honnour to Answer the first Immediatly, had I not been in daily expectation to receive the Commission for the Black Princess, which your Excellency has been pleased to Promise to send in a few days & we want it very much to Listen [enlist?] the Crew.

The Promptitude with which your Excellency has sent the Condamnations for the good will & the 9. last Ransoms of our Black Prince, prompts my warmest thanks. These Condamnations & Letters to the admiralty have been forwarded on receit.

2. Dowlin, like Ryan, was a former Irish smuggler: Clark, *Ben Franklin's Privateers,* p. 5.

I have no Concern & know nothing about the Black Prince of Salem: your Excellency's kind enquiery thereon is an other obligation Confer'd on me.

Capt. Ryan & his officers did not fire at the good will with English Coulors, But at same Time observe they have always been decoy'd in this manner by the Ennemy, Because: Two guns are allowed thus, as ruse *de Guerre*. However, shou'd your Excellency order not to Practise it, your directions shall be obeied.

I beg Leave to express your Excellency my gratitude, for your favours to the Brave Mr. Ryan. I wish your Excellency wou'd grant him Protection to obtain him a Title in the Navy of the untited states & Secure thus this good officer to the american Government.

The Black Prince haveing finisht the Cruise, she has been Sold & I have bought her again yesterday at the admiralty. I shall refit her directly for three other months Cruise, & with the Same Crew, but under the Command of Mr. Pattrick Dowlin who was first Lieutenant on Board, & who is an honest Brave man & best qualified in every respect for this Command, & for all our Confidence, which, endeed, we ow him as a reward for his most essential Services on board. Mr. Ryan & all the Concerns beg Leave to recommand Mr. Dowlin to Your Excellency in the most favourable manner. Mr. Marchant has Taken a French Employ & has given up his Commission to Mr. Coffyn who sends it to your Excellency,[3] entreating to back it in margin to Mr. Pattrick Dowlin, & we think 'Twill be Legal thus, as Mr. Marchant is retired & 'Tis for the Same Cutter? Shou'd your Excellency Presume it not, we Beseech you will send me a fresh one as soon as possible, as the Vessell will be ready in a few days.

I have Contracted at Boulogne, where they Build as well as in England, for a fine Large Cutter to mount 22. Six & Nine Pounders, for Mr Ryan, who's health being a little altered, will stay ashore to see the work, which must be compleated in 4

---

3. The commission had been delivered to Marchant by Coffyn: XXIX, 495–6.

months fit for sea, & I Promise great Success with such a Vessell & Captain.[4]

The New Prisonners brot. here & those put ashoare in great Britain, & of which Mr. Coffyn sent your Excellency the Particulars,[5] will, we hope, enable to effect the Exchange of our 21. men whom we want greatly endeed.

I Left to Mr. Coffyn the Pleasure to advise your Excellency of all the Particulars relative to the arrival of the Black Prince.

The Lloyds List of the 28th. ulto. mentions the retaking of the Hopewell Capt. Bell, Prisonner here, our last Prise, by the Brilliant Privateer of Jersey & we loose there 6. men more.

I have the Honnour to be with greatest respect Honnourd Sir Your most obedient & most oblidged Humble Servant

J. TORRIS

P.S. I am this moment with the Letter your Excellency did me the honnour to write me the 5th. Inst.—[6] Tis full Time to fulfill your Excellency's wishes, & this very night I send my Correspondant at Morlaix,[7] a Copy of your Excellency's favour, & the Two Enclosed, with orders to send forthwith by the Coach, or any other Safe Conveyance, to your Excellency at Mr. Grand's at Paris, the Jappan'd Box mentd. Containing those Essential Papers, with the Key &c well Sealed— I request them to Purchase the Trunks as cheap as Possible, but not above £1000. *l.t.*[8]

Any orders from your Excellency will be obeyed with all the gratitude.

Endorsed: Torris, 8 Oct. 1779

4. Plans for the new vessel miscarried; see our annotation of Ryan's Oct. 8 letter.

5. On Oct. 3, above.

6. Actually the letter was from WTF, writing on his grandfather's behalf (Library of Congress). It requested Torris to allow the repurchase by their original owners of some trunks taken by the *Black Prince*. The trunks belonged to Mrs. Butler and contained bonds which John Holker had asked BF to retrieve: above, Oct. 2.

7. John Diot.

8. According to Holker, Mrs. Butler's goods were worth 50 pounds (equivalent to 1150 *l.t.*).

From Benjamin Vaughan

ALS: American Philosophical Society

My dearest sir,   London, Octr. 8th: 1779.
Mr Oliver has written me a letter from Barbadoes,[9] desiring me to procure from my connections letters to the French Governors of *Grenada* & *St. Vincents;*[1] in both which islands he has property, more particularly in the former. As I take for granted this hint was intended for *you,* and will be such as your opinion of him will induce to comply with; I take the liberty of asking for such letters; and, as after one letter is written, a duplicate can then be had with the mere trouble of an additional signature to a *copy;* I shall beg the farther of letters being sent by a French conveyance, and duplicates being sent to me for an English conveyance. The address will be sufficient, if the name of Richard Oliver Esq. with the respective island be mentioned.— The only letters I shall ask from you are for the *Oliver* connection, which I place to Mr Oliver's account, he being your friend; also for Mr Manning, father in law to President Laurens's son & who may chance also to be father in law to *one of your friends;*[2] and for our family.— Mr. Oliver's letters I suppose are now all finished, Mr Lovell's included; the letters for our family, I leave to your own suggestions, our concerns being all in Jamaica, & the letters not as yet apparently called for; Mr. Mannings letters will only be

9. Richard Oliver had returned to the West Indies in March to oversee his estates: XXIX, 43–4n.

1. The governor of St. Vincent was de Percin la Roche, who had led a force including some of the island's inhabitants during the French capture of the island on June 16: Ivor Waters, *The Unfortunate Valentine Morris* (Chepstow, England, 1964), pp. 66–9.

2. William Manning (1729–91) descended from a family that had been well-established in the West Indies since the time of Charles II: *DNB* under Henry Edward Manning. He moved to London from St. Kitts in late 1767 and became a partner in a merchant firm and Henry Laurens' business agent. His daughter Matilda married John Laurens: XXVII, 370n; Vere Langford Oliver, *The History of the Island of Antigua* ... (3 vols., London, 1894–99), II, 232. Manning's other daughter, Sarah, married Vaughan in 1781; the father had opposed the marriage until then, supposedly because Vaughan had no profession: *DNB* under Vaughan.

requested from you in case of accident to St. Kitts.—[3] I have a pacquet to send you on Sunday next,[4] and am my dearest sir, your ever devoted   BV.

Our affairs are here *semper eadem.*[5]

Notation: B. Vaughn Oct. 8. 79

To Arthur Lee[6]   Copy: Library of Congress

Sir   Passy, Oct. 9. 1779.

I have received no Answer relative to the Proposition you mention. Perhaps without waiting longer for an Answer, thro' Versailles it might be as well for you to apply directly to the Spanish ambassador for the Information you desire. With much Respect I have the honour to be Sir, Your most obedt. humble servant   BF

Honble. Arthur Lee Esq.

From Francis Coffyn: Two Letters

(I) and (II) ALS: American Philosophical Society

I.

Hond. Sir   Dunkerque Octor. 9th 1779

I beg leave to refer to the letter I had the honour to address your Excellency on the 3d. inst. being since deprived of your Excellencys favours, the purport of this is cheafly to inform your Excellency, that M. Stephen Merchant late Captain of the black prince has resign'd the command of Said privateer, and return'd me the Commission your Excellency was pleased to grant him, which, with the instructions, I Send here inclosed, and beg the favour of your Excellency to acknowledge the receipt. As Mr. Torris owner of Said privateer intends to give

3. St. Kitts (St. Christopher) had been threatened by d'Estaing's fleet in July; see our annotation of Bingham's Aug. 28 letter.
4. Oct. 10.
5. Always the same.
6. In response to Lee's of the previous day.

the command of her to M. Patrick Dowling, late first Lieutenant, he desired me to request your Excellency would endorse
or fill up the said Commission in favour of Mr. Patrick Dowling, mentioning in the margin or at the bottom that he has
reimplaced Capn. Merchant in the command, or if any blanck
Commissions are left, to grant him a new one.

Captain Marchant will sett off to morrow for Paris. I believe
he intends to return to America.[7]

The Edgar, Dromadary & Diamond which were Sent from
the Downs in quest of Capn. Jones Squadron, are (I am tol'd)
return'd to that station, the former Sail'd for Spithead to Join
Sir Chs. Hardys Fleet.

The black prince & Princess, are fitting out with all Expedition, I believe they will be ready for Sea in 10 or 12 days.

I have the honour to Subscribe myself with profound respect Your Excellencys most obedt & most devoted humble
Servant FRANS. COFFYN

Notation: F Coffyn. Oct 9. 1779

II.

Hond. Sir.   Dunkerque 9. Octor. 1779.

Captain Stephen Marchant having resign'd the command of
the Black Prince privateer, will Set off to morrow for Paris,
with an intend to return to America, he requested me to give
him a few lines to introduce him to your Excellency, which I
take the liberty to do, and to request your Excellency will
advise him in what manner he may proceed.

I have the honour to remain with due respect Your Excellency Most obedt & most humble Servant FRANS. COFFYN

Addressed: A Son Excellence / Monseigneur B Franklin, / Ministre plenipotentiaire des Etats / unis de l'Amerique Septentrionale / a la Cour de France / *à Passi*

Notation: F Coffyn. Oct 9. 1779

---

7. Marchant's hopes for a French command (if genuine) thus had proven
ephemeral. He returned to America on the *Mercury,* possibly after visiting
Passy: Clark, *Ben Franklin's Privateers,* pp. 91, 92n.

LS: American Philosophical Society

Ship Alliance off the Texel. 9 October 1779

May it please your excellency

I had the honour to write & transmitt some extracts of my Journal to you the 4th. Instant, & now inclose a plan of the engagement with the Serapis & Countess of Scarborough in the night of the 23 September.[8]

With respect to the present condition of this Ship, I am to inform your excellency that we have occasion for many Articles for Rigging & Stores, an Indent of which is making out to be sent to Messrs. Jean de Neufville et fils at Amsterdam,[9] that we have but 182 Officers & men belonging to her, out of which number 15 of my best men are on board the Serapis. I order'd my prize masters, who consist of all my masters mates & Midshipmen, excepting one of the latter & two of the former, to give your excellency the earliest information, when they should arrive, and you will please to order them with their men to repair on board the Alliance.

If your Excellency can obtain to have french deserters inlisted at Amsterdam, it might facillitate the manning this Ship, since fifty men more would be no great Complement for her.

This Ship did not sail well this last Cruize, her bottom was foul before she left L'Orient, and she was out of trim. If your Excellency would ship some Copper on board, to be put upon her at the place we are going to, it would be of great Service.

I have seen in a Recueil de Traites, Arrets, Ordonnances et Reglemens concernant la présente Guerre, Reglement concernant la Navigation des batimens Neutres en temps de guerre du 26 Juillet 1778. Articles 3d & 11th. will condemn the Swede I took last february, as a prize, for not producing all her papers; or at least will prevent her being paid damages, of which she makes such exorbitant demand, and the 6th. Article of the same, will Condemn the brig laden with wines.[1] This I should have noted before, had I seen them in Season.

8. See Landais, *Memorial,* pp. 37–43, for what probably are similar plans.

9. Landais had been given de Neufville's name by Dumas: *ibid.,* p. 46.

1. The first of these ships was the *Victoria,* the second, the *Three Friends.* The third article of the French regulations for neutral shipping declared

I have the Satisfaction to inform you that my Crew in general behaved well last Cruize & in the engagement of the 23d Ulto. and that I have two American Gentlemen of family Volunteers, one a Mr Spencer from So Carolina, who came over Captain of Marines & was carried into England sometime agoe; the other Mr. Ingraham, a young gentleman from Boston, who having a mind to make a Cruize, came on board at L'Orient & behaved so well as to demand my warmest recommendation to your Excellency,[2] & should any oppertunity offer it would give me the greatest pleasure to see their Merit rewarded. I remain with the greatest respect Your Excellency's Most obedient huml Servant   P: LANDAIS

P.S.[3] I am come today at Amsterdam (having not hear from any Body who I was to apply to for provision, and for Several things I want dealy & for refiting the Ship for sea at the Helder) to speak to Mr. Jean de Neuville and am Surprize to learn that he has Sent Some body down the Texel for to inquire the wants of all the Ships, but has not been heard of onboard the Alliance: I am very much affronted and insulted at hearing that Capn. Jones Dear to give out that I have fired upon his Ship desinged by in the ingeagment the Serapus.[4] He think to elude my resentment of his ill treatment to me the twenty four of August on board his Ship,[5] but I Beg of your

---

that all vessels which destroyed their papers would be treated as valid prizes, the eleventh that papers which were not found on board could not be used as evidence, and the sixth that the passports of enemy subjects would be treated as invalid except under specified conditions: Sir Francis Piggott and G.W.T. Omond, eds., *Documentary History of the Armed Neutralities, 1780 and 1800* (London, 1919), pp. 89–91.

2. The volunteers were John Spencer, who had accompanied Gillon to Europe (XXIX, 568–9n), and Nathaniel Ingraham: Landaïs, *Memorial,* p. 43.

3. In Landais' hand.

4. Jones himself directly made the accusation during a confrontation with Landais in an Amsterdam tavern. He declined Landais' suggestion that the two leave Dutch soil in order to fight a duel: Landais, *Memorial,* pp. 46–7.

5. Landais, *Memorial,* p. 28, gives his account of the contentious meeting of that date aboard the *Bonhomme Richard;* among other things Landais refused to accompany Jones's ship up the Limerick (Shannon) River and denied Jones's claim that BF had empowered him to take command of the *Alliance.*

OCTOBER 9, 1779

Excellency To order a Court of enquiry into the matter as Soon as possible.

His Excellency Dr. Franklin

Addressed: To / His Excellency Dr. Franklin / Minister plenipotentiary to the / United States of America / a Passy / near Paris

Notation: P. Landais. Oct 9. 1779

From Jean Meÿer

LS: American Philosophical Society

Monsieur   Dunkerque Ce 9. 8bre. 1779.

L'accueil gracieux que vous me fites, quand J'eus l'honneur de vous être presenté par Monsieur Le Professeur de Báer,[6] les offres généreuses que vous ÿ ajoutates de vôtre Crédit et de vôtre pouvoir dans les occasions où je pourrois en avoir besoin, m'enhardissent aujourd'hui d'avoir recours à vous, Monsieur, afin qu'il vous plaise en faire usage à mon egard dans les circonstances présentes. L'exposé suivant vous mettra à même de Juger si Je puis me flatter de meriter cette faveur:

En partant de La Bretagne Je laissois à Mons. Rion[7] de Brest ma procuration pour toucher la part qui me revenoit des Prises faites par la Fregate Ragnzer commandée par Le Sr. Jones, à bord de laquelle J'avois eté en qualité de Volontaire d'honneur. Je ecrivis en Juillet dernier a Mr. Rion ainsi qu'au Sieur Scheveighauson de Nantes pour m'Informer où en etoient mes affaires. Ces Messieurs me repondirent qu'ils avoient effectivement touché les fonds de la Vente des Prises faites par la ditte Frégate Ragnzer mais que n'etant pas chargés de rendre Compte à chacun des Captants Ils ne pouvoient le faire a mon egard sans y être autorisés par un ordre emané de vous, Monsieur. J'ose donc esperer, d'après les offres gracieux dont vous avez daigné m'honnorer, que non seulement vous voudrez bien m'accorder cet ordre, mais encore vous ressouvenir de la promesse que vous me fites d'ecrire au Congrès pour qu'il nous fit quelque gratifications.

6. In July, 1778; see XXVII, 84–5, where de Baër and Meÿer are both identified.

7. Pierre Rïou: XXVI, 419n.

508

Un François s'expliqueroit plus elégament que moi dans sa langue pour vous demander cette grace, mais Je doute, Monsieur qu'il en aye plus de reconnoissance qu'un suedois tel que Je Suis, et dont le souvenir du service que vous voudrez bien me rendre ne s'effaçera Jamais de mon Coeur. En attendant J'ai l'honneur de vous assurer qu'on ne sçauroit ajouter au profond respect, et à la parfaite vénération avec lesquels Je ferai gloire de me dire à Jamais Monsieur Vôtre très humble & très obeïssant Serviteur   J. Meÿer

officier au service de sa
Majesté Le Roÿ de suëde

Si vous daignez, Monsieur, m'honorer d'une reponse, vous m'obligerez de me l'addresser, chez Monsr. Thevenet le Je. Rûë du Moulin à Dunkerque.

Endorsed: answer'd Oct. 20.

Notation: J Meyer Nov 9. 79

To Francis Coffyn

Copy: Library of Congress

Sir   Passy, Oct. 10. 1779.

I have no objection to the taking the Parole of the Captains or Officers on Condition of the Security you mention.[8] But as the Prisoners taken by arm'd Vessels under our Colours are by giving me a means of exchanging so many of our Country men some satisfaction to me for the Trouble these Vessels occasion me in examining all the *Proces Verbaux,* making out the Judgment, answering Letters, and the Enormous Expense of Postage those Pacquets of Proces occasion to the States, it Seems just that the forfeiture in case of Breach of Parole should be made payable to me for the use of the united states, and if you are of the Same opinion, I wish the Bond or security may be so drawn.

As Soon as the Papers can be prepared which an Extraordinery Quantity of other Business has hitherto delayed, I Shall Send you what are necessary for the Princess.— It gave me

8. In Coffyn's of Oct. 3, above.

great Satisfaction to read the whole account of the Cruise of the Prince. I wish it had been more profitable to all concerned. It has certainly done greater Prejudice to the Enemy than could have been expected from so Small a force.

You will have heard of Comme. Jones's safe arrival in the Texel, after one of the most obstinate and bloody Conflicts that has happened this War. He has brought in the Ships of war Prises, and about 400. Prisoners.

I have the honour to be with much Esteem Sir your most obedient and most humble servant   BF.

M. Coffin.

To James Turing and Son   Copy: Library of Congress

Gentlemen,   Passy, Oct. 10. 1779.

I received the Letter you did me the honour of writing to me the 2. Instant, relating to the Capture of your Vessel by the General Mifflin, Capt. Babcock. I shall transmit by the first good Opportunity your Letter with the Papers it enclosed to the Government of the Massachusetts Bay, which is the State where the Owners of that Privateer reside, and where they have doubtless given bond with sureties as the Laws require, to make good all Damages occasioned by illegal Captures. The intention of the United States being to give no just Cause of Offence to neutral or friendly Nations, nor permit any which they can prevent or remedy. But as our our Dispatches in this time of War, may be intercepted or lost, and all Business is help'd by having an Agent on the Spot to forward it, I Suppose you will empower some person there to act for you, and send him Copies authenticated of all the Papers that Justify your Claim by several different Conveyances.— If you have no Correspondent in Boston, I would name to you Mr. Jonathan Williams Merchant there, who has the Character of an upright Man active and correct in Business.—[9] I have the honour to be Gentlemen &c.

Messrs. James Turing and son, Mershts. Middlebourg, holland.

9. On Oct. 28 the firm thanked BF and informed him they had invested Jonathan Williams, Sr., with full powers to obtain restitution of their prop-

From Stephen Sayre[1]

ALS: American Philosophical Society

Sir   Valenciens 10th octor. 1779[2]

From what I heard in Paris the day I came away, there seem'd a probability that the Captain who commands the Alliance Frigate would be dismiss'd. If that Event should take place, I should think myself happy to succeed him in the command of her.

I hope your Excellency can have no sort of apprehensions that I should in any shape, or under any circumstances, disgrace the American Flagg.

I am with great respect, your Excelcys. most obedt. & respectful Servt.   STEPHEN SAYRE

Notation: Sayre Mr. Stephen 10 Oct. 1779.—

From Benjamin Vaughan

ALS: American Philosophical Society

My dearest sir,   Oct. 10h., 1779.

Mr Thos. Oliver of Lowlayton, Mr Richd. Oliver's Cousin & the partner of Mr Lovel, thinks it adviseable to send the inclosed;[3] & as he seemed anxious about it, I did not prevent his satisfying his own mind & being also satisfied about *my* good wishes to the Alderman.

Being told that the Grenada people who went on Sunday, would take no letters I deferred preparing a copy of my analysis of Mr Crawford's book, and am caught unawares by this opportunity. You may perhaps have the book itself, but not

---

erty. They asked BF to forward letters to him and added that they had received a circular letter from Bache & Shee and would be happy to be of service to them. APS.

1. Sayre had last written BF from Amsterdam in June: XXIX, 653–5. He had since visited Passy where he had requested a letter of marque from BF for a warship he had proposed building (XXIX, 181–3, 639–40): BF to Dumas, Nov. 8, 1779 (Library of Congress).

2. Valenciennes is en route to Amsterdam; Sayre next wrote BF on Nov. 21 from there (APS).

3. Probably Thomas Oliver's letter of Oct. 8, above.

the other pacquet, at least without Mr Luard delays his departure.—⁴ By this time you will have received your own papers,
all but a material sentence or two in the Addenda & Corrigenda, and a corrected plate of Cotopaxi, taken from Bouguer,
who differs somewhat from Ulloa I find, but still more from
the English translator of Ulloa who makes sad *confusion* &
mistake, such as would have misled men more accurate than
myself.—⁵ But I have a singular confirmation in the interim
from Bouguer.

I am, as ever, my dearest sir, yours most devotedly &
gratefully   BV.

Nothing worth telling occurs to me at present.

Notation: B Vaughn Oct 10. 79

4. Luard carried a letter of introduction from Digges and a packet of
Vaughan's (see their letters to BF, both of Oct. 8). His departure was delayed at least until the 12th, on which day Samuel Vaughan & Son (Benjamin's father and probably his brother John: XXII, 71n) wrote, introducing
Luard as a "Gentleman whom we have long known." APS. See also Digges
to BF, Oct. 12 and 30, below.

5. Vaughan used an extensive bibliography for his commentary on BF's
paper on the aurora borealis (*Political, Miscellaneous and Philosophical Pieces,*
pp. 510–30.) To establish the fact that clouds have been observed well
above the congelation point on the tallest mountains, he drew on the works
of Pierre Bouguer (1698–1758) and Antonio de Ulloa (1716–95). The plate
he mentions (facing p. 522) is a reproduction of Bouguer's view in *La Figure
de la terre* . . . (Paris, 1749), facing p. cx, of the Peruvian volcano Cotopaxi
and its adjacent mountains, to which he added a cloud and a grid showing
height in both English and French measurements. To corroborate Bouguer's observations, he referred the reader (on p. 522n) to the partially
"misinterpreted" translation of Ulloa's *Relacion historica del viage a la América
Meridional* . . . (5 vols., Madrid, 1748), published in London as *A Voyage to
South America* . . . (2 vols., 1758).

To Wheeler Coit[6]

Copy: Library of Congress

Sir   Passy, Oct. 11. 1779.

I received yours dated april 15.[7] directed to the Commissioners and enclosing two Bils of Exchange N. 161 for 60. and N. 494 for 36 Dollars, being both Third Bills. The last viz, that for 36. Dollars will be paid but it ought to be endors'd Elisabeth Brown. The other for 60. Dollars has been paid; those mentioned in your Postcript as Sent by Messrs. Sterry and Murry I can Say nothing to, as you have not given their Numbers and Particular Values but only a general Amount of 540 Dollars. Please to inform me what is to be done with your 36. Dollars. I am, Sir, Your most obedient and most humble servt.

M. Wheeler Coit Mercht. Boston

To ———— Des Touches[8]

Copy: Library of Congress

Sir   Passy Oct. 11. 1779.

I duly received the Letter you did me the honour of writing to me the 4th. Instant,[9] together with the *Procedure d'Instruction* of the Ransom of the Sloop Limont, made by the American Privater the Black Prince, Capt. Stephen Merchant,[1] and am

---

6. Undoubtedly the Wheeler Coit (1739–96) of Preston, Conn., who handled several kinds of monetary transactions for individuals during this period: F.W. Chapman, comp., *The Coit Family* ... (Hartford, 1874), pp. 64–5; Worthington C. Ford, ed., *Commerce of Rhode Island 1726–1800*, vol. 2, *1775–1800* (Mass. Hist. Soc. *Collections,* LXX [1915]), 89–90.

7. Missing.

8. Or Destouches, as this chief clerk spells himself in a June 10, 1780, letter (University of Pa. Library). He is not to be confused with Le Roy's cousin Jean-Baptiste Destouches, a *conseiller* of the Dunkirk Admiralty and outfitter of privateers with whom BF later would have extensive contact.

9. Not located.

1. The *Limont* was captured on Sept. 10; paroles were accepted from five of her crewmen, while a sixth was taken hostage: Clark, *Ben Franklin's Privateers,* p. 85.

oblig'd to you for the care you took in sending the Same. With much Regard. I have the honour to be. Sir &c.

Mr. Des Touches Greffier en chef de l'amirauté De Dunkerque.

To Elizabeth Partridge

AL (draft): University of Pennsylvania Library

Passy, Oct. 11. 1779.

Your kind Letter,[2] my dear Friend, was long in coming; but it gave me the Pleasure of knowing that you had been well in October & January last. The Difficulty, Delay & Interruption of Correspondence with those I love, is one of the great Inconveniencies I find in living so far from home: but we must bear these & more, with Patience, if we can; if not, we must bear them as I do with Impatience.

You mention the Kindness of the French Ladies to me. I must explain that matter. This is the civilest Nation upon Earth. Your first Acquaintances endeavour to find out what you like, and they tell others. If 'tis understood that you like Mutton, dine where you will you find Mutton. Somebody, it seems, gave it out that I lov'd Ladies; and then every body presented me their Ladies (or the Ladies presented themselves) to be *embrac'd*, that is to have their Necks kiss'd. For as to kissing of Lips or Cheeks it is not the Mode here; the first is reckon'd rude, & the other may rub off the Paint. The French Ladies have however 1000 other ways of rendering themselves agreable; by their various Attentions and Civilities, & their sensible Conversation. 'Tis a delightful People to live with.

I thank you for the Boston Newspapers, tho' I see nothing so clearly in them as that your Printers do indeed want new Letters. They perfectly blind me in endeavouring to read them. If you should ever have any Secrets that you wish to be well kept, get them printed in those Papers. [*Deleted:* Here I wish my Enemies may vent all their Malice, in Libels and (*one*

2. Oct. 24, 1778, with a postscript of Jan. 2, 1779: XXVII, 620–2.

word illegible).] You enquire if Printers Types may be had here? Of all Sorts, very good, cheaper than in England, and of harder Metal.— I will see any Orders executed in that way that any of your Friends may think fit to send. They will doubtless send Money with their Orders. Very good Printing Ink is likewise to be had here.

I cannot by this Opportunity send the Miniature you desire; but I send you a little Head in China, more like, perhaps than the Painting would be. It may be set in a Locket, if you like it, cover'd with Glass, and may serve for the present. When Peace comes we may afford to be more extravagant. I send with it a Couple of Fatherly Kisses for you & your amiable Daughter; the whole wrapt up together in Cotton to be kept warm. Present my respectful Compliments to Mr Partridge. Adieu, my dear Child, & believe me ever Your affectionate

PAPAH

Mrs. Partridge

From Sir Charles William Blunt

ALS: American Philosophical Society

Dear Sir   11 Octr. 1779—

A very particular & worthy friend of mine Mr Luard having large concerns in the Island of Grenada, his private affairs & those of His family are deeply involved in the late capture of that Island. And its being judged advisable that he should visit Paris I thought it possible I might render my friend an essential service by a letter of recommendation to you. Trusting I shall not be thought to presume too much on old acquaintance & that degree of estimation you were always pleased to flatter me with, I beg leave in the warmest manner to bespeak in his favour your advice and such services as may be consistently in your power to afford him. If it shall please the Almighty that we live to see a cessation of the present calamities it will be no small happiness to me personally to thank you for your attention to this request. It will give you pleasure to be informed if you do not already know it, That we have at last brought the poor little Widows affairs to a happy conclusion. The balance of Interest is paid her & Bonds given for the principal at installments.[3]

I am Dear Sir Yr. most obedient humble Servt.

CHAS: WM: BLUNT

Notation: Chas. Blunt Oct 11. 79

From Tristram Dalton ALS: American Philosophical Society

Sir   Newburyport October 11th. 1779

Although triplicates of the enclosed have been forwarded to France,[4] yet, dubious if either Set have reached your Hands, I beg Leave, by so good an Opportunity as the French Frigate,[5] to trouble you with opening these—and, if nothing respecting the withinmentioned Loss is already done, to renew my Request in Behalf of the Owners—again asking your Excuse for this Interruption I remain with the utmost Deference and Respect, Sir Your most huml Servant   TRISTRAM DALTON

Honbe. Benjamin Franklin Esqre

Addressed: Honble. Benjamin Franklin Esqe / Minister Plenipotentiary of / the United States of North America / At / Versailles

Endorsed: Papers relating to the Fairplay Capt. Giddins Tristram Dalton Esq

From Isaac-Jean-Georges-Jonas Grand

ALS: American Philosophical Society

Monsieur   Amsterdam le 11 Octe. 1779

Jay l'honneur de vous Remetre cy Joint une Lettre qui m'a eté fort Recommandée pour Vous, quoiqu'a l'adresse de mon

3. Mary Hewson's inheritance from her aunt, Mrs. Tickell, had been in the process of settlement since 1775; see in particular XXII, 301n, XXVI, 360n.

4. Documents relating to the loss of this wealthy Newburyport merchant's brigantine, the *Fair Play,* Capt. Andrew Giddings, which had been mistakenly sunk by a French shore battery on Guadeloupe: XXIX, 486n.

5. The *Sensible,* which was returning JA to Europe; see Huntington's Oct. 16 letter; Butterfield, *John Adams Diary,* IV, 173–6.

frere;[6] elle m'a eté Remise ce matin; J'y en ajoute une autre que Jay Receu d'un Américain avec deux Paquets qui ne sont pas prêssés & qu'il ma dit de Vous envoyer par occasion;[7] J'espêre d'en etre le Porteur. Je Vous ai envoyé par Rouën, une boete du meilleur Kinkina[8] choisy, qui soit entré à Amsterdam dépuis 100 ans, Je souhaite que Vous n'en ayés pas besoin; ou qu'il serve à conserver Votre Santé aussi longtemps que mes Voeux le désirent.

Capn. Jones fait icy la plus grande Sensation, il ne m'a point fait lhonneur de me Venir Voir, M De Neufville s'en est emparé & le montre, comme une curiosité.

Jay l'honneur d'etre Tres Respectueusement Monsieur Votre tres humble & Tres obeissant Serviteur   GRAND

Notation: Grand. Amsterdam 11. 8bre. 1779.

From David Hartley: Two Letters

(I) ALS and copy:[9] American Philosophical Society; (II) ALS: American Philosophical Society; transcript: Library of Congress

I.

Dear Sir   Oct 11 1779

I have not yet got an answer from government relative to the proposition of Exchanging upon contract agrements in writing. I have renewed my application for an answer, &

6. Ferdinand Grand.

7. Gabriel Manigault of S.C. carried two paper parcels containing sections of Vaughan's edition of BF's writings for Grand to forward to BF: Digges to BF, Sept. 20, above, and Oct. 30, below, and Nov. 15 (APS).

8. The quinine was forwarded to BF on Oct. 15 by Trusson, receiver general for tobacco at Rouen (*Almanach royal* for 1779, p. 481 *bis*). He sent a case of twelve packets which had come to him from Horneca, Fizeaux & Cie. (in which Grand was a partner: XXVIII, 271n, 594) and for which he reimbursed them 2 *l.t.* 12 *s.* APS. BF's accounts record on Oct. 17 a payment of 3 *l.t.* 12 *s.* for transporting the bark from Rouen to Paris and 1 *l.t.* 16 *s.* for the porter who brought it from the *Grand Cerf:* Account XXIII (XXIX, 3).

BF thanked Trusson on Oct. 19, saying that he had received his letter and, separately, the "Box of Bark." Library of Congress.

9. The copy is a part of his second letter of Oct. 26, below.

therefore hope to have it soon.[1] In the mean, I wish to forward the Continuation of the Cartel by exchanges at Morlaix, as I mentioned to you in my last. If you will send me a passport for the Cartel ship to Morlaix, & inform me of the number of prisoners ready for exchange there, I will immediately apply to the board of Sick and Hurt to dispatch another Cargo of prisoners from England for the Exchange. Mr. Bell the first Commissioner told me the other day, that when they were informed of place & numbers, that they shd be ready to proceed with the Exchange. As to the other proposition of exchanging by written agreement, I presume that that must be referred to the first Ld of the Admiralty and to the Secretary of State.[2] The description of the person in whose favour I applied to you in my last letter is as follows—(Mr John Stephenson Master & owner of the Ship Sally a younger brother of the Trinity house & a freeman of Hull was taken on the 1st of July by a Lugger rigged privateer of Bretange named the Hawke Capt. Heden d'Polly of 6 one pounders 8 swivels and 38 men who carried him into Brest & he is now confined at Velse in Bretagne.) This is the description which has been transmitted to me.[3] If you cd facilitate his release I shd be much obliged to you as it wd be very agreeable to several of my friends at Hull.— Your affecte   DH

To Dr Franklin

II.

My Dear friend   October 11 1779

I send you a copy of a letter wch I writ to you on the 29th of June last.[4] I presume that you have received the original,

1. For the exchange of prisoners discharged at sea by written certificate see Hartley's of Sept. 18 and BF's of Oct. 8.

2. John Montagu, Earl of Sandwich, and Lord George Germain.

3. By the officers of the Hull Trinity House, who had sent the description to Hartley on Sept. 24. HTH Outletters, 1777–86. Hartley must have passed it on to Digges, who communicated it to BF in his letter of Oct. 12, below. On Nov. 9 BF informed Hartley that he expected to send Stephenson within a few days.

The capture by a French privateer of the *Sally* (en route to Hull) was reported in the July 27 issue of the *Courier de l'Europe* (VI [1779], p. 63).

4. XXIX, 767–70.

but not being quite sure of this I take another chance by sending you a copy. The Subject being peace, wch I know to be equally near to your heart as it is to mine, I am willing that you & I shd keep our reckoning together, that we may now & then take an observation, of the latitude & longitude of the Politicks of nations, thereby keeping a constant watch for any opportunity of approximating to Peace. I speak to you as to a Philosopher and a Philanthropist; for the principles of Philanthropy are the only true principles to steer by. Politicians may be wise men in their generation, but the Philanthropists will consider the policies of States & Statesmen, as the subordinate instruments of attaining the ends of general Philanthropy. Whether the State of things may appear promising or otherwise, in any particular period, or point of view, yet the final object is constantly the same; The labour is but little to keep a constant & attentive watch, and the Pearl is of great price. I think that a little of the Gothic rage for war is worn off among the Nations of Europe, & therefore I live in some degree of hope that opportunities may occur of forwarding the blessed work of Peace. At all events be assured of this on my part, that if any such opportunity shd occur within the circumscribed sphere of my abilities to forward it, that I shall not be found asleep.

The practicability of striking out acceptable terms of peace to all parties, does certainly from time to time lye at the Mercy of Events, therefore no man can answer for tomorrow, but at this day & hour I think the principles of the enclosed letter (wch was originally writ on the 29th of June last) do still remain in force, upon every ground of humanity reason & justice, therefore if I were to write a volume I cd add nothing new. You will ever find me the sincere and strenuous advocate for peace and ever Most affectionately yours   GB

To Dr. Franklin

From John Paul Jones

ALS: American Philosophical Society; copy: Library of Congress

Amsterdam Octr. 11th. 1779.

I had the honor to write your Excellency a line from the Hague on the 8th.— His Excellency the French Ambassador and the Agent have no doubt marked the situation of Affairs with respect to the Squadron, as concerned with this Government and with the Enemy.— I am doing every thing in my Power towards fulfiling the Advice which I have received from His Excellency, and as I am informed that Captain Cunningham is threatned with Unfair play by the British Government—I am determined to keep in my hands the Captain of the Serapis as an Hostage for Cunninghams release as a prisoner of War.— With respect to the other prisoners now in my hands, If the English Ambassador Sir J.Y. will give us Security *in his public Character* that an Equal number and denomination of Americans shall be Sent immediatly to France, I believe it will be good Policy to Let them at liberty here; and I shall endeavour indirectly to inform myself immediatly how that matter can be managed.—⁵ Landais is come up here and purposes after gadding about in this City to figure away at the Hague:— He continues to Affect an entire Independence of my Controul—And has given in here an Extraordinary demand for Supplies of every kind.— This famous demand however I have ventured to disaprove and to reduce to I believe a Tenth part of its first extent.— I hope to account to your Satisfaction for my reasons—among which is his having been so plentifully and so lately furnished.— I wish heartily that poor Cunningham (whom I am taught to regard as a Continental Officer) were exchanged; as with his assistance I could form a Court Martial, which I beleive you will see Unavoidable.— I go down to the Texel to Night and will from thence forward the Return of Killed & Wounded with the Prisoners.— I think the Prisoners will not fall much Short of

5. Meanwhile, Yorke was pressuring the Dutch government to arrest Jones and his squadron as pirates: *Gaz. de Leyde,* Oct. 15, 1779 (no. LXXXIII); Daniel A. Miller, *Sir Joseph Yorke and Anglo-Dutch Relations 1774–1780* (The Hague and Paris, 1970), pp. 78–83.

400—[6] And I hope my loss in Killed and Wounded will be less than I at first imagined.— I believe also that the Enemies loss will considerably exceed ours.

I am ever with Sentiments of the heighest Esteem and Respect Your Excellencies very Obliged & faithful Sert.

JNO P JONES

His Excellency Benjamin Franklin Esqr.

Notation: Capt: Jones Oct 11. 1779

From the Marquis de Lafayette

AL: American Philosophical Society

Dear Sir   havre 11th October 1779
The Matter I am going to write upon is of A delicate Nature, and Nothing But My Love for America, the sense I have of theyr interests, and the entire, unbounded Confidence, I trust on your friendship and secrecy could engage me to use with you on this subject all possible freedom.

From private intelligences, I am to suppose that a Negotiation has been propos'd, so far as to point out a place for a meeting of Plenipotentiary Ministers—[7] American Independency or a truce with the States are two points Which haughty Britain will Reluctantly Agree to, which France shall Never Recede from— But England will a least be oblig'd to Accept a Mediation, and I believe it is of an high Moment for America to know the Negotiations from theyr very Beggining.

If ever a Congress is fix'd upon it will be Compos'd of Mediator Ministers, and Envoys from the three Belligerant Courts— The Interests of the United States will be Chiefly in the hands of the french Minister or Ministers, if Many are sent.

Two Great inconveniences are to be fear'd on the Occasion— 1st. As our politicians Are throughly Acquainted with European and particularly with German Affairs, So they are totally Strangers to Commercial, Naval, Republican inter-

---

6. On Nov. 4 Jones reported to Dumas that the squadron had 504 prisoners: Bradford, *Jones Papers,* reel 4, no. 853.

7. Perhaps the same rumor recounted by Digges on Sept. 20. It was without foundation.

ests—how far Goes theyr ignorance on that head, (without Mentioning theyr Not knowing the Country where lies the present dispute) is obvious to Any one who has a Conversation with some of the Most Reputed Among them.

2dly As in such a Negotiation, Everyone Gives up some pretentions to be at lenght Conciliated on A Mutual scheme, our Gentlemen will be Apt to Make sacrifices which they Can't know the valüe of, and which England will seize with its usual skill on such Matters.

However Bound I am By what I have done and By what I intend to Do, to Military Profession and Glory, however far I am from desiring an Admittance into the Diplomatic Corps, I'll be very happy to serve My Country and America on such an Important occasion.[8]

Let absurd Reasonings say what they will, I think My Country's well fare is entirely United with the very interests of America—on the other hand, the love I Bear to the United states of which I May Consider Myself as a Citizen, has long Ago settled My heart on the happy scheme of American independency— Nay from the Part I have Acted Before all europe, and the little influence I May have had in My own Country, pride alone should engage me in the same interests for which love has long ago Requir'd all My Exertions. As from our European Prejudices, Birth is a thing Much thought of on such occasions, I Am the only one of My Rank (tho I Can't help laughing in Mentionning these Chance-Ranks Before an American Citizen) who is Acquainted With American Affairs.

In case A Negotiation is upon the Carpet, and You think My services May be Useful in that Capacity You Could *As from Yourself* tell Mr de Vergennes that You think it Consistent with the interests of the United states, that I Be or the Ambassador or One of them if Many are sent, who will be Nam'd for the Meeting.

M. de vergennes will I dare say be Glad to be earnestly induc'd By the American Minister to Do a thing which from

8. This was not Lafayette's first bid for a diplomatic mission. Two months prior to the present letter he had volunteered to carry a truce or peace treaty to America on behalf of Vergennes: Idzerda, *Lafayette Papers*, II, 300–2.

Affection and Esteem for me he would like very well, But which on Account of his diplomatic Band he Could not do from himself.

Don't answer my letter By the post and indeed it Needs no answer at all— You know My offer My zeal, My Means of serving America, and you will do what you think Consistent with the interest of *America,* and your friendship for me— I Beg the strictest secrecy, and expect you will be so kind as to Burn immediately this Confidential letter.[9]

Notation: La Fayette 11 Oct 79

From Jean de Neufville & fils

ALS: American Philosophical Society

High Honourable Sir!   Amsterdam the 11 October 1779.

As it hath been the favoúr of yoúr Excellency that we have found our Selfs honourd with the providing of the Squadron of Comandore J P. Jones Esqr. we thought it oúr duty again to assure yoúr Excellency that we will pay the utmost attention to this expedition; and obey his orders in every respect.

We were informed that Sr. Joseph York made private Aplications through Mrs Pey Rich and Wilkinsons[1] to the Admirallty, to have the wounded prisoners landed and taken care off, with all probability if once from board to claim them as British subjects;[2] we informd these above dearctly, Mr. Dúmas; Sr. Joseph York hath openly claimd the Prices; butt he could not do less, no attention we think will be pay'd there to.

It should be off importance even for the Vessells of this

9. This final paragraph was written in the margin.

1. Henri Pye Rich was the brother-in-law of the Dutch banker Louis Greffulhe; his banking firm of Pye Rich & Wilkinson was the London correspondent of the Dutch and Danish East India Companies: Lüthy, *Banque protestante,* II, 522–3, 601.

2. In mid-October the Dutch government finally agreed to Yorke's demand and authorized the wounded prisoners to be put ashore: Wharton, *Diplomatic Correspondence,* III, 370–2. The weather, however, was too stormy to permit the transfer: Daniel A. Miller, *Sir Joseph Yorke and Anglo-Dutch Relations 1774–1780* (The Hague and Paris, 1970), p. 81.

squadron if the prisoners could be given upp & in Exchange of as many Americans under Secúrity; Mr. Jones himself hath talk'd aboutt it;[3] we have mentiond it already to Mr. Dumas; butt do not think Sr. Joseph York could Consent to it withoút having positif orders from his Coúrt; and there perhaps this matter could only be brought aboút by the intercession of Yoúr Excellency; we hope Our Zeal for promoting every way the intrest of a caúse we are so glorioúsly concernd in, will apologize for making any mention there of.

We have the honoúr to be with all respectfull Regard High Honourable Sir Yoúr Excellencys most Devoted, obedient and most humble Servants.   JOHN DE NEUFVILLE & SON

[*In John Paul Jones's hand:*] In consequence of a Visit which the Admiralty are about to pay to the Texel I have been advised to remain here.—[4] I hope no time will thereby be lost as I have sent the necessary written directions to M. de Cottineau the Senior Officer. I am Your Excellencies most humble Servt

JNO P JONES

Notation: Neufville & fils Oct 11. 79

From Peter Collas[5]   ALS: American Philosophical Society

Honored Sir   Boston October 12th. 1779

   This goes per favr. of Monssr. De Changne[6] Captn. of the Sensible (French fregate) with a Small Casse Containing 24 Cake of Crown Soap that your worthy Sister made at Governor Green about Six weeks ago when I was present with Mrs. Collas.[7] Mrs. Mecom Desired me to Acquint you the Soap was not as white as she could wish, but as she has wrote you Since

---

   3. On the present date, above, Jones proposed the idea of an exchange to BF.

   4. Undoubtedly by La Vauguyon, who was anxious to have the squadron appear French; see our annotation of Jones to BF, Oct. 8.

   5. As far as we know, this is Collas' last letter to BF; for his continuing misadventures see Van Doren, *Franklin-Mecom,* pp. 206–7, 211, 223, 230, 285, 304.

   6. Bidé de Chavagnes: Butterfield, *John Adams Diary,* II, 379n.

   7. As was reported by Catharine Greene, above, Sept. 19.

concerning the same[8] I will Drop the Subject. Wilst I was at Greewich[9] we talkd about undertaking the bussness of Soap Making but we found that it would be Attended with a great Expence & uncertainty in getting the Meterials, & the Rising & falling of Our Currency would be an object much Against it. I Humbly thank you for your Kindness in wrighting Mr. Willms. to Suply Mrs. Mecom with mony Sufficent to undertake that bussnes,[1] I propose to lern of her the Art & follow the bussness when there is a better prospect & steadyness in the people & the Currency brought to its proper Value. I prepose Sailing this Day, Commander of a letter mart[2] that mounts ten Guns on a Short Cruse & then to N. Carolina for a Cargo for the Westindies.

I am Sorry to inform you that Our Markett here is Scarcly Sufficent to Suply three Quarters of the inhabitants Owing to a Regulated prise fix on Every Article, both Town & Country trays who'l have most of that Commodity, called paper Mony, which they have so much Despised & do Despise Still. I heard yesterday from Mrs. Mecom she was well & at Governor Green, Mrs. Collas Join me in love & Duty to your Subscribing As Ever your Most Humble & Obedient & Affectionat Nephew   PETER COLLAS

Addressed: Monssr. / Monssr. Franklin / Ministre Plenipotentere des Etats / Unies de la Merique / A Passy

From Thomas Digges   ALS: Historical Society of Pennsylvania

Dr Sir   Octo 12. 79
I wrote you by the same conveyance with this on the 8th. Int., and the detention the bearer has met with gives me an opportunity to forward a few more news papers; as well as to

8. Above, Sept. 12.
9. William and Catharine Greene lived near the village of East Greenwich, R.I.: William Greene Roelker, ed., *Benjamin Franklin and Catharine Ray Greene: Their Correspondence, 1755–1790* (Philadelphia, 1949), p. 30.
1. Apparently in one of the now-missing letters Williams answered on July 29 and Aug. 8, above.
2. The brigantine *Nancy:* Allen, *Mass. Privateers,* p. 226.

inform you that I have got things in such a way with Capn. C——m as to render his situation much more comfortable and easy to himself. I wish I had it in my power to say as much for His 193 Companions, who are become more than usually uneasy at their scanty allowance (wch from having a more griping Agent than that at Portso)³ has been rather hard on them lately. The detention of the Cartel too makes them despond and I fear it is but too true if Capn C——m had not been among them several would have been prevaild upon to Enter on bod. the Ships of their Enemy. Leiut. Wm. Picket & Adams whom I lately mentiond to you as deserving some little aid,⁴ drew up a petition in the name of the whole, to you, & sent it me for forwardance. It is meerly a prayer for some little pecuniary aid, & it is not necessary to forward it. Adams and Picket were both taken in men of war belonging to the United States.

Your friend Mr. B——⁵ was with me since I wrote you last. He wishes you much good &c. &c. & is looking out for an answer to His letter wherein He mentions a proposition to you about some blank copper meddals.

I have also a strong solicitation from our friend D—— H—— to describe to You the situation of a man whom He has, in a letter to You lately, solicited your aid to get releasd a man whom He is interested in the welfare of.— Mr John Stephenson a Younger Bror. of the Trinity House at Hull, a Freeman of Hull, and master of the Brig Sally; He was taken on the 1st. July 1779 by a luggar riggd Privateer of Bretagne named the Hawke Capn. Heden LePolly of six one pounders, Eight Swivels & 38 Men, and He was carryd into Brest, and now confined at Velse in Bretagne. It will answer a very good

3. William Cowdray, the keeper of Mill Prison, was notorious for drunken cruelty, lining his pockets with prisoners' funds, and providing inadequate rations: Kaminkow, *Mariners,* pp. xii-xiii.

4. He wrote about Adams on Oct. 8, above. William Pickett of Marblehead, Mass., was taken prisoner aboard the *Fancy* and committed to Mill Prison on Aug. 7, 1777. He eventually escaped. Kaminkow, *Mariners,* p. 151.

5. Edward Bridgen.

purpose to our friend if you can help towards the getting this man releasd.

There is no news yet from Ama— Adml Byron is arrivd in a single ship & *report* says that DEstaing has left his station for St Domingo from whence He is to go to America— Much fears about Jamaica & Adml. Byron is quite close mouthd about the disagreeable state of affairs in the West Indies.[6]

The Quebec Frigate 32 guns Capt. Fermor is blown up & only 17 men of the Crew savd it happend in an Engagement with a french frigate in the Channel.[7] I am with the highest esteem Dr Sir Yr obligd & ob Ser   T D

Addressed: A Monsieur / Monsieur B. Franklin / Passy

From Dumas

ALS: American Philosophical Society;
AL (draft): Algemeen Rijksarchief

Honoured & dear Sir   The Hague 12th. Oct. 1779.

The included paper will show your Excy. & Mr. De Cht. how affairs stand here concerning the Squadron.[8]

They will go out again, as soon as they shall be refitted, with which they go on at a great rate. It would not be prudent to write down here the place where they will be bound to.[9] You will hear of it in time. The Captain of the Alliance, I fear,

---

6. Byron handed over his command to Adm. Hyde Parker on Aug. 23: W.M. James, *The British Navy in Adversity: a Study of the War of American Independence* (London, 1926), p. 154. He landed in Portsmouth aboard the *Maidstone* on Oct. 10, and arrived in London that evening: *The General Advertiser, and Morning Intelligencer,* Oct. 12, 1779.

7. Capt. George Farmer (1732–79) met the *Surveillante,* 26, off Ushant on Oct. 6, and after a three-hour battle the *Quebec* caught fire. To recognize his gallant conduct the Board of Admiralty provided a pension for his family and requested that a baronetcy be conferred upon his eldest son. *DNB.*

8. Dumas enclosed extracts of his Oct. 9 and 10 letters to Jones (Bradford, *Jones Papers,* reel 4, nos. 763, 766), which relayed advice for Jones to sail as soon as possible and warned him not to land his wounded prisoners unless an exchange or some other security was arranged.

9. Dunkirk, where La Vauguyon wished the squadron to sail as soon as it was ready: La Vauguyon to Sartine, Oct. 8 (AAE).

is not a good man, & has done much mischief, & not well behaved.

You will receive a Letter from Commodore Jones in the paquet of the Gd. Facteur, dispatched the 8th Oct.[1]

The appearance of the Commodore at Amsterdam has been exceedingly agreeable to the people of that City. We have almost been smothered at the Exchange & in the Streets, by an innumerable multitude, overjoy'd & mad to See the vanquisher of the English. They applauded him, & bowed down to his feets, ready to kiss them.[2]

I am ever with great respect, Honoured & dear Sir yr. most obedient & humble servant   DUMAS

I hope my last Letters from the Helder are come safe to yr. hands. Sir Joseph's memorial delivered to their H.M., if I can get to day a copy of it, will be join'd here. This Memorial is to claim the Serapis & the Scarborough as being no legal prizes; being taken by rebels, & by a Subject of the English King.[3]

His Ency. B. Franklin

Addressed: His Excellency / B. Franklin, Esqr., Min. Plenipy. / of the United States, &c. / *Passy.*/.

Notation: Dumas Octr. 12. 1779

From James Lovell[4]

LS: Massachusetts Historical Society; copy and transcript: National Archives

Oct 12–79

To Doctor Franklin

Mr. Gerard having been particularly applied to relative to the Affairs of M. Du Coudray by the Heirs has the original Certif-

1. Either Jones's of the 8th or of the 3rd.

2. Jones received an ovation at the theater; while returning home from the stock exchange he was followed by a cheering crowd: Morison, *Jones,* pp. 254–6.

3. Yorke's memoir of Oct. 8 to the States General ("H. M." for "High Mightinesses") called Jones a rebel and a pirate: *Gaz. de Leyde,* issue of Oct. 15 (no. LXXXIII).

4. Writing no doubt on behalf of the committee for foreign affairs.

icate of which this is the Triple; but Doctr. Franklin will mark out for himself a Line of Conduct referring properly to the Civility due to Mr. Gerard and the Interest of Mr. Du Coudray's Heirs.[5]   JAMES LOVELL

Addressed: Mr. Gerard[6]

Endorsed: relating to M. de Coudray

From Margaret E. Stevens[7]

ALS: American Philosophical Society

New Norfolk Street Grosvenor Square
Dear Sir/   October 12th 1779
I am sensible the favor I am about to ask of you require many apoligizes, & yet when I consider that you are never so happy as when you have an opportunity of shewing your humanity, & of communicating happiness to others: I flatter myself you will pardon the liberty I take; As I was the other day expressing the sense I had of the politeness, & civility I receiv'd from you during my stay at Paris; a Gentleman entreated I wou'd entercede with you, in behalf of a Mr. Currie, who was a Captn. of an english privateer, & is now a prisoner at Tours in Turenne;[8] he wishes much to have him exchanged, & if that is not to be done, that he may have leave of

5. Lovell enclosed a declaration that Maj. Gen. Philippe-Jean-Baptiste Tronson du Coudray had been drowned crossing the Schuylkill River on Sept. 16, 1777 (for which see xxv, 220–1), along with an attested copy of a congressional resolution ordering that he be interred with honors of war (*JCC*, VIII, 751); this enclosure is also at the Mass. Hist. Soc. The declaration apparently had been precipitated by a financial claim of du Coudray's heirs, which on Sept. 9 had been referred to the Board of Treasury; eventually they were paid 14,886 *l.t.* 6 *s.* 1 *d.*: *JCC*, xv, 1041; xxi, 1014.

6. Gérard, returning to Europe aboard the *Confederacy,* agreed to carry letters to France: the committee for foreign affairs to BF, Oct. 14, below.

7. A native of Beaufort, S.C., she had visited Paris in June, 1778, returning to London the following February: xxvi, 684; xxviii, 459.

8. Digges describes an Alexander Currie who commanded the merchant ship *Henry* (owned by Hartley's cousin Samuel Hartley) and was taken on Oct. 31, 1778, by the *Vengeance.* He had been carried into Brest and was now at Tours. Elias and Finch, *Letters of Digges,* pp. 84, 102n.

absence to return to England; be so good therefore dear Sir to interest yourself in favor of Mr. Currie, if what I have asked is proper to be granted, & if not to excuse my error; & to beleive me to be with the greatest respect Dear Sir, Your Most obedient, & Sincere Humble Sert   M: E: STEVENS

please to present my best Compts. to Mr. Franklin

Addressed: A Monsieur / Monsieur Franklin / à Passy

Notation: Stevens Oct. 12. 1779.

From the Committee for Foreign Affairs

> ALS: Historical Society of Pennsylvania; copy and transcript: National Archives

Sir   Octr. 14th. 1779 Philada.
    By a letter of July 16th. the Superscription of Letters to "Our great faithful beloved Friend & Ally" was submitted to yr. Judgement. You ought however to be told Mr. Gerard has one to deliver directed in the same manner, the double of which you herewith receive, to be kept for him, to serve in case he may have been forced to sink his Papers.
    The Opportunity by him from this Port being so good I only now send a few of the latest Prints and Journals large Packages being on board the Confederacy. Your most humble Servant   JAMES LOVELL
                    for the Comtee of forgn. Affrs

Honble. Doctor Franklin.

Addressed: Honorable / Doctor Franklin

Endorsed: J. Lovell

From the Marquis de Lafayette

> ALS: American Philosophical Society

Dear Sir   havre 14th October 1779
    From the Sight of this hand writing, you will, I dare say, expect some dissertation on Military, Political, and in a word

on Public Affairs— how far you are from guessing the object of My letter will clearly Appear in a little time.

I am not a *scavant,* My Good friend, I am nothing But a Rough soldier, and would hardly do for a Committee-Man, tho you know it don't Alwaïs suppose A Great share of Learning—learning, however, is not totally stranger to the family, and from the duke d'Ayen a worthy member in the french Academy of sciences,[9] I have Got A Reccommendation, Which I have the honor of forwarding to You.

Doctor Noemer Counsellor of the City of Ziericzée, And A Member to the Academy of Zeland,[1] has from his Calculations found out that Men were born to be free, and that freedom was to be perfectly Enjoy'd But upon American shores—in Consequence thereof he wants immediately to Embark for, and settle in A Country where one May be bless'd with the healthy air of liberty— I have been applied to for a letter of Reccommendation to You And An other to Congress.

Whenever I will send them An officer, I Make Bold to say that out of Esteem for My opinion, they will Give him A Commission in the Army— Whenever I May Beg theyr favors for a friend of Mine, I know that out of theyr particular Goodness for me, they will show him All possible Attention— But if I am to Reccommend Doctor Noemer on account of his Learning, I think it very useful that My praises be Backed with some attestation from Mr Benjamin franklin.

Inclos'd I have the honor to send You My letter to Congress,[2] which, when the Gentleman will Waït on You, I Beg You would deliver to him, and also, upon your knowledge of his Merit, favor him with such a Reccommendation from you as you may think fit for his good Reception in America.

---

9. The duc d'Ayen, Lafayette's father-in-law, was selected as an *académicien honoraire* in 1777 and served as vice president in 1779: *Index biographique des membres et correspondants de l'académie des sciences du 22 décembre 1666 au 15 novembre 1954* (Paris, 1954), pp. 380–1.

1. Pieter or Petrus van Noemer, a physician and author: A.J. Van der Aa, ed., *Biographisch Woordenboek der Nederlanden* (7 vols., Haarlem, 1852–78, reprinted, Amsterdam, 1969). He had already written BF directly: XXIX, 53.

2. His Oct. 14 letter of introduction to the president of Congress (National Archives).

With the Greatest impatience I waït for intelligences from Count d'estaing, and Most heartly I will thank You for any news[3] that you will Get on his operations in America— I hope that in Concert with My heroïc friend, he will Rather Contract the Arms of the British tyrant and his faithfull incendiary soldiers, so that our people may perhaps be By this time in possession of Newyork— When I say *our,* I Mean the Americans, and under that same denomination I us'd in America to Mean the french, so that whatever of Both Countries I am in, I am at once Both Speaking as a foreigner, and spoken of as a Citizen.

With the most sincere affection, and high Regard, I have the honor to be Dear Sir Yours   LAFAYETTE

Notation: La Fayette Oct 14. 1779

From Richard Price   ALS: American Philosophical Society

Dear Sir/   Newington-Green Oct 14th: 1779

Will you be so good as to get the inclosed letter convey'd to Mr A——r Lee, if he is near you and it can be done easily? If not, be so good as to burn it. Being obliged for particular reasons to avoid politics, it is a short acknowledgmt: of the favour he did me by a letter I received from him at the beginning of last Summer, and contains nothing of much importance.

I received the greatest pleasure from the note which you Sent me by Mr J——s and Mr P——se.[4] They were much gratified by your kind notice of them— Dr Priestley is well, and much engaged in prosecuting his Experimts on air. Dr Ingenhouz, by whose hands this is convey'd, has lately been warmly employ'd in the Same pursuit. He will tell you what great Success he has met with.[5] The Society of honest whigs[6] which you used to honour with your company, are Soon to

---

3. First written as "intelligence", which has been lined through.
4. William Jones and John Paradise: XXIX, 524n, 570–1n.
5. See Priestley's letter of Sept. 27. Ingenhousz wrote on Nov. 18 from Brussels, forwarding the present letter and a book from Price. APS.
6. The Club of Honest Whigs: XI, 98n.

renew their meetings for the winter; and you will undoubtedly be one of the first Subjects of our conversation— I Spent in August Some time with an amiable family near Winchester.[7] The house in the garden that you used to frequent often brot: you to our remembrance. You can Scarcely imagine with what respect and affection you are talked of there— I have heard, with particular concern of the death of Dr Winthrop.[8] To this we are all destined, but the virtuous will be happy in better regions. The clouds gather frightfully over this country. I am waiting for the issue with anxiety, but at the Same time with much complacency in the reflexion, that at this most important period I have endeavoured to act the part of a faithful and good citizen— Accept, my dear Friend, these lines as a testimony of my very affectionate remembrance. May heaven preserve you and grant you the best enjoymts. With great regard, I am ever yours   R. PRICE

Notation: R Price Oct 14 1779

From Jean Rousseaux[9]   ALS: American Philosophical Society

Monsieur.   A Wakefield. Le 14. octobre 1779
Je me fait l'honneur de vous Ecrire cette lettre Pour vous prié davoir la bonte de me faire L'honneur de vouloir me rendre le Service de vous interesse Pour moy au Sujet de mon Echange. Jespere Monsieur cette grace de vous nayant personne qui puise mieu faire cela que vous: aupres de mon ministre. Jespere Monsieur que vous ne moublier Pas. Ayant deja Servit au Service du congre et ayant ette pris Sur lexemton Capt. henry Jonchon ainsy Monsieur jay ette assey Malheureux. de reste 6. moy en prison a plimouth et Jespere cette grace de vous. Jay ette pris Sur le Compte de mourepas[1] de Dunkurque en qualite de premie Lieutenant Jespere Monsieur

7. The Shipleys.
8. Dr. John Winthrop died on May 3: XXIX, 438.
9. A former officer from the continental brig *Lexington,* Capt. Henry Johnson: XXVI, 147–8; XXVIII, 514–15, 636–7; XXIX, 4, 173. He wrote again on Dec. 1 to ask BF's assistance. APS.
1. *Maurepas* or the *Comte de Maurepas,* a French privateer: XXVIII, 107, 591.

que vous ne Moublire Pas et vous en aure toute Les obligation posible.

Jay Lhonneur dettre avec respect Monsieur Votre tres heumble et tres obt. Serviteur   JEAN ROUSSEAUX

Addressed: A Monsieur. / Monsieur le Docteur / franquelin Embassadeur des /Ameriquain a / Passy

Notation: Jean Rousseau

From Sartine: Two Letters

(I) LS: American Philosophical Society; copy: Library of Congress; (II) copy: Library of Congress

I.

Versailles le 14. 8bre. 1779.

Mr. L'Amiral,[2] Monsieur, m'a fait passer un memoire qui lui à été adressé par le nommé françois Vermeille qui represente que s'etant embarqué sur le Corsaire Americain le Revanche en 1777. il fut mis avec sept autres Marins sur une prise qu'ils conduisoient à Bilbao lorsqu'ils ont été repris par deux fregates Angloises,[3] qu'a leur retour d'Angleterre ils ont reclamé votre Autorité pour obtenir les parts qui leur reviennent sur les 14 prises que ce Corsaire à faites pendant la même croisiere qui à été de trois mois; Mais que le Sieur Coffin Armateur de ce Corsaire loin de s'empresser à exécuter les ordres que vous lui avez sans doute donné à cet egard, refuse constamment de payer ces parts de prise. Je vous prie Monsieur de vouloir bien me faire connoître ce que vous pensez de la reclamation du Sieur Vermeille, jattendrai votre réponse pour faire part à Mr. L'Amiral des esperances que son protegé doit avoir, et des suites qu'il doit attendre de sa reclamation.

2. Louis-Jean-Marie de Bourbon, duc de Penthièvre (1725–93), the son of one of Louis XIV's illegitimate children, was the senior officer of the navy although he had never commanded a ship: Larousse.

3. The *Revenge* had made several cruises in Spanish waters in 1777 and 1778, but lacking the enclosure we are unable from this description to ascertain on which of her prizes Vermeille and his shipmates were captured; see Neeser, *Conyngham,* pp. xxxix-xlv and the list of prizes facing p. 152.

J'ai l'honneur dêtre avec un trés parfait attachement Monsieur votre trés humble et trés obeissant serviteur.

DE SARTINE

Pour francklin

Endorsed: answer'd

Notation: De Sartine 8bre 19. Prises

II.

à Versailles le 14. 8bre. 1779.

Je suis persuadé, Monsieur, que vous n'aurez pas eté moins touché que moi de la perte d'un grand nombre de Volontaires François qui ont été tués dans le Combat du Bon-homme Richard contre le Vaisseau de Guerre Anglois la Seraphie.[4] Cet événement est d'autant plus facheux, qu'il paroit que si la Fregate Americaine l'Alliance avoit secondé le Bon homme Richard, en combatant en même tems, l'avantage remporté par le Commodore Jones auroit été plus prompt auroit couté moins de monde, et n'auroit pas mis le Bonhomme Richard dans le Cas de couler bas trente six heures après le Combat. Le Capitaine de cette fregate ayant tenu une Conduite tres extraordinaire, je ne doute pas, Monsieur, que vous ne lui mandiez de se rendre auprès de vous pour en rendre compte et que dans le cas où vous reconnoitrez que c'est par sa faute que la victoire a couté tant de sang, vous ne jugiez a propos d'en informer le Congrès, afin qu'il fasse rayer ce Capitaine de dessus la liste des officiers de sa Marine.

J'ai l'honneur d'être avec une parfaite consideration, Monsieur, Votre tres humble et très obeissant Serviteur.

Je connois ce Capitaine pour une bien mauvaise tête.

(signé) DE SARTINE

---

4. At least 27 Frenchmen aboard the *Bonhomme Richard* (including officers) were killed and 42 wounded: Augustus C. Buell, *Paul Jones, Founder of the American Navy: a History* (2 vols., New York, 1906), II, 410–11. According to Morison, *Jones,* p. 205, the crew contained 137 French marines and 36 French "landsmen."

From Jonathan Williams, Sr.

ALS: American Philosophical Society

Hond. sr— Boston Octr. the 14. 1779

The Bearer mr. Jeremiah Allen[5] a neighbour & a most worthy acquaintance of ours, comes to France Partley on Business & on pleasure, I take the Liberty to Recommend him warmly to your Civilities Which will ad to the many Obligations allready Confer'd on Your Dutyfull Nephew & Hble Servant

JONA WILLIAMS

Doctr. Benja Franklin Esqr

Notation: Jona. Williams. Boston Oct 14. 1779

To Francis Coffyn

Copy: Library of Congress

Sir Passy, Oct. 15. 1779.

Inclosed I Send you the Commissions desired for the Black Prince and The Black Princess.[6] You will be so good as to fill up the Blanks properly and take the Bonds from the Parties, of which I Send one only, not having time to copy it: but that may be done with you for the other Vessel. I have the honour to be Sir &c.

M. Coffin.

To Dumas

Copy: Library of Congress

Dear sir Passy, Oct. 15. 1779.

I write this Line just to acknowledge the Recepit of your greable Favours of the 2d. 3d. & 6th. Instant. I hope you are

---

5. A merchant hoping to establish business connections in Spain and France, he traveled to Europe aboard the *Sensible* with the Adams party. JA said of him, "There is a Softness, and a Melancholly, in his face, which indicates a Goodness": Butterfield, *Adams Correspondence,* III, 246n; Butterfield, *John Adams Diary,* II, 402.

6. Clark believes that BF sent new commissions rather than altering Marchant's old one (as Torris and Coffyn had suggested) out of concern for the

now well with your family, and that I shall soon hear from you what Part your Governement takes with regard to our Little Squadron. I am ever Your's affectionately

Mr. Dumas.

To John Paul Jones

LS:[7] National Archives; copies: Library of Congress (two), National Archives (two); extract: National Archives

Dear Sir,   Passy Oct. 15. 1779.
I received the Account of your Cruize & Engagement with the Serapis, which you did me the honour to send me from the Texel.[8] I have since received your Favour of the 8th from Amsterdam. For some Days after the Arrival of your Express scarce any thing was talked of at Paris and Versailles but your cool Conduct and persevering Bravery during that terrible Conflict. You may believe that the Impression on my Mind was not less strong than that on others, but I do not chuse to say in a Letter to yourself all I think on such an Occasion.

The Ministry are much dissatisfied with Captain Landais, and M. De Sartine has signified to me in writing that it is expected I should send for him to Paris and call him to Account for his Conduct, particularly for deferring so long the coming to your Assistance, by which means, it is supposed the States lost more of their valuable Citizens, and the King lost many of his Subjects Volunteers in your Ship, together with the Ship itself.[9] I have accordingly written to him this Day acquainting him that he is charged with Disobedience of Orders in the Cruise and Neglect of his Duty in the Engagement; that a Court Martial being at this time inconvenient if not impracticable, I would give him an earlier Opportunity of offering what he has to say in his Justification, and for that purpose

---

safety of the recipient: *Ben Franklin's Privateers,* p. 100. Bad weather held the two privateers in port until December: *ibid.*, pp. 102–3.

7. In WTF's hand.
8. Above, Oct. 3.
9. See Sartine's second letter of Oct. 14.

direct him to render himself immediately here, bringing with him such Papers or Testimonies as he may think useful in his Defence. I know not whether he will obey my Orders, nor what the Ministry will do with him if he comes; but I suspect that they may by some of their concise Operations save the Trouble of a Court martial.[1] It will be well however for you to furnish me with what you may judge proper to support the Charges against him, that I may be able to give a just and clear Account of the Affair to Congress. In the meantime, it will be necessary, if he should refuse to come, that you should put him under an Arrest, and in that Case as well as if he comes, that you should either appoint some Person to command his Ship or take it upon yourself; for I know of no Person to recommend to you as fit for that Station.

I am uneasy about your Prisoners. I wish they were safe in France. You will then have compleated the glorious Work of giving Liberty to all the Americans that have so long languished for it in the British Prisons: for there are not so many there as you have now taken.

I have the Pleasure to inform you that the two Prizes sent to Norway are safely arrived at Berghen.

With the highest Esteem, I am Dear Sir, Your most obedient & most humble Servant   B FRANKLIN

I am sorry for your Misunderstanding with M. de C. who has a great Regard for you

(Private.)

Honble. Comme: Jones.

Endorsed: From Doctr. Franklin Octor: 15. 1779. No. 25. Private

---

1. Perhaps a reference to *lettres de cachet,* used in 1777 to imprison William Hodge in the Bastille (XXIV, 414).

To Landais

Copies: Harvard University Library, Library of Congress[2]

Sir,   Passy Oct. 15th. 1779

I receivd the Letter you did me the honour of writing to me the 4th. inst. with an Abstract of your Journal; I thank you for your care in sending it so early, & I congratulate you on the success of your cruize.

But I am sorry to find, there are charges against you for disobedience of Orders, & also that the Ministry here think the great loss among the King's subjects viz. the french Volunteers on board the Bon-homme Richard, was owing to your not coming up sooner to her assistance, as it is supposed you might have done. M. De Sartine has in consequence written to me, that it is expected I shoud cause an immediate enquiry to be made into your conduct. A Court martial is the regular way if you choose it. But as that may occasion a long discussion, & be in many respects at this time inconvenient to the Service, I have (with the advice too of your friend M. de Chaumont) thought it better to give you an opportunity of justifying yourself, both to the Ministry & to me, by coming directly to Paris which I do hereby accordingly desire (or to use a stronger expression as you may think such necessary to justify your leaving your ship, I do require) that you render yourself here as soon as possible. I need not advise you to bring with you, such Papers & Testimonies as you may think proper for your justification. And will only add that you may be sure of finding in me every disposition to do that justice of your character which it shall appear to merit. I have the honor, &c

signed B FRANKLIN

Honble. Capt. Landais

P.S. I have the pleasure to acquaint you that the two Prizes you sent to Norway are safely arrived at Bergen.

---

2. The one at Harvard is in Ludwell Lee's hand. That at the Library of Congress lacks the postscript. We have not located the recipient's copy but it has been printed (with its date mistranscribed as Oct. 14) in Landais, *Memorial,* p. 47.

I certify this to be a true Copy from the original

LUDWELL LEE

To Jean de Neufville & fils

LS:[3] National Archives; copy: Library of Congress

Gentlemen,   Passy Oct. 15. 1779

I received the Letter you did me the honour to write to me the 7th. Instant, acquainting me with the Arrival of Commodore Jones at Amsterdam, for which I am obliged to you, as well as for the friendly Reception and Assistance you have afforded that brave Officer. I suppose M. de Chaumont who is your Correspondent, and had the Care of equipping that Squadron, writes to you on the Subject of the Supplies it may want. I hope it will not, thro' the Influence of the English, meet with any unfriendly Treatment from your Governt. America will remember, and one Day be in a Condition to return with Gratitude, the Kindnesses she receives from other Nations in her infant State.

Your Friend M. Dumas being here at the time, and in Correspondence with you, I communicated to him my Sentiments on your Proposition concerning the Loan, which made it less necessary for me to write to you, as I should otherwise have done, that the Terms were such as I could not agree to, as they exceeded my Orders and were otherwise impracticable, and that I had long given over all Expectation of a Loan from Holland while other Powers gave so much higher Interest.

I have the honour to be, Gentlemen, Your most obedient & most humble Servant   B FRANKLIN

Messrs J. Neufville et Son.

Addressed: A Messieurs/ Messieurs Jean de Neufville et Fils. / Negociants, / a Amsterdam

Notations: 1779 franklin 30 7ber / Franklin

---

3. In WTF's hand.

From Silas Deane

ALS: American Philosophical Society

Dear Sir   Head Quarters[4] 15th Octo. 1779

This will be handed to you by Mons. Colomb, who came out to America with the Marquiss de la Fayette,[5] & has served with Reputation in the Army of the United States, and now returns to Visit his Country, and Freinds, I take therefore the Liberty to introduce him to your Acquaintence and to refer you to him for Information of the State of Our Army, and its Operations. I set out for Philadelphia tomorrow, and hope for the pleasure of embracing you in health at Paris in the course of the Winter[6] meantime I remain with the most sincere Respect and Attachment Dear Sir Your most Obedient and Very Humle. Servt.   SILAS DEANE

His Excellency B Franklin Esqr.

Notation: Silas Deane Head Quarters 15 Oct. 1779

From the Board of Treasury

ALS: Historical Society of Pennsylvania

Sir,   Treasury Office Philadelphia Otober 16. 1779.—

I have the Honer of informing you that two Setts of Exchange four Bills to each Sett for 900 Livres Tournois each No 1 in Faver of Nicholas Fouquet and No 2 in Faver of Mark Fouquet payable at thirty Days Sight have been this Day drawn upon you pursuant to the enclosed Act of Congress of

---

4. At West Point. On Oct. 15 Deane also wrote Col. Samuel Webb, datelining his letter from nearby Murderer's Creek: *Deane Papers,* IV, 108.

5. Pierre Colomb (b. 1754), a Continental Army captain, had been captured the previous winter at Savannah. He returned to France in November, apparently for good, but his combat days were not over; he became a *général de brigade* in 1793 after service against the Prussians: XXVIII, 384–5; Bodinier, *Dictionnaire; DBF.* Deane is apparently confusing him with Lafayette's aide-de-camp Louis Saint-Ange Morel de la Colombe (1755-*c.*1799), who also appears in Bodinier, *Dictionnaire.*

6. Deane told Webb that after a short stay in Philadelphia he would travel to Virginia, where he would embark for Europe.

the 12th. Instant;[7] and I am directed by the Board of Treasury to request that you will honer them as soon as Circumstances will permit.

I have the honer to be, Sir, with the greatest Respect Your most obedient, Humble Servant   ROB. TROUP.
                                                     Secretary.

To The honorable Benjamin Franklin Esqr. Minister Plenipotentiary of the United States of America at the Court of France.

From Samuel Huntington[8]

LS:[9] Library of Congress; partial copy: National Archives

Sir,   Philadelphia Octr. 16. 1779.
Congress have appointed the honble. John Jay esq minister plenipotentiary for negotiating a treaty of amity and commerce and of alliance between his Catholic Majesty and the united states of America And the honble. John Adams esqr. minister plenipotentiary for negotiating a treaty of peace and a treaty of commerce with Great Britain.[1]

7. The enclosure is also at the Hist. Soc. of Pa. This resolution (*JCC,* xv, 1165) states that Nicolas and Marc Fouquet had been employed in the service of the United States for two years supervising the manufacture of gunpowder and saltpetre and had recommended themselves to the favorable opinion of Congress. It directed that bills of exchange for 900 *l.t.* be delivered to them in addition to the sum mentioned in their contract with the Board of War and Ordnance. The latter sum was 6,000 *l.t.* due to Nicolas Fouquet (*JCC,* xv, 1154). BF noted on the enclosure that N. Fouquet was owed 6,000 *l.t.,* and that M. Fouquet was owed 900 *l.t.* For the father and son see XXVII, 207n.

8. In his new capacity as president of Congress. On Oct. 16 Huntington also signed the instructions to BF which we print under the date of Aug. 14. The present letter was drafted by a congressional committee consisting of Henry Laurens, Daniel of St. Thomas Jenifer, Woodbury Langdon, John Witherspoon, and James Lovell: *JCC,* xv, 1167–8, 1179–81, 1182–3.

9. In the hand of Charles Thomson, secretary of Congress. The copy lacks the final paragraph.

1. The election of Adams and Jay on Sept. 27 was the result of a compromise between political factions in Congress. BF was nominated as peace commissioner, but then-President of Congress Jay objected: H. James Hen-

The honble. William Carmichael esqr. is appointed secretary to the first and the honble Francis Dana esqr secretary to the last mentioned embassy.[2]

Mr Jay and Mr Carmichael will embark on board the Confederacy, continental ship of war now in the Delaware ready to sail for France. Mr Adams and Mr Dana will probably take their passage on board Le Sensible, one of his most Christian Majesty's frigates in the harbour of Boston.

The salaries annexed to these appointments respectively are two thousand five hundred pounds sterling per annum to the ministers and one thousand pounds sterling to the secretaries.[3] An in order to enable these gentlemen to enter without embarassment, upon the duties of their several functions, I am authorised by an act of Congress of the 15 instant, a certified copy of which will accompany this, to request you Sir, to take the most effectual means for supplying them with two thousand Louis d'ors in distributions proportioned to their respective salaries and to assure you on the faith of Congress that speedy and proper measures will be adopted both for repaying that sum and for establishing a fund for the future support of all the embassies of these united states in Europe.[4]

You will likewise find enclosed a certified copy of an act of Congress of the 4th. instant, by which you will be informed that your Salary is also to be two thousand five hundred pounds sterling per annum, and that John Laurens esqr. a

---

derson, *Party Politics in the Continental Congress* (New York, St. Louis, San Francisco, 1974), pp. 208–10; Jack N. Rakove, *The Beginnings of National Politics: an Interpretive History of the Continental Congress* (New York, 1979), p. 258.

2. For their nomination and election see *JCC*, xv, 1115, 1127–8; Smith, *Letters*, XIII, 586.

3. In a tie vote Congress on Oct. 4 failed to pass a resolution to pay BF, JA, and Jay £3,000 per annum: *JCC*, xv, 1143–4. BF's annual salary as commissioner had been 11,428 *l.t.* (approximately £500) plus "reasonable expences": *JCC*, xiv, 928.

4. The enclosure (*JCC*, xv, 1179–80) is among BF's papers at the APS, as are the other enclosures, noted below. He endorsed it "Resolution of Congress Oct. 15. 1779 That Messrs Jay & Adams be furnish'd each with 1000 Louis d'Or And that the Sum be replac'd."

member of the house of representatives for the state of South Carolina and lieut col. in the army of the united states is appointed by Congress to be secretary to the minister plenipotentiary at the court of France.[5] I have the honour to be Sr. Your obedient humble Servt   SAML. HUNTINGTON
President

Honble. B. Franklin Esqr.

Endorsed: Honble. S. Huntington Esq President. Letter Oct. 16. 79 Recd June 12. 1780—Salaries

To Tristram Dalton

Copy: Library of Congress

Sir   Passy, Oct. 17. 1779

I received Lately your Letter of the 13th. of may,[6] with the Papers relative to the Loss of the Brigantine fairplay. I had on the first Intelligence of that accident from the west Indies, made application to the Minister of the marine in favour of the sufferers, and received from him the answer of which I formerly Sent you a Copy;[7] but as that may have miscarried, I

5. Laurens was nominated by Elbridge Gerry and was elected on Sept. 29 by the vote of eleven states: *JCC,* xv, 1115, 1128; Smith, *Letters,* xiii, 586. On the same day Congress elected Joshua Johnson to audit the accounts of the American diplomats in Europe: *JCC,* xiv, 929; xv, 1126; Smith, *Letters,* xiii, 349n, 586–7. BF endorsed the notice of Laurens' appointment and of the Oct. 4 resolution fixing his salary, "Resolution of Congrss Sept. 29 & Oct. 4. 1779. Secretary elected / Allowance to Plenipotentiary & Secretary, established." The last enclosure is a copy of the Congressional resolutions of Aug. 6 (recommending the appointment of someone to examine American accounts in Europe) and of Sept. 29 appointing Johnson. BF's endorsement reads "Resolution of Congress, Aug. 6 and Sept. 29. 1779. Accounts Mr. Johnsons Appt.—". There is also a copy in L'Air de Lamotte's hand. Laurens declined his appointment (*JCC,* xv, 1366); Johnson accepted but four months later refused to undertake the audit (to BF, Feb. 29 and July 1, 1780, APS).

6. xxix, 486–8.

7. Acting on information received from William Bingham, BF on April 29 had written Sartine on behalf of the ship's crew; Sartine on May 26 promised an indemnity and later the same day BF informed the committee for foreign affairs: xxix, 546, 560. This, however, is the first extant letter from BF to Dalton.

now enclose another. I hope you have received or will soon receive in consequence of this kings order to the Governor of Guadeloupe, the Compensation desired. With much regard, I have the honour to be Sir Your &c.

Tristram Dalton Esqe. Newbury Port, Massachusets bay.

To the Eastern Navy Board

Copy: Library of Congress

Gentlemen,   Passy, Oct. 17. 1779.

I received the Letters you did me the honour of writing to me the 30th of July and 18th. of August last, by the Mercury Packet Boat and by a french Cutter, the other Dispatches Capt. Samson was entrusted with, came all Safe to hand; and I Should have dipatch'd him sooner, if I had not found it necessary to detain him in order to Send by him to Congress some Advices of Importance which could not be Sooner obtained.

The Cruise of our Little American Squadron under Commodore Jones, intended partly to intercept the Baltic Trade, has had some success tho' not all that was hoped for. The Coasts of Britain and Ireland have been greatly alarmed, apprehending Descents, it being Supposed that he had land forces with him. This has put the Enemy to much Expence in marching Troops from place to Place. Several valuable Prizes have been made of Merchant ships, particularly two one from London 300 Tons and 84 men, with 22 Guns laden with naval Stores for Quebec; the other from Liverpool bound to New York and Jamaica of 22 Guns and 87 men, laden with provisions and Bale Goods.[8] These two are safely arrived at Bergen in Norway; two Smaller Prizes are arrived in france, and a Number of Colliers have been burnt or ransomed. The Baltic fleet was met with and the two men of War who convoyed them viz. the serapis a new ship of 44 Guns and the Countess of Scarborough of 20. Guns are taken, after a long and bloody engagement, and are brought into the Texel. But the merchant Ships escaped during the conflict for which the alliance and

---

8. The *Betsy* and *Union*.

one of the other Ships[9] are blamed whether Justly or not may be enquired into. Our Commodore's Ship was so shatter'd that she could not be kept afloat, and the People being all taken out of her she Sunk the Second Day after the Engagement.— The rest of the Squadron are refitting in the Texel from which neutral Place they will be obliged soon to depart with their prizes and Prisoners near 400. I wish they may arrive safe in france for I suppose the English will endeavour to intercept them. Jones's Bravery and conduct in the Action has gain'd him great honour.

I condole with you on the Loss of your Armament against Penobscot; but I Suppose the Sugar ships[1] Since taken and brought into your Port have more than compensated the Expence tho' not the disappointment of the well intended Expedition. The Congress write for Naval Stores. I have acquainted them[2] that I have Lately been informed, that stores for fitting out two 36 Gun frigates, which we brought here and sent out two Years ago are still lying in the Warehouses of Mr. Carrabas, at Cape françois, having been forgotten there or never sent for. Perhaps you may obtain them. The Quebec Ship if we can get her safe home will afford a large Supply.

I am much oblig'd to you for the Newspapers. I Shall direct Mr. Schweighauser to send you an account of the advances made to the officers of the alliance, if he has not already done it. With great Respect, I have the honour to be Gentlemen &c.

Honourable the Commissioners of the Navy for the Eastern Department. Boston.

9. The *Vengeance;* Jones criticized her captain in his Oct. 3 letter.
1. *I.e.,* the ships from the Jamaica convoy brought into Boston by the *Providence, Queen of France,* and *Ranger.*
2. Above, Oct. 4.

To James Lovell

LS:[3] National Archives (two); AL (draft): Library of Congress; copy: Library of Congress; transcript: National Archives

Sir,   Passy Oct. 17. 1779.

The foregoing is a Copy of my last. I have now before me your several Favours therein mentioned, viz of June 13. July 9 & 16. and Augt. 6.[4]

I received the Journals of Congress from Jany. 1st. to June 12. which you took care to send me: But the Vols 1. & 2d which you mention are not yet come to hand. I hear they are at Madrid. I know not how they came there, nor how well to get them from thence. Perhaps you can easier send me another Set.

As I hear of the Arrival of the Chevalier de la Luzerne, by whom I wrote a long Letter to your Committee,[5] I presume you have received it, and that it is not now necessary to send more Copies. By this Opportunity I write largely to the President.[6]

You ask, "will no one under a Commission from the United States" &c.[7] Inclosed I send you a Copy of the Instructions I gave to Commodore Jones, when it was intended to send with him some Transports and Troops to make Descents in England.[8] Had not the Scheme been alter'd, by the more general One of a grand Invasion, I know he would have endeavour'd to put some considerable Towns to a high Ransom or have burnt them. He sailed without the Troops; but he nevertheless would have attempted Leith, and went into the Firth of Edinburgh with that Intention; but a sudden hard Gale of Wind, forced him out again.— The late Provocations by the burning

---

3. We print from the one in WTF's hand. The other is in L'Air de Lamotte's hand, with the complimentary close, inside address, and "Copy" added by BF. It bears the notation, "recd. May 13. 1780," and must have gone with the letters Lafayette carried in March.

4. His most recent letter was Sept. 30. The June 13 letter is in XXIX, 683, and the remainder are above.

5. XXIX, 547–61.

6. Above, Oct. 4.

7. In the committee for foreign affairs' letter of July 16.

8. XXIX, 386–7.

of Fairfield and other Towns, added to the preceding, have at length demolish'd all my Moderation; and were such another Expedition to be concerted, I think so much of that Disposition would not appear in the Instructions. But I see so many Inconveniences in mixing the two Nations together that I cannot encourage any farther Proposal of the kind. This has ended better than I expected, and yet a mortal Difference has arisen between Captains Jones & Landais, that makes me very uneasy about the Consequences. I send you the Journal of the Cruise.[9]

I am glad to understand that the Congress will appoint some Person here to audit our Accounts.[1] Mine will give but little Trouble, and I wish much to have them settled.[2] And for the future I hope I shall have none to settle but what relate to my Expences.

The Quarrel you mention between Mr Deane and Mr Lee[3] I have never meddled with, and have no Intention to take any Part in it whatever. I had and still have a very good Opinion of Mr Deane for his Zeal and Activity in the Service of his Country: I also thought him a Man of Integrity. But if he has embezzled Public Money, or traded with it on his Private Account, or employed it in Stock-jobbing, all which I understand he is charged with, I give him up. As yet I think him innocent. But he and his Accusers are able to plead their own Causes, and Time will show what we ought to think of them.[4]

I send you with this a Piece written by a learned Friend of mine on the Taxation of Free States, which I imagine may give you some Pleasure.[5] Also a late Royal Edict for abolishing the

9. After "Cruise" in the draft is written (and deleted) "as written to me by Capt. Jones". BF must have enclosed Jones's Oct. 3 letter.

1. Joshua Johnson; see our annotation of President Huntington's Oct. 16 letter.

2. In the draft after "Settl'd": "and never to have any more to settle except those of my Expences."

3. In his letter of Aug. 6.

4. In the draft this sentence originally read, "He is able to plead his own Cause, and Time will show what we ought to think of him, and of his Accusers."

5. Sir William Meredith, *Historical Remarks on the Taxation of Free States* ... (London, 1778). BF had once listed Meredith among the friends to America

Remains of Slavery in this Kingdom.[6] Who would have thought a few Years since, that we should live to see a King of France giving Freedom to Slaves, while a King of England is endeavouring to make Slaves of Freemen!

There is much talk all over Europe of an approaching Peace by the mediation of Russia & Holland: I have no Information of it to be depended on, and believe we ought to lay our Account on another Campaign. For which I hope you will receive in time the Supplies demanded. Nothing is wanting on my Part to forward them: And I have the Satisfaction to assure you that I do not find the Regard of this Court for the Congress and its Servant in any respect diminished.

We have just heard from Norway that two of the most valuable Prizes taken by the Alliance Capt. Landais, in the Squadron of Come. Jones, are safe arrived at Bergen: viz The Ship from London to Quebec laden with Naval Stores; and that from Liverpool to New York and Jamaica. They were Letter of marque, of 22 Guns & 84 Men each. I wish we may get them safe to America.

The Squadron itself is got into Holland with the two Prize Men of War, where they are all refitting. Great Damage has been done to the English Coal Trade, and 400 Prisoners have been taken, which will more than redeem the rest of our People from their Captivity in England; if we can get them safe from Holland to France: but I suppose the English will endeavour to intercept us, and recover their Ships if possible.

With great Esteem for yourself and the Committee, I have the Honour to be, Sir, Your most obedient & most humble Servant.   B FRANKLIN

Honble. James Lovell Esqr.

---

in the House of Commons (XIII, 170) and he proved to be still one; on June 11, 1779, he moved in the Commons for peace with America: XXIX, 668–9n.

6. In August Louis issued an edict registered in Parlement on Aug. 10, abolishing the right of *mainmorte* and servitude in France. For a report on it see the *Ga‡. de Leyde,* Aug. 20, 1779 (no. LXVII). The Sept. 3 issue of the *Courier de l'Europe,* VI (1779), 146–7, prints the edict in full.

Endorsed: Letter from Doctr. Franklin Passey Septr. 30th-Oct. 17 1779 to J Lovell Reced March 4th. 1780 and refd. to the Comee. for foreign Affairs—[7]

To the Massachusetts Delegates to Congress

LS:[8] Yale University Library; copy: Library of Congress

Gentlemen,   Passy, Oct. 17. 1779.

I have lately received the Letter you did me the honour of writing to me the 7th of May last,[9] relating to the Loss of the Brigantine, *Fair Play.* I had before made the Application desired, and obtained an Order to the Governor of Guadaloupe for making the Compensation. I hope therefore that the Business is effected; but if any Difficulties have arisen, and any farther Steps are necessary to be taken here I will readily endeavour to do what may be desired of me, having the greatest Regard to your Recommendation.

I have the Honour to be, with much Esteem, Gentlemen, Your most obedient & most humble Servant   B FRANKLIN

To Messrs. S. Adams, E. Gerry, James Lovell, and S. Holton Esqrs.

Endorsed by James Lovell: Octr. 17. 1779 From Doctr. Franklin respectg. the Brigne. *Fair Play.* in answer. recd Mar. 4th: 1780

From Richard Bache   ALS: American Philosophical Society

Dear & Hond: sir   Philadelphia October 17. 1779

Mr Gerard having been detained thus long, affords me an opportunity of informing you that Sally has presented us with another fine Boy;[1] she was safely Delivered on Thursday the

7. This was received in the same packet as BF's Oct. 4 letter to the president of Congress so it too must have been brought by the *Mercury:* Smith, *Letters,* XIV, 459n.

8. In WTF's hand.

9. Actually, the letter (XXIX, 480–1) was dated May 12.

1. Louis Bache (1779–1819), the fifth of Richard and Sarah's children. Gérard, whom Sally had wished to be the child's godfather, left Philadelphia on the 18th: Meng, *Despatches of Gérard,* p. 902n.

7th. Instant, and I have the pleasure to tell you, that she and the baby are as well as we could wish or expect— Miss Sally Duffield is now with us, she sends Compliments to you & Temple— Yours of the 6th. June has been delivered by M de la Serre, whom I have waited upon, and shall shew him every civility in my power—[2] The things are not yet come to hand from Boston, they are daily expected but it has been some disapointment to us, that they did not arrive before Sally kept her Room; however, with the assistance of our friends, we have made a shift— We intend to call our little Stranger Lewis, with this view, that we may frequently be put in mind of our *August Ally,* and as often contemplate the Virtues of the *Protector of the Rights of Mankind*— I am with sincere Love & Duty Your affectionate son   RICH: BACHE

Dr. Franklin

Addressed: His Excellency / Dr. Benjamin Franklin / Minister Plenipotentiary from / the United States of No: America at the Court / of / Versailles

Endorsed: R Bache Oct 17. 1779 recd June 12. 1780

From Coder

ALS: American Philosophical Society

Monsieur le Docteur   Paris ce 17e. 8bre. 1779

Recevez avec bonté mes remercimens et ceux de mon digne frere, pour l'interet que vous avez bien voulu prendre dans le tems à son affaire auprès de Mr. de Sartine. Ce ministre doit voir avec bien de l'etonnement, ainsi que tous les Courtisans qu'un officier aussi subalterne que mon frere vis a vis Mr. D'argout, soit sorti d'un conseil de guerre si avantageusement, surtout le gouverneur sous les yeux duquel il a été tenu n'ayant rien negligé pour le corrompre.

---

2. We have not found such a letter. BF had written on June 2: XXIX, 597–600. Arsène-Guillaume-Joseph Barbier de La Serre came to America with Rochambeau in 1780 and remained there after the war, but we have found no evidence of a prior visit: Bodinier, *Dictionnaire* (under Barbier); *Jefferson Papers,* VIII, 448–9; IX, 523–4.

Cet évenement, Monsieur, me prouve que la vertu n'est pas encore bannie du coeur de tous mes compatriotes.

Lisez, je vous en conjure, le memoire cy joint et si vous avez occasion de le faire recommander à Mr. De Sartine vous mobligerez infiniment.[3]

Vous connoissez, homme juste et vertueux, mon respecteux attachement pour vous et mon desir sincere de servir vos concitoyens et leur juste cause de toutes mes ressourses et de tout mon sang.

Je suis avec veneration Monsieur le Docteur Votre tres humble et tres obeissant serviteur   CODERC

Notation: Coder Paris 17. 8bre. 1779.

From the Chevalier de Kéralio

ALS: American Philosophical Society

A Forbach, Le 17e. 8bre 1779.
Arrivé à vingt Lieues de Forbach, je me suis empressé de venir rendre mon hommage à La personne du monde qui a le plus de droits sur mon respect, mon dévouement et ma reconnoissance.[4] Il y a huit jours, Monsieur, que j'ai Le bonheur de vivre près d'elle, de la voir, de l'entendre, de l'admirer. Combien de fois déja vous avés été le sujet de nos conversations! Avec quelle effusion de coeur nous avons admiré en vous Le grand Homme, L'homme aimable, le citoyen vertüeux. Que n'est-il ici, me disoit notre céleste amie? Il y jouiroit de la liberté qu'il

---

3. The undated memoir, two tightly packed pages, is at the APS. Coder rejoices briefly at his brother's vindication by the *Conseil de Guerre,* then proceeds to enumerate the family's grievances: the two houses in St. Domingue in ruins, slaves scattered, debts unpaid, another brother left practically blind on the Ile de France (Mauritius) because of an attempted poisoning, an octogenarian mother living in poverty, and so many calamities as a result of the brothers' attempts to serve King and country. The memorialist finally urges Sartine to reimburse the brother for his fare, grant him his back pay, and make sure he is restored to active duty.

4. The comtesse de Forbach, duchesse douairière de Deux-Ponts.

a donnée a sa patrie: des soins trop importants vous retiennent et c'est à nous à vous aller Trouver; il est possible que Mad. La Douariere ait dans peu le bonheur de vous revoir; elle s'en fait une grande fête et me charge de vous Le dire et de vous assurer de sa tendre amitié. Si elle quitte sa demeure, je ne tarderai pas à La Suivre, autrement je ne serai à paris que du 20e au 25e du mois prochain: en attendant et supposé que vos affaires vous laissent un instant, veuillés donner de vos nouvelles aux amis les plus vrais que vous ayés dans le monde. Apprenés nous que nos braves alliés ont enfin secoué Le joug de leur maratre, et soyés bien certain que nous serons heureux de votre bonheur.

Rendés toujours justice, je vous en supplie, à L'attachement inviolable et à la vénération profonde avec Laquelle je suis, Monsieur Votre tres humble et très obéissant serviteur

LE CHE. DE KERALIO

Permettés que Mr. votre fils trouve ici les assurances de notre sincere amitié.

Notre Bonne amie me charge encore une fois de vous renouveller l'hommage de sa tendre amitié et vous prie de faire parvenir la Lettre ci jointe à Son neveu.[5]

Notation: Keralio Oct 17. 79

From Sartine

Copy: Library of Congress

Versailles le 17. 8bre. 1779.

J'ai reçu, Monsieur, la lettre que vous m'avez fait l'honneur de m'écrire le 28. du mois der [dernier]. Le Roi à qui j'ai rendu Compte de la demande que vous me faites de permettre au Batiment parlementaire destiné à l'Echange des Prisonniers Americains et Anglois, d'aborder dans le port de Morlaix, a bien voulu consentir à lui accorder cette permission; J'ai l'honneur de vous envoyer en Conséquence le passeport necessaire au Bâtiment.

5. Jean-Baptiste de Fontevieux, then fighting in America: xxv, 314n.

J'ai l'honneur d'être avec la consideration la plus distinguée, Monsieur, votre tres humble et très obeissant Serviteur.

(signé) DE SARTINE.

M. Franklin

From ——— Joyce[6]   AL: American Philosophical Society

Thursday Morng [before October 18, 1779][7]

Miss Joyce presents her best respects to Docter Franklin sends him a letter Inclosed to her from Lisbon— Mr. & Mrs. D'arcy[8] desires their most affte Compliments to Docter Franklin Mr. D'arcy's Ammendment still continues.

Addressed: A Monsieur / Monsieur Franklin / a / Passy

To William Gordon   Copy: Library of Congress

Dear sir   Passy, Oct. 18. 1779.

I received but the other day your favour of feby. 4.[9] It has been round by the West Indies. The Letter it inclos'd for Mr. Parker is forwarded.

I forwarded to you lately a Letter from your friend Mr. Samuel Taber in Holland.[1] Your mistaking his name and calling him Jonathan occasioned one of your Letters to wander and be opened before it got to his hands. I suppose you must know long before this time, that we have lost good Mr. Sowden.[2]

6. Possibly a niece who lived with the d'Arcys: Butterfield, *Adams Correspondence,* III, 182.

7. The date of the comte d'Arcy's death; *Index biographique des membres et correspondants de l'Académie des sciences* . . . (Paris, 1954), pp. 15–16. It was reported in Bachaumont, *Mémoires secrets,* XIV, 232, 287.

8. D'Arcy had married his much younger niece, a Miss d'Arcy, in 1777. In 1783 she married Thomas Talbot. From a folder on d'Arcy in the archives of the *Académie des sciences.*

9. XXVIII, 467–8.

1. Tabor's covering letter to BF is above, Aug. 16.

2. In August of 1778 Hannah Sowden had asked BF to notify Gordon of her father's death: XXVII, 203–4.

The Account you gave of the Lucky arrival of Provisions at Boston, was very pleasing.—³ I beg you will continue to write me Intelligence of what happens in your publick affairs. All go well here, and I am with great Esteem. Revd. Sir Y. m. o. &c

Revd. M. Gordon.

From Richard Bache

ALS: American Philosophical Society

Dear & Hond. Sir   Philadelphia Octr. 18, 1779
   Finding that Mr. Jay, who is appointed Minister Plenipotentiary to the Court of Madrid, goes with Mr. Gerard by way of France, and probably will stop at Paris a short time, I commit this, with the inclosed, and a packet of Magazines to his care; He carries his Lady with him, the Daughter of Governor Livingston,⁴ she is a fine sensible Woman, and will do honor to her native Country— I need not recommend them to your particular notice & regards, as I am confident they will [*torn:* almost] certainly meet with them, as they meet with you. I am ever Dear sir Your affectionate son   RICH. BACHE

Dr. Franklin

Addressed: His Excellency / Dr. Benjamin Franklin / Minister Plenipotentiary from the United States / of No: America at the Court of / Versailles. / Favored by his Excelly / John Jay Esqr.

Endorsed: R. Bache Oct. 18—79 recd June 12, 1780

From James Cuming

ALS: American Philosophical Society

Sir   L'Orient 18th. 8bre. 1779
   I am honoured with your letter of the 30th. Ulto.—
   It gives me particular pleasure to hear you have receiv'd

---

3. XXIX, 438–40.
4. Sarah Van Brugh Livingston (1756–1802), the daughter of William Livingston (governor of New Jersey from 1776 to 1790), had married John Jay in 1774. The Jay party which accompanied Gérard to Europe also included two secretaries, William Carmichael and Henry Brockholst Livings-

several packets—making no doubt but those to my care were among them.—

Permit me to return you thanks for your desire of accomodating me.—

Sir John Lambert at Paris[5] advises me that all the Bills I sent him on the Hble. the Commissrs: are accepted among which were those drawn in favour of Mr. Tharp— Nevertheless I take the liberty to Inclose you Mr. Tharps letter—

The purchase of the Cargo for the Sloop Pap Called me to distant parts of the Country which prevented my answering you before—

I shall deliver the letter directed to Mr Lovell to the Captn. of the Sloop Pap with particular directions to comply with your desire in distroying it in case of necessity—

I have the Honour to be Your Excellencies—Most Obt. Hble. Servt.   JAS. CUMING

Addressed: His Excellency / Benjamin Franklin Esqr. / at / Passy

Notation: Jas: Cuming Oct 18. 79

From Dumas   ALS: American Philosophical Society

Monsieur   Amst. 18e. Oct. 1779

Voici, dans la Gazette de Leide, le Mémoire de Sir Joseph.[6] L'Avis de l'Amirauté là-dessus, dont nous sommes fort contents notre Ami & moi, est que l'on observera à l'égard de cette Escadre, le Reglement fait par cette Rep. en 1756 à l'égard des vaisseaux de guerre & armateurs de toutes les Puissances étrangeres. Cet avis a été fait commissorial, pour

---

ton, and John Jay's twelve-year-old nephew, Peter Jay Munro: Richard B. Morris, ed., *John Jay, the Making of a Revolutionary: Unpublished Papers, 1745–1780* (New York, Evanston, and San Francisco, 1975), pp. 123–4, 651.

5. An English baronet and Paris banker: XIX, 189n; Lüthy, *Banque protestante,* II, 320; *Almanach des marchands,* p. 374.

6. The issue enclosed was that of Oct. 15; see our annotation of Dumas' Oct. 12 letter. A copy of the article about Yorke's memorial is among BF's papers at the APS.

servir de base à la résolution qu'on prendra quant à la réponse à faire au Mémoire.

Il est bon cependant que cette Escadre reparte incessamment, pour plusieurs raisons. 1.° Il ne faut pas abuser de la bonne volonté des gens ici: ils l'ont montrée; cela suffit pour une premiere fois. 2. Les équipages, déjà foibles, s'affoibliront de plus en plus par la désertion entre autres.[7] 3.° On ne voit pas de trop bon oeil en ce pays, tant de malades entassés, & la malpropreté qui regne sur ces vaisseaux; & l'on craint de là quelque infection.[8] Cela me fait presser tant que je puis le radoub & l'approvisionnement, afin qu'ils puissent faire voile pour Dunkerke, où ils pourront se debarrasser de leurs malades et prisonniers, & prendre du monde fraix pour compléter leurs équipages. Je suis avec le plus respectueux attachement Monsieur Votre très-humble & très obéissant serviteur

DUMAS

Passy à Son Exc. Mr. Franklin

Addressed: His Excellency / B. Franklin, Esqr. / Min. plenip. of the United / States &c. / Passy.

Notation: Dumas Octr. 18. 1779.

From Gourlade & Moylan

ALS:[9] American Philosophical Society

Honord Sir   L'Orient 18 Octobr: 1779

We received a letter from our friend Cap. Jones dated on board the ship of war Seraphis 3d. Inst. at Anchor off the Texel, giving us the very pleasing acct. of his victory of the 23d. Sepr. last[1] and desiring us to forwd. through your hands,

---

7. For desertion from the *Serapis* see Dumas to BF, Oct. 22, below.

8. On Oct. 18 Dumas wrote Jones to warn him of rumors about the filthy condition of the *Serapis* (including unremoved pieces of corpses); in reply Jones said that the ship "is now and shall be kept clean": Bradford, *Jones Papers,* reel 4, nos. 786, 802.

9. In Moylan's hand.

1. In this letter (Bradford, *Jones Papers,* reel 4, no. 747) Jones accused the *Alliance* of repeatedly firing on the *Bonhomme Richard.*

any letters we might have received for him: in complyance therwith, we inclose you a packet for him[2] wch. we pray you will convey to his hands in the speediest manner possible.

We have the honor to be respectfully Honord sir Your most obt hle sts GOURLADE & MOYLAN

Notation: Gourlade & Moylan Oct 18. 79

From Danniel Stuart

ALS: American Philosophical Society

Worthy sir Dinan Prison 8ber 18th 1779

I beg leave to be troublesome in laying my case before & hope you will See me redressed. I am a native of Philladelphia & was taken prisoner by the English & was in prison there for two years & at the end of which I Contrived to Escape out of prison,[3] & then entered in the french service on Board a privateer. I took the liberty of getting into a Boat at St. Malloes to go to granville in order to receive my Prize monny. I was taken up & clapt into a Black hole in that place, & kept me there for 20 days & then sent me to st. Malloes where I was kept in a Black hole for 80 days— living on Bread & Watter, I was Sent to this place last week & am now Confined with English prisoners. I Expect warthy Sir you will write to the Commissiarry of this place to order me my liberty that I may go on Board to Serve My own Country Tho' I have been 6 months on Board a french Privateer called the America. She belongs to Munsieur morisot(?) in granvill, I never received a farthing for my service & I hope you may put me in the way of being payd, I am Sir your most obdt sert DANNIEL STUART

Addressed: A / Monsr / Monsieur Le Docteur / franklin envoy des / Etat unis de l'amerique / à Paris

Notation: Danl. Stuart 18 Oct 79

---

2. This packet must have contained a now-missing Oct. 15 letter from the firm to Jones; see Bradford, *Jones Papers,* reel 4, no. 859 for Jones's response.

3. He had been committed to Forton prison on Aug. 8, 1777: Kaminkow, *Mariners.*

To Georges Grand

Copy: Library of Congress

Dear sir   Passy, Oct. 19. 1779.

I received your favour of the 11th: Inst: and the Bark you have been so good as to procure for me is also come safe to hand. You have obliged me exceedingly by this friendly attention. If it helps, as you wish to prolong my life, it will at the same time prolong my Remembrance of your kindness.— I am glad to understand that you have Thought of a Visit to Paris. It will always be a pleasure to me to see a friend I so much esteem.— I hope M. de St. Simon has received the Books I ordered for him from England: They were to pass through your hands.[4]

I wonder Capt. Jones has not been to see you, as I think he had the honour of being known to you here. The furnishing of his Squadron you are sensible is not with me.— With great and Sincere Esteem, I have the honour to be Dear Sir Your &c.

Sir G. Grand.

To David Hartley

LS:[5] M.D.A.F.H.H. Hartley Russell, on deposit in the Berkshire Record Office (1955); copy and transcript: Library of Congress

Dear Sir,   Passy Oct. 19. 1779.

Having just received the Passport desired for the Cartel to make use of the Port of Morlaix, I take this first Opportunity of sending it to you,[6] in hopes of releasing by more expeditious Voyages the poor Prisoners on both Sides before the Severity of Winter comes on. Besides those released on Parole, we have now more English Prisoners than you have Americans. In those Releases we have relied on the honour &

---

4. The books went through the Netherlands because the marquis resided in Utrecht: XXIX, 498n.

5. In WTF's hand.

6. Sartine had sent it on the 17th, above, and BF acknowledged it on the 19th, below.

Humanity of the Board and I am persuaded we shall not find ourselves deceived. You will always see me ready in every Step that may soften the Rigours of War to give the first Demonstrations of that Confidence which naturally opens by Degrees the way to Peace. With great Esteem and Affection I am ever Dear Sir, Your most obedient & most humble Servant

B FRANKLIN

D. Hartley Esqr.

(Duplicate)

Endorsed: DF Oct 19 1779

To John Holker

Copy: Library of Congress

Dear sir   Passy Oct. 19. 1779.

Immediately on the Receipt of your Letter,[7] I wrote to the Owner of the Black Prince at Dunkirk who informed me that my application was in time, and that he would give Orders directly to have the Box of Papers Sent to me; and he has Since wrote that he will order the Trunks of Clothes to be purchased as much under 1000 livres as may be.—[8] I hope you Continue well and hearty. Make my affectionate Respects acceptable to Mrs. Holker, and believe me ever, with great Esteem. Dear sir Your m. o. and m. h. S.

M. Holker.

To the Marquis de Lafayette

Copy: Library of Congress

Dear Sir   Passy, Oct 19. 1779.

Nothing of the Proposals you mention[9] has been communicated to me, and I therefore question their Existance.

---

7. Of Oct. 2, above.

8. See Torris' postscript to his Oct. 8 letter, where he mentions having just received the letter regarding the trunks. Torris answered WTF on Oct. 14; he repeated what he had told BF and requested WTF's good offices in obtaining from BF commissions for the *Black Prince* and *Black Princess*. APS.

9. In his Oct. 11 letter.

But should Such a thing be, there is certainly no one whom I should more wish to see concern'd in the management than the Person you mention, as he is Throughly acquainted with the Subject, and a hearty friend to Those concerned. Accordingly I should immediatly take the step advis'd to Engage him. With the Highest Esteem and affection, I am. Dear sir, &c.

M. De La fayette.

To Sartine: Two Letters

(I) and (II) Copy: Library of Congress

I.

Passy, Oct. 19. 1779.

I received the Letter your Excellency did me the honour of writing to me the 14th. Inst. relating to the Claim of françois Vermeille to be payd Wages and prize money due to him from Capt. Cunyngham, Commander of the Revenge Privateer. I find on Enquiry that the Said Vermeille and several other french Sailors who Said they had belonged to that Vessel, having been a long time imprisoned in England, were exchanged by the Last Cartel. When they pass'd thro' this Place on their Return to Dunkirk, I gave them some Money to help them on their Journey,[1] and advis'd them to apply to Mr. Coffin our Present agent there, who I Supposed could inform them who it was that did the Business of equiping Capt. Cunnyngham, and must therefore know what men were Shipt on what terms, what they had received in advance and what Prizes were taken (of all which I was totally ignorant) and by that means ascertain their Claims, in which I desired Mr Coffin to assist them so that I might take the proper Means of obtaining for them what is their Due. Mr. Coffin wrote me a Letter in answer to

1. Between Aug. 2 and 4, BF had given Vermeille and seven of his former shipmates 12 *l.t.* apiece to aid their return to Dunkirk: Account VI (XXIII, 21); Alphabetical List of Escaped Prisoners. His Cash Book (Account XVI, XXVI, 3) on Oct. 24 records a payment of 24 *l.t.* as "Charity to one of Capt Conyngham's People, Sergeant of his Marines, to help him home having been a Prisoner."

my Request; of which I inclose a Copy—[2] Mr. Deane and Mr. Hodge who were concerned in that Enterprise are neither of them at present in france, But Mr. Deane is soon expected here. Capt. Conyngham is now a Prisoner in England, but I hope will soon be exchanged and appear here, Nothing is more just than that These Men should be paid what is Really due to them, but as I had no Concern in the affair, and never Saw any Account of the Prizes taken, and know nothing of the agreement made with the Sailors, it is impossible for me to adjust their Claims. All I can do is to communicate them to the proper Persons, and Solicit which I Shall do warmly that justice be done. With great Respect, I am your Excellency's most obedt.

M. De Sartine.

II.

Sir   Passy, Oct. 19. 1779.
 I am much obliged to your Excellency for so Speedily procuring for me the Passport desired, for the Cartel ship to make use of the Port of Morlaix, and am very thankful to his Majesty for his Goodness in so readily granting it as I now hope soon to have by that means the rest of our American Prisoners at Liberty who will then be ready to act against the Common Enemy. With the greatest Respect, I am &c.

Mr. De Sartine

From Adam Crossley ALS: American Philosophical Society

Honoured Sir   De Nan Castle Octr. 19th—1779
 I know not how to Appoligize for taking the Liberty of writing to you. The Necessity and Hardship of my Case must Plead my Excuse. I am by Birth an American, and a Subject of the United States, and as such I Apply to your Goodness for putting me in Possession of that, which by the Priviledge of my Country I am Intitled to— It was my Misfortune to be

---

2. Above, Oct. 3.

taken last May in the Kitty Brigg Homeward Bound from Kales, in Spain, to Boston in New England, (which is the place of my Birth) By the Childers Armed Brigg, and Carried into Gibralter as a Prisoner of War—and in July following I was sent on Board the Fanny Brigg Henry McNamarra Commander, in Order to take my Passage to some prison in England. In our Passage to England we were taken by the La Concorde a French Frigate, Off Ushant,—a Cercumstance that gave me much Pleasure, as I hoped by that means to gain my Liberty. I Accordingly Apply'd to the Captain and shew'd him my Certificate (signed by Admerall Duffs Secretary) of my being sent over to England as a Prisoner And was told by him that if I would do duty on Board the Frigate I should be set at Liberty on our Arival in Brest and a Certificate given me to go to some Place where there were some of my own Country Vessels when I might go Home. On our Arival in Brest I Claimed my Liberty According to Promise And was told that I should have it, if I would Enter for the Next Cruse which I Absolutely refusing, was sent with the rest of the Prisoners to De Nan Where I now am. I hope Your Goodness will be kind Enough to Interfere in my behalf and Get me my Liberty and give me a pass to go to my own Country which is my most Ardent Desire— And Wait with the Utmost Impatiance for the result of your Goodness— And beg leave to Subscribe Myself with all Due Submission— Honoured Sir Yr Most Obedt. Hble Servt: ADM CROSSLEY

Addressed: The Honourable Dr Franklin / Plenepotentary to the United / States of America / At / Paris

Notations: A Crossley Oct 9. 79 / Adm Crosley De nan Castle Oct. 9. 79

From John G. Frazer
ALS: American Philosophical Society

Honoured Sir, Bordeaux 19th. October 1779.

I am agoing to America Immediately in a very large Ship well Armed & Man'd—if you have any commands (and will inclose them to Mr. John Bonfield American Agent here) I will

with the greatest pleasure take particular care of them— The
Fleet will depart from this the last of the Month, or the beginning of the next at furthest.

I wrote to you some time ago at the request of Mr. Cradock
Taylor, a Country man of mine now Prisioner at Aix, to assure
you that he is no imposter &c. but a native of Virginia, and I
am sure as true to his Country as any one in it he has lately
wrote me that a Cartel is settled for the exchange of prisioners
between Port-Mahon, and Marseilles, and that he must be exchanged, if not released as an American, which he hopes &
begs you will be good enough to have done for he writes me
that it is much against his inclination, or desire, ever to return
to the English Service, which he was at first forced into—
please to excuse the liberty I take in writing to you upon this
subject, for I really cannot help fealing for my Friend, Acquaintance, and Countryman, give me leave Sir, to wish you
your Health, and a happy sight of your Native Land once
more—if it may be ever your desire, or wishes, to return to
it— I hope we shall soon have peace and plenty in every part
of the Free & Independent States of America. I have the Honour to be with the greatest respect, Your Excellency's Most
Obedient, and, Most Humble Servant   JOHN G. FRAZER

Addressed: His Excellency / Benjamin Franklin Esqr. / Minister
Plenipotentiary / to the United States of America / at Passy, /
near, Paris

Notation: J. G. Frazer. Oct 19. 1779

From "Comte" Julius de Montfort de Prat

ALS: American Philosophical Society

ruë montmartre vis avis celle du Croissant a Paris
Sir   Ce 19 8bre. 1779

As I am at present at Paris on some Besonies, I Shall be
much obliged to you for Sending to me my Plan on the general Education of the distinguished american youth, your Exellency will be good Enough, I hope, for letting me Know
What is wanted in the plan to obtain the approbation of the

high rulers of the united states & to take the must proper means to perform well the wants(?) of a true citizen of america Such as I desire to be & such as I Should desire to render every individual Living in that happy independent country.

As soon as I shall receive The plan with your observations, I'll correct it accordingly & Shall take a new copy of it.

I hopes, sir, that your Excellency constantly animated by the public good, will be kind enough to me to recommend an institution So much wanted in the united states & only capable, indeed, to create greatness in a republican citizen of our newly rised empire.

Be pleased, sir to take your proper time to examine my plan; such an important affair is to be looked on as very serious & too much precipitation must be feard.[3]

I am with the highest respect and esteem Sir, your Most obedient humble servant   JULS. CT. MONTFORT.

Addressed: A Son Excellence / Monsieur Le Docteur franklin / ministre plénipotentiaire des Etats unis / de L'amérique a La Cour de france / A Passy

Notation: Count Montfort Oct 19. 79

To Jonathan Loring Austin   Copy: Library of Congress

Sir   Passy, Oct 20. 1779

I received your several favours of June 10. July 12. and 27.[4] It Gave me Pleasure to hear of your Safe arrival in your native Country; and I am obliged to you for the Intelligence your Letters contain which I hope you will continue and for the newspapers. This Campaign in Europe has not been so active

---

3. The writer, to whom BF lent Priestley's work on education (XXVIII, 178; XXIX, 453), sent a note to WTF on the same day, asking him to add his observations to BF's on the *Plan d'Education* and to correct its English. He conveys the feelings of admiration that WTF evoked in a charming young woman with whom they both dined and predicts that, though a provincial at present, she will make her mark in Paris (APS). She may have been the "de Stenay" who inquired about WTF's health on a "jeudi matin," also mentioning Montfort and his ideas which would benefit America. APS.

4. For the first of these see XXIX, 656–7; the others are above.

as was Expected owing to contrary winds and other accidents which a long time prevented the junction of the french and Spanish fleets and afterwards the Meeting with that of the English. But something may yet be done before wenter. The American flag has however disturbed the Britich Coasts interrupted their home trade a good Deal, and allarmed them with apprehensions of Descents, in different places: Our Little Squadron under Commodore Jones has also lately taken two of their men of War, and brought them into holland with near 400 Prisoners which will be a means I hope of delivering the rest of our Countrymen who are confined in English Prisons. Here is nothing worth your Acceptance that one can propose to you.[5] I wish you Success in any Business you may undertake, being with much Regard. Sir Your most obedient and most humble servant

My Grandson presents his Respects.

Mr. Austin.

To Meÿer   Copy: Library of Congress

Sir   Passy, Oct. 20. 1779.
    I received the Letter you did me the honour of writing to me dated the 9th. Instant. I am quite unacquainted with the affairs of the Ranger, and never had anything to do with the Payment of Shares of her Prizes to any Person whatever: I cannot therefore understand Mr. Schweighhauser's referring you to me; but I will write to him about it. I have the honour to be, Sir Your most. o. & m. h. s.[6]

Mr. Meyer

5. Austin had volunteered to return to Europe should it be "serviceable": xxix, 657.
6. We have no record of BF's writing to Schweighauser on the matter. Meÿer later appealed to Jones, who provided him with a certificate of service, dated March 5, 1780, which he hoped Schweighauser would not dare dispute. Bradford, *Jones Papers*, reel 5, no. 1006.

From ——— Stadel[7] ALS: American Philosophical Society

Paris ce 20 8bre 1779

J'ai L'honneur de vous Joindre Monsieur un Projet que m'a remis un Colonel au service de Sa Majesté Le Roy de Prusse, et qu'il né veut se nommer avant de scavoir, s'il y à moyen de faire L'entreprise qu'il Propose.[8] Je sçai qu'il est en mesme de remplir ce qu'il avance, et que ces Terres qu'il Possedent en Allemagne, il sont plus que suffisant pour remplir çes Engagements. Le Roy de Prusse à sçeu tirer partie puisqu'il y a fournit tout un Regiment et encorre en outre 800 hommes dans La derniere Guerre. Vous sçavoit Monsieur que Les Nouveau Regiments, ont estez en partie incorporer Les autres Congediès à La Paix, cela fait de mécontentement, et Pourra d'autant mieux servir à Procurer ce que L'on dessire, d'autant plus qu'il vise Principalement sur La Criculture [l'Agriculture?] et Population hors de la Guerre, il reste à scavoir si vous Le trouvoit Monsieur de Convenance pour Messieurs Les Etats unis de L'amerique, ou non, c'est de quoy j'ose Vous suplier Monsieur de me faire part, à ce fin de ne point arretter Monsieur Le Colonel qui est venu incognito & ne trouvant pas que cela puisse avoir Lieu repartira de suite pour s'en retourner en attendant J'ai L'honneur d'être avec La Consideration La plus parfaitte & distingue Monsieur Votre tres humble & tres obbeissant Serviteur[9]   STADEL

à L'hotel de Chartre rue de vieux Augustins

7. A merchant from Strasbourg: XXVII, 228; XXVIII, 351–2, 583.

8. The Prussian colonel proposes to raise a regiment, battalion, or legion which at war's end could serve as settlers such as troops in Austrian service do. This enclosure, in Stadel's hand, is at the APS.

9. BF answered the same day; a copy of that letter is at the Library of Congress. He thanked Stadel for the proposal to raise a regiment but explained, "The Congress I believe have never had any Intention of raising Troops in Europe and transporting them to America: the Expence would be too great for them, and the Difficulty extreme as the English Command their Seas, and would often intercept their transports." Lacking authorization for such a project, he cannot offer any encouragement. Please present his thanks to the officer who made the proposition.

567

Addressed: A Monsieur / Monsieur de Francklin / Envoyè Extraordinaire des Etats des / Provinces Unies de L'amerique / à Passÿ

Notation: Stadel.

To the Committee of Commerce

Copy: Library of Congress

Gentlemen   Passy Oct. 21. 1779.
I received the honour of yours dated the 21st. of july containing an Extract of Mr. Pollocks Letter to you, in which he mentions his Drafts on Mr. Delap for 10,897. Dollars and his Expectation that in case of any difficulty I will See those Bills paid. I Should certainly do every thing in my power to support the credit of the States and of every Person acting under their authority: But I have been So exhausted by great and unexpected Drafts and Expences, that I am glad those Bills have never been proposed to me, as I could not have taken upon my Self to pay them. And I beg that you would not in future have any dependance of that kind upon me, without knowing before hand from me that I Shall be able to do what is desired. I hope you will excuse my giving this Caution which is forc'd from me, by the Distress and Anxiety Such occasional and unforeseen demands have occasioned me. I have the honour to be Gentlemen,

Commercial Committee of Congress Philada.

From Jean de Neufville & fils

ALS: American Philosophical Society

High Honourable Sir   Amsterdam the 21th. Oct: 1779
May we begg leave to troúble the attention of your Excellency, and ask his assistance for oúr selfs and oúr American frinds, in a misfortúne the last English maill Acquaints ús With: Those are the Circúmstances by extracts oút of a letter

from Capn. Moses Grinnell[1] fm. Boston to oúr adress. "On the 17 Sept: I was drove on shore at shetland in a violent gaill of wind, and fell into the hands of a tender laying there, with all my Letters and bills of Exchange"

he says further

"I had many bills that was payable to yoú and some to Mr. Oliver Smith

Mr. James Jarvis

Mr. Thomas Knox"[2]

"All them is in Capn. Hunters hands with the Letters, and I think he will try to gett them pay'd to him, so you will guard against it."

We are in great hopes none of those bills should yett have appeard, or, if properly endorsed, that at least those to oúr order shall not have been made over to any other or the hand-writing should have strúck your Excellencys attention, bútt how this may be, we flatter oúr selfs and tranquillized oúr frinds, as with all morall probability, that those bills none of them Can yett be payd, and that then we might prevent it, as they should be falsely endorsed by false handwritings; we wish oúr supposition may prove trúe; and even that they may not have tryed for it; bútt what is a Schotsman and even an Englishman not Capable off? As we have proofs of they not paying ransom bills fr. Vessells duely taken, So may we begg from yoúr Excellency that none of such bills may be payd except they should have passed through our hands, as we have agreed with those frends they may concern. With the Squadron of Comodor Jones every thing goes right and clever as it should do, we have gott a permission to ketch his desertors, bútt we need not enter into particulars as Mr Dumas will Cer-

1. Captain of the *Sally and Becky* of Boston: xxviii, 608.

2. Smith is perhaps Col. Oliver Smith of the Connecticut militia: Francis B. Heitman and Robert H. Kelby, compilers, *Historical Register of Officers of the Continental Army* . . . (rev. ed., Baltimore, 1982), p. 506. There are several merchants named John Jarvis, but our guess is that this one was from Boston: Allen, *Mass. Privateers,* pp. 114, 188. We suspect Knox too was from Boston: Allen, *Mass. Privateers,* p. 179; Mass. Hist. Soc. *Proc.,* 1st ser., xx (1882–3), 11.

tainly inform Yoúr Excellency aboút them.[3] We have beggd a line from him to Yoúr Excellency fr. Capn. Robbinson, who setts out next week to pay his respects to the Plenipotentiary Minister of his country he hath escaped oút of gale, where he went into to save his Sons from being pressed. One of them is still in prison, and is worthy to be recomanded in Case of exchanging prisoners.

This we dare mention likewise in favoúr of Capn. Moses Grinnell oúr last that now was taken, and likely will be carried into Edenbúrg;

We dare recomand oúr Selfs to the protection of yoúr Excelly and have the honoúr to be with the highest Regard. High Honourable Sir! Your Excellency's most obedient and most devoted Servants.   JOHN DE NEUFVILLE & SON.

P.S. By the way of France, we have received some remittces. in the Letters Mr. David Sears had orderd ús to open in his absence, as he is returnd to Boston;[4] bútt he not being able thús to endorse them, we múst leave it to Yoúr Excellency how we shall proceed there with; we have endorsed the same however to oúr frends Mr. Mallet Le Royer & Mallet fils de Paris,[5] they are endorsed by Mr. Ebenezer Dorr[6] to said Mr. David Sears consisting in

No. 163. dated	3 June	$18.	No. 530 dated	1st June	$ 60
257. —	17 —	24.	443 —	17 —	60
28. —	1 —	24.	453 —	12 fev	120
302 —	3. —	30.	182 —	17 June	120
306. —	17 —	30.	524 —	1 June	120
169. —	12 Feby.	30.			

$636 in all

Notation: Neufville John 21. Oct. 1779.

3. He did so the following day.

4. Sears had announced his impending return the preceding June: XXIX, 662–30.

5. For the banking firm of Mallet, Le Royer & Mallet fils see Lüthy, *Banque protestante,* II, 270–1.

6. Probably the longtime patriot from Roxbury who appears in *JCC,* I, 36n; he was also involved in financing privateering ventures: Allen, *Mass. Privateers,* pp. 103, 198, 256.

From Jean-Jacques de Lafreté

AL: American Philosophical Society

Paris ce 22. 8bre. 1779.

Mr. Lafreté a l'honneur de presenter son Respect à Monsieur franklin, et de le remercier des piéces qu'il a eu la bonte de lui envoyer. Mr. holkier lui en demande d'autres, qu'il prie instamment Monsieur franklin, de vouloir bien certiffier véritables et conformes aux originaux qu'il a lhonneur de lui communiquer.[7] Il le prie ensuite de vouloir bien faire partir ces trois duplicata, et de les mettre dans Ses Dêpeches Si cela est possible. Madme. De lafreté le prie d'agréer Ses Respectueux complimens.

Addressed: A Monsieur / Monsieur franklin / Ministre Plenipotentiaire des / Etats ünis, / à Passy

Notation: Lafreté, Paris 22. Octobre 1779.

To Robert Morris

LS:[8] Yale University Library; copy: Library of Congress

Dear Sir,   Passy Oct. 22. 1779.

My Friend, M. De la Freté, having a considerable Property in the Hands of M. De Rouillac & Co. at Edenton in N. Carolina[9] has sent a Power of attorney to M. Holker to recover the same for him. If you can in any way assist M. Holker in effecting this Business, you will very much oblige Dear Sir, Your most obedient & most humble Servant.   B Franklin

Honble. Robt. Morris Esq.

Addressed: Honble Robt. Morris Esqr / Member of Congress / at Philadelphia

7. BF this day certified a power of attorney in his friend Lafreté's proceedings against the bankrupt firm of Reculès de Basmarein & Raimbaux: XXVIII, 566n. The following day he certified to the authenticity of a shipping agreement between Lafreté and the firm (two copies of which are at the Yale University Library).

8. In WTF's hand.

9. Roulhac represented Reculès de Basmarein & Raimbaux: XXVIII, 566n.

To Sartine

Copy: Library of Congress

Sir   Passy Oct. 22. 1779.

The Enclos'd Papers containing much information of the State of the garrison at St. John's in Newfound land, and of the fortifications there. The Loss of Military Stores by the late great Fire &c &c. I thought it my Duty to communicate them to your Excellency[1] as they may be of use if perhaps an attempt against that Place Should be intended.[2] They were taken in one of our late Prizes coming from thence.[3] And It seems to me not probable that the Loss of Stores can be supplied before next year— With the greatest Respect I am your Excelly.

Mr. De Sartine.

From Richard Brocklesby[4]

ALS: American Philosophical Society

Dear Sr.   London 22nd Octobr. 1779

I never before presumed to give you the trouble of a letter in these miserable times, nor should I have done it at present when your Cause is so high & ours so low; but on the behalf of suffering humanity I adventure to bespeak your well known good Offices, & to tell you, that a worthy friend of mine Mr Croft a Banker in Pall Mall[5] has a favorite Son Lieutent Rich-

---

1. On May 15, 1779, a storehouse at St. John's was destroyed by fire. A list of the supplies that had been in it (dated six days later and addressed to the British Board of Ordnance) is among BF's papers at the APS. So too are more than half a dozen other documents sent from Newfoundland to the Board of Ordnance between March 31 and July 28; BF apparently made for Sartine copies of some or all of them.

2. There would have been precedent for such a move: in a surprise attack the French had seized St. Johns in June, 1762, doing more than £1,000,000 damage: G. Lacour-Gayet, *La marine militaire de la France sous le règne de Louis XV* (2nd ed., Paris, 1910), pp. 388–9.

3. Perhaps the *Fortune,* one of Jones's prizes.

4. Brocklesby (1722–97) was a physician, a friend of Burke and Johnson, and a fellow of the Royal Society: *DNB.*

5. Probably Richard Croft (d. 1793) of the firm of Crofts, Devaynes, Roberts, and Dawes: F.G. Hilton Price, *A Handbook of London Bankers* . . .

ard Croft of the 20th Regiment of Foot a Prisoner, now at Charlotteville in Virginia,[6] whose letters wch I have seen give such a deplorable representation of his past condition in his Captivity wth some circumstances particular in his case, that the philanthropy of my Nature, where friendship is concernd, induces me now to implore your good offices in his favor to facilitate his Exchange & release from Captivity on the establishd terms agreed by each party. Prudence forbids me to enlarge farther than to assure you I shall ever gratefully acknowledge whatever kindness you can procure for this Gentleman & I will only add that no one can venerate you more than Dr Sr your most Affecte & faithful Hle Servt.

RICHARD BROCKLESBY

Addressed: To / His Excellency / Benjamin Franklin Esqr. / &c &c &c / at / Paris

Notation: Brocklesby 22 Oct. 1779.

From Dumas

ALS: American Philosophical Society

Monsieur, Amst. 22 Oct. 1779.

Les Extraits ci-joints[7] vous donneront une idée de ce que nous faisons ici, & de l'état où est notre Escadre.

(London, 1876, reprinted New York, 1970), p. 48, 169; Lewis, *Walpole Correspondence,* XLIII, 280.

6. Croft was probably a young man as he received his commission only in September, 1775. He was still a prisoner in Virginia in November, 1780: Worthington C. Ford, comp., *British Officers Serving in the American Revolution 1774–1783* (Brooklyn, 1897), p. 54; *Jefferson Papers,* IV, 120.

7. Dumas enclosed extracts from the following letters, which we summarize:

Capt. Cottineau of the *Pallas* to Dumas, Texel, Oct. 14. This afternoon I responded to distress signals from the *Serapis* by trying to send my ship's boat, loaded with sailors and soldiers, but was prevented by the wind and tide. Lt. Stack of the *Serapis* arrived and used the boat to pursue a number of his ship's crewmen who had seized a Dutch *boot.* We pursued them to shore and Mr. Stack ran after them. I feared we would be compromised so I tried to recall my boat and that of the *Countess of Scarborough,* but he persisted. Fifteen of the deserters have been retaken, five were drowned,

Je suis très-content de la maniere d'agir de Mr. De Neufville dans cette affaire.

Il n'y a pas de résolution prise encore sur la réponse que l'on donnera au Mémoire de Mr. D'York. Mais il y a une autre, à ce que l'on vient de me dire, qui embrouille plus que jamais l'affaire des convois illimités, & qui a engagé Amsterdam & Harlem a protester de nouveau.[8]

J'espere qu'à la fin de la Semaine prochaine notre Escadre sera entierement réparée, & en état de remettre en mer.

---

one had his arm shattered by a bullet, and five are at large. They are Frenchmen, aged 22 to 30, who now are en route to Amsterdam. Will it not be possible to arrest and return them? (For Stack's account of the incident see Bradford, *Jones Papers,* reel 10, no. 2046).

Duc de la Vauguyon to Dumas, Oct. 18. By firing on the deserters Jones has committed an imprudence which can have very harmful consequences. I hope you and de Neufville will do all you can with the commandant of the roadstead and the Admiralty. Consult with the local authorities about reclaiming the deserters and follow their advice exactly. Inform me of the effect this very ill-considered act of Jones has caused. It has exerted a very bad effect here, capable of doing him infinite harm. If he did not give the order himself, I believe he should punish very severely the person responsible.

La Vauguyon to Dumas, Oct. 20. I am surprised not to have received a response from you.

Dumas to La Vauguyon, morning of Oct. 21. De Neufville has shown no lack of sagacity or zeal. Last evening the deserters were apprehended without incident. I believe they will be returned under guard this evening. I have written to find out what is happening at the Texel.

Dumas to La Vauguyon, evening of Oct. 21. A minor formality will delay the return of the deserters until tomorrow or the day after. You can be tranquil about what happened at the Texel. Far from complaining about our people, the commandant of the roadstead is very content with them.

Jones to Dumas, Oct. 21. We have moved the squadron into a safe harbor. The affair of the deserters has been misrepresented. They were recaptured while they were swimming, except for five of them, who were not pursued. The commandant of the roadstead, given a report, was perfectly satisfied, and even thanked the officers for the delicacy of their proceeding. (The full letter is reproduced in Bradford, *Jones Papers,* reel 4, no. 802.)

8. On Oct. 25 the States General responded to Yorke's memoir by confirming the Admiralty's decision not to hand over Jones's squadron to the British; see Dumas to BF of that date. La Vauguyon, encouraged by recent developments, believed the Dutch would offer convoy protection for naval stores: Fauchille, *Diplomatie française,* pp. 172–3.

Je suis avec le plus respectueux attachement, Monsieur Votre très-humble & très obéissant serviteur   DUMAS

Vous aurez bien la bonté, Monsieur, de communiquer tout cela à Mr. De Chaumont.

Passy à S. Exc. Mr. Franklin &c.

Addressed: His Excellency / B. Franklin, Esqr., Min. Plenip. / of the United States / *Passy.*/.

Notation: Dumas. Oct. 22. 1779

From ——— Gratien[9]   ALS: American Philosophical Society

Monseigneur   Morlaix 22e 8bre. 1779.

Monsr John Diot, faisant Et agissant Pour Messrs Chs Torris[1] & Compagnie De Dunkerque, armateurs Du prince noir, ma representé, que cetoit le vœu de votre excellence et qu'il Desiroit En son particulier, qu'il fut vendu pour Une somme De Mille Livres, a Made. Buttler, Les Effets contenus En plusieurs malles Trouvés à Bord du Dublin, navire anglais pris Et amené en ce port.[2]

Il m'a eté impossible D'acceder a cette Demande. 1° sans un consentement Juridique, non seulement des cointeressés, mais même Des Equipages preneurs qui y ont Egalement Droit, Et Dont nous Devons soigner les Interets.

2d.° Il Seroit fort Difficile De Distinguer Dans ce moment, ce qui peut appartenir a Made. Buttler, La pluspart Des malles Etant sans adresses.

Au surplus ce que nous pouvons presumer etre a cette Dame Excede de beaucoup en valeur Le prix offert.

Je Suis Donc arresté par ces circonstances Et mon Desir D'obliger Devient Impuissant par Tant de Contrariétés.

J'ay L'honneur De Donner avis, à votre excellence de mes

9. A member of the Admiralty court at Morlaix who had been in communication with BF about other prizes: XXIX, 215, 368.
1. Charles Torris was a silent partner in his brother John's firm: Clark, *Ben Franklin's Privateers,* p. 23.
2. See John Torris' Oct. 8 letter for his orders about the effects.

observations, qui fondés sur La Justice et L'impossibilité, Doivent obtenir aveu.

Je Suis avec Un Profond Respect. Monseigneur Vôtre Très humble Et Très obeissant Serviteur GRATIEN

Lieut Genl De L'amirauté

Notation: Gratier 22 Oct 79

From the Crew of the *Alliance:* Affidavit[3]

Printed in Pierre Landais, *Memorial, to Justify Peter Landai's Conduct during the Late War* (Boston, 1784) pp. 50–1.

On board the Alliance, Texel,

May it please you Excellency, Oct. 23, 1779.

To bear the humble representation and petition of the Mariners and Marines on board the Continental ship Alliance.

---

3. Landais, learning that he had been summoned to Paris to answer charges, apparently solicited this letter; see his of Oct. 24. He also prepared a statement concerning his activities during the Battle off Flamborough Head, which included sketches showing the positions of the various naval units during the different phases of the action: Landais, *Memorial,* pp. 34–43. These sketches were certified by fifteen officers and volunteers of the *Alliance,* who also signed an affidavit testifying that the officers had seen no signal but the one for chase, that the *Bonhomme Richard* failed to answer the *Alliance*'s hail, and that Landais had given orders to the gunners to take care not to fire on the *Bonhomme Richard* and had clearly indicated which of the contending ships was which, the colors of them being visible. They also explained that twice they had gone within musket shot of the *Serapis*'s stern and once her bow, that they had lost neither opportunity nor time in coming to the *Bonhomme Richard*'s assistance, and that they had seen the *Serapis* on fire and the *Countess of Scarborough* raking the *Bonhomme Richard.* Finally they certified that the *Alliance*'s crew had been very attentive to orders and had executed them immediately to the satisfaction of all the officers. This affidavit was certified by WTF to be an exact copy and bears the notation "Certificate given to Capt. Landais by the Officers of the Alliance." University of Pa. Library. Landais made another copy which is at the same repository. Both state that the original had been written on Oct. 21 on the back of the sketches of the engagement. The printed version of the affidavit (Landais, *Memorial,* p. 43) lacks the final paragraph.

Honored S I R,

We have been surprised with the information that our honored commander, Peter Landais, Esq; has been impeached of cowardice to your Excellency, relative to his conduct on the 23d day of September last.— We would beg your Excellency's indulgeance while we humbly represent, that we conceive it don't become us to enter into the particulars of his conduct, yet we would wish to say, the said Peter Landais, Esq; behaved through the whole of that day, and especially in the time of the action with his Britanic Majesty's ships the Serapis and Countess of Scarborough, with the utmost magnanimity, prudence, and vigilence of a wise and resolute commander, and that he took all the possible methods in so calm a time, and in the night, to distress the enemy, and to help our friend.

Therefore we flatter ourselves and trust, that upon an impartial investigation of his conduct, these things will appear so plain to your Excellency as to remove all the dishonourable aspersions of the malignant.

We would further beg your Excellency's clemency while we say we humbly conceive almost all of us have long since fulfilled our obligations to the said ship Alliance, and we look upon it a great hardship that we are detained in a foreign country on board the said ship, and should think it an addition to our present uneasiness to have a new commander appointed over us.— We would humbly pray your Excellency to consider our long absence from our distressed country and families, many of us by a tedious confinement in a British prison; and if it should appear consistent with your Excellency's duty, and the interest of our country, that you should order us home, where, we humbly conceive, our suffering country may receive much greater service from your Excellency's and our country's devoted humble servants.

PAUL NOYES,	NICHOLAS WORD-BURY,	JOSEPH FREDERICK,
ROBERT EMBLETON,	JAMES BOUIRD,	GEORGE ALLEN,
ELIAS HASTINE,	HENRY WRIGH-TINGTON,	JACOB NUTTER,

ALEXANDER AN-
GUISH,
JAMES COLLITON,
ROBERT CAIDER,
JOHN MAZY(?),
SAMUEL BAWL,
JOHN KEILY,
JOHN THOMAS,
NATHANIEL
WARNER,
JOHN M. BLAIN
JAMES YOUNG,
ALEXANDER TAY-
LOR,
WILLIAM CUN-
NINGHAM,
CHARLES M.
CHASTNEY,
JOHN LEAK,
SAMUEL GERCHALL,
DANIEL BUMSTOCK,
JOHN FORESTER,
JAMES MOZAN,
SAMUEL DALE,
EBENEZER EDWARD,

JOSEPH MAZARY.

CHARLES HOWARD,

JOHN BEGRAM,
JAMES PORTER,
THOMAS WATCH,
MICHAEL BAPTIST,
JOHN DIMOND,
CHARLES FORBES,
JOHN SPRINGS,

JOSEPH STILL,
GEORGE FE(?),
JOHN KELLY,

JAMES POOR,

GILLAM VEIL,

JOHN ORR,
EBENEZER(?),
DANIEL JACKSON,
WILLIAM BOCKS
JOHN PARE,
JOHN RICK,
JOSEPH SHILLAHOW,

BENJAMIN YOULIN,

AUBUR(?) BEN-
NETT,
ADDL(?) FAZEN,
JOSEPH BLAWT,
RICHARD OWEN,
WILLIAM STOAPER,
JAMES DICKASON,
JOSEPH STICKER,
THOMAS BAILY,

NATHAN PORTER,
EBENEZER BROWN,
JOHN SIMPSON,

WILLIAM SHACK-
FORD,
THOMAS MITONY,

JOHN SMITH,
THOMAS LEWIS,
We, whose names
are here written,
do attest this
a true copy.
NATHANIEL INGRA-
HAM,
JOHN SPENCER.[4]

P.S. We, whose names are above, can attest, from the common conversation on board the ship, that the foregoing sentiments expressed, are the sentiments of all in our rank on board, but the shortness of the time, the business of the ship, many sick, and many on board Captain Jones, is the only reasons why more have not affixed their names.[5]

4. Ingraham and Spencer were volunteers who also signed the officers' affidavit.

5. Landais claimed that virtually the only people not to sign were twenty-seven sick men, thirty crewmen then on board the *Serapis,* and various prize crews: Landais, *Memorial,* p. 51.

From Girardot, Haller & Cie.

L:[6] American Philosophical Society

Sir   Paris 23 Octr 1779

Mr. Wm. Bingley a native of Rotterdam bearer of these, and who has been upwards of nine years Continually in our Business, having Acquitted himself in evry department he has undertaken to our utmost Satisfaction, and being desirous of proceeding to America for several Reasons, which he will communicate to you/: we beg leave to introduce him to you as a person who quits us to our Regret.

It is in your power Sir to Render him very essential service, and what ever instruction, Advice or introduction you may be pleased to favor him with, shall be esteemd as a great obligation conferrd on them who will allways be desirous of giving you convincing proofs of their Sincere esteem and attachment, having the honor to Stile themselves on All occasions Sir Your mt obedt hble servts   GIRARDOT HALLER

To his Excy. The honb. B. Franklin Esqr:—

Addressed: To / his Excelly. The honble. / B Franklin / Passy

Notation: Girard or Challers 23 Oct 79

To Vergennes

AL: Archives du Ministère des affaires étrangères

Passy, Oct. 24. 1779.

Mr Franklin presents his Respects to M. le Comte de Vergennes, and begs leave to lay before his Excellency the enclos'd Letter from Messieurs Alexanders,[7] and to request he would be pleased to give it a little of his Attention.

---

6. Written and signed by a clerk.

7. William and his brother Alexander John, who had recently arrived from Grenada, where he had been engaged in a lengthy legal dispute on behalf of the family: XXII, 521–2n; XXIV, 199; XXIX, 689. Lord Macartney, the former British governor of Grenada, had ordered the Alexanders' properties on the island sequestered, overturning a jury decision in their favor. The French capture of the island had transferred the case to the French courts and the Alexanders' opponent, the banking firm of Walpole & Elli-

From Landais

ALS: American Philosophical Society; copy: Harvard University Library

Please Your Excellency The Helder the 24th October 1779.

I received the 22d Inst the letter you did me the honour of writing to me the 15th It. and would have complye'd with Your order inclose'd in it immediatly had I not been detain'd aboard one day to over hauld my papers, and when I came ashore I thought I wanted but half an our of time for to have a Certificate from under the hand of Mr de Cottineau Capn of the Pallas,[8] I fund him So ill that he was neither to be Spoke to, or Seen; I have been Ever Since waiting for a moment of relif but it is not come yet! I do'nt know what to do, to go without that paper I may want it, to Stay longer I am afraid Your Excellency or the french Minister would think I am delaying, but I will do as I have allways done, for the best, for to fullful Your order and follow Your advice, and go So Soon as Possible[9] being fully Confident of Your doing justice. I am with Respect Your Excellency's Most Obeidient Most humble Servant   P: LANDAIS

P.S. I hope Mr DuNeufville will aford me with the money I Shall want for the journey, or else I could not Proceed.

---

son (allied with the Bank of England in the case), asked the French council of state to confirm Macartney's decision: Price, *France and the Chesapeake*, II, 698–9. BF enclosed a memorandum from the two brothers claiming the case against them was fraudulent and asking that they be permitted to use the proceeds from the Grenada estates to satisfy the other creditors of the family.

8. Several weeks later Cottineau sent Chaumont a memoir about the events off Flamborough Head supporting Landais' contention that the *Alliance* had raked not the *Bonhomme Richard*, but the *Serapis*. Schaeper, *Battle off Flamborough Head*, pp. 83–5, gives a translation; see also our annotation of Jones's Oct. 3 letter to BF. Jones may have destroyed an earlier letter from Cottineau to him, because it did not support his, Jones's, position: Schaeper, *Battle off Flamborough Head*, pp. 58–9.

9. On Oct. 22 Landais informed Jones that he had turned over command of the *Alliance* to Lt. James Degge and was preparing to leave for Paris:

His Excellency Bn. Franklin Minister Plenipotentiary of the united States of America

Notation: P. Landais 24 Oct 79

From Charles-François Le Brun

ALS: American Philosophical Society

honble. Sir   Paris rüe de vaugirard 8ber. 25th. 1779.

Messrs. delagoanere & Co.[1] from coruña desire me to inquire whether Mr. A. Lee is still the deputy of the congress for the court of Spain. 'Tis very Long Since they have not been honour'd with his correspondence; and they Seem to have Some piece of information which they would communicate to the person appointed for that department.

The Silence of Mr. A.L. his Staying at paris when things Seem'd to be ripe for his appearing at madrid in his public caracter, the rumours which have been Spread of his being recall'd induc'd them to think it would be rather improper to write to him without a certitude that he acts still in the Same capacity.

They are very uneasy on account of that brave Capt. Coningham[2] and entreat me to get what Light I can on the fate of a man who here inspired with the highest esteem and friendship. I hope you'll be so kind as to Let me Know what sort of answer I can make to them.

I am with the highest regard and most deserved respect honble. Sir, your most humble and obedient Servant

LE BRUN

Notation: Le Brun 25. Oct. 1779.—

Bradford, *Jones Papers,* reel 4, no. 810; reel 10, no. 2045. He left Amsterdam about Nov. 3 and arrived in Paris on the 8th: Dumas to BF, Nov. 5 (APS); Landais, *Memorial,* p. 51.

1. About whom Le Brun had written BF in 1777: XXIV, 541–2.

2. Whom the firm had assisted during his lengthy stay in Spain: Neeser, *Conyngham,* pp. 108–9 and following.

To Le Brun
Copy: Library of Congress

Sir   Passy Oct. 25. 1779.

Mr. Arthur Lee has not been recalled the States in Congress being equally divided on the Question; but he has mentioned to me his Intention of returning immediately to America as no certain Provision has been made for his support in Spain.[3]

Capt. Conyngham was sent to England in Irons to be try'd for his Life as a Pirate. The Congress ordered some English Prisoners of equal Rank to be put in Irons by way of Reprisal to abide his fate.[4] Since his arrival in England, his Irons have been taken off and he is treated as the other Prisoners, and will probably Soon be exhang'd. Here are a Number of frenchmen that had serv'd with him and being put on Board one of his Prizes afterwards carried into England, were kept Prisoners there till Lately when we exhang'd them. They demand their Wages and a Share of his Prises.[5] I Shall be oblig'd to Messrs. de Lagoaner for any Information they may be pleased to Send me what has been done with the Produce of those Prizes sold in Spain. With great Regard, I have the honour to be &c

M. Le Brun

To Jane Mecom
LS:[6] American Philosophical Society; copy:[7] South Carolina Historical Society

Dear Sister,   Passy Oct. 25. 1779.

I received your kind Letter of Feb. 14. the Contents of which gave me a kind of melancholy Satisfaction. The greater Ease you will now enjoy makes some Compensation in my Mind for the uncomfortable Circumstance that brought it

---

3. Above, Sept. 26. Four states had voted to recall Lee, but four others were opposed, and four divided equally: *JCC,* XIV, 542–3.

4. See BF to Nesbitt, Sept. 29.

5. BF had told Coffyn he thought the claims should be backed by testimony: above, Sept. 28.

6. In WTF's hand.

7. In the hand of L'Air de Lamotte, corrected and signed by BF.

about. I hope you will have no more Afflictions of that kind, and that after so long and stormy a Day your Evening may be serene & pleasant.[8]

Yours of June 23d by Mr Watson is also come safe to hand.[9] The Description you give of your present Situation is pleasing. I rejoice to hear you have so much Comfort in your Grandaughter and her good Husband. Give my Love to them.

The Account you had from Jona. Williams of the Vogue I am in here, has some Truth in it. Perhaps few Strangers in France have had the good Fortune to be so universally popular: But the Story you allude to, which was in the News Papers, mentioning "mechanic Rust," &ca. is totally without Foundation. The English Papers frequently take those Liberties with me. I remember to have once counted seven Paragraphs relating to me that came by one Post, all of which were Lies except one that only mentioned my living in the same House with Mr Deane.— This Popularity has occasioned so many Paintings, Busto's, Medals & Prints to be made of me, and distributed throughout the Kingdom, that my Face is now almost as well known as that of the Moon. But one is not to expect being always in Fassion. I hope however to preserve, while I stay, the Regard you mention of the French Ladies, for their Society and Conversation when I have time to enjoy it, is extreamly agreable.

The Enemy have been very near you indeed. When only at the Distance of a Mile you must have been much alarm'd. We have given Them a little Taste of this Disturbance upon their own Coasts this Summer; And tho' we have burnt none of their Towns, we have occasioned a good deal of Terror & Bustle in many of them, as they immagined our Commodore Jones had 4000. Troops with him for Descents. He has however taken and destroyed upwards of twenty Sail of their Merchantmen or Colliers, with two Men of War, and is arrived safe in Holland with 400. Prisoners.[1] Had not contrary Winds and Accidents prevented it, the intended Invasion of England

---

8. The affliction was the death of her son Peter Mecom (XXVIII, 541–2).

9. XXIX, 722–5.

1. The copyist omitted the last two words; BF interlined, "them & 500 Prisoners."

with the combined Fleet and a great Army might have taken Place, and have made the English feel a little more of that kind of Distress they have so wantonly caused in America.

I come now to your last of July 27. I am glad to learn by it that my dear Sister continued in good Health and good Spirits; and that she had learnt not to be afraid of her Friend Fresh Air.

You will do me a great deal of Pleasure in sending me as You propose, some Crown Soap, the very best that can be made. I shall have an Opportunity of obliging some Friends with it, who very much admire the little Specimens I have been able to give them. With the tenderest Affection I am ever, my Dear Sister, Your very loving Brother.   B FRANKLIN

My Love to Mr & Mrs. Greene & to my young Friend Ray. Temple desires me to present you his Affectionate Respects.

Mrs. Meacome.

To Richard Peters   Copy: Library of Congress

Sir   Passy, Oct. 25.[–27] 1779.
    With great Difficulty and after much Enquiry my Correspondent in England found out the residence of your honoured father and furnished him by my orders with an hundred Pounds sterling.— I have a Letter from him acknowledging the Receipt of it; and he writes one to you which I forward by this Conveyance.[2] He desires me to give you my sentiments what Channel may be best for you to use in making future Remittances. I know none better, than to vest what you send in Congress interest Bills which if you transmit to me, I will take care to remit the accounts to him in a Bill upon England. I request you to send me in the same Bills the Sum I have already advanced as above, by the first opportunity as I have many occasions for Money here. Make my Compliments ac-

2. See William Peters to BF, Aug. 12. BF recorded in his Cash Book (see XXVI, 3) on Oct. 24 a payment for, "Richard Peters Dr for 100£ Sterling advanc'd by me to his Father in England, thru Mr Digges."

ceptable to Mrs. Peters, and believe me to be with great Esteem Your sincere friend and most obedient humble servant.

P.S. Oct. 27. I have this Day drawn on you at 10 Days sight for twenty five Louis in favour of Mr. De Carné Trecesson[3] which drafts I make no Doubt will be duly honoured.

Richard Peters Esqe.

To Jonathan Williams, Sr.

LS:[4] Yale University Library

Dear Cousin   Passy, Oct. 25. 1779.

I received your kind Letters of July 29, and August 8. It was a great satisfaction to me to learn that my Dear Sister, was relieved from that continual Distress She had so long labour'd under.— I know not whether my Proposal with regard to Mr. Collais employing himself in making Crown Soap, is Likely to be exceuted by him to Advantage: Perhaps he may not have Activity and Acuteness enough: You and my Sister can judge of that better than me. I wish however that one good Boiling of it may be made and sent me. It will be useful to me in obliging Friends with it; and I shall thankfully refund what

3. Louis-Marie-Victor Carné de Trécesson (b. 1759) had gone to America in 1778 to serve as a volunteer in La Rouërie's legion, then as aide-de-camp to General du Portail. In May, 1779, he left to rejoin the Armagnac regiment in Martinique: Lasseray, *Les Français,* I, 144–6. BF's Cash Book, under the date of Oct. 27, states that he "Received of M. le Comte de Chateaugiron, Twenty-five Louis, for which I gave him my Draft on Mr. Richard Peters at Phila. payable to Mr Carné de Trecession ... 600—." On April 28, 1780, Peters informed Trécesson that BF, under the assumption Trécesson was still in Col. Armand's corps, had sent to him there a letter advising him of the arrangement. Peters, however, could not pay the twenty-five *louis* until an endorsed bill was presented. William Bingham in Martinique would no doubt cheerfully negotiate the affair. APS.

4. In the hand of L'Air de Lamotte, whose mistranscription of the last word ("Unite" instead of "Uncle") is typical. As the address indicates, this was one of the copies BF had his new secretary make for Lafayette to bring to America. The address sheet, and the notation, "Duplicate," are in WTF's hand.

you may advance on that Account for me, in any manner you may order.

I received the young Gentleman M Watson wiith such Civilities as were in my Power, on your Recommendation.[5] He is gone down to Nantes.

I am now to congratulate you on the Marriage of your Son Jonathan to a very amiable young Lady, Miss Marianne Alexander, Daughter of a friend of mine, who will I am persuaded make him a good Wife and a pleasing Compagnion as her Conversation is very Sensible and engaging. He will Doubtless give you other particulars.

I am always glad to hear of your Welfare, and that of your Family, to whom my Love and blessing. I am as ever, Your affectionate Unite   B FRANKLIN

Jonathan Williams Esqe.

(Duplicate)

Addressed: To / Jonathan Williams Esqr / Merchant, / Boston / Favd by the Marqs / De la Fayette

From Benjamin Franklin Bache[6]

ALS: American Philosophical Society

My Dear grand Papa   Geneve 25 octobre 1779
    I am very glad that you write to me very often I pray you too continu it I am very sorry because I have not put the date to my letres but I will put it to the fust letre I have recived your print and accept it Mr Marignac has bought me a

---

5. BF indeed spared no efforts to welcome young Elkanah Watson, extending him an introduction to Vergennes, an invitation to dine at the Chaumonts, and an invitation to jw's wedding, before sending him to Nantes with American and French dispatches for the *Mercury:* Winslow C. Watson, *Men and Times of the Revolution; or, Memoirs of Elkanah Watson* . . . (New York, 1856), pp. 86–93.

6. This letter, only the first half of which is in English, reflects the degree to which French dominates his syntax. We have deciphered what we could of his near-phonetic spellings.

dictionary[7] I am very glad that you will send my some books inglith the scolars have leave ventuige [the advantage?] Jexlaine(?) selecte historie profaine and writ it ad phedre's fables[8] the exercises of mister Mercier.[9] My dear grandpapa tell my cosin that I can not write to him but wen I will have some time I will write to him I have nothing to say to you for the present.

I am your afectionaite son.   B. F. B.

J'ai reçu Mon cher grand papa la lettre que vous m'aves envoyée de mon cher papa elle m'a fait grand plaisir et si vous souhaites que je lui ecrive je lui ecrirai Me Cramer De Long a beaucoup de bontés pour moi je vais y coucher le samedi au soir et je viens le lundi matin Mr et Me Marignac vous presentent bien leurs respects Mr Marignac m'a mené ches Me Artaud[1] qui ma fait beaucoup de politesses et m'a invité pour diner jeudi prochain. Je ne saurois vous dire, Mon cher grand papa, quel plaisir m'a fait votre portrait! c'est une obligation de plus que j'ai à Mon cousin, à qui je fais mille amitiès.

Notation: B. f. B. Geneve 25. Octbre. 1779.

7. The bill for BFB's schooling dated Oct. 5, above, includes a "Dictionnaire Anglois en 2 Volumes."

8. A popular work in schools; several 18th-century school editions of the *Fables* are listed in the catalogues of the British Museum and the Bibliothèque Nationale, and in Antoine-Alexandre Barbier, *Dictionnaire des ouvrages anonymes* (4 vols., Paris, 1872–79).

9. An earlier schooling bill (XXIX, 347–9) lists "Themes Mercier" among the books M. Marignac purchased for the newly enrolled BFB. The author of these books may be Nicolas Mercier, a 17th-century professor at the collège de Navarre whose *Manuel des grammairiens* became a classic for the teaching of Latin and was reprinted throughout the 18th century. He was also the author of *Vocabulaire françois-latin, pour les thèmes de M. le professeur Mercier:* Hoefer, ed., *Nouvelle biographie générale* (46 vols., Paris, 1855–66).

1. Born Agathe Silvestre and married to Jérémie Arthaud, a banker, she was the sister of Mme Ferdinand Grand. Lüthy, *Banque protestante,* II, 339. The Silvestre family was from Vevey, on the Lake of Geneva.

From Dumas

ALS: American Philosophical Society; AL (draft): Algemeen Rijksarchief

Monsieur, Amsterdam 25e. Octob. 1779

Les affaires de notre Escadre vont très-bien à Lahaie. Voici ce que l'on m'en apprend de très-bonne part, le 23.

"Les Etats d'Hollde. ont adopté unanimement l'Avis des Amirautés, qui est parfaitement conforme à celui du College particulier d'Amsterdam, dont vous avez eu connoissance. Vraisemblablement la Résolution de la Province sera confirmée Lundi par celle des Etats-Généraux, & la réponse, très satisfaisante pour le Congrès, remise à Sir J. Y."[2]

Je viens de voir chez mon ami le Libraire Rey, une Lettre d'un Libraire de Londres (Elmsly)[3] qui lui dit entre autres: *Notre commerce, notre Argent, notre Honneur, Tout va au diable.*

Permettez que je présente ici mes respects à Mr. De Chaumont. Cette Lettre doit le rassurer sur les dispositions des Amirautés ici, dont il étoit en peine.

Dès que je pourrai avoir la résolution des Et. Gx. & la réponse à Mr. Y——, je vous la ferai parvenir.

Je suis avec le plus respectueux attachement, Monsieur Votre très-humble & très obéissant serviteur DUMAS

Je ne sais plus, Monsieur, quelle excuse alléguer à *notre Ami,* quand il me demande si je n'ai pas encore reçu de retour notre projet de Traité.[4]

P.S. Mr. Sayre est venu me demander, si je n'avois pas reçu de votre part, Monsieur, des Lettres de marques pour lui en blanc. Je lui ai dit que non. Il craint, Monsieur, que vous n'ayiez oublié la promesse que vous lui aviez faite, dit-il, à cet égard; & il me prie de vous en faire souvenir comme d'une

2. On Monday, Oct. 25, the States General replied to Yorke that it would not pass judgment on the ownership or legality of Jones's prizes, but would authorize the Admiralty of Amsterdam to compel Jones's ships to put to sea as soon as possible: *Annual Register* for 1779, pp. 429–30; Daniel A. Miller, *Sir Joseph Yorke and Anglo-Dutch Relations 1774–1780* (The Hague and Paris, 1970), p. 81.

3. Most probably the famous bookseller Peter Elmsley or Elmsly: XIX, 343n.

4. See Dumas to BF, Sept. 21.

chose dont il est pressé. J'ai vu le vaisseau que l'on bâtit ici d'après son modele. Il est déjà fort avancé.

Passy à Son Exc. M. Franklin

Addressed: à Son Excellence / Monsieur B. Franklin, Esqr. / Min. Plénip. des Etats-Unis / &c. &c. / *Passy.*/.

Notation: Dumas Octr. 25. 1779

From Jean de Neufville & fils

ALS: American Philosophical Society

High Honourable Sir!   Amsterdam the 25th. October 1779

We acknowledge with the greatest regard yoúr Excellencys last favoúr of the 15th., and will be very anxious in execúting to satisfaction the orders Mr. De Chaumont and Mr. Dumas gave and will give ús for the supplies of the American Squadron. We hope we may likewise meet there in with the approbation of your Excellency;

What the influence of the English might have operated withoút the opposition and leading firmness of the City of Amsterdam, we dare scarcely Conjecture; bútt as matters stand, presume to say, that The United States of America will meet with every friendly treatment; we long ago ponderated the Consequences of their inflúence and may rejoice, as we hope before long, in the so múch desired Union of the two Sister Republicqs; and if that beauty might bestow one day or other her favoúrs to some private Admirers in Our Citÿ, we never will desist from Courting her with the útmost Assidúity, may we owe our Triúmph over so many rivals, as she will attract by her continually encreasing Charm to the influence of yoúr Excellency and trúe Fatherly power.

Mr. Dumas acquainted ús with the dispositions of Yoúr Excellencÿ about the Loan in Holland, as not expecting any thing could be efectuated there in as yett; the reqúired subscription we make free to avow, was yett to large for the Cirúmstances, bútt at the same time we were pretty sure, that now and then we should have mett, and we have, with some Patrioticq spirits, disposed to assist the caúse of Liberty in that way; thoúgh the intrest was under that of others; we wish again, at any opportúnity of this kind to convince yoúr Excellency of the Warmth of our attachment, as

We have the honor to be with the highest regard High Honourable Sir. Yoúr Excellencys most Obedient and most devoted Servants   JOHN DE NEUFVILLE & SON

Notation: Neufville John & son—25. Oct. 1779.

From Cradock Taylor   ALS: American Philosophical Society

Sir,   Aix in Provance Octbr. 25th. 1779
I Yesterday Recd. a letter from Mr. Gregoire informing me that your Excellency has no objection to giveing me my liberty provided you were assured that I was raly an American.

Inclosed I send you three Letters I have receivd. from Mr Frazier which is all I can do to convince you[5] Mr. Frazier has likewise informed me that he has acquainted your Excellency fully who (& what) I am; the most of the Officers who were Prisoners in this place are Exchangd, & there is a Cartell expected every Day for the exchange of the rest of us but for my part I am determind. sooner than go in the English Service again; to go in the French provided there is no possabillity of my returning to my Native Country which I can't help thinking veary hard. Mr. Gregoire has likewise Informed me your Excellencyes reason for not Answering my letters yet I hope

5. Letters from Frazer to Taylor dated June 7 (XXIX, 771n), Sept. 15, and Oct. 18, are among BF's papers at the APS. In the one of Sept. 15 Frazer explains that he has written fully (to BF, Sept. 7, above) about Taylor's plight and hopes the young man will soon obtain his liberty. If he does, let him lose no time in reaching Bordeaux, traveling light but bringing his sea books and his quadrant. On Oct. 18 Frazer expresses surprise that Taylor's letters to Passy go unanswered and promises to write BF again. He advises the unfortunate prisoner not to be exchanged as an Englishman: if he does not wish to go home, as Frazer first suggested, he should enter French service.

The present letter must have persuaded BF of Taylor's truthfulness; on Nov. 1 the American minister wrote him that he would try to secure his discharge right away. Library of Congress.

Sir You will Condesend to answer this as it is the last I shall persume to trouble you with.

I am Sir with all due Respect your Excellencies most Obbdt. Humbl. Servt.,   CRADOCK TAYLOR

Addressed: To / His Excellency Benjn. Franklin / Esqr. Plenopitry. to the / United States of America / Parris

Notation: Cradoc Taylor 25 Oct 79

From De Chezaulx   Press copy:[6] Library of Congress

Monsieur   à Berghen en Norvege le 26. 8bre. 1779.

Il m'est douloureux au dela de toute expression d'avoir à vous informer aujourdhui que les deux prises *The Betsey* & *The Union* (faites par la fregate l'Alliance Capne. Landais & conduites en ce port) ont été ces jours-ci restituées aux Anglois en vertu d'une resolution emanée du Roi de Dk. resolution injuste & contraire aux droits des gens. Nous sommes ici, Monsieur dans la plus grande consternation, parceque je ne m'attendois rien moins qu'à un tel événement.

J'ai l'honneur de vous remettre ci-jointe, Monsieur, la traduction de cette singulière resolution, qui m'a été communiquée,[7] laquelle m'a d'autant plus surpris que M. Caillard chargé des affaires du Roi à Copenhague me mande par sa lettre du 9 de ce mois, qu'il avoit eté en conference avec le ministère Danois; mais qu'il n'avoit pu obtenir la permission qu'il avoit sollicitée pour la vente des dites prises, & que par consequent elles auroient ordre de reprendre la mer. On voit

6. In the hand of William Short, Jefferson's secretary. The document is virtually illegible in places, and we have supplied in brackets those readings of which we remain uncertain.

7. On Oct. 16 Bager, grand bailiff of Bergen, notified de Chezaulx of the government's ruling of two weeks earlier. De Chezaulx sent BF a French translation (Library of Congress), which BF incorporated in a Dec. 22 petition to Danish Foreign Minister Andreas Peter von Bernstorff (Wharton, *Diplomatic Correspondence,* III, 433–5). The ruling stated that King Christian VII had ordered the ships and cargoes liberated because he had not yet recognized the independence of the colonies associated against England and hence the vessels could not be considered good and lawful prizes. For the British reaction see Stevens, *Facsimiles,* x, no. 1031.

que ce ministre n'a eu aucune connoissance de la resolution de cette cour du 2. 8bre. puisqu'il n'en fait pas mention.

Je m'etois toujours attendû que par le moyen de la negociation nous auroit gagné du tems & que dans l'intervalle la frégate l'Alliance, ou quelque autre batiment de l'escadre de M. Jones seroient entré en ce port, & que nous aurions pû prendre des arrangements pour renforcer les equipages de ces prises à l'effet de leur faire reprendre la mer sous leur escorte, ou enfin que j'aurois pû avoir le tems de recevoir vos ordres, sans lesquels je ne pouvais rien faire, parceque l'ordre par écrit du Capne. Landais donné aux officiers chargés du commandement de ces prises leur prescrit de les conduire à Berghen. Je ne pouvois rien prendre sur moi.

Quand ces prises arrivérent au bas de la riviere je fus obligé de leur envoyer du monde pour les aider à monter à la ville, ètant très faible d'equipage, elles ne pouvoient donc dans cet etat reprendre la mer que dans le cas ou les gouverneurs ici auroient eu ordre de leur refuser l'entrée. Nous comptions ainsi que je l'ai deja dit, avoir eu le tems de recevoir vos ordres; car il n'etoit pas a présumer que la cour de Dk. eut pris une resolution hostile à leur égard, celle que j'attendois ne pouvait etre au pis aller, qu'un ordre aux gouverneurs ici de leur faire reprendre la mer, sur le fondement que l'indépendance des Etats-Unis n'étoit encore pas reconnue par la Cour Danoise.

Je me propose de vous envoyer, Monsieur, par le courier prochain un memoire detaillé de la conduite que j'ai tenue, & de toutes mes operations relativement a ces prises. J'ai fait protester aux officiers contre la violence qui leur a été faite, & tous dommages & interets pour y avoir recours en son tems, à l'effet que l'on puisse se procurer par les voyes que l'on jugera convenables le dedommagement de cette perte considérable & la satisfaction due aux Etats-Unis. Vous recevrez aussi, Monsieur, l'expedition de ce protêt en bonne & due forme.

Jai fait tout ce qui m'a été possible pour retarder l'operation et [l'executoire?] des gouverneurs Danois; mais je n'ai rien pu obtenir. On s'est emparé des batiments de leurs cargaisons et de leurs inventaires au nom du Roi de Dk., & livraison dans toutes les formes a été faite au consul d'Angleterre. Je me suis pourvu en justice pour obtenir en payement des frais faits ici à la charge des dits navires & de leur équipages [?] à son alt. Rale [Royale?]. Nous verrons ce qui sera décidé.

Jai également exigé du gouvernement que puisque l'on avoit degradé les equipages Américains il etoit bien juste que l'on pourvût à leur subsistance, leur passage & leur [confort?] pour les rendre ou mettre en état de retourner dans leur patrie; mais je n'ai rien pû obtenir. On me laisse le soin d'y pourvoir. Ces èquipages engendraient ici beaucoup de frais & de dépense. Je vous suplie de vouloir bien me faire connoître vos intentions à cet egard.

La valeur de ces deux prises que l'on vous enleve injustement, est au moins de £40,000 sterling indépendamment des frais, & l'argent deboursé par le banquier M Dankert Dn Krohn, dont je vous remettrai le compte.

Le tems nous apprendra, Monsieur, comment la cour de Danemark se retirera de la fausse demarche qu'elle a faite & hazardée au prejudice du droit des gens. Il y a peut-etre une convention secrete entre elle & l'Angleterre relativement aux prises des Américains: cependant il n'en a rien transpiré, & je l'ignore.

Le courier prochain nous apportera peut être, le même ordre à l'egard de la prise *Le Charming Polly*.[8] Cependant je vais faire diligence pour le mettre en etat de sortir avant qu'il parvienne aux gouverneurs. Mais il y a apparence qu'ils s'y opposent. J'aurai l'honneur de vous informer, Monsieur, par le courier prochain du suivi, comme aussi de tout ce qui me paraitra meriter votre attention.

J'ai l'honneur d'etre &c.   (signé) DECHEZAULX

P.S. Le consul anglois[9] n'a point de monde. Il faut qu'il en fasse venir d'Angleterre. Je ne prevois pas que ces batiments soient

---

8. Another of Landais' prizes, a brig which arrived in Bergen on Oct. 20 and was turned over to the British two weeks later: Thomas Fitzgerald to Jones, Oct. 2, 1783, Bradford, *Jones Papers*, reel 7, no. 1479.

9. John Wallace: *The Court and City Register . . .* for 1779 (London, n.d.), p. 94.

en etat de sortir d'ici avant deux mois & peut-être trois. Il faudroit tâcher de sen emparer en sortant d'ici.

Notation: (Copy. W Short, Secy)

From Henrÿ du Bois   ALS: American Philosophical Society

Monsieur   Amsterdam le 26. 8bre. 1779.

L'audience dont vous avez daigné m'honnorer a mon dernier voyage a Costi, m'a fait chercher les occasions de vous être utile, ainsi qu'a tous vos Compatriotes que les Circonstances ou les affaires ont Conduit ici; Je compte d'y avoir en quelque sorte satisfait, en donnant a plusieurs americains échapés des prisons d'angleterre et venus en notre ville, tous les secours et les Connoissances qui ont dépendu de moi, pour les mettre a portée de retourner tranquillement chez eux;[1] et j'ai la satisfaction de pouvoir me flatter d'avoir acquis la Confiance de tous les Capitaines arrivés cette Campagne, même du Capitaine Paul Jones, qui pendant son sejour ici, ma honnoré de sa visite et fait espérer la préférence dans tout ce qu'il aurait besoin de relatif a mon Commerce. Si sans préjudicier a vos amis d'ici, vous voulussiez, Monsieur, m'honnorer de quelque part dans la distribution de vos ordres et Commissions, Je ne négligerai rien, pour y repondre et m'en rendre digne par mon empressement a vous être utile et vous prouver le profond respect avec lequel J'ai lhonneur d'être Monsieur Votre très humble et très obéissant serviteur   Henrÿ du Bois

---

1. For the assistance previously provided escaped American prisoners by the Amsterdam linen, lace, and haberdashery merchant see xxv, 158n; xxviii, 607–8. Dubois continued to aid escaped prisoners; for an example see Bradford, *Jones Papers,* reel 5, no. 927.

From David Hartley: Two Letters

(I) ALS: American Philosophical Society; transcript: Library of Congress; (II) ALS: American Philosophical Society; copy:[2] Historical Society of Pennsylvania

I.

My Dear friend   October 26 1779

I have communicated the Substance of yours of the 8th instant to the Board & when I receive their answer I will transmitt it to you. I am very anxious to hear again from you of M De Sartine's consent to the passport to Morlaix that we may get our Cartel ship on float again. With respect to the admission of the written contracts I am sorry for the delay of the answer. I have renewed my application for an Answer upon transmitting the additional Contracts wch you sent me in your last letter.

I shall be much obliged to you for your assistance in the Case of Capt. Stephenson not only as an agreeable thing to myself being a request coming to me from some very particular friends of mine who are of great weight & importance to me but because little *douceurs* of that kind contribute to soften asperities, & may in the end produce very great good. I have had another application of the same kind from a friend of mine at Hull Mr Thomas Browne an Elder Brother of the Trinity house at Hull. His Son was taken on board the armed ship the Countess of Scarbrough.[3] He writ to me to desire that I wd apply to you in his favour if it was in your power either to obtain his release or an easy Confinement. There is nothing that I set my heart upon so much as to cultivate the interven-

2. In Digges's hand.

3. Thomas Brown, or Browne (d. 1795/6), was a leading citizen of Hull. He became an elder brother, or member of the governors of the Trinity House in 1777 and served as a warden during 1778–79. Information kindly supplied by the Hull Trinity House archivist.

Almost 700 prisoners had come from the *Serapis,* the *Countess of Scarborough,* and other ships captured by John Paul Jones: Schaeper, *Battle off Flamborough Head,* p. 63. On Feb. 2, 1780, BF wrote Hartley that the prisoners taken from the *Countess of Scarborough* had been exchanged in Holland and that he hoped Browne's son was home (Library of Congress).

tion of any good offices to prevent and to abate animosities between the people of Great Britain & America. That is an object wch is never out of my thoughts.— Your affate. DH.

to Dr. Franklin—

P.S.[4] According to yr. request I send you the particulars of Capn. C——ms situation. He was taken by an Engs Frigate near Bermudas in May, kept in Irons on board Her, for some weeks at sea & in the port of N York, then put on board the Grantham Packet & brought in Her *all the way Irond* to Falmo. abot. the 9 July removd from this Packet to Pendennis Castle, where He was kept in Irons & deprivd any open converse but with the Goaler. As soon as this was known here, a friend of yrs. informd the Board of sick & hurt of His situation & bad treatment, & petitiond for His removal to Mill Prison there to wait the common fate of His Countrymen. The petition was granted, & a Sloop of war carryd Him to Plymo. where His Irons were taken off and where he still is in the same situation with others. As He was exceedingly, nay shamefully, bare of Cloaths during His voyage to & from N York, as soon as things could be got into Prison to Him he was comfortably clad, & in this respect, as well as small supplys of a few guineas at a time to procure him tolerable food (for the Prison allowance is very scanty) He is now tolerably well off & has a communication with his friends; He being allowd to talk to them at the Grate of the Prison. He was harshly treated on board the man of war & the packet, & very ill used while at N York; but as his situation is now much better & rather more comfortable, I think it is but right it should be made known in America, In order that the three officers confind in the Goal of Phila. '*to abide His fate*' may also meet with better treatment from their keepers. There is no knowing to what lengths of mischief acts of retaliation may be carryd— there seems a disposition at present in this Country, to treat Prisoners better than heretofore; and I am given to believe there will be no unfair proceeding against any individual taken

4. The postscript is in Digges's hand.

in War and brought *here,* that will authorise retaliation in America.

Addressed: To Dr Franklin

II.

My Dear friend   October 26 1779

I understand from a friend of ours that by a letter from you he thinks that you have not received the letters wch I have writ to you lately on the Subject of the Exchange of prisoners. I therefore send you the Copies. I have indeed been surprized at not having had any answers from you wch makes me likewise doubt whether my letters since the beginning of September may not have miscarried—[5]

These are the Copies to wch. I have nothing to add but that as soon as I receive your answers I will do every thing in my power to proceed with farthar Exchanges— I have writ to you another letter of October 11 wch was to be sent to you by a private hand—

Your affecte   DH

To Dr. Franklin—

To Samuel Cooper

LS:[6] Henry E. Huntington Library; ALS (draft) and copy: Library of Congress

Dear Sir   Passy Oct. 27. 1779.

It is a long time Since I have had the Pleasure of hearing from you.[7] The Intelligence you were us'd to favour me with, was often useful to our Affairs. I hope I have not lost your friendship, together with your Correspondence. Our Excellent Mr. Winthrop I see is gone.[8] He was one of those old friends

---

5. Hartley here copied his letters of Sept. 1 and 18 and the first one of Oct. 11, all above. The friend was Digges.

6. In the hand of L'Air de Lamotte and marked "Copy" by BF.

7. The latest extant letters from the Boston clergyman are those of Jan. 4, brought by Lafayette on the *Alliance:* XXVIII, 338–40.

8. See Richard Price's letter of Oct. 14.

for the sake of whose Society I wish'd to return and to spend the Small Remnant[9] of my Days in New England. A few more such Deaths will make me a Stranger in my own Country—The Loss of friends is the Tax a Man pays for Living long himself. I find it a heavy one: for I pay it, not in depreciated Paper, but in Sterling Gold.[1]

You will see by the Newspapers that we have given some Disturbance to the British Coasts this Year. One little Privateer of Dunkerque, the Black Prince, with a Congress Commission and a few Americans mixed with Irish and English Smugglers, went round their Islands and took 37 Prizes in less than 3 Months. The little Squadron of Commodore Jones under the Same Commissions and Colours, has alarm'd those Coasts exceedingly, occasion'd a good deal of internal Expence, done great Damage to their Trade, and taken two fregates, with 500, Prisoners. He is now with his principal Prizes in Holland, where he is pretty well received, but must quit that neutral Country as soon as his Damages are repaired—The English watch with a superior Force, his coming out, but we hope he will manage so as to escape their Vigilance. Few Actions[2] at Sea have demonstrated such steady cool determined Bravery, as that of Jones in taking the Serapis.

There has been much Rumour this Summer throughout Europe, of an approaching Peace thro' the mediation of Russia and Holland; but it is understood to arise from the Invention of Stock jobbers and others interested in propagating Such an Opinion.[3] England seems not to be yet sufficiently humbled, to acknowledge the Independence of the American States, or to treat with them on that Footing; and our friends will not make a Peace on any other. So we shall probably See another Campaign.

By the Invoices I have seen and heard of, Sent hither with Congress Interest Bills of Exchange to purchase Goods, it Should seem that there is not so great a Want of Necessaries as of superfluities among our People. It is difficult to conceive

9. The preceding two words replace "Remainder" in the draft.
1. What follows the colon was added in BF's hand.
2. Replaces "Commanders" in the draft.
3. For the rumor see Digges's Sept. 20 and Lafayette's Oct. 11 letters.

that your Distresses can be great, when one sees, that much the greatest part of that Money is Lavish'd in Modes, Gewgaws, and Tea! Is it impossible for us to become wiser, when by Simple Economy and avoiding unnecessary Expences we might more than defray the Charge of the War— We export solid Provision of all kinds which is necessary for the subsistance of Man, and we import fashions, Luxuries, and Trifles. Such trade may enrich the Traders, but never the Country.

The Good Will of all Europe to our Cause, as being the Cause of Liberty which is the Cause of Mankind, Still continues, as does the universal Wish to see the English Pride humiliated, and their Power curtailed.— Those Circumstances are encouraging, and give hopes of a happy Issue. Which may God grant, and that you my friend, may live long a Blessing to your Country.

I am ever, Yours most affectionately   B FRANKLIN

Revd Dr: Cooper.

Copy

To Joseph Palmer

LS:[4] American Philosophical Society; copy: Library of Congress

Sir   Passy. Oct. 27. 1779.

I received your favour of Aug. 3. by your Nephew, who after Staying here a few Weeks, went for England, where I hope he has had a happy Meeting with his family and friends. I should very readily have Supply'd him with Money as you desired, if he had wanted it.— He appears an amiable young Man and his Return must give great Pleasure to his father.

I was glad to learn that you continue well, being with great Esteem Sir, Your most obedient and most humble servant
                                                B FRANKLIN

J. Palmer, Esq.

4. In the hand of L'Air de Lamotte.

Addressed: To / J. Palmer Esquire / German Town / Massts. Bay.

Endorsed: His Excellency Benja Franklin Esqr: Octor: 1779.

Notation: Lafayette M.g.[5]

To Elizabeth Temple

Copy: Library of Congress

Madam,   Passy, Oct. 27. 1779.

I received your favour of July 30. with a Letter enclos'd for Mr. Temple. He came to Holland as I heard and went from thence to England, but has not written to me, nor do I know where he resides, So as to direct your Letter to him properly.[6] But I Shall have an oportunity in a few Days of Sending it by a friend, who will find him out and deliver it—[7] Please to present my Respects to your Good father and mother, whom I much wish again to see, and believe me to be with Sincere Regard. Madam, Your most obedient humble servant   BF.

Mrs. Temple, Boston.

From Gourlade & Moylan

ALS:[8] American Philosophical Society

Hond. Sir   L'Orient 27th. Octr. 1779

Mr. Louis Le Grand,[9] a principal Merchant of Havre de Grace and our very perticular friend, writes us, that he is very

---

5. Lafayette's frank is on the back cover. The letter is one of the duplicates BF sent to America with the marquis; see our annotation of BF to Lovell, Sept. 30.

6. Richard Bennett Lloyd had informed WTF in July that John Temple was "still in England" on some business that Lloyd could not determine. Temple claimed to have written BF from Holland: Lloyd to WTF, July 15, APS. On Oct. 30, below, Digges confirmed Temple's presence in London.

7. The friend was Peter Luard, who said that he would endeavor to locate Temple: BF to Digges, Nov. 17, Library of Congress.

8. In Moylan's hand.

9. Louis Legrand & Cie. was one of the Le Havre outfitters most active in trans-Atlantic trade: Pierre Dardel, *Navires et marchandises dans les ports de Rouen et du Havre au XVIIIe siècle* (Paris, 1963), p. 409n.

anxious to be of the number of those who have the honor of your personal acquaintance. This gentleman has invariably shewn a particular attachment to the cause of the United States of America, and has been of great utility to us, in procuring seamen for the late Bonhomme Richard. From those motives, and our request, of your civilitys in his favor, we flatter ourselves he will be indulged on the like or any other occasion you will find us sincerely Honord sir Your most obe. & most humble Servts.   GOURLADE & MOYLAN

The Honorable Benj: Franklin at Passy

Addressed: The Honorable / Doctor Benj: Franklin / Plenipotentiary Minister / from the United States of / America at the Court of / Versailles, at his Hotel / In Passy./.

Notation: Gourlade et Moylan 27. Oct. 1779.

To Browns & Collinson[1]   Copy: Library of Congress

Gentlemen,   Passy, Oct. 28. 1779.
    I send you enclos'd a Bill of Exchange for 100£ sterling, with which please to credit my Account.[2] With great Esteem, I am Gentlemen y. m. o. & m. h. s.

Messrs. Browns and Collinson.

To John Diot   Copy: Library of Congress

Sir   Passy, Oct. 28. 1779.
    I received your favour of the 22d Instant. inclosing the Packet of Mr. Butlers and Mr. Galwey's Papers with the receipt for those sent to Mr. Clonard, and am extreamly oblig'd by your Care in sending them.[3] As to the Trunks of Clothes, as they are advertised for sale, it seems to be best that the Person

---

1. BF maintained a small account with his London bankers: XXIII, 18n.
2. These were funds which BF intended to cover William Caslon's bill for type. See BF to Fizeaux, Grand & Cie., Oct. 29, below.
3. As far as we know, BF did not retain copies of Diot's letter or any of its enclosures when he forwarded them to John Holker (see the following

who desires to have them, and to whom I have sent the advertisement, should get some one to bid for them. With great Regard I have the honour to be. Sir, &c.

M. Diot.

To John Holker

Copy: Library of Congress

Dear sir   Passy, Oct. 28. 1779.

Inclos'd I send you a Packet I have just received from Morlaix, containing some of the Papers you requested me to recover, and a Receipt for the Rest—[4] You Will see what Mr. Diot says about the Trunks of Clothes. It will be best I imagine for the person who desires to have them, if he knows which they are, to Describe them to Mr. Diot or some other Person, and order them to be bid for at the Sale.— I received a Quantity of Excellent apple Gelly but no Letter. If it was for me, 1000 Thanks, to good Made. Holker.[5] I am ever, my dear friend Your most affectionately

Mr. Holker.

To Robert Montgomery

LS:[6] American Philosophical Society; copy: Library of Congress

Sir,   Passy Oct. 28. 1779—

When you first wrote to me of the Vexations you received at Alicant,[7] I communicated your Letter to M. le Comte d'Aranda, requesting his Interposition for your Relief. He let me understand (thro' M. Grand) that there was no doubt but

---

letter). Jean, comte Sutton de Clonard had recommended Marchant to BF: XXIX, 474–5.

4. See the preceding document. Holker had requested the papers on Oct. 2, above.

5. On Oct. 20 BF paid 1 *l.t.* for the shipment of the jelly and tipped the porter who had brought it from Paris 1 *l.t.* 8 *s.:* Account XXIII, XXIX, 3.

6. In WTF's hand.

7. XXIX, 746–7.

you would receive it from the Court, as soon as it should be known that you were an American. This I had afterwards the Satisfaction to learn from yourself had actually happen'd. But when in a subsequent Letter you informed me that those Vexations were renewed, I began to apprehend there might be something in your Case or Conduct that I did not understand; And I am still at a Loss to conceive how the Certificate given you by me & Mr. Adams jointly can receive greater Force by my acknowledging it. And with all the good Will Spain has manifested in many Instances for the Americans in general, I am surprized that you in particular should meet with so much Unkindness, unless you had given some Offence or some Cause for Suspicion. For these Reasons I postponed answering some of your Letters, 'till I should be better acquainted with your Character, and with the Circumstances. I will however apply again to the Spanish Ambassador here as soon as he returns from Brest, where he is at present, and from whence he is expected in a few Days,[8] and I will request that agreable to the Certificate you have received from the Commissioners here you may be considered and treated as an American, unless the Court has some good Reasons to consider you in another Light.

I am, Sir, Your most obedient humble Servant

B FRANKLIN

M. Montgomery.

Endorsed: Passy 28 Octr. 1779 B Franklin Received the 15th Nov Answd the 20th Ditto

Notation: B Franklin

8. Ambassador Aranda had been at Brest to supervise the Spanish contingent of the combined fleet. He was returning to Paris to avoid the risk of contracting the disease infecting the fleet: Vergennes to Montmorin, Oct. 29, 1779 (AAE).

To Daniel Roberdeau

Copy: Library of Congress

Dear sir   Passy, Oct. 28. 1779.

I received the Copy of your Letter dated Jany. 5.⁹ inclosing a Letter for your Name sake at Haguenace, which I have forwarded.

With this I send you a Letter I received from a Gentleman at Bordeaux, who has married a Lady of your Name.¹ I am ever with Sincere Esteem Dear sir Your most obedient and most humble servant

Hon. D. Roberdeau Esqe.

From Dumas

ALS: American Philosophical Society²

Dear, Honoured Sir   Amst. 28 Octob. 1779

I wrote to you last ordinary,³ that the States of Holland had unanimously adopted te advice of their several colleges of Admiralty, concerning the admission of the American Squadron on the same footing as those of *all other foreign powers*. Now I am happy to tell your Excy., that the States General have confirmed this resolution, & that they are now making up an answer to the Memorial of Sir J. Y. which will be as unpleasing to the King his Master, as it must be agreeable to Congress. I congratulate Your Excy. with all my heart with this happy turn of affairs; & I must insist again, on this occasion, that you will be so good as to return me the project of a Treaty, with your remarks, in order to bring it to perfection. For you see, Sir, by this Instance, that things can happen where it would be *à propos* to propose incessantly such a project here.

Mr. Robinson Captain of an American Mercht. Ship taken lately by the English, has escaped with one of his Sons, & proposes to go to France, & present himself to you with a

9. XXVIII, 354–5. Since writing that letter Roberdeau had resigned from Congress: Burnett, *Letters,* IV, lxi.

1. Not located.

2. A one-sentence summary of the letter, made by Dumas, is at the Algemeen Rijksarchief.

3. Above, Oct. 25.

recommendation of Mr. De Neufville, Who prays me to recommend him also to yr. Exc. as a very brave man, which I do with pleasure.[4] Poor George Dandin![5] To see the American colours flying in those Ports among those of *other forein powers,* will break half his heart. I am with great respect Dear, honoured Sir Your most obedient & humble servant   DUMAS

I am hastening to the Hague, where the gd. factor desires to shew me some Letters received from yr. quarters.

His Excy. B. Franklin

Addressed: To his Excellency / B. Franklin, Esqr., Min. / Plenip. of the united States / *Passy./.*

Notation: Mr. Dumas, Amst. Oct. 28. 1779

From Joshua Johnson   ALS: American Philosophical Society

Sir.   Nantes 28 Octo. 1779

I did myself the Honour to address you the 23 & 29 April and the 11 May[6] to nither of which have I been favoured with an Answer, as the first was on the Business of the State I had sanguine hopes of hearing from you and which would have better enabled me to have wrote the Governor & Council on that Subject. I now trouble you to inform me whether under the Treaty of Alliance between France & America any American taking a Home & Settling in France is esteemed a Subject to his Catholick Majesty and whether they are liable to the Caputation Tax & Soldiers Quartered on them, your explanation will not only oblige me but determine me in my continuance in this Country or not.—[7] An American Vessell is a few Days arrived in this River from Baltimore she left that City on

4. De Neufville had recommended the captain himself: above, Oct. 21.

5. The suspicious husband in Molière's *George Dandin ou le Mari confondu.*

6. The first of these letters is missing, the others are in XXIX, 397, 470. From Johnson's subsequent description the missing letter presumably was related to his attempts to procure military supplies for the state of Maryland: XXIX, 223, 415–17, 678.

7. We assume that Article XIII of the Treaty of Commerce (XXV, 606–7) by freeing Americans from an inheritance tax levied on aliens thereby gave

the 28 of that Month and the Capes of Virginia the 20th September. The Capn. had heard nothing of Count De Estangs being on the Coast. Inclosed I forward three News Papers all that he brought with him— I have the Honour to be with great regard. Sir. Your most Obedt. Hb'le Servant

JOSHUA JOHNSON

His Excellency Benjamin Franklin Esqr. Passy.

Addressed: His Excellency / Benjamin Franklin Esqr. / Plenipotentiary of the thirteen / United States / Passey / Proche Paris.

Notation: J. Johnson Oct 28. 79

From John Locke[8]

ALS: American Philosophical Society

Righit honarabil   Nants octobar the 28 A1779
    Being undar and unhappy Setate I now make bold to trobel your honar with theas fue Lynes beging your honars a sis tans as I am an a mary Can and your honar the one Ly Parsin that I have to a Ply tue now. In the fust Plays may it Pleas your honar I sald from a mary cah In a brig belong to Mr Aron lopas and mr fransis Roch[9] whairof I was mis forting ly takin by an In glish man of wor and Carid to Porchmath whair I was some time a Prisnor but In the Cos of 13 months I obtaind my lebbarty & went doun to London thinking to Git a passag to amary whair of Sune aftar I got thair I was takin with the Small Pox which not onely maid me Poor In Pors but

grounds for questioning whether Americans should enjoy the exemptions of aliens from quartering troops and paying the *capitation* (poll tax).

8. A whaling captain from Cape Cod who had been captured a year earlier; see his letter of Nov. 10, 1778 (XXVIII, 74–5).

9. Francis Rotch of Nantucket, along with Aaron Lopez of Newport and others, had been trying to establish a London branch of the Southern Whale Fishery. In September, 1775, they organized a fleet out of Nantucket which was to deliver their oil directly to London. A number of these vessels were captured by the Royal Navy and brought into Portsmouth, where they were released only after Rotch arrived in London to intervene. Edouard A. Stackpole, *Whales & Destiny* . . . (Amherst, Mass., 1972), pp. 7–9.

Like wise brote me In det and great Ly be hollen to my frends whair of I was a blige to go a whaling out of London which is the Reasin now of my beeing hear a Prisnor my vessil Sur was ond In London by Mr. Thomas Powal mr Sansom and Docktor Williams[1] I rote tue Letters to you When that Eye fust wos brot In to frans but Resevd no ansor.[2] I Like wis rote one Letter to Capt. Landais of the a Lyans friggit beging his a Sistans for me to your honar I like wise Resevid no ansor from him. I then watid with Patians for a Long time and Eand Con Cludid that I Coold not have a ny a sistans I then broke my Parole from whair I was and went to Nans to Seea Some of my Countrymen as thinking Some of them wold Stand my frend and a sist me which thay all seeam to bee as four as lyes In thair Powar but on fortinate Lye I have got takin up and Poot to Prisson hear In nans and hear I must Re main Rite honarabil without you well a sist me I wos Sur born In a mary Ca and all the frends that I have In the world is thair and that is the Country that Eye will fite for and help to Suport as Long as Life Last I have Lyke wise a sisted Every one of my Countrymen as fur as Lay In my Powar or my ability wold ad mit of I got a noumbar of from the Inglish men of wor and Carid them a whaling so that thay Shoold not fite a gaenst thair Country So I Con Clude Sur your most obedeant humbil Sarvant   JOHN LOCKE

All that I Crave Rite honarabil is my Lybbarty So that I Can help Support my Country and Self thair fore I hope your honar will Releave a poor distresed Country man out of this Cold Loth soum Prison whair I am thus I Cant Reman Long

Notation: Locke John 18 Oct. 1779.

1. Griffith Williams, the London surgeon and ship owner who had corresponded with BF on the subject of Americans taken in the Southern Whale Fishery, had listed Thomas Powell and ——— Sansom as members of the fishery who had been generous to American prisoners. (Undated list, Hist. Soc. of Pa.) Williams and Powell were named as owners of the whaleship on which Thomas Pottar was captured in 1778. See XXVII, 491, 653–4, 666–8.
2. The only surviving letter is the one cited above.

From Simeon Samson

LS: American Philosophical Society

Sr   Nants 28th October 1779

As Mr. Watson waited on your Excellency with the Dispatches I had the honor to bring for you from Congress I did not write you untill the 7 Inst:[3] when the Mercury was Clean'd and Ready for the Sea then acquainted your excellency with the same and that I was waiting your orders which was my Instructions from the Honble. Navy board at Boston & not having the honor to have an Answer from you I naturely supose my Letter never came to hand— Sr. I take this opportunity to acquaint you with the same & that the Mercury has been dropt down the River this 18 days past ready to Sail at the shortest notice having been Clean'd for some time I find my Ships Bottom begins to fowl very fast the season of the Year approaching that to gett a Passage on the coast of America often is attended with great difficulty the Mercury being a small Vessell & very low in the Water naturly will be more Exposed then a larger Ship these Circumstances considerd makes me Anxious to have your approbation for my Departure—[4]

Sr. I am Your most Obdt: Huml Servt: at Command—

SIMN SAMSON

To His Excellency Benja: Francklin Esqr:

P.S. I have to acquaint your honor there is severall Americans here that have been lately Prisoners Officers & Seamen being Intirely destitute of Money & short of Clothing supported at the Expence of the Continent while here they would be very glad of a Passage wch: I am freely willing to give them on my part wth: proviser the Continent will aford them Provisions & Stores they are such men as we want in America and about Eight in number. I should be very glad to have some Directions from you with Respect to this Matter—

I have the Honor to be Sr. Your Most Obdt: Servt—

S SAMSON

3. Missing.
4. BF's approval crossed this letter in the mail: BF to Schweighauser, below, Oct. 30.

Addressed: His Excellency Benja: Francklin Esqr: / Piercy— near— / Paris

Notation: Saml. Sampson 28 Oct 79

To Dumas

Copy: Library of Congress

Dear sir   Passy Oct. 29. 1779.
    I received yours of the 18th. and 22 & communicated them to Mr. Chaumont as you desired.— I am glad to Learn that the affair of firing at the Deserters has had no worse Consequences. I wish to know whether Letters I sent sometime since to Comme. Jones and Captain Landais under your Cover, came to hand as you Expect they will sail by the End of this Week. I do not now write to the Commodore. If he should be still with you, present my cordial Respects and good Wishes. I am ever, my dear friend. Your sincerly.   BF.
Mr. Dumas.

To Fizeaux, Grand & Cie.

Copy: Library of Congress

The following letter is the earliest dated clue in Franklin's papers to a meeting in Passy which, at the time, left virtually no trace, but which resulted in Franklin's quietly ordering a substantial quantity of British printing supplies. The meeting, which took place in June, 1779, was with two of London's leading suppliers: William Caslon III, the typefounder, and the stationer James Woodmason.
    Caslon and Woodmason had traveled to Paris in mid-June at the suggestion of Lord Shelburne, in order to try to sell their goods to Caron de Beaumarchais. The playwright, who was preparing to launch a complete edition of Voltaire's works, had asked Shelburne's advice on the selection of a typeface and paper, as British printing supplies were so far superior to the French.[5]
    Shelburne sent Caslon and Woodmason to Paris with a letter of

---

5. See Morton, *Beaumarchais Correspondance,* I, xxiii-xxiv; Brian N. Morton, "Beaumarchais et le prospectus de l'édition de Kehl," *Studies on Voltaire and the Eighteenth Century,* LXXXI (1971), 133–8; John Dreyfus, "The Baskerville Punches 1750–1950," *The Library,* 5th ser., V (1951), 32–3.

introduction to his close friend, the abbé Morellet. Morellet, in turn, directed the pair to Beaumarchais, sometime around June 25.[6] Although Beaumarchais ultimately rejected Caslon's type (he bought the Baskerville foundry instead), Caslon had some success at the home of Benjamin Franklin, his family's old friend and client, and neighbor of Morellet.

Franklin had known three generations of Caslons. As a Philadelphia printer he had ordered type from the famous Caslon the elder, and as of 1753 dealt with his successor, Caslon the younger. During his years in England, Franklin continued to patronize Caslon II, whose son William attended school with Temple. After his father's death in 1778, William Caslon III helped his mother run the foundry, and fourteen years later, established an independent shop.[7]

Morellet had never seen type or paper to rival what the two Englishmen were offering. Caslon's type lived up to its reputation. As for the vellum-like wove paper brought by Woodmason, manufactured according to a technique unknown in Europe, its smooth surface seemed the perfect medium on which to display the delicate English typefaces.[8] Morellet engaged his visitors in long discussions of printers' arts. Franklin was undoubtedly present at some of these conversations.[9]

Among Franklin's papers at the American Philosophical Society is an undated list in his hand, entitled, "Order to M. Caslon." We believe that this is a copy of an order handed directly to Caslon in

6. Dorothy Medlin, Jean-Claude David, Paul LeClerc, eds., *Lettres d'André Morellet* (1 vol. to date, Oxford, 1991—), I, 396.

7. *DNB;* John Findlay McRae, *Two Centuries of Typefounding* . . . (London, 1920), pp. 61–2. For BF's initial dealings with the grandfather and father, see III, 14; V, 82–3.

8. Wove paper, invented in China, was rediscovered in England around 1750, by either John Baskerville or James Whatman. Its first British appearance was in Baskerville's highly acclaimed edition of Virgil (Birmingham, 1757), to which BF subscribed: VIII, 53; IX, 257. Whatman's paper mill was the primary manufacturer of wove paper, and by 1780, Woodmason was Whatman's chief distributor. Dard Hunter, *Papermaking* (2nd ed., New York, 1947), pp. 125–8; Thomas Balston, *James Whatman, Father & Son* (New York and London, 1979), pp. 51–2.

9. Medlin *et al., Lettres d'André Morellet,* I, 396–7. In his letter to Shelburne of [c. June 25], just cited, Morellet also wrote of a new, as yet unannounced discovery: a smaller, less expensive, printing press. This was the machine invented by the abbé Rochon, based on an idea of BF's, which Rochon would present to the *académie des sciences* on Aug. 19, 1780. *Procès-verbaux,* XCIX, 206.

late June, with instructions that it be shipped to Amsterdam. This type, we presume, is the subject of the letter printed below. The list is as follows:

100 lbs. Five Lines Pica ⎱ all Roman if no Italic
80 lbs. Four Line Pica ⎰
60 lbs. French Canon Rom & Ital
60 lbs. Two Lines Great Primmer Rom & Ital
60 lbs. Two Lines English
60 lbs. Two Lines Pica Rom & Ital
80 lbs. Double Pica No 2 Rom & Ital
100 lbs. Paragon
300 lbs. Great Primmer Rom & Ital
___
860
12 Ream of large fine thick Post

In late November or early December, Franklin ordered from Caslon an additional 96 pounds of Two Line Double Pica, to be sent, as this was, care of his Amsterdam bankers.[1] The initial order, packed in eight boxes, arrived in Passy in April, 1780. The second order, which filled one box, was sent on January 27; we have no record of its arrival.[2]

Although these boxes were stored in the Passy print shop, the type does not seem to have been used in France.[3] Franklin apparently talked about sending it to America, yet the boxes were still at Passy when Benny Bache packed the printing equipment in 1785, and the type is listed in Franklin's inventory of Passy fonts made after his return to Philadelphia.[4] It was inherited by Benny Bache, and exhibited on his specimen sheet for the Market Street printing office.[5]

A portion of Woodmason's paper, on the other hand, had an im-

1. Caslon to WTF, Dec. 7, 1779, APS.

2. BF to Fizeaux, Grand & Cie., April 23, 1780, Library of Congress; Caslon to WTF, March 10, 1780, APS.

3. The boxes of type appear on an inventory of Jan. 27, 1781 (APS), but the type is not evident on any extant issue of the Passy press.

4. Hints that the type was destined for America can be found in letters from Caslon and Henry Grand, March 10 and 14, 1780. BFB's notation from 1785 is on the inventory cited above; BF's later inventory is undated. All documents cited here are at the APS.

5. A facsimile of the specimen accompanies [Douglas Crawford McMurtrie], *Benjamin Franklin, Typefounder* (New York, 1925).

mediate and particular application. Franklin ordered two of the reams to be marbled, expressly for the certificates he would issue for installments of French government loans, the first of which had arrived on June 10.[6] The paper took longer to manufacture than the type had; it was ready at the end of December, and would not arrive in Passy until the end of May, 1780. What Franklin did with the unmarbled balance of this order may yet become clear as the present edition continues.

Gentlemen,   Passy, Oct. 29. 1779.

I have advice from England that 8 boxes of Printing Characters are sent from London, to your Care for me, If they are arrived, I request you would ship them to Rouen, address'd to Mr. Holker here. I suppose you have Dutch Vessels frequently going there. Their Value is about 100£ sterling, which I desire you to get insur'd.[7] Whatever Charges you are at, I shall repay with Thanks. I have the honour to be, with great Esteem, Gentlemen Y. m. o. & m. h. s.

Messrs. Fizeaux & Grand

To Jean-Charles-Pierre Lenoir[8]   Copy: Library of Congress

Sir   Passy, Oct. 29. 1779.

One of the Persons you had Notice of from Caen named Smith,[9] has just now been with me. He Says, the other Watt,[1]

6. Woodmason to BF, [Dec. 25] (APS); BF to Ferdinand Grand, May 30, 1780 (Dibner Library of the History of Science and Technology, Smithsonian Institution). See also our annotation to the French loan certificate, Sept. 16, above, and XXIX, 594n.

7. BF paid for the order out of personal funds; the previous day he had sent £100 to be deposited with his London banker (to Browns & Collinson, Oct. 28, above). The total came to £70.8.0: BF to Brown, Collinson & Tritton, Jan. 10, 1780, APS.

8. The head of the Paris police.

9. Probably Capt. Granville Smith of Grayson's regiment, who had resigned his commission on July 15, 1778: Heitman, *Register of Officers*, p. 370; E.M. Sanchez-Saavedra, comp., *A Guide to Virginia Military Organizations in the American Revolution, 1774–1787* (Richmond, 1978), p. 74. In a Nov. 10 letter to BF (APS) Lafayette recommended him as a former army officer now in partnership with Brig. Gen. Scott (*i.e.,* Charles Scott, for whom see

has been and continues ill, Since their arrival at Paris which is the reason of their not coming to me sooner. They have no Letters for me. But he Show'd me one for the Marquis de la fayette; & he desired a Pass from me to go to Havre in order to deliver it. As I know nothing of him or his Companion, and look upon it as a frivolous Errand, The going to havre to deliver a Letter which he might as well send per Post, I refus'd to give him a Pass. And yet the man seems rather too weak and silly to be concern'd in any Plot.

I examin'd him about Virginia, and find him so much acquainted with that Country, that I have no doubt of his having been there. He Says they are come over with commercial Purposes; that he is to go back, and Watt to Stay here, and that they are employ'd by a Coll Scot in Virginia. I think it may be well to observe them farther and If I learn any thing more of them, I Shall immediately communicate it.

With great Respect I have the honour to be. Sir.

Mr. Le Noir.

To Jean de Neufville & fils

LS:[2] National Archives; copy: Library of Congress

Sir,   Passy Oct. 29. 1779.

I received your respected Favour of the 21. Inst. and shall take what Care I can that the Bills endors'd to you, and taken by the English, be not paid without your Endorsement. The others which you mention that have come to your Hands in

---

the *DAB*). Granville Smith later became deputy quartermaster of Virginia: *Jefferson Papers*, IV, 327, 445n.

1. Probably Capt. John Watts of the 1st Continental Light Dragoons, largely disbanded in early 1779. A Virginian like Smith and Scott, he later served as a lieutenant colonel of light dragoons: Heitman, *Register of Officers*, p. 424; Sanchez-Saavedra, *Guide to Virginia Military Organizations*, p. 103; Harold C. Syrett *et al.*, eds., *The Papers of Alexander Hamilton* (27 vols., New York and London, 1961–87), XXIV, 82n. Lafayette recommended him as well. If our identifications of Smith and Watts are correct they did not spend long in Europe.

2. In WTF's hand. The copy is misdated Oct. 19.

Mr Sears's Letters, have already been presented, & tho' not endorsed by him will be accepted on your Engagement of being answerable to me for the Amount, in Case M. Sears should disapprove of it. I am glad to hear that the Affairs of Comme Jones under your Management go well. With great Regard, I have the honour to be, Sir, Your most obedient & most humble Servant.   B FRANKLIN

Messrs Neufville & Son—

From Dumas   ALS: American Philosophical Society[3]

Dear, Honoured Sir   at the Hague Oct. 29th. 1779
   I send you herewith a Copy[4] of the advice of the College of Admiralty at Amsterdam, which adopted by the other Colleges, has proved the Base of the Resolution taken since by the province of Holland, & confirmed by their H. M.[5] It is a translation made by the privy Secretary of the French Ambassador, his Excy having been so good as to give me a Copy of it. I expect from *our friend* a copy of the Resolution, which I shall translate immediately myself for your use.
   I have concerted with the *gd. facteur* a visit I am to pay to the G. P. when it is done, I shall not fail to acquaint yr. Excy with the Success I hope from this step.
   I have but the time to acknowledge the favour of the Extract of a Letter from Newfoundland, just received from my very dear & amiable friend Mr. Wm. Franklin, being in great haste, ever Dear & honoured Sir, yr. most humble, obedient and respectful servant   DUMAS

   3. A brief summary of this letter, made by Dumas, is at the Algemeen Rijksarchief.
   4. Actually a copy, in Dumas' hand, of a French translation. It is with this covering letter at the APS. The Amsterdam college of admiralty requested the States General's permission for the American squadron to disembark its sick and wounded. For an English translation see Wharton, *Diplomatic Correspondence*, III, 370–1.
   5. High Mightinesses, *i.e.,* the States General, which did grant the permission: Wharton, *Diplomatic Correspondence*, III, 371–2.

Addressed: His Excellency / B. Franklin, Esqr., Min. Plenip. / of the United States, &c. / *Passy.* /.

Notation: Dumas Octr. 29. 1779

From John Holker

ALS: American Philosophical Society

Dear Sir Rouen 29 Octobr 1779

I Received your agreeable leter of the 19 and one yesterday handing me the Peapers belonging to Mrs Butler, which you have been so good as to procure me, I have sent the whole to Mr. Garvey to be forwarded to the Oners, and he writes me that it wont be in his power to give any Intelegence Regarding the weareing apparil, that belonged to Mrs Butler, as they have not sent him a list of what they containe, or any explenation about the trunks by which he Immagins it wont be prudent to make any purchas as Mrs Butlers objects air mixed with those of the Rest of the People on Board. I have praid Mr. Garvey to write to your Corrospondence on the Subject so as to give you no More Truble, and I know must thanke you for what you have allredy had & beg youl excuse the liberty I have tooke which I should not have don had I not been convinced of your friendship for me & mine; and I beg upon every occasion youl not speare me as no man alive has more Regard, or more your Intrest at heart than my Self & beg youl permit me to be with Respect & consideration Dear Sir your Most Obed & very humble sert J HOLKER

I shall pay all the expences you have been at when I have the pleasur to see you.

P.S. my wife presents you her complements & is glad you found the apple Gelly good, & has more at your Servis If it will be agreeable

Notation: J Holker Oct 29. 1779

From Joseph Varage

ALS: American Philosophical Society

Excelence.   a Lorient Le 29. octobre 1779.

J'ai L'honneur de vous Envoyer les Signeaux de reconnois-
sances que nous avions fait et Convenus avec Mr. Jones avant
nôtre depart de ce port. Je les avois ouvert et recachetés Ensuite, pour faire le Signal a un Batiment duquél J'etois Envuë
apres que Mr. Jones m'eut quité le 26. aoust dernier.[6]

J'aurois desiré, Excelence, que Mr. Jones eut resté sur les
parages des Blasques à l'ouest d'Irlande ou Il mi laissa par
l'effet d'un coup de vent qu'il l'obligea de laisser Courrir vent
arriere, mais Je me flate de trouver quelque Jour de nouvelles
occasions qui En me metant a même de donner des marques
de ma reconnoissance aux Etats unis me fourniront Encore les
moyens de vous assurer du trés profond respect avec Ce que
Je Suis, Excelence Vôtre tres humble et tres ôbeissant serviteur   VARAGE

Notation: Varage Oct 29. 79

From Vergennes

L (draft):[7] Archives du Ministère des affaires étrangères

                        A Versailles le 29 8bre 1779.

J'ai reçu, M, la lettre de Mrs. John et William Alexander que
vous m'avez fait l'honneur de m'addresser Le 24. de ce mois;
je l'ay fait passer à M. de Sartine, afin qu'il puisse[8] mettre sous
les yeux du Roi et de Son Conseil les moyens de defense des
Sr. Alexander, lorsqu'il fera le raport de la reqte. de M. Walpole: ne doutez pas, M, que la discution dont il sagît ne soit
jugée d'après les règles de la plus parfaite équité./

M. franklin

---

6. Varage's cutter, the *Cerf,* became separated from Jones's squadron
while reconnoitering the Irish coast. By now the *Cerf* had been disarmed
and her crew taken aboard two French ships of the line: Moylan to Jones,
Oct. 18, Bradford, *Jones Papers,* reel 4, no. 787.

7. In the hand of Gérard de Rayneval.

8. At this point the words "rendre compte au" have been lined through.

616

From Wilhelm Augustine von Steuben[9]

LS and translation:[1] American Philosophical Society

Custrin, dans le marché neuf
Monsieur l'ambassadeur   le 29. 8bre. 1779.—

Vôtre Excellence voudra bien me pardonner avec bonté Si je recourre de nouveau à Elle. Mon fils frederic Wilhelm von Steuben m'à marqué quil s'étoit engagé en Septembre 1777. au Service amériquain en qualité de General, & il m'à addressé à Mr. de Beaumarchais.[2] Cependant depuis lors je n'ay reçû aucune nouvelle ny réponce. Comme par ce moyen je Suis dans l'incertitude, je prie trés humblement vôtre Excellence d'avoir la bonté de m'apprendre par quelques lignes Si mon fils est encore en vie, ou ce qui en est avec luy. Il ne peut être autrement que ces Circonstances ne vous soyent Connuës. J'ay bientôt 81. ans & ma femme 73. ans Jespére que vous voudrés bien ne pas refuser cette grace à deux Viellards.

Je suis avec la plus grande Consideration De vôtre Excellence Le très humble & très obeisst. servt.[3]

signé W.H. VON STEÚBEN—
Major & chevalier de l'ordre du Mérite.—

To Schweighauser

Copy: Library of Congress

Sir   Passy, Oct. 30. 1779.

The Last I had the honour of receiving from you was without date, But it contain'd your additional Explication or Rea-

---

9. A highly-decorated former major in the Prussian army, this von Steuben (1699–1783) was living in retirement at the post of Cüstrin, where he had been joint commandant: Friedrich Kapp, *The Life of Frederick William von Steuben* . . . (New York, 1859), pp. 42–3.

1. The LS is in German. We print from the French translation because BF undoubtedly used it in drafting the response described below. The complimentary close and dateline of the LS are in von Steuben's shaky hand.

2. Who had provided passage to America for the son: Morton, *Beaumarchais Correspondance*, III, 131–2n.

3. On Nov. 6 he sent another letter (in German; it and a French translation are at the APS) asking BF to forward a letter to his son. According to

son in support of the second one per Cent. with which I acquiesce. I do not find that you have yet rectified the Charge of 5. per Ct. on more than one of the Cargoes of Tobacco.[4]

I now send the remainder of the Dispatches for Capt. Samson, wishing him a Good Voyage.[5] Those Parcels which are marked, to be Sunk in cas of Capture, and all not marked News-papers he is to keep in a Separate Bag, containing a sufficient Weight, to be ready for that purpose. I hope he will not be too late to arrive in Boston. But if he Should find the Winds and Weather more favourable, he may go to the Southward, and make the Port most convenient. I am with great Regard. Sir y. m. ob. and m. h. S.

P.S. You will take a Recipit from Capt. Samson when you deliver him the Dispatches. They are in 14 Parcells and are already number'd.[6]

M. Schweighauser

From Thomas Digges   ALS: Historical Society of Pennsylvania

Dr Sir   Octor 30. 1779

Since I wrote you by Mr. Luard the 8 & 12th. Int. (and in these letters took the liberty to introduce Mr Luard to you) I

BF's letterbook (Library of Congress) he responded on Nov. 27: "I received your Letters of the 28th October and 6th: Instant. General Steuben was well and much esteem'd by the Congress when the last Advices left America. I shall forward the Letters you send to him by the first Opportunities." BF apparently had not yet received the general's Sept. 28 letter, above.

4. Very few letters from Schweighauser to BF are extant and we have found none which answers this description. BF discussed Schweighauser's commission at length in his Sept. 17 letter to him, above.

5. On Oct. 28 BF decided to wait no longer to send his dispatches; see the postscript to his letter to John Jay begun on Oct. 4. It then took some three months for Samson's *Mercury* to reach America.

6. Among BF's papers at the University of Pa. Library is an undated list in WTF's hand. It reads:

gave you a line by common post the 20th. past,[7] giving an accot. that an amn. Privateer caled the Gen Glover was taken by the frigate wch. brot over Adml. Byron from Antigua abot. the 20th Sept.; This vessel soon after her sailing from No Carolina fell in with DEstaigns fleet & was with the fleet the 13. 14. & 15 Sept off the Coasts of No Carolina, 24 Ships of the line frigates &c— they had a fair wind, & were steering Noward. Byron is much blamd for not sending this prize Express to New York with advices that DEstaign was on the Coast & steering Noward. It seems that his appearance there will be a great surprize to Clintons army. The latest accots. from that quarter is the 17th. Sept. there were then 4,000 men ready for an Expedition soward— The intelligent here say that 2,000 of them were going to Quebec, and one to garrison Pensacola agt. the Spaniards. Notwithstanding DEstaigns move of situation we are much in fear for Jama. Two Regts. of the new raisd Corps will be sent there on bod. the fleet wch. sails abot

---

List of Dispatches, sent by the Mercury Packet, Capt. Sampson. Numbers.
1. To the honble. J. Jay Esqr. President of Congress
2. To the honble. the President of Congress.
3. To Do——— News Papers———
4 For the honble James Lovell Esq.
5. Do———
6. To the honble the Committee for Foreign Affairs
7. Do——— News Papers———
8. To the honble the Commissioners of the Navy for the Eastern Department— Boston
9. To his Exy the Chevr. de la Luzerne
10 To the honble Robert Morris Esq.
11 Thomas Payne Esqr—
12 Richd Bache Esqr.
13 To Do———
14 A Monsr Holker Consul de France

The verso bears WTF's notation, "List of Dispatches sent by the *Mercury*" and, lined out by a later hand, "I acknowledge to have received the above fourteen Parcells of Mr. Jonathan Williams junior. At Nantes this [*blank*] Day of [*blank*]."
7. Missing.

the 12 or 15 next month Rodney with 4 or 5 ships of the line & abot 30 merchantm will compose this fleet, & the troops are to be put on board the common merchant ships.[8]

Mr. S——y[9] who was lately with you was detaind sometime on his way & only arrivd last week. He will go in a few days with a large Cargoe.

By this conveyance there will be forwarded some duplicates of letters from our friend DH which He supposes have not got regularly to hand, at least those wch. are the most material & which relate to the Excha. of Prisoners—[1] The crew of the Genl Glover Privateer has added 60 to the numbers in Forton which make them 206 there and 193 at Plymo. As yet there is no appearance of the Cartel moving, & the agents say she is only stopt for want of the French passport— Mr. H and myself are in dayly hopes it will soon arrive; I am very much plagued with their solicitations, & in keeping them quiet. I believe had it not been for Capt C——m,[2] many of those in mill prison would have enterd into the service of the navy here, to which they have had strong temptation from want & the large bountys offerd them.

I have forwarded & got supplyd to Capt. C——m thirty odd pounds. I wrote you before that I had drawn on G——d for fifty pounds the 27th last month for the purpose of help to Capt. C——m. G——d (altho I wrote him to present the bill to you) writes to the person who negotiated it here, that it

8. Clinton was preparing to move his troops toward the Carolinas when on Sept. 15 he received a plea for help from officers in Jamaica alarmed by d'Estaing's position at St. Domingue. Cornwallis was ordered to go south with 4,000 reinforcements but was stopped on the 24th by news that d'Estaing was off the coast of Georgia. Cut off from their navy, 55,000 British troops were temporarily isolated in groups from Quebec to Tobago. Adm. Sir George Brydges Rodney (1719–92), who had been living in Paris to escape the debts he had run up in England, in September, 1779, was given command of a convoy to the Leeward Islands via Gibraltar. It did not put to sea until the end of the year. Mackesy, *War for America*, pp. 275–6, 309–13, 319–20; *DNB*.

9. Cyprian Sterry.

1. See Hartley's second letter of Oct. 26.

2. Gustavus Conyngham. "G——d" in the next paragraph is Ferdinand Grand.

was not paid or presentd for want of advice; and I am yet uninformd whether it is paid or not & consequently without the money. I remitted a second to the same bill abot. a fortnight ago, and wrote him as I had before done that my bills on you, were by *Your order;* and desird they might be presented to you before any Ansr. might be given as to protest or acceptance &c—this I thought was advice enough, but he does not seem to think so.

I now inclose You two american Loan Office Bills, the property of a man who is in want in mill prison. One is for 80 the other 36 Dollars making in the whole four hundred & Eighty Livres. If they are good, be pleased to mention so to me in a common letter directed Mr Wm. Singleton Church Nandos Coffee House; and Mr Luard will bear the amot. of them to me provided He has not left Paris—or I dare say Mr W——lp——e will take the trouble of it when He may return.[3] By any such oppery. I should be glad of a name to direct to you under cover to Monr G——d, wch may be safer than your own. There are many little trifling occurrances here that may be useful for you to know, & wch I can communicate safely by that means, but when sent immedy. to *You* they will be stopt in the Post Office where letters *lately* have undergone a stricter scrutiny than heretofore. I should be very thankful for a line by common post as soon as this gets to hand, to know whether the poor Prisoners bills herewith inclosd are good or not. Yr. Letter may be directed a Monr. Monr. Wm Singleton Church, Nandos Coffee Ho.

I find by yours of the 7th (recd. since I sat down to write this letter) that some of my letters have miscarryd; for I think I have in two or three mentiond the particular situation and present treatment of Capt. C——m.— He was taken in May by an Engs Frigate, sent to & kept in Irons on board the sd. frigate at N York till put on board the Grantham Packet wch. arrivd at Falmo. the 8th July in a passage of only 17 days.— He was sent directly (*Irond*) to Pendennis Castle & denied pen

3. In his letter of Nov. 15 (Hist. Soc. of Pa.), Digges identified the owner of the bills as John Calef. Commander of the schooner *Hawk,* Calef had been committed to Mill Prison on May 10 and eventually escaped: Claghorn, *Naval Officers,* p. 47. W——lp——e is Thomas Walpole.

& Ink or to speak to any one but the Goaler. As a Mr Milligan from Maryld. was a passenger in the packet, I very soon heard of Capt C—— situation, & wrote four or five times to a freind of mine in Falmo. to give him every necessary help, but this could not be done there, as no one was allowd to speak to him, & my friend being fearful to trust the Goaler, & not on the spot while he was removing, He was put on board a Sloop of war much in want of Cloaths & refreshment. As soon as I was certain of His confinement & situation, I got a freind to solicit the Board of sick & hurt to have his Irons taken of & get him removd to Mill Prison; the request was granted, tho in such a manner as left me at a loss to know if he was gone a cruise in the ship from falmouth, or impressd as a Seaman; however he got a letter from me the 20th. of Augt. since which He has been as comfortably situated as his place of confinement will admit, & I have had many letters full of thanks from him, & the last very expressive of gratitude to You for yr. offer of assistance, which has been got to him by little & little above thirty pounds, & for which you shall hereafter have his receipts. As it has been principally laid out by a frd. of mine in Plymo.[4] in purchasing Him Cloaths (of which He was *extreemly* bare) and other comforts, I have not yet recd the accots, & indeed shall not until I hear his wants have been amply satisfyd. He deserves this & much more from Me, & I most cordially wish I had it more in my power to comply with the frequent solicitations I have from that and another quarter. I have spent so much that I really *must* stop; This is the case with some others here, and as our Subscripn. is in the last fifty, God knows what will become of these poor fellows when it is gone & if the Cartel should be stopt. The last five rects and your intimation are before the Board of Sick & hurt, & we are hopeing dayly for an Ansr. I wish the Texel scheme may be acceptd, but altho humanity to the suffering Prisoners there may point it out, I have little Expectation it will; because the pride of these Gentry may prevent it.

I gave your message to Mr. R——pe & He was extreemly thankful. I did not observe by his manner that he meant soon

4. Rev. Robert Heath; see Digges's letter of Sept. 20.

to take a journey.[5] By his recommendation a Mr. D. Williams sent me two books of His Lectures, which He requested might be forwarded to You.[6] They are gone by a like conveyance to the two paper parcels I lately forwarded to Mr Grand at Amm. (who acknowleges the Rect. of them to Me) I mean those from Mr. V——n.[7] When you get them, it will be a satisfaction to Mr. V. to hear they are got safe, & I shall be glad to hear of the safe arrival of the books.

I find by a letter from Mr. I——d[8] He is now at Amm. ready to embark for Ama. I suppose in consequence of some late resolves. I am sorry for the motives or purposes for wch. He is going to Ama.; that Country has enough to do without entering into further & fatal broils— Some folks seem to like living in hot water.

His friend J. T——e is still here; I see him now & then, but can make nothing out as to what he is about. I beleive he brought over something like a whisper, and is now seemingly much displeasd at the manner it has been treatd. Our friend DH says he is perfectly honest and right, but in these times of peril & false appearances I keep a distance & live but among a few; one of these is honest little B——g——n who is in some expectation of hearing from you I beleive on the subject of some copper meddals. I wish you all success & happiness & am with the highest esteem Yr. very obligd & ob Sert.

ALEXR. HAMMILTON

Addressed: A Monsieur Monsieur B. Franklin / Passy

Notation: Digges Oct 30 79

---

5. Rudolph Erich Raspe did not accept BF's offer of hospitality but continued his scholarly endeavors in Cambridge, and by the following year was in even more dire financial straits: Timothy L.S. Sprigge *et al.,* eds., *The Correspondence of Jeremy Bentham* (9 vols. to date, 1968—) II, 346, 506.

6. Rev. David Williams, *Lectures on the Universal Principles and Duties of Religion and Morality* (2 vols., London, 1779): XXVII, 355.

7. Vaughan's edition of BF's writings, forwarded via Georges Grand in Amsterdam.

8. Ralph Izard. The initials Digges uses in the next paragraph stand for John Temple and Edward Bridgen.

From Pierre-François-André Méchain[9]

ALS: American Philosophical Society

Monsieur   à paris le 30. 8bre. 1779

Je prens la liberté de vous adresser une lettre de M. le Marquis de la fayette en faveur de M. de Noemer Docteur en Médecine et Conseiller de la ville de Ziric-zée en Zélande;[1] ce savant a dessein de s'établir dans les Etats unis de l'amerique, je crois même quil a deja eu l'honneur de vous etre presenté, Monsieur, par M. l'abbé rozier, pour vous supplier de vouloir bien lui accorder votre recommandation. Je me suis engagé de solliciter pour lui la même grace auprès de M. de lafayette, mais en attendant la reponse M. de Noemer a etè obligè de retourner en Zélande ou je dois la lui envoyer.

Je recois, en arrivant de la Campagne, les lettres de M. de la fayette qui Contiennent celle ci pour vous Monsieur, laquelle en renferme une autre de lui pour le Congrès Américain selon ce quil me fait lhonneur de me mander.[2] Je vous supplie, Monsieur, de vouloir bien ordonner quelle soit remise à la poste à mon adresse, afin que je puisse la faire parvenir à M. de Noemer, pour qui sans doute, toutes difficultés seront applanies et qui sera certain dun plein succés si vous daignez joindre votre puissante protection à celle de M. de lafayette. J'ai trop craint d'abuser de vos momens precieux pour oser vous presenter cette lettre moi meme etant d'ailleurs encore plus admirateur des savans que Connu deux.

---

9. Méchain (1744–1804), hydrographer at the naval ministry's *dépôt des cartes,* was a future member of the Académie des sciences and a distinguished astronomer. He discovered and calculated orbits for numerous comets, and was appointed in 1790 to calculate fundamental geodetic measurements of southern France based on the new unit of length, the meter. Charles Coulston Gillespie *et al.,* eds., *Dictionary of Scientific Biography* (18 vols., New York, 1970–90), IX, 250–1.

1. Lafayette's letter of Oct. 14, above.

2. For Lafayette's letter to Congress see our annotation of his letter cited above.

Je suis avec un très profond respect Monsieur votre trés humble et très obeissant serviteur

MECHAIN
astronome hydrographe du Depôt de la Marine vielle rue du temple

Notation: Mechaine Oct 30 79.

From Officers of the American Squadron: Affidavit[3]

DS: National Archives; copies: University of Pennsylvania Library,[4] National Archives

[October 30, 1779]

The officers Who are Knowing to the following facts, Will please to mention them in full unequivocal terms in their Certificates.

1. The Captain of the alliance did not take the Steps in his power to prevent his Ship from getting foul of the Bonhomme

3. On Nov. 15 BF began an inquiry into Landais' conduct while serving with Jones's squadron, the minutes of which are at the University of Pa. Library. He had to suspend the hearings until Nov. 24, however, because of his ill health. (He had been ill in October, too; on Oct. 27 Turgot reported him recovered: Schelle, *Œuvres de Turgot,* v, 602.) During the interim he received this and a number of other affidavits which Jones had forwarded him on Nov. 13. (Jones's covering letter of that date is at the APS.) Because Jones could not attend BF suspended the hearings again after one meeting, but two days later he did present Landais a copy of the charges presented in the present document: minutes of the inquiry; Landais, *Memorial,* pp. 57, 60. Landais' response to these charges is at the University of Pa. Library and like the inquiry minutes will be printed in volume 31. Jones also solicited affidavits, dated between Oct. 23 and Nov. 13, from Nathaniel Fanning, John Mayrant, Robert Coram, Capt. Philippe-Nicolas Ricot, Henry Lunt, Pierre Vinet, and other officers of the *Vengeance* (a copy of which at the University of Pa. Library bears BF's endorsement), Edward Stack, J.W. Linthwaite, John Spencer, and Matthew Mease: Bradford, *Jones Papers,* reel 4, no. 871; reel 10, nos. 2047–54, 2056, 2058.

4. In the hand of L'Air de Lamotte and bearing BF's notations, "Charges against Capt. Landais, from Comme Jones / certified & attested by sundry officers." Both copies contain an introductory statement which differs from the one printed below. It reads:

Richard in the Bay of Biscay;[5] for instead of putting his helm a Weather, and bearing up to make Way for his Commanding officer (Which Was his Duty) he left the deck for to load his pistols.

2.   When in Chace of a Ship (Supposed an English East india man) on the   Day of August 1779. Captn: Landais did not do his utmost to overtake that ship, Which he might easily have done before night; but put his helm a Weather and bore away Sundry times in the day after Alliance had gained the Wake of the chace and was overtaking her Very fast.—

3.   Captain Landais beheaved With Disrespect and Impertinence towards the Commander in Chief of the Squadron on frequent occasions—

4.   He disobeyed his Signals—

5.   He Very Seldom answered any of them—

6.   He Expressed his fears and apprehensions of being taken on the Coast of Ireland, and insisted on Leaving Sight of it immediatly When We had Cruised there only two days—

7.   His Separation from the Squadron the first time must have happened Either thro' ignorance or design, because tho' he distinctly Saw the Signal for the Course before night. Yet he altered it first two and then four points of the Compass before morning—

8.   His Separation from the Squadron the Second time must also have happened thro' ignorance or design, because the Wind being at N.W. and the other Ships to *his Knowledge* laying too and being a Stern of the Alliance—What less than

---

WE THE OFFICERS &c. &c. of the American Squadron, Now at the Texel, this 30th. Day of Octr: 1779. do attest and declare on our Words of honor as Gentlemen; that all the following Articles Which We Suscribe respecting the Conduct of Peter Landais Captain of the American frigatte Alliance, are really and truely matters of fact; in Witness Whereof We here unto sign our names and qualities; and will, at anytime hereafter, be Ready to prove the Same upon oath if Required.

Like the other affidavits solicited by Jones, the officers' affidavit was published in a pamphlet, [John Paul Jones], *Charges and Proofs Respecting the Conduct of Peter Landais* (New York, 1787), which has been reproduced in Bradford, *Jones Papers,* reel 9, no. 1921.

5. XXVIII, 709n.

Separation Could be the Consequence of his obstinacy in ordering the Weather main brace to be hauled in and the Ship to
be Steered S.W. and S.W.B.S. in the trough of the Sea, Which
Was done from ten at night till morning: and he Would not
then permit the Ship to be tacked in order to rejoin the Squadron as was proposed to him by the officers.—

9. On the morning of the 23. of September When the B. h.
R. after being off the Spurn Came in Sight of the Alliance and
Pallas off flamborough head, Captn. Landais distinctly told
Captn. Cottineau, that if it Was, as it appeared, a fifty guns
Ship; they must run away: altho' he must have been Sure that
the Pallas *from her heavy Sailing* must have fallen a Sacrifice.

10. In the afternoon of the Same day, Captn. Landais paid
no attention to Signals, particularly the Signal of preparation
and for the Line Which Was made With great Care and Very
distinctly on board the B. h. R.—

11. Altho' the Alliance was a Long Way a head of the B. h.
R., When bearing down on the Baltic fleet, yet Captn. Landais
lay out of gun Shot to Windward, and until the B. h. R. had
passed by and Closely engaged the Serapis, and then instead
of Comming to close action with the Countess of Scarborough the Alliance fired at Very Long Shot—

12. He continued to Windward and a Considerable time
after the action began, fell a Stern and Spoke the Pallas; Leaving the Countess of Scarborough in the Wake of the Ships
engaged, and at free Liberty to rake the B. h. R.—

13. After the B. h. R. and Serapis Were made fast along Side
of Each other, as in the margin[6] (Which Was not done till an
hour after the Engagement began) Captn. Landais, *out of mus-
quet Shot* Raked the B. h. R. With Cross bar and grape Shot
&ca. Which Killed a number of men, dismounted Sundry
guns, put out the side Lights and Silenced all the 12. pounders—

14. The alliance then Ran down towards the Pallas and
Countess of Scarborough that Were at the time Engaged at a
Considerable distance to Leeward of the B. h. R. and Serapis,

6. In the margin is a small drawing of the two ships showing the *Serapis'*
anchor and indicating the wind direction.

and Captn. Landais hovered about there out of gun Shot and Without firing till Some time after the Countess of Scarborough had Struck, and then bore down under his top Sails and Spoke first the prize, and then the Pallas asking a number of questions—

15.   At Last Captn. Landais made Sail under his top's Sails to Work up to Windward, but made tacks before he (Being Within the Range of grape Shot, and *at the Longuest* three quarters of an hour before the Serapis struck) fired a Second broadside into the B. h. R.'s Larboard quarter, the Latter part Whereof Was fired When the Alliance was not more than three points abaft the B. h. R.'s beam, altho' many tongues had Cryed from the B. h. R. that Captn. Landais Was firing into the Wrong Ship, and prayed him to Lay the Enemy along Side; three Large Signal Lanthorns With proper Signal Wax Candles in them, and Well Lighted had also previously to his firing been hung over the bow quarter and Wraist of the B. h. R. in a horisontal Line, which Was the Signal of reconnaissance, and the Ships, the one having a heigh poop and being all black, the other having a low Stern With yellow Sides, Were Easily distinguishable it being full moon—

16.   The alliance then passed at a Very Considerable distance along the larboard or off Side of the B. h. R. and having tacked and gained the Wind ran down again to Leeward, and in Crossing the B. h. R.'s bow Captn. Landais Racked her With a third broad Side after being Constantly Called to from the B. h. R. not to fire, but to Lay the Enemy along Side.

17.   Sundry men Were Killed and Wounded by the broadsides mentioned in the two Last articles—

18.   Captain Landais never passed on the off Side of the Serapis, nor Could that Ship Ever bring a gun to bear on the Alliance at any time during the Engagement—

19.   The Leakes of the B. h. R. Increased much after being fired upon by the Alliance; and as the most dangerous Shot Which the B. h. R. received under Water Were under the Larboard bow and quarter, they must have come from the Alliance, for the Serapis Was on the other Side.

20.   Several people on board the Alliance told Captn. Landais

at different times, that he fired upon the Wrong Ship, others refused to fire.—

21. The alliance only fired three Vollies, while Within gun Shot of the B. h. R. and Serapis—

22. The morning after the Engagement Captn. Landais acknowledged on board the Serapis that he Raked Each time With grape Shot, which he Knew Would Scatter—

23. Captain Landais has acknowledged Since the action that he Would have thought it no harm if the B. h. R. had struck for it Would have given him an opportunity to retake her and to take the Serapis—

24. He has frequently declared that he Was the only American in the Squadron, and that he was not under the Orders of Captn. Jones.

25. In Comming into the texel, he declared that if Captn. Jones Should hoist a broad pendant, he Would *to Vex him* hoist another—

I attest the Articles Number 2. 4. 5. 10. 11. 15. 16. and 22. to be matters of fact, and I believe all the rest.

> ROBERT CORAM Midshipman of the late
> Ship of War the Bonhomme Richard

I attest the articles number, 2. 3. 4. 5. 6. 10. 11. 13. 15. 16. 17. 19. 21. 22. to be matters of fact, and I belive all the rest.

> J. W. LINTHWAITE Midshipman of the Late
> ship of war the Bon Homme Richard

I attest the articles Number, 2. 3. 4. 5. 6. 10. 11. 13. 15. 16. 17. 19. 21. 22. to be matters of fact, and I believe all the rest.

> JOHN MAYRANT. Midshipman of the late
> Ship of War the Bon H Richard

I attest the Articles Number, 1. 2. 3. 4. 5. 6. 7. 8. 10. 13. 15. 16. 17. 18. 19. 20. 22. 23. & 24. to be matters of fact, and I believe all the rest.

> LT. COL. WUIBERT. american Engineer and
> Commanding officer of the Volunteers on
> board Serapis late of the Bon Homme
> Richard.

I attest the Articles Number, 2. 3. 11. to be matters of Fact, & I believe all the rest.   BENJN. STUBBS Midshipman of the Late
            Ship of War the Bon H. Richard

I attest the Articles Number, 2. 3. 4. 5. 6. 10. 11. 13. 15. 16. & 17. to be Matters of Fact & I believe all the Rest.
                    THOS. POTTER Midshipman of the late Ship
                    of War the Bon H. Richard

I attest the Articles Number, 2. 3. 4. 5. 10. 11. 13. 15. & 19. to be Matters of Fact & I believe all the Rest.
                    NATHL. FANNING Midshipman of the late
                    Ship of War the Bon H. Richard

I attest the Articles, 3. 4. 5. 10. 11. 13. 15. 16. 17. 19. & 21 to be Matters of fact & I believe all the Rest.
                    THOS. LUNDY Midshipman of the late
                    Ship of War the Bon H. Richd:

I attest the Articles Number, 2. 3. 4. 5. 6. 10. 11. 13. 15. 16. & 17. to be Matters of Fact and I believe all the Rest.
                    BEAUMONT GROUBE Midn. of the late Ship
                    of War the Bon H. Richd.

We attest the Articles Number, 2. 3. 4. 5. 7. 8. 11. 12. 18.* 20. & 21. to be matters of Fact.
                    JAMES DEGGE Liet.
                    JOHN LARCHAR JUNR. Masters Mate
                    on board the Alliance
                    JOHN BUCKLEY Master

*N.B. The Alliance never pass'd on the offside of the Serapis

I attest the Articles 2. 3. 4. 5. 10. 11. 15. 16. 17. 18. 23. to be matters of fact
                    STACK Lt. of Walsh's Regt. and Offer. of
                    Volunteers on Board the Bon Homme
                    Richard by congé from Court

I attest the Articles 2. 3. 4. 5. 6. 10. 11. 13. 15. 19. 23. 24. to be matters of fact   MACARTHY offr. of Walsh's Regiment and Lt
                    of Voluteers on board the Bonhomme
                    Richard

I atestte Les Articles 11. 12. 14. & 24. quant à l'article 4. j'ai connoissance quil à refusé d'obeir aux Signaux de se rendre à bord du bonhomme Richard, et relativement à l'article 9. je me rappelle quil me dit Si c'est un vaissau au dessus de 50 Canons nous n'avons que le parti de la fuitte.

DE COTTINEAU DE KERLOGUEN.
Capne de La Pallas[7]

I attest the Articles 2. 5. 11. 12. 20. 22. to be matters of fact.
M. PARKE Capt. of Marines on board the American Frigate Alliance.

I attest the Articles 2. 3. 4. 5. 15. 16. 17. 18. 19. 21. to be matters of fact RICHARD DALE, Lieutenant of the late Ship of War the Bon Homme Richard.

I Attest the Articles 2. 3. 4. 5. 11. 14. 22. to be matters of fact.
HENRY LUNT Lieutenant of the late Ship of War the Bon Homme Richard

I Attest the Articles 2. 3. 4. 5. 10. 11. 13. 15. 16. 17. 18. 19. 21. to be matters of fact SAMUEL STACY Master of the late Ship of War the Bon Homme Richard.

Notation: Articles respecting the behavior of Captain Landais since we left l'orient. October 30th. 1779.

From Thomas O'Gorman

ALS: American Philosophical Society

Tonnerre 30th.
Dear Doctor and best of Excellencies.　　　8ber. 1779.
I embrace the first moment I have enjoyed since the vintage to present you my best respects and to acquaint you of the quantity and quality of our late crop of Wine. The quantity

7. Cottineau later wrote to Landais to explain his testimony; an English translation is printed in Landais, *Memorial,* pp. 81–2.

has not answer'd our expectations, the vintage affords not quite a one third of a full crop, but the quality is excellent.

As your Excellency flattered me with the hope of having the honour to furnish you duely with your provision of Wine, I shall let you have at the rate of 300 *l.t.* the muid or two casks the first growth of 1776 both of red and white wine such as I furnish to the nobility of England, and the second growth of Sd. year for your ordinary at 220 *l.t.* The first will amount to no more than 1 *l.t.* 2*s.* per bottle and the Second to about 15 sols delivered at your hotel at Passy.[8]

I should be glad to know your Commands as soon as possible as I have wrote circular letters to all my correspondants with the intent to empty my cellars of all my old wine before my speedy departure for England.

I flatter my self that the Count Destaing, who I am credibly informed steared his course towards New York, has 'ere now sufficiently revenged on Admiral Colliers the destruction of the American fleet at Penobscot. I hope likewise that in Concert with General Washington he will oblidge the Royalist to evacuate New York & Rhode-Island. I beg you'l inform me of whatever good News you have from the other side of the Atlantic. You know my sincere good Wishes for the Cause and my ardent desire of becoming one day or other a good subject of yours. I hope you'l aid my endavours for that purpose and back my postulation with M. de Sartine.[9] Please to present my best compliments to young M. Franklin and beleive me to remain with the greatest Deference Dr. Doctor your Excellency's Most devoted and humble Servant

LE CHEVR. O GORMAN

P.S. My Sister in Law[1] presents you with her Respectful Compliments. She is well and amuses herself with embellishing her

---

8. In the spring of 1778, the chevalier had sent BF enough wine to fill 900 bottles: XXVI, 87–8. The present letter may have prompted another order, since on March 11, 1780, BF paid O'Gorman's account 150 *l.t.* for a cask of burgundy: Account XXIII, XXIX, p.3.

9. For an account of those memoranda to the naval minister see XXVI, 471n.

1. The chevalier d'Eon (XXV, 515n), then in exile in Tonnerre (Burgundy) where he/she had an estate.

Domaine and preparing a good and Comfortable habitation for herself. She and I would be very happy to receive you and your grandson in this Country, but we can hardly expect a visit from you in your present Situation; when America is quite free, which I hope will be Soon, then you'l be able to take the amusement of a good vintage with us and make your observations on the Culture of vineyards./.

his excellency Doctor Franklin.

Notation: Chevr: Gormon Oct 13 79

From Dumas

ALS: American Philosophical Society; AL (draft); Algemeen Rijksarchief

Dear, honoured Sir   Lahaie 31e. Oct. 1779.

I send you herewith copy of the Letter I received yesterday, with a loose Seal, from his Exc. the french Ambassador, & which I forwarded the Same day with another of mine, of which also I join an Extract.[2] If we can but get safe our Squadron to Dunkirk, then it must be acknowledged that the Sending of it in a Dutch Port, has produced an admirable effect, & does in every respect the greatest honour to the politic views of him who has imagined it. If our brave Commodore Should be taken or Killed, the same effect would subsist, but at a dear rate.

Our friend has not yet been able to procure me the Resolution, which I must have, to translate it, & then pay a visit to the g. P. He has sent me in the meantime another Resolution of late, 13 pages in folio, concerning the unlimited convoys, a matter, which I think will remain undecided, till this war is over. If I had any leisure, or rather the help of a Secretary, I should send you a translation of it, for it is a curious piece,

---

2. Dumas enclosed extracts from La Vauguyon's of Oct. 29 to Jones (telling him that orders from Sartine about his future destination would be awaiting him at Dunkirk), from Dumas' of Oct. 30 to Jones (a covering letter for the former), and from Jones's of Oct. 21 to Dumas (about the attempted mass desertion from his squadron). All are reproduced in full in Bradford, *Jones Papers,* reel 4, nos. 830, 834, 802.

which would give you a clear idea of the artifices of our cunctators, & of the marine circumstances of this rep.

Mr. Izard is at Amsterdam. I don't know his business there.[3] He & Mr. Neufville have exchanged a visit each. I have not seen him.

There is a vessel building at Amsterdam, after the pattern of Mr. Sayre, at the expence of some merchants there. Tuesday to come the States of Holland will resume their Assembly.

I think, Sir, I have forgotten to tell you of a very great desertion of people from the Serapis, not less than 25 Men at once.[4] 15 of whom have been retaken on the spot before they reached te Shore, 5 are drowned, & 5 we have got arrested at Amsterdam by authority of the Magistrate, & sent them back on board. The Magistrate of Amsterdam, as well as the commanding Officer of the road have behaved very friendly on this occasion.

I am with very great respect, ever Dear & honoured Sir your most obedient & humble servant   DUMAS

Passy à Son E. Mr. Franklin

Addressed: His Excellency / B. Franklin, Esqr. Min. Plenip. / of the United States, &c. / *Passy. /* .

Notation: Dumas. Octr. 29. 1779

From Sartine   Copy: Archives Nationales

A Versailles le 31. Octobre 1779.
M. de sartine fait ses complimens à Monsieur franklin, et a l'honneur de le prévenir qu'il vient d'etre rendû un Arrêt du Conseil portant que la Requête du Sr. Walpole[5] sera communiquée aux Srs. Alexander pour y répondre dans la quinzaine;

3. Izard was hoping to find a passage to St. Eustatius, from whence travelers often found ships for America: Wharton, *Diplomatic Correspondence,* III, 447. When his efforts proved futile, he returned to Paris.

4. Dumas did send an account of the incident with his Oct. 22 letter to BF.

5. Thomas Walpole of Walpole & Ellison, Alexander John and William Alexander's opponent in the case of the Alexanders' properties in Grenada.

les choses demeurant en même état où elles étoient avant l'Ordonnance de M le Comte de Durat⁶ les Srs. Alexandre ont écrit à M le Comte de Vergennes qu'ils consentoient à la continuation du séquestre de leurs Biens.⁷

A M. franklin à Passy

6. The French governor of Grenada.

7. Sartine notified Vergennes as well on the 31st: Archives Nationales. The council continued the sequestration, the Alexanders appealed to the French courts, and Thomas Walpole eventually came to France to contest them. The case reverted to the English courts after the end of the war and dragged on until 1790, a multinational equivalent of Charles Dickens' Jarndyce and Jarndyce: Price, *France and the Chesapeake,* II, 699–700; Namier and Brooke, *House of Commons,* III, 600–1.

Index

Arms. *See* Muskets; Supplies, military
Army, American: in Illinois country, 65: south, 96, 105–6, 110, 112, 114, 147, 161, 178, 183, 185, 204, 209–10, 220–1, 234, 266, 268, 306, 399: N.Y., R.I., 221, 632; Lafayette wishes to return to, 100, 271, 424, 483; Gérard visits, praises, 185n; reportedly is strong, 186; campaigns against Iroquois, 186n; La Luzerne praises zeal, success of, 281; J. Smith, Sterry to procure supplies for, 304, 393; French serving in, 363; attacks Stony Point, 365–6, 405, 413, 416n, 423–4, 432: Paulus Hook, 416n; regulations for, sent by Steuben, 412; compared to European armies, 412–13; officers leave, claiming Americans do not love French, 469–70; takes the offensive, says Digges, 493; information on, to be provided by Colomb, 541. *See also* Regiments, American
Army, British: atrocities committed by, lxi, 96, 100n, 110, 115n, 116–17, 118–19, 183–4, 405, 430, 483, 547–8; occupies Philadelphia (1778), lxiii; in N.Y., R.I., 11n, 209, 266, 378, 619, 632: Illinois country, 65: Natchez and Manchac, 65–6: West Indies, 117–22, 265, 378, 619: America, to be lent troops from West Indies, 122n: Britain, reacts to rumors that Jones squadron has troops, 471; expedition to Va. by, 22–3, 99, 183, 185, 234; military operations in S.C., Ga. by, 96, 105–6, 110, 112, 114, 147, 161, 178, 183, 185, 204, 209–10, 220–1, 234, 266, 268, 306, 307, 399, 493–4; threatens Pa., 99–100; during Indians by, 100; during Seven Years' War, 321n; gloomy prospects of, 493–4; at Quebec, 619. *See also* Penobscot Bay; Stony Point
Army, Dutch, 337n, 338n
Army, French: in attempted invasion of England, 98–100, 186, 276, 467, 584; in West Indies, 117–20, 424; aboard d'Estaing's squadron, 266; impression of Lafayette's sword on, 271; compared to American, 412–13
Army, Prussian, 412–13, 566–7
Army, Spanish, 22, 24–6
Arnold, Gen. Benedict: toast to, at Independence Day banquet, 46

Arnoux, ———, abbé (xxv, 382): attends Independence Day banquet, 44; and Chalut invite BF, WTF to dine, 236; notifies BF of arrival of quinine, 250n; inquires after BF's health, asks to borrow *Courier de l'Europe*, 434; letters from Chalut and, 236, 434
Arthaud, Agathe Silvestre: invites BFB to dine, 587
Arthaud, Jérémie (Agathe's husband), 587n
Artisans: in Philadelphia, affected by rising prices, lxiii; in BF's foundry, salaries of, 3
Assemblée de charité, 295
Auer, Deacon M.: asks assistance in recovering money, 189–90; letter from, 189–90
Aurora borealis: BF's paper on, in Vaughan's edition, 66, 175, 512n: Priestley praises, 408; Vaughan observes, will write about, 381
Aurore (French frigate), 25
Austin, Jonathan Loring (xxv, 103n): reports on British cruelties, lxi, 96; sends news of British defeat at Charleston, 96, 147: greetings to WTF, 96–7; forwards newspapers, letter for JA, 96–7, 147–8; Knox carries letter of, 96–7, 147–8; introduces W. Knox, 147–8; BF acknowledges letters from, has nothing to offer, 565–6; mentioned, 126n; letters from, 96–7, 147–8; letter to, 565–6
Autroche, baron d', 355
Aval, ———, 481
Aycard, ——— (sculptor): identified, 196n; inquires about missing statue, 196–7; letter from, 196–7
Ayen, Jean-Paul-François de Noailles, duc d' (Lafayette's father-in-law), 531

Babcock, Capt. George Waith, 103–4, 127–8, 136, 140, 211, 246, 437–8, 510
Bachaumont, Louis Petit de, *et al. See Mémoires secrets*
Bache, Benjamin Franklin: educated in Geneva, 107, 241, 242, 244, 248, 333, 365, 480–1, 586–7; RB fails to hear from, 193; and Deane, Cochran, 241: Cramers, Marignac, 241, 242, 248, 480–1, 586–7; books for, 241, 587; urged to behave, be cheerful, 241; happy disposition of, 248;

Bache, Benjamin Franklin (*continued*)
family of, worries about distance from
BF, 327, 333, 365; compared to sister,
335; Greenes send greetings to, 375;
bills for, 480–1; scolded for not dating
letters, 586; sends thanks for portrait,
586–7; entertained by Marignacs, Mme
Arthaud, 587; inherits Caslon type, 611;
mentioned, 149; letter from, 586–7; letter to, 241–2
Bache, Elizabeth (Eliza, Betsy) (RB and SB's
daughter), 194, 241, 335, 352
Bache, Louis (RB and SB's son), 194, 550–1
Bache, Richard (BF's son-in-law, XIV,
136n): Vatteville recommended to, 107;
writes J. Mecom, 149; WTF, 350: BFB,
587; and C. Schneider, 190n; sends
circular letters for Bache & Shee,
193–4, 364–5: bills, inquires about goods,
200–1, 333: letter, magazines with
Jay, 555; brother of, 200, 363; in good
health, 241; heads subscription assemblies, 333–4; business ventures of,
335; sells BF's printing office, 363–4;
is pleased with BF's reports of BFB,
365; praises Gérard, 366; waits on La
Luzerne, 398; Duclos de Vulmer recommended to, 407n, 423; reports
birth of son, 550–1; and SB, await
shipment from Boston, 551; BF sends
dispatches to, on *Mercury,* 619n; letters
from, 193–4, 200–1, 363–6, 550–1, 555;
letters to, 107, 423
Bache, Sarah Franklin (Sally): sends news
of family, friends, lxiii, 350–3, 397–8;
criticized by BF, defends herself, lxiii–
lxiv, 333–5, 352; reports on scarcity of
goods in Philadelphia, lxiii–lxiv, 332–6,
351–2; reports patience and linen worn
out, lxiv, 351; not opposed to Phelps's
plan to help citizens of Charlestown,
81; pregnancy, childbirth of, 194, 397,
550–1; in good health, 241; gives Hopkinson BF medallion, 299; friendship
with Gérard, 299, 366, 550n; writes J.
Mecom, 327, 375: BFB, 365; sends squirrel skins to WTF, 332–3, 350–1, 366; asks
WTF to send goods from France, 351–2;
claims is too old to go without cap, 352;
flannel cloth for, 398; sends *U.S. Magazine,* news of Blair family, 432–3; Amelia

Barry asks after, 490; letters from, 332–
6, 350–3, 397–8, 432–3
Bache, William (RB and SB's son), 194, 241,
333, 350, 352
Bache & Shee (Philadelphia merchant
firm, XXVIII, 552–3n): circular letters for,
193, 364–5, 383, 435, 511n
Baër, Frédéric-Charles de, 508
Bager, —— (grand bailiff of Ber-
gen), 591n
Bailey, Francis (printer), 432–3
Bailly, Jean-Sylvain: identified, 387; re-
quests permission to visit with Mme de
Beauharnais, 387; letter from, 387–8
Baily, Thomas: letter from, *inter alia,*
576–8
Baird, Col. James Gardiner: returns to En-
gland, 209–10, 221
Balance of power: as French war objec-
tive, 226
Bale goods, 143, 255
Baltic Sea: convoy from, 452n, 469
Baltimore, Md.: tobacco shipped from,
179; ship from, arrives at Nantes, 605–6
Bancroft, Edward: accused of mismanag-
ing American affairs, 58n; examines
Ross's accounts, 197–8
Bankers, French: and American loan,
206–7, 219
Bank of England, 580n
Baptist, Michael: letter from, *inter alia,*
576–8
Barbados, 118n, 120
Barbé de Marbois. *See* Marbois
Barbeu-Dubourg, Jacques (BF's former
editor, XV, 112–13): refutes "Morals of
Chess," 18, 19–20; attends Independence Day banquet, 18, 44; gives BF brochure from Honoré, 74; and Boyer de la
Croix, 81: Cadet de Vaux, 112: Lalande
recommend Raggi, 132–3, 164: Agatange Le Roy, 164: F. Grand, 206, 225:
liqueurs from Martinique, 165; asks con-
sulship for Grégoire, 164–5, 225: introduction for Duclos de Vulmer, 406–7;
awaits BF works, 165; inquires about
Gen. Lincoln, Gen. Prevost, 165: about
loan, 206–7, 219: about vacant lands in
America, 207, 219–20; BF to visit, dine
with D.-C. Cochin, 340–1, 406–7; desires answer from JW, 341; letter from

Peru, 250n

Peruvian bark. *See* Quinine

Peter I (the Great), Czar of Russia, 248n

Peters, Richard (Richard's son), 352n

Peters, Richard (secretary of continental board of war, XXIII, 274n): seeks aid for father, lviii, 95, 218, 584; Vatteville recommended to, 95; and SB, 352; father's letter forwarded to, 485; BF's draft on, payable to Carné de Trécesson, 585n; letters to, 95, 584–5

Peters, Sarah Robinson (Richard's wife): greetings to, 95, 352–3, 584–5; gives birth to son, 352–3

Peters, William (Richard's father): search for, lviii, 57n, 95, 485, 584; wishes to, draws on BF, lviii, 57, 95, 106, 208, 220, 290–1, 301, 584; and Digges, 57, 106, 208, 220, 290–1, 301, 485, 584; sends news, encloses letter, 217–19; letter from, 217–19

Petrie, Samuel (merchant, XXIV, 543n): attends Independence Day banquet, 44; accused of stockjobbing, 180n; and proposed duel with W. Lee, 180–1n; requests passport, 180–1; called one of "Council at Passy," 181n; writes Vergennes, 181n; letter from, 180–1

Phaedrus (Phèdre), 587

Pharmaceuticals: purchased in Netherlands for BF, 264. *See also* Quinine

Phelps, Charles: presents scheme to aid citizens of Charlestown, Mass., 81

Philadelphia: celebrates capture of Grenada, lvi–lvii, 194: American independence, 44; regulation of prices in, lxiii, 307, 395; British occupy, leave, lxiii, 364; Bond comments on social revolution in, lxiii, 395; hardship of wartime life in, lxiii–lxiv, 333–5, 351–2; *General Mercer* insured for trip to, 108; McCraken wishes to emigrate to, 166; ships from France arrive in, 193; La Luzerne proceeds to, 199n, 281n, 299, 350, 372, 479n; Inglis writes from, 233n; difficulty of manning ships at, 235; *Deane* cruises out of, 235n; Tathwell paroled in, 280; Gérard sends plants for Nolin from, 285–6; ship from, taken to Lisbon, 286n; Howe's campaign against, 303n; Becker & Saltzmann urged to send cargo to,

321; BFB's print shop at, 347; Radical Party seizes of control of, 395; inhabitants of, petition Congress for Conyngham, 415n; expense of congressional delegates living in, 422; Deane leaves for, 541; British officers confined in jail at, 596

Phoenix (Phianix) (sloop), 38, 39n

Physiocrats, 384

Picardy, 425n

Pickesgill, Samuel (British prisoner), 143

Pickett, William (prisoner): identified, 526n; Digges writes on behalf of, 526

Piercy, Capt. Thomas, 477

Pigault de Beÿmont, ——— (commission seeker), 53

Pillat Delacoupe, ———: wishes to cash bills of exchange, 77

Piquet (card game): compared to chess, 20

Pitot, ——— (American agent in Morlaix, XXIX, 90n), 224

Place Vendôme, 250n

Plan d'Education (Montfort de Prat), 564–5

Plants: Gérard sends to Nolin, have not arrived, 285–6; of Cochin's garden, BF invited to view, 340. *See also* Vegetation

Plymouth, England: prisoners at, 16n, 220; cartel ship takes prisoners from, 29n, 410: expected to return to, 59; British navy off, 134; Marchant takes brig *Ann* on its way to, 255; Conyngham moved to, 291; French prisoner at, 533. *See also* Mill Prison

Plymouth (Plimouth) (American privateer): captures Spanish ships, 102

Poems: sent BF, 82; to be recited at masonic ceremony, 238; BF and Hopkinson exchange, 298

Point-No-Point, Pa., 394n

Poland: BF aids abbé from, 3

Police de Paris dévoilée, La (Manuel), 157n

Political, Miscellaneous and Philosophical Pieces (BF): Vaughan works on, 66n, 175–6, 379, 381, 504, 512, 623; motto for frontispiece of, 175

Politics: Hopkinson comments on party disputes in, 298; Steuben cautions against divisions in, 413

Pollard, Walter (XXVIII, 5n): receives assistance from BF, 129n; father of, 129–30;

Wellis, Capt. John (British prisoner), 143
Welsh, James: assumes business of Duff &
Welsh, 233
Welsh, John: offers services, forwards let-
ter, 233; letter from, 233
Welsh poetry, 165
Wernier, Hartsinck & Wernier (Amster-
dam merchants): seek relations with
American merchants, 77
Wesselowsky, ——— (Catherine Delon-
Cramer's father), 248n
West, Col. ———: returns to England,
209–10, 221
West Indies, British: military, naval opera-
tions in, lvi–lvii, 23–5, 117–22, 129,
193–4, 204–5, 208, 265, 267–8, 271, 309,
485–6, 497, 527, 619–20; Congress pro-
poses burning towns in, 115–16; British
money loaned to merchants of, 176;
convoys to, from, 205, 208, 620; poor
state of affairs in, 378, 494, 527. See also
Antigua; Barbados; Dominica; Grenada;
Jamaica; St. Christopher; St. Lucia; St.
Vincent; Tobago
West Indies, French: convoy for, 235n, 268;
reinforcements for, 424; Irish beef for,
437; d'Estaing returns part of fleet to,
497. See also Guadeloupe; Martinique;
St. Domingue
West Point: Washington, La Luzerne meet
at, 479n; Deane writes from, 541
Wethersfield, Conn.: threatened attack on,
110n
Whale fishery: southern, 606n, 607n
Whaling ships, British: Americans forced
to serve on, 607
Wharton, Joseph, Jr. (Samuel's brother,
XXVII, 229n), 193, 394, 398
Wharton, Samuel (merchant, XI, 187–8n):
attends Independence Day banquet, 44;
sends papers, intelligence, 88, 112, 114–
15, 134, 145, 204–5, 257; moves from
London to Paris, 88n; and T., R. Burdy,
113, 176, 181n: Hutchins, treasonable
correspondence, 291–2, 302–3, 376–7;
effects of, to be sent, 176; called one of
"Council at Passy," 181n; notation in
hand of, 181n; examines Ross's accounts, 197–8; seeks depositions for
Neaves, 198; sends papers, reports on
price of copper, 418; does not receive in-

telligence from England, says BF, 485;
mentioned, 193n; letters from, 88–9,
112, 114–15, 134, 145, 198–9, 204–5,
257, 418
Whatman, James, 610n
Wheat, 310
Whipple, William (congressional delegate,
XXIII, 339n), 115n, 183n
White, Lt. Thomas (prisoner), 59, 136–7
White, Thomas (prizemaster), 336, 339n,
340n, 342
Wikoff, Turnbull & Co., 287
Wilkes, John, 499n
Wilkinson, Thomas (prisoner), 42
William V, Prince of Orange (stadholder of
Netherlands): political activities of, 59–
60, 338n; Dumas' code name for, 60n
Williams, David (clergyman): sends Lec-
tures on the Universal Principles ... to be
forwarded to BF, 623
Williams, Grace (JW's mother), 314n
Williams, Dr. Griffith, 607
Williams, Hugh (British prisoner), 144
Williams, John, 362
Williams, Jonathan, Jr. (BF's grandnephew,
I, lviii): courtship, marriage of, lvii, lxii,
153n, 263n, 276n, 313–17, 586; and WTF,
lxii, 137n, 284n, 497n: A. Lee, 9n, 123:
Schweighauser, 18, 70, 284n, 314–15:
A.J. Alexander, 103: prisoner exchange,
103–4, 127–8: W. Alexander, 128, 331:
care of prisoners, 163, 355: RB, 193,
200–1, 366: Greene family, 375, 478–9:
conveyance for packet of engravings,
497n; accounts of, merchants' committee examines, 9, 17–18, 70, 123, 128,
151–3, 263–4, 314–15, 349, 413–14, 464;
investigates complaints of Spanish ambassador, 70, 102, 127; sends Schweighauser copy of Babcock's receipt for
ransomed British prisoners, 140n: bills,
201, 331, 333: accounts, promises to
send paper, 349: accounts, memorial to
Congress, 413n: story about BF to J. Mecom, 583; commission charged by, on
work done for commissioners, 151–2;
forwards news from America, 177–8:
letter to Lovell, 194; shares responsibility for delaying letter to Lovell, 194n;
ship of, arrives in Boston, 200; in Lorient, proceeds to Passy, Nantes, 263n;